American
Stud

Contributions in American Studies

Series Editor: Robert H. Walker

American Studies

TOPICS
and
SOURCES

Robert H. Walker
Editor

Contributions in American Studies, Number 24

GREENWOOD PRESS
Westport, Connecticut • London, England

Library of Congress Cataloging in Publication Data

Main entry under title:

American studies: Topics and Sources

    (Contributions in American studies; no. 24)
    "These essays have appeared or will appear in American Studies international."
    Includes bibliographies and indexes.
    CONTENTS: American studies and traditional topics: Sklar, R. Cultural
history and American studies. Ahlstrom, S. E. A bibliography of religious history
in its American setting. Stone, A. E. Autobiography and American culture. [etc.]
    1. American studies--United States--Addresses, essays, lectures. I. Walker,
Robert Harris,
1924-   II. American studies international.
E175.8.A584   973'.07'2   75-35675
ISBN 0-8371-8559-9

Library of Congress Catalog Card Number: 75-35675
ISBN: 0-8371-8559-9

First published in 1976

Greenwood Press, a division of Williamhouse-Regency Inc.
51 Riverside Avenue, Westport, Connecticut 06880

Printed in the United States of America

Contents

Introduction

These essays have appeared or will appear in *American Studies International*, a journal addressed to an international community of individuals interested in the study of the United States and its colonial precondition. Founded as an informal newsletter among senior Fulbright-Hays grantees, its pages have regularly announced meetings, exchange opportunities, and similar items of more than national interest. The journal languished for a while, following the retirement of its founder, and was resurrected in 1970 as a more formal publication including regular bibliographic essays.

The topics for these essays were chosen with an eye toward current importance. We have paid special attention to areas of expanding definition where publication sometimes proceeds at so frenzied a pace that even the specialist is overwhelmed. Some topics were chosen because of their obvious utility; others because of repeated requests from abroad. The authors of these essays were asked to concentrate on identifying materials available outside the United States or readily transportable, such as microforms and paperbacks.

Not much to our surprise we soon discovered that these essays were being heavily used at home as well as overseas. Not only were beleaguered graduate students looking for a marked trail through a forest of publications, but highly professional scholars also searched for a method for catching up in fields outside their own specialty. Since American studies has always been an expanding concept, there has been a continuous need for charting its growth.

The bicentennial years suggest to us, therefore, not so much a compulsive review of the American Revolution as a convenient impetus for the continuing search for useful perceptions of American culture. These essays lead in that direction. They lead to materials written or compiled mostly by Americans, to works that are neither consistently favorable nor unfavorable, neither fastidiously objective nor wildly opinionated. The only thing they unarguably show is an ever-increasing interest in the study of the United States.

The attitude underlying works about America in the last decade is not easy to summarize. It is not the buoyant vigor of the turn of the century when the nation first shouldered her way into the cast of world powers. It has not been an iconoclastic, "debunking" mood as prevailed in the 1920s. Nor has it been a "hail and farewell" salutation addressed to a traditional America that was not to have survived a Great Depression or an age of consumer-directed technology. The point of view has even passed beyond those sober appraisals of the years following World War II when citizens and scholars grappled with the inevitability of global responsibilities.

The assumptions of the last decade are most like those of the late Progressive years when a kind of stock-taking (as Parrington called it) was underway. Artists and scholars show an almost equal interest in past, present, and future. Revisions and counter-revisions succeed one another not with a passion for the destruction of an older view but with an interest in a deeper understanding. The history of a race or region is rescued from one stereotype not to be returned to another but to be revealed as a complex entity resistant to oversimple categorizations. We are not hypnotized by our contemporaries into imagining that a great age of objectivity has arrived—data banks and scientific methods notwithstanding. We do sense a reassuring degree of open-mindedness concerning the sums to be taken when the evidence is added together.

We do not regard these collected essays as comprising an ideal totality. There are other topics to be covered, further problems to be encountered. We hope that this group, brought together in 1975, will be useful during these days of the re-examination of American civilization. By the time the Bicentennial of Yorktown has rolled around, we hope to have another bundle of equally useful works.

We have arranged these essays in three parts, opening with a group that shows the bibliographer's estimate of what the American studies approach has meant within more or less traditional areas. The second group includes those topics that—while not entirely original—represent a new stress as well as a scope of attention not usually associated with a single department or discipline. The third short section is devoted to three pragmatic essays that offer a guide to archives, periodicals, and books across the whole spectrum of American studies. Within each section the essays appear in the order in which they were originally published. Each author was given the opportunity to update his essay immediately prior to publication; most authors did so.

If we have not divided American studies into twenty equal parts, neither have we sought to define this subject in any rigid way. Yet it is impossible to assemble so many good essays without observing the comment they make on directions in American studies; in fact several of the essays explicitly direct attention to a "new" or "neglected" discipline within our general purview. What are these directions, new and old?

The first part of this collection makes it easy to observe that many important contributions still come from the established disciplines. Whether the work be in religion, geography, or literature, it contributes obviously and importantly to the improved understanding of an aspect of the culture. But it is also true that something called an American studies approach may distinguish the contributors to this volume from some of their colleagues. This approach is first defined by a concern with mutuality of interest across the lines of specialization. The geographer wants to know whether his generalizations are useful to the economist. He therefore offers them in terms readily understandable outside the specialist's tight-knit frame of reference. Conversely, he hopes the economist will react in terms he can appreciate.

American studies also defines itself through its interest in the people of the United States. There is less stress on great ideas than on their effects. Merle Curti exemplified this viewpoint when he carefully called his major work "a *social* history of American thought" (italics ours). Indeed, Curti and his kindred spirits can be usefully understood as continuing that academic revolution begun by those early social historians who called for fewer kings and more commoners in the recorded past.

Part I shows American studies influencing traditional subjects toward a kind of academic populism; it shows an effort toward making investigations readily assimilable. Part II shows this and more. Although the message is by no means buried, it signifies more against the background of recent academic history.

Looking only at internal academic causes, one could say that American studies originated in order to merge some insights in literary history with others in social history, and—incidentally in all but the political sense—to impart validity to the study of American subjects. These two interests, history and literature, merged not along an uninterrupted chronological line, but in response to stress on certain subjects where each needed the other: protest, conformity, values. Thus, although the governing discipline was that of history, the approach came soon to focus on certain problems of social understanding and documentation. Social scientists and aestheticians brought with them commitments to other kinds of continuity; but they penetrated American studies only when they helped shed light on such topics of established interest as the distribution of wealth, the assimilation of minorities, and the identification of socially useful symbols.

American studies was ready and waiting, therefore, when the academic world became involved with certain subjects that had more to do with problems than with departments: the city, ecology, subcultural identities. It would not be correct to say that American studies absorbed the movements directed at such problems. American studies helped spark some of these interests and clearly accepted them as ways of expanding its own agenda. Part II makes this abundantly clear.

Also clear is the expansion of the boundaries of American studies as a general rule of behavior. But is there a lesson in method beyond the simple commitment to grow? Have the humanists resisted the quantifiers? Has cultural anthropology won over all? Has some long-awaited fusion come about? Although this collection furnished some support for each of these alternatives, there appears to be one generalization that overrides them all: namely, that method has been subordinated to materials; or, to put this matter less succinctly, that the philosophy of method has been de-emphasized while scholarly practice has led to methods that are relatively simple, natural, and unselfconscious.

The example of urban studies may serve as a case in point. Few of us are comfortable with a neologism like "urbanology." Yet this coinage represents a true need to find a term that would indicate neither a historian, a planner, a demographer, or a sociologist. It is true that the student of the city needs to learn about his subject from poets and engineers, architects and political bosses, census takers and social workers—but without accepting the controlling discipline that may organize the experiences of any one of them. What does he do? Does he manage to work under the constraints of something called an interdiscipline? Not likely. Does he invent a new discipline of his own? Probably not.

What can be observed is the tendency of a number of scholars to become generalists within a limited, nontraditional field of study. Such scholars master a number of disciplines well enough to extract the lore recorded under these controls. They then assemble this information with constant reference to a specific topic (the city is the example here; the observations apply to regional studies, minority studies, and many other topics). Some of their conclusions may be structured with little regard for time coordinates in a social science manner. Some may rely on the historian's chronological perspectives. Some may make use of aesthetic, imaginative, or metaphorical insights. In any case, the methods grow out of the materials in ways that seem almost unavoidable. Conversely, it seems rare in the annals of an expanding American studies to find scholars approaching large topics with method in hand, predetermining to bend the materials to fit that shape, come what may.

These observations will surprise some chroniclers of American studies, including the one who sets them down. We had not held to the likelihood of a single American studies method, nor to the blanket, undiscriminating, and hopelessly vague rationale of interdisciplinary studies. But we had by no means foreseen the apparent rout of the methodologist at the hands of the worker in the topical fields. If the present trends have been accurately observed, they do not predict any new set of catacombs as rigid and intricate as the older stones beneath the ivy. They may, on the other hand, describe a movement that refuses to be tyrannized by artificial and arbitrary ideas of order.

Acknowledgments

Acknowledgments begin with a statement of gratitude to the authors of these essays. The editors appreciate their respect for the limitations of space and time as well as their willingness to adjust their imaginations to the needs of their audience. The journal that played the central role in collecting them was founded by Trusten Russell, supported by the Cultural Affairs branch of the State Department, and administered until recently by the National Academy of Sciences. We thank the many individuals so helpfully supportive, especially John Landgraf, who oversaw the reestablishment and enlargement of the journal, and Maria Stevens, who has seen us through a difficult transition. The journal is now published at the American Studies Program, George Washington University.

The editorial "we" in the foregoing paragraphs has been used with a deliberate sense of the plural. The editor of this volume, who has served as Consulting Editor of the journal since its rebirth, gratefully records the important contributions of three successive journal editors: Brian Svikhart, who helped establish new patterns; Ronald Fonte, who carried on the next two years; and William Bate, who has not only been a most effective journal editor since July 1974, but has also handled many of the details in assembling this volume including the comprehensive bibliography and index.

Robert H. Walker
Editor
June 1975

Part I
American Studies
and Traditional Topics

Cultural History and American Studies: Past, Present and Future

by Robert Sklar

The oldest question in American Studies is still the freshest question: How can we understand the lives of men and women in society, their behavior, their institutions, their words and images, their beliefs? What is this thing they have made of their earthly existence, their culture? American Studies has never lacked for prophets and seers to expound the reasons for studying American culture past, present, future, as a whole. If all their essays were laid end to end they would build a bridge between the humanities and the social sciences. This is not to belittle their always illuminating and sometimes inspiring efforts. Yet the creation of a cultural history remains as always a hope, a promise, a possibility— and a necessity.

There is evidence now, however, that the task of developing a whole cultural history approach to American Studies is being tackled with new energy and perhaps even with new understanding. The sources of this resurgent interest stem from the dynamics of change in the past decade which have greatly altered the way academic scholars and Americans at large perceive their own society. The foundations of a successful effort to study the whole culture of the United States may very well lie in this major reorientation of consciousness which has not yet run its course.

During the 1960s the premises of an optimistic and largely uncritical American cultural consensus were shattered. Where most Americans had once perceived a society of affluence and well-being, many now began to see poverty and malnutrition. Where most Americans had accepted their nation's military and economic role in the world as benevolent and necessary, many now began to regard it as destructive and imperialistic. Where it had been generally assumed that eco-

3

nomic and material growth were the signs of a thriving society, many now sensed that growth meant pollution and ecological crisis. Where it had been expected that assimilation and an end to discrimination were rapidly being achieved, many began to find identity and pride in heightened racial and sexual consciousness, confrontation, and separation. Groups which had seemed only peripherally or covertly or inconsequentially a part of American culture—blacks, Chicanos, Puerto Ricans, Indians, women, homosexuals—demanded to be recognized as part of the whole culture of the United States, as well as asserting their rights to create their own histories and determine their own cultural role.

The vitality, ferment, and conflict of the 1960s have had a salutary effect on American Studies. Looking back a decade ago, one can see unmistakable signs that the American Studies movement was preparing to settle into premature middle age. The ambitions of youth seemed impossible to fulfill, the tasks of maturity seemed a little stale and unproductive, but at least they were respectable and time-filling. But the shock of cultural change jolted American Studies out of its impending complacency. If we were truly committed to the present and future of American culture as well as the past, then new cultural attitudes and expressions had to find a place in our teaching and scholarship. More important yet, if there were voices throughout American society calling for new perspectives on the whole culture in which they lived, could American Studies stand idly by, saying, "We tried it once, it didn't work"? The mandate to understand the whole culture was thrust back upon us.

American Studies was not completely unprepared for the shifts in emphasis that the outward events of cultural change were to call forth. There were already signs that the ends of some scholarly paths were rapidly being reached, and indications as well that new roads were opening up. The study of expression, of ideas and images, myths and symbols, had dominated literary and historical study of American culture for more than three decades. It had produced enduring works of scholarship by Henry Nash Smith, R. W. B. Lewis, Perry Miller,

Marti Friedlander

Robert Sklar is Professor of History at the University of Michigan, Ann Arbor. A former Vice-President of the American Studies Association, Mr. Sklar has been Visiting Professor of History at the University of Aukland, New Zealand, and was a Fulbright lecturer at the University of Tokyo and Sophia University, Japan, in 1971. During the academic year 1975-76, Mr. Sklar was Distinguished Visiting Professor of American Civilization at Bard College, Annandale-on-Hudson, New York. He is the editor of The Plastic Age: 1917-1930, *and the author of* F. Scott Fitzgerald: The Last Laocoon, *and of* Movie-Made America.

F. O. Matthiessen, and several others. But there was a growing sense that the methods of literary and intellectual history no longer possessed the explanatory power to answer the questions American Studies scholars wished to ask. In retrospect, the work that marked a turning point was Leo Marx's important study, *The Machine in the Garden: Technology and the Pastoral Ideal in America* (1964). Marx's conclusion suggests that the values and perceptions of literary expression need to be placed in a broader social context than that which literary analysis can provide. Larzer Ziff's informative work, *The American 1890s: Life and Times of a Lost Generation* (1966) seemed to demonstrate Marx's point; it described the dilemmas of a generation of writers but could find no explanation for their collective behavior other than individual failing. American Studies had once assumed that society could be understood by studying the lives and works of writers and intellectuals; it was becoming increasingly clear instead that writers and intellectuals could not be understood without studying social institutions and social relationships.

The Study of . . . Everything?

Until the mid-1960s the study of society, whether through sociological or historical methods, had not played as large a role in American Studies as the study of literature and ideas. The specialized techniques and vocabularies of academic sociology had erected a formidable barrier, preventing humanists from getting a clear view of social structure and social change; and social history had seemed to fragment into sub-specialties such as labor, cities, immigration, religion, and education, further obstructing a sense of the whole. About a decade ago, however, the urban historians began to take the lead in breaking down the boundaries that separated American Studies scholars from social questions. On a smaller scale they were finding it possible to study whole social and cultural environments. And several of the most innovative urban historians combined a background or interest in multidisciplinary American Studies with training in quantitative methods. Among the many useful recent works of urban history, Stephan Thernstrom's *Poverty and Progress: Social Mobility in a Nineteenth Century City* (1964) and two books by Sam Bass Warner, Jr., *Streetcar Suburbs: The Process of Growth in Boston, 1870-1900* (1962) and *The Private City: Philadelphia in Three Periods of Growth* (1968), pointed the way toward a successful integration of cultural phenomena—ideas, attitudes, beliefs, myths, and symbols—with the structure of social institutions.

Perhaps it would be useful at this point to define more precisely what I mean by *culture* and *cultural history*. I use *culture,* of course, in the anthropological sense rather than the "high" cultural ideal expressed by Matthew Arnold as "the best which has been thought and said in the world." An entire book by the anthropologists A. L. Kroeber and Clyde Kluckhohn, *Culture: A Critical Review of Concepts and Definitions* (1952), was devoted to exploring the meanings of the word. One of the most succinct anthropological definitions is Dorothy Lee's in her *Freedom and Culture* (1959): " . . . culture is a symbolic system which transforms the physical reality, what is *there*, into experienced reality." Lee's idea of a "symbolic system" is related to Kenneth Boulding's use of the word "image," in his *The Image: Knowledge in Life and Society* (1956), as part of general systems theory. They do not mean simply the symbols and images of literature and rhetoric, with which American Studies scholars are already familiar. Their symbolic systems and images denote all that men and women have made of their world—their politics, their economics, their families, their work, their gestures and movements, their machines, their art and artifacts, their . . . everything.

Everything? Is this the mandate of the cultural historian, to study *everything?* One should bear in mind William James' warning that the human mind has no power of universal intuition, that it is "a necessity laid upon us to limit our view." He cites the example of a naval captain who might lose a battle if by reason of excessive "thoroughness" he took the moldy biscuit in the storeroom into his plans. Here precisely is the issue for cultural historians, who are fortunately not in the position of a naval captain directing the battle. Perhaps to the cultural historian that moldy biscuit provides more accurate clues—to the nature of the culture which outfitted that ship, to the lives of its citizens, to the reason why that ship is out there fighting that battle anyway—than the tactical considerations of the captain on the bridge. The cultural historian's mind, like every other human's, must make choices and set limits. Yet we may have to look at every aspect of a culture before deciding which elements are important for our understanding of how our special subject develops, changes, or works.

There is at present no coherent theory of culture that provides us with easy solutions to the problems of how cultures are formed, or that places the various institutions and expressions of culture in rank order of importance. Few students of culture fully accept Karl Marx's view that economic relationships are the underlying substructure of culture and consciousness is its superstructure, any more than they fully accept Marshall McLuhan's idea that technological change and media forms determine the nature of consciousness. It is evident rather that consciousness and social, economic, and technological structures interact, creating and transforming one another in processes of growth, change, and decay. American Studies scholars have devoted most of their energies in the past generation to understanding consciousness divorced from social structure, and predominately a limited area of consciousness at that——the consciousness of artists and intellectuals. There is now a growing sense, as I have suggested, that the coin must be turned on its head—not that consciousness should be abandoned, of course, but that the boundaries we have set up be opened to include much of the culture that has been overlooked, and that consciousness and social structure be united in the same range of vision. This is what I mean by cultural history. Out of its concrete expression in books and articles shall come a new understanding of the structure of American culture and the ways that culture has been and is now being transformed.

Influential Studies of Culture as a Whole

Cultural history of course has its own history, and one aspect of the shift toward a broader view of culture in recent years has been a revived interest in the traditions of cultural study in the United States. The most important work of revaluation, itself a major contribution to cultural history, is Maurice R. Stein's study of sociologists and American community life, *The Eclipse of Com-*

munity: An Interpretation of American Studies (1960). Another valuable work, focusing on literary historians and critics, is Richard Ruland's *The Rediscovery of American Literature: Premises of Critical Taste, 1900-1940* (1967). Richard Hofstadter creates humane and perceptive portraits of three influential historians of the American cultural past in his *The Progressive Historians: Turner, Beard, Parrington* (1968). We also need to take a new look at the cultural studies of Constance Rourke and Lewis Mumford.

The sociologists, critics, and historians covered in these works flourished principally before the First World War and in the years between the wars. After 1940 the new criticism and the history of ideas dominated academic scholarship of American cultural expression. Over the past generation the number of efforts to grasp the nature of American culture as a whole can almost be counted on the fingers of both hands. One could cite works by Lewis Hartz, Oscar and Mary Handlin, William Appleman Williams, David Riesman, Richard Hofstadter, David Potter, and Daniel Boorstin, among others, which presented interesting and often controversial viewpoints, but none has had a widespread formative influence on how other scholars perceive the past and organize their teaching and research—certainly not comparable to the impact of Turner, Beard, and Parrington on scholarship and society. One of the most challenging of recent studies to come out of this group is Hartz's *The Founding of New Societies: Studies in the History of the United States, Latin America, South Africa, Canada, and Australia* (1964), which places United States historical development in the comparative context of other new societies; four other historians also contributed chapters to the book.

A younger generation of cultural historians has so far taken on the task of grasping the whole culture only within chronologically limited boundaries. One such collective effort which will eventually encompass the entire span of American cultural history is The American Culture Series, under the general editorship of Neil Harris, eight volumes of original sources with interpretative introductions designed to widen the scope of cultural studies and place cultural expression within a social and technological context. Five volumes appeared in 1970: David Grimsted, ed., *Notions of the Americans: 1820-1860;* Alan Trachtenberg, ed., *Democratic Vistas: 1860-1880;* Neil Harris, ed., *The Land of Contrasts, 1880-1901;* Roderick Nash, ed., *The Call of the Wild: 1900-1916;* and Robert Sklar, ed., *The Plastic Age: 1917-1930.*

Another collective effort, *The Development of an American Culture* (1970), edited by Stanley Coban and Lorman Ratner, contains a number of valuable essays more in the traditions of intellectual history than of cultural history as I have defined it. There are more useful approaches to cultural history in a collection not specifically devoted to it, Barton J. Bernstein, eds., *Towards a New Past: Dissenting Essays in American History* (1968), especially essays by Jesse Lemisch, Staughton Lynd, Michael A. Lebowitz, Eugene D. Genovese, and Stephan Thernstrom. Finally, in a series of history texts Robert Wiebe's *The Search for Order: 1877-1920* (1967) makes an impressive effort to build a general history of his period on the foundation of a whole cultural history, relating politics, economics, diplomacy, and ideas to an interpretation of social structure and cultural consciousness.

Impressive Period Studies

In recent years historians of the American colonial era have been particularly successful in moving toward an understanding of their period of culture as a whole. The masterful intellectual histories of Perry Miller have served as their foundation for investigating how theology and idealogy were embodied in family and social structures, work and play. Edmund Morgan's *The Puritan Family* (1944) was the first and still one of the most valuable of these studies. More recently Richard L. Bushman has written an important study of social change, *Puritan to Yankee: Character and Social Order in Connecticut, 1690-1765* (1967), and there have been several innovations of social structure in New England towns, including Darrett Rutman's *Winthrop's Boston* (1965), John Demos' *A Little Commonwealth: Family Life in Plymouth Colony* (1970), and Kenneth Lockridge's *A New England Town: The First Hundred Years* (1970), on Dedham, Massachusetts. One of the most suggestive works bringing social science perspectives to bear on early American culture in Kai T. Erikson, *Wayward Puritans: A Study in the Sociology of Deviance* (1966). Race in early American culture is broadly and impressively discussed in Winthrop D. Jordan *White Over Black: American Attitudes Toward the Negro, 1550-1812* (1968).

For the nineteenth century, William R. Taylor's *Cavalier and Yankee: The Old South and the American National Character* (1961) remains a valuable effort to relate the myth and symbol method of cultural analysis more directly to social behavior and institutions. In his posthumously published *The Life of the Mind in America, From the Revolution to the Civil War* (1965), and particularly in his discussion of the legal system, Perry Miller demonstrated his extraordinary skill at extracting meanings for the whole culture out of materials generally overlooked by culture historians. Recent important works on the slave system and its role in creating consciousness and social conflict include Eugene D. Genovese's *The Political Economy of Slavery: Studies in the Economy and Society of the Slave South* (1965) and Aileen Kraditor's *Means and Ends in American Abolitionism: Garrison and His Critics on Strategy and Tactics* (1967). For literary studies, the culmination of the effort to elucidate the mythic structure of American literature came in Leslie A. Fiedler's *Love and Death in the American Novel* (1960), a work which does not speak directly about society but constantly offers suggestive hypotheses about the roots of social behavior. Since Fiedler the most significant study of American Literature I know of is Richard Poirier's *A World Elsewhere: The Place of Style in American Literature* (1966), a work which illuminates the forging of styles out of fundamental social perceptions. Among recent studies of American expansion in the nineteenth century, William Appleman Williams' *The Roots of the Modern American Empire: A Study of the Growth and Shaping of Social Consciousness in a Marketplace Society* (1969) is a major effort to relate foreign policies to cultural perceptions and ideologies.

Studies in twentieth-century cultural history have so far lacked a firm grasp on the nature of social structure and social change in mass technological societies. Many of the most illuminating books have been philosophical or polemical works which have reported on or helped to shape the cultural transformations of the 1960s—among them Herbert Marcuse's *One-Dimensional Man: Studies in the Ideology of Advanced Industrial Society* (1964, Marshall McLuhan's *Understanding Media: The Extensions of Man* (1964), and Theodore Roszak's *The*

Making of a Counter Culture: Reflections on the Technocratic Society and its Youthful Opposition (1969). One could list a great many valuable specialized studies on aspects of twentieth-century culture and society, but scholars, teachers, and students in cultural history still require broader and more unifying perspectives. Besides Marcuse, McLuhan, and Roszak, recent works which provide important insights into twentieth-century cultural transformations include Elting E. Morison, *Men, Machines, and Modern Times* (1966), Kenneth F. Boulding, *The Meaning of the Twentieth Century* (1964), John Kenneth Galbraith, *The New Industrial State* (1967), Paul A. Baran and Paul M. Sweezy, *Monopoly Capital: An Essay on the American Economic and Social Order* (1966), and Lewis Mumford, *The Myth of the Machine: Technics and Human Development* (1967) and *The Pentagon of Power: The Myth of the Machine, V. II* (1970).

And what of the future? Given the difficulties of coming to grips with the present, is it likely that cultural historians, or the American Studies movement more broadly conceived, can provide useful knowledge and insights to the public debates over the future course of American society and culture? We have produced no Norman O. Brown or Buckminister Fuller to offer provocative insights into the nature of human civilization or the destiny of Spaceship Earth. Yet as Kenneth Boulding has written, "We can grow in knowledge and begin to apply the human mind to the critique of the *ends* of man and his social systems, just as we can to the improvement of *means*. . . . As our power increases, the question of *what* we want to do with it acquires overriding importance." For those of us in American Studies and cultural history who have taken on the task of understanding the ends, the desires, the social systems of American men and women past, present, and future, the responsibility—and the opportunity—seem abundantly clear.

A Bibliography of Religious History in Its American Setting

by Sydney E. Ahlstrom

The historiography on religion in America reached classic stature almost from the first and continued to be important in every subsequent period, though it was often marked by a strong polemical spirit. For similar reasons the greater part of American intellectual history, including philosophy, has been pervaded by religious or theological concerns. During the nineteenth century the historiography begins to exhibit a more critical spirit, though only in the twentieth century do any great number of historians break out of denominational or Protestant channels.

Author's Note: The books listed here are by express intention overwhelmingly available in paper editions. Because all are deemed to be of very considerable significance for present-day interpretation, space has been saved by giving the original date of publication in brackets, and by omitting (usually) the name of the original publisher. Many of the works are published in paper edition at the outset. Works which are at present available only in hardcover are marked **. Because paper editions constantly become or cease to be available, readers should regularly consult Paperback Books in Print, published semi-annually by R. R. Bowker Co., 1180 Sixth Avenue, New York, 10036. It also gives the full name and address of each publisher. The following abbreviations of frequently-cited publishers are used: BM–Bobbs-Merrill; Chic–Chicago University Press; Col–Columbia University Press; Cr–Crowell; Doub–Doubleday and Co.; G&D–Grosset & Dunlap; Ginn–Ginn-Blaisdell; HBJ–Harcourt, Brace, Jovanovich; HM–Houghton-Mifflin; H&R–Harper & Row; HR&W–Holt, Rinehart, and Winston; H&W–Hill and Wang; LB&P–Little, Brown, and Price; Max–Macmillan; Mich–University of Michigan Press; NAL–New American Library; NCUP–North Carolina University Press; Oxf–Oxford University Press; PH–Prentice-Hall; PUP–Princeton University Press; Quad–Quadrangle Books; Ran–Random House; Ron–Ronald Press; and U.P.-following a name, University Press.

Especially notable among the early colonial works are the *History of Plymouth Colony* by Governor Wm. Bradford (1590–1657), which was not published until 1856 (modern version, Ran.**); and Cotton Mather's *Magnalia Christi Americana* [1702], soon to appear in a new critical edition (Harvard U.P.**). Standing between these early works and the emergence of a more objective tradition is Robert Baird's *Religion in America* [1844], which provides a broad synoptic account, though from a fervently Protestant viewpoint (critical abridgment, H. W. Bowden, ed., H&R). More impressive examples of the 19th-century historical revival are Francis Parkman's multi-volume account of the rivalry of France and England in North America, and George Bancroft's equally large *History of the United States to 1789* [Boston, 1852], both of which deal extensively with religious subjects. Documenting the historiographical situation as of the 1890's is the 13-volume *American Church History Series*, Philip Schaff, gen. ed., which contains denominational histories, a general history, large bibliographies, and a survey of the churches at the century's end (out of print).

During the last three or four decades, however, the historiography of religion in America experienced a very noticeable renaissance. The reason for this heightened interest lies, no doubt, in a growing awareness that a people's moral and spiritual development, as well as its religious thought, is essential to an understanding of even such seemingly remote topics as party politics and foreign policy. This awareness, moreover, has had the effect of attracting historians from outside the traditional circle of "church historians" who often saw history chiefly as a means for the upbuilding or defense of their own tradition. A final factor has been a growing conviction that the values and animating concerns of most national leaders as well as the great movements and experiences of a country have many important and inescapable religious dimensions. In any event, it must be said at the outset that the bibliography that follows has been compiled with these comprehensive notions of religious history in mind. The great majority of the works listed were written or edited in the last 10 or 15

Mr. Ahlstrom is Professor of Modern Church History and American History, and Director of Graduate Studies in the Department of Religious Studies, at Yale University, New Haven. From 1967 to 1971 he was Chairman of Yale's American Studies Program. He has served as a Fulbright lecturer to the University of Strasbourg and to the Kyoto American Studies Seminar, and has been a faculty member of the Salzburg Seminar in American Studies. Mr. Ahlstrom's many publications include Theology in America, "The Puritan Ethic and the Spirit of American Democracy," The Shaping of American Religion, The American Protestant Encounter With World Religion, *and* Continental Influence on American Christian Thought. *His most recent book,* A Religious History of the American People, *was published in 1972 by Yale University Press.*

Yale News Bureau

years, and nearly all of them provide extensive bibliographical guidance to the problems they address.

General Surveys of Religion

The most complete and helpful bibliography of religion in America is by Nelson R. Burr, in the last two volumes of James W. Smith and A. Leland Jamison, eds., *Religion in American Life*, 4 vols. [PUP**, 1961]. This series also contains two volumes of important essays on American religion, theology, and philosophy. The best recent survey is Winthrop S. Hudson, *Religion in America* [Scribner, 1965]. Robert T. Handy *et al* have edited a large collection of documents, *American Christianity*, 2 vols. [Scribner**, 1960] which is almost indispensable for those who lack large library resources. Also invaluable is Edwin S. Gaustad's *Historical Atlas of Religion in America* [H&R**, 1962], as is his brief and well-illustrated *Religious History of America* (H&R**). Sydney E. Ahlstrom's *A Religious History of the American People* [Yale U.P.**, 1972] is the most comprehensive account, and contains a 35-page bibliography. Robert T. Handy's recent *A Christian America* [Oxf**, 1971] is a valuable and well-annotated survey of Protestant efforts to win and transform the U.S.A. Two extremely useful collections of documents on American religious history, both with a strong Protestant emphasis, are Edwin S. Gaustad, ed., *Religious Issues in American History* (H&R) [1968] and Robert L. Ferm, ed., *Issues in American Protestantism* (Doub-Anchor) [1969]. For information on nearly all American churches, see Frank S. Mead, *Handbook of Denominations in the U.S.* (Abingdon, 4th ed.) [1965] and F. E. Mayer, *Religious Bodies of America* (Concordia) [1956].

Specific Traditions

Among the best accounts of specific traditions are Nathan Glazer, *American Judaism* (Chic) [1957]; Franklin E. Frazier, *The Negro Church in America* (Schocken) [1949]; Martin E. Marty, *Righteous Empire: The Protestant Experience in America* (Dial) [1970]; Sydney E. Ahlstrom, *Theology in America: The Major Protestant Voices from Puritanism to Neo-orthodoxy* (BM) [1967]; Sidney E. Mead, *The Lively Experiment* [H&R**, 1963]; Andrew M. Greeley, *The Catholic Experience* (Doub-Image) [1967]; and two works by John Tracy Ellis: *American Catholicism* (Chic, 1969 ed.) [1956], and *Catholics in Colonial America* [Helicon**, 1965]. On large denominations often slighted in general surveys, see William W. Manross, *The Episcopal Church in America* [AMS**, 1950], and A. R. Wentz, *A Basic History of Lutheranism in America* [Fortress**, 1955].

On two widely known movements that are often, and with much justice, seen as distinctive American contributions to world religion, see Thomas O'Dea, *The Mormons* (Chic) [1957]; Fawn Brodie, *No Man Knows My History* (Ran) [1935], a biography of Joseph Smith, the founder of the Church of Jesus Christ of Latter-Day Saints; Robert Peel, *Mary Baker Eddy* 2 vols. [HR&W**, Vol. 1, 1966; Vol. 2, 1971] and Edwin F. Dakin, *Mrs. Eddy* (G&D) [1930]. See also Charles Braden's *Spirits in Rebellion* [Southern Methodist U.P.** 1963] on related religious movements.

On four vigorous streams of Protestant emphasis that have developed with special force in the U.S. and been extended to all parts of the world see: John T. Nichol, *Pentecostalism* (H&R) [1966]; Marley Cole, *Jehovah's Witnesses* [Vantage** 1955]; C. Norman Kraus, *Dispensationalism in America* [John Knox** 1958]; Donald Meyer, *The Positive Thinkers from Mary Baker Eddy to Norman Vincent Peale* (Doub-Anchor) [1965].

For interesting comparisons see H. H. Walsh, *The Christian Church in Canada* [Toronto: Ryerson Press, 1956**].

Important enough to be singled out as a separate tradition is the American form of "civil religion," which has gradually developed since early Puritan times. Among many works on this powerful stream of American patriotic piety see especially: Conrad Cherry, *God's New Israel* (PH) [1971]; Winthrop Hudson, *Nationalism and Religion in America* (H&R) [1970]; Ernest L. Tuveson, *Redeemer Nation* [Chic** 1968]; Elwyn A. Smith, *The Religion of the Republic* [Fortress** 1970]; R. W. B. Lewis, *The American Adam* (Chic) [1955]; and Henry Nash Smith, *Virgin Land* (Ran) [1957] and Paul C. Nagel's two works, *One Nation Indivisible* [Oxf** 1964] and *This Sacred Trust* [Oxf** 1971].

Intellectual History and the History of Philosophy

On American philosophy the most comprehensive and bibliographically valuable general account is Herbert W. Schneider's *History of American Philosophy* [Col** 1963], with its companion volume, Joseph L. Blau, ed., *American Philosophical Addresses* [Col** 1946], both of which give large place to religious thinkers. Morton White, *Science and Sentiment in America* [Oxf** 1972] is a major recent interpretation. More technical, and with strong emphasis on the last century is William H. Werkmeister, *History of Philosophical Ideas in America* [Ron** 1949]. Available in paper editions are Joseph L. Blau, *Men and Movements in American Philosophy* (PH) [1952]; Morris R. Cohen, *American Thought: A Critical Sketch* (Mac) [1954]; Robert Roth, *American Religious Philosophy* (HBJ) [1967]; Robert C. Whittemore, *Makers of the American Mind* (Apollo) [1964]; Wm. H. Marnell, *Man-Made Morals: Four Philosophies That Shaped America* (Doub-Anchor) [1966]; and Paul K. Conkin, *Puritanism to Pragmatism* (Dodd, Mead) [1968]. Among a fair number of anthologies of American philosophic thought are Walter G. Muelder and L. Sears, eds., *The Development of American Philosophy* [HM** 1960]; and Max H. Fisch, *Classic American Philosophers* (Appleton) [1961].

The major intellectual histories are Merle Curti, *The Growth of American Thought* [H&R** 1943]; Ralph H. Gabriel, *The Course of American Democratic Thought* [Ron** 1940]; and Stow Persons, *American Minds* (HR&W) [1958]. Cushing Stout, ed., *Intellectual History in America*, 2 vols. (H&R) [1968] contains a valuable collection of interpretive essays. Among several excellent one-volume United States histories are John Blum *et al*, *The National Experience* [HBJ** 1963]; T. C. Cochran *et al*, *The Democratic Experience* (Scott Foresman) [1968]; and Carl N. Degler, *Out of Our Past* (H&R) [1959].

Also surveying the whole range of American history in ways of special relevance for religious and intellectual history are David B. Davis, ed., *Fear of Conspiracy* [Cornell U.P.** 1971]; Richard Hofstadter, *Anti-Intellectualism in America* (Ran) [1964]; and Thomas F. Gossett, *Race: The History of an Idea in*

America (S. Methodist U.P.) [1963]. Still very useful on changing cultural conditions, including religion, is Arthur M. Schlesinger and D. R. Fox, *A History of American Life*, 13 vols. (reprint ed., Quad) [1950]. Invaluable on nearly all phases of American thinking is the very large *American Heritage Series*, Leonard Levy, gen. ed. (BM).

The Reformation and the Puritan Background

Very basic in shaping the character of American moral and religious history is the Anglo-American Puritan movement, which has also received the most intensive study of all fields in American history. The European background is surveyed by Roland H. Bainton, *The Reformation of the 16th Century* (Beacon) [1952]; Harold J. Grimm, *The Reformation Era* [Mac** 1954]; John T. McNeill, *The Nature and History of Calvinism* (Oxf) [1954]; Conrad Bergendoff, *The Lutheran Tradition* [Concordia** 1967]; and Max Weber, *The Protestant Ethic and the Rise of Capitalism* (Scribner) [1930].

On Puritanism see Alan Simpson, *Puritanism in Old and New England* (Chic) [1955]; Darrett B. Rutman, *American Puritanism* (Lippincott) [1970]; Wm. B. Haller, *The Rise of Puritanism* (H&R) [1938]; Perry Miller, *Errand Into the Wilderness* (H&R) [1956] and *Orthodoxy in Massachusetts* (H&R) [1934]; Edmund S. Morgan, *Visible Saints* (Cornell U.P.) [1965], *Roger Williams: The Church and the State* (HBJ) [1967] and *The Puritan Dilemma* (LB&P) [1958].

The following collections of primary and/or secondary literature on Puritanism are very fine: Perry Miller & Thomas H. Johnson, eds., *The Puritans*, 2 vols. (H&R) [1938]; Williston Walker, ed., *Creeds and Platforms of Congregationalism* (Pilgrim) [1893]; Alden T. Vaughan, ed., *The Puritan Tradition in America, 1620-1730* (H&R) [1972]; David D. Hall, ed., *Puritanism in 17th Century Massachusetts* (HR&W) [1968]; Richard Reinitz, *Tensions in American Puritanism* (Wiley) [1970]. See also Hugh Barbour, *The Quakers in Puritan England* [Yale U.P.** 1964]; Rufus Jones, *The Quakers in the American Colonies* (Norton) [1911]; and Catherine O. Peare, *William Penn* (Mich) [1968]. Of obvious importance are the most widely read Puritan authors: George Fox, *Journal* (Putnam); John Bunyan, *Pilgrim's Progress* (HM); and John Milton *Selected Works* (Doub-Anchor).

The Great Awakening in Colonial America

The colonial religious revival of the 18th century was largely a continuation of Puritan history, and it has likewise received much scholarly attention. Among major accounts see Edwin S. Gaustad, *The Great Awakening in New England* (H&R) [1957]; Charles H. Maxson, *The Great Awakening in the Middle Colonies* [Peter Smith** 1958]; Wesley M. Gewehr, *The Great Awakening in Virginia* [Peter Smith** 1930]; and C. C. Goen, *Revivalism and Separatism in New England* (Yale U.P.) [1962]. James B. Tanis, *Life of T. J. Frelinghuysen* [J. Nijhoff, Netherlands** 1968] provides a vital insight into the Dutch contribution as does Ernst Stoeffler, *The Rise of Evangelical Pietism* [Leiden, Holland: Brill** 1965]. See also the following: Darrett Rutman, ed., *The Great Awakening: Event and Exegesis* (Wiley) [1970]; Perry Miller and Alan Heimart, eds., *The Great Awakening*, (BM) [1966]; and David S. Lovejoy, ed., *Religious Enthusiasm and The Great Awakening* (PH) [1969].

The first major philosophical figure in American history is Jonathan Edwards, who was also an active participant in the Great Awakening. On Edwards see Ola Winslow's biography (Collier) [1941] and her volume of selections (NAL) [1966], as well as the following important studies of his thought: Conrad Cherry, *The Theology of Jonathan Edwards* (Anchor) [1966] and Edward H. Davidson, *Jonathan Edwards* (Mac) [1966]. David Levin has edited a fine *Profile* (H&W) [1969], while Clarence H. Faust and Thomas H. Johnson have compiled the best book of *Representative Selections* (H&W) [1962]. Editions of various individual works are also available in paperback. Many editions of Edwards' *Works* have appeared over the years, the best being that of Sereno Dwight (10 vols.) [1822] and the Worcester or New York editions (4 vols.) [1843]. The first four volumes of a new Yale U.P. edition are in print.

The Enlightenment and the Revolutionary Era

In *The Puritan Mind* (Mich) [1958], Herbert Schneider traces various movements of thought down to the Revolutionary generation, as does Gerald R. Cragg in *From Puritanism to the Age of Reason* (Cambridge U.P.) [1966] for the Anglican tradition. In *Religion and the American Mind from the Great Awakening to the Revolution* [Harvard U.P.** 1966] Alan Heimert stresses the link between the revivals and the Revolution. Bernard Bailyn's *The Ideological Origins of the American Revolution* [Harvard U.P.** 1967] is a masterful study. Documents illustrating these trends have been edited by Peter N. Carroll, *Religion and the Coming of the Revolution* (Ginn) [1967]; Cedric Cowing, ed., *The Great Awakening and the Revolution* (Rand-McNally) [1971]; and Merrill Jensen, ed., *Tracts of the American Revolution* (BM) [1966]. Carl Bridenbaugh stresses the fear of Anglican episcopacy as a cause of the Revolution in *Mitre and Sceptre* (Oxf) [1962].

On the nature and impact of the Revolution as well as its religious dimensions see Gordon Wood, *The Creation of the American Republic* (NCUP) [1970]; Edmund S. Morgan, ed., *The American Revolution: Two Centuries of Interpretation* (PH) [1965]; John R. Howe, ed., *The Role of Ideology in the American Revolution* (H&R) [1970]; Daniel Boorstin, *The Lost World of Thomas Jefferson* (Beacon) [1948]; Robert R. Palmer, *The Age of the Democratic Revolutions*, 2 vols. (PUP) [vol. 1, 1969; vol. 2, 1970]; Peter Gay, *The Enlightenment: The Rise of Modern Paganism* (Knopf) [1966]; and Ernest Cassirer, *The Philosophy of the Enlightment* (Beacon) [1951]. In this same context see Conrad Wright, *The Beginnings of Unitarianism* (Beacon) [1955]. On the nation's founders as thinkers see Alfred O. Aldridge, *Benjamin Franklin and Nature's God* [Duke U.P.** 1967]; Gilbert Chinard, *Thomas Jefferson* (Mich) [1926]; Neil Riemer, ed., *James Madison* (Washington Square) [1968]; Zoltan Haraszti, *John Adams* (Harvard U.P.) [1952]; and Carl L. Becker, *The Declaration of Independence* (Ran) [1922].

Ante-Bellum Protestantism

The period 1800–1860 was a time of maximum cultural influence for the evangelical Protestant tradition, with revivalism as its major strategy and voluntary associations as its chief mode for reforming American society, though it maintained itself as a strong majoritarian movement down to the 1920s, and to a lesser degree even to the 1960s. Surveying this broad movement are Robert T.

Handy, *A Christian America* [Oxf** 1971]; Bernard A. Weisberger, *They Gathered at the River* (Quad) [1966], a history of revivalism; Wm. G. McLoughlin, *Modern Revivalism* [Ron** 1959], as well as his *Isaac Backus and the American Pietistic Tradition* (LB&P) [1967], and his anthology of documents, *The American Evangelicals* (H&R) [1968]. On the ante-bellum evangelicals see Timothy L. Smith, *Revivalism and Social Reform* (H&R) [1957]; Clifford S. Griffin, *Their Brothers Keeper* [Rutgers U.P.** 1960] as well as his *Ferment of Reform* (Cr) [1967], a survey of books and issues; and Charles I. Foster, *Errand of Mercy: The Evangelical United Front* [NCUP** 1960].

On nativism and anti-Catholicism to 1860, see Ray Allen Billington, *The Protestant Crusade* (Quad) [1938]. Alice F. Tyler, *Freedom's Ferment* (H&R) [1944] is an especially comprehensive survey of evangelicalism and reform. Marvin Meyers, *The Jacksonian Persuasion* (Stanford U.P.) [1957] and John W. Ward, *Andrew Jackson: Symbol of an Age* (Oxf) [1962] illuminate the "secular" ethos of the age, though the next section on the South, slavery, abolitionism, and the Civil War deals with the nation's primary moral dilemma during this period. On the culture of the early national period three French observers have given important accounts: G. Jean de Crèvecoeur, *Letters of an American Farmer* (Penguin) [1782]; Michel Chevalier, *Society, Manners and Politics in the United States* (Doub-Anchor) [1839]; and most famous of all, Alexis de Toqueville, *Democracy in America*, 2 vols. (Schocken) [vol. 1, 1835; vol. 2, 1840].

Sectional Conflict and the Civil War

The disruption of the Union over slavery is the central event in the moral and spiritual history of the American people, not only because it led to a devastating civil war, but because it fully exposed the paradox of racist oppression and democratic egalitarian ideals. If isolated from this "American dilemma" the country's history will remain an insoluable conundrum.

On the transmission of this problem from Europe and Africa to the Americas see David B. Davis, *The Problem of Slavery in Western Culture* (Cornell U.P.) [1966]; Winthrop Jordan, *White Over Black* (Penguin) [1968]; and Basil Davidson, *The African Slave Trade* (LB&P) [1961]. On the institutionalization of slavery and the molding of a "slavocracy" in the South see three excellent collections of interpretive writing: Allen Weinstein and Frank O. Gatell, eds., *American Negro Slavery* (Oxf) [1968]; Monroe J. Billington, *The South* (HR&W) [1969]; and Edwin C. Rozwenc, *The Causes of the American Civil War* (Heath) [1961]. Among many important monographs on the South are Eugene Genovese, *The Political Economy of Slavery* (Ran) [1965]; Kenneth M. Stampp, *The Peculiar Institution* (Ran) [1956]; Wilbur J. Cash, *The Mind of the South* (Doub-Anchor) [1950]; Frederick L. Olmsted's pre-war observations, *The Slave States*, H. Wish, ed. (Putnam) [1856]; Donald G. Mathews, *Methodism and Slavery* [PUP** 1965]; James M. Silver, *Confederate Morale and Church Propaganda* (Norton) [1967]; Samuel S. Hill, *Southern Churches in Crisis* (Beacon) [1968]; and Harriet Beecher Stowe's classic protest novel of 1852, *Uncle Tom's Cabin* (NAL, H&R, *et al*).

On the anti-slavery movement see Louis Filler, *The Crusade Against Slavery* (H&R) [1960]; Dwight L. Dumond, *Antislavery* (Norton) [1961]; Gilbert H. Barnes, *The Anti-Slavery Impulse* (HB) [1957]; Aileen S. Kraditor, *Means and Ends in American Abolitionism* (Ran) [1969]; and Martin S. Duberman, ed., *The Anti-Slavery Vanguard* (PUP) [1965].

On the War and Reconstruction see Kenneth M. Stampp, *And The War Came* (Chic) [1950], and his *The Era of Reconstruction* (Ran) [1965]; J. G. Randall and D. Donald, *The Civil War and Reconstruction* [Heath** 1961]; Charles Crowe's fine collection of essays, *The Age of Civil War and Reconstruction, 1830–1900* (Dorsey) [1966]; Thomas J. Pressley, *Americans Interpret Their Civil War* (Mac) [1965]; George M. Fredrickson, *The Inner Civil War* (H&R) [1965]; and Wm. J. Wolf, *The Religion of Abraham Lincoln* (Pilgrim) [1963].

Black Religion Since 1865

For a full century after Emancipation the churches have been the chief institutional channel for the maintenance of the Afro-American tradition. E. Franklin Frazier, *The Negro Church in America* (Schocken) [1964] is a succinct survey; but see also W. E. B. DuBois, *The Souls of Black Folk* (Fawcett) [1903]; Benjamin E. Mays, *The Negro's God* (Atheneum) [1938]; August Meier, *Negro Thought in America* (Mich) [1963]; and two anthologies edited by August Meier *et al*, *Black Nationalism in America* (BM) [1971] and *Negro Protest Thought in the 20th Century* (BM) [1971]; Arthur H. Fauset, *Black Gods of the Metropolis* (Penn. U.P.) [1944]; E. U. Essien-Udom, *Black Nationalism* (Dell) [1962] on the Black Muslims; James H. Cone, *Black Theology and Black Power* (Seabury) [1969]; *The Autobiography of Malcolm X* (Grove) [1965]; S. P. Fullinwider, *The Mind and Mood of Black America* (Dorsey) [1969]; and H. M. Nelsen *et al* eds., *The Black Church in America* [Basic Bks** 1971].

Clifton H. Johnson, Ed., *God Struck Me Dead* (Pilgrim) [1969] contains conversion accounts of ex-slaves. The following biographies and autobiographies of great black leaders are valuable: Booker T. Washington, *Up From Slavery* (Bantam) [1933]; Samuel R. Spencer, *Booker T. Washington* (LB&P) [1955]; W. E. B. DuBois, *Dusk of Dawn* (Schocken) [1940]; Elliott M. Rudwick, *W. E. B. DuBois* (Atheneum) [1969]; William Miller, *Martin Luther King* (Avon) [1968]; and Martin L. King, Jr.'s *The Strength to Love* (Pocket Books) [1963] which contains sermons and an autobiographical account.

From the Gilded Age to World War I

As efforts to "reconstruct" the South passed into history the nation faced many new social problems. Outstanding on the social and governmental background is Robert H. Wiebe's *The Search for Order* (H&W) [1966]. Perry Miller's thoughtful anthology, *American Thought: The Civil War to World War I* (HR&W) [1954], illustrates the age's diverse intellectual currents, while Henry S. Commager's *The American Mind* (Yale U.P.) [1950] sets these thinkers in their historical context. See also Paul Carter, *The Spiritual Crisis of the Gilded Age* [Northern Illinois U.P.** 1971].

In the new industrial and urban world which began to emerge in the North, a new movement of Protestant social reform arose on the foundations supplied by the country's Puritan heritage, pre–war reform activities, and the anti-slavery crusade. This Social Gospel movement is surveyed in two excellent works: Henry F. May, *Protestant Churches and Industrial America* (H&R) [1963], and Charles H. Hopkins, *The Rise of the Social Gospel in American Protestantism* (Yale U.P.) [1940]. This movement, however, is part of a larger "liberal movement" in theology which is, in fact, a major feature of the entire century's religious intellectualism. The union of liberalism and social concern is illustrated in W. J. Rauschenbush's classic of 1907, *Christianity and the Social Crisis* (H&R).

The Rise of Religious Liberalism—1700-1900

Liberal religion began to emerge in America as the Puritan impulse lost its primal vitality. One sees it emerging in the thought of the foremost Puritan spokesman, Cotton Mather, a selection of whose works has been edited by Kenneth B. Murdock (Hafner) [1960]. Jonathan Edwards represents another modernizing phase (see above). Joseph Haroutunian has given a brilliant account of the way Edward's followers advanced the process of liberalization in his *Piety Versus Moralism* (H&R, Intro. by S. E. Ahlstrom) [1964]. On the background for this trend see the works on the Enlightenment and the Founding Fathers listed above.

More obvious was the rise of Unitarianism, whose full philosophic development is treated in Daniel W. Howe's *The Unitarian Conscience* [Harvard** 1970]. Within this movement, however, transcendentalism and other forms of romantic modernism arose. They are described or excellently anthologized in Octavius B. Frothingham, *Transcendentalism in New England* (Penn U.P., introduction with bibliography by S. E. Ahlstrom) [1876]; Perry Miller, ed., *The Transcendentalists* (Harvard U.P.) [1950]; as well as his *The American Transcendentalists* (Doub-Anchor) [1957]; and George Hochfield, ed., *Selected Writings of the American Transcendentalists* (NAL). In the widely available poetic and fictional works of the most widely-read literary figures of the period one sees other aspects of this impulse (see works on and by Emerson, Thoreau, Melville, Hawthorne, Whitman, Dickinson, Longfellow, Lowell, Whittier, Bryant, *et al.*).

The real father of Protestant liberalism was Horace Bushnell, whose *Christian Nurture* is available in paperback (Yale U.P.) [1888]. Barbara Cross' *Horace Bushnell* [Chic** 1958] is the most recent critical biography. Contributing to this trend were controversial developments in science and scholarship: the new geology, evolutionary biology, biblical criticism and the historical study of world religions. See Charles C. Gillispie, *Genesis and Geology* (H&R) [1951], even though it deals primarily with Britain; J. W. Brown, *The Rise of Biblical Criticism in America* [Wesleyan U.P.** 1969]; John C. Greene, *The Death of Adam* (NAL) [1959], and his *Darwin and the Modern World View* (NAL) [1961]; Richard Hofstadter, *Social Darwinism* (Beacon) [1955]; and Phillip Wiener, *Evolution and the Founders of Pragmatism* [Harvard U.P.** 1949]. For selections from the ensuing debates see George Daniels, ed., *Darwinism Comes to America* (Ginn) [1969], and R. Jackson Wilson, *Darwinism and the American Intellectual* (Dorsey) [1970]. Kenneth Cauthen, *The Impact of Liberalism* [H&R** 1962] is the best study of the new theology. W. R. Hutchinson, ed., *American Protestant Thought: The Liberal Era* [1968] (H&R) (out of print) is the most satisfactory anthology.

The Golden Age of American Philosophy—1875-1930

Because theology inescapably deals with virtually all of the major concerns of philosophy the two disciplines are always closely related; and during the later 19th century this inter–relationship became especially close, with the religious philosophies of William James and Rosiah Royce becoming especially relevant. For the best overview of this period when philosophers moved strongly into American academic life see John E. Smith, *The Spirit of American Philosophy* (Oxf) [1966]. Ralph B. Perry, *The Thought and Character of William James*, 2 vols. [LB** 1936] is a classic work on the man and his contemporaries. Another angle of vision is provided by R. C. Lyon, ed., *Santayana on America* (HBJ), [1968] and several anthologies, of which Amelie Rorty's *Pragmatic Philosophy* (Doub-Anchor) [1966] is perhaps the most comprehensive, though it under-estimates the significance of the idealists, especially Josiah Royce. Morton White's *Social Thought in America* (Beacon) [1957] treats the "revolt against formalism" in an important group of the period's social thinkers; paperback editions of works by James, Royce, Peirce, Dewey, and Mead are in print. See also Henry A. Pochmann, *German Culture in America* (Wisconsin U.P.) [1953]; Loyd Easton, *Hegel's First American Followers* [Ohio U.P.** 1966]; James H. Nichols, *Romanticism in American Theology* [Chic** 1961] as well as his an-thology of writings by Philip Schaff and J. W. Nevin, *The Mercersburg Theology* [Oxf** 1966]. On trends of the 20th century see the general histories of American philosophy cited above, and Yervant H. Krikorian, *Naturalism and the Human Spirit* [Col** 1944].

Immigration and Group Conflict

The United States, of course, is a nation of immigrants, and the cumulative, collective trauma of that experience, plus the added unsettlement caused by constant internal migration, constitutes a major factor in the shaping of Ameri-can religion, as well as the national character. This *Völkerwanderung*, probably the greatest in world history, has been surveyed by Carl Wittke in *We Who Built America* (W. Reserve U.P.) [rev. ed. 1964]; Marcus L. Hansen, *The Atlantic Migration* (H&R) [1951]; and Oscar Handlin, *The Uprooted* (G&D) [1952]. Pre-Civil War ethnic conflict is considered in R. A. Billington, *The Protestant Crusade* (Quad) [1938], and the period since 1865 in John Higham, *Strangers in the Land* (Atheneum) [1955].

Notable with regard to late 19th century Catholicism are two accounts of the grappling of the Roman Catholic Church with American conditions: Thomas T. McAvoy, *The Great Crisis in American Catholic History* (Notre Dame; una-bridged) [Regnery** 1957]; and Robert Cross, *The Emergence of Liberal Catholicism in America* (Quad) [1958]. The emergence of Catholic social con-cern in the 20th century is ably studied in Aaron I. Abell, *American Catholicism and Social Action* [Hanover** 1960], and David J. O'Brien, *American Catholi-cism and Social Reform* [Oxf** 1968], as well as Philip Gleason's book *The Conservative Reformers* [Notre Dame U.P.** 1968] on German-American Catholics.

The most valuable interpretations of Jewish adaptations are sociological in character: Louis Wirth, *The Ghetto* (Chic) [1928]; Marshall Sklare, *Conservative Judaism: A Modern Religious Movement* [Free** 1972]; and Will Herberg, *Prot-estant, Catholic, Jew* (Doub–Anchor) [1955], which carries the narrative of America's three great faiths down to the 1950s. Daniel Moynihan and Nathan Glazer in *Beyond the Melting Pot* (MIT U.P.) [1970] carry the matter down another decade when the "melting pot" theory of acculturation was being widely questioned.

Protestant Conflict and the Rise of Fundamentalism 1875-1940

The trend to modern appropriations of science, scholarship, critical philoso-phy, and social reform, as well as the routinization and *embourgeoisement* of religious life, led to the rise of sectarianism and other forms of dissent. During the past century controversy and schism have tended to make the conservative-liberal rift fundamental to American Protestantism. The old "evangelical united front" of pre-Civil War days gradually collapsed, with the members of the Federal Council of Churches (1908) constituting the "progressive" or cooperative group, and the National Association of Evangelicals (1941) the "fundamentalist" or "Evangelical" party.

Conservative Protestantism and the emergence of various distinct religious impulses that have made a great impact with their active missionary efforts abroad are considered in the following volumes: Ernest H. Sandeen, *Towards a Historical Interpretation of Fundamentalism* (Fortress) [1968]; Ernest R. Sandeen, *Roots of Fundamentalism* (Chic) [1970]; John L. Peters, *American Methodism and Christian Perfection* [Abingdon** 1956]; John T. Nichol, *Pentacostalism* (H&R) [1966]; C. Norman Kraus, *Dispensationalism in America* [John Knox** 1958]; Marley Cole, *Jehovah's Witnesses* [Vantage** 1955]; Norman F. Furniss, *The Fundamentalist Controversy, 1918-1930* (Shoe String) [1954]; Louis Gasper, *The Fundamentalist Movement Since 1930* [Humanities** 1963]; and J. Gresham Machen's "classic" attack on liberalism, *Christianity and Liberalism* (Eerdman's) [1923]. The Fundamentalist controversy is surveyed by Gail Kennedy, ed., *Evolution and Religion* (DC Heath) [1956]. The best account of the 20th-century controversy is Williard B. Gatewood, *Controversy in the Twenties* [Vanderbilt** 1969], but see also Ray Ginger, *Six Days or Forever* (Quad) [1958], on the same events. Closely related are Andrew Sinclair's *Era of Excess* (H&R) [1962] and Jos. R. Gusfield, *Symbolic Crusade: Status Politics and the American Temperance Movement* (Illinois U.P.) [1963] on the prohibition movement.

Toward Post-Protestant America: 1920-1970s

The impact of the wars of 1898 and 1914, the "boom" of the Twenties, followed by the Depression, the New Deal, and World War II have obviously had enormous consequences for religion, though only certain major works can be mentioned, more or less in the chronological order of the periods they treat: K. M. MacKenzie, *The Robe and the Sword* [Public Affairs** 1961] on Methodism and the War with Spain; Ray Abrams, *Preachers Present Arms* [Herald** 1933] on World War I; Frederick L. Allen, *Only Yesterday* (Bantum) [1931] on the twenties and *Since Yesterday* (Bantam) [1940] on the thirties. Three fine works consider the inter-war years: Paul A. Carter, *The Decline and Revival of the Social Gospel* [Cornell** 1956]; Donald Meyer, *The Protestant Search for Political Realism* [California U.P.** 1960]; and Robert M. Miller, *American Protestant and Social Issues* [NCUP** 1958]. On this period also see the many works in paper editions on and by the major thinkers of the Neo-Orthodox movement in American theology, especially Reinhold Niebuhr, H. Richard Niebuhr, and Paul Tillich.

During this period the American philosophic tradition became increasingly reclusive, concerning itself with logical and analytic problems, though John Dewey (1859-1952) remained active almost to the end of his life. The post-World War II religious ethos is effectively surveyed in Will Herberg's *Protestant, Catholic, Jew* (Doub-Anchor) [1955] and Martin Marty's *The New Shape of*

American Religion [H&R** 1959]. Some of its major interests are illustrated in the immensely popular books of Norman Vincent Peale, Joshua Loth Liebman, and Anne Morrow Lindbergh. The best introduction to the peace-of-mind interest that flourished in the 1950s is Donald Meyer, *The Positive Thinkers: From Mary Baker Eddy to Norman Vincent Peale* (Doub-Anchor) [1965].

After 1960, however, a distinctly radical turn in ethics, theology, and social criticism began to be manifested. It was often inspired by Dietrich Bonhoeffer, Nietzsche, the Marxians (notably the interpretations of Hegel, Marx, and Freud by Herbert Marcuse), and the protest literature provoked by the multiple problems of racial injustice, urban decay, youth alienation, and, above all, by the war in Southeast Asia. On the period since 1960 there has been a wealth of commentary on every major theme. Two collections of essays are especially valuable: James M. Gustafson, ed., *The Sixties: Radical Change in Religion* (Annals of the American Academy of Social and Political Science, No. 387), and Martin Marty and Dean Peerman, eds., *New Theology No. 8* (Mac; 8 volumes, 1964-71). The best account of radical theology and its American background is Frederick Sontag and John Roth, *The American Religious Experience* [H&R** 1972].

Three widely-read accounts of the new moral and spiritual atmosphere are Theodore Roszak, *The Making of a Counterculture* (Doub-Anchor) [1964]; Charles Reich, *The Greening of America* (Bantam) [1970]; and Jean-Francois Revel, *Without Marx or Jesus: The New American Revolution* [Doub.** 1971]. Also valuable are Jacob Needleman's *The New Religions* (Doub) [1970]; and the Trappist mysticism of Thomas Merton's many books, including *Mysticism and Zen Masters* (Dell) [1957] and *The New Man* (NAL) [1971]. Jacob Neusner's *American Judaism: Adventure in Modernity* (PH) [1972] describes the later phases of Judaism, while Richard Rubenstein provided a radical statement of its theological predicament in *After Auschwitz* (BM) [1966]. On Roman Catholicism in America since Vaticanum II see Thomas O'Dea's two books, *American Catholic Dilemma* (Sheed & Ward) [1958] and *The Catholic Crisis* (Beacon) [1969]; J. F. Scheuer *et al*, *The De-Romanization of the American Catholic* (NAL) [1966]; John O'Conner, *The People Versus Rome: The Radical Split in American Catholicism* [Ran** 1969]; and Aelred Graham's autobiographical reflections, *The End of Religion* [HBJ** 1971].

On new currents of evangelicalism, see Ronald M. Enroth *et al*, *The Jesus People: Old-Time Religion in the Age of Aquarius* (Eerdman's) [1972].

Autobiography and American Culture

by Albert E. Stone

One of the striking and promising developments in recent American studies is the new exploration of autobiography. This concern, a product largely of the past decade, is currently being pursued with an energy and sophistication which virtually constitute a rediscovery of the manifold possibilities of the genre. As cultural documents providing unique insights into history, cultural change, social and individual experience and identity, autobiographies have of course long been used by social scientists and historians. As prime forms of the American imagination also, personal narratives engage the attention of literary critics and scholars for whom Franklin, Thoreau, Henry Adams, and Gertrude Stein are distinctive names, among others, in the history of American self-consciousness. Both groups, humanists and scientists, find in the 6377 items listed in Kaplan's *A Bibliography of American Autobiographies* (1), its more selective predecessor, Lillard's *American Life in Autobiography* (2), and in a more specialized successor, Brignano's *Black Americans in Autobiography* (3), a wealth of cultural information quite literally unparalleled in other sources. Moreover the number of autobiographies increases almost astronomically; it has been estimated that more than 10,000 life stories by Americans have now been published in the United States. Hardly a week passes but the newspapers announce that another American like Frank Sinatra or Gwendolyn Brooks has written his or her story.

"This most democratic province in the republic of letters," as William Dean Howells called it in 1909, is open to all; nearly anyone, it seems, who writes "the sincere relation of what he has been and done and felt and thought" (4) can find an audience. To this genre therefore have been drawn public and private figures: poets, philosophers, and prizefighters; actresses, artists, political activists; statesmen and penitentiary prisoners; financiers and football players; Quakers and Black Muslims; immigrants and Indians. The range of personality, experience, and occupation reflected in the varieties of American autobiography is as diverse as American life itself. Barriers of literacy, education, and taste which usually divide a culture into "low" and "high" seem almost to disappear in this case. As Lillard reminds us, "autobiography is as near as mankind gets to a unified, lasting, prima facie version of what happens in an individuals's lifetime."

Paperbacks and Autobiography

Because of the widespread and natural interest in a form of literature so varied, personal, and illuminating, paperback publishers thrive on autobiography. The availability of classic, new, and long-neglected autobiographies in relatively inexpensive editions is one factor in the increased attention paid by readers, teachers, and scholars. Sales of such works have so increased of late that traditional estimates of readership as a reflection of cultural significance or influence have been upset. Thus it is probably more dangerous to cite sales figures as meaningful indices of the importance of autobiographies than is the case for most other documents. Benjamin Franklin's *Autobiography* (5), the book that begins the modern American tradition and which remains one of the most famous works in American literature, may not have sold as many copies as *The Autobiography of Malcolm X* (6), the most powerful of recent autobiographies and, as Carol Ohmann has pointed out, a literary descendant in important respects of Franklin's masterpiece (7). Both, however, may be eclipsed by books riding the crest of a purely temporary popularity.

Hence such memoirs and autobiographies as footballer Jerry Kramer's *Instant Replay* (8) or entertainer Sammy Davis, Jr.'s *Yes I Can* (9) have an apparent significance but actually offer limited insights to the cultural critic. How to distinguish the permanently valuable from the Madison Avenue product of the moment, how to establish, for instance, the immense superiority of an Indian autobiography like *Black Elk Speaks* (10) over an imitation like *The Memoirs of*

Mr. Stone is Professor of English and American Studies at Emory University, Atlanta, Georgia. He was educated at Yale University, where he taught in the American Studies program until 1962. The author of The Innocent Eye: Childhood in Mark Twain's Imagination, *he also is editor of works of Crèvecoeur, James and Twain, and has published articles on Frost, Robert Lowell, Frederick Douglass, and Louis Sullivan. In 1965 the Danforth Foundation presented him an E. Harris Harbison Award for Gifted Teaching. Mr. Stone was Fulbright lecturer at the Charles University, Prague, in 1968-69, and served on the Advisory Committee on American Studies of the CIEP as well as on the editorial board of AS:AIN from 1970-74.*

Chief Red Fox (11), or of Shirley MacLaine's *Don't Fall Off the Mountain* (12) over *Yes I Can*, calls not only for familiarity with the range of American auto-biographies now available but also for an awareness of essential definitions, dis-tinctions, and standards in this fast-changing field. Fortunately these criteria—not all of which are highbrow or academic—are now being established by a number of scholars who approach autobiography freshly from a variety of fruitful perspec-tives, including traditional English and European literary criticism, historical American Studies, social psychology and psychoanalysis, Black Studies, and Women's Studies.

What Is Autobiography?

Before any distinctively American emphases or aspects of autobiography can be posited, some general definitions are needed as bench-marks. These may be found in abundance in classic discussions of autobiography by Georg Misch (13), André Maurois (14), Arthur Melville Clark (15), Wayne Shumaker (16), Georges Gusdorf (17), Roy Pascal (18), Jean Starobinski (19), and James Olney (20). Among these critics—most of them British or European in origin or focus—there is a wide agreement that autobiography, as roughly distinguished from journal, diary, memoir, or reminiscence, is the retrospective account of an individual's life, or a significant part thereof, written by that person with the avowed intent of telling the truthful story of his or her public and private experience. Hence autobiography describes a content not a form. Three hazy areas can at once be detected in this consensus definition, each of potential importance for American autobiography. These are: "a significant part thereof"; "written by that person"; and "avowed truth." Given the pace of modern experience and the still widely shared belief (or fiction) that ordinary individuals can participate meaningfully in extraordinary events, many topical autobiographies or memoirs continue to appear. Sometimes it is difficult to detect any generic difference between, for instance, two contemporary works like Kramer's *Instant Replay* and Norman Mailer's *The Armies of the Night* (21). Both chronicle brief portions of their authors' recent lives. Yet Kramer's subtitle, *The Green Bay Packer Diary*, justly removes it from the category of autobiography, whereas Mailer's even more restricted narrative of the October, 1967 peace march on the Pentagon is authen-tic autobiography. At least, there are two persuasive critics, Richard Gilman (22) and Warner Berthoff (23), who argue the case for Mailer.

A second problem for the student of American autobiography is that of authorship. Many modern autobiographies, though not "written by that person," make available the experience of inarticulate lives. This discovery of previously mute voices in American history is, in fact, a signal development of contempo-rary American studies. Are such books to be denied the status of "true autobiog-raphy"? So many slick and superficial fabrications of pseudo-identity and ex-perience have been published that one is tempted to reply yes categorically—until one turns to *The Autobiography of Malcolm X*, or *Black Elk Speaks*, or *The Life of Nate Shaw* (24). Each is a kind of collaboration yet each recreates vividly and powerfully the personality of a singular man. Other triumphs over the ghost-writer suggest that readers should proceed case by case and not by rule.

A brilliant essay by F. R. Hart takes precisely this empirical, inductive approach in discussing the knotty problem of "truth" in autobiography (25). Taking issue with Shumaker and others who insist that autobiographers always intend to be taken as writing nothing that is not literally and factually true, Hart Quotes Ernest Renan ("ce qu'on dit de soi est toujours poésie") and cites many autobiographers who acknowledge the necessarily fictive element in the genre. Nevertheless, in reference to Nabokov's *Speak, Memory* (26), perhaps the most evocative immigrant or emigre autobiography ever written, Hart properly observes "The historicity of the recreation is imperative, *even though* the autobiographer knows the terrible elusiveness of that historicity." Autobiography *is* a species of history but it is at the same time a form of fiction; like history, it is descriptive and subject to verification, but like fiction it is inventive and lays claim to veracity. The reader of autobiography knows that he can never wholly separate the two, any more than the author has. What he must learn, then, is a sophisticated reality-testing, a point argued by Norman N. Holland in an essay important for the psychoanalysis of non-fiction. "Any given paragraph could be fiction or non-fiction—it is our different expectations from fiction and non-fiction rather than the texts as such that differentiate our degrees of involvement. Non-fiction usually asks us to do more reality-testing than fiction." (27) Though all readers may not share Holland's Freudianism, most would recognize that autobiography overlaps history, literature, and psychology and can be properly understood only by reference to the coinciding concerns and criteria of all three disciplines. Thus it is a natural interdisciplinary study.

Autobiography and American History and Myth

One of the first historical dimensions of autobiography as an American act is a fact James M. Cox emphasizes in an important essay (28): the very term "autobiography" in its modern sense was coined only in 1809, and the new phenomenon to which Robert Southey applied it was a product of what R.R. Palmer calls the Age of the Democratic Revolutions. Franklin shares with Rousseau the honor of creating the modern autobiography. Its two classic forms—the memoir and the confession—persist in their two original titles. But both form and content were transformed into secular, private, democratic, and psychological modes by the American and the Frenchman. Each invented the literary analogue to the revolutionary changes occurring in their respective societies. Even earlier than Franklin, however, the spiritual autobiographies composed by Puritan and Quaker colonists had assumed a subtly different content if not a distinct form from European prototypes. In *Spiritual Autobiography in Early America* (29) Daniel B. Shea, Jr. examines a number of the colonial followers of Bunyan and Fox, including Thomas Shepard (30), Jonathan Edwards (31), and John Woolman (32). Shea concludes that these proto-Americans departed very early from the narrow narrative of conversion and confession; their autobiographical accounts often include a very wide range of experience that bore on their spiritual condition. The same inclusive approach can be seen in the first great black autobiography associated with American letters, *The Life of Olaudah Equiano, or Gustavus Vassa, the African* (33). Conversion, adventure, and abolitionist propaganda are almost equally prominent themes in this remarkable Nigerian's story.

Cox's thesis that America and autobiography arose together and under the stimulus of similar forces suggests that this democratic genre has closer, more immediate linkages to political and historical events and ideologies than do fiction, poetry, or drama. Light on this hypothesis is thrown by checking in Kaplan and the other bibliographies the publication dates for a number of important autobiographies. An unusual clustering does seem to occur at the time of the American Revolution (Woolman, Franklin, Crèvecoeur (34), Vassa); in the immediately pre-Civil War era (slaves' narratives, Thoreau (35), Whitman (36), Cartwright (37)); just before and after World War I (Henry Adams (38), Mark Twain (39), Henry James (40), Mary Antin (41), Andrew Carnegie (42), Alexander Berkman (43), Theodore Dreiser (44), Louis Sullivan (45)); during the Great Depression (Gertrude Stein (46), Black Elk, Lincoln Steffens (47), Clarence Darrow (48), W. E. B. DuBois (49)); and in the post-World War II era (Richard Wright (50), Thomas Merton (51), Conrad Aiken (52), Nabokov, Whittaker Chambers (53), Malcolm X, Claude Brown (54), Mailer, Maya Angelou (55), Eldridge Cleaver (56)). Conversely, periods of *relative* social or political calm—pre-Stamp Act America, the early nineteenth century, the Gilded Age—seem to have been times when fewer important autobiographies appeared. Yet Robert Cantwell in an essay (57) on the spate of autobiographies appearing around 1938 warns of the dangers of making such simple connections between artifacts and eras. Because autobiography is, in Starobinski's terms, both past history and present discourse it is at least a double reflection of attitudes and values. Thus the *Personal Memoirs of Ulysses S. Grant* (58), which appeared in 1885, is a far more significant document of the Civil War than of the Gilded Age, to which Grant makes scarcely a single reference. On the other hand, Lucy Larcom's *A New England Girlhood* (1889) (59) chronicles family life in the Massachusetts of the 1820s and 30s, but her nostalgia and gentle feminism reflect values more properly shared with Howells and Sarah Orne Jewett.

Another way to relate autobiography and history is proposed and argued in a pioneering essay by William C. Spengemann and L. R. Lundquist (60). These critics assert that because autobiography is imaginative art it "has nothing to do with factual truth," so cannot be read descriptively to illuminate historical events or eras. The truth and therefore the utility of autobiography is instead mythic; "the writer explains his life by depicting himself according to culturally evaluated images of character. As he turns his private experience into language he assumes one of the many identities outlined in the myth and so asserts his connection with his culture." Spengemann and Lundquist describe "the" American myth as "a pilgrimage from imperfection to perfection." As the adaptation of Christian mythology to the changing problems and possibilities of American experience, this increasingly secular myth defines roles for Americans which are assumed and acted out in exemplary autobiographies of our culture: the Prophet (Whitman, Mailer); the Hero (Franklin, Carnegie); the Villain (P. T. Barnum (61), Whittaker Chambers); the Outsider or Outcast (Mae West (62), Caryl Chessman (63)); the Disenchanted (Scott Fitzgerald (64)). Thus autobiographical form and content are controlled by pervasive cultural belief in "an integrated, continuing personality which transcends the limitations of time and

space and unites all of one's apparently contradictory experiences into an identifiable whole. This notion of individual identity, in fact, may well be the central
belief of our culture. With all its ramifications—personal responsibility, individual
destiny, dissent, vocation and so forth—it forms the core of our being and the
fabric of our history."

This is a broad and challenging thesis, but rests upon the prescriptively con-
fining assumption that all really significant autobiographers have settled upon a
central self or a culturally-defined role. For Spengemann and Lundquist, the
writer "must adopt some consistent, overriding view of himself and his part.
He must identify the 'I' which unites all his past experiences." A critic like Hart
might argue that writing autobiography is sometimes a more protean act of
self-discovery or self-transcendence, many of whose American monuments display discontinuities and fragmentations of self and society more clearly than
consistent identities and clearly defined roles. Moreover, psychologists and psy-
chistrists would doubtless disagree with the to-them simplistic definition of
"identity" employed by these myth-critics of American autobiography.

Certain aspects of autobiography as history remain unexplored or have only
recently come in for critical attention. One of the most important of these is the
complex relationship between biography and autobiography, their respective
claims to credence, their comparative utility for the historian. I know of no
theoretical or comprehensive discussion of this dimension of American life-writ-
ings, no book or essay which domesticates and tests the generalizations of
Maurois and Pascal. One response to this gap is for the student to contrast exemplary biographies of those persons who have also written important autobiographies. Particularly fruitful subjects for such comparisons would include Ernest
Samuels' three-volume biography of Adams (65) and the *Education*, Leon Edel's
Henry James: The Untried Years, 1843-1870 (66) and *A Small Boy and Others*,
and Michel Fabre's *The Unfinished Quest of Richard Wright* (67) and *Black Boy*.
That many historians have consciously or unconsciously avoided autobiographies
in historical research is discussed in an interesting appendix to John W. Blassingame's *The Slave Community: Plantation Life in the Antebellum South* (68).

Autobiography and American Literature

At present there is no critical or comprehensive history of American autobiography as a branch of American Literature. Several recent books and a number of essays offer partial views of the whole landscape or detailed looks at
particular works, but no inclusive study has yet been written. (American scholars reputedly at work on such a project include Cox, Robert F. Sayre, Spengemann and Lundquist, Herbert Liebowitz, and A. E. Stone. There are no doubt
others.) Cox's essay (28) is presently the best brief discussion but treats only
Franklin, Thoreau, Whitman, and Adams, with a final glance at Gertrude Stein.

A far fuller treatment of Franklin, Adams, and James is provided by Sayre's
excellent work, *The Examined Self* (69). Sayre rejects the reduction of autobiography to biography and history, attempts instead what he calls proper "autobiographical criticism." This entails not merely tracking "fictional" episodes
back to their "real life" sources but, more importantly, relating each part of an

autobiography to the writer's changing need for appropriate form and image. Sayre's analysis draws illuminating parallels between the forms of fiction and autobiography (as in the picaresque Part One of Franklin's *Autobiography*) and suggests themes and techniques shared by the novels and autobiographies of James and by the histories of Adams and his *Education*, which is probably the richest of all American autobiographies. Sayre's approach offers many opportunities for considering representations of American experience in more purely literary terms than Spengemann and Lundquist employ. Thus works like James's *A Small Boy and Others* and *Notes of a Son and Brother* might be seen as imaginative re-creations of childhood and youth to be stylistically and structurally compared to similar narratives by Lucy Larcom, Louis Sullivan, Richard Wright, or James Baldwin (70) but also to novels like *The Adventures of Tom Sawyer* and *What Maisie Knew*.

This imaginative and comparative approach is carried even further by David L. Minter in *The Interpreted Design* (71). Here Minter traces a recurrent theme, design, and metaphor in American fiction and personal narrative—the juxtaposition of two characters, a man of bold design who acts and another man of reflective consciousness through whom the story of the active other is interpreted. In fiction the classic examples are *The Blithedale Romance, The Great Gatsby,* and *Absalom! Absalom!* In autobiography Jonathan Edwards, Franklin, Thoreau, and Adams model their life-stories on this pattern. This emphasis upon design in life and art leads Minter to read Part Two of Franklin's *Autobiography*, in which the plan for moral perfection is recounted, as the book's core. Through the eyes of the older observing Franklin we see both the idealism and the naif egotism of the younger man who tries on one active role after another in search of both worldly success and the humility of Jesus and Socrates. Similarly, Adams as an older writer looks back on the little mannikin who is his historical self and in recording the failure of his attempts to master history and nature makes of the *Education* a work of consummate art, a "supreme no to chaos and disorder." A somewhat similar treatment of time, as both concrete present and in transcendent perspective, is found in John Lynen's *The Design of the Present* (72), which offers a sensitive reading of the personal histories of Edwards and Franklin in thematic-temporal terms which might well be applied to Adams as well.

Aside from Cox, Sayre, Minter, and (passingly) Lynen, there remains chiefly a growing list of individual essays, chapters, and introductions which examine American autobiographers as separate works of art. Many of these critiques are couched in cultural rather than narrowly aesthetic terms. In this their various authors often reflect the influence of American Studies or Black Studies as well as the inevitably interdisciplinary nature of autobiography itself. What follows is a selective sampling of useful commentaries on certain of the best-known types and examples of American autobiographies.

Of the many studies of Franklin published in recent years those by Charles Sanford (73), David Levin (74), and John William Ward (75) should prove particularly illuminating, but no reader should neglect the riches of the Yale paperbound edition with its extensive historical and biographical materials. Franklin, Shepard, and Vassa are compared thematically in a recent essay by A. E. Stone (76). Significant discussions of the eighty-odd slave narratives published in pre-Civil War America have been contributed by Charles H. Nichols (77), Arna Bontemps (78), Gilbert Osofsky (79), John F. Bayliss (80), and

Houston A. Baker, Jr. (81). Certain of these narratives stand out for their imaginative recreation of the horrors of slavery, the excitement of escape, the achievement of freedom and manhood. Historians and critics, both black and white, return most often to the narratives of Vassa, Frederick Douglass (82), Henry Bibb (78), Solomon Northup (78), Josiah Henson (83), Charlotte Forten (84), and Harriet Jacobs (85).

No one has contributed more than J. C. Levenson to the appreciation of the *Education of Henry Adams* (86)—except Ernest Samuels, whose Riverside Edition of the *Education* (38) is the best available paperback. A brilliant recent study of Gertrude Stein and her several autobiographies is found in Richard Bridgman's *Gertrude Stein in Pieces* (78). Richard Wright's *Black Boy*, the most poetically powerful of all black autobiographies, has been perceptively discussed by several critics including Ralph Ellison (88), George E. Kent (89), and Robert Bone (90). *Black Elk Speaks* is most easily approached through Sayre's sympathetic essay in *College English* (91), but a valuable religious-anthropological perspective is provided by Joseph E. Brown's *The Sacred Pipe* (92). The subtle nature of Conrad Aiken's *Ushant*, at once an autobiography, essay, and novel, is traced by Jay Martin (93).

Although *The Autobiography of Malcolm X* is now widely appreciated as the imaginative equal of *Black Boy*, its special literary form and relations to earlier black writing have not yet been fully explored. Warner Berthoff (23) and David Demarest (94) have written of it from a white perspective but another white critic Richard Gilman (22) has argued vehemently that proper criticism of books like *Malcolm X* and Cleaver's *Soul on Ice* must come from black critics. Malcolm's impact on black poets and novelists has been enormous but the critical evaluations Gilman wants are less numerous. Materials for such appreciation may be found in John H. Clark's *Malcolm X* which contains an interesting essay by the young Egyptian-American scholar, A. M. Elmessiri (95). One possible reason for the delay in black literary discussions of autobiographies like Malcolm X's may be that many militant black intellectuals remain profoundly suspicious not only of formal literary criticism but also of autobiography itself as a traditional European genre explicitly committed to a kind of individualism which can be seen as a white cultural threat to black consciousness and community. V. S. Pritchett, the British critic, has commented on a similar ideological attack on Western autobiography by Communist writers. Such works in this view necessarily glorify the private ego and thus are proof of bourgeois social decadence. Pritchett disagrees, asserting instead that autobiographies are significant expressions of a "revolutionary" consciousness and "the necessary civilising force in mass society." (96) Thus literary analysis of autobiography shades imperceptibly into ideology, and the cultural critic can refine his awareness of the inevitability of this fact by reading Frederick Crew's thoughtful essay "Do Literary Studies Have an Ideology?" (97).

Autobiography and the Social Sciences

Psychology, psychoanalysis, anthropology, and sociology are the social sciences, besides history, which are most directly involved in the subjective dimension of culture. The proper use of human documents in the discovery and testing of social data and generalizations has been an issue since at least the publication in 1927 of Thomas and Znaniecki's *The Polish Peasant in Europe and America* (98), one part of which is the analysis of an autobiography by one Wladek, a Polish immigrant to the United, States. Thomas and Znaniecki's famous description of autobiography as "the *perfect* type of sociological material" has since been criticized, most acutely by Herbert Blumer (99). Despite their fullness of detail about the personal experience of social process, autobiographies can never meet, either singly or in collection, the three criteria for scientific evidence: representativeness, adequacy, reliability. Moreover, as Blumer points out, a document as individual and imaginatively self-contained as autobiography bears a curious double relationship to any scientific theory. Speaking of Thomas and Znaniecki's theory of "social becoming" in light of Wladek's autobiography, Blumer observes "while the experiences have a tough independent character which enables them to be a test of a theoretical conception, at other times they seem, metaphorically speaking, to be helpless before the imposition of a theoretical view." Blumer concludes that while personal narratives lend themselves to diverse interpretations, they grow less satisfactory as evidence as the interpretation grows more abstract or general. "At best, these materials only enable one to make a *case* for the theoretical interpretation."

Gordon Allport accepts Blumer's critique but still vigorously defends the use of autobiography as a legitimate and necessary idiographic tool for the scientist. In *The Nature of Personality*, particularly in the challenging final essay "Personality: A Problem for Science or a Problem for Art?" (100), Allport counters arguments of the scientific objectivists and urges the use of various quantitative and non-quantitative methods of validation of theory by means of autobiographies. His case is extended in *The Use of Personal Documents in Psychological Science* (101), in which he concludes: "Acquaintance with the particular case, a sense of its patterned character and its individualized laws of action, stand at the gateway of generalized knowledge and at its terminus at the point of application. . . . The positivist who dreads the subjectivity of the process of understanding needs as much as does the intuitionist to settle down to the task of finding out how his own mind, the most sensitive recording machine in existence, is capable of registering multiple variables and discerning relationships between them."

One promising technique for doing this which has been developed since Allport and Blumer first wrote is value analysis. The pioneering study is R. K. White's examination of Richard Wright's *Black Boy* (102) by means of alternating impressionistic and statistical analyses. White redraws the picture of Wright's youthful personality in the light of both sorts of readings, in comparison to eight very different white life-stories, all within a Freudian framework. Like Blumer, White accepts *Black Boy's* imaginative integrity which he sees as fitting, evading, and testing his hypotheses. His analysis, however, has limitations. Thus White downplays the issue of fundamental differences in identity and psychosocial development between black and white Americans. (This important area is being explored, through insights derived in part from black autobiographies, by Erikson (103), Silberman (104), Hauser (105), and Franklin (106).) Also, White tends to ignore the historical dimensions of Wright's autobiography. For example, he underestimates the influence of Wright's Communist experiences in the 1930s as a factor affecting the narrative's treatment of family, black community, and self in *Black Boy*. To be sure, the biographical riches of Fabre's masterful biography (67) were not available in 1947.

Although anthropology is also a biographically-based science, many American anthropologists once neglected life-histories as idiographic instruments. With the recent emphasis on culture-and-personality studies, however, more anthropologists are now following the lead of Kardiner, Hallowell, Oscar Lewis and others in using biographies and autobiographies as significant sources in the study of internalization and motivation. L. L. Langness presents the best case for the relevance of autobiography in *Life History in Anthropological Science* (107).

In the present day interface of history and psychology along several fronts, the pre-eminent figure is Erik Erikson, whose *Childhood and Society* (108) still provides one of the most flexible neo-Freudian contexts for studying American autobiographies. Erikson's studies of Luther and Gandhi, too, are built upon a deep and sensitive awareness of individual experience as somatic, social, and historical and of individual expression as conditioned by form, language, and convention. "There is always some naive self-revelation in any outpouring of autobiographic data," he says of Gandhi's *Autobiography*. "Yet each given medium (diary, conversation, or autobiography) has its own formal laws and serves tradition and personal style. As to unconscious motivation, we must always remember that the autobiographer has not agreed to a therapeutic contract by which he promises to put into words his "free associations" so that we may help him to compare them with inner and outer 'reality.' " (109) Erikson enumerates the factors to be considered in thus "helping" an autobiographer: one must keep in mind *"the stage of the recorder's life,"* and *"the course of his whole life history"* and the *"historical process"* of which any moment is but a stage. Moreover, the interpreter must never forget that he himself is subject to the *"mood of his own life"* and heir to a given *"lineage of conceptualization." Gandhi's Truth* (110) demonstrates Erikson's own mastery of these factors to illuminate both a man and his autobiography.

Erikson's continuing interest as scientist and humanist has been in human identity, its cultural determinants and manifold expressions. As autobiography is one of these expressions, his and others' explorations of identity are of major significance for any scientific reading of personal narratives. Two of the many theoreticians of human identity who offer particularly cogent generalizations for the student of autobiography are Heinz Lichtenstein (111) and Phyllis Greenacre (112). The latter has offered some very promising generalizations about the psychology of the genius-as-autobiographer. Another interesting scientific perspective, that of the ecologist, is provided by Edith Cobb (113).

Finding links between individual and group experience is as much the historian's task as the sociologist's or the psychologist's, and many American historians today find Erikson the most stimulating exemplar of fresh ways to "do history" in connection with psychoanalysis. Psycho-history has emerged as a sub-discipline with an understandable interest in personal documents and a variety of techniques for their use. H. Stuart Hughes summarizes in *History as Art and as Science* (114) the coinciding concerns of history and psychoanalysis: both "believe in the radical subjectivity of human understanding"; both seek for systematic generalizations for dealing with individual consciousness as the "final datum, the bedrock of what we know." Hughes concludes that historians and psychoanalysts "have finally realized that the individual can be understood in his full cultural context only if his spiritual biography is viewed in relation to the lives of others with whom he has deep-seated emotional affinities; . . . the path to the fuller understanding of the individual lies through the group—and vice versa. In both cases, the explanation of motive runs from the single human being to others comparable to him, and then back to the individual once more, as the ramifying thought and action of both are gradually illuminated. This reciprocal method is the ultimate concern that history and psychoanalysis share." Hughes's reference to the importance of "spiritual biography" in tracing this process suggests that autobiography will continue to play a central role in future developments of American history as a bridge between the social sciences and the literary arts, as all these disciplines seek to further comprehension of American culture.

A Note on Periodicals

In addition to traditional journals serving the disciplines and professional associations of literature, history, and social sciences, there are several others which the student of American autobiography should consult. Besides those with an obvious interdisciplinary focus—e.g., *American Quarterly, Literature & Psychology, Phylon, The Black Scholar*—there are some more recent journals of special relevance: *Genre, History and Theory, New Literary History, Journal of Interdisciplinary History, Critical Inquiry.*

Bibliography

The following works are referred to in the essay. Paperback editions are indicated by an asterisk (*).

1. Louis Kaplan, *A Bibliography of American Autobiographies* (Madison, Wisc., University of Wisconsin Press, 1961).

2. Richard G. Lillard, *American Life in Autobiography, A Descriptive Guide* (Stanford, Stanford University Press, 1956).

3. Russell C. Brignano, *Black Americans in Autobiography: An Annotated Bibliography of Autobiographies and Autobiographical Books Written Since the Civil War* (Durham, Duke University Press, 1974).

4. W. D. Howells, "Editor's Easy Chair," *Harper's Monthly* 119 (October 1909), 798.

*5. *The Autobiography of Benjamin Franklin,* eds. L. W. Labaree, R. L. Ketcham, H. C. Boatfield, H. H. Fineman (New Haven, Yale University Press, 1964).

*6. Malcolm X and Alex Haley, *The Autobiography of Malcolm X* (New York, Grove Press, 1966).

7. C. Ohmann, *"The Autobiography of Malcolm X:* A Revolutionary Use of the Franklin Tradition," *American Quarterly* 22 (Summer, 1970), 131-49.

*8. J. Kramer, *Instant Replay: The Green Bay Packer Diary,* ed. Dick Schaap (New York, New American Library, 1968).

*9. Sammy Davis, Jr. and Jane and Burt Boyar, *Yes I Can, The Story of Sammy Davis, Jr.* (New York, Pocket Books, 1966).

*10. *Black Elk Speaks, Being the Life Story of a Holy Man of the Oglala Sioux* as told through John G. Neihardt (New York, Pocket Books, 1972).

*11. *The Memoirs of Chief Red Fox* (Greenwich, Conn., Fawcett, 1971).

*12. Shirley MacLaine, *Don't Fall Off the Mountain* (New York, Bantam, 1970).

13. G. Misch, *The History of Autobiography in Antiquity* (Cambridge, Harvard University Press, 1951), vol. 1, chap. 1.

14. André Maurois, *Aspects of Biography,* trans. S. C. Roberts (New York, Ungar, 1966).

15. A. M. Clark, *Autobiography, Its Genesis and Phases* (Edinburgh, 1935; Folcroft Press, 1969).

16. W. Shumaker, *English Autobiography: Its Emergence, Materials, and Forms* (Berkeley, University of California Press, 1954).

17. G. Gusdorf, "Conditions et limites de l'autobiographie," in *Formen der Selbstdarstellung,* eds. G. Reichenkron & E. Haase (Berlin, Duncker & Humblot, 1956), 105-23.

18. R. Pascal, *Design and Truth in Autobiography* (Cambridge, Harvard University Press, 1960).

19. J. Starobinski, "The Style of Autobiography," in *Literary Style, A Symposium,* ed. S. B. Chatman (New York, Oxford University Press, 1971), 285-96.

20. J. Olney, *Metaphors of Self: The Meaning of Autobiography* (Princeton, Princeton University Press, 1972).

*21. N. Mailer, *The Armies of the Night: History as a Novel, The Novel as History* (New York, New American Library, 1968).

*22. R. Gilman, *The Confusion of Realms* (New York, Random House, Vintage, 1970).

23. W. Berthoff, "Witness and Testament: Two Contemporary Classics," in *Aspects of Narrative,* ed. J. H. Miller (New York, Columbia University Press, 1971), 173-98.

24. Theodore Rosengarten, *The Life of Nate Shaw* (New York, A. A. Knopf, 1974).

25. Francis Russell Hart, "Notes for an Anatomy of Modern Autobiography," *New Literary History* 1 (Spring, 1970), 485-511.

*26. Vladimir Nabokov, *Speak, Memory, An Autobiography Revisited* (New York, Putnam, 1966).

27. N. N. Holland, "Prose and Minds: A Psychoanalytic Approach to Non-Fiction," in *The Art of Victorian Prose,* eds. G. Levine & W. Madden (New York, Oxford University Press, 1968), 314-37.

28. J. M. Cox, "Autobiography and America," in *Aspects of Narrative,* op. cit., 143-72.

29. D. B. Shea, Jr., *Spiritual Autobiography in Early America* (Princeton, Princeton University Press, 1968).

30. *God's Plot: The Paradoxes of Puritan Piety; being The Autobiography & Journal of Thomas Shepard,* ed. M. McGiffert (Amherst, University of Massachusetts Press, 1972).

*31. J. Edwards, *Personal Narrative* in *The American Tradition in Literature,* eds. S. Bradley, R. C. Beatty, E. H. Long (New York, W. W. Norton, 1967), I, 124-36.

*32. J. Woolman, *The Journal of John Woolman* (New York, Corinth Books, 1961).

*33. *The Life of Olaudah Equiano, or Gustavus Vassa, the African, Written by Himself,* in *Great Slave Narratives,* ed. A. Bontemps (Boston, Beacon Press, 1969).

*34. M. G. St.-Jean de Crèvecoeur, *Letters from an American Farmer and Sketches of XVIII-Century America,* ed. A. E. Stone (New York, New American Library, 1963).

*35. H. D. Thoreau, *The Variorum Walden,* ed. W. Harding (New York, Washington Square Press, 1968).

*36. W. Whitman, *Specimen Days,* ed. A. Kazin (Boston, D. R. Godine, 1971).

 37. *The Autobiography of Peter Cartwright* (New York & Nashville, Abingdon Press, 1956).

*38. *The Education of Henry Adams,* ed. E. Samuels (Boston, Houghton Miffin, Riverside, 1973.

 39. M. Twain (Samuel Langhorne Clemens), *Mark Twain's Autobiography,* ed. A. B. Paine (New York, Harper, 1924); *Mark Twain in Eruption,* ed. B. DeVoto (New York, Putnam, 1968); *The Autobiography of Mark Twain,* ed. C. Neider (New York, Harper, 1959).

 40. *Henry James: Autobiography,* ed. F. W. Dupee (New York, Criterion Books, 1956).

*41. M. Antin, *The Promised Land* (Boston, Houghton Mifflin, Sentry Edition, 1969).

 42. A. Carnegie, *Autobiography of Andrew Carnegie* (Boston, Houghton Mifflin, 1920).

*43. A. Berkman, *Prison Memoirs of an Anarchist* (New York, Schocken Books, 1970).

*44. T. Dreiser, *Dawn; A Book About Myself* (Greenwich, Conn., Fawcett, 1965).

*45. L. Sullivan, *The Autobiography of an Idea* (New York, Dover Publications, 1956).

*46. G. Stein, *The Autobiography of Alice B. Toklas* (New York, Random House, Vintage, 1960); *Everybody's Autobiography* (New York, Vintage, 1973).

*47. L. Steffens, *The Autobiography of Lincoln Steffens* (New York, Harbrace, 1968) 2 vols.

*48. C. Darrow, *The Story of My Life* (New York, Scribner's, 1960).

*49. W.E.B. DuBois, *Dusk of Dawn: An Essay Toward an Autobiography of a Race Concept* (New York, Schocken Books, 1968); *The Autobiography of W.E.B. DuBois: A Soliloquy on Viewing My Life from the Last Decade of its First Century* (New York, International Publisher, 1969).

*50. R. Wright, *Black Boy, A Record of Childhood and Youth* (New York, Harper & Row, 1966).

*51. T. Merton, *The Seven Storey Mountain* (New York, New American Library, 1948).

*52. C. Aiken, *Ushant, An Essay* (Cleveland & New York, Meridian Books, 1962).

*53. W. Chambers, *Witness* (Chicago, Regnery, 1969).

*54. C. Brown, *Manchild in the Promised Land* (New York, New American Library, 1965).

*55. M. Angelou, *I Know Why the Caged Bird Sings* (New York, Bantam Books, 1969).

*56. E. Cleaver, *Soul on Ice* (New York, Dell, 1970).

 57. R. Cantwell, "The Autobiographers," *New Republic* 94 (27 April, 1938), 354-56.

*58. U.S. Grant, *Personal Memoirs of Ulysses S. Grant,* ed. E. H. Long (New York, Grosset & Dunlap, Universal Library, 1962).

*59. L. Larcom, *A New England Girlhood* (New York, Corinth Books, 1961).

60. W. C. Spengemann & L. R. Lundquist, "Autobiography and the American Myth," *American Quarterly* 17 (Fall, 1965), 92-110.

61. Phineas T. Barnum, *The Life of P. T. Barnum, Written by Himself* (Buffalo, Courier Co., 1888).

62. M. West, *Goodness Had Nothing to Do With It* (Englewood Cliffs, N.J. Prentice-Hall 1959).

63. Caryl Chessman, *Cell 2455, Death Row* (New York, Prentice-Hall, 1954).

*64. F. Scott Fitzgerald, *The Crack-Up,* ed. E. Wilson (Norfolk, Conn., New Directions, 1956).

65. E. Samuels, *The Young Henry Adams* (Cambridge, Belknap Press of Harvard University Press, 1948); *Henry Adams: The Middle Years* (1958); *Henry Adams: The Major Phase* (1964).

66. L. Edel, *Henry James: The Untried Years, 1843-1870* (Philadelphia, Lippincott, 1953).

67. M. Fabre, *The Unfinished Quest of Richard Wright* (New York, Morrow, 1973).

*68. J. W. Blassingame, *The Slave Community: Plantation Life in the Antebellum South* (New York, Oxford University Press, 1972).

69. R.F. Sayre, *The Examined Self: Benjamin Franklin, Henry Adams, Henry James* (Princeton, Princeton University Press, 1964).

*70 J. Baldwin, *Notes of a Native Son* (Boston, Beacon Press, 1957); *Nobody Knows My Name* (New York, Dell, 1963); *The Fire Next Time* (New York, Dell, 1970).

71. D. L. Minter, *The Interpreted Design as a Structural Principle in American Prose* (New Haven, Yale University Press, 1969).

72. J. F. Lynen, *The Design of the Present: Essays on Time and Form in American Literature* (New Haven, Yale University Press, 1969).

73. C. L. Sanford, *The Quest for Paradise: Europe and the American Moral Imagination* (Urbana, University of Illinois Press, 1961).

74. D. Levin, *In Defense of Historical Literature* (New York, Hill & Wang, 1967).

75. J. W. Ward, "Who Was Benjamin Franklin?" *American Scholar* 32 (Autumn, 1963), 541-53.

76. A. E. Stone, "The Sea and the Self: Travel as Experience and Metaphor in Early American Autobiography," *Genre* 7 (September, 1974).

*77. C. H. Nichols, *Many Thousand Gone: The Ex-Slaves' Account of Their Bondage and Freedom* (Bloomington, Indiana University Press, 1969).

*78. *Great Slave Narratives,* ed. A. Bontemps (Boston, Beacon Press, 1969).

*79. G. Osofsky, *Puttin' On Ole Massa, The Slave Narratives of Henry Bibb, William Wells Brown, and Solomon Northup* (New York, Harper Torchbooks, 1969).

*80. J. F. Bayliss, *Black Slave Narratives* (New York, Macmillan, 1970).

81. H. A. Baker, Jr., *Long Black Song: Essays in Black American Literature and Culture* (Charlottesville, University Press of Virginia, 1972).

*82. F. Douglass, *Narrative of the Life of Frederick Douglass, An American Slave, Written by Himself,* ed. B. Quarles (Cambridge, Harvard University Press, 1960).

*83. J. Henson, *Father Henson's Story of His Own Life* (New York, Corinth Books, 1962).

*84. C. L. Forten, *Journal of Charlotte L. Forten: A Free Negro in the Slave Era* (New York, Macmillan, Collier Books, 1961).

*85. H. Jacobs (pseudonym, Linda Brent), *Incidents in the Life of a Slave Girl* (New York, Harcourt Brace Jovanovich, Harvest Book, 1973).

*86. J. C. Levenson, *The Mind and Art of Henry Adams* (Stanford, Stanford University Press, 1968).

87. R. Bridgman, *Gertrude Stein in Pieces* (New York, Oxford University Press, 1970).

*88. R. Ellison, *Shadow and Act* (New York, Random House, Vintage Books, 1972).

89. G. E. Kent, "Richard Wright: Blackness and the Adventure of Western Culture," *CLA Journal* 12 (1969), 322-43.

*90. R. Bone, *Richard Wright* (Minneapolis, University of Minnesota Press, 1969).

91. R. F. Sayre, "Vision and Experience in *Black Elk Speaks*," *College English,* 32 (February, 1971), 509-535.

*92. J. E. Brown, *The Sacred Pipe: Black Elk's Account of the Seven Rites of the Oglala Sioux* (New York, Penguin Books, 1971).

93. J. Martin, *Conrad Aiken, A Life of His Art* (Princeton, Princeton University Press, 1962).

94. D. P. Demarest, Jr., "*The Autobiography of Malcolm X:* Beyond Didacticism," *CLA Journal* 16 (December, 1972), 179-87.

95. *Malcolm X: The Man and his Times,* ed. J. H. Clarke (New York, Macmillan, 1969).

96. V. S. Pritchett, "All About Ourselves," *New Statesman & Nation* 51 (26 May, 1956), 601-602.

97. F. C. Crews, "Do Literary Studies Have an Ideology?" *PMLA* 85 (May, 1970), 423-28.

98. W. I. Thomas & F. Znaniecki, *The Polish Peasant in Europe and America* (New York, A. A. Knopf, 1927), 2 vols.

99. H. Blumer, *Critiques of Research in the Social Sciences: 1. An Appraisal of Thomas and Znaniecki's "The Polish Peasant in Europe and America"* (New York, Social Science Research Council, 1939).

100. G. Allport, *The Nature of Personality: Selected Papers* (Cambridge, Addison-Wesley Press, 1950).

*101. ————, *The Use of Personal Documents in Psychological Science* (New York, Social Science Research Council, 1942).

102. Ralph K. White, "*Black Boy:* A Value-Analysis," *Journal of Abnormal and Social Psychology* 42 (October, 1947), 440-61.

103. E. Erikson, "The Concept of Identity in Race Relations: Notes and Queries," in *The Negro American,* eds. T. Parsons & K. B. Clark (Boston, Houghton Mifflin, 1966), 227-53; "Race and the Wider Identity," in *Identity: Youth and Crisis* (New York, W. W. Norton, 1968), 295-320; "A Memorandum on Identity and Negro Youth," *Journal of Social Issues* 20 (October, 1964), 29-42.

*104. C. Silberman, *Crisis in Black and White* (New York, Random House, Vintage Books, 1964).

105. Stuart T. Hauser, *Black and White Identity Formation: Studies in the Psychosocial Development of Lower Socioeconomic Class Adolescent Boys* (New York, John Wiley, 1971), chap. 1.

106. Vincent P. Franklin, "Slavery, Personality, and Black Culture—Some Theoretical Issues," *Phylon* 35 (March, 1974), 54-63.

*107. L. L. Langness, *The Life History in Anthropological Science* (New York, Holt, Rinehart & Winston, 1965).

*108. E. Erikson, *Childhood and Society,* rev. ed. (New York, W. W. Norton, 1963).

109. ———— "Gandhi's *Autobiography:* The Leader as a Child," *American Scholar* 35 (Autumn, 1966), 632-46.

110. ————, *Gandhi's Truth* (New York, W. W. Norton, 1969).

111. H. Lichtenstein, "Identity and Sexuality: A Study of their Relationship in Man," *Journal of the American Psychoanalytic Association* 9 (1961) 179-260; "The Dilemma of Human Identity," *JAPA* 11 (1963), 173-223.

112. P. Greenacre, *Emotional Growth: Psychoanalytic Studies of the Gifted and a Great Variety of Other Individuals* (New York, International University Press, 1971), 2 vols.

113. E. Cobb, "The Ecology of Imagination in Childhood," in *The Subversive Science,* eds. P. Shepard & D. McKinley (Boston, Houghton Mifflin, 1969), 122-32.

*114. H. S. Hughes, *History as Art and as Science: Twin Vistas on the Past* (New York, Harper & Row, 1964).

Interpreting Nineteenth-Century American Literature

by Arlin Turner

Aids to the study, understanding, and interpretation of American Literature are plentiful nowadays, and are growing steadily in numbers and usefulness. The abundance of such aids could not have been foretold half a century ago, considering, for one thing, the reluctance Americans showed long after independence to think of their literature as separate rather than as a segment of British literature, and considering also the pattern of literary studies normal in American colleges and universities, in which even today the national literature appears usually as one field in a department devoted mainly to the study of British language and literature.

American authors themselves—perhaps more persistently than the authors of other major literatures—have responded with a self-consciousness (national, regional, ethnic, or social) that has leavened their work with an acute awareness of the time, place, and circumstances of their American experience. This self-consciousness is reflected in our minor and major writers; in our literary critics and scholars; and, moreover, in the tendency of each era to interpret and to evaluate earlier works anew by its own theories and tastes. Such reassessments of the literary past according to criteria of the moment have been the more persuasive because the major literary theorists, critics, and interpreters of an era have been often the major poets or novelists: William Cullen Bryant and Edgar Allan Poe, for example, or William Dean Howells and Henry James, T. S. Eliot, Wallace Stevens, John Crowe Ransom, and Robert Penn Warren.

National Self-Consciousness

American Literature in the nineteenth century developed a national seif-consciousness: poets and novelists felt compelled to fill needs within their own nation, and critics tended to identify national needs and to evaluate literary works according to their success in meeting those needs. During the Early Republic, if American authors were optimistic, they aimed at a literature appropriate to the achievement and the prospects of the new nation; if they feared the new form of government would fail, they saw literary works as forces toward the survival of the nation. A prediction by James Kirke Paulding in 1831 might have been heard at any time during the first century of national existence: "Assuredly the time will arrive when the American people will take pride in a literature of their own and realize that a National Literature is a National Power." Pretensions often outran accomplishments, though not so far, probably, as foreign travelers and some native critics said.

No author could forget that he was an American, nor that his writings and their acceptance would both be affected by that fact. Charles Brockden Brown, one of the earliest to write without political or other immediate didactic purpose, brought the novel and the Gothic romance from Europe at the turn of the nineteenth century and made conscious adjustments to the new land. Even though William Cullen Bryant spoke of literature more often in a universal rather than a parochial sense, he nevertheless showed himself consciously an American author. In spite of—or perhaps because of—Washington Irving's long residence in

Mr. Turner is editor of American Literature *and James B. Duke Professor of English at Duke University, Durham, North Carolina. He has served as chairman of the Advisory Committee on American Studies of the Council for International Exchange of Scholars and as a Visiting Fulbright Professor to the Universities of Western Australia and Hull, England. He also has taught at the Universities of Montreal and Bombay, and has received Guggenheim and National Endowment for the Humanities Senior fellowships, and also A.C.L.S. and Huntington Library research grants. Mr. Turner's numerous other positions in American Studies have included chairmanship of the American Literature Section of the Modern Language Association, the vice presidency of the American Studies Association, and the presidency of the Southeastern American Studies Association. He has published chiefly on Hawthorne and George W. Cable; his book,* George W. Cable: A Biography *won the Southern Historical Association award for the best book in Southern history for 1956–57.*

Europe and the compatability he felt with the English gentry, his sketches and tales, his narratives of western exploration, and his biography of Washington suggest that he remembered the question Crèvecoeur had asked before the Revolution: "What Is an American?" Similarly, James Fenimore Cooper, William Gilmore Simms, and John Pendleton Kennedy, while following in the tracks of Sir Walter Scott and other romance writers of Europe, consciously undertook to define American character and the American experience.

The need to speak self-consciously as an American had its most urgent statements in the period called the Renaissance of American letters. Speaking from personal and literary positions and in tones of language that were by no means identical, Ralph Waldo Emerson, in his essay "The American Scholar" (1837), and Herman Melville, in his review of Hawthorne's *Moses from an Old Manse* (1850), exhorted their literary compatriots to stand on their own feet. Following in this tradition, Walt Whitman sounded his "barbaric yawp" and continued the rest of his life an apostle of what he considered distinctly American in outlook and poetic form.

Whitman's call, it should be noted, was not the same as that sounded earlier in the century. Taking for granted the permanence of the new nation and the inclusiveness of its revolution against the past, he asked for yet additional growth and freedom for the American as the representative modern. But the habit of national self-consciousness remained after Whitman, as European travelers writing about America, offering ignorant prejudice at one extreme and acute insight at the other, were quick to note. Far into the century, American authors, like James Russell Lowell in his essay of 1869, "On a Certain Condescension in Foreigners," were answering Sydney Smith's query of 1820: who reads an American book?

Whether prompted by adverse criticism from abroad or by faith in American democracy as an agency of private and public good, authors tended in the nineteenth century to speak in tones of pride and confidence—not excluding Hawthorne, Melville and others who were not comfortable with the extreme Nationalists—the social millenialists or the philosophical optimists—so ubiquitous in their times. Later writers, beginning with the wild demurrers of Henry James and reaching new levels of protest and derision in the later expatriates, would employ different tones. But Americans would continue the habit of writing and judging works not simply as individual specimens of literary art, but as pieces integral to a total social entity, whether of a nation or a smaller unit; novels, poems, or plays would be seen in relation to social movements or developments. This generalization may apply even more conspicuously to the writings prominent in our own time, in which experiments with contents and techniques, challenges to norms of taste and decorum, and advocacy of political, social, and religious causes reflect probably a sharper awareness of time, place, and issues, and a greater allegiance to considerations normally not thought to be literary, than in any earlier period of our literature.

It is worth remarking also that instead of the approach through "set" books and authors common to literary study in European schools and universities, the approach in America is most often through a movement, a development, a genre, a region, or a period. In non-academic as well as academic interpretation, literature is thus viewed in a network of relationships, purposes, influences, and results; and the interpretation of a work may change sharply when the cultural context in which it appeared is understood differently, or when a new era has brought a new critical approach.

The Personal Voice

It would be a mistake to imply that the personal voice of a literary interpreter is normally lost in the voice of his age. He, like the poet or the novelist, will blend his voice with that prevalent in his time; and the greater his gifts, the more his individual voice is likely to remain audible. Henry James's book on Hawthorne in the English Men of Letters series (1879) was a product of the age of realism, to be sure, but it was also a product of James's own idiosyncrasies. Vernon L. Parrington's *Main Currents in American Thought* (New York: Harcourt, Brace, 1927-1930), to cite another instance, reflects the Jeffersonian liberalism and the emphasis on economic and social forces prevalent at the time, but maintains also the author's distinctive outlook. The great respect paid to F. O. Matthiessen since his *American Renaissance* (New York: Oxford University Press) appeared in 1941 is due not only to his learning, perceptiveness, and balance, but also to the deftness with which he fused the literary outlook of the preceding decade with the outlook that was evolving and became dominant in the new decade—the 1930s sought human and social values in the context of the current scene; the 1940s shifted emphasis to literary artistry considered in a frame of aesthetic universals. The authors Matthiessen chose for study (Emerson, Thoreau, Hawthorne, Melville, and Whitman) were well suited to his purpose.

Sectional and Regional Consciousness

The fifty years of sectional strife and war in the middle of the nineteenth century gave special coloring and shape—or distortion—to literary endeavors: extremes in the debate on slavery; individual responses to the war, as in the poems of Walt Whitman and Henry Timrod; voices of reconciliation after the fighting had closed; and massive literary production afterward, especially Civil War novels. Even Emily Dickinson could not close the war out entirely, nor could Mark Twain; and readers and critics read through glasses tinted like those of the authors. In later times, interpretation of literature from the Civil War era experienced revisionism comparable to that well known in the political and social history of the era. A late revisionist in this area was Edmund Wilson, who in a book entitled *Patriotic Gore* (New York: Oxford University Press, 1962), brought his large gifts as a literary critic and his lesser, often idiosyncratic, gifts as a social historian to bear on a score of literary authors whose lives and works were touched by the war.

Well before the sectional antagonisms arising in the 1830s had soured the Era of Good Feeling, literature had begun to portray local particularities of character, manners, speech, and hereditary lore. What was peculiar to Dutch New York, for example, Down East New England, or the Southwest frontier was delineated with sympathy or good humor or kindly satire. Self-consciousness, here local or regional, continued important. A writer sketching a "natural" character or recounting an outlandish anecdote would know whether he was writing for the local weekly newspaper or a national periodical. The backwoods

humorists realized that the low characters, illiterate speech, indelicacy, and ir-
reverence they employed moved them outside the bounds of polite literature,
with the consequence that they sometimes added a double measure of indelicacy
and extravagance, to emphasize their rebellion.

The humorists of the old Southwest had readers in their own time, but slight
literary respectability. William Gilmore Simms, always ready to hear or to tell a
raucous yarn, said of a collection of frontier humorous tales published in 1849
that it was just the book to read on a boat or a train, but not a book to take into
the house at the end of the journey. It was nearly a hundred years after the
backwoods American humor flourished that it first became known in literary
study. F. J. Meine (*Tall Tales of the Southwest,* New York: Knopf, 1930) and
Constance Rourke (*American Humor,* New York: Harcourt, Brace, 1931; paper,
Doubleday Anchor Books) initiated a study that has uncovered a rich lore in the
Old Southwest, in oral tradition and unliterary writing; has shown the importance of that lore to Mark Twain, William Faulkner, and many others; and has
given the early humorists a literary station that would have astonished them.

Most important among the works that have rehabilitated and reinterpreted the
native humor is Walter Blair's *Native American Humor* (New York: American
Book, 1937; paper, San Francisco: Chandler Publishing, 1960). Other general
treatments are Bernard DeVoto, *Mark Twain's America* (New York: Little,
Brown, 1932); Mody C. Boatright, *Folk Laughter on the American Frontier*
(New York: Macmillan, 1949); Kenneth Lynn, *Mark Twain and Southwestern
Humor* (Boston: Little, Brown, 1959); Willard Thorp, *American Humorists* (No.
42 in the University of Minnesota Pamphlets on American Writers, 1964);
Jesse Bier, *The Rise and Fall of American Humor* (New York: Holt, Rinehart
and Winston, 1968); and Richard Hauck, *A Cheerful Nihilism: Confidence and
"the Absurd" in American Humorous Fiction* (Bloomington: Indiana University
Press, 1971). Anthologists have provided samples of the humorous writings:
Brom Weber, *An Anthology of American Humor* (New York: Crowell, 1962);
Hennig Cohen and William B. Dillingham, *Humor of the Old Southwest* (Boston:
Houghton Mifflin, 1964); Kenneth Lynn, *The Comic Tradition in America* (New
York: Doubleday Anchor Books, 1958). And several critical biographies of indi-
vidual humorists have contributed depth and perspective to our view of the
native humor: John Donald Wade, *Augustus Baldwin Longstreet: A Study of the
Development of Culture in the South* (New York: Macmillan, 1924; Athens:
University of Georgia Press, 1969); John Q. Anderson, *Louisiana Swamp Doc-
tor: The Life and Writings of Henry Clay Lewis* (Baton Rouge: Louisiana State
University Press, 1962); Milton R. Rickels, *Thomas Bangs Thorpe* (Baton Rouge:
Louisiana State University Press, 1962) and *George Washington Harris* (New
York: Twayne, 1965). Norris W. Yates has studied humorists of the present
century with special reference to their heritage from the earlier tradition: *The
American Humorists: Conscience of the Twentieth Century* (Ames: Iowa State
University Press, 1964), and *William T. Porter and the Spirit of the Times* (Baton
Rouge: Louisiana State University Press, 1957).

No other portion of our literary past has been so thoroughly redeemed from
oblivion and interpreted so thoroughly *de novo* as the ante-bellum humor, but
other examples of repeated reassessment can be cited—local color fiction, for
example. Following the Civil War, the sympathetic portrayal of local peculiari-

ties was resumed with a far greater knowledge and curiosity about remote sections than ever before, and with a desire to promote tolerance between the North and the South. Magazine fiction of the West, the South, and the East won popular and critical approval, but later estimates have noted that authors like Bret Harte of novels and stories intended primarily to exploit the remote and the odd rarely surpassed in achievement the level of their intentions. Local color collections such as Harry R. Warfel and G. Harrison Crians, *American Local-Color Stories* (New York: American Book, 1941) and Claude M. Simpson, *The Local Colorists: American Short Stories, 1857–1900* (New York: Harper, 1960), contain mainly lesser authors; in major authors, such as Mark Twain, other elements are likely to be more important than the local. Local colorists often combined an awareness of sectional differences with their close observation of others; e.g., Bret Harte's western miners, Joel Chandler Harris's plantation Negroes and mountaineers, and Sarah Orne Jewett's rural and small-town New Englanders. These writings have been evaluated anew for the social history of a section they record, or for more strictly literary qualities. For example, a recent book by Merrill Maguire Skaggs, *The Folk of Southern Fiction: A Study of Local Color Tradition* (Athens: University of Georgia Press, 1972) surveys local color fiction written in the Southern region with particular attention to the portrayal of the yeoman farmers.

Realism and American Literature

My discussion thus far has dealt with tendencies, trends, or vogues in which the directing force was consciousness of the nation or a region. Howellsian realism, dominant on the literary scene from 1870 to 1890, was a full-scale literary movement, involving both materials and techniques, developing a body of theory and criticism, and enlisting the major authors of the period. Not since Hawthorne and Poe had works been subjected to such distinctly literary considerations. Recent interpretative biographies of William Dean Howells (by Edwin H. Cady, Syracuse, N.Y.: Syracuse University Press, two volumes, 1956–1958) and Henry James (by Leon Edel, Philadelphia: Lippincott, five volumes, 1953–1972), taken together, furnish definitions, principles, and examples from the two authors who dominated the novel and the criticism of fiction in their time. In the extremes of Howellsian glorification of the commonplace and Jamesian insulation of characters from the workaday world, the realistic novels lost something of the immediacy, if not the urgency, American readers customarily demanded. Because Howells was so conscious of his fiction as a commentary on the distortions apparent in that actual world, the commonplace in some of his novels is anything but common.

Starting with the goal of naturalness in portraying man in his ordinary environment, but impressed with the new scientific thought, including the social, psychological, philosophical, and aesthetic implications, the group of authors who produced the amalgam of materials, attitudes and techniques called naturalism were themselves re-interpreting literary realism before its vogue had passed. What in Frank Norris and Stephen Crane began as extension of realistic materials and techniques became in others, such as Theodore Dreiser and Upton Sinclair, conscious revolt. This example of the abruptness of change in literary criteria and literary interpretations is accented by the sharp alterations apparent in the fiction and the criticism written by Howells himself.

Uncertainty of definition and delineation—and as a consequence uncertainty of evaluation—remained beyond the age of realism and naturalism in the late nineteenth and early twentieth centuries. Several important studies of the past twenty years can be cited to illustrate the clarification, reinterpretation, and reassessment that one literary era may provide for an earlier one. Among the broader studies are Warner Berthoff, *The Ferment of Realism: American Literature, 1884-1919* (New York: Free Press, 1965); Donald Pizer, *Realism and Naturalism in Nineteenth-Century American Literature* (Carbondale: Southern Illinois University Press, 1966); and Jay Martin, *Harvests of Change: American Literature, 1865-1914* (Englewood Cliffs, N.J.: Prentice Hall, 1967). More restricted investigations include Lars Åhnebrink, *The Beginnings of Naturalism in American Fiction* (Uppsala, Sweden, 1950); Everett Carter, *Howells and the Age of Realism* (Philadelphia: Lippincott, 1954); Charles Child Walcutt, *American Literary Naturalism, A Divided Stream* (Minneapolis: University of Minnesota Press, 1956); Robert Falk, *The Victorian Mode in American Fiction, 1865-1885* (East Lansing: Michigan State University Press, 1965); and Larzer Ziff, *The American 1890's: Life and Times of a Lost Generation* (New York: Viking, 1966). The journal *American Literary Realism* (1967-) limits itself to the years 1870-1910 and gives special attention to bibliography. Similar journals might be cited for many other areas of literary study.

New Levels of Scholarly Research

As every age writes the literary history of its past, new interpretations evolve, which leave former interpretations along with the poetry, novels, plays and other records of the earlier age, subject to reinterpretation. The facts, insights, and suggestions encased in earlier interpretations remain useful, as is the information on other arts and the composite background of the earlier period. But of primary importance to any interpretation is, of course, the literary work itself, in an accurate text and accompanied by appropriate bibliographical and other factual information. This is the kind of information being furnished today in such an abundance as never before. If technological advancements in our generation are making textual editors and bibliographers instead of interpreters and critics of our literature, as may seem to be the case, no one can object to the editions and bibliographies being produced—for they become available to scholars and critics of this and following generations.

Several collateral developments have spurred the growth and distribution of aids to literary study: the paperback revolution, for one; the expansion of university presses; the multiplication of scholarly and critical journals; the underwriting of literary research and writing by societies, educational institutions, and foundations; the preparation of indexes, concordances, and bibliographies; the establishment and distribution of dependable texts of the major authors; and the publication of authors' letters and notebooks.

There have been no more than hints thus far of the ways in which literary study may benefit as the age of the computer advances. The Modern Language Association has begun the storing of bibliographies and abstracts for later sorting and printing out to meet special needs. The American Bibliographical Center, Santa Barbara, California, is well along in a program of Automation of Bibliography through Computerization. Under the title *America: History and Life,* abstracts and indexes are now printed quarterly from computer print-out; stored entries are flagged so as to permit retrieval for demand bibliographies and selective dissemination. Besides the now regular use of computers for making concordances and for comparing stylistic elements in a known sample and in an unknown sample to determine authorship, collation by computer has been employed in the editing of a literary text. (See William M. Gibson and George R. Petty, Jr. *Project Occult: The Ordered Computer Collation of an Unprepared Literary Text.* New York: New York University Press, 1970).

American literary scholarship has profited through several important cooperative efforts. The pioneering cooperative literary history, *The Cambridge History of American Literature* (New York: Macmillan, four volumes, 1917–1920), has been followed by *The Literary History of the United States* (two volumes of history and a volume of bibliography, New York: Macmillan, 1948), the work of more than fifty hands. The American Literature Section (formerly Group) of the Modern Language Association has sponsored a number of joint undertakings and has found that large bibliographical and editorial projects yield especially well to such efforts. Since its founding in 1929 the journal *American Literature* has been published by the Duke University Press in cooperation with the American Literature Section. Through an editorial board and a bibliographer elected from its members, the Section (without fiscal obligations) is able to direct editorial policy and make sure that the journal serves the changing needs of scholarship. The quarterly lists of "Articles on American Literature Appearing in Current Periodicals" (brought together by Lewis Leary in two volumes: for the years 1900-1950 [1954] and for the years 1950–1967 [1970] Durham, N.C.: Duke University Press) along with the book reviews and book notes, inform the readers of *American Literature* about current publications more promptly than occasional lists or annual lists such as those published by the Modern Language Association (*MLA International Bibliography of Books and Articles on the Modern Languages and Literature*), the Modern Humanities Research Association (*Annual Bibliography of English Language and Literature*), and the English Association (*The Year's Work in English Studies*).

The American Literature Section sponsors also an analytical and evaluation bibliography, *American Literary Scholarship.* Prepared annually by some eighteen scholars of the Section since 1963 and running to over four hundred pages a year, it is published in cloth for the trade and in paper for free distribution to members of the Section. Another major bibliography to be credited to the American Literature Section is *Eight American Authors,* published by the Modern Language Association in 1956, the work of eight scholars writing evaluative essays on eight major authors. It was reissued with a supplement in 1962 by W. W. Norton; a new edition appeared in 1972, with the essays rewritten and brought up to date. These works sponsored by the American Literature Section testify to an awareness of the scholar's perennial cry for current bibliography. The bibliographical volume of the *Literary History of the United States* (New York: Macmillan, 1948) has been extended by supplements in 1960 and 1972.

Other evaluative bibliographies cooperatively prepared are *Fifteen Modern American Authors,* edited by Jackson R. Bryer (Durham, N.C.: Duke University

Press, 1969); *Fifteen American Authors before 1900,* edited by Robert A. Rees and Earl N. Harbert (Madison: University of Wisconsin Press, 1971); and *A Bibliographical Guide to the Study of Southern Literature,* edited by Louis D. Rubin, Jr. (Baton Rouge: Louisiana State University Press, 1969). Literary bibliographies are available for many of the states; others are devoted to regions or special types of American writing. On one restricted topic of collateral use in literary study, the following bibliographies might be listed (all published at Norman: University of Oklahoma Press): Walter S. Campbell, *The Book Lover's Southwest: A Guide to Good Reading* (1955) and two books by Ramon F. Adams: *Six Guns and Saddle Leather: A Bibliography of Pamphlets on Western Outlaws and Gunmen* (1954) and *The Rampaging Herd: A Bibliography of Books and Pamphlets on Men and Events in the Cattle Industry* (1959).

Such lists can be extended, and many seem to argue that the greatest riches for American literary study—and greater year by year—are in bibliography. Jacob Blanck's majesterial *Bibliography of American Literature* (New Haven, Conn.: Yale University Press, 1955-) has now reached volume six and Thomas William Parsons. Lyle H. Wright, after publishing the three volumes of his bibliography *American Fiction,* modestly subtitled "A Contribution toward a Bibliography" (San Marino, Calif.: Huntington Library, I, 1774–1850 [1939 and 1948]; II, 1851–1875 [1957]; III, 1876–1900 [1966]), brought out in 1969 a revised and augmented edition of "Wright I," as the first volume is reverently called. The Charles Evans bibliography (twelve volumes, 1903–1934) was reprinted in 1941; and several supplementary and auxiliary volumes have followed.

Those needing guidance for initial steps in American literary study might begin with Charles H. Nilson's *Bibliography of Bibliographies in American Literature* (New York: Bowker, 1970). Several directories and lists published by the Swallow Press of Chicago will illustrate the guides to the criticism of American Literature that are available: Donna Gerstenberger and George Hendrick, *The American Novel: A Checklist of Twentieth Century Criticism* (volume I: from 1900 to 1959, 1960, volume II: from 1960 to 1968, 1970); by the same compilers, *Third Directory of Periodicals Publishing Articles on English and American Literature and Language* (1970; the two preceding directories appeared in 1959 and 1965); Arthur Coleman and Garry R. Tyler, *Drama Criticism: A Checklist of Interpretation Since 1940 of English and American Plays* (1966); Joseph Kuntz, *Poetry Explication: A Checklist of Interpretation since 1925 of British and American Poems* (revised edition, 1962); Jarvis Thurston and others, *Short Fiction Criticism: A Checklist of Interpretation since 1925 of Stories and Novelettes* (1960). The Goldentree Bibliographies series (New York: Appleton-Century-Crofts, paper) includes the following volumes on American subjects and announces others to come: Blake Nevius, *The American Novel: Sinclair Lewis to the Present* (1970), and Darwin T. Turner, *Afro-American Writers* (1970).

Compilers and publishers have been comparably generous in furnishing bibliographies of individual authors. Patricia Pate Havlice, *Index to American Authors' Bibliographies* (Metuchen, N.J.: Scarecrow Press, 1971), is likely to be especially useful, since it lists only bibliographies that are printed in periodicals and consequently are omitted from most lists. Alan Swallow issued from his press at Denver, in thin volumes, a series of bibliographies of lesser authors, including, as examples, Hart Crane in 1955 and Yvor Winters in 1959. Other publishers have initiated series of individual bibliographies: Kent State University Press, for example, and the Charles E. Merrill Company. Especially welcome are the lists that describe and evaluate the items, such as *A Checklist of Hawthorne Criticism, 1951–1966* (Hartford, Conn.: Transcendental Books, 1967), by Buford Jones, and *Hawthorne, Melville, Stephen Crane: A Critical Bibliography* (New York: Free Press, 1971), by Theodore L. Gross and Stanley Wertheim.

The most extensive collective effort in American literary scholarship is the editing of texts being done under the aegis of the Center for Editions of American Authors, an agency of the Modern Language Association. The achievements to the present have far exceeded what seemed likely in the beginning exploratory and planning sessions held in 1962: the adoption of plans by the MLA; the establishment of the CEAA office, with its director and supervisory committee; the formulation of editorial policies and procedures; the enlistment of scores of literary and textual scholars as editors and consultants; the provision of Federal financing through the National Endowment for the Humanities; the publication thus far of texts for nearly a hundred works by a dozen authors; and the prospect of including complete or selected works by all major authors of the nineteenth century. Since the "best possible texts" thus produced are now available (under conditions stipulated by the Center) for reproduction by other publishers, they can be expected to become widely available (often in paper covers) and in normal attrition to replace other texts.

Editorial matter accompanying the CEAA texts is restricted mainly to technical and factual information, leaving each succeeding generation to furnish its own interpretation and criticism. Those furnishing the interpretation and criticism, in the immediate or the remote future, will profit from these texts and the other aids—bibliographical, historical, and technical—that are being supplied in growing abundance.

CEAA Published and Forthcoming Volumes
(CEAA Seals Awarded Through 27 November 1974)

FUNDED EDITIONS

● STEPHEN CRANE
University Press of Virginia

Bowery Tales	*Tales, Sketches, and Reports*
Tales of Whilomville	*The Red Badge of Courage**
Tales of War	*Poems**
Tales of Adventure	*Third Violet - Active Service**
The O'Ruddy	**Edition complete**
Reports of War	

● RALPH WALDO EMERSON
(THE JOURNALS)
Harvard University Press

Volume VII	1838-42	Volume XI	1848-51*
Volume VIII	1841-43	Volume XII	1836-62*
Volume IX	1843-47	**Volumes I-VI were published without**
Volume X	1847-49	**the seal**

*Sealed, but not published.

● RALPH WALDO EMERSON
(THE WORKS)
Harvard University Press
Nature, Addresses, and *Lectures*

● NATHANIEL HAWTHORNE
Ohio State University Press
The Scarlet Letter   *A Wonder Book* and *Tanglewood*
The House of the Seven Gables   *Tales*
The Blithedale Romance and   *American Notebooks*
  Fanshawe   *Twice-Told Tales*
The Marble Faun   *Snow Image*
Our Old Home   *Mosses from an Old Manse*
True Stories

● WILLIAM DEAN HOWELLS
Indiana University Press
The Shadow of a Dream and   *Indian Summer*
  An Imperative Duty   *The Leatherwood God* *
The Kentons   *A Hazard of New Fortunes* *
Their Wedding Journey   *April Hopes* *
Literary Friends and   *The Quality of Mercy* *
  Acquaintances   *Modern Instance* *
Altrurian Romances   *The Minister's Charge* *
Son of Royal Langbrith   *Letters I* *
Years of My Youth *   *Criticism I* *
The Rise of Silas Lapham   *Criticism III* *
A Chance Acquaintance   *Selected Novelle* *

● WASHINGTON IRVING
University of Wisconsin Press
Journals and Notebooks, 1803-06   *Astoria* *
  (Vol. I)   *Bracebridge Hall* *
Journals and Notebooks, 1819-27   *Bonneville* *
  (Vol. III)   *The Sketch Book of Geoffrey*
Mahomet   *Crayon, Gent.* *
The Alhambra *   *Life of George Washington* *
Oldstyle-Salmagundi *   *Letters I* *

● HENRY DAVID THOREAU
Princeton University Press
Walden   *Reform Papers*
The Maine Woods   *Early Essays and Miscellanies* *

● MARK TWAIN PAPERS
University of California Press
Which Was the Dream? and Other   *Hannibal, Huck & Tom*
  Symbolic Writings of the Later   *Fables of Man*
  Years   *Notebooks I* *
Letters to His Publishers   *Notebooks II* *
Correspondence with Henry   *Notebooks III* *
  Huttleston Rogers   *Satires and Burlesques* published
Mysterious Stranger Manuscripts   without the seal

● MARK TWAIN WORKS
  University of California Press
  Roughing It   *Innocents Abroad* *
  What Is Man?   *Early Tales and Sketches* (4 vols.) *

● WALT WHITMAN
  New York University Press
  Diaries and Daybook *   *Early Poems and the Fiction*
  published without the seal: *Prose Works 1892: Specimen Days*
  Correspondence 1842-67   *Prose Works 1892: Collected and*
  Correspondence 1868-75   *Other Prose*
  Correspondence 1876-85   *Leaves of Grass*
  Correspondence 1890-92

ASSOCIATED EDITIONS

● CHARLES BROCKDEN BROWN
  Wieland *

● JOHN DEWEY
  Southern Illinois University Press   *Early Essays and the Study of Ethics*
  Early Works   *Early Essays*
  Early Essays and Leibniz's   *Middle Works*
      New Essays   *Essays, The School and Society,*
  Psychology   and *The Educational Situation* *
  Early Essays and Outlines of a   *Essays, Studies in Logical Theory,*
      Critical Theory of Ethics   and *The Child and the Curriculum* *

● WILLIAM JAMES
  Pragmatism *
  The Meaning of Truth *

● HERMAN MELVILLE
  Northwestern University Press
  Typee   *Mardi*
  Omoo   *Pierre*
  Redburn   *The Confidence Man* *
  White-Jacket

● WILLIAM GILMORE SIMMS
  University of South Carolina Press
  Voltmeier   *Stories and Tales*
  As Good as a Comedy and   *Joscelyn* *
      Paddy McGann

Illustrations of the American Earth: A Bibliographical Essay on the Cultural Geography of the United States

by G. S. Dunbar

More than fifty years ago, a French geographer defined human geography as the study of the progressive humanization of the surface of the earth. In this essay I shall be concerned with the humanization of the American earth—first the Indianization, then the Europeanization and Africanization, and finally, through synthesis of all the earlier elements, the Americanization of the area that is now the United States. These matters are not, of course, exclusively the domain of geography but are shared with all other branches of the social sciences and humanities; indeed, they form the common focus for all fields in American Studies. To Crèvecoeur's question, "What, then, is the American, this new man?," we might add, "What is America, this new land?" To a very great extent, man made the land, and perhaps to a certain extent the land made man, but we do not yet have the proper tools and techniques to be able to come to grips with this question. In the study of man–land relationships geographers now emphasize man, whereas, two generations ago, the land would have been given a central role in shaping human events.

In writing this essay I have been helped enormously by the almost providential appearance of a new book, *The Cultural Geography of the United States* by Wilbur Zelinsky (Prentice-Hall, 1973 pb). I have also been aided by bibliographies provided by my colleague Tom McKnight of UCLA and by Peirce Lewis, Zelinsky's colleague at the Pennsylvania State University. Although academic geographers make much of the differences among human, cultural, and social geography in their intramural debates, we can spare these somewhat arcane distinctions and concern ourselves with any and all works which illustrate the variety and complexity of the American landscape. In order to understand how the cultural (human, manmade, or artificial) landscapes of the United States came into being, it is necessary to seek historical explanations, and so a fair sample of the work of American historical geographers is included in this essay.

Atlases and Journals

There are a number of good atlases—state, regional, and national—but none is so well done, so comprehensive, or so expensive as *The National Atlas of the United States*, edited by Arch Gerlach (U. S. Geological Survey, 1970). The best historical atlas is still Charles Paullin's *Atlas of the Historical Geography of the United States*, edited by John K. Wright (Carnegie Institution and American Geographical Society, 1932). The U. S. Department of Agriculture has recently produced *The Look of Our Land—An Airphoto Atlas of the Rural United States* (5 vols., 1970–1971), a useful compilation for the teacher of geography.

There is no journal which is devoted strictly to American geography, in the manner of the *Journal of American History* and the regional and state historical journals, but articles on American geography are scattered widely through the literature. The journal *Landscape*, unfortunately now moribund, has for over twenty years published vividly impressionistic but largely undocumented articles which illustrate land and life in all parts of the world, with emphasis on the United States. Three special issues are of particular importance: "The Farm Scene" (Spring 1957), "The Small City" (Autumn 1957), and "The Countryside" (Spring 1959). Many of the trenchant essays of *Landscape's* founder and first editor, J. B. Jackson, have been gathered into a book, *Landscapes* edited by Ervin Zube (University of Massachusetts, 1970 pb).

Geographies of the United States and Its Major Regions

In 1936 W. L. G. Joerg wrote a splendid history of the regional exposition of North America (*GR*, October 1936), but unfortunately he has had no imitators. Most of the current textbooks treat all of "Anglo-America," i.e., North America north of Mexico, but some, such as Zelinsky's new book and Robert Estall's *Modern Geography of the United States* (Penguin, 1972 pb), only cover the United States. Ralph Brown's *Historical Geography of the United States* (Harcourt Brace, 1948) covers the period 1600–1870 and gives the background necessary for the understanding of the present landscape. The textbooks on Anglo-America are necessarily quite superficial, partly because they attempt to cover

---

[Author's Note: Wherever possible, I have indicated books that are available in paperback (pb). It can be assumed that most of the books published or reprinted in the last half–dozen years or so are still available from the publishers. As a space-saver I have abbreviated the names of the two leading American geographical journals, the *Annals of the Association of American Geographers (AAAG)* and the *Geographical Review (GR)*. I depart from normal *AS:AIN* practice and cite articles as well as books because many of the most important topics have not yet been given book-length treatment by geographers. Although I emphasize the work of card-carrying geographers, I cite the best works irrespective of the academic affiliations of their authors. I hope that the crypto-geographers will not mind being co-opted for such a noble purpose.]

an area of more than seven million square miles, and they are rather unsatisfying to cultural or historical geographers because they do not have much time depth. An exception is J. Wreford Watson's *North America, Its Countries and Regions* (Praeger, 1968), which manages to combine depth and breadth. Another excellent text is *The United States and Canada: A Regional Geography* by William Mead and Eric Brown (Hillary, 1962 pb). Most of the other texts treat the contemporary geography and present sober data rather than evocative description. Among the best are *Regional Geography of Anglo-America* by Langdon White, Edwin Foscue, and Tom McKnight (Prentice-Hall, 4th ed., 1974, *North America* by John Paterson (Oxford, 4th ed. 1970), and *The Anglo-American Realm* by Otis Starkey and Lewis Robinson (McGraw-Hill, 1969).

It is interesting to note that Estall, Watson, Mead, Brown, and Paterson are all British geographers. Outsiders can often comprehend a monumental task and write more insightfully than the natives can. Part of the explanation may lie in the fact that geographers, like anthropologists, seem to get more prestige from working in foreign parts. Many American cultural geographers have devoted their attention to other parts of the globe, while leaving the mother country in comparative neglect. For example, my colleague Joseph Spencer is best known for his work in Asia and for his textbooks in cultural geography (e.g., *Introducing Cultural Geography* by J. E. Spencer and William Thomas, Wiley, 1973), but he began his professional career with a study of southwestern Utah.

The sections or larger regions of the United States have all had able expositors. Among works by geographers I should like to mention *The South: Its Economic-Geographic Development* by Almon Parkins (Wiley, 1938, recently reprinted by Greenwood), *The Southeastern United States* by John Fraser Hart (Van Nostrand, 1967 pb), *The Northeastern United States* by Lewis Alexander

Mr. Dunbar is Professor of Geography at the University of California, Los Angeles. He has served as Fulbright senior research scholar at the University of Dacca, Bangladesh, chairman of

Photo: UC/Santa Barbara

the Department of Geography at the University of Virginia, and visiting professor in Ahmadu Bello University, Nigeria. His teaching and research interests lie in the general realms of historical and cultural geography and the history of geography. He is currently at work on a biography of the French geographer-anarchist, Elisée Reclus (1830-1905).

(Van Nostrand, 1967 pb), *The North American Midwest: A Regional Geography* edited by John Garland (Wiley, 1955), *The North Central United States* by Wallace Akin (Van Nostrand, 1968 pb), *The Pacific Northwest: An Overall Appreciation* edited by Otis Freeman and Howard Martin (Wiley, 2nd ed. 1954), *California and the Southwest* edited by Clifford Zierer (Wiley, 1956), and *Southwest: Three Peoples in Geographical Change, 1600-1970* by D. W. Meinig (Oxford, 1971 pb). Of these books, Meinig's is of particular importance because of its cultural-historical orientation. Meinig's other works are also of special interest: *The Great Columbia Plain* (University of Washington, 1968), *Imperial Texas* (University of Texas, 1968), and an article, "The Mormon Culture Region," *AAAG*, June 1965.

Of the many state geographies, those which I think merit special attention are *Geography of New York State* edited by John Thompson (Syracuse University, 1966), *Virginia in Our Century* by Jean Gottmann (University Press of Virginia, 1969), *Minnesota's Changing Geography* by John Borchert (University of Minnesota, 1959), and *Louisiana: Its Land and People* by Fred Kniffen (Louisiana State University, 1968). The last two were written for schoolchildren but can very profitably be used by more mature readers. I wish that James Parsons' tantalizingly brief essay, "The Uniqueness of California" (*American Quarterly*, Spring 1955), had been expanded to book size.

There are a number of studies of areas that are of less-than-state size, and the best of these, in my biased view, are patently historical: *Colonial North Carolina in the Eighteenth Century* by Roy Merrens (University of North Carolina, 1964), and *The Best Poor Man's Country: A Geographical Study of Early Southeastern Pennsylvania* by James Lemon (Johns Hopkins, 1972). Lauren Post's delightful book–*Cajun Sketches* (Louisiana State University, 1962), offers a glimpse of what life is like in one of America's most distinctive culture areas, French Louisiana. Terry Jordan has described nineteenth-century Texas in several articles and a book, *German Seed in Texas Soil* (University of Texas, 1966). A special issue of *AAAG* (September 1959), "Man, Time and Space in Southern California" edited by William Thomas, describes the past, present, and future of "the patio of America." A new book, *Regions of the United States* edited by John Fraser Hart (Harper-Row, 1973 pb), consists of papers published in the June 1972 issue of *AAAG*. These papers do not collectively cover the whole United States, and some are essentially topical, rather than regional studies. I should like to cite Hart's own paper on the Midwest, Peirce Lewis' on small town life, Meinig's on the Wests (*sic*), and Cotton Mather's on the Great Plains as being the most interesting papers illustrating the cultural geography of the United States.

The works of crypto-geographers often contain excellent geography, and I should like to mention specifically *The Great Plains* by Walter Prescott Webb, (Ginn, 1931 and many subsequent reprintings), *Human Geography of the South* by Rupert Vance (University of North Carolina, 1932, repr. by Russell 1968), *Great Basin Kingdom* by Leonard Arrington (Harvard, 1958, pb repr. by Nebraska 1966), *The Great Plains in Transition* by C. F. Kraenzel (Oklahoma, 1955, pb repr. 1970), and *The Grassland of North America* by James Malin (pub. by author, 1947, repr. by Peter Smith 1967). It has always puzzled me that the

Great Plains should get the lion's share, and now the imbalance is being aggra-vated by a recent conference at the University of Nebraska, "Images of the Plains," which may result in the best book of all.

Humanization of the American Earth

The Indianization of North America has already been treated in an *AS:AIN* article by Wilcomb Washburn [*AS:AIN* XI, #1, p. 25ff.], but it might be worth-while to mention some works which stress such geographically important themes as the provenience, numbers, settlement forms, and economic activities of the American Indians. Geographers will still find much of value in *Cultural and Natural Areas of Native North America* by A. L. Kroeber (University of Cali-fornia, 1939). Perhaps the best modern text is *The Indians of North America* by Harold Driver (University of Chicago, 2nd ed. 1969 pb), but geographers will also want to consult the parent work—*Comparative Studies of North American Indians* by Driver and William Massey (American Philosophical Society, 1957 pb).

Questions surrounding the late Pleistocene entry of man into North America are explored in *The Quaternary of the United States* edited by H. E. Wright and David Frey (Princeton, 1965) and *The Bering Land Bridge* edited by David Hop-kins (Stanford, 1967), but one must go to journal articles for the latest develop-ments in this fast-changing field. The conservative estimates by James Mooney and A. L. Kroeber of the pre-Conquest population north of Mexico have been re-vised from about one million to 10-12 million. See especially a paper by Henry Dobyns in the October 1966 issue of *Current Anthropology*. Cultural geogra-phers, notably the late Erhard Rostlund (e.g., *AAAG*, December 1960), have written articles on the role of the Indian as an agent of landscape change, but more should be done in this rewarding area. Sam Hilliard has produced a series of maps illustrating Indian land cessions (*AAAG*, June 1972), and Elliot Mc-Intire, Imre Sutton, and Donald Ballas have written about modern reservations, but a comprehensive geographical overview of Indian life in the United States, past and present, is needed. An interesting article which treats the Indian con-tribution to American culture is that of the anthropologist Irving Hallowell in *American Anthropologist* (April 1957).

The Africanization of the United States is as old and in certain areas as signifi-cant as the Europeanization, but documentation has been scarce because of the circumstances which brought most of the Africans to these shores. Most books on immigrants stress the European elements and barely mention the African, if at all. Philip Curtin has provided a convenient compendium of data on African immigration, *The Atlantic Slave Trade: A Census* (University of Wisconsin, 1969 pb), but these figures must be given life and meaning. So far, geographical studies of Afro-Americans have emphasized their numbers—e.g., books on the modern ghettos such as *The Black Ghetto* by Harold Rose (McGraw-Hill, 1971 pb) and *Geography of the Ghetto* ed. by Harold Rose (Northern Illinois University, 1972) and articles on the distribution of the Black population in modern times (Fraser Hart in *AAAG*, September 1960) or pre-Civil War days (Zelinsky on the Free Negroes in *Population Studies*, March 1950)—but studies of their diet, settle-ment forms, and economic activities should also be made.

Although the Europeanization of North America may have begun as early as the eleventh century (Helge Ingstad, *Westward to Vinland*, Harper-Row 1972 pb), the story properly begins in the sixteenth century. The full significance of the initial discoveries is made manifest by J. H. Parry, *The Age of Reconnaissance* (World, 1964, NAL pb), and for detail one should turn to S. E. Morison, *The European Discovery of America: The Northern Voyages, A. D. 500–1600* (Oxford, 1971). Geographers will want to consult *Sixteenth Century North America* by Carl Sauer (University of California 1971) and *European Impressions of the New England Coast, 1497–1620* by Douglas McManis (Chicago Geography Research Papers, 1972).

There are several good histories of the Colonial era, but historians do not usually give adequate coverage of the topics geographers are interested in. An exception is T. J. Wertenbaker's *The Founding of American Civilization: The Middle Colonies* (Scribner's, 1938, repr. by Cooper Square). Settlement morphology is treated in John Reps' *The Making of Urban America* (Princeton, 1965) and in Glenn Trewartha's article, "Types of Rural Settlement in Colonial America," *GR*, October 1946. The best book-length studies of any colonial areas by geographers are the two aforementioned works by Roy Merrens and James Lemon on eighteenth-century North Carolina and Pennsylvania, respectively. A masterful essay by Robert Mitchell on the initial peopling of the Shenandoah Valley of Virginia in *AAAG* (September 1972) has significance for other frontier regions as well.

American population before the first census (1790) is treated in two books by historians, *American Population before the Federal Census of 1790* by Evarts Greene and Virginia Harrington (Columbia, 1932; repr. by Peter Smith 1966) and *Population Distribution in Colonial America* by Stella Sutherland (Columbia, 1936; repr. by AMS 1966), but the best cartographic treatment of the subject is that of the geographer Herman Friis, *A Series of Population Maps of the Colonies and the United States, 1625–1790* (American Geographical Society, 1940 pb; rev. ed. 1968). Seventeenth- and eighteenth-century economic activities are treated in the general histories, in the standard agricultural histories such as *History of Agriculture in the Southern United States to 1860* by Lewis Gray (Carnegie Institution, 1932; repr. by Peter Smith 1958) and *History of Agriculture in the Northern United States, 1620-1860* by Percey Bidwell and John Falconer (Carnegie Institution, 1925; repr. Peter Smith), and in such works as *Tobacco Coast* by A. P. Middleton (Mariner's Museum, 1953) and *Economic History of Virginia in the Seventeenth Century* by P. A. Bruce (Macmillan, 1896; repr. by Johnson 1966).

The characteristics of the early Spanish and French settlements within the boundaries of the present-day United States are fairly well known, thanks to scholars such as Herbert Bolton, John McDermott, and Jack Holmes, but much more can be done. Geographers have not contributed significantly to the study of the Spanish and French colonial era, with the exception of Louis Gentilcore's studies of California missions and of Vincennes, Indiana (*AAAG*, March 1961 and September 1957) and portions of Carl Sauer's *The Geography of the Ozark Highland of Missouri* (University of Chicago, 1920) and Almon Parkins' *Historical Geography of Detroit* (Michigan Historical Commission, 1918; repr. Kennikat 1970). For New Netherland and New Sweden we must turn to such works as *New York Beginnings* by Thomas Condon (New York University, 1968) and *Dutch Explorers, Traders and Settlers in the Delaware Valley* by C. A. Weslager (University of Pennsylvania, 1964). Many interesting possibilities await the geographer here. Peter Wacker has found some of them in his *The Musconetcong Valley of New Jersey* (Rutgers, 1968).

Americanization of the Land

The process of Americanization—the blending of the European, African, and Indian elements—surely began early in the sixteenth century but became obvious by the time of the Revolution. Thenceforth, although the cultural landscapes of the United States have superficially resembled European prototypes, they in fact represent a uniquely American synthesis.

The nineteenth- and twentieth-centuries are, of course, richer in data for geographers than the earlier centuries. Population data since 1790 are readily available in Census Bureau publications, but skill is needed to make these data come alive. Demographers have provided important comprehensive studies, such as *The Changing Population of the United States* by Conrad and Irene Taeuber (Wiley, 1958) and *The Population of the United States* by Donald Bogue (Free Press, 1959). Among geographers, Wilbur Zelinsky has made the most numerous and successful studies in population geography; see, for example, his paper, "Changes in the Geographic Pattern of Rural Population in the United States, 1790-1960" (*GR*, October 1962).

The morphology of nineteenth- and twentieth-century settlements has been treated in books by architectural historians such as John Reps (cited above) and also in articles by the dean of American cultural geographers, Fred Kniffen. See especially his "Louisiana House Types" (*AAAG*, December 1936), "Folk Housing: Key to Diffusion" (*AAAG*, September 1965), and, with Henry Glassie, "Building in Wood in the Eastern United States: A Time-Place Perspective" (*GR*, January 1966). Glassie has also written *Pattern in the Material Culture of the Eastern United States* (University of Pennsylvania, 1968; rev. ed. 1971 pb), an eclectic catalogue not only of building techniques but also of just about every other aspect of material culture. Interesting papers on house types, barns, fences, and field patterns have been provided by geographers such as Wilbur Zelinsky, Roger Trindell, Peter Wacker, Fraser Hart, Cotton Mather, Joseph Spencer, Hallock Raup, and John Rickert. American hamlets and farmsteads were treated by Glenn Trewartha in *AAAG* (March 1943 and September 1948).

Studies of larger settlements, up to the largest cities, abound, but few convey a feeling of what it is like to live there. A recent exception, which shows fruitful collaboration between a geographer and an historian, is *Chicago: Growth of a Metropolis* by Harold Mayer and Richard Wade (University of Chicago, 1969). Two recent textbooks, *The American City: An Urban Geography* by Raymond Murphy (McGraw-Hill, 1966) and *North American Cities* by Maurice Yeates and Barry Garner (Harper-Row, 1971), cover the contemporary cityscape thoroughly but are deficient in cultural and historical geographical description. Jean Gottmann's urban studies should be mentioned, especially his book *Megalopolis* (Twentieth Century Fund, 1961; repr. by MIT 1964 pb) and an article, "Why the Skyscraper?" (*GR*, April 1966). A geographical study which combines good statistical and historical description is David Ward's *Cities and Immigrants: A Geography of Change in Nineteenth-Century America* (Oxford, 1971 pb).

The great waves of European immigration in the century before 1920 are sketched in Maldwyn Jones's *American Immigration* (University of Chicago, 1960 pb). Immigration from Mexico, chiefly in the twentieth century, is treated in *North from Mexico* by Carey McWilliams (Lippincott, 1948; repr. by Greenwood) and *The Mexican-American People, the Nation's Second Largest Minority* by Leo Grebler *et al.* (Free Press, 1970). See also Meinig's *Southwest* (cited above) and Richard Nostrand's paper, "The Hispanic-American Borderland: Delimitation of an American Culture Region" (*AAAG*, December 1970).

Perhaps the most striking single cultural feature in the American landscape is the "checkerboard" or "gridiron" pattern, especially in the lands surveyed after 1785 in the Midwest and West, but a great deal of rectangularity and linearity is also evident in the Eastern Seaboard as well. Such rectangularity reflects the relative recency and homogeneity of the settlement of the United States. It demonstrates how completely the aboriginal patterns have been replaced by newer forms. The American land systems and patterns have been described in the aforementioned works of John Reps, Glenn Trewartha, and Ralph Brown, and also in an excellent monograph by F. J. Marschner, *Land Use and Its Patterns in the United States* (U. S. Department of Agriculture, 1959 pb). William Pattison has written on the *Beginnings of the American Rectangular Land Survey System, 1784-1800* (Chicago Geography Research Papers, 1957 pb), and studies of the way in which the system worked in Ohio and Minnesota have been made by Norman Thrower and Hildegard Johnson, respectively (*Original Survey and Land Subdivision,* Rand McNally, 1966; and "Rational and Ecological Aspects of the Quarter Section: An Example from Minnesota," *GR*, July 1957). This "striking example of geometry triumphant over physical geography," as Pattison called it, is particularly noticeable to airborne visitors, and, indeed, it may be the first visible sign of "intelligent" life as the Earth is approached from space.

The varieties of American religious experience, so ably documented by Sydney Ahlstrom in a recent *AS:AIN* article, are only beginning to attract attention from geographers. The historian Edwin Gaustad has produced an excellent *Historical Atlas of Religion in America* (Harper-Row, 1962), but I prefer the maps of the distribution of denominations in Wilbur Zelinsky's article, "An Approach to the Religious Geography of the United States: Patterns of Church Membership in 1952," *AAAG*, June 1961. I hope that a geographer will mine the nuggets of social geography in Whitney Cross' *The Burned-Over District* (Cornell University, 1950; repr. Harper-Row, 1965 pb) and bring them together in a truly geographical study. A neglected aspect of the geography of religion has been the study of cemeteries, those invaluable palimpsests which tell us so much about the living as well as the dead. Cemeteries have been given some attention in articles in *Landscape* by J. B. Jackson (Winter 1967-68) and Donald Jeane (Spring-Summer 1969) and in *AAAG* by Richard Francaviglia (September 1971), but more such studies are needed.

Other aspects of social geography, such as folklore, foodways, and forms of recreation, have been treated by E. Joan Wilson Miller ("The Ozark Culture Region as Revealed by Traditional Materials," *AAAG*, March 1968), Sam Hilliard (*Hog Meat and Hoecake: Food Supply in the Old South, 1840-1860*, Southern Illinois University 1972), and John Rooney ("Up from the Mines and out from the Prairies: Some Geographical Implications of Football in the United States," *GR*, October 1969). This literature is rather meager but high in quality, and one hopes that other geographers will look beyond the purely economic aspects of human behavior and will consider other possible explanations. Edward Ullman pointed out the need for this wider view in his paper, "Amenities as a Factor in Regional Growth" (*GR*, January 1954), but economic geographers have been slow to follow his lead. In this sensitive age when all people are becoming less interested in sheer economic growth than in improved social well-being, geographers are responding with timely books and articles—e.g., *The Geography of Poverty in the United States* by Richard Morrill and Ernest Woldenberg (McGraw-Hill, 1972 pb), *The Geography of Social Well-Being in the United States* by David M. Smith (McGraw-Hill, 1973 pb), and "Race and Socioeconomic Well-Being: A Geographical Analysis of the Mississippi Case" by Mark Lowry (*GR*, October 1970). Such studies have so far emphasized quantitative description, and some subjective leavening would be helpful.

Some Concluding Remarks

It appears that the questions "What is the American?" and "What is America?" are inextricably entwined, and they cannot be satisfactorily answered by scholars from a single discipline, whether it be cultural geography, history, or whatever, but they can be approached from the interdisciplinary viewpoint of American Studies. There have been a number of attempts to capture the essence of American character, such as the works of Denis Brogan, Geoffrey Gorer, André Siegfried, and John Greenway, all surely familiar to readers of this journal, but none of these wholly satisfies the geographer's desire for a treatment of the American land (the *humanized* land) as well as of the American people. One such study was produced by David Lowenthal, "The American Scene" (*GR*, January 1968), and I hope that Lowenthal or a kindred spirit will expand these themes to book length. The notorious *géographe malgré lui* George Stewart has put geographers in his debt with a number of excellent books, among which I should like to single out *U. S. 40* (Houghton Mifflin, 1953) and *American Ways of Life* (Doubleday, 1954 pb; repr. Russell 1971). Another crypto-geographer, Eric Sloane, has delightfully described the American landscape in a series of books published by Wilfred Funk over the last two decades—*American Barns and Covered Bridges* (1954), *Our Vanishing Landscape* (1955), *American Yesterday* (1956), *The Seasons of America Past* (1958), etc.—although he sometimes sacrifices accuracy for vividness.

It is possible to combine accuracy, clarity, excellent illustration, and even humor; Wilbur Zelinsky has done just that in his *Cultural Geography of the United States*. It is the best book that I could recommend to overseas geographers or to non-geographers for an overview of American geography—not only geography (the landscape itself) but geography (the academic discipline). He may be wrong about the origin of bourbon whiskey, but no author is perfect—and authors of bibliographical essays least of all!

The American Presidency:
A Bibliographical Essay

by Kenneth Davison

Every nation possesses a cultural treasure that it values above everything else. In England, the national treasure consists of a splendid library and the superb collections of papyri, manuscripts, and historical objects carefully-preserved in the British Museum. For the French, the most valuable material objects are probably the magnificent stained glass windows of Chartres Cathedral. The secret of their coloring process is lost forever. They are literally unique.

The American people have a treasure too. On March 16, 1963, President John F. Kennedy announced his unqualified support of a ten million dollar program to preserve major United States historical documents. To fund the project, he endorsed legislation proposed by the National Historical Publications Commission [National Archives] to secure five million dollars from the Federal Government and five million dollars from private sources over a ten-year period (1963-1973). The money was needed, the NHPC said, to stimulate the collection, editing, and publication of great historical documents not readily available to the public.

Since the Kennedy pronouncement, the National Historical Publications Commission has pursued three courses of action:

1. Five projects, enjoying the highest priority, to publish the papers of the Adams family, Benjamin Franklin, Alexander Hamilton, Thomas Jefferson, and James Madison, are being financed through to completion by means of capital funds granted by private donors directly to sponsoring institutions, with the income generated, if any, to be available in perpetuity to finance similar projects after the primary ventures have been completed.

2. To permit it to plan a realistic ten-year program, including assistance to other projects in progress, being proposed, or needed, the Commission requested a minimum of one million dollars a year for a grant-in-aid program, such funds to be provided about equally from private sources and the Congress. These grants are intended, through matching offers and other devices, to stimulate and increase the donation of funds from other sources. It was recommended that a part of the money sought from Congress be used to complete a Documentary History of the Constitution and the First Ten Amendments, and to finance the editing and publishing of the Records of the First Congress.

3. Legislation was passed to authorize such a grant-in-aid program and to permit payment of the expenses of occasional special advisory committees to study and review specific proposals to guarantee wise and impartial administration of the whole program.

Since many of the more important projects and publishing programs endorsed by National Historical Publications Commission concern presidential papers, the following comments are limited to a discussion of the nation's presidential archives.

Presidential Row

These archives, commonly called "Presidential Row," were once located exclusively in Washington, D. C. Today, however, they literally span the continent from Massachusetts to California. The original "Presidential Row" occupies one corner on the third floor of the Library of Congress Annex Building. Imagine a corridor two-hundred feet long with twenty-one bays, each eighty feet in depth with six tiers of shelves—for such is the depository of the most personal belongings of twenty-three men who have served as President of the United States from George Washington to Calvin Coolidge. All told, these presidential papers comprise some two million items. Close at hand are eighteen million other papers of

Mr. Davison is Professor of History and American Studies, and Chairman of the American Studies Department, at Heidelberg College, Tiffin, Ohio. A specialist on the American Presidency and Presidential papers, he has delivered conference papers on the Presidency in America and Europe, written numerous book reviews, and published articles on Hayes and Arthur; his book, The Presidency of Rutherford B. Hayes *(1972) won the Ohioana Library Association History Medal. Mr. Davison is also editor of the* Ohio Academy of History Newsletter *and National Treasurer of the American Studies Association. An active association member, he has served as President of the Ohio-Indiana ASA and has written "Notes on Financial Aid to Graduate Students" for the summer supplement of* American Quarterly *since 1962.*

Heidelberg College

men and women at one time associated with these twenty-three American presidents. The twenty million documents constitute much of the raw material of American history. As President Truman once observed: "There's the United States for you—they tell the whole story." Out of them, scholars, historians, and writers have composed the life story of the Federal Republic, and the biographies of the men and women who have guided America's destiny.

"Presidential Row" in the Library of Congress contains ninety-five per cent of all George Washington manuscripts in existence, and 15,000 Lincoln Papers. The real value of such a collection is, of course, not monetary, but rests upon the fact that America's heritage is bound up in them. They are unique—literally irreplaceable—and consequently carefully guarded and protected from fire and destruction. Like the beautiful windows of Chartres Cathedral, America's presidential papers were removed to a place of greater safety during World Wars I and II. Few visitors, not even specialists in the field, are ever admitted to "Presidential Row." Instead, scholars are permitted to use the priceless documents under the watchful eye of a uniformed guard in the reading room of the Library of Congress Manuscript Division.

"Presidential Row" has been expanding ever since 1815 when the first collection of Presidential papers was purchased by the Government. Today it goes far beyond the Library of Congress collection, because White House staffs of the twentieth century, aided by the typewriter, carbon paper, dictaphone, tape recorder and telephone, and mimeograph and photocopying equipment, have swelled the files of modern Presidents to millions of items.

The largest collection of Presidential Papers outside of the Library of Congress, other than the Presidential libraries, which are really archival operations, is owned by the great Henry E. Huntington Library at San Marino, California, where researchers will find such items as Washington's cash book, Jefferson's diary of daily expenses while traveling to the Continental Congress (while there, he would write the Declaration of Independence), and a White House account book, 1805-1809, kept by Jefferson's majordomo. The Massachusetts Historical Society, first of its type in the new nation, has a half-million Adams Family Papers, including 50,000 manuscripts of John Adams, 150,000 in the handwriting of John Quincy Adams, 10,000 associated with Jefferson, and 600 from the pen of George Washington. The Historical Society of Pennsylvania keeps the Buchanan Papers, about 25,000 in all. The Illinois Historical Library at Springfield treasures 1,300 Lincoln items.

Presidential Projects

In the past two decades, a great effort has been quietly underway to enable the American people to repossess their historical heritage and to make the contents of their presidential papers more accessible and better understood by all Americans.

The starting point in the new emphasis on presidential research was the publication by Princeton University Press in 1950 of the first volume in a projected fifty-two-volume set of the papers of Thomas Jefferson, superbly edited by

Julian Boyd and his team of assistants. When presented with his complimentary copy, President Truman, an avid reader of American history and biography, was so impressed that he immediately directed that the National Historical Publications Commissions be revitalized, so that the papers of other American leaders might be similarly printed in well-edited volumes. A master list was prepared, and many of these projects are now well under way, financed by foundations and private sources, with university press cooperation.

Five of the projects as noted above have received major attention, namely the Jefferson, Hamilton, Franklin, Madison, and Adams Papers. Numerous volumes in each series have already been published. Their scope is enormous. Heretofore, only about fifteen per cent of Jefferson's Papers have been available in print. The Adams Family Papers total one-half million items. Only a few of the eighty volumes projected have been issued, but some 300,000 of the Adams Papers covering 250 years of American history are already available on 608 microfilm reels. Better yet, they may also be used on interlibrary loan for the modest expense of postage.

Meanwhile, other projects are in progress: Wilson Papers at Princeton; Andrew Johnson Papers at the University of Tennessee; Polk Papers at Vanderbilt; Garfield Papers at Michigan State; Hayes Papers at Heidelberg College; Grant Papers at Southern Illinois University. Clay and Calhoun editions are also underway, plus many more. It is a very exciting time for historical scholarship. After all these intervening years, scholars are getting, for the first time, definitive editions of public and private papers upon which to base solid historical investigation.

A second boon to modern presidential research was the announcement in the Fall of 1954 of a new series published by the Government Printing Office for the National Archives called "The Public Papers of the Presidents of the United States." This series fills a need of scholars engaged in evaluating contemporary presidents. All of the Eisenhower, Truman, Kennedy, and Johnson volumes have been published, plus the first three of the Nixon era. Franklin D. Roosevelt's *Public Papers and Addresses* were printed commercially in 1938–1950. For the period from Washington to Coolidge, a useful but incomplete and less documented set, *Messages and Papers of the Presidents* edited by James D. Richardson is available.

Presidential Libraries

A third development stimulating presidential research was the passage of the Presidential Libraries Act in 1955. Under the terms of this law, the General Services Administration, the Government agency having supervision of the National Archives, received authority to accept and to maintain, when offered as a gift, any Presidential Library and its holdings, and the power to enter into arrangements for the preservation and maintenance of collections of other Presidential Papers tendered to the Government, even if they were housed in buildings not likely to become the property of the Government, as is still the case with certain Hoover Papers which remain at Stanford University. The United States now operates six Presidential Libraries: Hoover (West Branch, Iowa);

Franklin D. Roosevelt (Hyde Park, New York); Truman (Independence, Missouri); Eisenhower (Abilene, Kansas); Kennedy (in temporary quarters at Waltham, Massachusetts); and Lyndon B. Johnson (Austin, Texas). A seventh one is in the planning stage in California for the Nixon Papers with the help of archivists who have been working with the White House staff since the early months of the first Nixon administration. After nearly two centuries, the nation has discovered a satisfactory way to preserve the historical records of the most unique organ of democratic government, the Presidency.

The prototype of the presidential library idea is in Fremont, Ohio. For there, amid the mighty trees of President Hayes' Spiegel Grove estate, is situated the oldest presidential library museum in America, and the only one not operated by the Federal Government. Instead, it is maintained jointly by the State of Ohio and the Hayes Foundation. The Hayes Library, located just inside the north entrance of the beautifully-wooded twenty-five acre estate, contains an item-indexed collection of 150,000 manuscripts (plus 500,000 more of other men and women), 50,000 photographs, the President's private library of 10,000 volumes, and thousands of books and articles—all deserving the greater attention which will come with the approaching centennial of the Hayes presidency.

It is not fully understood and appreciated by the public that the papers acquired by a President during his term of office are his personal property, and that he has the power to do with them as he wishes. (As of July 25, 1969, it is no longer possible to claim a tax deduction for the donation of such papers). Although valuable simply for the autographs they contain, they are immensely important as a record of an administration and a people. What a President does with his papers is therefore of considerable public concern. And it is much harder for him to make adequate provision for them today than it was earlier. Washington could store his papers at Mount Vernon in packing cases and even consider building a small library for them, but Franklin Roosevelt's personal papers consist of four and one-half million items, and fill 500 five-drawer file cabinets. The total manuscript holdings of the Roosevelt Library are estimated today to be in excess of twenty million. Truman's papers run less because of his shorter tenure, and Eisenhower's are about the same. Kennedy's papers accumulated at a far more rapid rate. President Hoover received about 400 letters a day; Franklin Roosevelt got about 4000. John F. Kennedy normally received about 6000 each day. The management of collections of this size is beyond the resources of any one individual. The presidential library provides trained personnel, affords security against fire, theft, and careless handling, and insures the integrity of the papers.

The Hoover Library at Brithplace Park in West Branch, Iowa opened in August 1962, but it has had good use by scholars only in the last three years. Mr. Hoover's papers as Secretary of Commerce and President have been moved from Stanford University, although the many other documents he collected literally by the ton on his world travels will remain in Palo Alto, California in the Hoover Library of War, Revolution and Peace. They constitute one of the finest collections of first hand records documenting the political, economic, and social changes of the twentieth century. This makes President Hoover unique— the only Chief Executive with two buildings for his Papers.

The Truman Library, dedicated in 1957, contains over eight million papers, and is constantly augmenting its collection by gathering the private papers of President Truman's associates in government. Mr. Truman personally donated seventeen million dollars worth of papers and mementoes to get the library started. The Eisenhower Library, dedicated in May 1962, is open to limited research.

The Franklin D. Roosevelt Library is the oldest Presidential Library administered by the Federal Government, and dates from a 1939 joint resolution of Congress. The Library was formally dedicated and opened to the public in 1941 and it is the most fully developed one in terms of researchers, total projects, and published works based on its holdings.

After President Kennedy's death in 1963, the nucleus of a John F. Kennedy Library was created in the National Archives, and temporarily moved in 1969 to the Federal Records Center in Waltham, Massachusetts, where the first papers were opened to researchers in 1970. Some of the more than three-hundred Oral History interviews are also available for use. A permanent home for the Kennedy Library is now in progress in Cambridge, Massachusetts.

In May, 1971, the Lyndon B. Johnson Library at Austin, Texas was dedicated. The first of its thirty-one million pages of documents (those dealing with education) were opened to qualified persons in January, 1972. Ordinarily a presidential library is opened to general research within six to seven years of the time when a President completes his term of office.

The fourth method of encouraging presidential research in recent years was the passage of a law by Congress in August, 1957, directing the Librarian of Congress to arrange, microfilm, and index the Presidential Papers. The purpose of the legislation was twofold: 1) To provide greater security through the wide distribution of copies of the microfilm, and, 2) To facilitate the use of the papers by scholars and others.

An appropriation of $620,000 was made in August, 1958, and the project began in the same month. Twenty-one of the twenty-three collections have been filmed and twenty-one indexed. The remaining Jefferson and Garfield projects are in progress. Reels may be purchased or borrowed from the Library of Congress. A complete microfilm set of all the Presidential Papers in the Library of Congress will cost about $20,500. Any one may gain direct access to America's heritage for about 24¢ [U. S. mailing price] which is the cost of mailing a single microfilm reel. [Inquiries about ordering microfilm sets may be addressed to Photoduplication Service, Department C-136, Library of Congress, Washington, D.C. 20540. For Interlibrary loan, write to Chief, Loan Division, Library of Congress.—Ed.]

What are the results of this increased emphasis on Presidential Papers and research? The pace of scholarship has been enormously accelerated. Many books and articles have appeared based upon the new opportunities. In mid-November, 1962, Page Smith of the University of California published a two-volume study of John Adams, the first biography ever written based upon thorough use of the Adams documents. Over ninety percent of Franklin Roosevelt's Papers are open to researchers. Thus Roosevelt scholarship is already at the same stage as Woodrow Wilson scholarship. Both Frank Freidel and Arthur M. Schlesinger, Jr.

have completed three volumes of their respective studies of Roosevelt and they have other volumes in progress. Arthur Link of Princeton has published five volumes on Wilson to 1917 but has interrupted his biographical work to edit the Public Papers of Woodrow Wilson. Irving Brant began a one-volume biography of James Madison in 1941 which he finished twenty years later in six volumes. Dumas Malone of the University of Virginia has completed four volumes of his masterful account of Jefferson's career to the year 1805. Margaret Leech won a second Pulitzer Prize in 1959 with a beautifully written and researched study of the McKinley years. Since then she has been at work on a Garfield biography. At the Hayes Library in Fremont, Ohio, some five hundred research topics are investigated each year. Historians are not unmindful of their new opportunities.

Until the present generation, the literature on the office of the American presidency was extremely limited. During the entire first century and a half of the national experience (1789-1939), only fifteen titles on the presidency appeared, but in the single election year of 1960, an additional fifteen books were published, most of them of enduring value. Since 1960, the quantity and quality of research and publication on presidential history and contemporary presidential politics has expanded at an extraordinary rate. Many excellent articles and monographs, detailed histories and biographies, as well as source books are now readily available to students and scholars of American civilization.

Contemporary Sources on the Presidency

For contemporary analysis of the presidency, a good place to begin is with the government documents:

1. *Federal Register* (Washington, D. C.: Government Printing Office, 1936–). Published five times each week. Includes presidential executive orders, proclamations, reorganization plans, and rules and regulations issued by executive departments and agencies.

2. *Weekly Compilation of Presidential Documents* (Washington, D. C.: Government Printing Office, 1965–). Published every Monday by the Office of the Federal Register. Contains presidents' addresses, remarks, announcements, appointments and nominations, executive orders, memoranda, meetings with foreign leaders, and proclamations, as well as reports to the president, released by the White House up to 5:00 P.M. the preceding Friday.

3. *Public Papers of the Presidents of the United States* (Washington, D. C.: Government Printing Office, 1958–). A series inaugurated by publication of the 1957 Eisenhower volume. Now complete for Truman (1945-53); Eisenhower (1953-61); Kennedy (1961-63); Johnson (1963-69); and Nixon (1969-71).

4. *United States Government Organization Manual* (Washington, D. C.: Government Printing Office, 1935–). An annual publication which describes the current organization and functions of each of the departments and agencies in the executive branch, as well as the legislative and judicial branches. It also is helpful in understanding the transfer of responsibilities from discontinued or reorganized government agencies.

5. *Monthly Catalogue of U. S. Government Publications* (Washington, D. C.: Government Printing Office, 1895—). The basic index to the thousands of pamphlets, books, and periodicals published by the Government Printing Office, still the largest paperback publisher in the U. S.

6. Schmeckebier, Laurence F., and Eastin, Ray B. *Government Publications and Their Use* 2nd rev. ed. (Washington: The Brookings Institution, 1969). The best guide to government publications. Especially helpful in explaining the rapid changes and growth in the number of such publications in recent years; also calls attention to many special series.

In addition to the Presidential Libraries discussed earlier, three private organizations conduct extensive research, publication, and other activities relating to the study of the contemporary presidency:

1. The Brookings Institution, 1775 Massachusetts Avenue, N.W., Washington, D. C. 20036, is an independent research organization founded in 1927 to aid in the development of sound public policies and to promote public understanding of issues of national importance. Among its recent publications are five volumes in a new series called "Studies in Presidential Selection" (1970—) entitled *Voting for President; Financing Presidential Campaigns; The Convention Problem; Perspectives on Presidential Selection;* and *Convention Decisions and Voting Records.*

2. Congressional Quarterly, Inc., 1735 K Street, N.W., Washington, D.C. 20006. Publisher of *Congressional Quarterly Weekly Report* (Washington: Congressional Quarterly, Inc:, 1945—). The most authoritative and easy to use source of information on Congress. The president's position on all major legislation and roll call votes is given, plus his messages to Congress, press conferences, and vetoes. An annual digest is published under the title *Congressional Quarterly Almanac.* Other special publications include: *Congress and the Nation,* a resumé of congressional and presidential actions from 1945 to 1972; the semi-annual *Congressional Quarterly Guide to Current American Government;* and the weekly *Editorial Research Reports* on current controversial issues.

3. Center for the Study of the Presidency, 926 Fifth Avenue, New York, New York 10021. Formerly the Library of Presidential Papers, the Center conducts several outstanding lectures and symposia each year, featuring distinguished political scientists and leaders of government. It issues a quarterly newsletter, the *Center House Bulletin,* excellent annotated bibliographies on the Presidency, and occasional books including conference proceedings. The first two volumes, both edited by R. Gordon Hoxie, are: *The White House: Organization and Operations: Proceedings of the 1970 Montauk Symposium* (New York: Center for the Study of the Presidency, 1971), and *The Presidency of the 1970's: Proceedings of the 1971 Montauk Symposium* (New York: Center for the Study of the Presidency, 1973).

Certain newspapers have built a reputation for excellent coverage and interpretation of events. *The New York Times* maintains a consistently high standard of independent political reporting. It normally prints complete texts of all important presidential statements. The *Christian Science Monitor* is strong on international news coverage and political analysis. The *Washington Post* has frequently won acclaim for its investigative reporting, while the *Wall Street Journal* is the nation's best known paper for financial and business affairs.

Magazines and professional journals frequently carry articles bearing directly on the contemporary presidency. Of these, the most prestigious are *The American Political Service Review* (Menasha, Wisconsin: American Political Science Association, 1906–) and *Foreign Affairs* (New York: Council on Foreign Relations, 1922–).

The Political Science Quarterly (New York: Columbia University 1886–) and the *Public Administration Review* (Washington: American Society for Public Administration, 1940–) also frequently feature articles and book reviews on the Presidency. Presidential Papers are often mentioned or discussed in *Prologue, the Journal of the National Archives* (Washington: National Archives, 1969–) and *The American Archivist* (Washington, D.C.: Society of American Archivists, 1938–) which devotes a section in each issue to recent manuscript accessions by the presidential libraries. A new magazine, the *Washington Monthly* (Washington: Washington Monthly Co., 1969–) offers a liberal interpretation of the contemporary scene which may be counter-balanced by William F. Buckley's conservative *National Review* (Bristol, Connecticut: National Review, Inc., 1955–).

General Bibliographical Guidance

For basic bibliographical guidance in the study of the Presidency, three tools are available. Donald H. Mugridge (comp.) *The Presidents of the U.S., 1789–1962: A Selected List of References* (Washington: Library of Congress, 1963) is an annotated listing of 1453 items pertaining to the presidency and individual presidents, including their writings as well as writings about them or their administrations. An excellent way to keep abreast of current presidential literature is to subscribe to the Library of Congress Card Service which automatically insures monthly notification of all new titles catalogued by the nation's leading reference library. Finally, a recent dissertation by David Alan Heslop, *The Presidency and Political Science: A Critique of the Work of Political Scientists in Three Areas of Presidential Politics* (Ann Arbor: University Microfilms, Inc., 1969) offers a fundamental survey of the more important books and articles dealing with the President as chief legislator, administrative chief, and party leader.

A good encyclopedia volume of personal and comparative data on all American chief executives through Lyndon B. Johnson is provided by Joseph Nathan Kane, *Facts About the Presidents: A Compilation of Biographical and Historical Data* 2nd edition (New York: H. W. Wilson, 1968). Another excellent source is Howard F. Bremer, editor, *Presidential Chronology Series* 32 vols. (Dobbs-Ferry, N.Y.: Oceana Publications Inc., 1968–72).

Many unusual and entertaining facts about Presidents are to be found in Don Smith, *Peculiarities of the Presidents, Strange and Intimate Facts Not Found in History* (Van Wert, Ohio: Wilkinson Printing Co., 1938). Famous presidential statements may be traced through Caroline Harnsberger, *Treasury of Presidential Quotations* (Chicago: Follett Publishing Co., 1964).

Campaign and election data is readily available in Donald E. Cooke, *Atlas of the Presidents* (Maplewood, N.J.: Hammond Inc., 1967); the Congressional Quarterly Service special publication, *Presidential Candidates from 1788 to 1964, including third parties, 1832-1964* (Washington, 1964); Svend Petersen, *A Statistical History of the American Presidential Elections* (New York: Ungar, 1963); and Richard M. Scammon (ed.), *America at the Polls: a Handbook of American Presidential Election Statistics, 1920-1964* (Pittsburgh: University of Pittsburgh Press, 1965).

Useful reference collections of important presidential speeches are assembled in the Library of Congress Legislative Reference Service volume, *Inaugural Addresses of the Presidents of the U.S. from George Washington, 1789 to John F. Kennedy, 1961* (Washington: Government Printing Office 1961); and Fred L. Israel (ed.), *The State of the Union Messages of the Presidents, 1790-1966* 3 Vols. (New York: Chelsea House, 1966).

Diaries and Autobiographies

Only five presidents kept diaries which cover the presidential period:

Washington, George. *Diaries, 1748-1799.* Edited by John C. Fitzpatrick. (Boston: Houghton Mifflin, 1925).

Adams, John Quincy. *Memoirs . . . comprising portions of his Diary from 1795 to 1848.* 12 Vols. Edited by Charles Francis Adams. (Philadelphia: Lippincott, 1874-77).

Polk, James K. *The Diary of James K. Polk During His Presidency, 1845 to 1849.* Edited and annotated by Milo Milton Quaife. 4 Vols. (Chicago: McClurg, 1910).

Hayes, Rutherford B. *Hayes: The Diary of a President, 1875-1881, Covering the Disputed Election, the End of Reconstruction, and the Beginning of Civil Service.* Edited by T. Harry Williams (New York: D. McKay Co., 1964).

Garfield, James A. *The Diary of James A. Garfield.* Edited by Harry James Brown and Frederick D. Williams. 3 Vols. (East Lansing: Michigan State University, 1967—).

Of a dozen presidents who have prepared autobiographical accounts, only five are significant for their reflections on the presidency. Theodore Roosevelt's *Autobiography* (New York: Macmillan, 1913) is outstanding. Hoover's three-volume *Memoirs* (New York: Macmillan, 1951-52) and Truman's two-volume *Memoirs* (Garden City, New York: Doubleday, 1955-56) broke fresh ground and remain primary sources of considerable value. Eisenhower's *Mandate for Change, 1953-1956: The White House Years,* and *Waging Peace, 1956-1961: The White House Years* (Garden City, New York: Doubleday & Co., 1963-65) continued the tradition. Lyndon B. Johnson's *The Vantage Point: Perspectives of the Presidency: 1963-1969* (New York: Holt, Rinehart and Winston, 1971) is helpful on understanding some aspects of the decision-making process in the modern presidency.

Recordings and Pictorial Works

A few documentary recordings, especially concerning presidents since Grover Cleveland, deserve mention:

Election Songs of the United States (New York: Folkways Records, 1960).

FDR Speaks. 6 records (Washington: Washington Records, Inc., 1960).

Four Days that Shocked the World (New York: Colpix Records, 1964).

If I'm Elected (New York: Heritage, 1953).

The Inaugural Addresses of Franklin D. Roosevelt, Harry S. Truman, Dwight D. Eisenhower, and *John F. Kennedy* 3 records (New Rochelle, N.Y.: Spoken Arts, Inc., 1962)

The Invention of the Presidency (New York: American Heritage Publishing Co., 1968).

I Can Hear It Now: The Sixties (New York: Columbia Records, 1970).

Years of Lightning, Day of Drums (Hollywood, Cal.: Capitol Records, Inc., 1966).

Of the many pictorial works on the American Presidency, a few are notably outstanding. The White House Historical Association booklets, *The Living White House* (Washington; 1966) and *The White House: an Historic Guide* (Washington, 1969) are both inexpensive and authoritative. Herbert R. Collins details presidential vehicles in his delightful *Presidents on Wheels* (Washington: Acropolis Books, 1971). Margaret Bassett offers brief biographical vignettes and excellent pictures in her *Profiles and Portraits of American Presidents and Their Wives* (Freeport, Maine: The Bond Wheelwright Company, 1969).

The two best general pictorial treatments of the presidency are Kenneth W. Leish, *The American Heritage Pictorial History of the Presidents,* 2 Volumes (New York: American Heritage Publishing Co., 1968) and Stefan Lorant's superb *The Glorious Burden: the American Presidency* (New York: Harper & Row, 1968), a revision of his earlier *The Presidency: a pictorial history of presidential elections from Washington to Truman* (New York: Macmillan, 1951).

General Histories

The best general surveys of the historical development and present position of the presidency may be found in Wilfred E. Binkley's masterful *The Man in the White House: His Powers and Duties* rev. ed. (New York: Harper Colophon Books, 1964) and *President and Congress* 3rd. rev. ed. (New York: Vintage Books, 1962); Clinton Rossiter's highly readable *The American Presidency* 2nd ed. (New York: Harcourt, Brace, & Co., 1960); and Sidney Hyman's careful study, *The American President* (New York: Harper, 1954). Interesting anecdotes and comparative appraisals presented in lively fashion are the hallmark of both Thomas A. Bailey, *Presidential Greatness: The Image and the Man from George Washington to the Present* (New York: Appleton-Century-Crofts, 1966) and Holman Hamilton, *White House Images and Realities* (Gainesville: University of Florida Press, 1958).

Morton Borden (ed.) *America's Ten Greatest Presidents* (Chicago: Rand McNally, 1961) and Richard Hofstader, *The American Political Tradition and the Men Who Made It* (New York: Knopf, 1948) present provocative interpretations of the more famous American presidents. Asa E. Martin, *After the White House* (State College, Pa.: Penns Valley Publishers, 1951) traces the careers of America's retired presidents in an interesting manner.

The definitive analysis of the office of President is provided in Edward S. Corwin, *The President: Office and Powers,* 4th ed. (New York: New York University

Press, 1957) and Louis W. Koenig, *The Chief Executive,* rev. ed. (New York: Harcourt Brace, & World, 1968).

Comparative studies of the presidential office are offered by Harold Laski, *The American Presidency* (New York: Harper & Brothers, 1940) and Joseph E. Kallenbach, *The American Chief Executive: The Presidency and the Governorship* (New York: Harper & Row, 1966). The classic study of the functioning of the executive branch is the four-volume administrative history series by Leonard D. White, *The Federalists, a Study in Administrative History; The Jeffersonians, 1801-29, The Jacksonians, 1829-61,* and *the Republican Era, 1869-1901,* (Macmillan, 1948-1958).

For the intentions of the Founding Fathers with respect to the Presidency, see *The Enduring Federalist,* edited and analyzed by Charles A. Beard (Garden City, N.Y.: Doubleday & Co., Inc., 1948). For an analysis of how the President may effectively use his great powers see: Richard E. Neustadt, *Presidential Power, the Politics of Leadership* (New York: John Wiley, 1960).

Contrasting contemporary judgments on the future of the presidential office, by former White House aides, are given by George E. Reedy in his two books, *The Twilight of the Presidency* (New York: The World Publishing Co., 1970) and *The Presidency in Flux* (New York: Columbia University Press, 1973); by Emmet John Hughes, *The Living Presidency* (New York: Coward, McCann & Geoghegan, Inc., 1973), and very recently by Arthur M. Schlesinger, Jr., *The Imperial Presidency* (Cambridge: Houghton-Mifflin, 1973).

A basic introduction to party history is provided in Wilfred E. Binkley, *American Political Parties: Their Natural History* 4th ed. enlarged (New York: Alfred A. Knopf, 1963). For more of a political science approach, see the standard work by V. O. Key, *Politics, Parties and Pressure Groups* (New York: Thomas Y. Crowell, 1964). The nominating process is analyzed with great care in Paul T. David, *et al, The Politics of National Party Conventions* (Washington: Brookings Institution, 1960). Individual conventions are scrutinized with mathematical accuracy and tables in Richard E. Bain and Judith H. Parris, *Convention Decisions and Voting Records* (Washington: The Brookings Institution, 1973). Possible reforms in the presidential selection system and the convention nominating process in an age of television are considered in Judith H. Parris, *The Convention Problem* (Washington: The Brookings Institution, 1972) and Donald R. Matthews (ed.), *Perspectives on Presidential Selection* (Washington, D.C.: The Brookings Institution, 1973).

Thorough summaries of presidential campaigns and elections are available in Herbert Eaton, *Presidential Timber* (New York: The Free Press of Glencoe, 1964); Eugene H. Roseboom, *A History of Presidential Elections* (New York: The Macmillan Company, 1957); and Arthur M. Schlesinger, Jr., *History of American Presidential Elections, 1789–1968.* 4 vols. (New York: Chelsea House, 1971). The very real threat of increasing campaign costs to democratic electoral processes, and possible reforms is examined in Delmer D. Dunn, *Financing Presidential Campaigns* (Washington, D.C.: The Brookings Institution, 1972).

A good historical introduction to the electoral college system is Lucius Wilmerding, *The Electoral College* (New Brunswick, N.J.: Rutgers University Press, 1958). Two modern reappraisals of the system with alternative suggestions for reform are: Wallace S. Sayre and Judith H. Parris, *Voting for President: The Electoral College and the American Political System* (Washington: The Brookings Institution, 1970) and Neal R. Peirce, *The Peoples' President: The Electoral College in American History and the Direct-Vote Alternative* (New York: Simon and Schuster, 1972).

A spirited history of defeated presidential aspirants is contained in Irving Stone, *They Also Ran: The Story of the Men Who Were Defeated for the Presidency* (Garden City, N.Y.: Doubleday & Co., Inc., 1945).

Students interested in inauguration events will find a good guide to the literature in Ruth S. Freitag, *Presidential Inaugurations: A Selected List of References*. Third edition, revised and enlarged. (Washington: The Library of Congress, 1969). Pictorial books of interest are *The Inaugural Story, 1789-1969* (New York: American Heritage Publishing Co., 1969), and Louise Durbin, *Inaugural Cavalcade* (New York: Dodd, Mead & Co., 1971).

Monographs on Special Aspects

Excellent monographs on many special aspects of the modern presidency have been published during the past two decades. With the increasing complexity of government, an institutionalized presidency has developed to rival the older cabinet system. The only recent book on the cabinet is Richard F. Fenno's *The President's Cabinet: An Analysis in the Period from Wilson to Eisenhower* (Cambridge: Harvard University Press, 1959). Just one book has appeared on a particular president's cabinet, but it is a very fine study: Burton J. Hendrick, *Lincoln's War Cabinet* (Boston: Little, Brown, 1946).

The new trend toward studies of other presidential advisors and staff began with Louis W. Koenig's, *The Invisible Presidency* (New York: Rinehart, 1960), a case study of seven influential "favorites" from Washington's Alexander Hamilton to Eisenhower's Sherman Adams. Patrick Anderson continues the practice in his light-hearted, *The President's Men* (Garden City, N.Y.: Doubleday & Co., Inc., 1968). A much more sophisticated, generalized approach is Thomas E. Cronin and Sanford D. Greenberg (eds.), *The Presidential Advisory System* (New York: Harper and Row, 1969). Recent special studies include: Norman C. Thomas and Hans W. Baade, (eds.), *The Institutionalized Presidency* (Dobbs Ferry, N.Y.: Oceana Publications, 1972); Joseph Coffey and Vincent P. Rock, *The Presidential Staff* (Washington: National Planning Association, 1961), and Frank Popper, *The President's Commissions* (New York: Twentieth Century Fund, 1970).

No one as yet has made a comprehensive study of presidential private secretaries, but several of the latter have written interesting accounts of their superiors. Especially recommended are: Grace G. Tully, *F.D.R., My Boss* (New York: Scribner, 1949); Evelyn Lincoln, *My Twelve Years with John F. Kennedy* (New York: David McKay Co., Inc., 1965); and Lady Bird Johnson's Press Secretary, Liz Carpenter, *Ruffles and Flourishes* (Garden City, N.Y.: Doubleday & Co., Inc., 1970).

The standard work on presidential press relations is James E. Pollard, *The Presidents and the Press* (New York: Macmillan, 1947). A brief account emphasizing the recent period is Meyer L. Stein, *When Presidents Meet the Press* (New

York: Messner, 1969). A pioneering book that also gives attention to presidential speech-writing and use of radio and television media is Elmer E. Cornwell, Jr., *Presidential Leadership of Public Opinion* (Bloomington: Indiana University Press, 1965). Pierre Salinger, *With Kennedy* (Garden City, N.Y.: Doubleday and Co., Inc., 1966) includes some excellent comments on press relations by President Kennedy's press secretary.

Presidential views on racial questions are surveyed in George Sinkler, *The Racial Attitudes of American Presidents from Abraham Lincoln to Theodore Roosevelt* (Garden City, N.Y.: Doubleday & Co., Inc., 1971). Less comprehensive is Melvin Steinfield, *Our Racist Presidents: from Washington to Nixon* (San Ramon, California: Consensus Publishers, 1972).

Law and order issues are discussed in Bennett Milton Rich, *The Presidents and Civil Disorder* (Washington: Brookings Institution, 1941) and Ruth Morgan, *The President and Civil Rights: Policy-making by Executive Order* (New York: St. Martins' Press, Inc., 1970).

The President's role as commander-in-chief is reviewed through eight case studies from Madison to Eisenhower in Ernest R: May (ed.), *The Ultimate Decision* (New York: George Braziller, 1960). Nathan D. Grundstein, *Presidential Delegation of Authority in Wartime* (Pittsburgh: University of Pittsburgh Press, 1961) is also instructive.

Possible reorganization of the Executive branch is the theme of Herman Finer, *The Presidency: Crisis and Regeneration* (Chicago: University of Chicago, 1960). and Rexford G. Tugwell, *The Enlargement of the Presidency* (Garden City, N.Y.: Doubleday, 1960).

Dorothy Louise Tomkins, *Presidential Succession, a Bibliography, rev. ed.* (Berkeley: Institute of Governmental Studies, University of California, 1965) provides a starting point for yet another area of contemporary concern. The older standard work is by Ruth Silva, *Presidential Succession* (Ann Arbor: University of Michigan Press, 1951). Senator Birch Bayh recently headed a committee investigation of the problem with a resulting book, *One Heartbeat Away: Presidential Disability and Succession* (Indianapolis: Bobbs-Merrill, Inc., 1968). Studies of specific succession crises of the past are summarized in Richard Hansen, *The Year We Had No President* (Lincoln: University of Nebraska Press, 1962), and John D. Feerick, *From Failing Hands: The Story of Presidential Succession* (New York: Fordham University Press, 1965).

Authoritative monographs on the vice-presidency are Louis C. Hatch, *A History of the Vice-Presidency of the United States,* revised and edited by Earl L. Shoup (New York: American Historical Society, 1934), and Irving G. Williams, *The Rise of the Vice Presidency* (Washington: Public Affairs Press, 1956).

A book which greatly influenced President Kennedy's administration is Laurin L. Henry, *Presidential Transitions* (Washington: Brookings Institution, 1960) which describes four transitions from one presidential administration to another in which a change of party was involved, from 1912-13 to 1952-53. The Eisenhower-Kennedy transfer of power is detailed in Paul T. David (ed.), *The Presidential Election and Transition, 1960–1961* (Washington: Brookings Institution, 1961).

The physical and health histories of the various Presidents is given in a fascinating series of medical profiles by a Los Angeles surgeon, Rudolph Marx, in his

The Health of the Presidents (New York: Putnam, 1961). The work of the Secret Service in protecting the person of the president is the subject of two books: U. E. Baughman, *Secret Service Chief* (New York: Harper, 1961), and Edmund W. Starling, *Starling of the White House* (New York: Simon and Schuster, 1946). The best overall history of attempted and successful presidential assassinations is Robert J. Donovan, *The Assassins* (New York: Popular Library, 1964).

The religious affiliations and convictions of the Presidents are set forth in Bliss Isely, *The Presidents: Men of Faith* (Boston: W. A. Wilde Co., 1953) and Olga Jones, *Churches of the Presidents in Washington.* Second enlarged edition. (New York: Exposition Press, 1961). Peter Odegard documents the historic impact of religion in his *Religion and Politics* (New York: Oceana Publications, 1960), while Robert S. Alley concerns himself with the twentieth century story in *So Help Me God: Religion and the Presidency: Wilson to Nixon* (Richmond, Virginia: John Knox Press, 1972).

Edmund Lindop and Joseph Jares, *White House Sportsmen* (Boston: Houghton Mifflin, 1964) catalogues the leisure time pursuits of the Presidents.

White House social history is the subject of several volumes. One of the best is still Bess Furman, *White House Profile, a Social History of the White House, Its Occupants and Its Festivities* (Indianapolis: Bobbs Merrill, 1951). A fine pictorial and personal history of the first families is Amy La Follette Jensen, *The White House and Its Thirty-Four Families* (New York: McGraw-Hill, 1970). Of the various collective biographies of presidential wives, the student should especially consult Mary O. Whitten, *First First Ladies, 1789–1865, a Study of the Wives of the Early Presidents* (New York: Hastings House, 1948) and Ona Griffin Jeffries, *In and Out of the White House, from Washington to the Eisenhowers; an Intimate Glimpse into the Social and Domestic Aspects of the Presidential Life* (New York: W. Funk, 1960). Claudia ("Lady Bird") Johnson has provided her memoirs in *A White House Diary* (New York: Holt, Rinehart and Winston, 1970).

Biographical Studies

In recommending each of the following titles, I have sought to apply three basic criteria: sound scholarship; eminent readability; and emphasis upon the presidential years.

1. George Washington (1789–1797):

Flexner, James Thomas. *George Washington and the New Nation (1783–1793)* and *George Washington: Anguish and Farewell (1793–1799).* Volumes III and IV. (Boston: Little, Brown, 1969–1972). Comprehensive treatment with both praise and blame.

Freeman, Douglas Southall. *George Washington: A Biography.* 7 Vols. (New York: Scribner's Sons, 1948–1957). Classic study emphasizing Washington's human qualities. Volume seven was written by two of Freeman's associates, John Alexander Carroll and Mary Wells Ashworth. A one-volume abridgement, *Washington,* by Richard Harwell was issued in 1968 by Scribner's.

2. John Adams (1797–1801):

Chinard, Gilbert. *Honest John Adams* (Boston: Little, Brown, 1933). Good for Adams' political philosophy.

Smith, Page. *John Adams.* 2 Vols. (Garden City, N.Y.: Doubleday, 1962). Authoritative, but harder reading. First comprehensive biography based upon the Adams Papers opened in 1952.

3. Thomas Jefferson (1801–1809):

Malone, Dumas. *Jefferson and His Time.* 4 Vols. (Boston: Little, Brown, 1948–1970). Definitive treatment by a master historian.

Peterson, Merrill D. *Thomas Jefferson and the New Nation.* (New York: Oxford University Press, 1970). Stresses the many contributions of Jefferson to the nation.

4. James Madison (1809–1817)

Brant, Irving. *The Fourth President: A Life of James Madison.* (Indianapolis: Bobbs-Merrill, 1970). Abridgement of the author's earlier (1941–1961) six-volume life of Madison. Definitive and sympathetic.

Ketcham, Ralph. *James Madison: A Biography.* (New York: Macmillan, 1971). Most recent study. Massive detail and thorough acquaintance with source materials.

5. James Monroe (1817–1825)

Ammon, Harry. *James Monroè: The Quest for National Identity.* (New York: McGraw-Hill Book Co., 1971). Especially good on Monroe's relationship with Jefferson and Madison.

Cresson, William P. *James Monroe.* (Chapel Hill: University of North Carolina, 1946). Strong on foreign affairs.

Dangerfield, George. *The Era of Good Feelings.* (New York: Harcourt, Brace and Company, 1952). Excellent personal and political history covering the years, 1814–1829.

6. John Quincy Adams (1825–1829)

Bemis, Samuel Flagg. *John Quincy Adams and the Foundations of American Foreign Policy* and *John Quincy Adams and the Union.* (New York: Knopf, 1949–1956). Pulitzer Prize winner. One of President Kennedy's favorite biographies. Bemis had access to the Adams Papers.

7. Andrew Jackson (1829–1837)

James, Marquis. *The Life of Andrew Jackson.* (Indianapolis: Bobbs Merrill, 1938). Well-written. Strong on personal and family life.

Schlesinger, Jr., Arthur M. *The Age of Jackson.* (Boston: Little, Brown, 1945). Pulitzer Prize winner. Pictures Jackson as an intelligent as well as courageous champion of the laborer and the farmer against speculative capital and entrenched privilege.

8. Martin Van Buren (1837-1841)

Curtis, James C. *The Fox at Bay: Martin Van Buren and the Presidency, 1837-1841.* (Lexington: The University Press of Kentucky, 1970). The first detailed examination of the Van Buren presidency.

Van Deusen, Glyndon G. *The Jacksonian Era. 1828-1848.* (New York: Harper, 1959). Good synthesis of many monographs on the period.

9. William Henry Harrison (1841)

Cleaves, Freeman. *Old Tippencanoe: William Henry Harrison and His Time.* (New York: Scribner, 1939). Standard treatment.

Gunderson, Robert Gray. *The Log-Cabin Campaign.* (Lexington: University of Kentucky Press, 1957). Colorful accounts of famous Whig triumph in which they outwitted the Democrats.

10. John Tyler (1841-1845)

Chitwood, Oliver Perry. *John Tyler, Champion of the Old South.* (New York: Appleton-Century, 1939). Very favorable interpretation based on family papers.

Seager, Robert. *And Tyler Too.* (New York: McGraw-Hill Book Co., 1963). Excellent social history of President Tyler, his wife Julia Gardner, and their large family.

11. James K. Polk (1845-1849)

McCormac, Eugene Irving. *James K. Polk, A Political Biography.* (Berkeley: University of California Press, 1922). The only complete biography to date.

Sellers, Charles Grier. *James K. Polk, Jacksonian, 1795-1843* and *James K. Polk, Continentalist, 1843-1846.* (Princeton: Princeton University Press, 1957-1966). Authoritative. Will become the standard work when completed.

12. Zachary Taylor (1849-1850)

Dyer, Brainerd. *Zachary Taylor.* (Baton Rouge: Louisiana State University, 1946). Especially good on Taylor's executive-legislative struggle.

Hamilton, Holman. *Zachary Taylor.* 2 vols. (Indianapolis: Bobbs Merrill, 1941-1951). Admirable, well-researched and written study based upon twenty years' work.

13. Millard Fillmore (1850-1853)

Rayback, Robert J. *Millard Fillmore: Biography of a President.* (Buffalo: H. Stewart, 1959). Readable. Dispels image of Fillmore as an anti-Catholic bigot.

14. Franklin Pierce (1853-1857)

Nichols, Roy F. *Franklin Pierce, Young Hickory of the Granite Hills.* 2nd ed. (Philadelphia: University of Pennsylvania Press, 1958). Excellent scholarship by one of the great masters of nineteenth century American political history.

15. James Buchanan (1857-1861)

Klein, Philip Shriver. *President James Buchanan, A Biography.* (University Park, Pa.: Pennsylvania State University, 1962). Definitive, yet very readable.

Nichols, Roy F. *The Disruption of American Democracy.* (New York: Macmillan, 1948). Pulitzer Prize winner. Excellent vignettes of major and minor political leaders. Outstanding analysis of the party process.

16. Abraham Lincoln (1861-1865)

Randall, James Garfield. *Lincoln, the President.* 4 vols. (Dodd, Mead, 1945-1955). Critical and yet sympathetic. Pictures Lincoln as a moderate liberal.

Sandburg, Carl. *Abraham Lincoln: The War Years.* 4 vols. (New York: Harcourt Brace, 1939). Excellent. Stresses Lincoln's human qualities.

Thomas, Benjamin P. *Abraham Lincoln, A Biography.* (New York: Knopf, 1952). The standard one volume treatment.

17. Andrew Johnson (1865-1869)

Lomask, Milton. *Andrew Johnson: President on Trial.* (New York: Farrar, Straus, and Giroux, 1960). A readable account concentrating on the presidential period. A good overall, up-to-date biography of Andrew Johnson is still needed.

McKitrick, Eric L. *Andrew Johnson and Reconstruction.* (Chicago: University of Chicago, 1960). The best account of President Johnson's struggles with the Radical Republicans and hostile Democrats.

18. Ulysses S. Grant (1869-1877)

Hesseltine, William B. *Ulysses S. Grant, Politician.* (New York: Dodd, Mead, 1935). The standard biography. Favorable.

Nevins, Allan. *Hamilton Fish: the Inner History of the Grant Administration.* (New York: Dodd, Mead, 1936). Solid political history from the vantage point of Grant's key cabinet officer and Secretary of State for eight years.

19. Rutherford B. Hayes (1877-1881)

Barnard, Harry. *Rutherford B. Hayes and His America.* (Indianapolis: Bobbs Merrill, 1954). Excellent on the disputed election of 1876 and the family background of President Hayes. Limited discussion of presidential period.

Davison, Kenneth E. *The Presidency of Rutherford B. Hayes.* (Westport, Conn.: Greenwood Press, 1972). Standard work. New material on Hayes' early life, nomination for President, White House staff, Indian policy, use of executive power, and travels.

20. James A. Garfield (1881)

Caldwell, Robert G. *James A. Garfield, Party Chieftain.* (New York: Dodd, Mead, 1931). Still the standard one volume work.

Smith, Theodore Clarke. *The Life and Letters of James Abram Garfield.* 2 vols. (New Haven: Yale University Press, 1925). Good for details on Garfield's early years.

21. Chester A. Arthur (1881–1885)
Howe, George Frederick. *Chester A. Arthur: A Quarter-Century of Machine Politics.* (New York: Dodd, Mead, 1934). The only existing twentieth century biography. Limited by paucity of Arthur Papers.
Reeves, Thomas C. *The Gentleman Boss.* (New York: Knopf, forthcoming). Destined to be the standard biography. Based upon intensive research and new manuscript finds.

22. Grover Cleveland (1885–1889; 1893–1897)
Merrill, Horace Samuel. *Bourbon Leader: Grover Cleveland and the Democratic Party.* (Boston: Little, Brown, 1957). A well-written brief biography.
Nevins, Allan. *Grover Cleveland, A Study in Courage.* (New York: Dodd, Mead, 1932). Pulitzer Prize winner. Definitive.

23. Benjamin Harrison (1889–1893)
Sievers, Harry J. *Benjamin Harrison: Hoosier Warrior, 1833-1865.* (Chicago: Henry Regnery Co., 1952); *Benjamin Harrison: Hoosier Statesman, 1865-1888* (New York: University Publishers, 1959); *Benjamin Harrison, Hoosier President, 1888-1901* (Indianapolis: Bobbs Merrill, 1968). The first comprehensive biography based upon intensive use of the Harrison Papers.

24. William McKinley (1897–1901)
Leech, Margaret. *In the Days of McKinley.* (New York: Harper, 1959). Pulitzer Prize winner. Gives a balanced view of McKinley's presidency. Excellent personal vignettes, especially of Mrs. McKinley.
Morgan, H. Wayne. *William McKinley and His America.* (Syracuse: Syracuse University Press, 1963). Particularly strong on McKinley as a political leader and President.

25. Theodore Roosevelt (1901–1909)
Blum, John Morton. *The Republican Roosevelt.* (Cambridge: Harvard University Press, 1954). A very good brief political biography.
Gatewood, Jr., Willard B. *Theodore Roosevelt and the Art of Controversy.* (Baton Rouge: Louisiana State University Press, 1970). An examination of seven episodes from the Roosevelt years in the White House.
Harbaugh, William Henry. *The Life and Times of Theodore Roosevelt.* Revised edition. (New York: Collier Books, 1963). A solid book, emphasizing Roosevelt the man and the political leader.
Lorant, Stefan. *The Life and Times of Theodore Roosevelt.* (Garden City, N.Y.: Doubleday, 1959). A superb pictorial biography seventeen years in the making.
Mowry, George F. *The Era of Theodore Roosevelt, 1900-1912.* (New York: Harper, 1958). Excellent treatment of Roosevelt's philosophy and policies as a national leader.
Pringle, Henry F. *Theodore Roosevelt, A Biography.* (New York: Harcourt, Brace, 1931). Pulitzer Prize winner. Well grounded in the sources.

26. William Howard Taft (1909-1913)

Coletta, Paolo E. *The Presidency of William Howard Taft.* (Lawrence: The University Press of Kansas, 1973). The first volume in a new series on presidential administrations.

Pringle, Henry F. *The Life and Times of William Howard Taft, A Biography.* 2 vols. (New York: Farrar and Rinehart, 1939). Definitive. Based on Taft Papers in the Library of Congress.

27. Woodrow Wilson (1913-1921)

Bailey, Thomas A. *Woodrow Wilson and the Lost Peace* (New York: Macmillan, 1944) and *Woodrow Wilson and the Great Betrayal* (New York: Macmillan, 1945). Highly readable accounts of Wilson's inflexibility at the time of the fight for the League of Nations.

Baker, Ray Stannard. *Woodrow Wilson: Life and Letters.* 8 vols. (Garden City, N.Y.: Doubleday, Doran & Co., 1927-1939). Authorized biography. Very informative first-hand volumes by Wilson's literary executor.

Link, Arthur S. *Woodrow Wilson.* 5 vols. (Princeton: Princeton University Press, 1947-1965). Critical, but far from hostile biography, destined to be the definitive account when the series, now up to 1917, is completed.

Smith, Gene. *When the Cheering Stopped: the Last Years of Woodrow Wilson.* (New York: William Morrow and Company, 1964). Fascinating account of Wilson's last years and crippling illness, based upon documents found after his widow's death.

28. Warren G. Harding (1921-1923)

Downes, Randolph C. *The Rise of Warren Gamaliel Harding, 1865-1920.* (Columbus: The Ohio State University Press, 1970). The best account of Harding's career before he became President. Based upon the recently opened Harding Papers in the Ohio Historical Society.

Murray, Robert. *The Harding Era: Warren G. Harding and His Administration.* (Minneapolis: University of Minnesota Press, 1969). The most up-to-date and scholarly account of the Harding Presidency.

29. Calvin Coolidge (1923-1929)

Fuess, Claude. *Calvin Coolidge, the Man from Vermont.* (Boston: Little, Brown, 1940). Interesting and well-written, but uncritical.

McCoy, Donald R. *Calvin Coolidge: The Quiet President.* (New York: Macmillan, 1967). A recent reassessment well researched and presented.

White, William Allen. *A Puritan in Babylon.* (New York: Macmillan, 1938). A sardonic view of Coolidge's shortcomings.

30. Herbert Hoover (1929-1933)

Warren, Harris G. *Herbert Hoover and the Great Depression.* (New York: Oxford University Press, 1959). The best secondary account, but written without access to the Hoover Papers. A definitive Hoover biography has not yet appeared.

31. Franklin D. Roosevelt (1933-1945)

Burns, James MacGregor. *Roosevelt: The Lion and the Fox* (New York: Harcourt, Brace & Co., 1956) and *Roosevelt: The Soldier of Freedom* (New York: Harcourt, Brace Jovanovich, Inc., 1970). The first scholarly biography, informative and critical, of President Roosevelt. Excellent descriptions of the political scene.

Freidel, Frank. *Franklin D. Roosevelt.* 4 vols. (Boston: Little, Brown, 1952–1973). Excellent biography to July 1933. To be completed in three more volumes.

Lash, Joseph. *Eleanor and Franklin.* (New York: W. W. Norton & Co., 1971). Personal and family history based upon Eleanor Roosevelt's Papers.

Leuchtenburg, William E. *Franklin D. Roosevelt and the New Deal, 1932–1940.* (New York: Harper & Row, 1963). The best short account of the New Deal.

Schlesinger, Jr., Arthur M. *The Age of Roosevelt.* 3 vols. (Cambridge: Houghton-Mifflin, 1957-1960). An exciting series which carries the account to 1936.

32. Harry S. Truman (1945-1953)

Phillips, Cabell. *The Truman Presidency.* (New York: Macmillan, 1966). A journalistic study of the two Truman administrations with modest use of the Truman Papers.

Rudoni, Dorothy June. *Harry S. Truman: A Study in Presidential Perspective.* (Ann Arbor: University Microfilms, 1969). An examination of the ideas and forces which shaped President Truman's concept of the presidential office.

Steinberg, Alfred. *The Man from Missouri: the Life and Times of Harry S. Truman.* (New York: Putnam, 1962). The best of the earlier books on Truman.

Truman, Margaret. *Harry S. Truman.* (New York: William Morrow & Co., 1972). Interesting for its personal history and the Truman-Roosevelt relationship.

33. Dwight D. Eisenhower (1953-1961)

Adams, Sherman. *Firsthand Report: the Story of the Eisenhower Administration.* (New York: Harper, 1961). Governor Adams functioned as President Eisenhower's White House Chief of Staff.

Donovan, Robert J. *Eisenhower: the Inside Story.* (New York: Harper, 1956). Authorized account of the first Eisenhower administration by a well-known journalist given access to the White House.

Hughes, Emmet John. *The Ordeal of Power: a Political Memoir of the Eisenhower Years.* (New York: Atheneum, 1963). A critical account by a former Eisenhower speech-writer who was allowed to sit in on a number of Cabinet meetings.

Parmet, Herbert S. *Eisenhower and the American Crusades.* New York: Macmillan, 1972). First major assessment of the Eisenhower administrations based on interviews, oral history recordings, and manuscript sources.

34. John F. Kennedy (1961-1963)

Burns, James MacGregor. *John Kennedy: A Political Profile.* (New York: Harcourt, Brace & World, 1960). The best account of Kennedy's life before he became President. Based upon interviews and family papers,

Donald, Aida Dipace (ed.). *John F. Kennedy and the New Frontier.* (New York: Hill and Wang, 1966). A collection of essays and early appraisals of President Kennedy.

Manchester, William R. *Portrait of a President: John F. Kennedy in Profile.* Rev. ed. (Boston: Little, Brown, 1967). The original edition of this book led to the choice of Manchester by the Kennedy family to write the account of Kennedy's assassination.

Schlesinger, Jr., Arthur M. *A Thousand Days: John F. Kennedy in the White House.* Cambridge: Houghton Mifflin Company, 1965. An important memoir by a distinguished historian and Kennedy Special Assistant, 1961–1963. The best work on Kennedy as President.

Sorenson, Theodore C. *Kennedy.* (New York: Harper and Row, 1965). A superb account of decision-making by John F. Kennedy as Senator (1953–61) and President (1961–63) by his closest assistant and speech-writer.

White, Theodore H. *The Making of the President, 1960.* (New York: Atheneum Publishers, 1961). The first and best of White's four detailed accounts of presidential campaigns from 1960 to 1972.

35. Lyndon B. Johnson (1963–1969)

Goldman, Eric. *The Tragedy of Lyndon Johnson.* (New York: Knopf, 1969). A memoir by Johnson's disillusioned "intellectual-in-residence."

Steinberg, Alfred. *Sam Johnson's Boy: A Close-up of the President from Texas.* (New York: Macmillan, 1968). Uncomplimentary, but exhaustively researched and well-written.

White, William S. *The Professional: Lyndon B. Johnson.* (Cambridge: Houghton Mifflin, 1964). Favorable brief biography.

36. Nixon, Richard M. (1969-1974)

Evans, Rowland, and Novak, Robert D. *Nixon in the White House.* (New York: Random House, 1971). A journalistic account of the first Nixon administration.

Mazlish, Bruce. *In Search of Nixon: A Psychohistorical Inquiry.* (Baltimore: Penguin Books, Inc., 1973). A fascinating effort to probe President Nixon's personality.

Mazo, Earl and Hess, Stephen. *Nixon: A Political Portrait* (New York: Harper & Row, 1968). A rewritten version of Earl Mazo's earlier *Richard Nixon: A Political and Personal Portrait.* (New York: Harper, 1959).

Wills, Garry. *Nixon Agonistes: The Crisis of the Self-Made Man.* (Boston: Houghton Mifflin, 1970). An analysis of President Nixon's methods and ideology.

Source Materials for the
History of American Cartography *

by John A. Wolter

The following source materials are selected from a large and diverse group of publications which deal in whole or in part with the history of American cartography. Titles included are, of course, the result of personal bias and the reader may not agree with all of the author's inclusions.** It was interesting to find so many publications available but so few of any real comprehensiveness, particularly in the general monographic literature. This probably says a good deal about the present state of the art.

A selective and definitive work similar to Wright and Platt's *Aids to Geographical Research*[1] is needed within the near future. The sheer size, dispersion, and exponential growth of the literature demands that a better form of bibliographic control, particularly for literature produced in this country, be instituted to cope with this "information explosion."

---

*An earlier version of this paper appeared in the SLA Geography and Map Division *Bulletin*, No. 88, June 1972.

**This is the substance of a lecture given for the past three years to the Library of Congress-George Washington University graduate seminar in American Thought and Culture. Seminar participants had scant knowledge of maps and mapping, let alone of bibliographies and other finding aids in cartographic history. Because of this I decided to limit the discussion to those works which could be considered basic to any study of the development of American cartography. In addition I wanted to cover all forms of publication, *i.e.*, monographs, bibliographies, indexes, catalogs, periodicals, serials, and facsimiles to show the great diversity in style and type presently available and, most importantly, to lead the student to other similar publications. I also felt that these works could and should be found in most college and university libraries.

The titles included have been divided, for ease of discussion, into the following categories: 1) general monographs, 2) regional bibliographies, 3) bibliographies, indexes and catalogs, 4) serials and periodicals, 5) globes, and 6) facsimile maps and atlases.

General Monographs

Several monographs on cartographic history have been published since World War II. Of particular interest are the sections devoted to the history of American cartography in the following works.

Leo Bagrow's *Die Geschichte der Kartographie,*[2] the English-language edition of which was edited by the late R. A. Skelton, one of this century's foremost cartographic historians, was published in 1964 as the *History of Cartography.*[3] Although the section on America covers less than two pages, the illustrations and reproductions of maps are good, and the bibliography and list of cartographers are important. The larger German language edition should also be consulted. It should be emphasized that this work and the following works are general introductions. A definitive monograph on American cartographic history has yet to be published.

Lloyd Brown's *Story of Maps,*[4] published in 1949, is a general introduction to the history of mapmaking with more emphasis on the development of techniques (*e.g.,* instrumentation, latitude, longitude, the chronometer, air photos, etc.) than on exploration and discovery. It does, however, include an extensive bibliography and many valuable notes. America is again slighted, with the emphasis on ancient, medieval, and early modern cartography.

Gerald Crone's *Maps and Their Makers: An Introduction to the History of Cartography,*[5] 4th edition, 1968, is a brief, but very well-written work. It is highly recommended as an authoritative introduction to the history of cartography. There are notes and bibliographic references following each chapter. A list of early

Photo by The Library of Congress

Mr. Wolter is Assistant Chief, Geography and Map Division, Library of Congress, and the Library's deputy to the U.S. Board on Geographic Names. He is a member of the U.S. National Committee for the International Geographical Union and U.S. member of the Working Group for the History of Cartography of the International Cartographic Association. Mr. Wolter is presently serving as Secretary-Treasurer of the Society for the History of Discoveries and is a Director of the Cartography Division, American Congress on Surveying and Mapping. He has lectured on geographic and cartographic history and bibliography at the University of Minnesota and for the Library of Congress' George Washington University seminar on American Thought and Culture. His publications are, for the most part, in the above fields; in addition, he serves as an advisory editor for Cartographica, Surveying and Mapping *and* The American Cartographer.

maps (appendix II) and a note on library collections in Great Britain are also included. Sections on "The Cartography of the Great Discoveries," "Topographical Mapping in the Fifteenth and Sixteenth Centuries," and "The British Contribution" are particularly valuable. The history of North American cartography is treated with the growth of cartographic knowledge of the entire world in several chapters.

Explorers' Maps,[6] subtitled *Chapters in the Cartographical Record of Geographical Discovery,* is a reprint, with appropriate revision, of 14 articles which appeared from 1953 to 1956 in the *Geographical Magazine,* a popular British periodical. A new edition of *Explorers' Maps,* in slightly enlarged format, was published by Spring Books in 1970. This book, by R. A. Skelton, can be regarded as a pictorial companion to histories of exploration. The maps are carefully chosen and effectively reproduced. Chapter XII, entitled "North America From Sea to Sea," summarizes the cartography of North America, with reproductions of John Smith's 1612 *Map of Virginia,* Champlain's *Map of New France,* 1632, and several important 18th century maps. The notes for each chapter are informative and interesting.

R. V. Tooley's *Maps and Map-makers,*[7] 4th edition, 1970, is written for both the student and the collector. The section on America, although brief, is valuable for its extensive bibliography with more than 120 citations.

Maps and Man[64] by Norman J. W. Thrower was first published in 1972. The author deals with the historical development of cartography and its relationship to cultural and scientific history. This is the first really new and up-to-date history of cartography in all its varied forms. American cartography is treated in several chapters as a part of general development. The text is excellent and very readable and the book is a complement and supplement to G. R. Crone's previously cited *Maps and Their Makers.*

Landmarks of Mapmaking, An Illustrated Survey of Maps and Mapmakers,[8] by Charles Bricker, a large, beautifully illustrated, and well-written cartographic history, was published by Elsevier in 1968. Maps were selected by Tooley and the preface was written by Crone. It was also published by Thames and Hudson, London, in 1969, with the title *A History of Cartography: 2500 Years of Maps and Mapmakers.*[9] "The Americas" section is illustrated with many sketches and facsimiles of maps, some in color. However, as with most cartographic histories, it stops short in the latter part of the 18th century.

Identification of old and rare maps is a major problem area in the history of cartography. Some assistance is given in Raymond Lister's *How to Identify Old Maps and Globes . . . ,*[10] published in Great Britain and the United States in 1964. It also includes useful information on reproduction methods and mapmakers of note. Appended to the volume is Edward Heawood's "The Use of Watermarks in Dating Old Maps and Documents," which is reprinted from the 1924 volume of the *Geographical Journal.*

Armando Cortesão, one of the leading cartographic historians, published in 1969 the first volume of a projected three-volume work entitled *History of Portuguese Cartography.*[11] Volume I, which covers the period to the 14th century, is attractively produced in a limited edition of 1,000 copies. Cortesão divides cartographic history into four periods: 1) Classical Cartography, 2) Medieval Cartography, 3) Modern Cartography, and 4) Contemporary Cartography. Volume

11 (1971) includes chapters on the 14th and 15th centuries and on navigation and navigational instruments. This promises to be one of the most significant cartographic histories published since Bagrow/Skelton's *History of Cartography*[12] cited above.

William P. Cumming, David B. Quinn, and the late Raleigh A. Skelton have co-authored *The Discovery of North America*,[13] volume 1. This outstandingly beautiful book, published in 1971, reconstructs, by means of numerous color plates and monochrome illustrations, the visual record of the European discovery of this continent.

Regional Bibliographies

Several of the more important North American regional cartobibliographies, well-established references as well as some volumes of more recent vintage, are described under this heading.

Justin Winsor's *Narrative and Critical History of America*,[14] in eight volumes, published in 1889, is so well illustrated with sketches and facsimiles of early maps that it might be called a "Narrative Critical and Cartographic History." As such it is highly recommended.

Samuel Eliot Morison's *The European Discovery of America: The Northern Voyages A.D. 500-1600*,[15] published in 1971 and the second volume, *The European Discovery of America: The Southern Voyages 1492-1616*,[66] published in 1974, supplement the first several volumes of Winsor. They are both excellent and comprehensive reviews. Like others of Admiral Morison's books, the two volumes of *European Discovery* are a delight to read.

Carl I Wheat's *Mapping the Transmississippi West*,[16] published in five volumes between 1957 and 1960, is a monumental work. Volume I presents a general background and "a narrative discussion of the growth and spread of knowledge concerning the Transmississippi region over the period 1540–1804. . . ." This is a comprehensive cartobibliography with many fine reproductions. Wheat treats the growth of geographical knowledge as portrayed in the maps he describes. His bibliographic descriptions are not always good, and he pays no attention to the mechanics of map production at different periods, *i.e.*, engraving, wax engraving, lithography, etc., but it is truly a landmark work in American cartographic history.

W. P. Cumming's *The Southeast in Early Maps, An Annotated Check List of Printed and Manuscript Regional and Local Maps of Southeastern North America during the Colonial Period*[17] is also an excellent reference. The illustrations are well done and the text is informative. Henry R. Wagner's *The Cartography of the Northwest Coast of America to the Year 1800*,[18] which covers roughly the same time span as Cumming, is important for western North America.

One of the earliest trans-Appalachian settled areas is described in Lloyd A. Brown's *Early Maps of the Ohio Valley. . . .*[19] Although not a definitive historical work it is nonetheless an interesting summarization. The choice of maps which illustrate the book is particularly good. As Brown states, "this book is primarily a picture book containing a brief review and summary of the cartographic record left by men who first explored and mapped the region of the Ohio." It includes maps made by Indians and Colonials from 1673 to 1783.

An extremely valuable check list of maps and charts was published in 1969 by Yale University Press. Wheat and Brun's *Maps and Charts Published in America before 1800: A Bibliography*[20] reflects the gradual growth of the American press prior to 1800. Described are maps and charts published separately, as well as those used as illustrations in books and pamphlets, atlases, gazetteers, almanacs, and periodicals.

The Iconography of Manhattan Island, 1498-1909[21] offers more than its title promises. Published in New York, 1915-1920, and reproduced in facsimile by Arno Press in 1967, the six volumes contain a wealth of geographic information in text, maps, plans, and views. Of particular interest are volume two, which deals in part with the entire North American coast, and volume six, which contains valuable information on individual maps and mapmakers.

Emerson Fite and Archibald Freeman compiled, and Harvard University Press published, in 1926, *A Book of Old Maps, Delineating American History from the Earliest Days Down to the Close of the Revolutionary War.*[22] The title explains its scope. The book includes excellent reproductions and explanatory text on facing pages, beginning with Ptolemy in the 2d century A.D. and ending with Mitchell's *A Map of the British Colonies in North America,* 1755. In 1969 Dover Publications brought out a paperback reprint edition with new plates for several of the maps.[23] Arno Press also produced a 1969 edition reprinted from a copy in the collections of the New York Public Library with a facsimile of the Vinland Map and additional notes supplementing the original text.[24]

A most inclusive study of maps relating to early American history is Henry Harrisse's *The Discovery of North America. . . .*[25] First published in 1892, it was reissued in a facsimile edition by N. Israel, Amsterdam, in 1961. Harrisse described and analyzed some 250 maps or globes, existing or lost, constructed before the year 1536. Biographical accounts, voyage chronologies, and "A copious list of the original names of American regions. . ." are also included. This is an indispensable work for the period.

Louis Karpinski, a mathematics professor at the University of Michigan, during the early decades of this century compiled an excellent *Bibliography of the Printed Maps of Michigan 1804-1880. . . .*[26] It includes notes on individual mapmakers, maps, and on copyright law and its relation to mapmaking.

The Map Collectors' Series, discussed below under "Serial Literature," has included some studies of important maps, among them Coolie Verner's *Smith's Virginia and its Derivatives; A Cartobibliographical Study of the Diffusion of Geographical Knowledge*[27] which is significant for its content and technique. The study of Captain John Smith and his 1612 Virginia map has been a long-time interest of Professor Verner and his contributions to cartobibliography are important. Cartographic history seems to appeal to a wide range of scholars. Academic geographers in this country, with some few noteworthy exceptions, have little interest in the history of cartography, particularly American cartographic history.

A number of significant works dealing with Canadian cartographic history have been published. One of the more recent efforts is Don W. Thomson's *Men and Meridians: The History of Surveying and Mapping in Canada.*[28] Volume I was published in 1966, and the third and last volume in 1968. Volume I includes chapters on "Early Surveying and Mapping in the United States" and "International Boundary Surveys." The other volumes deal with surveyors, surveying instruments, ancient and modern surveying techniques, modern mapping, thematic maps, among other topics. It is a government-sponsored research project. The writing is good, the illustrations superb, and the price reasonable.

A collection of nine papers by W. F. Ganong entitled *Crucial Maps in the Early Cartography and Place-name Nomenclature of the Atlantic Coast of Canada*[29] was published by the University of Toronto Press in 1964. The papers, which originally appeared in the Royal Society of Canada *Transactions,* deal with the cartographic history of the Maritimes. A comprehensive work that complements Ganong was compiled by T. E. Layng, Chief of the Map Division in the National Archives of Canada, *Sixteenth Century Maps Relating to Canada, A Check-list and Bibliography,*[30] published in 1965. The introduction to early Canadian cartography is particularly interesting and informative. The volume includes lists of Agnese and other Italian atlases of the sixteenth century, as well as a comprehensive bibliography.

General Bibliographies, Indexes, and Catalogs

General bibliographies and indexes of historical cartography are available in many different formats, including an increasing number of printed catalogs of United States and foreign map collections. A recent example is the New York Public Library's *Dictionary Catalog of the Map Division,*[31] in ten volumes, published in 1971. This excellent research tool, which contains approximately 175,000 cards, lists, in addition to maps and charts, some 6,000 atlases and approximately 11,000 volumes including reference books relating to maps and map making. Analytical entries are included for maps and articles from collections housed in other divisions of the library.

An important addition to the list of bibliographic indexes and catalogs is the *Guide to Cartographic Records in the National Archives.*[63] First published in 1971, the *Guide* contains descriptions of some 560 unit entries which include the more than 1,600,000 maps and approximately 2,250,000 aerial photographs which were in the National Archives as of July 1, 1966. This is one of the most valuable reference works in the field of cartographic history to be published in the last two decades. A number of cartographic record inventories and special lists which supplement the *Guide* have also been published during the last few years.

Special collections in universities and colleges also house important cartographic materials. The Bancroft Library of the University of California, for example, has had its dictionary catalog of "... maps from the 16th to the 20th century..." published in 1964 as the *Bancroft Library Index to Printed Maps.*[32]

The British Museum *Catalogue of Printed Maps, Charts, and Plans*[33] was published in 1967. This 15-volume work "contains entries for maps, atlases, globes, and related materials, (including literature on them...)." This major cartobibliographic reference aid is supplemented by *Accessions: Main Entries Only,*[34] published irregularly since 1964. A related work, the catalog of Manuscript Maps, Charts and Plans, and Topographical Drawings in the British Museum,[35] in three volumes, first published in 1844, was reprinted in 1962.

The Library of Congress Geography and Map Division has for several decades published cartobibliographic works describing important parts of its collections. Of particular value is Philip Lee Phillips' *List of Geographical Atlases,*[36] the first volume of which appeared in 1909. Volume 4, published in 1920, ended his contribution. Subsequent volumes (published in 1974) have been compiled by Clara Egli LeGear. Phillips' *A List of Maps of America in the Library of Congress, Preceded by a List of Works Relating to Cartography*[37] was published in 1901. The *List . . .* includes approximately 18,435 titles in an alphabetical arrangement and comprises the maps of America in the Library of Congress at the time a separate Division of Maps was established in 1897.

Mrs. LeGear's *United States Atlases. . . ,*[38] published in 1950, is a list of national, state, county, city and regional atlases in the collections of the Library of Congress. It includes atlases dated from 1776 to 1950 and is a most important and valuable compilation for the period. *United States Atlases . . . ,* Volume 2,[39] published in 1953, lists additional atlases located in the Library of Congress, and in some 184 cooperating libraries, to 1953.

An excellent guide to general works on historical cartography, which includes citations to monographs and serial literature as well as to bibliographies, is Walter W. Ristow's *Guide to the History of Cartography,*[40] 1973.

The Lowery Collection; a Descriptive List of Maps of the Spanish Possessions Within the Present Limits of the United States, 1502–1820,[65] edited by P. L. Phillips and published in 1912, is an annotated bibliography of some 700 maps. It includes a substantial number of references to source material and is well indexed.

General bibliographies of geography also contain references of interest to the historical cartographer. The American Geographical Society *Research Catalogue*[41] (1923–1961), published in 1962, is retrospective, and the citations to historical cartographic materials, which appear in both the topical and regional sections, include many references to works published before 1923. It is kept up to date by *Current Geographical Publications,*[42] which has the same classified arrangement. This periodical bibliography has been published since 1938, in 10 issues a year, with about 5,000 annual entries, of which approximately 250 are cartographic.

Wright and Platt's *Aids to Geographical Research,*[43] 2d edition, 1947 (reprinted in 1971 by Greenwood Press), now out of date, is still one of the best general guides. The sections on "Maps and Cartography" and its regional sections are particularly valuable. The entire work contains much of historical, regional, and topical interest.

Several useful directories of map collections have been published during the last decade. The second edition of *Map Collections in the United States and Canada, A Directory*[67] describes some 475 collections. The first edition, compiled in 1953, was released in 1954, and included information on 428 collections. *A Directory of Canadian Map Collections . . .*[68] was published in 1969. The information contained in these compilations, including notes on early maps and important regional collections, is most important to cartographic research. An article describing the growth, structure and present size of the most important collections in the United States and Europe, "Geographical Libraries and Map Collections,"[69] was published in 1973.

Serials and Periodicals

With the exception of reviews in the cartography sections of the *Geographisches Jahrbuch,*[44] which appeared at irregular intervals, there had been no concerted effort to collect, classify, and disseminate cartographic information on an international scale, until the beginning of this century. It should be noted that the *Jahrbuch* review articles summarized the literature of a subject for a given period of time. There was also much historical cartographic information in the regional reviews which generally appeared at two to three year intervals. Most *Jahrbuch* reviews to 1908 were limited to publications on map projections and map reading techniques. After this date there was more attention to the toal cartographic literature. A more recent trend includes a shift in emphasis to works on thematic cartography with consequently less on historical cartography, reflecting the increasing importance of thematic maps in the general field of cartography.

Herman Haack, among others, contributed much of bibliographical significance during the first four decades of this century. His contributions to cartobibliography ceased in 1942 with publication of Volume 57 of the *Geographisches Jahrbuch.* No sections on cartography have been published in this serial since 1968. A reprint publisher is reorganizing the 57 volumes into a new subject and area format. All sections on cartography will, reportedly, be published in three separate volumes. This will be an improvement over the original arrangement and, more importantly, will make this monumental bibliographic work once again available.

The wartime gap in bibliographic coverage was filled, in quite thorough fashion, with Hans Kosack and Karl-Heinz Meine's *Die Kartographie 1943–1954; eine bibliographische Ubersicht.*[45] Section C, pages 28–39, entitled "Geschichte der Kartographie," contains references to several hundred monograph and serial sources, and is accompanied by a short introductory essay. The subsection on pages 28–31 contains, among 102 references, several to the United States from sources as varied as the *Canadian Geographical Journal* and the *Papers of the Bibliographical Society of America*. Other sections, subdivided chronologically, also contain many references, particularly to maps of the sixteenth through nineteenth centuries. There is an alphabetical index of authors and a list of the several hundred cited periodicals. A comparison of this work with Haack's reviews in the *Geographisches Jahrbuch* shows a fundamental difference in that individual maps are not cited in Kosack-Meine, except for monographs on historical maps, the number of which had grown enormously. It is interesting that *Die Kartographie* contains more than ten pages on historical cartography.

In 1957, under the auspices of the Institut für Landeskunde and Die Deutsche Gesellschaft für Kartographie, the first issue of *Bibliotheca Cartographica*[46] appeared. This important new serial of international scope supplements *Die Kartographie,* and is current at this writing. The latter two publications index a significant portion of the post-war world's cartographic literature and are indispensable research tools for the historian of cartography.

The serial literature on American cartography is dispersed in many publications. Most useful for our purposes are the bibliographical, geographical, and historical serials, particularly those of a regional, state, or local nature. David Woodward of the Newberry Library has recently compiled a "Bibliography of Papers on History of Cartography . . ."[47] found in this type of publication, but much more remains to be done.

There is no *one* current serial bibliographic source for the historical cartography of North America, although the journal *Imago Mundi*[48] carries a bibliographical section entitled "Chronicle" which describes in some detail the current historical cartographic activities in the United States as well as in other countries. *Imago Mundi* has been published since 1935, although publication was suspended from 1940–46 and 1957–58. It is an annual devoted exclusively to scholarly studies in the history of cartography. Twenty five issues have been published to 1971. The journal is well illustrated with reproductions of early maps and also contains news, reviews, and bibliography. Only two articles dealing with nineteenth century maps of America have so far been included, and only fourteen articles devoted to American cartographic history have been published in *Imago Mundi*. Publication is irregular with, at times, two or three years elapsing between issues. It is, nonetheless, the best serial source for articles dealing with the history of cartography. The first seven issues have been reprinted. The others are all currently available. A supplemental *Imago Mundi* series is devoted to publication of facsimile maps and cartobibliographies, all issues of which are still in print.

Acta Cartographica; A Series of Monographs and Studies on the History of Cartography, Reprinted from Periodicals since 1800[49] is a series of unabridged reprints from about 150 of the foremost European and American historical and geographical journals, and from monographs and reports. It should be noted that 72 of the 288 articles in the first fifteen volumes are in English and of these several deal with America. A number of articles in French and German also deal specifically with America. This reprint serial includes excellent source material, particularly for those who do not have access to library collections of the periodicals in which the articles initially appeared. It would be helpful if summaries in English, German, French and Italian were provided. *Acta Cartographica* may be too expensive ($65.00 per year) for the individual scholar, but college, university, and reference libraries should subscribe to it.

The Map Collectors' Circle: Map Collectors' Series,[50] a British publication, begun in 1963, is another important serial source. The stated aim is to stimulate interest in, and publish material on, early printed maps, atlases, and cartographers. Most issues are devoted to one topic, bibliography, or area and are well illustrated.

The Library of Congress Geography and Map Division has maintained for many years a card catalog of the world's cartographic literature. It includes citations to articles, monographs, reviews, serials, and bibliographies dealing with all phases of cartography. The *Bibliography of Cartography,* as it is known, is of particular importance for research in American cartographic history. It was first microfilmed, through 1969, on 29 reels, to make it available to researchers and other libraries. The microfilm format was, however, awkward to use.

In 1973 G. K. Hall and Company published the card catalog in book form as *The Bibliography of Cartography.*[51] The five volumes of this important work reproduce some 90,000 cards relating to the literature of cartography published from the early 19th century through 1971. Supplemental volumes which will include several thousand cards not reproduced in the above work are under consideration.

Globes

Those whose interest lies in other cartographic formats, particularly globes, armillary spheres, etc., will refer to *Der Globusfreund,*[52] an annual serial published in Vienna since 1952. This excellent publication, devoted solely to the study of historical and modern globes, includes articles, illustrations, bibliographies, and biographical sketches.

The late Ena L. Yonge compiled in 1968 *A Catalog of Early Globes, Made Prior to 1850 and Conserved in the United States. . . .*[53] Listed are approximately 400 globes, orreries and armillary spheres made by some 93 globemakers. Brief biographical sketches are included.

A comprehensive work, with an extensive bibliography and an index of globemakers with locations of globes, is Edward Luther Stevenson's *Terrestrial and Celestial Globes; Their History and Construction. . . ,*[54] published in 1921 for the Hispanic Society of America by the Yale University Press. The history of globe making in the United States still awaits a definitive text.

Facsimile Maps and Atlases

The history of cartography is best studied and interpreted through contemporary maps and charts. Although there are many collections of early cartographic materials in this country, few are comprehensive enough to satisfy the requirements of research which spans long periods of time and large geographic areas. Noteworthy exceptions are the collections of the Geography and Map Division of the Library of Congress, the National Archives, New York Public Library, American Geographical Society, Harvard and Yale Universities, and the Newberry, Clements and Bancroft libraries. These collections, however, are not easily accessible to the researcher in the hinterlands and some provision must be made for those who cannot personally visit them. As noted above, useful cartobibliographies and catalogs have been published, but more remains to be done to make these collections, particularly the Federal ones, more accessible to scholars of American cartographic history.

An increase in facsimile map and atlas production in recent decades has made available much of the important cartographic materials of the last few centuries. Facsimile reproduction of cartographic rarities is not a new development, for facsimile maps have been published since the latter part of the 16th century. It wasn't until the mid-19th century, however, that mechanically produced facsimiles (lithographed and engraved) were available for the most distinctive maps of the early period. These techniques permitted large numbers of facsimiles to be produced at relatively low cost, particularly those using the various applications of lithography.[55]

The study of cartographic history was greatly advanced by publication, in 1889, of Nordenskiöld's *Facsimile Atlas,*[56] which includes reproductions of 51 historical maps, all but one of which are full-scale facsimiles. It also includes small maps in the text section. Photolithography was the reproduction medium used in this famous facsimile atlas. In 1897 Nordenskiöld published the *Periplus: An Essay on the Early History of Charts and Sailing Directions,*[57] which he regarded as a continuation of his *Facsimile Atlas.* In 1961 Kraus Reprint Corporation produced a facsimile of the *Facsimile Atlas* as did Dover Publications in 1973 and in 1967 Burt Franklin reproduced the *Periplus. . . .*

The Geography and Map Division of the Library of Congress has a collection of hand-drawn facsimile maps produced during the mid-19th century by Johann Georg Kohl. This distinctive collection, which came to the Library from the Department of State in 1903, was first described by Justin Winsor. Winsor's list, with a supplemental index by P. L. Phillips, was reprinted as *The Kohl Collection (Now in L.C.) of Maps Relating to America,*[58] by the Library of Congress in 1904. It is a unique assemblage of copies of 474 early printed and manuscript maps.

Many cartographic facsimiles have been issued by Theatrum Orbis Terrarum Publishing Company, including, among other atlases, the 1513 *Ptolemy.*[59] T.O.T. publications are, for the most part, uncolored photo-offset facsimile atlases reproduced on good paper from the best copies available. They are not bound as well as they might be. Color facsimiles of rare atlases are also available from other publishers.

Many single maps and charts have also been published in facsimile in this country, including Hermann's *Virginia and Maryland (1673)*[60] by the John Carter Brown Library, and Abel Buell's *New and Correct Map of the United States of America (1783)*[61] by the New Jersey Historical Society.

A list of currently available facsimiles is included in the third revised edition, with supplement, of *Facsimiles of Rare Historical Maps,*[62] which has been compiled by Walter W. Ristow for a number of years.

Old maps are interesting, not only to historians and antiquarians, but also, because of their lettering, illumination, fanciful cartouches, or fanciful depiction, to many other persons with a great variety of backgrounds. The great increase in prices for rare maps and atlases has made them prohibitively expensive for most libraries; thus the facsimile publication will become increasingly important in the future. The increase in facsimile map and atlas publication, if it can be taken as indicative of increased interest in American historical cartography, is encouraging to those of us who are working in this field.

Cited Works

1. Wright, John K., and Platt, Elizabeth T. *Aids to Geographical Research.* 2d ed. rev. New York, American Geographical Society, 1947. 331 p. (American Geographical Society Research series number 22). Reprinted in 1971 by Greenwood Press, Westport, Connecticut.

2. Bagrow, Leo. *Die Geschichte der Kartographie.* Berlin, Safari-Verlag, 1951. 383 p. See also by the same author, *Meister der Kartographie.* Berlin, Safari-Verlag, 1963. 579 p. [Based on the English edition by R. A. Skelton].

3. Bagrow, Leo. *History of Cartography.* Revised and enlarged by R. A. Skelton. Cambridge, Harvard University Press, 1964. 312 p.

4. Brown, Lloyd A. *The Story of Maps.* Boston, Little, Brown, 1949. 397 p.   •

5. Crone, Gerald R. *Maps and Their Makers; An Introduction to the History of Cartography.* 4th rev. ed. London, Hutchinson, 1968. 181 p.

6. Skelton, Raleigh A. *Explorers' Maps; Chapters in the Cartographic Record of Geographical Discovery.* [New ed.] Feltham, New York, Spring Books, 1970. 337 p.

7. Tooley, R. V. *Maps and Map-Makers.* 4th ed. London, Batsford, 1970. 140 p.

8. Bricker, Charles. *Landmarks of Map-Making; An Illustrated Survey of Maps and Mapmakers.* Maps chosen and displayed by R. V. Tooley, text written by Charles Bricker, preface by Gerald R. Crone. Amsterdam, Brussels, Elsevier, 1968. 276 p.

9. Bricker, Charles. *A History of Cartography: 2500 Years of Maps and Map-makers.* Maps chosen and displayed by R. V. Tooley, text by Charles Bricker, preface by Gerald R. Crone. London, Thames and Hudson, 1969. 276 p.

10. Lister, Raymond. *How to Identify Old Maps and Globes, with a List of Cartographers, Engravers, Publishers, and Printers Concerned with Printed Maps and Globes from c. 1500 to c. 1850.* Hamden, Conn., Archon Books, London, G. Bell, 1965. 256 p.

11. Cortesão, Armando. *History of Portuguese Cartography.* Lisbon, Portugal, Junta de Investigaçoes do Ultramar, 1969. v. 1. (Agrupamento de Estudos de Cartografia Antiga. [Publicacoes] 6).

12. Bagrow, *op. cit.*

13. Cumming, William P., Quinn, David B., and Skelton, Raleigh A. *The Discovery of North America.* New York, American Heritage Press, 1972. 304 p.

14. Winsor, Justin. *Narrative and Critical History of America.* Boston, Houghton, Mifflin, (1884–89). 8 v.

15. Morison, Samuel Eliot. *The European Discovery of America; The Northern Voyages A.D. 500–1600.* New York, Oxford University Press, 1971. 712 p.

16. Wheat, Carl I. *Mapping the Transmississippi West, 1540–1880.* San Francisco, Institute of Historical Cartography, 1957–60. 5 v.

17. Cumming, William P. *The Southeast in Early Maps, with an Annotated Check List of Printed and Manuscript Regional and Local Maps of Southeastern North America during the Colonial Period.* Chapel Hill, University of North Carolina Press [1962]. 284 p.

18. Wagner, Henry R. *The Cartography of the Northwest Coast of America to the Year 1800.* Amsterdam, N. Israel,1968. Reprint of the Berkeley,University of California Press,1937 ed. 2 v. in1.

19. Brown, Lloyd A. *Early Maps of the Ohio Valley; A Selection of Maps, Plans, and Views Made by Indians and Colonials from 1673 to 1783.* [Pittsburgh], University of Pittsburgh Press [1959]. 132 p.

20. Wheat, James C., and Brun, Christian F. *Maps and Charts Published in America Before 1800, A Bibliography.* New Haven and London, Yale University Press, 1969. 215 p.

21. Stokes, Isaac. *The Iconography of Manhattan Island, 1498–1909.* New York, Arno Press [1967]. 6 v. Reprint of 1915–1920 ed.

22. Fite, Emerson D., and Freeman, Archibald. *A Book of Old Maps, Delineating American History from the Earliest Days Down to the Close of the Revolutionary War.* Cambridge, Harvard University Press, 1926. 299 p.

23. *Ibid.* New York, Dover Publications, 1969. 299 p.

24. *Ibid.* New York, Arno Press, 1969.

25. Harrisse, Henry. *The Discovery of North America; A Critical Documentary, and Historic Investigation, with an Essay on the Early Cartography of the New World, including Descriptions of Two Hundred and Fifty Maps or Globes Existing or Lost, Constructed before the Year 1536; to which are added a Chronology of One Hundred Voyages Westward, Projected, Attempted, or Accomplished between 1431 and 1504; Biographical Accounts of the Three Hundred Pilots who First Crossed the Atlantic; and a Copious List of the Original Names of American Regions, Caciqueships, Mountains, Islands, Capes, Gulfs, Rivers, Towns and Harbours.* London, H. Stevens & Sons, 1892. 802 p. Reprinted in 1961 by N. Israel, Amsterdam.

26. Karpinski, Louis C. *Bibliography of the Printed Maps of Michigan, 1804–1880, with a Series of over One Hundred Reproductions of Maps Constituting an Historical Atlas of the Great Lakes and Michigan.* Lansing, Michigan Historical Commission, 1931. 539 p.

27. Verner, Coolie. *Smith's Virginia and Its Derivatives; A Cartobibliographical Study of the Diffusion of Geographical Knowledge.* London, Map Collectors Circle, 1968. 40 p. (Map Collectors' Series, no. 45).

28. Thomson, Don W. *Men and Meridians; The History of Surveying and Mapping in Canada.* Ottawa, R. Duhamel, Queen's Printer, 1966–69. 3 v.

29. Ganong, William F. *Crucial Maps in the Early Cartography and Place-Nomenclature of the Atlantic Coast of Canada.* With an introduction, commentary, and map notes by Theodore E. Layng. Toronto, University of Toronto Press, 1964. 511 p.

30. Canada. Public Archives. *Sixteenth-century Maps Relating to Canada, A Check-list and Bibliography.* Compiled by T.E. Layng. Ottawa, Public Archives of Canada, 1965. 203 p.

31. New York Public Library. Research Libraries. *Dictionary Catalog of the Map Division.* Boston, G. K. Hall, 1971. 10 v.

32. California, University. Bancroft Library. *Index to Printed Maps.* Boston, G. K. Hall, 1964. 519 p.

33. British Museum. Department of Printed Books. Map Room. *Catalogue of Printed Maps, Charts and Plans.* Photolithographic edition complete to 1964. London, Trustees of the British Museum, 1967. 15 v.

34. British Museum. Department of Printed Books. Map Room. *Accessions: Main Entries Only.* n.s., 1964–.

35. British Museum. Department of Manuscripts. *Catalogue of the Manuscript Maps, Charts, and Plans, and of the Topographical Drawings in the British Museum.* London, British Museum, 1844–61. 3 v. Reprinted, 1962.

36. U.S. Library of Congress. Map Division. *A List of Geographical Atlases in the Library of Congress, with Bibliographical Notes.* Compiled under the direction of Philip Lee Phillips F.R.G.S. . . . Washington, Government Printing Office, v. 1–4, 1909–20; v. 5, 1958, and v. 6, 1963 and v. 7, 1973, compiled by Clara E. LeGear. v. 8 in press.

37. U.S. Library of Congress. Map Division. *A List of Maps of America in the Library of Congress, Preceded by a List of Works Relating to Cartography.* by P. Lee Phillips. Washington, Government Printing Office, 1901. 1137 p.

38. U.S. Library of Congress. Map Division. *United States Atlases; A List of National, State, County, City and Regional Atlases in the Library of Congress.* Compiled by Clara Egli LeGear. Washington, Government Printing Office, 1950–53. 2 v. (A reprint edition of volume one was published by Arno Press in 1971.)

39. *Ibid.,* v. 2.

40. Ristow, Walter W. *Guide to the History of Cartography: an Annotated List of References on the History of Maps and Map Making.* Washington, D.C., Library of Congress, 1973. 96 p.

41. American Geographical Society. *Research Catalogue.* Boston, G. K. Hall & Co., 1962. 15 v. with map supplement.

42. *Current Geographical Publications: Additions to the Research Catalogue of the American Geographical Society.* (American Geographical Society of New York). New York, New York. 1– (1938–). Monthly (except July and August). Annual index.

43. *Op. cit.*

44. *Geographisches Jahrbuch.* Gotha, v. 1–58, no. 1 (1866–1943); v. 58, no. 2– (1943/47–). Irregular. Index: v. 1–40. 1866–1925, in v. 40, v. 52 (1937).

45. Kosack, Hans Peter, and Meine, Karl-Heinz. *Die Kartographie, 1943–1954, eine bibliographische Übersicht.* Lahr/Schwarzwald, Astra Verlag, 1955. 216 p. (Kartographische Schriftenreihe, Band 4).

46. *Bibliotheca Cartographica. Bibliographie des kartographischen Schrifttums; bibliography of cartographic literature; bibliographie de la litterature cartographique.* (Institut für Landeskunde and Deutsche Gesellschaft für Kartographie). Bad Godesberg. 1– (1957–). Irregular.

47. Woodward, David. *A Bibliography of Papers on History of Cartography in American Periodicals of Bibliographical Interest Found in the Libraries of the University of Wisconsin.* Madison, Wisconsin, University of Wisconsin, Geography Dept., Jan. 1968. 13 1.

48. *Imago Mundi: A Review of Early Cartography.* Leyden, etc. 1– (1935). Irregular. Suspended 1940–46, 1957–58. Subtitle varies.

49. *Acta Cartographica: A Series of Monographs and Studies on the History of Cartography Reprinted from Periodicals Since 1800.* Amsterdam. 1– (1967–). 3 nos. a year.

50. Map Collectors' Circle. *Map Collectors' Series.* London, Map Collectors' Circle, Durrent House, 1963–. Irregular. 8–10 issues per year.

51. U.S. Library of Congress. Geography and Map Division. *The Bibliography of Cartography.* Boston, G.K. Hall & Company, 1973. 5 vols.

52. *Der Globusfreund.* Vienna. 1– (1952–). Annual.

53. Yonge, Ena L. *A Catalogue of Early Globes, Made Prior to 1850 and Conserved in the United States; A Preliminary Listing.* New York, (American Geographical Society Library Series, no. 6). 1968. 118 p.

54. Stevenson, Edward L. *Terrestrial and Celestial Globes; Their History and Construction, Including a Consideration of Their Value as Aids in the Study of Geography and Astronomy.* New Haven, Published for the Hispanic Society of America by the Yale University Press, 1921. 2 v. (Publications of the Hispanic Society of America, no. 86).

55. The reader is referred to the excellent summary of facsimile publishing in Walter W. Ristow's "Recent Facsimile Maps and Atlases." *Library of Congress Quarterly Journal,* v. 24 (July 1967), pp. 213–229.

56. Nordenskiöld, Nils Adolf Erik, *friherre. Facsimile-Atlas to the Early History of Cartography with Reproductions of the Most Important Maps Printed in the XV and XVI Centuries.* Translated from the Swedish original by J. A. Ekelof and C. R. Markham. Stockholm. [author], 1889. 141 p. 51 plates. (Reprinted by Kraus Reprint Corp., New York, 1961 and Dover Publications, New York, 1973.)

57. Nordenskiold, Nils Adolf Erik, *friherre. Periplus; An Essay on the Early History of Charts and Sailing Directions Translated from the Swedish Original by Francis A. Bather with Numerous Reproductions of Old Charts and Maps.* Stockholm, Norstedt, 1897. 208 p. 97 illus., maps. (Reprinted by Burt Franklin, New York, 1967).

58. Kohl, Johann Georg. *The Kohl Collection (Now in the Library of Congress) of Maps Relating to America.* Washington, GPO, 1904. 189 p. (Reprint from Bibliographical contributions to the Library of Harvard University, no. 19).

59. Ptolemaeus, Claudius. *Geographia.* Strassburg, 1513. With an introduction by R. A. Skelton. Amsterdam, Theatrum Orbis Terrarum, 1966. xxii, [360] p.

60. Hermann, Augustine. *Virginia and Maryland as it is Planted and Inhabited This Present Year 1670.* London, 1673. Collotype reproduction from original in John Carter Brown Library. On four sheets, each 16 x 19 inches. With descriptive text.

61. Buell, Abel. *A new and correct map of the United States of North America layd down from the latest observations and best authorities, agreeable to the Peace of 1783, humbly inscribed to His Excellency the Governor and Company of the State of Connecticut.* New Haven, Abel Buell

[1784]. Collotype reproduction from original in the collections of the N.J. Historical Society, 1963. Colored. On 4 sheets, overall measurement, 44 x 49 in.

62. U.S. Library of Congress. Geography and Map Division. *Facsimiles of Rare Historical Maps.* 3rd rev. ed. Compiled by Walter W. Ristow. Washington, 1968. 20 p. *Supplement,* 1971. 5 p.

63. U.S. National Archives and Record Service. *Guide to Cartographic Records in the National Archives.* Washington, Government Printing Office, 1971. 444 p.

64. Thrower, Norman J.W. *Maps and Man: An Examination of Cartography in Relation to Culture and Civilization.* Englewood Cliffs, N.J., Prentice-Hall, 1972. 184 p.

65. Lowery, Woodbury. *The Lowery Collection; a Descriptive List of Maps of the Spanish Possessions Within the Present Limits of the United States, 1502–1820.* Edited with notes by Philip Lee Phillips. F.R.G.S. Chief, Division of Maps and Charts. Washington, Govt. Print. Off., 1912. 567 p.

66. *The European Discovery of America: The Southern Voyages: 1492-1616,* New York, Oxford University Press, 1974, 775 p.

67. Special Libraries Association, Geography and Map Division, Directory Revision Committee, *Map Collections in the United States and Canada, A Directory,* 2nd ed., David Carrington, chairman, Special Libraries Assoc., New York, 1970, 176 p. (see also 1954 edition, 352 pp.)

68. *Directory of Canadian Map Collections. Repertoire des Collections de Cartes Canadiennes,* compiled by Joan Winearls and Yves Tessier, Assoc. Canadian Map Lib., Montreal, 1969, 72 pp., illus., index.

69. Wolter, John A. "Geographical Libraries and Map Collections,"*Encyclopedia of Library and Information Science,* v. 9, 1973, p. 236-266.

Revolution in American Education: A Bibliographical Essay

by John A. Hague and Diane E. Lea

Historically, Americans have believed that education was essential to freedom, democracy and success. To expect to be ignorant and free was, as Jefferson put it, "to expect what never was and never will be." To expect uneducated citizens to govern themselves was folly, and to expect ignorant people to be upwardly mobile denied the laws of reason.

The world in which education became essential to upward mobility, liberal democracy and personal freedom was, as far as America was concerned, characterized by physical expansion, the rapid movement of people, and the steady conversion of material resources into goods and services. In that kind of world, what people needed first and foremost was ambition; that came with the territory. It was the job of the school to attach such ambition to manageable goals and to provide its students with the skills which would further their success and the knowledge which would enhance their capacities for self-government.

The assumptions upon which these ideals rested were clear. The world was rational. Since people had rational capabilities which could be developed they could, if properly trained, manage their freedom in such a way that their pursuit of happiness and the well-being of society were simultaneously furthered.

Nevertheless, there was always tension between personal and social goals. Men who believed that an understanding of Greek, Latin and the Bible was essential for responsible citizenship did not surrender easily to demands that the curriculum should accommodate a growing population. Moreover, the growing specialization of modern society forced heated debates over general education and the functions of the vocational school. Nevertheless, an educational system emerged which (a) accommodated a growing population and (b) reflected the confidence of the American people that solutions could be found to personal and collective problems which were both just and equitable.

John Dewey (*Democracy and Education*, New York, Macmillan, 1916; *School and Society*, Chicago, University of Chicago Press, 1900, revised edition, 1953), despite his criticisms of educational procedures, carried this system faithfully into the twentieth century. Indeed, a whole series of books, some highly critical, nevertheless continued to place a heavy burden on the schools and to insist that sound education and the good society were synonomous.

Things came to a head in the years following World War II. The Harvard report on General Education sounded the alarm and raised questions about the survival power of liberal education in a specialized society (*General Education in a Free Society*, Cambridge, Harvard University Press, 1945). Global challenges, meanwhile, posed new threats to the security of the United States, and in 1957 Sputnik confronted Americans with the possibility that they might not have enough trained scientists, engineers and technicians to insure their survival. The response was swift. Powered by grants from the Carnegie Corporation, James Bryant Conant and his collaborators produced six notable books between 1959 and 1967 (*The American High School Today: a First Report to Interested Citizens*, 1st edition, New York, McGraw-Hill, 1959; *Recommendations for Education in the Junior High School Years: a Memorandum to School Board*, 1st edition, Princeton, New Jersey, Educational Testing Service, 1960; *Slums and Suburbs: a Commentary on Schools in Metropolitan Areas*, New York, McGraw-Hill, 1961; *The Education of American Teachers*, New York, McGraw-Hill, 1963; *Shaping Educational Policy*, 1st edition, New York, McGraw-Hill, 1964; *The Comprehensive High School: a Second Report to Interested Citizens*, 1st edition,

Mr. Hague is Professor of American Studies and Chairman of the Department at Stetson University. Educated at Princeton and Yale, he is a member of Phi Beta Kappa and a former Woodrow Wilson Fellow. In addition to his teaching activities, Mr. Hague has served as Vice President of the American Studies Association (1972), and is presently the Director of the National American Studies Faculty.

Diane E. Lea received both A.B. and M.A. degrees from Stetson University where she served as a Social Sciences Graduate Fellow in 1968. A member of both the American Association of Museums and the American Association for State and Local History, she is President of the Chapel Hill Preservation Society, and is currently serving as a full-time consultant to the Community Museum Program, National American Studies Faculty, in DeLand, Florida.

New York, McGraw-Hill, 1967). Jerome Bruner (*The Process of Education,* New York, Vantage, 1960) argued that it was possible to teach any subject to any age group if one understood the structure of the subject and developed a logical conceptual scheme based on that structure. In essence, Conant, Bruner and others were arguing that American schools suffered from a dearth of effective teaching materials, insufficient public support, and inadequately trained teachers.

The Federal Government, through the National Science Foundation and the Department of Health, Education and Welfare, subsidized the development of new courses and publications. For example, the Physical Science Study Committee produced a text (*Physics,* Heath, 1960) which updated and upgraded the teaching of physics in secondary schools. HEW, in 1960 and 1961, produced a series of paperback pamphlets entitled *New Dimensions in Higher Education* which spurred innovation and independent study in American colleges and universities.

Meanwhile events were taking shape within American society which greatly intensified the pressures affecting educational institutions. Gunnar Myrdal, with assistance from Richard Sterner and Arnold Rose, wrote *An American Dilemma* in 1944 (New York, Harper) and produced massive evidence to document the fact that a caste system excluded Negroes from participation in the mainstream of American society. As blacks and whites revolted in the 50s and 60s, a large number of books illustrated the devastating effects which segregated schools had on American society and laid down new guidelines for equal opportunity. Some representative books are

Robin Murphy Williams, Ed., *Schools in Transition: Community Experiences in Desegregation,* Chapel Hill, University of North Carolina Press, 1954.

Don Shoemaker, Ed., Southern Education Reporting Service, *With All Deliberate Speed: Segregation-Desegregation in Southern Schools,* 1st edition, New York, Harper, 1957.

John William Gardner, *Excellence: Can we be Equal And Excellent, too?,* New York, Harper, 1961.

John Kenneth Morland, *Token Desegregation and Beyond,* Atlanta, New York, Southern Regional Council, Anti-Defamation League of B'nai B'rith, 1963.

Kenneth Bancroft Clark, *Prejudice and Your Child,* 2nd edition, Boston, Beacon Press, 1963.

Robert Collins Smith, *They Closed Their Schools: Prince Edward County, Virginia, 1951–1964,* Chapel Hill, University of North Carolina Press, 1965.

Estelle Fuchs, *Pickets at the Gates,* New York, Free Press, 1966.

Daniel M. Berman, *It Is So Ordered: The Supreme Court Rules on School Segregation,* 1st edition, New York, Norton, 1966.

Eli Ginsberg, *The Middle-class Negro in the White Man's World,* New York, Columbia University Press, 1967.

Robert L. Crain, *The Politics of School Desegregation: Comparative Case Studies of Community Structure and Policy-making,* assisted by Morton Inger, Gerald A. McWorter, James J. Vanecko, Chicago, Aldine Publishing Company, 1968.

H. C. Hudgins, Jr., *The Warren Court and the Public Schools: An Analysis of Landmark Supreme Court Decisions,* Danville, Illinois, Interstate Printers & Publishers, 1970.

Frank Newman, *The Report on Higher Education,* Washington, D. C., Department of Health, Education, and Welfare, 1971.

Louis Lomax (*The Negro Revolt,* New York, Harpers, 1962) was one of the black educators who questioned whether the traditional American school could cope with the handicaps under which ghetto children grew up. In an interview recorded by the Center for the Study of Democratic Institutions and entitled "Have Slums, Will Travel" he argued that the environment of the ghetto was more powerful than the environment of the school. The only solution was to build boarding schools on the peripheries of the great cities, take children from their parents at the age of 3, and educate them in a wholly different environment.

Lomax's position is one which asserts that the school is the only institution which can bring health to a sick society. This position has received support from a variety of sources; notably, perhaps, from B. F. Skinner. In *The Technology of Teaching,* (New York, Appleton-Century-Crofts, 1968) and more powerfully in *Beyond Freedom and Dignity* (New York, Knopf, 1971) Skinner asserts that scholars know enough about the learning process to educate children who will in fact acquire the traits which humane teachers want them to want. In a somewhat related vein Harry S. Broudy has argued that the schools suffer from the absence of truly professional teachers. Broudy's book, *The Real World of the Public Schools,* (New York, Harcourt Brace Jovanovich, Inc., 1972) contends that it is possible to utilize creatively the resources of a technological society if we will train a small cadre of teachers who combine professional mastery of learning theory and practice with a classical liberal education.

Skinner, Lomax, and Broudy are among those who, in some basic sense, believe in the existence of a real, rational world and who also believe that humans can adapt to such a world in a rational manner. They have few illusions about the problems which confront modern individuals, but they believe that rational strategies can be found which will enable us to cope with and triumph over even gigantic difficulties.

Broudy is reacting against a wide variety of authors who believe that some kind of counterculture must replace the sick culture in which we grow up. Paul Goodman wrote *Growing Up Absurd* in 1960 (New York, Random House). In the same year Alexander Sutherland Neill wrote *Summerhill: A Radical Approach to Child Rearing* (New York, Hart, 1960). Goodman's work was preceded by Erik Erikson's *Childhood and Society* (New York, Norton, 1950, paperback, 1963) and followed by Edgar Z. Friedenberg's *Coming of Age in America* (New York, Random House, 1965). In different ways these books describe how schools, parents and peers appear to victimize the inner life of youth. These authors share, however, at least one assumption with Broudy and Skinner. Their view of human nature is optimistic. They are, in a sense, the 20th century descendants of Jean Jacques Rousseau. They believe that children are born free and are enslaved and corrupted by adults and institutions. They believe that an enlightened, compassionate approach to teaching which gives children a chance to express and develop their creative bent will have a liberating and transformational effect.

Two streams of writing have emerged which characterize this twentieth century romanticism. One suggests a radical approach to teaching which maximizes emphasis upon affective elements in education but which preserves the school as a basic institution in modern society. The other insists that school is dead and proposes in answer to the conviction that institutions enslave the abolishment of formal educational institutions.

Neil Postman and Charles Weingartner have published a series of books (now available as Dell paperbacks) which belong to the first tradition. The most famous of these is *Teaching as a Subversive Activity* (New York, Dell Publishing Company, 1966). Others are *The Soft Revolution: A Student Handbook for Turning Schools Around* (New York, Delacorte Press, 1971) and *The School Book: For People Who Want to Know What the Hollering is All About* (New York, Delacorte Press, 1973). *The School Book* is an index to educational resources, especially to underground and little magazines put out by teachers and students. It is modeled after a Scandinavian counterpart—*The Little Red School Book* by Soren Hansen and Jasper Jensen (New York, Pocket Books, 1971). Another famous book which describes many of the most prominent innovative educational programs is Charles E. Silberman's *Crisis in the Classroom* (New York, Random House, 1970). Still others are

Herbert Kohl, *The Open Classroom,* New York, New York Review; distributed by Random House, 1969.

Joseph Featherstone, *Schools Where Children Learn,* New York, Liveright, 1971.

Shelly Umans, *The Management of Education: A Systematic Design for Educational Revolution,* Garden City, N. Y., Anchor Books, Doubleday, 1971.

Jonathan Kozol. *Free Schools,* Boston, Houghton Mifflin, 1972.

Ewald B. Nyquist and Gene Hawes, *Open Education: A Sourcebook for Parents and Teachers,* New York, Bantam, 1972.

Jeffrey Shrank, *Teaching Human Beings: 101 Subversive Activities for the Classroom,* Boston, Beacon Press, 1972.

Theodore R. Sizer, *Places for Learning, Places for Joy,* Cambridge, Massachusetts, Harvard University Press, 1973.

A final volume in this tradition which has had an important effect upon educational pedagogy is a book edited by Benjamin Samuel Bloom, et al, *Taxonomy of Educational Objectives: The Classification of Educational Goals* (New York, Longmans, Green, 1956).

The more radical approach also has a distinguished list of authors. Michael Katz wrote *Class, Bureaucracy and Schools: The Illusion of Educational Change in America* (New York, Praeger) in 1971 and, as the sub-title suggests, argued that educational change was illusory; that the schools simply provide a massive indoctrination into the mores and values of the establishment. A much more famous, earlier work is Ivan Illich's *Deschooling Society* (New York, Harper & Row, 1971). In this book and also in one entitled *Tools for Conviviality* (New York, Harper and Row, 1973) Illich contends that no matter what approach teachers take to education, they only manipulate their pupils. Nevertheless, Illich believes that education can transcend manipulation if we change our attitudes and use "convivial" tools which are available to all. Also in the "school is dead" tradition is Everett Reimer's *School is Dead: Alternatives in Education* (Garden City, Doubleday, 1971).

The two traditions, taken together, define a revisionist approach to the role of the school in society. They assume that the traditional school is failing both to nurture the talents of individuals and to make equal opportunity in America a reality. They differ in their attitudes toward institutionalized education.

In 1972 Christopher Jencks and his associates reported the results of a three-year study by the Harvard Center for Educational Policy Research in a volume entitled *Inequality: A Reassessment of the Effect of Family and Schooling in America* (New York, Basic Books, 1972). Jencks also took issue with those who have championed education as the instrument for providing equal opportunity to American youth. The Jencks volume, which has been vigorously debated (See *Harvard Educational Review,* February, 1973, volume 43, no. 1), offers evidence to support the thesis that schools simply cannot bear the brunt of making equal opportunity effective. If America wants to achieve this ideal, the authors argue, it must do so by means of social legislation rather than by leaving the task to educational institutions. Nevertheless, the Jencks study does not propose the abandonment of educational institutions. It suggests that schools can address themselves to a variety of educational objectives and achieve valuable results. What they cannot do is solve the problem of inequality.

Higher education did not escape the turmoil of the 1960s nor the efforts of re-visionists to redefine the role and the mission of colleges and universities. In 1963 John Gardner made a plea for more imaginative education in *Self-Renewal: The Individual and the Innovative Society* (New York, Harper and Row, 1963). Theodore Roszak edited *The Dissenting Academy* in 1967 (New York, Random House) and chastised the learned professions as "grossly remiss in meeting any defensible standard of intellectual conscience." The contributors shared the conviction that "the central business of the academy is the public examination of man's life with respect to its moral quality." The following year Christopher Jencks and David Riesman published *The Academic Revolution* (New York, Doubleday, 1968). Attempting "a sociological and historical analysis of American higher education," the authors stressed the simultaneous coming of age of American universities with the emergence of a mass bureaucratic society, and raised questions about the capacity of the Academy to serve humane educational goals.

The questioning of the Academy did not go on simply on an academic level. Tensions which grew out of racism, the war in Vietnam and overcrowded campuses exploded in a variety of demonstrations and campus strikes in the latter half of the sixties. In addition, educational institutions found themselves squeezed by a combination of rising costs and dwindling enrollments. The result was that there began in the late sixties and early seventies what could be called the agonizing reappraisal of American higher education.

The Riesman and Jencks studies were, of course, part of the reappraisal. So also was a six-year study of higher education which the Carnegie Commission on Higher Education concluded in the fall of 1973. The final report describes a "crisis of confidence" which has affected all segments of education. "There has been," declared the Commission, "a basic erosion of affection for and interest in education, including higher education." Other landmark reports, published by McGraw Hill in both paperback and hard cover editions, include *Less Time, More Options: Education Beyond the High School; Higher Education and the Nation's Health: Policies for Medical and Dental Education; The Fourth Revolution: Instructional Technology in Higher Education; The Open Door Colleges: Policies for Community Colleges; The More Effective Use of Resources—An Imperative for Higher Education;* and *New Students and New Places: Policies for the Future Growth and Development of American Higher Education.* Others explore the relation between the university and its various constituencies, assess different kinds of colleges, examine the financial condition of universities and explore educational opportunities for a large number of people who do not fit the age and status stereotypes of most campus populations.

In 1971 the College Entrance Examination Board and the Educational Testing Service, backed by funds from the Carnegie Foundation, established a "Commission on Non-Traditional Study" to study the educational needs and demands which were not being met by traditional educational institutions. The Committee's report was published in 1973 in a volume entitled *Diversity by Design* (San Francisco, Jossey-Bass, 1973). The Committee found that there were nearly eighty million Americans who wanted to participate in some type of educational activity who were not currently involved in educational programs. These people wanted to pursue study in vocational areas, hobbies, general education, home and family life, personal development, public affairs, religious studies, and agriculture. The same individuals cited cost, time, age, home and job responsibilities, and inconvenient location as prime reasons for not pursuing their educational desires. The Commission offered fifty-seven specific recommendations which were designed to make education a lifelong experience. These recommendations, not surprisingly, call for new methods of finance, and much greater flexibility in the design and delivery of educational programs.

One of the Carnegie Commission sponsored research studies which appeared in 1973 lent, perhaps unwittingly, some support to the arguments of the Commission on Non-Traditional Study. The volume which resulted, *Academic Transformation: Seventeen Institutions Under Pressure* (David Riesman and Verne A. Stadtman, editors, New York, McGraw-Hill, 1973), is a collection of essays which describe what happened during the campus disorders of the sixties on seventeen campuses. While the assessments of what happened vary, the subtitle accurately suggests that the Academy is under great pressure to become more effective and more efficient.

Indeed many have argued that schools, whether secondary or collegiate, must pay less attention to credits, degrees, and particular age groupings. They must, according to this position, become learning centers which can be used by many different kinds of people to satisfy many different kinds of needs. The Commission on Non-Traditional Study makes clear that it believes that educational resources should be managed to serve individual rather than institutional needs. In a bureaucratic society these voices plead for programs that cater to individual preferences. Other volumes which make similar cases include Sir Eric Ashby's *Any Person, Any Study* (New York, McGraw-Hill, 1971); Samuel B. Gould and K. Patricia Cross's *Explorations in Non-Traditional Study* (San Francisco, Jossey-Bass, 1972); and Cyril Orvin Houle's *The External Degree* (San Francisco, Jossey-Bass, 1973).

There are a number of important observations which one can make about the volumes cited in this essay. Many were the products of conferences and commissions; in that sense they reflect a growing concern among educators and laymen about the quality of American education. One would not have found, before 1966, for example, a Project to Improve College Teaching sponsored jointly by the American Association of University Professors and the Association of

American Colleges. Such a group met, however, for a period of two years and produced a paperback volume entitled *The Recognition and Evaluation of Teaching* (Kenneth E. Eble, AAUP, Washington, 1970). Similarly we find a volume produced for The Urban Affairs Series sponsored by the Metropolitan Applied Research Center entitled *Racism and American Education: A Dialogue and Agenda for Action* (New York, Harper & Row, 1970). This book brought together the findings of the President's Commission for the Observance of Human Rights Year. Its title suggests a second generalization. Another major concern of the 1960s and 1970s deals with the question of the availability of educational programs. Who are left out? Who can take advantage of existing delivery systems and who are stymied in their efforts to pursue educational objectives?

A third area of concern has to do with educational objectives. Clearly one set of objectives is vocational in nature. People see themselves investing in an education in order to equip themselves to earn a living. Yet people are likely to spend less time earning a living in the 1970s than they did a generation earlier. Moreover, as costs have risen, people have re-asked age-old questions—questions which relate to inner resources, responsible citizenship, and personal happiness. Can education liberate people? renew them? transform them? What price must one pay for such an education?

A fourth issue has to do with relevance and freedom. As one goes through the educational literature of the sixties and seventies one is constantly bombarded with urgent pleas to make education responsive to communities and individuals; to teach in ways that speak to the real concerns and interests of students. Yet, increasingly, one discovers that even "relevant" curricula can be oppressive; student governance can be as unimaginative as any other governance [see Sylvia Berry Williams, *Hassling*, (Boston, Little Brown & Co.)]; and open schools can be as closed in their own way as traditional schools. In short the question of what liberates and causes real personal growth has not found an answer that can be easily institutionalized.

Yet, as Charles Silberman and others have pointed out, exciting alternatives are under way. One can point out that most of the "alternatives" are old, as Grace Rotzel reminds us in *The School in Rose Valley* (Baltimore, Johns Hopkins Press, 1971). Nevertheless, it can safely be said that a much greater number of educators than ever before are willing to admit to their failures and are simultaneously willing to explore new alternatives. In short, the quality and quantity of concern has risen, and, one suspects, many right questions are being asked.

One philosophical issue has not been resolved, however. Walter Lippmann once referred to the theory that children are naturally curious, intelligent, and benevolent as "the Jacobin Heresy." Another way of stating this heresy is to say that its proponents believe that virtues are passed on in the genes. Some of us believe, however, that if people must "be taught to hate" they must also be taught to love. Further, if the people who teach have, as seems likely, a mixture of selfish and altruistic motives, why should they expect or demand responses which do not include the same mixture? Can we not make education more flexible and imaginative without making impossible demands on those who participate in it? Perhaps, in the 1970's, our search should be for a pedagogy based on a realistic assessment of human nature.

American Workers
and American Studies

by James R. Wason

Although this essay is intended mainly to bring the interested scholar up to date in the field of labor history, it has been influenced by two observations on the pages of this journal as well as by some extended experiences as an American scholar working abroad. Libraries in American studies, it is clear, are still very near their beginning stages in many places. Therefore I have included the important old as well as the interesting new works. A second consideration results from those heartening signs that American studies is entering into a climate of cross-cultural studies. With this in mind I have given due consideration to our left-wing labor history as a subject of current interest both at home and abroad. Recent research has centered more on cross-cultural influences on the left than on the traditional American labor exceptionalism.

The fascinating complexities of cross-cultural studies can be illustrated by the case of Daniel De Leon, founder of America's oldest Marxist party, the Socialist Labor Party. He was also, and perhaps more importantly, the originator of the movement for industrial unionism, the face-to-face democracy of the work place. De Leon is representative of the international character of American labor. He was born in Curaçao in the Caribbean, the son of a surgeon in the Dutch army, and educated in Holland and Germany. Returning to the New World to New York, he moved across the political spectrum from membership in the Democratic Party, through the Knights of Labor, support of Edward Bellamy and Henry George, to Marxism. He was considered by Lenin to be the only socialist since Marx to have made any major contribution to socialist thought. Yet De Leon is the socialist who best expresses to the youthful enthusiasts of the New Left the dangers of Stalinism, the menace of concentrating power under socialism in the hands of an all-powerful state.

Perhaps here we move closer to the real meaning of American exceptionalism. An independent source of labor ideology need have little international significance. But as a source of both ideology and political power, American exceptionalism requires the consideration of the European left. For it is only in America that the "revolution of the twentieth century" can take place. And it is here that it has begun. We shall return to this at the end of the essay.

American Working People: Some General Sources

The first systematic students of American labor were members of that unique school of economic theoreticians, the American Institutionalists. The founder of the Wisconsin branch of this school was the first academician to write on American labor, Richard T. Ely, *The Labor Movement in America* (New York: Crowell Publishing, 1886). Economists dominated American writings on labor until after World War II, to the near complete exclusion of members of other disciplines. However, the Institutionalists, although several founders of the American Economic Association were numbered among them, used in their writings techniques drawn from several other disciplines: sociology, political science, history, psychology, anthropology, and the law.

The central figure of the Wisconsin School was John R. Commons. The two major works of this school on labor are both attributed to him, but are, in fact, the product of group research. The first is John R. Commons et al., eds., *A Documentary History of American Industrial Society,* 10 vols., (Cleveland, Ohio: Arthur H. Clark, 1910; reprinted, New York: Russell & Russell, 1958). This invaluable collection was the product, in part, of the work Commons and his

Dr. Wason is Lecturer in Economics and in History with the European Division of the University of Maryland. From 1962 to 1970, he was a Specialist in Labor Economics and Labor Relations with the Congressional Research Service of the Library of Congress, where he also served as a Consultant in Labor History to The George Washington University doctoral program in American Civilization. Dr. Wason received his Ph.D. in economics from The American University in Washington, D.C. In addition to his regular teaching program, he was actively engaged in making a physical survey of labor archives in Europe, having visited archives in Austria, Holland, Norway, Sweden, and Denmark during the summer of 1974.

associates did for the United States Industrial Commission. The second work is John R. Commons and Associates, *History of Labor in the United States,* 4 vols., (New York: The Macmillan Company, 1918, 1935). In the preface to the first two volumes, Commons lists no less than 33 persons, besides himself, as responsible for the research contained therein. The third and fourth volumes were authored and edited substantially by former students of Dr. Commons, volume 3 by Selig Perlman and Philip Taft, volume 4 by Don D. Lescohier and Elizabeth Brandeis.

More recent general works on American labor history are still largely derivative from the Wisconsin School. A major exception, by an outstanding Marxist scholar, is Philip S. Foner, *History of the Labor Movements in the United States,* 4 vols. (New York: International Publishers, 1947-65). This is a work in progress, extending down only to World War I. Based on extensive, original research, by itself it provides a parallel account to that of the Wisconsin tradition. Its orthodox, Leninist bias is easily discounted.

Conventional trade union history is well represented by Philip Taft, *Organized Labor in American History* (New York: Harper & Row, 1964). A volume in the Chicago History of American Civilization is the best recent short account: Henry Pelling, *American Labor* (Chicago: University of Chicago Press, 1960). Mr. Pelling is a British scholar. Two works are frequently used as textbooks in college-level courses in labor history: Foster Rhea Dulles, *Labor in America* (New York: Thomas Y. Crowell, 3rd ed., 1966), and Joseph G. Rayback, *A History of American Labor* (New York: The Free Press, rev. ed., 1966).

There are two recent bibliographies on American labor which complement one another. Maurice F. Neufeld, *A Representative Bibliography of American Labor History* (Ithaca, New York: Cornell University, New York State School of Industrial and Labor Relations, 1964) is updated but not replaced by James C. McBrearty, *American Labor History and Comparative Labor Movements, A Selected Bibliography* (Tucson, Arizona: The University of Arizona Press, 1973).

"There is no comprehensive up-to-date bibliographic essay on recent (American) labor historiography." This is true, but the essay from which the quotation comes is a very adequate substitute: Robert H. Zieger, "Workers and Scholars: Recent Trends in American Labor Historiography" *Labor History* 13 (Spring 1972): 245–66. Some additional similar references are: Thomas A. Krueger, "American Labor Historiography, Old and New: A Review Essay" *Journal of Social History* 4 (Spring 1971): 277–85; Paul Falor, "Working Class Historiography" *Radical America* 3 (March–April 1969): 56–68; and Irwin Unger, "The 'New Left' and American History: Some Recent Trends in United States Historiography" *American Historical Review* 72 (July 1967): 1255–57.

For the continuing bibliography of American labor there are several sources. *The Industrial and Labor Relations Review,* Cornell University, New York State School of Industrial and Labor Relations, issued quarterly, has a classified list of recently published books and articles, in addition to book reviews. *The Monthly Labor Review,* U.S. Department of Labor, Bureau of Labor Statistics, has book reviews and a list of books received. It is, in addition, by far the best and most convenient source for information on current events in labor, union conventions, legal decisions affecting labor, and labor statistics. *Industrial Relations,* University of California, Berkeley, Institute of Industrial Relations, issued three times a year, does not review books, but has excellent review articles, from time to time, on labor literature. Finally, *Labor History,* The Tamiment Institute, issued quarterly, has book reviews, an annual review of periodical references, and periodic reports on research in progress.

American Theories of the Labor Movement

There is no accepted theory of the labor movement at present in America. The best account of past theories, but limited to those of academics, is Mark Perlman, *Labor Union Theories in America: Background and Development* (Evanston, Illinois: Row, Peterson, 1958). Reference should also be made to two articles by Paul James McNulty: "Labor Market Analysis and the Development of Labor Economics," *Industrial and Labor Relations Review* 19 (July 1966): 538–48, and "Labor Problems and Labor Economics, the Roots of an Academic Discipline," *Labor History* 9 (Spring 1968): 239–61.

The standard theory of American labor was produced by the Wisconsin School, as well as the standard history. Much of this is scattered in the writing of John R. Commons, in prefaces and introductions of the above cited works. A convenient summary is John R. Commons, "American Shoemakers, 1648–1895: A Sketch of Industrial Evolution," *Quarterly Journal of Economics* 24 (November 1909): 39–84. To Commons, unions were economic institutions founded by workers as a response to their loss of control over local product markets caused by improvements in transportation and by the resulting specialization of labor, dividing the traditional functions of the craftsman as buyers of raw materials, manufacturer, and seller at retail among merchant capitalists, employers, and employees. Out of this breaking up of the traditional harmony of the local market came competition, wage cuts, and exploitation. The trade union was the means by which the exploited employee hoped to regain control of the labor market.

The most comprehensive account of the theory is Selig Perlman, *A Theory of the Labor Movement* (New York: Macmillan, 1928). Perlman's book has been widely criticised on two counts. First, his theory of the job-scarcity consciousness of the manual worker and his seeking for job control is no more than a generalization from the views of the craft unions of the American Federation of Labor in the time at which he wrote. And in the late 1920's these unions were weak and on the defensive. Second, Perlman's theory failed completely to anticipate the spread of unionization outside the craft field into the mass-production industries, which came with the rise of the CIO in the following decade.

For a recent and able defense of the Wisconsin theory and a reasonably objective review of its major critics see Robert Ozanne, "The Labor History and Labor Theory of John R. Commons: An Evaluation in the Light of Recent Trends and Criticism," in Gerald G. Somers, ed., *Labor, Management and Social Policy* (Madison, Wisconsin: University of Wisconsin Press, 1963). Despite the validity of some of the criticisms of the Commons-Perlman theory, no other nation of the West has produced a better model to explain union development in the process of industrialization. While Commons limited his theory to the United States, Perlman attempts to explain the development of the labor movement of the United States, England, Germany, and Russia.

While the need for a new theory of the labor movement has not been satisfied, several recent efforts are not without interest. One, published some years ago, made a necessary beginning by exploring the question of what a satisfactory theory should explain: John T. Dunlop, "The Development of Labor Organization: A Theoretical Framework" in Richard A. Lester and Joseph Shister, eds., *Insights into Labor Issues* (New York: Macmillan, 1948). Perhaps the major recent American contribution to theory stems from the massive "Four Universities" study of labor movements, world-wide. Professor Dunlop himself made a major contribution to this study: John T. Dunlop, *Industrial Relations Systems* (New York: Henry Holt, 1958). The summary report of this project is Clark Kerr, John T. Dunlop, Frederick Harbison, and Charles T. Myers, *Industrialism and Industrial Man* (Cambridge, Massachusetts: Harvard University Press, 1960). In this report, the industrialization process is viewed as determined by management elites, with the various labor movements as being no more than conditioned responses to the circumstances of the development of each national economy. Needless to say, while this is of unquestioned value to management theory, it has not won general acceptance as a theory of the labor movement. For a re-evaluation of their findings, see *idem*, "Postscript to 'Industrialism and Industrial Men,'" *International Labor Review* 103 (1971): 519–40.

The contribution of one other writer, distinctly outside the mainstream of labor theory, deserves mention. The late Frank Tannenbaum published two works on the labor movement: *The Labor Movement: Its Conservative Function and Social Consequences* (New York: Putnam, 1921) and *A Philosophy of Labor* (New York: Knopf, 1951). Both works reflect essentially the same point of view, despite differences in their policy conclusions. The earlier work reflects the interest of the early 1920's in worker control of the job, industrial democracy, and political pluralism; the latter the political blandness of the Eisenhower years. In each work, however, worker organizations, the type-case of which Tannenbaum considers to be the guild, are treated as an autonomous, essentially conservative force in society, but one which in its efforts to survive and to raise the share of labor is altering its social and economic bases. Tannenbaum's theories have not had a wide degree of acceptance. Yet, in the light of fairly general conditions of wage push and wage drift in Western society, he cannot be dismissed as clearly wrong.

Labor in Colonial America

At the time of their independence, the colonies were inhabited primarily by emigrants from Great Britain or the descendents of earlier emigrants from England, Scotland and Ireland. Most of the settlers came from working-class or peasant backgrounds, and a very large proportion reached the colonies only by paying for their passage by seven years of servitude as indentured servants. Few rich or successful Europeans sought a life on the North American frontier.

The laboring poor have a history, but it is badly documented and left largely unstudied. Immigration history is a comparatively new and rather sparse branch of historiography. Emigration history, the history of the failures, the exiles and paupers who deserted the homeland, is largely ignored by European scholars. And despite the large amount of work on the history of colonial America in both the United States and England, this remains the case. The Puritan Fathers of the Massachusetts Bay Colony have been honored as American ancestors for well over one hundred years, but only within the fairly recent past has anyone noted that they were largely cloth workers from East Anglia. The curious may refer to Nellis M. Crouse, "Causes of the Great Migration," *New England Quarterly* 5 (1937): 3–36. Indeed, the main source of information about colonial labor, the great body of colonial indentures, remains largely unstudied. It was on these and on court records that the only recent comprehensive account of colonial labor is based: Richard B. Morris, *Government and Labor in Early America* (New York: Columbia University Press, 1946). This is of interest, because the labor movements in America and Britain were parts of a common culture and must have common roots. To the extent conditions in the colonies required or permitted it, guilds on the British pattern appeared in the American colonies in the seventeenth century. In the eighteenth century one finds the same mobs, social protest, and political radicalism as in England. One finds the same trade unions.

In both areas, however, we lack comprehensive studies of trade union origins. It remains uncertain if there is continuity between the guilds and the unions. From being originally dated as appearing in both areas in the 1790's, research has pushed the dates for the appearance of some form of labor organization back to the seventeenth century in Massachusetts Bay Colony and to even earlier dates in England. A recent summary of this research is contained in Mary Roys Baker, "Anglo-Massachusetts Trade Union Roots, 1130–1790," *Labor History* 14 (Summer 1973): 352–96.

One of the few works about free craftsmen in the colonies is Carl Bridenbaugh, *The Colonial Craftsman* (New York: New York University Press, 1950). For other classes of white labor see: Abbott E. Smith, *Colonists in Bondage: White Servitude and Convict Labor in America, 1607–1776* (Chapel Hill, North Carolina: University of North Carolina Press, 1947), and Marcus W. Jernegan, *Laboring and Dependent Classes in Colonial America, 1607–1783* (New York: Frederick Ungar, 1931).

As it has generally, much work has been done in recent years with the problems of Black labor in Colonial America. The initial reference would have to be John Hope Franklin, *From Slavery to Freedom: A History of Negro Americans* (New York: Knopf, 3rd ed., 1967). This covers the colonial period in detail and has full and up-to-date bibliographies. A documentary history is Elizabeth Donnan, ed., *Documents Illustrative of the History of the Slave-Trade to the United States of America*, 4 vols., (Washington, D.C.: Carnegie Institution, 1935). We shall return to the history of the Black worker in America. Here we add three references of particular use for the colonial period: Herbert Aptheker, *American Negro Slave Revolts* (New York: Columbia University Press, 1943), David B. Davis, *The Problem of Slavery in Western Culture* (Ithaca, New York: Cornell University Press, 1966); and Winthrop D. Jordan, *White over Black, American Attitudes toward the Negro, 1550–1812* (Chapel Hill, North Carolina: University of North Carolina Press, 1968).

There are two areas of intellectual history which provide necessary background for the study of Colonial labor: puritanism and mercantilism. A few recent references to puritanism, which will provide ample additional bibliographic background are Larzer Ziff, *Puritanism in America: New Culture for a New World*

(New York: Viking, 1973); Michael Walzer, *The Revolution of the Saints, A Study of the Origins of Radical Politics* (New York: Atheneum, 1965); and Christopher Hill, *Society and Puritanism in Pre-Revolutionary England* (New York: Schocken Books, 1964). The classic study of labor under the mercantile system remains Edgar S. Furniss, *The Position of the Laborer in a System of Nationalism* (Boston: Houghton, Mifflin, 1920). However, recent research has placed greater stress on the benefits afforded labor by the mercantile state. For a convenient sampling of a literature still largely available only in periodicals, see D. C. Coleman, ed., *Revisions in Mercantilism* (London: Methuen, 1969).

Labor in an Age of Revolution, 1764–1819

That the political, rather than the economic, aspects of labor in this period have been studied should be corrected, for the period of the American Revolution appears to be the first time large numbers of trade unions surfaced, followed by a similar development during the Napoleonic Wars. Both seemingly were the result of wartime inflation, prosperity, and disruption of established economic relationships.

Most of the literature on the political history of labor in the period is to be found only in the periodicals. An exception is Pauline Maier, *From Resistance to Revolution, Colonial Radicals and the Development of American Opposition to Britain, 1765–1776* (New York: Knopf, 1972). Additional periodical references include: Robert J. Champagne, "Liberty Boys and Mechanics of New York City, 1764–1774," *Labor History* 8 (Spring 1967): 115–35; Jesse Lemisch, "Jack Tar in the Streets: Merchant Seamen in the Politics of Revolutionary America," *William and Mary Quarterly* (3rd series) 25 (1968): 371–405, and "Listening to the 'Inarticulate,' William Widger's Dream and the Loyalties of American Revolutionary Seamen in British Prisons," *Journal of Social History* 3 (1969): 1–29; Staughton Lynd, "The Mechanics in New York Politics 1774–1788," *Labor History* 5 (1964): 225–46; and Richard Walsh, "The Charleston Mechanics: A Brief Study, 1760–1776," *South Carolina Historical Magazine* 60 (1959): 123–44.

The labor organizations formed in this period were both economic and political in their objectives. This was, for example, the period of the formation of the Democratic-Republican clubs, of which Tammany Club of New York is a present-day survival. The only comprehensive study of these clubs is Eugene P. Link, *Democratic-Republican Societies, 1790–1800* (New York: Columbia Press, 1942).

A few older studies have touched on the economic aspects of unionism in the period: Ethelbert Stewart, "A Documentary History of the Early Organizations of Printers," *Bulletin of the Bureau of Labor, Document 61:* (1905): 857–1033. Washington, D.C.: G.P.O.; George A. Stevens, *New York Typographical Union No. 6: A Study of a Modern Trade Union and Its Predecessors* (Albany, New York: New York State Department of Labor, 1913); and Theodore W. Clocker, *Trade Unionism in Baltimore before the War of 1812* (Baltimore, Maryland: Johns Hopkins University, 1907).

But, again, for recent references to the political activities of labor in the period, one must turn to the periodical literature: Leonard Bernstein, "The Working

People of Philadelphia from Colonial Times to the General Strike of 1835,"
Pennsylvania Magazine of History and Biography 74 (1950): 332–39; Raymond
A. Mohl, "Poverty, Politics and the Mechanics of New York City, 1803," *Labor
History* 12 (1971): 38–51; David Montgomery, "The Working Classes of the
Pre-Industrial American City, 1780–1830," *Labor History* 9 (1968): 3–22; and
Alfred Young, "The Mechanics and the Jeffersonians, New York: 1789–1801,"
Labor History 5 (1964): 247–76.

"Workies" and Utopias, 1819–1840

There were two periods of utopian foundations before the Civil War. The first
began after the Panic of 1819 and extended into the 1830's. The second was a
new outburst in the depressed 40's. Many students have treated the pre-Civil
War utopian movements as one. One of the few writers to avoid this mistake is
Arthur E. Bestor, Jr., *Backwoods Utopias, the Sectarian and Owenite Phases of
Communitarian Socialism in America, 1663–1829* (Philadelphia: University of
Pennsylvania Press, 1950). This is the best book of the earlier utopian experi-
ments.

A major recent work on Owenism in Britain and the United States is J. F. C.
Harrison, *Quest for the New Moral World: Robert Owen and the Owenites in
Britain and America* (New York: Scribner, 1969). This has a very complete bibliography. A recent brief life of Robert Owen is Margaret Cole, *Robert Owen of
New Lanark, 1771–1858* (New York: Oxford University Press, 1953). The two-
hundredth anniversary of Owen's birth brought the publication of two volumes of
essays on Owen and Owenism: John Butt, ed., *Robert Owen, Prince of Cotton
Spinners* (London: David and Charles, 1971); and Sidney Pollard and John Salt,
eds., *Robert Owen, Prophet of the Poor* (London: Macmillan, 1971). The standard account of the Owenite settlement at New Harmony in Indiana remains
George B. Lockwood, *The New Harmony Movement* (New York: D. Appleton,
1905). (Note also the reference to Robert Dale Owen, below.)

Communitarian socialism in America is of interest not only as an early linking
of European and American social movements, but also because it was the form
in which socialism was first introduced to the young Engels and, through him, to
the young Marx. For this background, one may consult Lewis F. Feuer, "The
Alienated Americans and Their Influence on Marx and Engels" in *Marx and the
Intellectuals* (Garden City, New York: Anchor Books, 1969). From an article by
Marx, dated November, 1847, Feuer quotes: "Socialism and communism did not
originate in Germany, but in England, France, and North America."

However, American utopian colonies were not the only development in the
United States to influence the young Marx. Of far greater importance were the
workingmen's parties which developed in America in the late 1820's. These were
the first working class political parties in the world. Marx learned in 1843, from
secondary sources, of the New York party of 1829. He did not know of the earlier
party of 1828 in Philadelphia. Thus he wrote in 1845 in the German Ideology:
"They (the North Americans) have had, since 1829, their own social democratic
school." For an additional reference to the one by Feuer, cited above, see Maximilien Rubel, "Notes on Marx's Conception of Democracy," *New Politics* 1
(1962): 83-85. It was from the experience of these labor parties that the young

Marx derived his concept of the proletariat as the founder of independent political parties to take power in a socialist state. This vision, born of workingclass consciousness in America, adopted and recast by Marx and Engels, became the basis of scientific socialism.

The Jacksonian period was also one where trade unions revived and flourished. The present interest in labor in the period was set off by Arthur M. Schlesinger, Jr., *The Age of Jackson* (Boston: Little, Brown, 1945). In this work, Schlesinger drew a parallel between Andrew Jackson and Franklin Delano Roosevelt as leaders of the Democratic Party who assumed its leadership by organizing a coalition of Eastern workingmen. Western farmers, and Southern conservatives. Its publication set off a long and inconclusive wrangle over whether, in fact, the Eastern workingmen did support Jackson. The controversy led to a considerable amount of research on both labor and politics in the 1830's. Yet the nature of the movement of the producing classes in the period remains obscure. We still lack a definitive study of the history of labor in the period.

The trade union movement of the 1830's was clearly, in its economic aspects, a modern labor movement. The unions that arose in the period were formed to protect working people against the effects of rising prices, the spread in the use of machinery, and the growth of national markets. To use a contemporary French term the American union was a *résistance*. In retrospect, it would appear that in this period the modern American labor movement was founded. It was, as today, dedicated to maintaining, and, if possible, increasing the share of working people in the national wealth. And in this period we encounter most of the existing institutional forms of contemporary unionism, not only local unions, but city centrals, national trade unions, and the first experiments with national federations.

Although it badly needs a second edition, Arthur Schlesinger's book is still the best introduction to the period. References more specifically on the labor movement alone include: Walter E. Hugins, *Jacksonian Democracy and the Working Class: A Study of the New York Workingmen's Movement, 1829–1837* (Stanford, California: Stanford University Press, 1960); William A. Sullivan, *Industrial Worker in Pennsylvania, 1800–1840* (Harrisburg, Pennsylvania: Pennsylvania Historical and Museum Commission, 1955); and Edward Pessen, *Most Uncommon Jacksonians: the Radical Leaders of the Early Labor Movement* (Albany, New York: State University of New York Press, 1967). Two articles require citation: Louis H. Arky, "The Mechanics' Union of Trade Associations and the Formation of the Philadelphia Working Men's Movement," *Pennsylvania Magazine of History and Biography* 76 (April 1952): 142–76, and Edward Pessen, "The Egalitarian Myth and the American Social Reality: Wealth, Mobility and Equality in the Era of the Common Man," *American Historical Review* 76 (4) (1971): 989–1034.

Finally, three books relating the labor movement to the broader social aspects of the period: David Harris, *Social Origins in the United States, American Forerunners of Marx, 1817–1832* (Assen, the Netherlands: Van Gorcum, 1966); Edward Pessen, *Jacksonian America: Society, Personality and Politics* (Homewood, Illinois: Dorsey Press, 1969); and Richard William Leopold, *Robert Dale Owen, A Biography* (Cambridge, Massachusetts: Harvard University Press, 1940).

Industrialization and American Labor, 1840–1873

Our period of transit from an agrarian to an industrial economy began in the late 40's and early 50's, as in much of Western Europe. The Civil War, itself a result of American industrialization, interrupted and distorted the industrializing process, but set the stage for a rapid resumption in its aftermath, when the political changes wrought by the war favored an even more rapid pace of growth.

Three books cover the history of labor in this period of industrialization and nationalization quite well: Norman J. Ware, *The Industrial Worker, 1840–1860* (Boston: Houghton, Mifflin, 1924); David Montgomery, *Beyond Equality: Labor and the Radical Republicans, 1862–1872* (New York: Knopf, 1967); and Eric Foner, *Free Soil, Free Labor, Free Men: The Ideology of the Republican Party before the Civil War* (New York: Oxford University Press, 1970). For an evaluation of the struggle between the North and the South as a bourgeois social revolution, one may refer to Barrington Moore, *Origins of Dictatorship and Democracy* (Boston: Beacon Press, 1966). Additional references may be found in Moore's bibliography.

The late 30's and early 40's were a depressed period in the United States. Abroad the period was known as the "Hungry Forties." As with the earlier depression after 1819, this was a time for utopian experiments, inspired largely by the writings of Fourier and Cabet. Several older books are useful for this period: Alice Felt Tyler, *Freedom's Ferment: Phases of American Social History from the Revolution to the Outbreak of the Civil War* (Minneapolis: University of Minnesota Press, 1944); William A. Hinds, *American Communities and Cooperative Colonies* (Chicago: C. H. Kerr, 2nd ed., 1908); Charles Nordhoff, *Communistic Societies of the United States* (New York: Hillary House, 1895; 1960 reprint); John H. Noyes, *History of American Socialisms* (New York: Hillary House, 1870; 1961 reprint); and Lindsay Swift, *Brook Farm* (New York: Macmillan, 1900).

In this period of intermittent booms and slumps, the trade union movement advanced, but with repeated setbacks on the downswings. As national markets developed with the spread of water and rail transportation, the need for larger and stronger organizations on a permanent basis was learned from experience. It is to the 1850's that we trace the first national trade unions which have survived. The standard work on this development is Lloyd Ulman, *The Rise of the National Trade Union* (Cambridge, Massachusetts: Harvard University Press, 1955).

For an account of one of the first, nationally-important trade unions, the iron molders, and one of the first nationally-known labor leaders, see Jonathan Grossman, *William Sylvis: Pioneer of American Labor* (New York: Columbia University Press, 1945). It is significant that in a period of "pure-and-simple" trade unionism, an outstanding trade union leader like Sylvis should also be the leading organizer of the National Labor Union, a reform organization, advocating through legislation the eight-hour day, monetary reform, and producers cooperation. In addition to Montgomery, cited above, and Ware (1929), cited below, a valuable article here is Gerald N. Grob, "Reform Unionism: The National Labor Union," *Journal of Economic History* 14 (Spring 1954): 126–42.

For the economic background of a period when questions of land reform and monetary questions were of importance, some additional references are Helene

S. Zahler, *Eastern Workingmen and National Land Policy, 1829–1862* (New York: Columbia University Press, 1941); Robert P. Sharkey, *Money, Class, and Party: An Economic Study of Civil War and Reconstruction* (Baltimore: Johns Hopkins University Press, 1959); and Irwin Unger, *The Greenback Era, A Social and Political History of American Finance, 1865–1879* (Princeton, New Jersey: Princeton University Press, 1964).

For Black labor under slavery some general works include: Kenneth Stampp, *The Peculiar Institution: Slavery in the Ante-Bellum South* (New York: Knopf, 1956); Eugene D. Genovese, *The Political Economy of Slavery: Studies in the Economy and Society of the Slave South* (New York: Pantheon Books, 1965); Richard C. Wade, *Slavery in the Cities: The South, 1820–1860* (New York: Oxford University Press, 1964); and Leon F. Litwack, *North of Slavery: the Negro in the Free States, 1790–1860* (Chicago: University of Chicago Press, 1961). For the abolitionists a general reference is Louis Filler, *The Crusade Against Slavery, 1830–1860* (New York: Harper, 1960). For a recent work stressing their revolutionary nature see Martin B. Duberman, ed., *The Antislavery Vanguard: New Essays on the Abolitionists* (Princeton, New Jersey: Princeton University Press, 1965).

Two recent works on the Reconstruction are John Hope Franklin, *Reconstruction: After the Civil War* (Chicago: University of Chicago Press, 1961), and Kenneth M. Stampp, *The Era of Reconstruction, 1865–1877* (New York: Knopf, 1965).

Years of Depressed Growth and Violence, 1873–1899

The last quarter of the nineteenth century is a period of major interest today to scholars in various fields of historical writing. Partly this comes from a revived interest in the Victorian Era. More specifically, the current interest in aspects of social history, such as urban history and religious history, has led to work in the period. The roots of many of today's social problems are being sought in this crucial time of change from an agrarian to an urban culture. An example would be: Samuel P. Hays, *The Response to Industrialism, 1885–1914* (Chicago: University of Chicago Press, 1957); or, more graphically, Robert H. Walker, *Everyday Life in the Age of Enterprise* (New York: Putnam, 1968).

In this period big business rose to control the nation, using the spreading rail network to dominate a national market, driving out the self-employed and the small, local manufacturer. Competition was used to destroy competition. A restricted money supply and the accompanying fall in prices favored this process of consolidation. Hard money, hard men, and hard times were contemporaries. The labor movement, too, reacted to these changes. The last major labor organization to hope and work for independence for all workers was the Knights of Labor. Their program was to abolish the wage system and replace it with one of producers' cooperative workshops. The Knights failed and had all but disappeared by the turn of the century. In its place was Sam Gompers' labor aristocracy of skilled workers and its program of seeking for its members only "More, more, and still more." In this they echoed, however unconsciously, the aspiration and the greed of American business.

The possibility of an economic solution to the problems of working people died away as the frontiers of economic opportunity closed or were closed for farmers and self-employed craftsmen. The Eight-Hour Movement of the period is to be seen as a last desperate assertion by labor to a voice in setting the terms of its employment. With the death of the dream of an agrarian, democratic republic, and the failure of labor organizations to provide an economic solution to the economic problems of more than a handful of American workers, there arose demands for a political solution. In this period a variety of panaceas were advocated: greenbackism, the single tax, even colonies on the land. By the turn of the century most of these were discredited. Increasingly, workingmen came to accept that the possibilities for reform were divided between using the monopoly power of organized labor to win economic concessions for strategically-placed workers and the broader ideas of socialism.

The account of the death of the old labor movement is found in one of its aspects in the writings on the Knights of Labor. The most recent history is Gerald N. Grob, *Workers and Utopia: A Study of Ideological Conflict in the American Labor Movement, 1865–1900* (Evanston, Illinois: Northwestern University Press, 1961). The best account of the Knights remains Norman J. Ware, *The Labor Movement in the United States, 1860–1895* (New York: Vintage Books, 1929; 1964 reprint).

However, recent research into labor in these years has concerned itself as much with the social life of working people as with formal labor organizations. Some typical titles are Irwin Yellowitz, *The Position of the Worker in American Society 1865–1896* (Englewood Cliffs, New Jersey: Prentice-Hall, 1969) and Frederic Cople Jaher, ed., *The Age of Industrialism: Essays in Social Structure and Cultural Values,* (New York: Free Press, 1968). Herbert G. Gutman, in particular, has done much research into the social background and social relationships of the American working class in the Gilded Age. However, his publications are scattered among a variety of periodical and other, often obscure, sources. A sampling of some of his relatively more accessible articles includes "The Worker's Search for Power: Labor in the Gilded Age," in H. Wayne Morgan, ed., *The Gilded Age: A Reappraisal* (Syracuse, New York: Syracuse University Press, 1963); "Protestantism and the American Labor Movement: The Christian Spirit in the Gilded Age," *American Historical Review* 72 (October 1966): 74–101; and "Work, Culture, and Society in Industrializing America, 1815–1919," *American Historical Review* 78 (June 1973): 531–88. The latter article and its numerous footnote references are the best introduction to this new emphasis on the problems of adjustment of premodern working classes to industrialization. This interest in the social status and the social mobility of Americans in the nineteenth century is also reflected in the much-cited study by Stephan Thernstrom, *Poverty and Progress, Social Mobility in a Nineteenth-Century City* (Cambridge, Massachusetts: Harvard University Press, 1964). Thernstrom's research yields a seemingly less-favorable view of the status and prospects of American workers than appears in Gutman's articles, to date.

There has been a substantial amount of recent work on the general political, social, and economic background of post-Civil War America. This has concentrated on the labor and urban aspects of unrest in the period, correcting the earlier view of Populism as a rural movement only. In addition to the book edited by Jaher, cited above, there is Norman Pollack, *The Populist Response to Industrial America* (Cambridge, Massachusetts: Harvard University Press, 1962); Robert Higgs, *The Transformation of the American Economy, 1865–1914: An Essay in Interpretation* (New York: Wiley, 1972); Richard Hofstadter, *The Age of Reform* (New York: Knopf, 1955); Ray Ginger, *Age of Excess: American Life from the End of Reconstruction to World War I* (New York: Macmillan, 1965); Charles Hoffman, *The Depression of the Nineties: An Economic History* (Westport, Connecticut: Greenwood Press, 1971); and Chester McArthur Destler, *American Radicalism, 1865–1901* (New London, Connecticut: Connecticut College, 1946).

Works more narrowly concerned with the labor movement in this time of depression and revolt include Robert V. Bruce, *1877: Year of Violence* (Indianapolis: Bobbs-Merrill, 1959); Wayne G. Broehl, *The Molly Maguires* (Cambridge, Massachusetts: Harvard University Press, 1964); Donald S. McMurray, *Coxey's Army, A Study of the Industrial Army Movement of 1894* (Boston: Little, Brown, 1929); Henry David, *The History of the Haymarket Affair* (New York: Farrar & Rinehart, 1936); John A. Garraty, *Labor and Capital in the Gilded Age: 1883* (Boston: Little, Brown, 1969); Ray Ginger, *Altgeld's America: The Lincoln Ideal and Changing Realities* (New York: Funk & Wagnalls, 1958); Almont Lindsey, *The Pullman Strike* (Chicago: University of Chicago Press, 1942); Donald L. McMurry, *The Great Burlington Railroad Strike of 1888* (Cambridge, Massachusetts: Harvard University Press, 1956); Leon Wolff, *Lockout, the Story of the Homestead Strike of 1892* (New York: Harper & Row, 1965); Thomas G. Manning, *The Chicago Strike of 1894: Industrial Labor in the Late Nineteenth Century* (New York: Holt & Rinehart, 1960); and Larzer Ziff, *The American 1890's: Life and Times of a Lost Generation* (New York: Viking Press, 1966).

It is in this period that immigration appears for the first time as a major influence on the labor movement, a problem both for America and the unions. In addition to the general references cited above, there are: Charlotte Erickson, *American Industry and the European Immigrant, 1860–1885* (Cambridge, Massachusetts: Harvard University Press, 1957); Alexander Saxton, *The Indispensable Enemy: Labor and the Anti-Chinese Movement in California* (Berkeley, California: University of California Press, 1971); Rowland Berthoff, *British Immigrants in Industrial America, 1790–1950* (Cambridge, Massachusetts: Harvard University Press, 1953); Clifton K. Yearley, Jr., *Britons in American Labor: A History of the Influence of the United Kingdom Immigrants on American Labor, 1820–1914* (Baltimore: Johns Hopkins University Press, 1957); Donald B. Cole, *Immigrant City: Lawrence, Massachusetts, 1845–1921* (Chapel Hill, North Carolina: University of North Carolina Press, 1963); Gerd Korman, *Industrialization, Immigrants and Americanization: the View from Milwaukee, 1866–1921* (Madison, Wisconsin: State Historical Society of Wisconsin, 1967); and John Higham, *Strangers in the Land: Patterns of American Nativism, 1860–1925* (New Brunswick, New Jersey: Rutgers University Press, 1955).

America's continuing labor federation, the American Federation of Labor, was founded in this period. Older works on the Federation have been superseded by: Philip Taft, *The A. F. of L. in the Time of Gompers* (New York: Harper and Row, 1957); Bernard Mandel, *Samuel Gompers: A Biography* (Yellow Springs, Ohio:

Antioch Press, 1963); Gerald Emanuel Stearn, ed., *Gompers* (Englewood Cliffs, New Jersey: Prentice-Hall, 1971); and Stuart Bruce Kaufman, *Samuel Gompers and the Origins of the American Federation of Labor, 1848–1896* (Westport, Connecticut: Greenwood Press, 1973).

It was also in these years that the socialist movement in the United States took its modern form. For origins the best source, far broader in its scope than the title suggests, is Samuel Bernstein, *The First International in America* (New York: Augustus M. Kelley, 1962). Dated and hostile, but a massive source of information, with a huge bibliography, taking up the entire second volume, is Donald Drew Egbert and Stowe Persons, eds., *Socialism and American Life*, 2 vols. (Princeton, New Jersey: Princeton University Press, 1952). The long general history essay by Daniel Bell in this work has been revised and updated and published separately as *Marxian Socialism in the United States* (Princeton, New Jersey: Princeton University Press, 1967). For an account of the development of Marxist doctrine in the United States see: David Herreshoff, *American Disciples of Marx* (Detroit: Wayne State University Press, 1967).

The institutional history of American socialism is covered by Howard H. Quint, *The Forging of American Socialism* (Columbia, South Carolina: University of South Carolina Press, 1953), and David A. Shannon, *The Socialist Party in America* (New York: Macmillan, 1955). Two recent studies of the relations of organized labor and socialism are John H. M. Laslett, *Labor and the Left: A Study of Socialist and Radical Influences in the American Labor Movement, 1881–1924* (New York: Basic Books, 1970) and William M. Dick, *Labor and Socialism in America: The Gompers Era* (Port Washington, New York: Kennikat Press, 1972). The last of these is of value more for the period after 1900.

Progress and Reaction, 1900–1914

This so-called "Progressive Era" has received much attention in recent years, especially from the revisionist historians. Thus views of its nature are, at present, controverted. It is certainly true that in this period the legitimate aspirations of the labor movement were repressed. The open-shop drive after 1904, coupled with the widespread use of the labor injunction and a hostile judiciary, reduced the A. F. of L. unions to impotence and turned them toward political action. As abroad, left-wing labor movements flourished, combining radical ends with militant means. This was the period of the Socialist Trade and Labor Alliance of Daniel De Leon, the Industrial Workers of the World, the Western Federation of Miners of "Big Bill" Haywood, the Socialist Labor Party, the Social Democratic Party and the Socialist Party, brilliantly led by Eugene V. Debs.

It was a period of radical demands and radical acts of both workers and employers. The direct action of labor, boycotts, the general strike, free-speech agitations, and destructive violence, were met by repressions of the local police, vigilantes, and the use of troops to break strikes. This was the period when employers' associations like the National Association of Manufacturers, the Lake Carriers Association, the National Erectors Association, and the National Metal Trades Council were organized.

Some recent works on the Progressives, reflecting varying viewpoints, are: Otis L. Graham, *The Great Campaigns: Reform and War in America, 1900–1928*

(Englewood Cliffs, New Jersey: Prentice-Hall, 1971); Charles Forcey, *The Crossroads of Liberalism: Croly, Weyl, Lippmann and the Progressive Era, 1900-1925* (New York: Oxford University Press, 1961); James Gilbert, *Designing the Industrial State: Intellectual Pursuit of Collectivism in America, 1880-1940* (Chicago: Quadrangle Books, 1972); Christopher Lasch, *The New Radicalism in America, 1889-1963* (New York: Knopf, 1965); Robert H. Wiebe, *Businessmen and Reform: A Study of the Progressive Movement* (Cambridge, Massachusetts: Harvard University Press, 1962); and James Weinstein, *The Corporate Ideal in the Liberal State, 1900-1918* (Boston: Beacon Press, 1967).

For the American labor movement in this period, in addition to Taft (1957), cited above, see James O. Morris, *Conflict within the A. F. of L.: A Study of Craft versus Industrial Unionism, 1901-1938* (Ithaca, New York: Cornell University Press, 1958); Marc Karson, *American Labor Unions and Politics*, vol. 1 (1900-1918), (Carbondale, Illinois: Southern Illinois University Press, 1958); Graham Adams, Jr., *Age of Industrial Violence, 1900-1915: the Activities and Findings of the United States Commission on Industrial Relations* (New York: Columbia University Press, 1966); Irvin Yellowitz, *Labor and the Progressive Movement in New York State, 1876-1916* (Ithaca, New York: Cornell University Press, 1965); Melvyn Dubofsky, *When Workers Organize: New York City in the Progressive Era* (Amherst, Massachusetts: University of Massachusetts Press, 1968); Marguerite Green, *The National Civic Federation and the American Labor Movement, 1900-1925* (Washington, D.C.: Catholic University of America Press, 1956); Elsie Gluck, *John Mitchell, Miner: Labor's Bargain with the Gilded Age* (New York: John Day, 1929).

For the Industrial Workers of the World and the syndicalist labor movement before the war there are several recent references: John R. Conlin, *Big Bill Haywood and the Radical Union Movement* (Syracuse, New York: Syracuse University Press, 1969); Melvin Dubofsky, *We Shall Be All: A History of the Industrial Workers of the World* (Chicago: Quadrangle Books, 1969); Joseph R. Conlin, *Bread and Roses Too: Studies of the Wobblies* (Westport, Connecticut: Greenwood Press, 1969); Joyce L. Kornbluh, ed., *Rebel Voices: An IWW Anthology* (Ann Arbor, Michigan: University of Michigan Press, 1964); and Ralph Chaplin, *Wobbly: The Rough-and-Tumble Story of an American Radical* (Chicago: University of Chicago Press, 1948).

For some additional references to the socialist movement in this period see Ray Ginger, *The Bending Cross: A Biography of Eugene V. Debs* (New Brunswick, New Jersey: Rutgers University Press, 1949); Christopher Lasch, *The Agony of the American Left* (New York: Knopf, 1969); and Ira Kipnis, *The American Socialist Movement, 1871-1912* (New York: Columbia University Press, 1952).

War, "Normalcy," and Depression, 1914-1932

In historical perspective, these seemingly disparate years have taken on a certain unity. The nineteenth century ended in 1914. With it ended the classic period of world capitalism and European imperialism. The new world era, as yet unnamed, was ushered in by the war, the crumbling of four empires, and the Russian Revolution. These were followed by a worldwide resurgence of nationalism.

In the United States our traditional agrarian values became obsolescent, as rural Americans continued to flee the land for the cities. An even more significant indication of the closing of frontiers was the enactment by 1924 of legislation virtually cutting off foreign immigration. This closing of the American market to foreign labor was, in many ways, the most significant event in the labor history of the 1920's. For this, see Higham (1955), cited above.

American workers began the period experiencing a deep sense of unrest, aggravated by a persistent lack of employment. As abroad, the pre-war years in America had been years of social disorder and social revolt. The Socialist Party polled its highest vote for a presidential candidate in 1912. The unrest carried over into the war period (see, especially, Adams (1966), cited above). However, the war, even before America's involvement, brought a rising demand for labor, rising prices, and as labor shortages developed, rising wages. Organized labor achieved a degree of official recognition during the war. Representatives of the A. F. of L. and the railroad brotherhoods served on various boards and commissions, as the government co-opted labor into the administration. Wage and other concessions were made to head off strikes. The Wilson Administration also fostered worker representation in plants where unions did not exist by setting up shop-representation committees. Despite these efforts, wartime strikes were not entirely avoided.

At the same time, fears of strikes and the spectre of social revolution led to official repression of the labor left. The Socialist Party of America, almost alone among the socialist parties of the West, had opposed the war. The Industrial Workers of the World did likewise. Thus the same year that saw Sam Gompers and other right-wing labor leaders serving in Washington, saw Eugene V. Debs and Big Bill Haywood imprisoned and the offices of the Socialist Party and the IWW invaded and smashed by Federal marshals. The inflationary aftermath of the war unleashed a wave of unrest: the steel strike of 1919, the Seattle general strike, and the Boston police strike. A red scare swept the country. Oppression of the workers spread across the spectrum of labor from the left to the right. Despite the record of the standard unions in support of the war, all working-class organizations were now said to be tinged with red and condemned as "un-American."

The post-war recession started in the spring of 1920: production and employment falling rapidly, prices following them down. Organized business launched a new open-shop drive, christened the "American Plan," aimed at the destruction of organized labor. Strikes to preserve war-time gains in wages and union recognition were generally lost. Even the well-entrenched building trade unions suffered bruising defeats in such strongholds as New York, Chicago, and San Francisco. In 1924 the A. F. of L. and the Socialists both supported Robert M. LaFollette in his bid for the Presidency on the Progressive Party ticket. The election of 1924 was, however, the last gasp of the Progressive impulse. Thereafter, legal repression plus welfare capitalism kept the labor movement ineffectual in both economics and politics. The Twenties wound on to their climax—the Great Bull Market of 1929, followed by the Great Depression of the 1930's.

For labor's role in World War I several of the above references on the A. F. of L. are useful, especially Taft (1957). Two older references should be added: Alexander Bing, *War-Time Strikes and Their Adjustment* (New York: E. P. Dutton, 1921); and Gordon S. Watkins, *Labor Problems and Labor Administration in the United States during the World War*, 2 vols. (Urbana, Illinois: University of Illinois Press, 1920).

For the strike wave immediately after the war see David Brody, *Labor in Crisis: the Steel Strike of 1919* (Philadelphia: Lippincott, 1965); Colston E. Warne, ed., *The Steel Strike of 1919* (Boston: Heath, 1963); Melvin I. Urofsky, *Big Steel and the Wilson Administration: A Study of Business and Government Relations* (Columbus, Ohio: Ohio State University Press, 1969); Robert L. Friedheim, *The Seattle General Strike* (Seattle, Washington: University of Washington Press, 1964); and Gerald G. Eggert, *Railroad Labor Disputes: The Beginnings of Federal Strike Policy* (Ann Arbor, Michigan: University of Michigan Press, 1967).

For government efforts to suppress dissent see Robert K. Murray, *Red Scare: A Study in National Hysteria, 1919-1920* (Minneapolis: University of Minnesota Press, 1955) and, more generally, William Preston, Jr., *Aliens and Dissenters: Federal Suppression of Radicals, 1903-1933* (Cambridge, Massachusetts: Harvard University Press, 1963).

The international activities of the A. F. of L. in support of the war and in the peace settlement may be studied in Austin Van der Slice, *International Labor, Diplomacy and Peace, 1914-1919* (Philadelphia: University of Pennsylvania Press, 1941), and Frank L. Grubbs, Jr., *The Struggle for Labor Loyalty: Gompers, the A. F. of L. and the Pacifists, 1917-1920* (Durham, North Carolina: Duke University Press, 1968). More generally and more critically, see Ronald Radosh, *American Labor and United States Foreign Policy* (New York: Random House, 1969). A recent book of related interest is David Mitchell, *1919: Red Mirage, Elegy for a Lost Cause* (New York: Macmillan, 1970). The founding and the history of the International Labour Organization are covered in a recent work by Anthony Alcock, *A History of the ILO* (London: Macmillan, 1971).

For the split in the American socialist movement and the formation of the American Communist Party, in addition to Weinstein (1967), cited above, see Bernard K. Johnpoll, *Pacifist's Progress: Norman Thomas and the Decline of American Socialism* (Chicago: Quadrangle Books, 1970), and Theodore Draper, *The Roots of American Communism* (New York: The Viking Press, 1957). A lively general history of the Communist Party is Irving Howe and Lewis Coser, *The American Communist Party: A Critical History* (Boston: Beacon Press, 1967).

An excellent general history of American workers in the 20's and the Depression is Irving Bernstein, *The Lean Years: A History of the American Worker, 1920-1933* (Boston: Houghton, Mifflin, 1960). For the period after 1925: Philip Taft, *The A. F. of L. from the Death of Gompers to the Merger* (New York: Harper & Row, 1959). For political aspects see Robert H. Zieger, *Republicans and Labor, 1919-1929* (Lexington, Kentucky: University of Kentucky Press, 1969). The 1924 election is covered in Kenneth C. MacKay, *The Progressive Movement of 1924* (New York: Columbia University Press, 1947).

Industrial Unionism: Labor and the New Deal, 1933-1939

While the nature of the New Deal itself has become a matter of historical controversy, there is little dispute that it brought a major turning point in American labor history. In this period American unions were transformed. From one weak, stagnant movement on a narrowing craft base they grew into two strong, rival federations competing to organize the centers of corporate power in the mass-production industries and equally committed to an active political program and economic objectives. This rise of the CIO and the revival of the A. F. of L. were the most significant developments in American labor since the organization of the A. F. of L. in the 1880's.

Although the New Deal had in it undoubted elements of continuity, building as it did on the experience of the Populist and Progressive movements, innovation and experiment were equally characteristic of its programs. It pioneered, however reluctantly, in an active counter-cyclical fiscal policy, which later gained the designation of "Keynesian." This program of direct governmental intervention in the economy is now the basic program of the American labor movement, centering on a guarantee by the government of jobs and sustained income. When one recalls that in 1933 the A. F. of L. was opposed to such elementary forms of government intervention as minimum wages and unemployment compensation, this marks a truly significant broadening of the scope of labor's political interests.

The literature of the New Deal is already enormous. A good summary of the dispute about its nature and origins is Edwin C. Rozwenc, ed., *The New Deal: Revolution or Evolution?* (Boston: Heath, 1959). An excellent bibliographic essay is Frank Freidel, *The New Deal in Historical Perspective*, 2nd ed. (Washington, D.C.: American Historical Association, 1965). Some recent, critical evaluations include Paul K. Conkin, *The New Deal* (New York: Crowell, 1967); Alonzo T. Hamby, *The New Deal: Readings in Analysis and Interpretation* (New York: Weybright, 1969); and R. Alan Lawson, *The Failure of Independent Liberalism, 1930-1941* (New York: Putnam, 1971).

For another approach, there are three essays in John Braeman, Robert H. Bremner, and Everett Walters, eds., *Change and Continuity in Twentieth Century America* (Columbus, Ohio: Ohio State University Press, 1964): William E. Leuchtenburg, "The New Deal and the Analogue of War"; Richard S. Kirkendall, "The Great Depression: Another Watershed in American History?"; and David Brody, "The Emergence of Mass-Production Unionism."

The last article is also an excellent introduction to the history of American labor under the New Deal. The most detailed account is Irving Bernstein, *The Turbulent Years: A History of the American Workers, 1933-1941* (Boston: Houghton, Mifflin, 1970). Another volume, dealing with the non-institutional history during these years, is expected. This account has not made obsolete another excellent work by Irving Bernstein, *The New Deal Collective Bargaining Policy* (Berkeley, California: University of California Press, 1950). See also James Morris and Philip Taft (1959), cited above.

Another detailed account, based on the history of unionism in particular industries is Walter Galenson, *The CIO Challenge to the A. F. of L.: A History of the American Labor Movement, 1935-1941* (Cambridge, Massachusetts: Harvard University Press, 1960). A valuable series of essays is Milton Derber and Edwin Young, eds., *Labor and the New Deal* (Madison, Wisconsin: University of Wisconsin Press, 1957). A recent study is C. K. McFarland, *Roosevelt, Lewis and the New Deal, 1933-1940* (Fort Worth, Texas: Texas Christian University Press, 1970).

Detailed research into New Deal labor history is really just beginning. Some examples of the type of work underway are Jerold S. Auerbach, *Labor and Liberty: The LaFollette Committee and the New Deal* (Indianapolis, Indiana: Bobbs-Merrill, 1966); Sidney A. Fine, *The Automobile under the Blue Eagle* (Ann Arbor, Michigan: University of Michigan Press, 1963), and by the same author, *Sitdown: The General Motors Strike of 1936–1937* (Ann Arbor, Michigan: University of Michigan Press, 1969); and Harry A. Millis and E. C. Brown, *From the Wagner Act to Taft-Hartley: A Study of National Labor Policy and Labor Relations* (Chicago: University of Chicago Press, 1950). The revolution in economic thinking, called Keynesian, which was a development of the New Deal years, has also its own literature. Here we cite one recent title with a good bibliography: Donald Winch, *Economics and Policy, A Historical Survey* (London: Collins/Fontana, 1972).

The New Deal absorbed much of the right-wing of the Socialist Party. The Communist Party followed the tortuous line laid down for it in Moscow. It was, by turns, hostile to the New Deal, cooperative and co-opting in the United Front period, and isolationist after the signing of the Moscow Pact in August of 1939. In retrospect, although seen by some observers at the time, the high point of Communist influence in the West came with the Spanish Civil War and the formation of the International Brigades. This also marked the low point in New Deal diplomacy. It is probably incorrect to say that out of that bitter and confused struggle came the *concept* of an independent left. It is certainly true that the *need* for an independent left became clear as the struggle exposed successively anarchism, socialism, communism and democracy as the facades for national interest that they were. To many observers the only conviction to emerge from this polarizing episode was the conviction that fascism was an intolerable evil.

See Johnpoll, cited above, for socialism in this period. Two additional references on American Communism are David J. Saposs, *Communism in American Unions* (New York: McGraw-Hill, 1959), and David Shannon, *The Decline of American Communism* (New York: Viking Press, 1959). On the Spanish Civil War, see Hugh Thomas, *The Spanish Civil War* (New York: Harper & Row, 1963), and the references therein.

Labor Against Fascism and Communism, 1940–1955

The war to destroy fascism brought America, and American labor, however reluctantly, back into the world's arena. In some respects, the war completed and consolidated trends already underway in the labor movement. When the defense buildup restored the demand for labor, the unions rapidly completed the job of organizing the mass-production industries. By 1945, with few exceptions, practically all large private employers were organized. Trade union membership rose to roughly one-third of the non-agricultural labor force and remained at this proportion through the war years and beyond. This was done with the support of the Federal government, but at some cost to labor militancy. After Pearl Harbor, the prewar strike wave died as rapidly as did isolationism. When Hitler launched his attack on the U.S.S.R., the Communists became superpatriots, overnight. In or out of uniform, the working class enlisted, or was drafted, for the duration. The war also ended the depression. Unemployment, which had stood at ten million at the start of the defense build-up, fell to frictional levels. Keynes's thesis, that deficit spending by the government could restore and maintain prosperity, was convincingly confirmed. And after the war, pent-up demand, wartime savings, reconstruction spending, spending for industrial growth and Third World development, but, above all, for the Cold War, prevented the immediate return of any substantial amount of unemployment.

These experiences confirmed for American labor the correctness of the approach to policy it had developed as in 1936 and 1940, when it had entered actively into politics in support of the New Deal. Through its support of governmental spending it would assure full employment and economic growth; through collective bargaining it would maintain labor's share in a growing national income. This dual policy made it possible for American labor to pose a purely economic answer to the social question. Even abroad, in the post-war years, the question of nationalization was becoming a question of secondary importance, a matter of political expediency. In a sense, in the West socialism was considered to have died with fascism. For this one may refer to a work which attracted much attention at the time: Daniel Bell, *The End of Ideology* (New York: The Free Press, 1960).

The post-war political situation lent support to this economic program. The destruction of fascism left much of Europe open to the spread of Stalinism. This period of aggressive subversion in Europe was also the period of the end of colonial rule in most of Asia and Africa. Important as these events were, the development of a major independent Communist center in China in 1949 was the major event of this period. The Third World was opened to a variety of nationalistic regimes: democratic, but more often authoritarian; socialistic, but now as likely Maoist as Stalinist. The West reacted to the onset of the Cold War with the principle of containment. The early post-war internationalism of the U.N., and, in the labor field, the ILO, was first, supplemented, and then largely supplanted, by regional blocs. From the Marshall Plan for rebuilding Europe came the organizations for its economic and military defense, Atlantic Union, OEEC, OECD, NATO and, on the Continent, the European Common Market.

Both during and after the war, the American working people gave full support to America's policy. The results differed only in degree, not in kind, from labor's post-World War I experience. The Wagner Act, the principal New Deal measure for the protection of the rights of workers to organize and bargain collectively, was replaced by the Taft-Hartley Act, which was designed to immediately curb the further growth of unions and to prepare the way for the destruction of organized labor in the next major recession. The American Left, whether pro- or anti-communist was hunted down and all but destroyed in the witch-hunt led by Senator Joseph McCarthy. Labor unions ceased to grow. Thrown on the defensive, the A. F. of L. and the CIO composed their differences, compromised their principles, and united in 1955.

Although the period with which we are concerned lies from twenty to thirty-odd years in the past, the history of labor in the post-war years remains largely unwritten. The one monograph on labor's role in World War II is so good it appears to have discouraged further work: Joel Seidman, *American Labor from Defense to Reconversion* (Chicago: University of Chicago Press, 1953). Details and a contemporary flavor may be found in two older works: Colston E. Warne, ed., *War Labor Policies* (New York: Philosophical Library, 1943) and, by the same author, *Labor in Postwar America* (Brooklyn, New York: Rensen Press, 1949).

Wartime labor controls are usefully summed up in three official studies: Bureau of Labor Statistics, *Report on the Work of the National Defense Mediation Board, March 19, 1941–January 12, 1942* (Bulletin 714, Washington, D.C.: GPO, 1942) and *Problems and Policies of Dispute Settlement and Wage Stabilization during World War II* (Bulletin 1009, Washington, D.C.: GPO, 1950), and U.S. Department of Labor, *The National Wage Stabilization Board, January 1, 1946–February 24, 1947* (Washington, D.C.: GPO, 1947).

Two works cover the general history of labor in the immediate post-war period: Arthur F. McClure, *The Truman Administration and the Problems of Postwar Labor, 1945-1948* (Rutherford, New Jersey: Fairleigh Dickinson University Press, 1969) and Thomas R. Brooks, *Picket Lines and Bargaining Tables: Organized Labor Comes of Age, 1935–1955* (New York: Grosset and Dunlop, 1968). For the Taft-Hartley Act see Millis and Brown (1950), cited above.

The history of the Communist Party in the war and post-war years may be found in Theodore Draper, *American Communism and Soviet Russia* (New York: Viking, 1960) and Joseph R. Starobin, *American Communism in Crisis, 1943–1957* (Cambridge, Massachusetts: Harvard University Press, 1972). See also the references to Saposs (1959) and Shannon (1959), above.

The attack on the American left is covered in Earl Latham, *The Communist Controversy in Washington: From the New Deal to McCarthy* (Cambridge, Massachusetts: Harvard University Press, 1966); Michael Paul Rogin, *The Intellectuals and McCarthy: The Radical Spectre* (Cambridge, Massachusetts: Harvard University Press, 1967); and Michael Parenti, *The Anti-Communist Impulse* (New York: Random House, 1969).

Regrettably, not only have few studies been published of labor's role in foreign affairs, but even fewer have been objective. In part, this reflects a failure of the protagonists to take an objective view of their roles, and to write accordingly. As a result the works cited tend to be either official apologetics or left-wing criticism, with little in between.

In addition to the book by Radosh (1969) cited above there are: Lewis L. Lorwin, *The International Labor Movement* (New York: Harper, 1953); John P. Windmuller, *American Labor and the International Labor Movement, 1940–1953* (Ithaca, New York: The Institute of International Industrial and Labor Relations, Cornell University, 1954); George Morris, *The CIA and American Labor: The Subversion of the AFL-CIO's Foreign Policy* (New York: International Publishers, 1967); Alfred O. Hero, *The UAW and World Affairs* (Boston, Massachusetts: World Peace Foundation, 1965); the same, *The Reuther-Meany Foreign Policy Dispute* (Dobbs Ferry, New York: Oceana Publications, 1970). Two articles by John P. Windmuller should be added: "Foreign Affairs and the AFL-CIO," *Industrial and Labor Relations Review* 9 (1956): 419–432, and "The Foreign Policy Conflict in American Labor," *Political Science Quarterly* 82 (1967): 205–34. These articles and the above-cited book by Professor Windmuller are rare and all the more welcome exceptions to our above comments on objectivity.

Dry Rot and Ferment: Labor, 1956–1973

There are, of course, as with most controversial, live topics, numberless writings on labor in recent years. But without historical perspective, it is difficult to select. In reviewing these writings on American labor, we do at least learn what has attracted the attentions of students, even though volume is neither a necessary nor a sufficient criterion.

When we drew the line of 1955 as marking the end of a period, we had in mind the formation of the AFL-CIO as marking such an end, if not a beginning. Since then, despite much talk and writings on stagnation in the labor movement, the standard unions have fought off attacks and apathy, and made at least a beginning in organizing the growing service sector of the economy. After years when the structural shifts in the labor force weakened unions with their predominantly blue-collar membership, the growth of white-collar unionism and a major break-through in organizing government workers have shifted membership figures from a falling to a growing percentage of the labor force being organized.

The one book on the merger is Arthur Goldberg, *AFL-CIO: Labor United* (New York: McGraw-Hill, 1956). Some other recent books on labor, reflecting varying viewpoints and covering varying time-spans include: Jerold S. Auerbach, ed., *American Labor: The Twentieth Century* (Indianapolis, Indiana: Bobbs-Merrill, 1969); Derek C. Bok and John T. Dunlop, *Labor and the American Community* (New York: Simon and Schuster, 1970); Patricia Cayo Sexton and Brendon Sexton, *Blue Collars and Hard-Hats: The Working Class and the Future of American Politics* (New York: Random House, 1971); Sar A. Levitan, ed., *Blue Collar Workers: A Symposium on Middle America* (New York: McGraw-Hill, 1971); Jeremy Brecher, *Strike!* (San Francisco: Straight Arrow/World, 1972); and Sidney Lens, *The Labor Wars: from the Molly McGuires to the Sitdowns* (New York: Doubleday, 1973).

In recent years, structural trends and the resulting changes in job opportunities in the work force have attracted much attention to the study of manpower problems and labor markets. Among recent works in this field mention should be made of Leonard A. Lecht, *Manpower Needs for National Goals in the 1970's* (New York: Praeger, 1969), and Sar A. Levitan, Garth L. Mangum and Ray Marshall, *Human Resources and Labor Markets: Labor and Manpower in the American Economy* (New York: Harper and Row, 1972).

Employment of minority group members and questions of discrimination have motivated much of the writings on manpower. From among the voluminous books on Black workers the following are selected: F. Ray Marshall, *The Negro and Organized Labor* (New York: Wiley, 1965); same, *The Negro Worker* (New York: Random House, 1967); Louis A. Ferman, Joyce L. Kornbluh, and Joe A. Miller, comps., *Negroes and Jobs, A Book of Readings* (Ann Arbor, Michigan: University of Michigan Press, 1968); Julius Jacobson, ed., *The Negro and the American Labor Movement* (Garden City, New York: Anchor Books, 1968); Milton Cantor, ed., *Black Labor in America* (Westport, Connecticut: Negro Universities Press, 1969); and John H. Bracy, August Meier and Elliott Budwick, eds., *Black Workers and Organized Labor* (Belmont, California: Wadsworth Publishing Co., 1971).

Some additional references on the movement for equality by Blacks include:

James Boggs, *The American Revolution: Pages from a Negro Worker's Notebook* (New York: Monthly Review Press, 1963); same, *Racism and the Class Struggle: Further Pages from a Black Worker's Notebook* (New York: Monthly Review Press, 1970); Harold Cruse, *The Crisis of the Negro Intellectual* (New York: Morrow, 1967); and Stokely Carmichael and Charles V. Hamilton, *Black Power: The Politics of Liberation in America* (New York: Random House, 1968).

A second minority group, the Spanish-Americans, has attracted study both as a minority suffering discrimination and as one active in organizing a sector of the labor force, farm workers, not generally organized. Some useful references are Peter Matthiessen, *Sal Si Puedes: Cesar Chavez and the New American Revolution* (New York: Random House, 1969); John Gregory Dunne, *Delano: The Story of the California Grape Strike* (New York: Farrar, Strauss and Giroux, rev. ed., 1971); Mark Day, *Forty Acres: Cesar Chavez and the Farm Workers* (New York: Praeger, 1971); Stan Steiner, *La Raza: The Mexican Americans* (New York: Harper & Row, 1970); and Wayne Moquin and Charles Van Doren, eds., *A Documentary History of the Mexican Americans* (New York: Bantam Books, 1972).

Finally, the New Left, a broad and diffuse movement of social dissent, has touched on the labor movement at many points and produced a growing literature. As has been the case with students, women, and the above-mentioned minorities, underlying conditions which have produced this dissent are also present within the ranks of organized labor. This unrest has led to demands for a participatory plant-floor democracy, workers' control, and increased participation by the rank-and-file union membership in union government, the handling of grievances and the negotiation of contracts. The New Left is a topic in itself, and one badly documented and little studied as well. Two titles will provide initial orientation: a bibliography, James O'Brien, *A History of the New Left, 1960–1968* (Boston: New England Free Press, 1968), and a documentary history, Massimo Teodori, ed., *New Left: A Documentary History* (Indianapolis, Indiana: Bobbs-Merrill, 1970).

For the modern Marxist economic thinking, usually called again, political economy, a good selection will be found in R. C. Edwards, M. Reich, and T. E. Weisskopf, eds., *The Capitalist System* (Englewood Cliffs, New Jersey: Prentice-Hall, 1972). A cogent criticism of the economics of the New Left is Assar Lindbeck, *The Political Economy of the New Left-An Outsider's View* (New York: Harper & Row, 1971).

For the unrest in the unions and the movement for increased democracy, on and off the job, see Daniel Bell, *Work and Its Discontents* (Boston: Beacon Press, 1956); Gus Tyler, *The Political Imperative: The Corporate Character of Unions* (New York: Macmillan, 1968); Stanley H. Ruttenberg, *Manpower Challenge of the 1970's: Institutions and Social Change* (Baltimore: Johns Hopkins University Press, 1970); Milton Derber, *The American Idea of Industrial Democracy, 1865–1965* (Urbana, Illinois: University of Illinois Press, 1970); Harold L. Sheppard and Neal Q. Herrick, *Where Have All the Robots Gone? Worker Dissatisfaction in the 70's* (New York: Free Press, 1972); Burton Hall, *Autocracy and Insurgency in Organized Labor* (New York: Transaction Books, 1972); William A. Wesley and Margaret W. Wesley, *The Emerging Workers: Equality and Conflict in the Mass Consumption Society* (Montreal, Canada: McGill-Queen's University Press,

1971); and John Hutchinson, *The Imperfect Union: A History of Corruption in American Trade Unions* (New York: Dutton, 1970).

Several recent books on labor in politics have put an end to the myth that American labor is not and has not been politically active. These include J. David Greenstone, *Labor and American Politics* (New York: Knopf, 1969); Vivian Vale, *Labour in American Politics* (New York: Barnes & Noble, 1971); and Charles M. Rehmus and Doris B. McLaughlin, eds., *Labor and American Politics: A Book of Readings* (Ann Arbor, Michigan: University of Michigan Press, 1967).

The recent movement for workers' control or shop-floor democracy is based on syndicalist ideas, dating back to before World War I, but the movement itself is based on a widespread dissatisfaction with working conditions in industry: fatigue, environmental hazards, lack of safety, and boredom. Based on New Left ideals of individualism, democracy, and equality, this movement may well prove to be the cutting edge of world, as well as American, left unionism. A sampling of the already extensive literature should include: C. G. Benello and Dimitrius Roussopoulis, eds., *The Case for Participatory Democracy: Some Prospects for the Radical Society* (New York: Grossman Publishers, 1971); Gerry Hunnius, G. David Garson and John Case, eds., *Worker's Control: A Reader on Labor and Social Change* (New York: Vintage Books, 1973); Paul Blumberg, *Industrial Democracy: The Sociology of Participation* (New York: Schocken, 1969); Ken Coates and Tony Topham, eds., *Workers' Control* (London: Panther/Modern Society, 1970); Andre Gorz, *A Strategy for Labor* (Boston: Beacon Press, 1967); Carole Pateman, *Participation and Democratic Theory* (Cambridge, England: Cambridge University Press, 1970); Adolf Sturmthal, *Worker's Councils: A Study of Workplace Organization on Both Sides of the Iron Curtain* (Cambridge, Massachusetts: Harvard University Press, 1964); Jaroslav Vanek, *A General Theory of Labor-Managed Economies* (Ithaca, New York: Cornell University Press, 1970); and same, *The Participatory Economy* (Ithaca, New York: Cornell University Press, 1971).

Some recent references to two of the traditional groups on the Left include: Michael Harrington, *Socialism* (New York: Saturday Review Press, 1972); P. Anderson and R. Blackburn, *Toward Socialism* (London: New Left Review, 1965); James Joll, *The Anarchists* (Boston: Little-Brown, 1964); and David Apter and James Joll, eds., *Anarchism Today* (London: Macmillan, 1971).

Additionally, we might call attention to two books by Theodore Roszak which attempt to characterize and evaluate the New Left. These are *The Making of a Counter Culture* (New York: Doubleday, 1969) and *Where the Wasteland Ends: Politics and Transcendence in Post-Industrial Society* (New York: Doubleday, 1972). Second, for some underpinning: Daniel Bell, *The Coming of Post-Industrial Society* (New York: Basic Books, 1973).

Finally, it seems to us that the one writer with a legitimately hopeful view of America today and a foreign perspective is Jean-Francois Revel, *Without Marx or Jesus: The New American Revolution Has Begun* (New York: Doubleday, 1971). We telescope together Revel's first and final paragraphs: "The revolution of the twentieth century will take place in the United States. It is only there that it can happen. And it has already begun. . . . It is *the* revolution of our time. It is the only revolution that involves radical, moral, and practical opposition to the spirit of nationalism. It is the only revolution that, to that opposition, joins culture, economic and technological power, and a total affirmation of liberty for all in place of archaic prohibitions. It therefore offers the only possible escape for mankind today: the acceptance of technological civilization as a means and not as an end and—since we cannot be saved either by the destruction of the civilization or by its continuation—the development of the ability to reshape that civilization without annihilating it."

It has been said that Revel is a pamphleteer. He is; one in the tradition of Voltaire and Tom Paine. He sees America as being changed from within by social experimentation. To Europeans it is a laboratory of revolution in the same sense that eighteenth-century England was a laboratory for Voltaire. We end then on the note on which we began. America and American labor present greater opportunities for study from abroad than ever before. The world of our years is a world undergoing revolutionary change. To study, to write about this revolution, one must study, one must write about America.

Part II
New Accents
for American Studies

Man, Nature, and the Ecological Perspective

by Michael J. Lacey

The term *ecology* was coined a century ago by the German zoologist, Ernst Haeckel. Haeckel's aim was to establish a logical scheme for the life sciences, and he built his term on the Greek *oikos* ("home," "dwelling place") to refer to the relationships between organisms and their environment, both living and nonliving. The debut was modest, almost to a fault, and while the years that followed have witnessed the development of an intricate specialized history for the subject,[1] it is only in the very recent past that *ecology* has become a commonplace in serious discussions of the human condition. The population explosion, the unmanageable spread of cities, dwindling resources, pollution in all of its varieties, and the extinction of many forms of plant and animal life are different aspects of what often has been referred to as a pervasive ecological crisis. Reactions are widespread at elite levels. Over 500 bills dealing with environmental problems have been introduced into the 91st Congress. A spate of new journals have come into being within the last decade,[2] and even the popular media—television, newspapers, and magazines—have begun to devote sustained attention to the issue.[3] A major United Nations conference on the problems of the human environment is scheduled for 1972, and the International Biological Program, a global effort of basic research on the theme of man's survival in a changing world, now includes the participation of fifty-six nations in addition to the United States.

With its emphasis on interplay—on the interrelations among living things and conditions and processes—there appears to be an unlimited scope for ecology, and this has resulted in considerable confusion. Past efforts to define *human ecology* as a field of specific subject matter have been notably unsuccessful, and there is no single, unified body of thought to which one can refer for an authoritative briefing. The interplay between man and his environment, between the realm of nature and the realm of culture, is clearly too all-encompassing to allow easy definition. For scholars within the American Studies community, inured to the stress of an interdisciplinary frame of reference, possibly the most rewarding approach is to regard ecology as a theme that carries with it implications for many areas of inquiry.

The most important source for the theme in its modern context is found in the work of George Perkins Marsh (1801-1882), a distinguished American statesman and scholar. Marsh's public career included service as a member of Congress, minister to Turkey, and for the last twenty years of his life, as United States Minister to Italy. His scholarly interests were of the most catholic variety, and in his own time he had a considerable reputation as an English philologist and etymologist. His claim on today's attention, however, rests with the publication in 1864 of the monumental *Man and Nature; or Physical Geography as Modified by Human Action*,[4] which scholars in many fields, but particularly geography, anthropology, and ecology, regard as the first great work of synthesis in the modern period to examine in detail the impact of man on his environment.[5]

Mr. Lacey is Assistant to the Director of the Woodrow Wilson International Center for Scholars, Smithsonian Institution, Washington, D. C. He is a doctoral candidate in the American Studies Program of The George Washington University. Wallace D. Bowman, Deputy Director of the Environmental Policy Division of the Legislative Reference Service, Library of Congress, furnished valuable advice and criticism in the preparation of the article.

Marsh's point of view was original. Rather than regarding man as a passive creature subordinate to the mysterious workings of nature, he stressed the other side of the equation, maintaining that the cumulative effect of human activities in transforming the face of the earth was a force approaching geologic proportions. His treatment was limited primarily to western Europe and the Mediterranean Basin and his purpose was "to indicate the character and, approximately, the extent of the changes produced by human action in the physical conditions of the globe we inhabit; to point out the dangers of imprudence and the necessity of caution in all operations which, on a large scale, interfere with the spontaneous arrangements of the organic or the inorganic world; [and] to suggest the possibility and the importance of the restoration of disturbed harmonies and the material improvement of waste and exhausted regions . . ."[6] Using a wealth of evidence that he had drawn together from the technical writings of botanists, plant geographers, foresters, agronomists, meteorologists, and many others whose work is rarely mentioned in historical discourse, he discussed the increase in climatic contrasts resulting from deforestation, the revolution accomplished by man in plant and animal distributions throughout the world, the effects of agriculture on biotic communities, species extinction, soil erosion, unforseen changes in the regime of water supply, and a number of other topics with which we are now familiar. In the last revised edition of his work, he suggested a relationship between large urban masses and climatic conditions, an anticipation of present day studies.[7] Curiously, he paid scant attention to the problems of population and the consumption of nonrenewable resources, both of which are prominent in modern discussions.

In view of the scope of his subject, however, the sense of balance that Marsh brought to it was admirable indeed. While his research raised the possibility that "the earth is fast becoming an unfit home for its noblest inhabitant," and that "perhaps even extinction of the species"[8] was plausible, he admitted that his thesis had "no place in the general scheme of physical science, and is [a] matter of suggestion and speculation only, not of established and positive conclusion."[9] Nor did he content himself with impassioned pleas for conservation. Rather he looked forward to the gradual development of more powerful forms of knowledge and suggested, among other things, the national control of natural resources and the employment of land use plans based on the information that was then available.

Despite the fact that *Man and Nature* was widely discussed in both Europe and America, it is evident that the questions Marsh raised were lost in the shuffle of a vigorous, rapidly expanding civilization, understandably impressed with the accomplishments of its protean technology. Interest in his work has been rekindled in our own century as the problems he foresaw took on a more urgent character and became matters of widespread concern.[10]

Fifteen years ago a conference sponsored by the Wenner-Gren Foundation for Anthropological Research was held in Marsh's honor at Princeton, New Jersey, and the results of that meeting constitute a landmark in the history of interdisciplinary discussion. The symposium was a model of successful planning and a tribute to Dr. William Thomas, then Assistant Director of the Foundation. Three years were devoted to its preparation, the first of which was spent in researching the theme of man's impact on his environment. It was decided that the primary objective of the symposium was to be not merely the education of its participants, but the publication of the proceedings in a form that would be useful to scholars in oncoming generations. This decision required outlining not only a conference but a volume as well, which was to contain two things: a set of background papers, each stressing the contribution of a particular field of knowledge to the general theme, authored for an audience of non-specialists by scholars prominent in their fields, and an edited version of the discussions that would take place while the symposium was in progress. The theme was divided into three sections—"Retrospect," "Process," and "Prospect"—and three co-chairmen were appointed, each with responsibility for one of these aspects of the symposium. The co-chairmen were Professors Carl O. Sauer, then chairman of the Department of Geography, University of California at Berkeley, Marston Bates, an ecologist, then at the University of Michigan, and Lewis Mumford.

There were seventy participants at the conference, and fifty-three of them contributed papers. The papers were circulated to members months in advance so that the meeting itself could be devoted to interchange. Participants represented twenty-four different disciplines and nine countries in addition to the United States. The resultant volume, entitled *Man's Role in Changing the Face of the Earth*, edited by William L. Thomas, Jr., was published in 1956 by the University of Chicago Press. Nearly 1,200 pages in length, its organization and scope of coverage render it an excellent source book for non-specialists. The work as a whole is well illustrated and indexed, and the individual articles contain useful references.

Materials collected under the heading "Retrospect" dealt with man's tenure on the earth from pre-historic times to the present, of his rise to the status of ecological dominant, and included discussions of the antiquity and world expansion of human culture; cultural differences in the interpretation of natural resources; a survey of changing ideas of the habitable world within the western tradition; the effects of classical antiquity on the land; the role of fire as the first great force employed by man; early food producing populations; the clearing of woodlands in Europe; the ecology of peasant life in Western Europe; subsistence economies; commercial economies; the natural history of urbanization, and various related topics.

Sessions devoted to "Process" included a summary of environmental changes wrought by forces independent of man and consideration of those changes in which he is directly involved: his impact on the seas and upon coastlines; changes in the quantities and qualities of ground and surface waters; the alteration of climate in both the urban and rural contexts; slope and soil changes that result from human activity; the modification of biotic communities by fire, agriculture, grazing, the removal and introduction of species, and by other means; the ecology of wastes including problems of disposal, relations to disease, and the effects of fission material on air, soil, and living species; and lastly, urban-industrial demands on the land in terms of requirements for ores and minerals, ever-increasing amounts of space, and so on.

The third component of the symposium, entitled "Prospect," was concerned with the limits of the earth's resources, and considered the spiral of population; the possible limits of raw-material consumption; limitations to energy use; technological denudation; and man's adaptation to the earth in its bearing on his aesthetic, ethical, and legal values.

The "Marsh festival," to use Professor Sauer's phrase, was an attempt to provide an integrated basis for insights into the phenomenon of man's ecological dominance, and even the most lethargic reader of the proceedings emerges with the feeling that the processes of culture are indissolubly linked to those of the natural order, and vice versa. The history of the two converge. Given man's present capacity to effect massive environmental change, either deliberately or otherwise, it is unlikely that one can long be studied without reference to the other. Cultural adaptations vary—from primitive societies of hunter-gatherers to the extremely complex technological societies of western civilization—but the imprint of man is everywhere, from the uninhabited regions of the Arctic to the most remote stretches of the open sea.

Unfortunately, the perception that these two realms, each with a host of learned disciplines devoted to its analysis, inevitably "fit together" amounts to something less than an operative body of knowledge in its own right. When Marsh had reflected on the content of the new learning that was required, he clearly anticipated the focus of ecology, although the term itself was then unavailable. The future would require, he remarked, an understanding that embraced "not only the globe itself, but the living things which vegetate or move upon it, the varied influences they exert upon each other, the reciprocal action and reaction between them and the earth they inhabit. [11] Man's role in this grand design was obviously foremost in his mind, and to this day the relation between general ecology, with its emphasis on the structure and functioning of natural systems, and a number of other, independent fields of learning, lies at the heart of the matter.

The influence of ecological concepts on other fields of learning has been pronounced and seems to be increasing. Thus we read of the ecology of international relations, [12] the ecology of public administration, [13] the ecology of imagination, [14] and the politics of ecology. [15] If ecology then seems to flow over into all fields of learning, its basic principles and concepts become correspondingly more important, and at least a nodding acquaintance with some of its literature is essential. As in any science, its working vocabulary is rather rigid, and mixing it with the language of other disciplines can be hazardous.

From the viewpoint of ecology, life is the product of a delicate network of checks and balances which, in turn, are the products of evolution. The incredible diversity of life-forms that constitute this network is comprised functionally of producers, consumers, and decomposers, which utilize the mineral substances of often limited reservoirs of air, water, and land. The producers are the green plants, which, with the assistance of radiant energy from the sun, take up such substances as carbon dioxide, oxygen, water, nitrogen, sulfur, potassium, and phosphorus and transforms them into food. The plants, in turn, provide food for other forms of life. The consumers are the herbivores and carnivores, both types fitting into an intricate pattern of food chains and webs. The remains of both the producers and the consumers are then reduced by the decomposers—primarily bacteria and fungi—and returned to the land, water, and air.

A central concept of ecology is the *ecosystem*. Building upon the conventional levels of the organization of life [16]—molecules, cells, tissues, organs, organisms, populations, species, and communities—the vast assemblages of organisms mentioned above serve as interdependent communities of life-forms. These communities, when combined with the non-living environment, constitute ecosystems, the ultimate level of biological integration.[17]

The term was first proposed by the British plant-ecologist Arthur Tansley in 1935 as a means of focusing attention on living systems in their entirety, and it has proven to be an extremely fruitful contribution. [18] *Ecosystem* can be used to refer concretely to a specific situation or abstractly to a class. An island, a lake, or a pond, a forest, indeed, the earth itself, each can be regarded as an ecosystem. The term's significance lies in phenomena that are unique to its level of integration—energetics, nutrient cycling, species diversity, ecological regulation, and self-perpetuation—none of which can be understood simply by extrapolating knowledge gained from the lower levels.

Mention must also be made of self-regulation or *homeostasis* in ecological systems. Since both man-dominated ecosystems and those relatively free of his influence are subject to the same basic laws, such self-regulation has an important bearing on the general idea of the "balance of nature" that one so often encounters in discussion of current problems. The story is a very complicated one and systems-ecologists point out that present knowledge of the characteristics and mechanisms involved (i.e., community structure and dominance, species diversity, ecological niches, succession, energy flow and trophic structure, food webs, and biogeochemical cycles) is imperfect. The problem lies at the forefront of contemporary research, and a great deal depends on its solution—most notably the possibility of replacing our present behavior with the intelligent manipulation of ecosystems and the restoration of those now in a degraded condition.

The best known textbook on modern ecology (reportedly the one most used in college courses) is Eugene P. Odum's *Fundamentals of Ecology*, 2nd ed. (Philadelphia: Saunders, 1959). Another volume of Odum's, entitled *Ecology* (New York: Holt, Rinehart, and Winston, 1963), is very helpful because of its brevity (152 pp.) and purpose. Much more approachable than the *Fundamentals*, *Ecology* was written for a general audience and is organized around a series of pictorial or graphic models that illustrate the principles basic to an understanding of the subject. Peter Farb's *Ecology* (New York: Time Inc., 1963), a part of the *Life* Nature Library, is also effective in this connection.

The explosion of interest in the environment has presented a serious challenge to teachers of introductory biology on the college level, as they are often expected to sketch the grand design of the life sciences in terms that are meaningful to students who are working on a general liberal arts curriculum. A recent text by Robert B. Platt and George K. Reid, entitled *Bioscience* (New York: Reinhold Publishing, 1967), has been written with this difficulty in mind. While all due respect has been paid to the standard information on molecular and cellular biology, genetics, and evolution, the book is designed on a "levels-of-organization" framework and deals with the diversity of life, its organization into populations, communities, and ecosystems, with man as an integral part of the biosphere.

Reference must also be made to Charles Elton's classic *Animal Ecology*, [19] which first appeared in 1927 and earned for its author his designation as "the father of animal ecology." It remains of permanent value as a first-rate introduction to the subject, but is recommended here because of Elton's remarkable and refreshing ability as a writer. The clarity, grace, and good-humor found in this early effort are seldom encountered in later writings on ecology.

General ecology is fast becoming a prestigious discipline, quietly maturing within its own boundaries and taking on all the trappings of "big science." In the environmental planning explosion that lies ahead, however, the calm will disappear and the question of its relation to other branches of learning will become more acute. Each seems to have something to contribute. It was Elton who remarked, in discussing the disconcerting tendency of ecology to reach out in every direction, "that it might be worth while getting to know a little about geology or the movements of the moon or of a dog's tail, or the psychology of starlings, or of any of those apparently specialized and remote subjects which are always turning out to be at the basis of ecological problems enocuntered in the field." [20] When the field happens to be within the human sphere of influence, the need is multiplied a hundredfold.

Many disciplines have made humanizing claims upon ecology, and the following remarks are intended to introduce the reader to a few of the most obvious ones.

Geography, as protean and far-ranging a field as ecology itself, has a rich tradition that immediately comes to mind. There were more geographers in attendance at the Wenner-Gren symposium, mentioned earlier, than there were representatives from any other single discipline, and the basic paper on man as an ecological dominant was written by Carl O. Sauer. The structures of "human ecology" and "human geography" often seem to be interchangable, as witnessed by the recent publication of an anthology entitled *Geography as Human Ecology: Methodology by Example*. [21]

Problems of definition and method present serious obstacles. The equation of "environment" with "climate," as in Ellsworth Huntington's *Civilization and Climate* (1915) and *The Mainsprings of Civilization* (1945), has inevitably drawn fire from both social scientists, who fret over the specter of determinism, and from natural scientists, who are uncomfortable with simplified images of the environment. The historic controversy within geography on the issue of environmental determinism versus "probabilism" is the subject of a recent article by O. H. K. Spate.[22]

The problem in anthropology is a similar one and involves the question of whether culture can be explained exclusively on its own terms or only with the inclusion of an ecological frame of reference. Archeologists and physical anthropologists have always dealt with the possible effects of the physical environment on human evolution, and all classical ethnographies include descriptions of the climate, topography, flora and fauna of the area inhabited by the society under study. These descriptions, of course, do not amount to a triumph of synthesis. For an excellent discussion of studies that shed light on the controversy, see Betty Meggers' "Environmental Limitation on the Development of Culture," *American Anthropologist*, 56:801-824.

The only cultural anthropologist who has written extensively in recent years on the theoretical aspects of human ecology is Julian H. Steward. In his *Theory of Culture Change* (Urbana: University of Illinois, 1959), he proposes that the broad areas of human ecology be broken down into three categories: human ecology itself, which would be the concern of the human biologist; social ecology, which would be the domain of the sociologist or social anthropologist; and finally, cultural ecology, which would reflect the interests of the historian of culture. Steward points out that the method and theory on which these fields are dependent are quite different. For a detailed explanation of the concepts and procedures of cultural ecology, see Steward's essay under that heading in the *International Encyclopedia of the Social Sciences* (vol. 4, pp. 337-344). An earlier book by J. W. Bews, a British anthropologist, *Human Ecology*, (London: H. Milford, 1935) also provides perspective.

American sociology has had a long and tempestuous relationship with human ecology. In fact, the phrase itself is said to have its origins in that discipline. In 1924, McKenzie defined ecology as the study of the spatial and temporal relations of human beings as these were affected by the selective, distributive, and accomodative aspects of the environment.[23] In 1936, Robert Ezra Park explained that his use of the term was an attempt to operate between geography and economics and his emphasis was on the biotic or subsocial aspects of human social organization.[24] Here the term is now often referred to in connection with demography and urban geography.

The imagery of general ecology—the web of life, interdependent community, dominant species, and dynamic equilibrium—has been forced to double duty, and while the biologist may be flattered by this attention, he is likely to shudder at some of its results. Amos Hawley, probably the most prominent modern spokesman for the sociological tradition, has defined human ecology as a concern "with the general problem of organization conceived as an attribute of population—a point of view that has been shown to be consistent with a long-standing sociological tradition . . . Although the emphasis is centered on the functional system that develops in a population, it is not intended to exclude concern with spatial and temporal aspects; rather, these aspects are regarded as useful dimensions for the measurement of organization."[25]

By the term "community," for example, Hawley means a segment of human society, a "population which carries on its daily life in a given system of relationships."[26] An ecologist, on the other hand, defines a community as an assemblage of many different species of plants and animals that are interdependent.

The importance of the definition problem is easily discovered by comparing Hawley's *Human Ecology: A Theory of Community Structure* (New York: Ronald Press, 1950) with Lee R. Dice's *Man's Nature and Nature's Man: the Ecology of Human Communities* (Ann Arbor: University of Michigan, 1955). Dice is an ecologist, and the similarity between the books is limited to their titles.

An interesting attempt to sort out some of the difficulties between general ecology and sociology's rendition of human ecology is the subject of a paper by Otis Dudley Duncan entitled "From Social System to Ecosystem."[27] Duncan used a set of four categories—population, organization, environment, and technology (POET!) to describe ecosystem processes, his test case being air pollution in Los Angeles, California. After reviewing the Los Angeles situation, Duncan concluded that "social change and environmental modification occurred in the closest interdependence—so close, in fact, that the two 'levels' of change were *systematically* interrelated. Change on either level can be comprehended only by application of a conceptual scheme at least as encompassing as that of the ecosystem."[28] Perhaps something is in the wind. A very similar paper written by a plant-ecologist, Frank E. Egler,[29] concentrates on the pesticide controversy that followed the publication of Rachel Carson's *Silent Spring* in 1962. Egler claims that ecology has not risen to the needs of society, and to make his case he proposes a framework very much like Duncan's, though better documented and more carefully explained.

The humanities are not well represented in modern work on man's place in nature, despite the almost inexhaustible ramifications of a theme that now pervades every aspect of human life. Here also one finds bricks and mortar—essays on the history of agriculture, detailed monographs on the conservation movement, and studies on the concept of nature in the writings of the transcendentalists, for example—but practically no architecture. One strong exception is Clarence Glacken's *Traces On The Rhodian Shore: Nature and Culture in Western Thought from Ancient Times to the End of the Eighteenth Century*, (Berkeley: University of California, 1967). Glacken is presently chairman of the Department of Geography at Berkeley, and he has spent most of his academic life researching the history of ideas on man and his environment. *Traces on the Rhodian Shore* is the fruit of that effort, and it amounts to a major piece of scholarship. The volume records western man's changing response to three persistent questions. First, is the earth a purposefully made creation? Second, have its climates, its relief, the configuration of its continents influenced the moral and social nature of individuals, and have they had an influence in moulding the character and nature of human culture? Lastly, in his long tenure of the earth, in what manner has man changed it from its hypothetical pristine condition? Restated in terms of general ideas, the focus is on the idea of a designed earth, the idea of environmental influence, and the idea of man as a geographic agent.

It is unfortunate that Glacken stopped with the close of the eighteenth century, and one hopes that he will have much to say on later developments. The task is awesome. Specialization in the study of man, specialization in the study of ecology, technical research on the capacity of man to modify nature, generally of the ad hoc, how-to-do-it variety and written for an audience of practical men—all have their roots in the nineteenth century and all continue to the present day. The need for synthesis has never been greater.

A sampling of other works coming from the humanities, although much less ambitious and comprehensive than Glacken's, should also be mentioned because of their special relation to American studies. Arthur Ekirch's *Man and Nature in America* (New York: Columbia University, 1963), is a brief and readable discussion of some of the main currents in American history within the context of their relation to present environmental problems.

Nature and the American: Three Centuries of Changing Attitudes (Berkeley: University of California, 1957), by Hans Huth, is a useful survey of American attitudes to nature from the Puritan period to the conservation movement. Huth is Curator of Research at the Art Institute of Chicago, an unabashed nature lover, and his study has a strong conservationist flavor. He has drawn upon a very impressive array of primary sources and the work is beautifully illustrated with sixty-four black and white plates.

Leo Marx's *The Machine in the Garden: Technology and the Pastoral Ideal in America* (New York: Oxford University Press, 1967), is a literary theorist's sally into the field. Marx's thought-provoking essay traces the adaptation of the pastoral ideal to the conditions of the new world, its emergence as a distinctively American theory of society, and its subsequent transformation under the impact of industrialism.

A summary for this discussion would be rather awkward, and it seems wise at this point to borrow from Paul Shepard, who once remarked, "The ecology of man has no sacred core to guard from the Philistines. It will be healthiest perhaps when running out in all directions. Its practical significance may be the preservation of the earth and all its inhabitants."[30]

The following references are suggested as a guide to additional reading. None of them appears in the text, although each has a bearing on the ideas discussed there.

Adams, C. C. "Introductory Notes to a Symposium on Relation of Ecology to Human Welfare." *Ecological Monographs* 10 (1940): 307-310.
———. "The Relations of General Ecology to Human Ecology." *Ecology* 16 (1935): 316-335.

Balchin, William G. V., ed. *Geography and Man: A Practical Survey of the Life and Work of Man in Relation to His Natural Environment.* 2nd ed. 3 vols. London: New Era Publishing Co., 1955.

Bates, Marston. "Human Ecology." In *Anthropology Today: An Encyclopedic Inventory,* edited by A. L. Kroeber. Chicago: University of Chicago Press, 1953.

_____. *Man and Nature.* 2nd ed. Englewood Cliffs, N. J.: Prentice-Hall, Inc., 1964.

Note especially "Ecology and Economics," pp. 95-105.

_____. "The Human Ecosystem." In *Resources and Man*, Committee on Resources and Man of the Division of Earth Sciences, NAS-NRC. San Francisco: W. H. Freeman & Co., 1969.

Bertalanffy, Ludwig von. "General System Theory: A New Approach to Unity of Science." *Human Biology* 23 (December 1951): 302-361.

Boulding, Kenneth E. *Principles of Economic Policy.* Englewood Cliffs, N. J.: Prentice-Hall, Inc., 1958.

Note especially "The Ecological Approach in Economic Policy," pp. 14-20.

_____. "Economics and Ecology." In *Future Environments of North America*, edited by F. Fraser Darling and John P. Milton, pp. 225-234. Garden City, N. Y.: The Natural History Press, 1966.

_____. "Economics of the Coming Spaceship Earth." In *Environmental Quality in a Growing Economy*, pp. 3-14. Baltimore: Johns Hopkins Press, 1966.

Burke, Albert E. "Influence of Man Upon Nature—The Russian View: A Case Study." In *Man's Role in Changing the Face of the Earth*, edited by William L. Thomas and others, pp. 1035-1051. Chicago: University of Chicago Press, 1956.

Collingwood, Robin George. *The Idea of Nature.* Oxford: Clarendon Press, 1945.

Daedalus: "America's Changing Environment." XCVI (Fall 1967), Special issue.

Dansereau, Pierre. "Ecological Impact and Human Ecology." In *Future Environments of North America*, edited by F. Fraser Darling and John P. Milton, pp. 425-453. Garden City, N. Y.: The Natural History Press, 1966.

Darling, F. Fraser, ed. *West Highland Survey: An Essay in Human Ecology.* New York: Oxford University Press, 1955.

_____. "The Unity of Ecology." *The Advancement of Science* 20 (November 1963): 297-306.

_____. "A Wider Environment of Ecology and Conservation." *Daedalus* 96 (Fall 1967): 1003-1019.

de Jouvenel, Bertrand. "The Ecology of Social Ideas." In *The Art of Conjecture.* Translated by Nikita Lary, pp. 254-256. New York: Basic Books, 1967.

Dubos, Rene. "Environmental Biology." *Bioscience* 14 (January 1964): 11-14.

_____. "Humanistic Biology." *The American Scholar* 34 (Spring 1965): 179-198.

_____. *Man Adapting.* New Haven: Yale University Press, 1965.

_____. *So Human An Animal*. New York: Charles Scribner's Sons, 1970.

Duncan, Otis Dudley. "Social Organization and the Ecosystem." In *Handbook of Modern Sociology*, edited by Robert E. L. Faris, pp. 37-82. Chicago: Rand McNally & Co., 1964.

_____, and Schnore, Leo F. "Cultural, Behavioral, and Ecological Perspectives in the Study of Social Organization." *American Journal of Sociology* 65 (September 1959): 132-146.

Eyre, S. R. "Determinism and the Ecological Approach to Geography." *Geography* 49 (November 1964): 369-376.

Freilich, Morris. "Ecology and Culture: Environmental Determinism and the Ecological Approach in Anthropology." *Anthropological Quarterly* 40 (January 1967): 26-43.

Gettys, W. E. "Human Ecology and Social Theory." *Social Forces* 18 (May 1940): 469-476.

Gutkind, Erwin A. *Community and Environment: A Discourse on Social Ecology*. London: Watts, 1953.

Hawley, A. H. "Ecology and Human Ecology." *Social Forces* 22 (May 1944): 398-405.

Helm, June. "The Ecological Approach in Anthropology." *American Journal of Sociology* 67 (May 1962): 630-639.

Kates, Robert W., and Wohlwill, J. F., eds. "Man's Response to the Physical Environment." *The Journal of Social Issues* XXII (October 1966), Special issue.

Lewin, Kurt. "Psychological Ecology." In *Field Theory in Social Science*, edited by Darwin Cartwright, pp. 60-86. New York: Harper and Row, 1951.

Lowenthal, David, ed. "Environmental Perception and Behavior." University of Chicago Department of Geography Research Paper No. 109. Chicago: University of Chicago Press, 1967.

Lovejoy, Arthur O. *The Great Chain of Being: A Study of the History of an Idea*. Cambridge: Harvard University Press, 1936.

Malin, J. C. "Ecology and History." *Scientific Monthly* 70 (May 1950): 295-298.

Margalef, R. "On Certain Unifying Principles in Ecology." *The American Naturalist* 97 (November-December 1963): 357-374.

Nash, Roderick. *Wilderness and the American Mind*. New Haven: Yale University Press, 1967.

Pred, Allan. "The External Relations of Cities During 'Industrial Revolution'." University of Chicago Department of Geography Research Paper No. 76. Chicago: University of Chicago Press, 1962.

Reed, John F. "Ecology in Higher Education." *Bioscience* 14 (July 1964): 24.

Russett, Bruce M. "The Ecology of Future International Politics." *International Studies Quarterly* 11 (March 1967): 12-13.

Schnore, Leo F. "Social Morphology and Human Ecology." *American Journal of Sociology* 63 (May 1958): 620-634.

_____. "The Myth of Human Ecology." *Sociological Inquiry* 31 (Spring 1961): 128-139.

_____. *The Urban Scene: Human Ecology and Demography*. New York: The Free Press, 1965.

Schweitzer, Albert. *Out of My Life and Thought: An Autobiography*. Translated by C. T. Campion. New York: Henry Holt, 1933. See especially "Epilogue."

Sears, Paul B. "The Ecology of Man." In *Smithsonian Report for 1958-1959*, pp. 375-398. (Reprint of Condon Lecture, University of Oregon, 1957.)

_____. "Ecology: A Subversive Subject." *Bioscience* XIV (July 1964): 11-13.

_____. "Human Ecology: A Problem in Synthesis." *Science* CXX (December 10 1954): 959-963.

Slobodkin, Lawrence B. "Aspects of the Future of Ecology." *Bioscience* 18 (January 1968): 16-23.

Stauffer, Robert C. "Haeckel, Darwin, and Ecology." *The Quarterly Review of Biology* XXXII (June 1957): 138-144.

Stoddart, D. R. "Geography and the Ecological Approach: The Ecosystem as a Geographic Principle and Method." *Geography* L (July 1965): 242-251.

Teilhard de Chardin, Pierre. *The Phenomenon of Man*. Translated by Bernard Wall. New York: Harper and Row, 1961.

Udall, Stewart L. "The Ecology of Man and the Land Ethic." *Natural History* 74 (June-July 1965): 32-41.

Ward, Barbara. *Spaceship Earth*. New York: Columbia University Press, 1966.

Watt, Kenneth E. F., ed. *Systems Analysis in Ecology*. New York: Academic Press, 1966.

White, Lynn, Jr. "The Historical Roots of Our Ecological Crisis." *Science* 155 (March 10 1967): 1203-1207.

Willey, Basil. *The Eighteenth Century Background: Studies on the Idea of Nature in the Thought of the Period*. Boston: Beacon Press, 1961.

NOTES

[1] W. C. Allee, Alfred Emerson, Orlando Park, Thomas Park, and Karl P. Schmidt, eds., *Principles of Animal Ecology* (Philadelphia: Saunders, 1949). See the introduction and chapter one, which provide a comprehensive and detailed history of the development of ecology through the early 1940s.

[2] A representative sample includes *Design and Environment, Environment, Environment and Behavior, Environmental Science and Technology, Environmental Education,* and the *Journal of Applied Ecology*.

[3] The *New York Times* and *Christian Science Monitor* have environmental reporters; *Time* and *The Saturday Review* have regular environmental sections; The CBS Evening News has recently added an environmental feature.

[4] The most recent edition is David Lowenthal's *Man and Nature* (Cambridge: the Belknap Press of Harvard University Press, 1965). See also Lowenthal's biography, *George Perkins Marsh: Versatile Vermonter* (New York: Columbia University Press, 1958).

[5] See later discussion of Wenner-Gren Conference.

[6] Original edition, New York: Scribner, 1864, p. iii.

[7] Marsh, *The Earth as Modified by Human Action: A New Edition of "Man and Nature"* (New York: Charles Scribner's Sons, 1885), p. 473.

[8] Marsh, *Man and Nature* (1864), p. 44.

[9] Ibid., p. 10.

[10] For the rediscovery of Marsh, see Lewis Mumford's *The Brown Decades: A Study of the Arts in America, 1865-1895* (New York: Harcourt, Brace & Co., 1931), pp. 72-78. See also David Lowenthal's "George Perkins Marsh and the American Geographical Tradition," *Geographical Review* XLIII (2): 207-213.

[11] Marsh, *Man and Nature* (1864), p. 57.

[12] Harold H. and Margaret Sprout, *The Ecological Perspective on Human Affairs, With Special Reference to International Politics* (Princeton: Princeton University Press, 1965), 236 pp. See also *Man-Milieu Relationship Hypotheses in the Context of International Politics* (Princeton: Center for International Studies, Princeton University Press, 1965), by the same authors.

[13] Fred W. Riggs, *The Ecology of Public Administration* (New York: Asia Publishing House, 1962).

[14] Edith Cobb, "The Ecology of Imagination in Childhood," originally published in the Summer 1959 issue of *Daedalus*. The paper is reprinted in Paul Shepard and Daniel McKinley's excellent anthology, *The Subversive Science: Essays Toward an Ecology of Man* (New York: Houghton Mifflin Co., 1969). This collection contains an introduction and thirty-six carefully selected essays, each of which contains references. It also includes twelve pages of suggested readings that are not referred to in the text itself.

[15] Aldous Huxley, "The Politics of Ecology: The Question of Survival" (Santa Barbara: Center For the Study of Democratic Institutions, 1963). See also Huxley's "The Double Crisis" in *Themes and Variations* (New York: Harper, 1950), and Ernest Gruening's "The Political Ecology of Alaska," *Scientific Monthly* LXXIII (December, 1951): 376-386.

[16] For a discussion of the levels-of-organization concept, see S. Dillon Ripley and Helmut K. Buechner, "Ecosystem Science as a Point of Synthesis," Daedalus (Fall 1967): 1192-1199; also J. S. Rowe "The Level of Integration Concept and Ecology," *Ecology* 42 (April 1961): 420-427.

[17] For a discussion of the ecosystem concept, see F. R. Fosberg's "The Island Ecosystem," in *Man's Place in the Island Ecosystem: A Symposium*, ed. F. R. Fosberg (Bishop Museum Press, 1963). See also Francis C. Evans, "Ecosystem as the Basic Unit in Ecology," Science 123 (June 22 1956): 1127-1128.

[18] A. G. Tansley, "The Use and Abuse of Certain Vegetational Concepts and Terms," *Ecology* 16 (1935): 284-307.

[19] The most recent edition (London: Science Paperbacks, Methuen & Co., 1966) contains a special preface which was written by Elton in 1965. The reader is also referred to Elton's *The Ecology of Invasions by Animals and Plants* (New York: John Wiley & Sons, 1958). More than any single work in existence, this book establishes the scientific basis for conversation. In the last two chapters, entitled "The Reasons for Conversation" and "The Conversation of Variety," Elton has summarized six lines of evidence supporting the thesis that stability in ecological systems is a function of species diversity. It is primarily this concept that provides ecology with the ideological status of a resistance movement, highly critical of the concepts of "progress," "development," and the assumption that a constantly expanding economy (which requires an expanding market, labor force, intensified exploitation of resources, etc.) is a measure of national health.

[20] *Animal Ecology*, Science Paperbacks edition, p. 188.

[21] Edited by S. R. Eyre and G. R. J. Jones (London: Edward Arnold Ltd., 1966). In the introduction (pp. 1-29), the editors discuss the history that led to their choice of the title.

[22] O. H. K. Spate, "Environmentalism," *International Encyclopedia of the Social Sciences*, Vol. 4, ed. David L. Sills (New York:The Macmillan Co. and The Free Press, 1968), pp. 93-97.

[23] Roderick D. McKenzie, "The Ecological Approach to the Study of the Human Community," in ed. Robert E. Park, Ernest W. Burgess, and R. D. McKenzie, *The City* (Chicago: University of Chicago Press), pp. 63-79.

24"Human Ecology," *American Journal of Sociology* 42:1.

25Amos H. Hawley, "Human Ecology," *International Encyclopedia of the Social Sciences*, Vol. 4, pp. 328-337.

26Ibid., p. 331.

27*Sociological Inquiry* 31 (Spring 1961): 140-149.

28Ibid., p. 149.

29"Pesticides in Our Ecosystem," *American Scientist*, 52 (March 1964): 110-136. Reprinted in *The Subversive Science*, ed. Shepard & McKinley.

30"Whatever Happened to Human Ecology?" *Bioscience* (December 1967), p. 894.

The Black Revolution
in American Studies

by Saunders Redding

The concept "Black Studies," conceived in frustration and bitterness by an articulate and highly emotional minority, is of questionable validity as a scholarly discipline. It encompasses too much. It presumes no less than the universal social, cultural, and literary history of Blacks from pre-Islamic times to the present and the biological and anthropological linkage of all black people. It presumes, too, a genetic constant, although the theory of a genetic constant has been repudiated by the best scientific minds for a hundred years. The Black Studies concept is action-oriented, and to the extent that it is so oriented it is anti-intellectual. Represented in a mystique called "Negritude," it embraces a heavy, indeed, overriding emotional component that is referred to as "soul force," which force conditions ways of acting, feeling, and thinking that are distinctly racial and that characterize black people wherever they are and under whatever conditions they exist. All black men, therefore, are brothers both in the genetic and spiritual sense.

The advocates of this way of thinking have no corpus of cognitive knowledge to fall back on. They adduce the works of Marcus Garvey (whose recently discovered "lost papers" they cannot wait to get into), the romantic appeal of the Back-to-Africa movement, the position—which is grossly misunderstood—that Franz Fanon takes in *The Wretched of the Earth*, and various statements put forth by the self-exiled Stokely Carmichael. Fortunately few of the advocates of this way of thinking are professional academicians; they lack the authority to dilute the demanding intellectual endeavor that a mastery of black studies requires. This is not to say that they totally lack influence. They are of the Black Revolution, leaders and spokesmen for activist groups and political programs.

They speak their views from respectable platforms, and they publish them in the Black Muslim newspaper *Mohammed Speaks, Black World* (formerly *Negro Digest*), and *Ramparts.*

Many, and perhaps most, black scholars, who are also of the Revolution, neither condemn nor exculpate the non-academic revolutionaires. They say, truthfully enough, that there are emotional components and biases in all humanistic thought and learning, and, having defined them, the job of the academician is to modify or correct them by disseminating true knowledge. They say that Western learning begins from a bias that can be summarized as "Rah, rah, Whites!" and that, proceeding from this, white scholars generally have distorted facts, knowledge, and the truth by excluding Blacks from, or by defaming the role of Blacks in the history and culture of the Western world, and particularly the history and culture of America. Black scholars submit that this is likely due to the Whites' conscience-stricken realization that the ideals—social, political,

and religious: in short, humanitarian— which were and are set forth as the basis for human action and interaction, have been ignored; and the way to ease the abraded conscience is to write American history and to examine American civilization so as to exclude from consideration the victims of this falling away. White scholars have found justification for this exclusion in questionable theories, obsessively rationalized by some of the most eminent American minds from Thomas Jefferson to George F. Kennan, and in dubious psychological and social data and "proof" of black people's inherent inferiority.

This way of thinking has produced several interlocking complementary reactions and results, and black scholars and intellectuals have documented them in recent works that no honest

Professor Saunders Redding

Mr. Redding is Ernest I. White Professor of American Studies and Humane Letters at Cornell University, Ithaca, New York. Previously he held appointments as Professor of American Studies at The George Washington University and of English at Hampton Institute. He has been awarded a Rockefeller Fellowship and has twice been a Guggenheim Fellow. Mr. Redding served as Director of the Division of Research and Publication in the National Endowment for the Humanities, a member of the Editorial Board of American Scholar, and a member of the U.S. Committee for the First World Festival of Negro Art. He has lectured in India, Africa, and throughout the United States. His scholarly publications include No Day of Triumph, They Came in Chains, On Being Negro in America, An American in India, The Lonesome Road, and most recently, for USIA distribution overseas, The Negro.

student of American civilization should ignore. The scholarly caliber of John Hope Franklin's *From Slavery to Freedom* (now updated), of Benjamin Quarles' *The Negro in the Making of America*, and of Kenneth Clark's *Dark Ghetto* is very high. Less scholarly, but important to an understanding of the reactions and results mentioned above is Austin, Fenderson, and Nelson's *The Black Man and the Promise of America*. Then there are certain personal books and an official report: *Manchild in the Promised Land*, by Claude Brown; *Soul on Ice*, by Eldridge Cleaver; *The Autobiography of Malcolm X*; and the *Report of the National Advisory Commission on Civil Disorders*.

The results and the reactions that these books explore and document are social. They document the development and the operation of race prejudice. They present evidence of the American Whites' calculated avoidance of knowledge and learning about American Blacks. They give information about the operation of this willful ignorance in the day-to-day rounds of American life, and about the efforts of Blacks as individuals and as communities to accommodate and to moderate the ignorance of Whites, which is commonly called "racism."

A second result of the exclusion of black people from a role in the drama of American civilization and a place in American history is—or rather, was; for this is not new—the institution of courses in Negro history and literature in Negro high schools and colleges, where white supervision of curricula is minimal and careless. The tradition of studying Negro history and literature is more than a half century old. It goes back to W. E. B. DuBois, the black social historian who, believing that the solution to the "Negro problem was a matter of systematic investigation," tried to induce white institutions (notable the University of Pennsylvania and Harvard) to adopt black courses. He did not succeed, but he did inaugurate (in 1904) the Atlanta University Studies program, which focused on Negro material, and which annually published scholarly monographs and papers on the Negro. DuBois inspired Carter G. Woodson, also a Harvard Ph.D., who founded the Association for the Study of Negro Life and History in 1915, set up a company to publish books about blacks, edited and issued the quarterly *Journal of Negro History* (which the Association still issues), and himself wrote the texts—*The Negro in Our History* and *Negro Makers of History*—most widely used down to the Second World War.

A third result of the neglect of the black experience in American Studies is the Black Student Revolution—a social as well as an intellectual rebellion against the "irrelevance" of so much that passes for education in American institutions of higher learning. The social phase of the Black Student Revolution, like the instruction in black courses in Negro schools, goes back a long way—a fact which Harry Edwards' book, *Black Students*, an excellent account of contemporary temper and attitudes, fails to report on. It goes back to the 1920s. At Lincoln University, at Hampton Institute, and at Shaw University, private black colleges administered and faculty-staffed principally by Whites, students rebelled against the patronizing "missionary" attitudes of their white instructors and against the rigid "etiquette of race" that characterized all their relations with them. White administrators and instructors were said to feel that Blacks were not capable of really mastering the more demanding subjects, and that, perhaps excepting the manual arts, the subjects they were taught by the few black teachers—physical education, music, and a "folk variety of Negro history"—were not worth learning anyway. In short, the rebellion was against the inferior black status per se. The students demanded and gradually got more black administrators and teachers, a modification (at Hampton and Shaw) of the social rules that stigmatized them as irresponsible, sexually irrepressible "children," and increased respect as maturing human beings.

Not until the 1950s, when court decisions and steadily mounting pressures at home and abroad challenged the American status quo, and, among other things, made for a substantial increase in the enrollment of black students in predominantly white colleges—not until then did the intellectual phase of the Black Student Revolution begin to acquire definition. Even now, though, the definition is blurred by social factors and an emotional cloud cover and is rendered imprecise by the rhetoric of revolution. "Soul," "Black nationalism," "Black separatism," and "Black power" have been taken to mean what they seem to mean in the formation of Black Student Unions and Alliances and in the demand—bitterly ironic and cynical—on predominantly white campuses for autonomous Black Studies programs to be directed and taught by Blacks for black students only. In "The Role of Afro-American Education," one of the essays in *Basic Black: A Look at the Black Presence on Campus*, it is argued that "Black Studies must be taught from a black perspective. The spirit of blackness must pervade. . . . Black education must be based on both ideological and pedagogical blackness." The fact that one trained and practicing as a scholar can make such an argument is a measure of the extent to which emotionalism blurs, and, if not checked, will dilute the content that Black Studies must have if it is to attain respectability as a scholarly discipline.

Black Studies can attain that respectability. There are both black and white scholars—at Berkeley, Brown, Harvard, Michigan, Texas, and Yale—who believe this and are working toward that end. They seem agreed that "Black Studies" is a misnomer. They prefer Afro-American Studies, a title designating a body of potentially manageable knowledge focusing upon the experience of black people in America, in, specifically, what is now the United States. Afro-American Studies is not African Studies, which, thanks to the British universities and Berkeley, Boston University and predominantly black Howard University, has been deemed academically respectable for a decade. Afro-American Studies is not conceived as structurally dependent on other area studies, like Latin American Studies, for instance, which is also an independent discipline; or Caribbean Studies, which scholars at the University of the West Indies and the University of Puerto Rico are making distinct and independent.

All this is to say that Afro-American Studies is basically American Studies, an interdisciplinary major that must draw upon relevant knowledge and experience outside the United States. I have suggested elsewhere that a line of historical continuity and development peculiar to what is now the United States has generated a new breed of black man with a new "Americanized" orientation to life, with, demonstrably, a special culture and, one strongly suspects, a different psychological and emotional structure from that of his "brothers" in Africa, in South America, and in the Caribbean. Until scholars conscientiously pursue this line of development, American Studies will remain diminished and of questionable validity. Until this development is pursued, Americans will remain poorly equipped to deal with the problems that confront them. An intellectual pursuit—

any intellectual pursuit—serves a social function too. That, of course, is what education is all about. And when American students black and white complain about lack of "relevance," they are saying that education in America is not preparing them to serve an important social function, and they are saying this no matter what their definition of importance is.

Although the integration of Afro-American Studies with American Studies will probably require a new methodology for the measurable attainment of respectable scholarly performance and achievement, much of the material to be integrated is already at hand. Some of it was produced before the intellectual phase of the black student revolution got under way. The scholars who produced it were aiming at a revision of the American past; they were intent on correcting the errors of fact and the faults of interpretation of other American historians. C. Vann Woodward certainly had this in mind when he wrote *Reunion and Reaction, The Strange Career of Jim Crow*, and *The Burden of Southern History*. So did Leon Litwack in preparing *North of Slavery*, and Kenneth Stampp when he wrote *The Peculiar Institution*. Though all of these works, appearing in the late 1950s and early 1960s, draw upon sources that have been neglected by writers of "standard" American history, none of them begins to fill what American blacks feel to be the most urgent need—that is, the recreation of the American Blacks' history as separate from (but not independent of) the history of American Whites.

There have been efforts along this line, and they continue at a quickened pace. Scholars and intellectuals of both races have turned out more histories of black Americans in the past decade than in the preceding half century. Although Herbert Aptheker's *A Documentary History of the Negro* is good, the editor too often assumes that the collected documents can stand alone and independent of the historical background which produced them. Blaustein and Zangrando do not make this mistake in their more particularized *Civil Rights and the American Negro*, a compendium of legislative acts, court decisions, Executive Orders, and official public policy speeches documenting and illustrating the Negro's struggle for civil rights. The materials in *The Black American*, edited by Leslie H. Fishel, Jr. and Benjamin Quarles, are more discrete; some of them were chosen on the basis of non-historical criteria; but all relate directly or indirectly to the major themes of the book—"the primary role of the Negro in American history and the importance of the Negro's own history in America."

A different class of historical works—many of them first published years ago and now reprinted—were written, as Charles H. Wesley, who co-authored one of them, says, "to create a sense of pride on the one hand and appreciation on the other." In other words, they were written for black Americans. Only rarely do these books avoid the distortions that some of them purposely employ to counterbalance the distortions of white history. Only the very best of them is free of the intellectual and emotional parochialism that characterizes the race chauvinist. The best is Benjamin Brawley's *A Social History of the American Negro*, which is now reprinted after fifty years. Were it updated by a scholar as highly qualified as the original author was, *A Social History* would be all but indispensable. Markedly lesser achievements than Brawley's are Arnold Schuchter's *White Power: Black Freedom*, and recent collections of historical writings edited by Dwight Hoover (*Understanding Negro History*), by Ross Baker (*The Afro-*

American), by Bracey, Meier, and Rudwick (*Black Nationalism in America*), and by Charles E. Wynes (*The Negro in the South Since 1865*). Whether or not St. Clair Drake, a very perceptive black social scientist, is right in describing the "ultimate purpose" of historical works written specifically for the black American audience as "defining ourselves for ourselves" and "getting ourselves together—necessary conditions for an intelligent participation in a democratic society," one thing is certain: these works challenge contemporary scholarship in American Studies with the facts of black Americans' stolen past and contested future.

Upwards of thirty anthologies of literary writings by Blacks have been issued in the last twelve months. Many of these are quickies, collections of contemporary writings published in the hope of riding the wave of the fad for anything Black. Others are intended as textbooks in black literature courses, and the selections are representative of the development of Negro writing as art. Their editors establish both a critical and historical context. *On Being Black*, edited by Charles T. Davis and Daniel Walden has a brilliant critical introduction touching upon the "black aesthetic," and Addison Gayle's anthology, *Black Expression*, has an equally brilliant historical introduction. *Black Voices*, which was edited by Abraham Chapman, and *From the Ashes*, edited by Budd Schulberg, are important because they present work of a whole new crop of black writers heretofore unpublished.

Finally, there are current books that deal with the black American experience from the point of view of traditional scholarly disciplines. Using the methods and tools and providing the insights of psychology, sociology, economics, political science, and cultural anthropology, these books are responsive to the notion of the black American's "difference," and how that difference came to be. The books are "studies," but not all of them deserve the definition. The "black perspective" intrudes, as in Floyd McKissick's *3/5 of a Man*, which Justice William Douglas declares "a must," not because of its scholarly and objective examination of American jurisprudence as it affects the Negro, but because of its "mood . . . which reveals the depth of the anguish and anger in the Black community." In Grier and Poussaint's *Black Rage,* a study of the psychology of black youth, mood is restricted to the authors' introduction. And except for the somewhat sensational title, *The Forty Billion Dollar Negro*, the black perspective is entirely absent from Vivian Henderson's study of the black experience in the American economy.

Taken altogether, the books mentioned in this essay—and dozens not mentioned—are a measure of the deficiencies of most American Studies programs; of the extent to which American scholars have been either oblivious to or inexcusably mistaken about black Americans and the materials and substantive issues involving black Americans. These books suggest, too, the dimensions of the educational revolution that must take place in American Studies and that, hopefully, is now gathering momentum. Adversaries of the revolution have already surfaced, but they will scarcely prevail against the persistent work of even a small handful of dedicated scholars of both races who are rediscovering old, neglected historical facts, publishing and testing new theories in the social sciences, and devising new instruments of scholarly humanistic endeavor. The adversaries of the revolution in American Studies will scarcely prevail, either, against the demands for "relevance" by a great and growing number of students.

The Underdeveloped Discipline: Interdisciplinary Directions in American Urban History

by Dana F. White

In the early days of the Republic, America's premier city historian, New York's Diedrich Knickerbocker, established heroic standards for the craft.

> Thrice happy [he wrote], ... is this our renowned city in having incidents worthy of swelling the theme of history; and doubly thrice happy is it in having such an historian as myself to relate them. For after all, ... cities *of themselves* ... are nothing without an historian. It is the patient narrator who records their posterity as they rise,—who blazons forth the splendor of their noon-tide meridian,—who props their feeble memorials as they totter to decay,—who gathers together their scattered fragments as they rot,—and who piously, at length, collects their ashes into the mausoleum of his own work and rears a monument that will transmit their renown to all succeeding ages.
>
> What has been the fate of many fair cities of antiquity, whose nameless ruins encumber the plains of Europe and Asia, and awaken the fruitless inquiry of the traveller? They have sunk into dust and silence,—they have perished from remembrance for want of an historian! [Irving, 1809: 25]

During the 165 years since Washington Irving penned these satiric lines, scarcely one sizable American city has suffered "for want of an historian." Quite the contrary: most municipalities have had their "ashes" hauled many-a-time "into the mausoleum" of "local history." Although some of these studies have been first rate, the vast majority have been amateurish booster tracts and filiopietistic outpourings. The shelves of almost every big-city library in the land groan under their burden. What is more, particularly during the past twenty years, academic historians have marked out for themselves a special field in "urban history." They have conducted conferences on its nature, state, and future; they have set up an Urban History Group within the American Historical Association that publishes its own *Newsletter;* they have introduced undergraduate and graduate courses in the subject into college and university curricula; and they have written articles, and even texts, in "urban history." More recently still, beginning in the late 1960s, another generation of city historians has come forward to advance a "new urban history." The sheer bulk of this work—both the professional and the amateur—is sure to impress. And yet, at this stage in its evolution, American urban history is almost certain to be judged—depending, inevitably, upon one's perspective and disposition—as being either "underdeveloped" or "developing."

The Early Directions

When the Social Science Research Council published its survey of the state of urban studies among its member disciplines six years ago, the saddest tale of all was told of history. Urban historian Charles N. Glaab (1965) was able to report on the modest development of the craft from its early years to the date of his writing; however, his account stood in sharp contrast with those of the other social sciences. Specialists, both in the long-established fields (e.g., urban sociology and political science) and in the relatively-new ones (urban economics and geography) seemed more adept at establishing general theories and applying systematic analyses than did historians. Alongside of its sister social sciences, urban history appeared singularly eclectic, essentially unstructured, almost devoid of theory.

The long search for a theoretical framework for urban history was set in motion formally over thirty years ago when Arthur M. Schlesinger (1940) called upon his colleagues in the profession to unburden themselves of Turner's outdated frontier thesis and adopt, in its stead, an interpretation of American history along urban lines. Despite its obvious appeals of immediacy and innovation, Schlesinger's urban manifesto, as William Diamond (1941) was quick to point out, really begged the question. The manifesto replaced one unmanageable and, for all practical purposes, indefinable general *causal* force with still another, by substituting "city" for "frontier"; it also encouraged scores of undirected neophytes into a field without boundaries, across which many have been wandering aimlessly ever since. But their stories need not be repeated here, any more than should the historiography of the movement. For the basic outlines in the development of American urban history, from early amateurism to advanced expertise, have already been studied in satisfactory detail, perhaps best by Dwight W. Hoover (1968) in his summary analysis of "The Diverging Paths of American Urban History." In the present essay, the meandering paths will be avoided, so that recently-charted routes may be examined more carefully.

Recent Studies of Urban Growth

A History of Urban America, a compact and readable text, provides both a general survey of and a theoretical basis for beginning work in American urban history. Its aim, authors Charles Glaab and A. Theodore Brown (1967: i) explain, is "to use urban growth as the organizing theme in a study of the American past and to try to discover the historical meaning of that useful but elusive adjective, *urban*." Within the limits that they have set for themselves, Glaab and Brown have been remarkably successful. Their decision to devote eight of ten chapters to the commercial-industrial city of the nineteenth and early twentieth centuries, while sketching out the colonial and metropolitan stages in the remaining two chapters, is—given the secondary sources available to them at the time—both logical and defensible. What is less justifiable, specifically here, but also generally throughout the field, is their total reliance upon the written record to the complete exclusion of visual sources. For the physical dimension of cities, one must turn to that old standard, the *American Skyline* (Tunnard and Reed, 1955), and to John W. Reps' (1969) *Town Planning in Frontier America.* Neither, unfortunately, is entirely satisfactory. Despite its lively narrative and frequent flashes of brilliance, *American Skyline* is marred irreparably by its authors' obsession with the "Golden City," their own peculiar vision of "city beautiful" planning as an essential solution to the postwar urban crisis (a system as inappropriate for metropolitan America as would be a downtown coalition founded upon the divine rights of kings). Reps's survey of town planning from earliest colonial times—Spanish and French, as well as English—to the middle of the nineteenth century is, on the other hand, too narrowly focused upon how cities were established, rather than on what happened within them and to them; still, this is a valuable and a beautiful book, and it is one of the few works concerned specifically with the building of the physical city. Its detailed examinations of the plans of individual cities serve, moreover, to complement well the sweep of centuries as set forth in both *A History of Urban America* and *American Skyline.*

Dana F. White has held a joint appointment at Atlanta University and Emory University as Project Coordinator of the Interinstitutional Program in Social Change since the Fall quarter of 1970. Presently Associate Professor of Urban Studies, Mr. White teaches in the History Department and African and Afro-American Studies Program at Atlanta University and the Graduate Institute of the Liberal Arts at Emory. He was Visiting Professor during the Fall quarters of 1973 and 1974 in the Urban Design Program of Georgia Tech's School of Architecture. Before coming to Atlanta, he spent a year in residence at The Smithsonian Institution (1969-70); and before that he was a member of the History Department at the

Howard L. Preston

State University of New York at Buffalo (1965-69). Professor White's articles have appeared in such publications as Museum News, Technology and Culture, Urban Education, American Studies, *and the* South Atlantic Quarterly. *He edited the January 1974 special issue of* Urban Education, *entitled "Schools as City Shapers." His* Olmsted South: Old South Critic/ New South Planner *is forthcoming, and he is presently at work on a volume illustrating many of the ideas and concepts set forth here, entitled* Urban Structure, Atlanta. *His general field of study is American urban history; his special interest is in the structuring of the modern metropolis.*

Two recent collections of interpretive readings should also be included in any basic list of essential and readily available materials in the urban field. Together, Alexander B. Callow's (1969) *American Urban History* and Allen M. Wakstein's (1970) *The Urbanization of America* contain nearly all of the significant theoretical writings on the subject (including most of those mentioned here); in addition, both provide detailed and specialized articles on topics dealt with only in passing —if at all—by available texts. Wakstein's anthology is particularly valuable. *The Urbanization of America* is more than just a book title; it is also the unifying theme for a series of related topics (roughly chronological in their ordering), arranged to illustrate patterns of urban growth in the United States. Its thematic unity makes the Wakstein volume a valuable guide and handbook for the design of lecture courses and readings seminars in American urban history.

Classroom and Research Projects

The teaching of their subject has always attracted considerable attention among urban historians. Until 1969, when it became obvious to its editors that the saturation point had been reached, the Urban History Group *Newsletter* (1953–) regularly published course descriptions and syllabi, which, in turn, have been surveyed and evaluated both by Bayrd Still and Diana Klebanow (1969) and, more recently and also more critically, by Eric Lampard (1970). What is more, in June of this year, Dwight Hoover's (1971) *Teacher's Guide to American Urban History* is scheduled for publication. Advanced publicity notices promise "a complete program which can be included in the regular United States survey course or used for a special course in American urban history." This title includes information on theory, method, and a basic teacher's reference library of films, filmstrips, books, and simulation games. Various units include narrative, analysis, guidelines for classwork, and a selected bibliography of written and visual materials, supposedly arranged in an adaptable framework for the teacher. Allowing even for the customary hyperbole of advertising promotions, Dwight Hoover's book promises to be a valuable guide, indeed.

Information about research projects currently under way in urban history is also readily accessible. Since 1967, for example, the Urban History Group *Newsletter* has also published lengthy descriptions of dissertation research in progress as well as prospectuses for books and articles; its British counterpart, the *Urban History Newsletter* (1963–), contains an annual "Register of Research in Progress" and periodic surveys of the progress of urban history in various parts of the world. In the United States, the *Historical Methods Newsletter* (1967–) regularly provides valuable articles on new techniques in quantitative analysis, as well as a section given over to brief descriptions of work in progress. Thus, the three newsletters serve as clearing-houses for the exchange of ideas and information; more important still, they indicate shifts in emphasis and direction within the field, well before these changes are recognized and recorded elsewhere.

In Search of a Theory

There remains, of course, the formidable challenge of creating from this already-considerable body of work—what has been achieved to date, what is presently under way, what seems most likely to be done—a comprehensive and manageable theory (even theories) of urban history. The degree of difficulty involved in such an undertaking may, perhaps, best be seen in the published papers of two major conferences that were organized to meet this challenge: one in the United States (Handlin and Burchard, 1963), the other in Great Britain (Dyos, 1968).

The first, a conference sponsored by the Joint Center for Metropolitan Studies of Harvard and MIT in 1961, principally hosted scholars already well-established in the field or in related disciplines. Many of them, by that time, having behind them years of research experience, were more interested in general theory than they were in methodology. Consequently the Conference report, *The Historian and the City*, despite the excellence of many individual contributions, reads now like an abstract treatise, so far removed is much of it from the actual writing of urban history. In an essay on urban form, for example, Sir John Summerson (Handlin and Burchard, 1963: 165-66) suggested the following preparation for an historian studying the physical development of any one city:

> First, he must learn from the geographers the factors of site and situation and the general morphology of the city as it stands. Next he must take possession of whatever the political, economic, industrial and social historians can give him. After that he must master the whole corpus of topographical material—not only maps, but prints, drawings, photographs and descriptions of lost buildings. Last, he must know the city—know its modern face, its ancient monuments and equally, the scraps and fragments which are neither ancient nor monuments but [are] still significant and instructive flotsam from the past. When he has done all this he can begin (though I need hardly say that any historian not totally inhuman will have begun long before).

As the final parenthetical remark indicates, this advice was delivered with conscious irony; in fact, in the pages following, this very distinguished architectural historian begins himself to establish more reasonable limits for just such a hypothetical study. Still, by its very exaggeration, this same paragraph points up an essential failing, not only of this book, but also of many theoretical articles concerned with the writing of urban history. By concentrating upon *what* should be done, to the neglect of *how* it might actually be done, established historians tend often to demand too much and teach too little. They are therefore much less likely to inspire than they are to intimidate or infuriate.

At this stage in the development of the discipline, it might seem more logical to adopt an inductive approach, rather than the deductive: to begin with case studies before attempting to construct general theories. This was done quite well at the second conference noted above, sponsored by the British Urban History Group and held at the University of Leicester in 1966. *The Study of Urban History* (Dyos, 1968), its published proceedings, is comprised mainly of reports on research in progress; less than one-third of the book is given over to theoretical and bibliographical essays. While the projects reported on deal almost exclusively with British towns and cities, the Americanist will still find much to interest him in these pages. He will note obvious similarities between British studies of class stratification and American examinations of social mobility. At the same time, he will discover that cultural and social historians in Great Britain are paying more attention to the physical development of cities, especially to their individual characters and to their aesthetics, than are their colleagues in the States. (That this should be the case is all but inevitable, inasmuch as it is the "crisis of the cities" in this country that continues to attract attention and historians to the field, and its manifestations are more obviously "economic" and "social" than they are "geographic" or "aesthetic.") Still, these articles on the study of the physical city should prove to be most instructive for American readers, and the *The Study of Urban History* itself a valuable addition to any readings seminar or, for that matter, personal reference library. What is more, it points toward what may develop into an acceptable conceptual basis for urban history—a point that would be reached if and when two now-separate lines of investigation converge.

Quantification and "New Urban History"

One line of investigation is well represented by *Nineteenth-Century Cities: Essays in the New Urban History* (Thernstrom and Sennett, 1969), and is also the theme for several similar collections soon to be published. This "new urban history" differs from the "old" in its concentration more upon the processes of social development than on a straight chronological ordering of events, in its emphasis upon quantifiable evidence rather than on standard archival sources, and in its attention to the lower classes and ethnic or racial minorities too often "lost" in traditional accounts. This "sociological history" or "history from the ground up" was prefigured in Eric Lampard's (1961) "American Historians and the Study of Urbanization." Essentially, he called then for the abandonment of the "urban impact" or "problem" approach of the Turner-Schlesinger variety and the adoption, in its place, of a methodology based upon "the study of urbanization as a social process." Clearly, Lampard (1961: 49-50) urged then, "a serious social history of the United States ought to begin with a study of population."

In recent years, historical studies of city populations have dealt mainly with the incidences and processes of social mobility, particularly among racial or ethnic minorities and the lower classes. This emphasis upon patterns of mobility may be traced, at least in part, to the early influence of Stephan Thernstrom's (1964) investigation of several generations of unskilled laborers in nineteenth-century Newburyport, a study which soon became a model of its kind, as well as to his (Thernstrom, 1967 and 1968) theoretical writings on this same theme. Mobility studies seem also to answer current ideological needs. "The idea of the city as a social escalator," as Lampard (1968: 21) has pointed out, ". . may well be the consensus social scientist's substitute for the heroic 'rags to riches' myth propagated by nineteenth century individualists." Of course, there is more to the "new urban history" than mobility studies, but still there does not seem to be quite enough. Most critics of the movement, from hostile traditionalists to sympathetic innovators, have remarked on the "new urban history's" over-reliance on unrefined demographic data, the tedium imposed by the jargon in much of this writing, and its characteristic failure to deal with the human side of society—with, in a word, *soul*. Yet, despite these misgivings, which almost anyone outside the movement is bound to share to a greater or lesser degree, the real achievements of the "new urban history" must be recognized and applauded. For in their work with census schedules, city directories, voting lists, postal records, and the like, these young scholars have discovered a great deal about our cities pasts, have shaped sophisticated tools for further research, and have pointed out much that needs to be done before we can ever really understand what has happened in and to our cities. Just how singular has been its achievement is best apprehended when one recognizes that no other distinctive school or movement has as yet developed in the whole of American urban history. Yet, there are stirrings.

"City-Building" and Process Studies

The study of "urban structuring" would appear to be an even more promising line of investigation. Roy Lubove (1967: 34) has called it "the process of city-building over time" and has demonstrated its workings in his (Lubove, 1969) *Twentieth-Century Pittsburgh;* Charles Glaab (1967) has provided guidelines for future research along this line in his "Historical Perspective on Urban Development Schemes"; and Sam Bass Warner has attempted to build "a scaffolding for urban history" of this order in "If All the World Were Philadelphia" (1968a) and *The Private City* (1968b). What this movement within American urban history *is* remains difficult to define; what *is not* seems to be clear. "Urban structuring" or the "city-building process" is not the same as the "new urban history"; indeed, as Sam Warner (1970: 738) noted in his review of the Thernstrom and Sennett volume, "these essays are the new *social* history . . . Many . . . are not urban history because the urban dimensions of the subjects investigated were not a major concern for their authors." And these "urban dimensions" would necessarily include "the time, place, and role of . . . cities and towns in the larger context of the shifting national network of cities."

In his recent "Dimensions of Urban History," Eric Lampard (1970: 272-78) has identified for "city biographers and teachers of urban history" eleven *elements* essential for "an approach to the study of cities from the study of urbanization"—an updating, basically, of his (1961) "American Historians and the Study of Urbanization." With but one addition, they might well serve as guidelines for work on "urban structuring." The first four "fundamental" and "continuously interacting elements" in Lampard's scheme are population, topography, economy, and social organization; next come political process, civic leadership, and civic culture; then, there are a city's external relations, its image, and its foundations and workings in law; finally, there is the city as physical artifact. That "slippery concept," the "quality of urban life" (Dyos, 1969), rounds out this list of essential elements in the "city-building process" to an even dozen.

At first glance, this long inventory might appear to be a step backwards, a retreat to the lines established in those encyclopedic city histories endlessly churned out by dedicated antiquarians, those interminable laundry lists of social events and political happenings. But it is nothing of the sort. The thrust of this line of investigation is in the opposite direction: *away* from catch-all chronicles and *toward* an understanding of the urbanization process itself through the examination of those distinctive and significant patterns in one city's development that illuminate the larger outlines of American urban history. Selection is central to this approach: selection as practiced in Constance McLaughlin Green's (1957) *American Cities in the Growth of the Nation* and in Asa Briggs's (1963) *Victorian Cities*, in each of which a sequence of carefully-chosen case histories was assembled, so as best to illustrate the patterns of urban development at the national level—in one instance for the United States, in the other for Great Britain. Selection, too, as demonstrated in Sam Warner's (1968b) study of "privatism" during three key periods in Philadelphia's growth—"the town of 1770-1780," the big city of 1830-1860," and "the industrial metropolis of 1920-1930." Selection assures focus; it provides a measure of control over the vast quantities of material available for study; and, ultimately, it suggests topics and areas for comparative analysis.

Boston, one of our better-documented cities, will serve here as a case in point. To begin with, the broad outlines of its physical growth may be traced in Walter M. Whitehill's (1968) topographical history and in the Boston Society of Architects' (1970) recent photographic survey of both the historic city and the new. These two books provide the information and the basic resources (especially the maps in the latter) for a closer look at specific developmental patterns. For one thing, there was the pressing need to provide additional land for future growth, a challenge that Boston attempted to meet in two ways. First came land reclamation with the filling in of the Back Bay, the theme of a recent exhibition at Boston's Museum of Fine Arts (Back Bay Boston, 1969)—in itself a notable contribution to urban history (White, 1970)—and also the subject of Bainbridge Bunting's (1967) architectural history of the area. There followed the push outward into adjacent locales, a process described in Sam Warner's (1962) *Streetcar Suburbs* a book that soon proved itself to be a useful standard for comparative urban land-use histories (Ward, 1962). What was happening to the city's population during these years of rapid change may be determined, at least in part, from the class and ethnic analyses presented in *Nineteenth-Century Cities* (Thernstrom and Sennett, 1969: 125-64; 247-74), and from the accounts of the changing social balance in Roger Lane's (1967) *Policing the City*, Barbara M. Solomon's (1956) *Ancestors and Immigrants*, and Arthur Mann's (1954) *Yankee Reformers in the Urban Age*.

Bostonians themselves have also attracted considerable attention, from scholars and artists alike. Stages in the Irish "invasion" of the city, for example, have been examined in the historical works of Oscar Handlin (1959), William V. Shannon (1966), and Richard J. Whalen (1964); in the novels of Edwin O'Connor dealing with Mayor Curley (1956) and the Kennedys (1966); and in that remarkable apologia by James Michael "Himself" (1957), *I'd Do It Again: A Record of All My Uproarious Days*. Boston's Italian population is the subject of Herbert Gans's (1962) *The Urban Villagers* and, of course, much has been written, fact and fiction, about the city's Brahmin leadership. There are Cleveland Amory's (1947) *Proper Bostonians*, Leon Harris's (1967) scathing biography of Godfrey Lowell Cabot, and Helen Howe's (1965) moving portrayal of *The Gentle Americans* of that same generation; there are also William Dean Howells' (1885) *Silas Lapham*, John P. Marquand's (1937) *George Apley*, and all of Henry James's (1886) *Bostonians*. And this is a mere sample of the historical sources readily at hand for an introduction to the structuring of one American city.

The story of city building in Boston may even be carried on down to the recent urban past—that hard-to-handle historical time span during which, as Oscar Handlin (Handlin and Burchard, 1963: 24) has described it, "the urbanization of the whole society may be in process of destroying the distinctive role of the modern city." How metropolitan Boston has changed, is changing, and ought to change are the subjects of a number of interesting studies: Lloyd Rodwin's (1961) examination of middle-class housing throughout the metropolis; Christopher Rand's (1964) account of the suburban "brain drain" to *Cambridge, USA: Hub of a New World;* and the collected broadsides of Martin Meyerson and Edward Banfield (1966) on *Boston: The Job Ahead.* The changing cityscape as plotted out by Kevin Lynch (1960), and the regional transformation into *Megalopolis* as described by Jean Gottmann (1961). In addition, one might examine the quality of urban life as analyzed by Bernard Taper (1970) in *The Arts in Boston* and as experienced by David McCord (1948) in *About Boston: Sight, Sound, Flavor & Inflection.* Finally, one might look at the city's structure within a cross-cultural framework, as suggested by *Urban Dwelling Environments* (Caminos and others, 1969), in which sixteen localities—eight in Boston and eight in four Latin American cities—are compared imaginatively, if not always convincingly. Again, as with the standard historical sources, the range of available materials is wide.

The city chosen need not have been Boston. As the illustrations accompanying this essay suggest, it might just as well have been any other major American metropolis for which adequate introductory materials were available: Chicago (Mayer and Wade, 1969), Los Angeles (Fogelson, 1967), or New York (Kouwenhoven, 1953; Kaufman, 1970) readily come to mind. The city studied is less important than the approach taken, especially if investigations of "urban structuring" are ever to match and, finally, mesh together with those of the "new urban history." The end result, if and when the two lines meet, will be the real story of our cities—what happened, why and how it came about, and what it was like. At that point, the "underdeveloped discipline" will truly have come of age.

In the four years since this essay first appeared, the "underdeveloped discipline" has failed to "come of age." What has happened to it is still open for debate: whether, on the one side, we have more, albeit better of the same; or whether, as Sam Warner would have it, "our subdiscipline is really in deep trouble" (Bruce M. Stave, "A Conversation with Sam Bass Warner, Jr.," *Journal of Urban History,* I [November 1974], 92).

There has been a marked expansion in "Recent Studies of Urban Growth." Howard P. Chudacoff's *The Evolution of American Urban Society* (Englewood Cliffs, N.J.: Prentice-Hall, Inc., 1975), promoted by its publisher as an exploration into the "New Social History," is a compact and readable synthesis of the most significant recent research in American urban history. In the "Preface" Chudacoff rejects the standard "pathological" interpretations of the city, as advanced by earlier social scientists and echoed by many humanists, to posit a "functional point of view." "My purpose," he explains, "is to emphasize the overriding theme of urbanization—the process of growth and evolution. It is a theme that puts people at the center and that highlights the networks of interaction between urban dwellers and their environment" (p. viii). With so attractive a theme, with two of its nine chapters focusing on the contemporary metropolis, with its judicious sampling of visual materials, Chudacoff's volume should readily supplant Glaab and Brown's survey as the standard text in the field.

Sam Warner's *The Urban Wilderness: A History of the American City* (New York: Harper & Row, 1972) is, strictly speaking, neither text nor survey. Its "basic purpose," as its author describes it, "is to gather together what is now known about cities and to cast that knowledge in the form of a series of present-oriented historical essays which will give the reader a framework for understanding the giant and confusing urban world he must cope with" (p. 4). It is a book, paradoxically, that will be most enlightening for either the neophyte or the expert—those in between will have the most difficulty with it. It is a controversial book. Most of its reviewers have been overwhelmed by it, unwilling to face up to it as it is, and unable to put it into any familiar context. *The Urban Wilderness* is, in a word, "Mumfordian." As Warner himself points out: "A great deal has been learned since Lewis Mumford published his excellent *The Culture of Cities* in 1938, and it is time once again to portray the logic of our urban past" (p. 4). In concept, mood, and even format, *The Urban Wilderness* is *The Culture of Cities* updated. (In a curious way, it serves as a more fitting followup than Mumford's own *The City in History*.) How one responds to *The Urban Wilderness* may well depend on how one reacts to Mumford. On the one side, H. J. Dyos has warned that it is "a little fatuous to attempt too much and, in effect, to take on the whole history of cities at once. . . . At worst, it leads rapidly to 'the city in history', to unhistorical and even apocalyptic visions which, like Mumford's, convey all the images and excitement of a fireworks display that fizzles out in chilling caricature of actuality itself!" ("Agenda for Urban Historians," *The Study of Urban History*, H. J. Dyos, ed. [London: Edward Arnold, 1968], p. 9). On the other side there is Warner, who has described his initial (1950s) response to Mumford: "I read Mumford's *The Culture of Cities* and that just seemed . . . wow . . . that just seemed like so many exciting ideas" ("Conversation . . . ," *JUH,* 1 [November 1974], 89). Whatever the case, whether one is pro- or anti-Mumford or just plain undecided, *The Urban Wilderness* is an innovative and stimulating exploration into present-oriented history. As with all of Warner's work, it is required reading.

While few noteworthy texts have appeared in the past four years, large numbers of readers and anthologies have been published. Fortunately, although there has been a good deal of repetition in selection, a number of collections are conveniently distinguishable according to focus, theme, or period covered. Bayrd Still's *Urban America: A History with Documents* (Boston: Little, Brown and Company, 1974), for example, is a straightforward comprehensive anthology of, for the most part, brief primary sources that are linked together by the editor's running commentary. Raymond A. Mohl and James F. Richardson's *The Urban Experience: Themes in American History* (Belmont, Calif.: Wadsworth Publishing Co., Inc., 1973), on the other hand, is a collection of original essays that treat with the urbanization process, planning, race, ethnicity, labor, social welfare, religion, education, public administration, and politics. Kenneth T. Jackson and Stanley K. Schultz in their *Cities in American History* (New York: Alfred A. Knopf, 1972), have attempted to combine the original and the standard, with 11 of their contributions (from a total of 27) commissioned expressly for this volume. Jack Tager and Park Dixon Goist's *The Urban Vision: Selected Interpretations of the Modern American City* (Homewood, Ill.: The Dorsey Press, 1970), for its part, focuses chiefly upon the key theorists and shapers of the modern (1890 to 1965) metropolis—its planners, architects, social scientists, social and political reformers. More consciously interdisciplinary, more boldly experimental, more urban "studies" than "history," the following are worthy of attention: Alan Trachtenberg, Peter Neill, and Peter C. Bunnell, editors, *The City: American Experience* (New York: Oxford University Press, 1971); Susan Cahill and Michele F. Cooper, editors, *The Urban Reader* (Englewood Cliffs, N.J.: Prentice-Hall, Inc., 1971); and Michael E. Eliot Hurst, editor, *I Came to the City: Essays and Comments on the Urban Scene* (Boston: Houghton Mifflin Company, 1975). Perhaps these experiments with form and format in urban studies will encourage a similar taste for innovation in the traditionally more staid field of urban history.

Under the heading "Classroom and Research Projects," it is worth noting that much more attention has been paid to the latter than to the former during the past four years. Perhaps it is at this point that we ought to recall Sam Warner's warning that "our subdiscipline is really in deep trouble." For much of the élan seems to have gone out of the teaching of urban history. Admittedly, there is a success story to tell: the undergraduate survey of American urban history—the subject of most of the course descriptions and syllabi published in the Urban History Group *Newsletter* from 1953 to 1969, as well as of those circulated for discussion at numerous historical and American studies professional meetings—is now a part of the established curriculum in many colleges and universities. Nevertheless, there is also the story of failure: except for a scattering of graduate seminars, most of them the "special offerings" that "balance" the "teaching loads" of resident urbanists, there is little of urban history in the standard curriculum, especially at the undergraduate level. Seldom now does one learn of innovative offerings in the field, no longer are claims made for urban history "revolutionizing" undergraduate education. Instead, there seems to be more, perhaps better, of the same—with urban history comfortably "established" or "departmentalized." Conversely, of course, one might argue that the field is not in "deep trouble" but that, instead, it is exhibiting signs of disciplinary maturity. The debate is still open.

The research record is brighter. The inauguration in November 1974 of the *Journal of Urban History* as a quarterly publication was a significant addition to the field. Since only two numbers have appeared as of this writing, any definitive judgments would be premature; still, a few observations seem in order. To begin with, the *Journal* offers several innovative features: a coverage that promises to be international in scope; an indication that special thematic/topical numbers are in preparation; an editorial policy for essay reviews, much to be applauded now that the monthly *History: Review of New Books* is available to supplement the usual journal and newspaper reviews; and most important, a series of interviews with practicing urban historians, the first two of which—with Warner, then with

Stephan Thernstrom—make for fascinating reading. Concerning the six articles published in the first two numbers (three each), the following may be said: they covered a variety of topics, time periods, and locations; they were quite short (very probably following the policies set by SAGE Publications, publishers of more than twenty such journals and newsletters) with only one extending to full article length; they range from warmed-over versions of earlier work to solid new contributions in the field. For this reviewer, the article section of the *Journal* is its least promising feature. Compared, for example, with the early numbers of the *Journal of Interdisciplinary History* (even granted its more ambitious format and, it follows, larger budget), this section of the *Journal of Urban History* seems bland, without a distinguishing character to claim as its own. Whether its editors, all young and able practitioners in the field though they be, will prove able to commission or solicit sufficient fresh, quality material for four issues a year may also be questioned. If not, they might expand other sections of the *Journal*—for example, the review essays and/or interviews; then, again, they might turn to new features—such as detailed coverage of professional meetings and conferences (included previously in the British *Urban History Newsletter*); or, they might consider the inclusion of monographic contributions, along the lines of Herbert Gutman's 175-page "The World Two Cliometricians Made: A Review-Essay" of Fogel and Engerman's *Time on the Cross,* for the January 1975 issue of the *Journal of Negro History*. (This last classification, the specialized study between article- and book-length, seems especially appropriate for a publication like the *Journal*.) Given its specialized readership and limited pool of authors, the *Journal of Urban History* will have to chart its own path (street?, avenue?), resist the temptation of proving itself "respectable" according to the standards set by other historical journals, and prove itself the leader and innovator in the field.

The *Historical Methods Newsletter* and the Urban History Group *Newsletter* (USA) remain valuable sources for information on research method and work in progress; however, the *Urban History Newsletter* (UK) is no longer published. Its replacement, the *Urban History Yearbook*, boasts the same competent editor, H. J. Dyos, as well as the same point of origin, the University of Leicester. (Although its scope and significance for British history lie beyond the range of the present essay, both have been analyzed with customary flair and insight by Asa Briggs in his review of its first issue, that for 1974, in "History Goes to Town," *Times Literary Supplement*, December 27, 1974.) Since 1967, SAGE Publications has issued its "Urban Affairs Annual Reviews": two of these volumes were cited in the original version of this essay (Glaab, 1965 and Dyos, 1969); almost any number should contain something for the historian; and the 1973 volume, in particular, *The Urbanization of the Suburbs*, edited by Louis H. Masotti and Jeffrey K. Hadden, will be of special interest. The Council of Planning Librarians (Mrs. Mary Vance, Editor, Post Office Box 229, Monticello, Illinois 61856) lists among its substantial (and sometimes over-priced) inventory of "Exchange Bibliographies" several directly- and many indirectly-related to urban history; similarly, Xerox University Microfilms (300 North Zeeb Road, Ann Arbor, Michigan 48106) has recently issued *Urban Problems: A Catalog of Dissertations* (1974), which lists 1807 separate titles representing a wide range of topics under the general heading of urban studies. Since its September 1972 issue, finally, the *Journal of the American Institute of Planners* has published regularly, under the editorship of John L. Hancock, an important series of biographical analyses of major urban planners, builders, and theorists; historical and contemporary both. This series is already a major reference work in urban design and the history of city planning; what is more, it has begun bridging the gap between the design professions and the humanities.

Urban historians are still "In Search of a Theory," and Brian J. L. Berry may prove to be their best guide since Eric Lampard outlined "The History of Cities in the Economically Advanced Areas" twenty years ago (*Economic Development and Cultural Change*, III [Jan. 1955], 81-136) and Gideon Sjoberg described *The Preindustrial City: Past and Present* (Glencoe, Ill.: The Free Press, 1960), five years thereafter. In *The Human Consequences of Urbanization: Divergent Paths in the Urban Experience of the Twentieth Century* (New York: St. Martin's Press, 1973), Berry delivers even more than he seems to promise. His perspective is world-wide; it is, at the same time, comprehensive yet comprehensible; and, despite its subtitle, it deals intelligently with the nineteenth as well as the twentieth century. Although he challenges many of the basic hypotheses set forth by Lampard and Sjoberg, Berry shares their talent for generalization and synthesis. Thus, *The Human Consequences of Urbanization* stands as that rare commodity: a truly seminal conceptual construct of much of the best work of its own scholarly generation.

Another valuable synthesis by still another urban geographer/historian has appeared since "The Underdeveloped Discipline" was written. David Ward's *Cities and Immigrants: A Geography of Change in Nineteenth-Century America* (New York: Oxford University Press, 1971) is a "how to" book divided into two roughly-equal parts: the first (pp. 3-83) presents a general overview of the urbanization process at the national level; the second (pp. 85-150) examines the impact of urbanization upon the individual city and its various quarters and districts. Both halves of *Cities and Immigrants* have much to recommend them; still, the second part is the more original, it is the easier to comprehend, and it is the more likely to be of direct aid to the researcher in the field.

Blake McKelvey's *American Urbanization: A Comparative History* (Glenview, Ill.: Scott, Foresman and Company, 1973) is more difficult to categorize or summarize. Suffice it to say that it poses new and important questions concerning comparative analysis; that, as with all of McKelvey's work, it reflects prodigious reading and a singular talent for compression; and that, in all, it is a valuable and challenging essay into new areas, both for the reader and for the author himself— one of the "founding fathers" of American urban history. *The Victorian City: Images and Realities* (London: Routledge & Kegan Paul, 1973), edited by H. J. Dyos and Michael Wolff in two opulent volumes ($85 the set), for its part, is less comparative than suggestive, more "Victorian" than "City." All the same, it represents a landmark publication in urban history and should be examined (for its visual content alone) by any one seriously interested in the study of cities.

Indicative, perhaps, of the newly-gained professional recognition of "Quantification and the 'New Urban History' " was the award of the prestigious Bancroft Prize in American History for 1974 to Stephan Thernstrom's *The Other Bostonians: Poverty and Progress in the American Metropolis, 1880-1970* (Cambridge, Mass.: Harvard University Press, 1973). The second number of the *Jour-*

nal of Urban History (February 1975) sets this work within a thought-provoking framework: initially, with Bruce M. Stave's "A Conversation with Stephan Thernstrom" (pp. 189-215), an overview of Thernstrom's life-work, as well as speculations on his part concerning the future of the methodology that he has done so much to develop and promote; following this interview is Richard J. Hopkin's review essay, "Mobility and the New Urban History" (pp. 217-28), an attempt by a scholar committed to the "new urban history" to measure Thernstrom's latest work against two other major contributions in the field: Peter R. Knights's *The Plain People of Boston, 1830-1860: A Study in City Growth* (New York: Oxford University Press, 1971) and Howard P. Chudacoff's *Mobile Americans: Residential and Social Mobility in Omaha 1880-1920* (New York: Oxford University Press, 1972). As with Warner's *The Urban Wilderness,* the reader's predisposition toward this *type* of historical writing may very well determine his response to Thernstrom's *The Other Bostonians.* Still, what was claimed for Warner's work holds equally true for Thernstrom's: it is required reading for any one seriously interested in American urban history.

There is at work as of this writing, to slip into the jargon of the quantifiers, an "independent variable" that did not exist when "The Underdeveloped Discipline" was first published. And that is, quite simply, the academic furor over Robert W. Fogel and Stanley L. Engerman's *Time on the Cross: The Economics of American Negro Slavery*, 2 volumes (Boston: Little, Brown and Company, 1974). Fogel and Engerman's study, although it does devote one rather insignificant chapter to urban slavery, is beyond the range of this essay, but the mounting scholarly reaction to their claims for "Cliometrics" or "scientific history" is not. (Clio, the "metricians" should recognize, is not only the muse of history: she also claims dominion over Madison Avenue. The "Clio Awards" for "worldwide excellence in advertising" are held each spring in New York City.) After initially favorable reviews, a major promotional campaign in its behalf, and a series of scholarly meetings expressly convened to discuss its findings and implications, *Time on the Cross* became an academic *cause célèbre.* It has since been attacked as being simplistic, facist, and arrogant. (C. Vann Woodward, for example, after an early and positive review of Fogel and Engerman in the *New York Review of Books* [May 2, 1974]), has turned his attention again to our " 'psychohistorians,' our 'cliometricians,' and our crypto-analysts busy with their neat models, parameters, and hypotheses" and suggested that the study of "raw narrative, bereft as it is of 'insight,' might serve to expose them to the terrifying chaos and mystery of their intractable subject and disabuse them of some of their illusion of mastery" [March 6, 1975, p. 12]. Then, too, there is Herbert Gutman's monograph-review of "F+E" that takes up over 75% of the January 1975 issue of the *Journal of Negro History*.) Clearly and justifiably, as far as the present writer is concerned, a reaction against this brand of "Cliometrics" has set in; unfortunately, *Time on the Cross* has been taken by some to represent the direction of all quantitative history. It does not, and the "new urban history" ought not to be dragged into the hassle over "F+E." It has too much to contribute to our subdiscipline.

" 'City Building' and 'Urban Structuring' " might now be better demonstrated in Chicago. Harold M. Mayer and Richard C. Wade's *Chicago: Growth of a Metropolis* (Chicago: University of Chicago Press, 1969), very likely the finest collection of photographs on any one city in print, is now available in paperback.

Carl Condit's *Chicago: Building, Planning, and Urban Technology*, Volume I: *1910-1929*, Volume II: *1930-1970* (Chicago: University of Chicago Press, 1973 & 1974), originally conceived of and written as a single study, neatly supplements the Mayer and Wade volume; of even more significance, *Chicago* is the capstone of Condit's quarter-century study of the city that is truly his own. Finally, and conveniently, there is Thomas J. Schlereths' "Regional Studies in America: The Chicago Model," (see pp. 224-237, herein) which surveys the sources available, thus obviating the necessity for doing the same here.

Whether "in its general outlines, as well as in many of its specific dimensions, the Chicago story, 1871-1919, is the national story," as Thomas Schlereth asserts (p. 225), is open to question. That the record of its Black population has been viewed in like manner by most historians is, however, beyond doubt. The story of Afro-Americans in urban America, or in any one of its cities, has been written with one eye on Chicago and/or Harlem—as distinguished from New York, since Brooklyn has been largely ignored. The historiography of Black urbanization has been, until quite recently, a saga of the "rise of the ghetto."

It is time now, John W. Blassingame has suggested, for scholars to "take the blinders off and resist the temptation to read allegations of the all-pervasive present day pathology of a Newark or Harlem back into the nineteenth century" and "to ponder anew the meaning of the black urban experience."

> When [Blassingame continues] . . . scholars attempt to study the black community from the inside, focus on people rather than solely on real estate, analyze black hopes as well as black frustrations, and the solutions blacks proposed as well as the problems they faced, we will begin to understand the impact of urbanization on blacks. We need to know as much about black dreams as we do about white fears of blacks, as much about black institutions as housing patterns, black occupations as unemployment and black successes as black failures. Viewing the blacks in Savannah from this perspective suggests that nineteenth-century urban blacks had visions of the future which included self-determination, solving their social problems, educating their children and working and playing in ways which had little to do with later historians spinning fanciful theories (based on the European experience of Jews) about them being locked in "enduring ghettoes." They were building "enduring communities." ("Before the Ghetto: The Making of the Black Community in Savannah, Georgia, 1865-1880," *Journal of Social History*, VI [Summer 1973], 463-88; quotations here from pp. 483 and 484-85).

On the building of these "enduring communities," some of the old sources are still the best. W.E.B. Du Bois's *The Philadelphia Negro: A Social Study* of 1899 (New York: Schocken Books, 1967) and St. Clair Drake and Horace R. Cayton's *Black Metropolis: A Study of Negro Life in a Northern City* in 1945 (New York: Harcourt, Brace and World, Inc., 1970) are two classic social surveys that seem to offer the historian more with each reading. The single most valuable collection of basic sources is Hollis R. Lynch's impressive *The Black Urban Condition: A Documentary History, 1866-1971* (New York: Thomas Y. Crowell, 1973). The essential bibliography for Afro-American history is James M. McPherson and others, *Blacks in America: Bibliographical Essays* (Garden

City, N.Y.: Doubleday & Company, Inc., 1971); but a more recent source, such as Patrick Renshaw's "The Black Ghetto, 1890-1940," *Journal of American Studies*, VIII (April 1974), 41-59, might also be consulted.

Two very dissimilar studies that should facilitate research along the lines suggested by Blassingame are: George A. Davis and O. Fred Donaldson's *Blacks in the United States: A Geographic Perspective* (Boston: Houghton Mifflin, 1975), a work somewhat similar to, but neither as sophisticated nor as specifically urban as David Ward's *Cities and Immigrants*; and David Gordon Nielson's "Black Ethos: The Northern Urban Negro, 1890-1930" (unpublished Ph.D. dissertation, State University of New York at Binghamton, 1972), an able analysis of "the characteristic spirit woven into the web of northern black urban existence during the time, and how it changed" (p. ix). Two very dissimilar studies, indeed—the one geographic, the other literary. But that even such seemingly disparate approaches can be combined to create an original interdisciplinary perspective may be seen in Peter H. Wood's descriptions of early Charles Town in his brilliant *Black Majority: Negroes in Colonial South Carolina from 1670 through the Stono Rebellion* (New York: Alfred A. Knopf, 1974). Once again, *Black Majority* is not, strictly speaking, urban history. It does, nonetheless, set forth "an interdisciplinary route." "I am convinced," Wood confesses, "that any weaknesses which arise in my work from adopting this approach do not come from venturing too far, but rather from failing to proceed far enough" (p. xix).

An interdisciplinary route for urban history may well be the path out of the current "deep trouble," beyond mediocrity, to a true coming of age.

Suggested Reading

(The following documents are referred to by Mr. White in his original essay; those discussed in the postscript are included in the bibliography at the end of this volume. The asterisk indicates the availability of soft-cover editions.—Ed.)

*AMORY, Cleveland (1947) The Proper Bostonians. New York: Dutton.
*Back Bay Boston: The City as a Work of Art (1969). With Essays by Lewis Mumford and Walter M. Whitehill. Boston: Museum of Fine Arts.
*Boston Society of Architects (1970) Boston Architecture. Cambridge: MIT.
*BRIGGS, Asa (1963) Victorian Cities. New York: Harper & Row.
BUNTING, Bainbridge (1967) Houses of Boston's Back Bay: An Architectural History, 1840-1917. Cambridge: Harvard.
*CALLOW, Alexander B. (ed.) (1969) American Urban History: an Interpretive Reader with Commentaries. New York: Oxford.
CAMINOS, Horacio, John F. C. TURNER, and John A. STEFFIAN (1969) Urban Dwelling Environments: an Elementary Survey of Settlements for the Study of Design Determinants. Cambridge: MIT.
CURLEY, James Michael (1957) I'd Do It Again: A Record of All My Uproarious Years. Englewood Cliffs, N.J.: Prentice-Hall.
DIAMOND, William (1941) "On the Dangers of an Urban Interpretation of History." Pp. 67-108 in Eric F. Goldman (ed.) Historiography and Urbanization. Baltimore: Johns Hopkins. Reprinted in CALLOW, 1969.
DYOS, H. J. (ed.) (1968) The Study of Urban History. London: Edward Arnold.

_____(1969) "Some Historical Reflections on the Quality of Urban Life."
Pp. 31-60 in Henry J. Schmandt and Warner Bloomberg, Jr. (eds.) The Quality
of Urban Life. Beverly Hills, Calif.: Sage.

FOGELSON, Robert M. (1967) The Fragmented Metropolis: Los Angeles,
1850-1930. Cambridge: Harvard.

*GANS, Herbert J. (1962) The Urban Villagers: Group and Class in the Life of
Italian-Americans. New York: The Free Press.

GLAAB, Charles N. (1965) "The Historian and the American City: A Bibliographic Survey." Pp. 53-80 in Philip M. Hauser and Leo F. Schnore (eds.) The
Study of Urbanization. New York: Wiley. Reprinted in CALLOW, 1969.

_____(1967) "Historical Perspective on Urban Development Schemes. Pp. 197-
219 in Leo F. Schnore and Henry Fagin (eds.) Urban Research and Planning.
Beverley Hills, Calif.: Sage.

*_____and A. Theodore BROWN (1967) A History of Urban America. New
York: Macmillan.

*GOTTMANN, Jean (1961) Megalopolis: The Urbanized Northeastern Seaboard
of the United States. Cambridge: MIT.

*GREEN, Constance McLaughlin (1957) American Cities in the Growth of the
Nation. New York: Harper & Row.

*HANDLIN, Oscar (1959) Boston's Immigrants, a Study in Acculturation. (rev.
ed.) New York: Atheneum.

*_____and John BURCHARD (eds.) (1963) The Historian and the City. Cam-
bridge: MIT and Harvard.

HARRIS, Leon (1967) Only to God: The Extraordinary Life of Godfrey Lowell
Cabot. New York: Atheneum.

Historical Methods Newsletter (1967–) Department of History, University of
Pittsburgh. Communications to: Historical Methods Newsletter, Dept. of History, University of Pittsburgh, Pittsburgh, Pa. 15213.

HOOVER, Dwight W. (1968) "The Diverging Paths of American Urban History." American Quarterly 20 (Summer): 296-317. Reprinted in WAKSTEIN,
1970.

*_____(1971) Teacher's Guide to American Urban History. Chicago: Quadrangle.

HOWE, Helen (1965) The Gentle Americans 1864-1960: Biography of a Breed.
New York: Harper & Row.

*HOWELLS, William Dean (1885) The Rise of Silas Lapham. New York: Signet
edition.

*IRVING, Washington (1809) Knickerbocker's History of New York. New
York: Capricorn edition.

*JAMES, Henry (1886) The Bostonians. New York: Modern Library edition.

*KAUFMAN, Edgar, Jr. (ed.) (1970) The Rise of an American Architecture.
Essays by Henry-Russell Hitchcock, Albert Fein, Winston Weisman, and Vincent Scully. New York: Praeger.

KOUWENHOVEN, John A. (1953) The Columbia Historical Portrait of New
York: An Essay in Graphic History . . . Garden City, N. Y.: Doubleday.

LAMPARD, Eric E. (1961) "American Historians and the Study of Urbanization. American Historical Review 67 (October): 49-61. Reprinted in CALLOW,
1969.

_____(1968) Review of H. J. Dyos (ed.) The Study of Urban History. Urban History Newsletter No. 11 (December): 20-23.

_____(1970) "The Dimensions of Urban History: A Footnote to the 'Urban Crisis.' " Pacific Historical Review 39 (August): 261-78.

LANE, Roger (1967) Policing the City: Boston 1822-1885. Cambridge: Harvard.

LUBOVE, Roy (1967) "The Urbanization Process: An Approach to Historical Research." Journal of the American Institute of Planners 33 (January): 33-39. Reprinted in CALLOW, 1969.

*_____(1969) Twentieth-Century Pittsburgh: Government, Business, and Environmental Change. New York: Wiley.

*LYNCH, Kevin (1960) The Image of the City. Cambridge: MIT.

*McCORD, David (1948) About Boston: Sight, Sound, Flavor & Inflection. Boston: Little, Brown.

*MANN, Arthur M. (1954) Yankee Reformers in the Urban Age 1880-1900. New York: Harper & Row.

*MARQUAND, John P. (1937) The Late George Apley: A Novel in the Form of a Memoir. New York: Archway.

MAYER, Harold M., and Richard C. WADE (1969) Chicago: Growth of a Metropolis. Chicago: University of Chicago.

MEYERSON, Martin, and Edward C. BANFIELD (1966) Boston: The Job Ahead. Cambridge: Harvard.

*O'CONNOR, Edwin (1956) The Last Hurrah. New York: Bantam.

*_____(1966) All in the Family. New York: Bantam.

RAND, Christopher (1964) Cambridge, USA: Hub of a New World. New York: Oxford.

*REPS, John W. (1969) Town Planning in Frontier America. Princeton: Princeton University.

RODWIN, Lloyd (1961) Housing and Economic Progress: A Study of the Housing Experiences of Boston's Middle-Income Families. Cambridge: Harvard and MIT.

SCHLESINGER, Arthur M. (1940) "The City in American History." American Historical Review 27 (June): 43-66. Reprinted in CALLOW, 1969.

SHANNON, William V. (1966) The American Irish. New York: Macmillan.

SOLOMON, Barbara Miller (1956) Ancestors and Immigrants: a Changing New England Tradition. Cambridge: Harvard.

STILL, Bayrd, and Diana KLEBANOW (1969) "The Teaching of American Urban History." Journal of American History 55 (March): 843-47.

*TAPER, Bernard (1970) The Arts in Boston. Cambridge: Harvard.

*THERNSTROM, Stephan (1964) Poverty and Progress: Social Mobility in a Nineteenth-Century City. New York: Antheneum.

_____(1967) "Up from Slavery." Perspectives in American History 1: 434-39.

*_____(1968) "Urbanization, Migration, and Social Mobility in Late Nineteenth-Century America." Pp. 158-75 in Barton J. Bernstein (ed.) Towards a New Past: Dissenting Essays in American History. New York: Vintage. Reprinted in CALLOW, 1969.

*_____and Richard SENNETT (eds.) (1969) Nineteenth-Century Cities: Essays in the New Urban History. New Haven: Yale.

*TUNNARD, Christopher, and Henry Hope REED (1955) American Skyline: The Growth and Form of Our Cities and Towns. New York: Mentor.

Urban History Group Newsletter (1953—) Department of History, University of Wisconsin-Milwaukee. Communications to: Dept. of History, University of Wisconsin/Milwaukee, Milwaukee, Wisc. 53201.

*WAKSTEIN, Allen M. (ed.) (1970) The Urbanization of America: An Historical Anthology. Boston: Houghton Mifflin.

WARD, David (1962) "A Comparative Historical Geography of Streetcar Suburbs in Boston, Massachusetts and Leeds, England: 1850-1920." Annals of the Association of American Geographers 55 (Fall): 477-89.

WARNER, Sam Bass, Jr. (1962) Streetcar Suburbs: The Process of Growth in Boston, 1870-1900. New York: Antheneum.

——(1968a) "If All the World Were Philadelphia: A Scaffolding for Urban History, 1774-1930." American Historical Review 74 (October): 26-43. Reprinted in WAKSTEIN, 1970.

——(1968b) The Private City: Philadelphia in Three Periods of Its Growth. Philadelphia: University of Pennsylvania.

——(1970) Review of S. Thernstrom and R. Sennett (eds.) Nineteenth-Century Cities. Journal of American History 57 (December): 737-38.

*WHALEN, Richard J. (1964) The Founding Father: The Story of Joseph P. Kennedy. New York: New American Library.

WHITE, Dana F. (1970) " 'Back Bay Boston': A Museum Experiment with Urban History." Museum News 48 (March: 20-25.)

WHITEHILL, Walter Muir (1968) Boston, A Topographical History. (rev. ed.) Cambridge: Harvard.

Recent Trends in the Study of Popular Culture

by John G. Cawelti

The word of the modern, said Walt Whitman, is culture. But Whitman went on in *Democratic Vistas* to criticize the artificiality and elitism he associated with the nineteenth-century ideal of culture, insisting that America develop a broad democratic culture for all the people. Thus, the idea of popular culture has long been a part of American thought. With the development of modern mass communications and the new forms these media have helped bring to birth, the nature, development, and prospects of popular culture assumed an even greater significance. In recent years a younger generation of scholars has responded to the need for more understanding of the whole range of culture and has made the study of popular culture an increasingly respectable area of inquiry. The collection of essays edited by Ray Browne and Ronald Ambrosetti, *Popular Culture and Curricula* (1970) illustrates the number and variety of popular culture courses and programs that have sprung up in the past few years.

Studies in Popular Culture constitute a loose and baggy monster of an area, which involves several disciplines and a large range of potential subject-matter. A sampling of titles from a recent issue of the *Journal of Popular Culture* (Summer 1971) gives some idea of the variety of investigations now underway: "Racism, Formula, and Popular Fiction," "Baseball's Lost Centennial," "Subway Salvation, An Essay in 'Communications Theology'," "The Underground Press in America, 1955-70," "The Leisure Revolution: Recreation in the American City, 1820-1920," and "The Medium is the Message, Or Is It?: A Study of Nathanael West's Comic Strip Novel." Though one presumes that the area of "popular culture" is somewhat more delimited than that of "culture," at least in the latter's broadest anthropological sense, this does not give us much help in arriving at a more precise definition. Unfortunately, the term *popular* has almost as many different varieties of meaning as that notoriously ambiguous word *culture.* *Popular* can mean that which is most used, purchased, enjoyed or practiced by a large number of people. But *popular* can also refer to the culture of non-elite groups. Thus, working-class culture, middle-class culture, or various minority sub-cultures are commonly referred to as popular, and constitute a major area of interest for scholars in the field. It is, of course, quite possible for something to be popular in one sense and not in the other. Best-selling novels are clearly popular culture in our first sense, yet they do not form an important part of working-class culture since novels are purchased and read largely by members of the upper and middle classes. Still a third conception of popular culture defines it as culture which crosses class lines to become part of the life-style of all classes or subcultures in a particular society. This would be the case with highly success-ful television programs and films, for example, or with those musical groups like the Beatles who appealed to almost all groups in American and English society. Fourth, there is the definition of *popular* as the antithesis to the serious, i.e., those aspects of culture related to relaxation, recreation and entertainment and generally opposed to work on the one hand and Art with a capital *A* on the other. Cantor and Wertham state this conception of popular culture in their *History of Popular Culture* (1968):

> Popular culture may be seen as all those things man does and all those artifacts he creates for their own sake, all that diverts his mind and body from the sad business of life. Popular culture is really what people do when they are not working.

Finally, there is that conception of popular culture as defined by the content and character of those media of communication which reach the largest possible

Photo: David Travis

Mr. Cawelti is Professor of English and Chairman of the Committee on General Studies in the Humanities at the University of Chicago. Mr. Cawelti's books are Apostles of the Self-Made Man, The Six-Gun Mystique, *and* Sources of the American Republic. *He has published articles on American Studies and popular culture, and currently serves as Vice-President of the Popular Culture Association. He is working on a large study of some of the most important popular literary formulas, including the detective story, the western, and the spy story.*

publics—i.e., the mass media or mass communications, and the new cultural forms and processes that these media seem to be evolving.

There is enough connection between these various conceptions of popular culture to make the field, various and confused as it is, at least potentially a single area of study. But it will be some time, if ever, before any general theory or discipline of popular culture is likely to emerge. At the present time, studies in popular culture tend to follow one or more of five main subdivisions which have more or less developed out of the various conceptions of popular culture just described. (1) Studies in the popular arts; (2) Studies of popular behavior and attitudes; (3) Mass media and their cultural impact; (4) New trends in contemporary popular culture; (5) Theory of popular culture.

The Popular Arts

The popular arts consist of those media and forms which have a broad general appeal to members of most classes in the society. While some scholars feel that the popular arts, in the contemporary sense, did not come into existence until the widespread distribution of printing in the seventeenth and eighteenth centuries, others would argue that the contemporary popular arts exist in a tradition of popular entertainment at least as old as the mass spectacles of the Roman empire. Actually, our systematic knowledge of the popular artistic tradition in Western civilization is too fragmentary to resolve such questions. While a wealth of specialized studies of certain popular arts in particular periods exist, there is great need of a synthesis of this material. However, such a study would be a monumental and exhausting chore for an omnivorous scholar.

Our most comprehensive knowledge is of the popular arts of the nineteenth and twentieth centuries. Though systematic academic study has begun only recently, there is a long and significant tradition of criticism and analysis of the popular arts which flowered in the 1920s. Gilbert Seldes' pioneering book on *The Seven Lively Arts* (1924) remains one of the most sympathetic and perceptive analyses of some of the great creations of American popular art. Even the austerely intellectual T. S. Eliot wrote a brilliant essay on Marie Lloyd and the art of the English Music Hall, and George Orwell's studies of detective fiction and boys' weeklies are modern classics. Edmund Wilson, who vehemently denounced addicts of that great popular form, the mystery story, in the 1940s, wrote a number of marvelous essays on such topics as the Winter Garden Burlesque in the twenties. More recent landmarks in the tradition of criticism of the popular arts are Reuel Denney, *The Astonished Muse* (1957) which has a sociological orientation, and Robert Warshow, *The Immediate Experience* (1964) which continues the tradition of perceptive personal criticism, begun by Seldes.

In England, an important tradition of academic criticism of the popular arts was initiated by the work of Prof. and Mrs. F. R. Leavis. [Cf. R. R. Leavis and Denys Thompson, *Culture and Environment* (1933) and Q. D. Leavis, *Fiction and the Reading Public* (1932).] The English tradition has stressed the need for teaching discrimination between the valuable and the meretricious in the popular arts, and for making this kind of instruction a part of the school curriculum. Hall and Whannel, in their useful study of *The Popular Arts* (1965), sum up the central thesis of the English tradition:

It is, therefore, on a training in discrimination that we should place our emphasis. We should think of this as a training for a greater awareness, for a sharper attention to subtle meanings. In this sense it should be distinguished from 'raising the level of taste.' Tastechanging goes on all the time. Calendars with kittens in baskets are replaced by prints of Van Gogh's *Sunflowers* and these in turn by Buffet reproductions. But these shifts in fashion can take place without any great increase in pleasure or understanding. We must also stop talking about the various kinds of art and entertainment as if they were necessarily competitive. Popular music, for example has its own standards . . . If we can begin to recognize different aims and to assess varying achievements with defined limits we shall get rid of much of the mish-mash in between.

As a general discussion of the popular arts in relation to the fine arts, and as a practical series of proposals for making the study of the popular arts a feature of the elementary and secondary school curriculum, Hall and Whannel's *The Popular Arts* is an excellent introduction. Those interested in encountering some of the various kinds of criticism and analysis that have been applied to the popular arts can find a fairly representative spectrum in the following four anthologies: Rosenberg and White, *Mass Culture* (1957); Norman Jacobs, ed., *Culture for the Millions* (1961); Irving and Harriet Deer, *The Popular Arts* (1967); and David Manning White, *Pop Culture in America* (1970).

Though criticism of the popular arts has flourished for many years, it is only in the last two decades that trained historians have begun to write careful and systematic histories of the popular arts, as opposed to semi-popular accounts of some of the more colorful aspects of mass culture, which have long been available. Not surprisingly, the first area to be systematically investigated was popular literature, in Frank Luther Mott's *Golden Multitudes* (1947) and James D. Hart's *The Popular Book* (1950). Since that time there have been a number of important historical studies of various popular arts. Because the bibliography in this area is quite large and growing rapidly, I will mention only two studies which seem to exemplify in different ways what histories of particular popular arts can be at their best: David Grimsted's *Melodrama Unveiled: American Theater and Culture, 1800-1850* (1968), a superb work using traditional methods of literary and historical scholarship, and Albert McLean, *American Vaudeville as Ritual* (1965), a study which attempts to argue the thesis that vaudeville filled the cultural function of helping Americans, and particularly new immigrant groups, to adjust to the new social and psychological imperatives of urban industrial society.

From one point of view, popular culture is but an extension of the province of social history; as social history has evolved, it has escaped the patterns of political-economic periodization and has dealt more directly with the life and culture of the people. By the time of the History of American Life Series, Arthur M. Schlesinger (*The Rise of the City*) would include a chapter on "The Pursuit of Happiness" and Harold U. Faulkner (*The Quest for Social Justice*) on "The People at Play." Nelson M. Blake, who condensed this series into a single volume, has revised his work to include more discussion of "The American Spirit in Arts and Amusements," with specific focii such as "Music and the Machine" (*A History of American Life and Thought*). On a more humble but no less effective level was the English series by Marjorie and C.H.B. Quennell, ranging from *Everyday Life in the Old Stone Age* through more recent eras. A typical definition of popular culture is more readily fulfilled in works dealing with more modern periods. As this series crossed the Atlantic under the editorship of Louis B. Wright, it sponsored a series of works in which period interpretations rested heavily on the materials of popular culture.

Social historians sometimes focused on special aspects of popular culture (e.g., A. M. Schlesinger's study of etiquette books, *Learning How to Behave*), but. more commonly used popular culture as an extension of the traditional data for understanding a particular era, as in Carl Bode's *An Anatomy of American Popular Culture, 1840–60*, a work particularly valuable for its insights into the relation between the leading themes of the popular arts and dominant public attitudes. But it was the indefatigable Russel B. Nye who published in 1970 our first overview of the popular arts in America from the seventeenth century to the present, *The Unembarrassed Muse*. Nye's work, a massive compendium of information and interpretation is the best single introduction to this area of popular culture studies and cannot be recommended enough.

More specialized studies in the popular arts have tended to follow the lines of particular narrative genres or formulas such as the detective story, the Western, the spy story, science-fiction, the soap-opera, or the "gothic" romance. These story types comprise a major proportion of the material of the popular arts and they dominate popular fiction, film, and television. By a somewhat strained analogy, they can be called the ritual myths of the nineteenth and twentieth centuries. The enormous appeal of certain limited formulas as opposed to the infinite possible variety of stories, and the way in which these formulas have changed over the last two hundred years, pose both artistic and cultural questions. That certain narrative formulas have survived the evolution of popular culture suggests that there is some special kind of artfulness in their design. What is the nature of this art and how does it differ from the so-called "serious" novel? Which of the many writers and directors who have worked in these genres have used them to their fullest potential? What are the psychological and cultural reasons for the persistent appeal of certain genres? What do shifting genre patterns reveal about changing attitudes and feelings in the culture? These are the kinds of questions that engage the interest of students of popular formulas.

Though genre studies have long been one of the standard models of literary history, I believe that the honor for the first sustained study of a modern popular formula must go to the historian of detective fiction, Howard Haycraft, whose *Murder for Pleasure* (1941), is still a useful and charming work, though his cultural interpretations are dubious. Haycraft has also edited a very useful anthology of essays, *The Art of the Mystery Story* (1946), which includes classic discussions of the mystery story by some of its most eminent practitioners, including G. K. Chesterton, R. Austin Freeman, Dorothy Sayers and Raymond Chandler. Julian Symons' *The Detective Story in Britain* (1962), the essays on the hard-boiled detective story in David Madden, ed., *Tough Guy Writers of the Thirties* (1968), and the brilliant essay by W. H. Auden, "Guilty Vicarage: Notes on the Detective Story by an Addict" in *Harper's Magazine*, May 1948, pp. 406-12, reprinted in *The Dyer's Hand* (1962) are also important contributions to the interpretation of the detective story. For a fairly comprehensive bibliography of mystery fiction, the reader can consult two large recent volumes, *Who Done It?* by O. A. Hagen (1969) and Jacques Barzun and Wendell Taylor's *A Catalog of Crime* (1971).

Running quickly through a sampling of the more important studies of other genres: for the western, John G. Cawelti's *The Six-Gun Mystique* (1971) attempts to construct a theory of popular formulas and also has a useful bibliography. Particularly good on the western film are Fenin and Everson, *The Western: From Silents to Cinerama* (1962); Jim Kitses, *Horizons West* (1969); and Jean-Louis Rieupeyrout, *La Grande Aventure du Western* (1964). On the spy story, Ralph Harper, *The World of the Thriller* (Cleveland, 1969) is a philosophical and psychological exploration of the experience of the spy thriller. Science-fiction has a rapidly accumulating bibliography. Sam Moscowitz is the Howard Haycroft of "sci-fi"; his *Explorers of the Infinitive* (1963) and *Seekers of Tomorrow* (1966) are informative catalogs of the major trends and writers in science-fiction. More complex in their analytical approach are Kingsley Amis, *New Maps of Hell* (1960), Damon Knight, *Essays on Modern Science Fiction* (1956), and Robert Plank's fascinating psychological study, *The Emotional Significance of Imaginary Beings* (1968). Many other important popular formulas have not been as thoroughly investigated as mystery, the spy thriller, the western, and science-fiction. Our understanding of the popular arts would be greatly enhanced by solid inquiries into such genres as soap opera, "true confessions," the combat story, the horror story, the modern social romance (e.g., Harold Robbins, Grace Metalious, Jacqueline Susann, and others), the historical romance, the contemporary "gothic" romance, the situation comedy, and many other formulas.

Though I have concentrated my discussion mainly on the popular literary arts, these constitute only one portion of the popular arts which also include popular music, many forms of visual arts and especially what might be called the functional arts, ranging from advertising to interior design, from cookery to cosmetics and couture. In this area the reader should particularly consult the pioneering work of John Kouwenhoven, *Made in America* (1948), Russell Lynes, *The Tastemakers* (1954) and *The Domesticated Americans* (1963), as well as Marshall Fishwick and Ray Browne's fascinating *Icons of Popular Culture* (1970). For an excellent introductory bibliography on popular music, see pp. 431-433 of Nye's *The Unembarrassed Muse.*

Finally, in the area of the popular arts, there are many opportunities for significant research into individual creators who have worked in the major popular genres and whose work either achieves a high level of excellence or whose unusual popularity reflects some exceptional sense of the public's attitudes and emotional needs. While writers like Melville, James, Twain, Hemingway, Hawthorne, and Faulkner are discussed in voluminous outpourings of print, very little has been done with such figures of enormous popularity in their periods as Susan Warner, Augusta Jane, Evans Wilson, John B. McCutcheon, Harold Bell Wright, Zane Grey, Edna Ferber, Lloyd Douglas, Frank Yerby, Harold Robbins, or Erle Stanley Gardner, or with writers of considerable excellence who worked in popular genres such as Ernest Haycox, Dashiell Hammett, and Ross Macdonald. Fortunately, some of these omissions are being rectified. Richard Etulain of Idaho State University is working on a study of Ernest Haycox, and doctoral dissertations are underway on Ross Macdonald, Edna Ferber, and a number of other popular writers. In addition, a number of studies of individual figures have already been published. Examples are Philip Durham on Raymond Chandler, G. C. Ramsey on Agatha Christie, Kingsley Amis on Ian Fleming, Arthur Berger on Al Capp, and Robin Wood on the film directors Alfred Hitchcock, Howard Hawks, and Arthur Penn.

Popular Behavior and Attitudes

Just as the study of the popular arts relates to the history of the arts generally, the study of popular behavior shades over into history, sociology and anthropology. In general, the student of popular culture is primarily concerned with the history and sociology of recreation and entertainment, and with other areas such as politics or religion to the extent that they sometimes seem to resemble mass entertainments. Even such serious matters as crime and punishment can have a complex cultural significance as a center of popular interest, as Richard Altick has shown in his fascinating analysis of the nineteenth-century English public's obsession with murder trials, *Victorian Studies in Scarlet* (1970). Actually, aspects of popular behavior and attitudes have been widely studied by historians of different periods for many years. Some idea of the range of these investigations is apparent in the anthology edited by Norman Cantor and Michael Wertham, *The History of Popular Culture* (1968), which covers the field from the Greeks to the present day. Foster Rhea Dulles' *America Learns to Play* (1940) is a more specialized history of American recreation. No discussion of this area would be complete without mention of Leo Lowenthal's highly original work in the field of popular attitudes. Many of his important essays are included in the volume *Literature, Popular Culture, and Society* (1961). The current interest in popular behavior and attitudes has also strongly influenced the teaching of American Studies. At least two series of documentary anthologies designed for students and general readers interested in various periods of American civilization, have emphasized materials illustrative of popular culture: the Doubleday Anchor Documents in American Civilization Series edited by Hennig Cohen and John W. Ward, and the George Braziller series, The American Culture, edited by Neil Harris.

Closely related to the history of popular recreation and entertainment is the study of class cultures. Such studies attempt to isolate and analyze behavior and attitudes by social class or subculture. Much of the work inspired by what Saunders Redding called "The Black Revolution in American Studies" [see herein, pp. 146-151—Ed.] is of this type. There have also been a number of important studies of middle-class and working-class culture at various periods: Louis B. Wright's monumental *Middle-Class Culture in Elizabethan England* (1935); Louis James' *Fiction for the Working Man, 1830-50* (1963); R. K. Webb's *The British Working Class Reader 1790-1848* (1955); Richard Altick's *The English Common Reader* (1957); and Richard Hoggart's superb analysis of English working-class culture under the impact of new mass media, *The Uses of Literacy* (1957). Students of American popular culture have not yet turned their attention to the kind of systematic and sustained analysis of class cultures that have characterized their British counterparts, perhaps because class distinctions are more fluid and harder to pin down in American culture. However, this is a neglected area of investigation for which the English studies listed above can serve as initial models.

The study of leisure and mass entertainment has been primarily carried on by sociologists and their work in this area should be better known to students of American popular culture. A good introduction is the anthology *Mass Leisure*, edited by Eric Larrabee and Rolf Meyersohn (1958) and the more recent essay and bibliography by Meyersohn, "The Sociology of Leisure in the United States: Introduction and Bibliography, 1945-65," *Journal of Leisure Research* 1969, no. 1, pp. 53-68. Sebastian de Grazia's *Of Time, Work, and Leisure* (1962) examines the problem of leisure from a very broad philosophical and historical perspective and is one of the most outstanding works in this area. The sociology of entertainment is well represented by Harold Mendelsohn, *Mass Entertainment* (1966), and in Alvin Toffler, *The Culture Consumers* (1964).

Mass Media and Communications

In many ways the serious study of popular culture began with the investigation of the impact of the mass media of the late 1930s, an inquiry which was initially generated by concern over the role of the media as channels for political and social propaganda. Since that time enormous amounts of energy have been spent on media research from three rather different points of view: (a) by social scientists primarily interested in the cultural process and impact of the media, (b) by commercial interests concerned with the effectiveness of various uses of media for advertising, (c) by those with a professional or vocational interest in the operations of the media, such as teachers and historians of journalism and broadcasting. In addition, a large and growing literature of artistic interpretation and criticism has been stimulated by the media of film with its particular importance as an art form as well as a mode of mass communication. Finally, in the last decade the whole field of mass communication has had to come to grips with the theories of Marshall McLuhan and the approach to media study he represents. Other important scholars in this tradition are Harold Innis and Walter Ong. Obviously, students of popular culture should be aware of as many of the various kinds of media research as possible. Since space will not permit an adequate treatment of this large subject in this paper, I will confine myself to a few introductory suggestions.

I have found Joseph Klapper's *The Effects of Mass Communication* (1961) and Erik Barnouw's *Mass Communication* (1957) the most useful introductions to mass media research. Klapper's book is a summary of research with a large bibliography, while Barnouw provides a good introductory guide to the structure and functions of mass communications. Barnouw is also the author of a major contribution to the history of mass communications, the three volume *History of American Broadcasting* (1966, 1968, 1970). Another interesting approach to the problem of analyzing mass communications is suggested by William Stephenson in *The Play Theory of Mass Communication* (1967), which also contains an excellent bibliography. I do not know of any useful synthesis of the vast amount of commercial research into markets and audiences. Such a study would be of enormous value to students of popular culture. The work of Marshall McLuhan is readily available in his many publications, the most important of which to the student of popular culture are *The Mechanical Bride* (1951), *The Gutenberg Galaxy* (1964), and *Understanding Media* (1964). Since McLuhan's ideas are controversial—to put it mildly—the sensible student will want to consult some of the discussion, both positive and negative, which McLuhan's work has stimulated. A good collection is Raymond Rosenthal, ed., *McLuhan: Pro and Con* (1969).

Of many introductions to film and the special artistic problems of visual media, Ernest Lindgren, *The Art of the Film* (1970) is probably the best. For more complex treatments of film aesthetics, I recommend George Linden, *Reflections on the Screen* (1970), a serious philosophical attempt to differentiate film from other media, and Peter Wollen, *Signs and Meaning in the Cinema* (1969), a good discussion of three major conceptions of film aesthetics. For the history of the film, Kenneth Macgowan, *Behind the Screen* (1965) gives the best insight into the development of the techniques and organization of film production, while Gerald Mast, *A Short History of the Movies* (1971) is more a history of artistic expression. Arthur Knight, *The Liveliest Art* (1959) is perhaps the most general and engaging of brief film histories, though many of its judgments need to be qualified. For the study of the American film, Andrew Sarris, *American Cinema: Directors and Directions, 1929-1968* (1968), though quirky, is an indispensible catalogue of directors and films. Finally, the following works are among those with important insights into film as popular culture: Wolfenstein and Leites, *Movies: A Psychological Study* (1950); Leo C. Rosten, *Hollywood: The Movie Colony and the Movie Makers* (1941); Edgar Morin, *The Stars* (1960); Arthur McClure, ed., *The Movies: An American Idiom* (1971); and Richard Schickel, *The Disney Version* (1968).

The New Pop Culture

Perhaps the most striking cultural trend of recent years is the emergence of a new popular culture which synthesizes some of the traditional forms of popular culture with qualities from the elitist traditions of avant-garde art. This new synthesis manifests itself in many different forms. It appears in the new musical sophistication and social content of the style of popular music created by rock groups like the Beatles. We find it in the use of advertising, comic book and other commercial images by such contemporary artists as Oldenburg, Warhol, Lichtenstein, Wesselman, and many others, the so-called pop artists. Many recent novels and films make ironic and satirical use of traditional popular formulas of adventure and romance—Thomas Berger's "western" *Little Big Man*, made into a film by Arthur Penn, Hohn Bhorman's Kafkaesque gangster film, *Pointblank*, or Arthur Penn's *Bonnie and Clyde*, the savage satire on the epic of war in *Catch-22*, and Kurt Vonnegut's powerful allegories in the mode of traditional science-fiction are just a few examples. This new combination of elite and popular cultural traditions has also inspired the work of a younger generation of critics whose sensibilities reflect this new interest in certain aspects of popular culture. I find Tom Wolfe, Susan Sontag, and Benjamin DeMott the most consistently interesting of these new critics. A good anthology which focuses on the new popular music and illustrates some of the various modes of analysis employed by younger critics is Jonathan Eisen, ed., *The Age of Rock* (1969). There have also sprung up a large number of journals in newspaper format, commonly known as the "underground press" and including such papers as the *Berkeley Barb*, the *Chicago Seed*, and rock journals like *Rolling Stone* and *Crawdaddy*, which specialize in coverage of the new pop cultural scene.

Because of the immediate contemporaneity of these new trends, it is difficult to know whether they simply represent new fashions of the sort that have always cropped up in the history of popular culture, or whether they are symptoms of basic and lasting cultural changes. Recent books which analyze these new developments from various points of view are Leonard Meyer, *Music, the Arts and Ideas* (1967), Theodore Roszak, *The Making of a Counter-Culture* (1969), Charles Reich, *The Greening of America* (1970), and Alvin Toffler, *Future Shock* (1970).

Theories of Popular Culture

Like any other complex area of investigation, popular culture has been approached from a wide variety of theoretical perspectives. In many earlier investigations of popular forms and behavior there was a tendency to operate within various oversimplified theoretical frameworks on the assumption that the popular arts and forms of behavior were simply reflections of social or psychological needs that could easily be explained with the assistance of convenient Marxian or Freudian ideas. Thus, for some of the contributors to the Rosenberg and White anthology on *Mass Culture* (1957) the popular arts were simply opiates for the masses whose primary function was to keep a surly industrial proletariat tranquillized. In the Freudian vein, Martin Grotjahn in his *Beyond Laughter* (1957) saw the popular arts primarily in terms of sexual pathology, as an attempt to resolve oedipal conflicts that is doomed to repetitive failure because it fails to bring the root of the conflicts into consciousness. Both Freudian and Marxian perspectives have been very useful in the analysis of popular cultural materials when used with flexibility and openness. One of the most valuable studies of long-term trends in modern British culture, Raymond Williams' *The Long Revolution* (1960), uses essentially Marxian concepts of analysis. However, like any theoretical framework, Freudian and Marxian analysis in less skillful hands easily becomes dogmatically oversimplified or loosely subjective, or both. I have become convinced that the most fruitful procedure for students of popular culture is not to seek a single all-encompassing theory of popular culture, but to employ as many different analytical methods as possible and to seek ways of integrating these different perspectives. I have attempted to do this with the concept of popular formulas in *The Six-Gun Mystique* (1971) but I am sure that this is only one of many possible ways of bringing together the insights of several different disciplinary methods in the exploration of the forms of popular culture. In the next few years, students of popular culture will surely be exploring some of the new ideas and techniques of cultural analysis that have been developed in Europe, such as the structuralism of Levi-Strauss, the semiology of Roland Barthes. Barthes, himself, has done important work in the analysis of contemporary popular culture—cf. *Systeme de la Mode* (1967) and *Mythologies* (1957), and the comparative phenomenology of such scholars as Paul Ricoeur, [*The Symbolism of Evil* (1967)], Mircea Eliade [*Myth and Reality* (1963)] and Gaston Bachelard, [*The Poetics of Space* (1964) and *The Psychoanalysis of Fire* (1964)]. The recent American book I have found most provocative in its theoretical suggestions for the analysis of popular culture is Morse Peckham's *Art and Pornography* (New York, 1969) which attempts to construct an explanation of the enormous role of pornography in the history of popular culture.

It is too early to tell whether popular culture studies will develop as an independent discipline or will eventually be enfolded back into anthropology, cultural history, American studies and social psychology, but at the present time it is surely one of the liveliest and most stimulating areas on the American academic scene.

Suggested Readings

[All titles marked (*) are available in soft-cover editions. Note: Donald Druker is preparing a full-scale bibliography of studies in Popular Culture which will be published by the Bowling Green University Popular Press.]

*ALTICK, Richard. *The English Common Reader.* Chicago: University of Chicago Press, 1957.

_____. *Victorian Studies in Scarlet.* New York: Norton, 1970.

*AMIS, Kingsley. *The James Bond Dossier.* New York: New American Library, 1965.

_____. *New Maps of Hell.* New York: Harcourt, Brace. 1960.

AUDEN, W. H. *The Dyer's Hand.* New York: Random House, 1962.

BACHELARD, Gaston, *The Poetics of Reverie.* New York: Orion Press, 1969.

*_____. *The Poetics of Space.* New York: Orion Press, 1964.

_____. *The Psychoanalysis of Fire.* Boston: Beacon Press, 1964.

BARNOUW, Erik. *Mass Communication.* New York: Rinehart, 1957.

_____. *A History of American Broadcasting.* 3 vols. New York: Oxford University Press, 1966-1970.

BARTHES, Roland. *Mythologies.* Paris: Editions du Seuil, 1957.

_____. *Systeme de la Mode.* Paris: Editions du Seuil, 1967.

BARZUN, Jacques and Wendell Taylor. *Catalog of Crime.* New York: Harper and Row, 1971.

BERGER, Arthur A. *L'il Abner: A Study in American Satire.* New York: Twayne, 1970.

BLAKE, Nelson M. *A History of American Life and Thought.* New York: McGraw-Hill, 1963.

*BODE, Carl. *The Anatomy of American Popular Culture, 1840-1860.* Berkeley: University of California Press, 1960.

*BROWNE, Ray and Ronald Ambrosetti, eds. *Popular Culture and Curricula.* Bowling Green, Ohio: Bowling Green University Popular Press, 1970.

*CANTOR, Norman and Michael Wertham, eds. *The History of Popular Culture.* New York: Macmillan, 1968.

*CAWELTI, John G. *The Six-Gun Mystique.* Bowling Green, Ohio: Bowling Green University Popular Press, 1971.

*DEER, Irving and Harriet. *The Popular Arts.* New York: Scribner, 1967.

*DeGRAZIA, Sebastian. *Of Time, Work, and Leisure.* New York: The Twentieth Century Fund, 1962.

*DENNEY, Reuel. *The Astonished Muse.* Chicago: University of Chicago Press, 1957.

*DULLES, Foster Rhea. *America Learns to Play.* New York: Appleton-Century, 1940.

*DURHAM, Philip. *Down These Mean Streets a Man Must Go.* Chapel Hill, N.C.: University of North Carolina Press, 1966.

*EISEN, Jonathan, ed. *The Age of Rock.* New York: Vintage Books, 1969.

*ELIADE, Mircea, *Myth and Reality.* New York: Harper and Row, 1963.

ELIOT, T. S. *Selected Essays.* New York: Harcourt, Brace, 1950.

FENIN, George and William Everson. *The Western: From Silents to Cinerama.* New York: Orion Press, 1962.

*FISHWICK, Marshall and Ray Browne. *Icons of Popular Culture.* Bowling Green, Ohio: Bowling Green University Popular Press, 1970.

GRIMSTED, David. *Melodrama Unveiled: American Theater and Culture, 1800–1850.* Chicago: University of Chicago Press, 1968.

*GROTJAHN, Martin. *Beyond Laughter.* New York: McGraw-Hill, 1957.

HAGEN, O. A. *Who Done It?* New York: R. R. Bowker, 1969.

*HALL, Stuart and Paddy Whannel. *The Popular Arts.* New York: Pantheon, 1965.

HARPER, Ralph. *The World of the Thriller.* Cleveland: The Press of Case-Western Reserve University, 1969.

*HART, James, D. *The Popular Book.* New York: Oxford University Press, 1950.

*HAYCRAFT, Howard, ed. *The Art of the Mystery Story.* New York: Simon and Schuster, 1946.

_____. *Murder for Pleasure: The Life and Times of the Detective Story.* New York: Appleton-Century, 1941.

*HOGGART, Richard. *The Uses of Literacy.* Fairlawn, N.J.: Essential Books, 1957.

*JACOBS, Norman, ed. *Culture for the Millions?* Princeton, N.J.: Van Nostrant, 1961.

JAMES, Louis. *Fiction for the Working Man, 1830–50.* New York: Oxford University Press, 1963.

*KITSES, Jim. *Horizons West.* Bloomington: Indiana University Press, 1969.

KLAPPER, Joseph. *The Effects of Mass Communication.* Glencoe, Ill.: The Free Press, 1961.

*KNIGHT, Arthur. *The Liveliest Art.* New York: New American Library, 1959.

*KOUWENHOVEN, John. *Made in America.* Garden City, N.Y.: Doubleday, 1948.

LARRABEE, Eric and Rolf Meyersohn, eds. *Mass Leisure.* Glencoe, Ill.: The Free Press, 1958.

LEAVIS, F. R. and Denys Thompson. *Culture and Environment.* London: Chatto and Windus, 1933.

LEAVIS, Q. D. *Fiction and the Reading Public.* London: Chatto and Windus, 1932.

LINDEN, George W. *Reflections on the Screen.* Belmont, Calif.: Wadsworth, 1970.

*LINDGREN, Ernest. *The Art of the Film.* New York: Collier, 1970.

*LOWENTHAL, Leo. *Literature, Popular Culture, and Society.* Englewood Cliffs, N.J.: Prentice-Hall, 1961.

*LYNES, Russell. *The Tastemakers.* New York: Harper, 1954.

_____. *The Domesticated Americans.* New York: Harper and Row, 1963.

McCLURE, Arthur, ed. *The Movies: An American Idiom.* Cranbury, N.J.: Fairleigh Dickinson University Press, 1971.

*MACGOWAN, Kenneth. *Behind the Screen.* New York: Delta, 1965.

McLEAN, Albert. *American Vaudeville as Ritual.* Lexington, Ky.: University of Kentucky Press, 1965.

*McLUHAN, Marshall. *The Mechanical Bride.* New York: Vanguard Press, 1951.

*_____. *The Gutenberg Galaxy.* Toronto: University of Toronto Press, 1964.

*_____. *Understanding Media.* New York: McGraw-Hill, 1964.

MADDEN, David, ed. *Tough Guy Writers of the Thirties.* Carbondale, Ill.: Southern Illinois University Press, 1968.

*MAST, Gerald. *A Short History of the Movies.* New York: Pegasus, 1971.

*MENDELSOHN, Harold. *Mass Entertainment.* New Haven: College and University Press, 1966.

*MEYER, Leonard B. *Music, the Arts, and Ideas.* Chicago: University of Chicago Press, 1967.

MEYERSOHN, Rolf. "The Sociology of Leisure in the United States: Introduction and Bibliography, 1945–1965." *Journal of Leisure Research* 1 (1969) pp. 53–68.

*MORIN, Edgar. *The Stars.* New York: Grove Press, 1960.

*MOSCOWITZ, Samuel. *Explorers of the Infinitive.* Cleveland: World Publishing Co., 1963.

*_____. *Seekers of Tomorrow.* Cleveland: World Publishing Co., 1966.

MOTT, Frank Luther. *Golden Multitudes.* New York: Macmillan, 1947.

NYE, Russel B. *The Unembarrassed Muse.* New York: The Dial Press, 1970.

*ORWELL, George. *Shooting an Elephant and Other Essays.* New York: Harcourt, Brace, 1950.

PECKHAM, Morse. *Art and Pornography.* New York: Basic Books, 1969.

PLANK, Robert. *The Emotional Significance of Imaginary Beings.* Springfield, Ill.: Thomas, 1968.

RAMSEY, Gordon C. *Agatha Christie, Mistress of Murder.* New York: Collins, 1968.

*RICOEUR, Paul. *The Symbolism of Evil.* Boston: Beacon Press, 1967.

*RIEUPEYROUT, Jean-Louis. *La Grande Aventure du Western.* Paris: Editions du Cerf, 1964.

*ROSENTHAL, Raymond, ed. *McLuhan: Pro and Con.* Baltimore: Penguin, 1969.

*ROSENBERG, Bernard and David Manning White. *Mass Culture.* Glencoe, Ill.: The Free Press, 1957.

ROSTEN, Leo, C. *Hollywood: The Movie Colony and the Movie Makers.* New York: Harcourt, Brace, 1941.

*ROSZAK, Theodore. *The Making of a Counter-Culture.* Garden City, N.Y.: Doubleday, 1969.

*SARRIS, Andrew. *American Cinema: Directors and Directions, 1929–1968.* New York: Dutton, 1968.

*SCHICKEL, Richard. *The Disney Version.* New York: Simon and Schuster, 1968.

SCHLESINGER, Arthur M. and Dixon R. Fox. *A History of American Life.* 13 vols. New York: Macmillan, 1927–48.

*SELDES, Gilbert. *The Seven Lively Arts.* New York: Harper and Brothers, 1924.

*SONTAG, Susan. *Against Interpretation.* New York: Farrar, Strauss and Giroux, 1966.

*_____.*Styles of Radical Will.* New York: Farrar, Strauss and Giroux, 1969.

STEPHENSON, William. *The Play Theory of Mass Communication.* Chicago: University of Chicago Press, 1967.

*SYMONS, Julian. *The Detective Story in Britain.* London: Longmans, Green, 1962.

*TOFFLER, Alvin. *The Culture Consumers.* New York: Macmillan, 1964.

*_____. *Future Shock.* New York: Random House, 1970.

*WARSHOW, Robert. *The Immediate Experience.* Garden City, N.Y.: Doubleday, 1964.

WEBB, R. K. *The British Working Class Reader, 1790–1848.* London: Allen and Unwin, 1955.

*WHITE, David Manning. *Pop Culture in America.* Chicago: Quadrangle Books, 1970.

*WILLIAMS, Raymond. *The Long Revolution.* London: Chatto and Windus, 1960.

*WILSON, Edmund. *Classics and Commercials.* New York: Farrar, Strauss, 1950.

*_____. *The Shores of Light.* New York: Farrar, Strauss and Young, 1952.

*WOLFE, Tom. *Kandy-kolored Tangerine-flake Streamline Baby.* New York: Farrar, Strauss and Giroux, 1965.

*_____. *The Pump House Gang.* New York: Farrar, Strauss and Giroux, 1968.

*WOLFENSTEIN, Martha and Nathan Leites. *Movies: A Psychological Study.* Glencoe, Ill.: The Free Press, 1950.

*WOLLEN, Peter. *Signs and Meaning in the Cinema.* Bloomington: Indiana University Press, 1969.

*WOOD, Robin. *Hitchcock's Films.* New York: Barnes, 1965.

*_____. *Howard Hawks.* Garden City. N.Y.: Doubleday, 1968.

*_____. *Arthur Penn.* New York: Praeger, 1969.

WRIGHT, Louis B. *Middle-Class Culture in Elizabethan England.* Chapel Hill, N.C.: University of North Carolina Press, 1935.

_____, ed. Life in America Series. Volumes on the frontier and colonial America (Wright); nineteenth century (Robert H. Walker); twentieth century (John W. Dodds). New York: Putnam, 1965–67. Some volumes now available in softcover edition from Capricorn.

American Things:
A Neglected Material Culture

by Harold Skramstad

During the past decade American museums have been accused of a variety of sins, ranging from elitism and antiquarianism to sensationalism and neglect of traditional collecting responsibilities. In the heat of the attack on museums for all the things they have not done, and in some cases probably can never do, very little attention has been given the role that the museum, its collections, and its particular point of view, can play in the study of American civilization.

The association between the museum and the university has always been a rather uneasy one. Most traditional historians, and many of their colleagues in American Studies programs, see the museum as a collecting agency where objects with either antiquarian or artistic value are preserved. Unfortunately this perspective is not without validity. On the other hand, the museum curator sees the work of his academic counterpart as overly theoretical, lacking the solidity and specification provided by contact with objects. Because of this, neither institution has been able to reach its full potential.

Only recently have some historians begun to go beyond the written word, to look at "things" or "material culture," as important to the study of American civilization. Among the most important and influential of these was the architectural historian Sigfried Giedion, whose *Mechanization Takes Command* (1948) was significant in its use of everyday objects as primary evidence for his study of the impact of mechanization on Western history. Even more important was the fact that Giedion concerned himself with the effect of mechanization on patterns of everyday life rather than with its impact on great thinkers or literary men. Giedion introduced his "contribution to anonymous history" by writing,

We shall deal here with humble things, things not usually granted earnest consideration, or at least not valued for their historical import. But no more in history than in painting is it the impressiveness of the subject that matters. The sun is mirrored even in a coffee spoon.

In their aggregate, the humble objects of which we shall speak have shaken our mode of living to its very roots. Modest things of daily life, they accumulate into forces acting upon whoever moves within the orbit of our civilization.

The slow shaping of daily life is of equal importance to the explosions of history; for, in the anonymous life, the particles accumulate into an explosive force. Tools and objects are outgrowths of fundamental attitudes to the world. These attitudes set the course followed by thought and action. Every problem, every picture, every invention, is founded on a specific attitude. . . .

For the historian there are no banal things. Like the scientist, the historian does not take anything for granted. He has to see objects not as they appear to the daily user, but as the inventor saw them when they first took shape. He needs the unworn eyes of contemporaries, to whom they appeared marvelous or frightening. At the same time, he has to establish their constellations before and after, and thus establish their meaning.

Giedion's approach, with its very important implications, generally went unnoticed among American historians. Except for the work of such men as Thomas Jefferson Wertenbaker (1938) and Daniel Boorstin (1965), few historians have chosen to go beyond the obvious written sources available to them. Ironically, museums also ignored the import of Giedion's message. Often oblivious to the rich potential inherent in their collections they continued to see the objects in their custody as antiquities valuable for historical or personal associations, or as art objects with a self-contained artistic worth.

The American Studies equivalent of Giedion's work was John Kouwenhoven's *Made in America: The Arts in Modern American Civilization* (1948). Kouwen-

Harold Skramstad is currently the Director of the Chicago Historical Society, Chicago, Illinois. Previously he served as Special Assistant to the Director, The National Museum of History and Technology, Smithsonian Institution, Washington, D.C., and as the Assistant Director of the Smithsonian's graduate program in American Studies. He has in addition taught American Studies at The George Washington University. His research interests include the general study of material aspects of American civilization, the history of American architecture and building art, and the physical development of American cities. Mr. Skramstad's scholarly articles and reviews have appeared in Technology and Culture, The Records of the Columbia Historical Society, The Journal of the Society of Architectural Historians, Museum News, *and* Isis.

hoven used information gleaned from objects as well as from more traditional sources in the formulation of his hypothesis about vernacular and genteel culture in the United States. Both Giedion and Kouwenhoven highlighted the two areas in which the study of objects have the greatest potential for the American historian: cultural history and the history of American technology. In the case of cultural history, a close recording and interpretation of material culture can provide insights into the life of the common man who, while dominant numerically, leaves little or no written record of his existence, and whose activities do not produce a self-conscious literary record.

The Decorative Arts and Architecture

There have been many fragmentary attempts to interpret specific aspects of American culture through the study of material objects, but usually such studies have focused on a particular class of object, rather than on its connection with the rest of society. The decorative arts have been better studied than any other class of objects, since they have been more widely collected and saved by museums because of their antique value. E. McClung Fleming's "Early American Decorative Arts as Social Documents" (1958) set out a number of avenues of research which might be followed in the interpretation of the material object, but unfortunately these have been primarily pursued by art historians, whose first interest is artistic and esthetic, only secondarily viewing the object as an indicator of a "fundamental attitude toward the world." Another basic starting point for exploration of either the fine or decorative arts in America is *The Arts in Early America* (1965). This volume includes an excellent essay by Walter Whitehill on the problems of evaluating the physical objects of the arts, as well as an extensively annotated bibliography. Two serial publications, the annual *Winterthur Portfolio* and the random *Contributions of the Museum of History and Technology* [since August 1969, published as *Smithsonian Studies in History and Technology*], provide the best continuing source of studies on the decorative arts, although to some extent the *Portfolio's* value is limited by its almost exclusive concern with the material culture of elite society and its overall perspective is that of art history rather than cultural history.

Next to the decorative arts, architecture has received the most attention from object-oriented historians. A number of early studies of American architecture— Kimball (1922), Kelly (1924), Waterman (1932), Hitchcock (1939), Shurtleff (1939), and Forman (1948)—made extensive use of first hand experience with the buildings they studied. Hitchcock's study, however, is the only one to go much beyond a descriptive cataloging process, to make useful interpretive statements from the research. His findings broadened the scope of the study of architectural history considerably. Instead of following the well-beaten track to monumental public architecture or quaint colonial homes, studied and restudied by generations of art historians, Hitchcock's field exposure to a wide variety of American structures led him to observe that, "it is in three fields that our achievement is surest and most widely recognized: our industrial architecture, our commercial architecture, and our suburban middle class homes." More recent studies such as Garvan (1951), Bunting (1967), and Barley (1963) have extended the range of architectural studies in rural and urban environments, making extensive use of firsthand study of structures from the point of view of the cultural historian.

While scholarship concerning the decorative arts and architecture has at least begun to make use of material objects, the humbler objects of everyday life generally remain reglected. Students of American folklife have paid some attention to the material culture of everyday life and a stimulating introduction to the relationship of material folklife to American Studies can be found in Glassie (1968) and Dorson (1971). Glassie's study is especially useful in showing the pitfalls of making generalizations from a small body of diverse information; this fault is still a major drawback to most studies of American material culture.

Interpreting America Through its "Things"

Since monographic studies utilizing American material culture are so few and far between, there has been little attempt to interpret the whole of American civilization through the medium of physical objects. The closest thing to such an attempt is Alan Gowans' *Images of American Living: Four Centuries of Architecture and Furniture as Cultural Expression*. Gowans' highly interpretive study is both imaginative and controversial. Beginning with the basic point of view of an art historian, Gowans attempts to read from objects not only their visual meaning, but also the motivations and cultural forces which produced them. In order to interpret American society on a broad scale, Gowans has tried to deal with a large body of physical evidence. However, he tends to use objects studied primarily by art historians as the basis for his generalizations: fine chairs, architect designed houses, et cetera. He transfers artistic judgements into cultural judgements too easily and thus we see a "decadent" work of art quickly become a causal factor in a decadent society. Such generalizations raise the question of whether Gowans' judgements are formed from the objects themselves, or whether the objects are merely illustrative of generalizations gleaned from more traditional written sources.

The study of material objects, while extending the range of American cultural history, is in fact the starting point for any consideration of American technology and its relationship to the rest of society. The technologist's output has always been expressed in things rather than words, and an accurate interpretation of the history of American technology is impossible unless the historian is willing, and able, to confront these objects—whether they be machine tools, bridges, or steam engines.

The most useful introduction to the study of the material culture of American technology is Brooke Hindle's essay, "The Exhilaration of Early American Technology," which appears in *Technology in Early America* (1966). In his essay Hindle asks, "Is it not necessary for the historian to come to terms with the internal life of technology before he seeks to assign title as inventor or to confer other accolades? This requires an end to the prejudice against the 'hardware historian.' It requires an effort to see through the eyes and feel through the hands of the craftsman and mechanic. The social relations of technology must not be neglected; they represent the historian's highest goal, but they are attainable only after the historian has developed a direct understanding of the men and their works." Here Hindle's attitude is much the same as Giedion's; both are asking historians to break down the barrier between words and things. Both feel that historians must develop the same critical sense toward objects that they now use in their study of the written record.

There are, however, some real differences in the nature of material evidence and written evidence which conspire to keep them apart. One of the most important of these is simple availability. While generation after generation of Americans have carefully saved the written record of political events, literary efforts, entrepreneurial activities, and the like, much of the material remains of American civilization has been used up, allowed to wear out, been changed beyond recognition, or destroyed. Only those objects having artistic or antiquarian value have been saved. For this reason most museum collections of objects comprise a very select sample of the material culture of the American past, usually representing only the highest levels of society. Moreover, those museum collections of artifacts which do exist are inadequately catalogued or otherwise recorded. Few museums publish guides to their collections and there is no equivalent of the *National Union Catalog of Manuscript Collections* to guide the historian interested in the study of objects. Lucius Ellsworth's "Directory of Artifact Collections" in Hindle (1966) briefly lists the resources of a number of museums whose subject interests cover the history of technology, providing a good beginning—but it is only a beginning. There is no equivalent listing of museum resources for cultural history. The great bulk of material culture remains uncollected and undiscovered in the field. It is through the process of recording, documenting, and interpreting of this mass of evidence, that the great potential of studying American material culture lies. Only when the cultural or technological historian has a sufficient amount of evidence about a particular class of object to be able to evaluate it properly and generalize from it, be it silver spoons, steam engines, or slave pottery, will the study of objects come of age.

Special research skills must be utilized in order to accomplish this task. Aerial photography is required to locate unrecorded and undocumented sites, whether cultural or technological. Mechanical drawing skills are necessary to record accurately such large objects as buildings so that when the object itself is gone, a usable record will remain. Specialized excavation techniques are required to unearth the information that lies buried beneath the soil. For the study of objects, such skills are just as important as foreign languages are to the historian of comparative culture and as knowledge of the complex language of land patents land grants is to the historian of the colonial period.

Historical and Industrial Archaeology

Two examples of rapidly developing research methods employing combinations of such special skills are historical and industrial archaeology. Both historical and industrial archaeology offer a systematic method of discovering and recording information found in the material remains of the American past. Historical archaeology provides one of the most potentially useful methods for discovering the day to day physical fabric of the past. It is this aspect of American society that is still almost totally neglected due to the dearth of written evidence concerning the pattern of life of the common man who left no diary, never participated in public life, and who never ran afoul of the legal system. The only things he left behind were the material fragments of his life, and when these are pieced together at least a partial sense of his activities will emerge.

In the last several decades, archaeology, with its useful modifications of anthropological techniques, has become recognized as an important tool for the cultural historian (Harrington, 1955). As a result there has been a wholesale assault on colonial and early nineteenth-century archaeological sites in the United States, resulting in a number of useful publications: Cotter and Hudson (1957), Cotter (1959), and Noël Hume, (1969-70). The two volumes by Ivor Noël Hume, *Historical Archaeology* (1969) and *A Guide to the Artifacts of Colonial America* (1969) provide the best starting point for a consideration of the techniques and philosophy of historical archaeology. Another of Noël Hume's works, *Here Lies Virginia: An Archaeologist's View of Colonial Life and History* (1963), provides a model study of the unique kinds of insights available to the historian through study of physical remains. Noël Hume is the first to acknowledge, however, that historical archaeology is merely a tool, not an end in itself, and that the "object itself is of secondary importance. . . . The objects that we dig up are merely clues to the story of past events, pieces of a jigsaw puzzle which, when correctly fitted together, recreate a picture of life as it was lived. . . . "

A familiarity with industrial archaeology provides for the historian of technology the same broadening of scope that historical archaeology gives the cultural historian. Industrial archaeology provides a systematic method of documenting and studying the physical remains of America's industrial and technological past which for the most part are still above ground. To the industrial archaeologist, special recording and interpreting skills such as photography, mechanical drawing, and the history of materials are critical. The size and scale of many technological objects such as bridges, factories and mills, make accurate record keeping imperative, as such artifacts seldom find their way into museums. The best general introductions to the field of industrial archaeology, although oriented to English sites, are the works of Kenneth Hudson, *Industrial Archaeology* (1964) and *Handbook for Industrial Archaeologists* (1967); the best American studies are Robert Vogel's "Industrial Archaeology" (1967) and *The New England Textile Mill Survey* (1972).

Many of the techniques used in historical and industrial archaeology can be useful in the study of other classes of material objects, most prominent among these being architecture. Slowly but surely the study of American architecture is passing from the hands of art historians to a new breed of historian whose approach to the study of buildings is that they are primarily containers of people and events. To these historians, a close examination and recording of the physical fabric of a particular structure is essential to their research. While several theoretical frameworks exist for such studies—Demos (1970) and Rappaport (1969)—there has not yet been enough good fieldwork to result in any significant new publications.

As the documentation of American material culture increases, institutions must rise to the challenge of preserving and making it available for study. The Historic American Buildings Survey and the much more recent Historic American Engineering Record, both housed at the Library of Congress, provide unique sources of documentation of architectural and technological artifacts. Unfortunately there is no such repository or clearing house for the information gleaned from archaeological sites. Museums must broaden their collecting efforts to embrace the entire range of American civilization, and they must make this information easily accessible to scholars of every type.

Academic Object-Orientation

Although still in its infancy, there are many signs that the study of American material culture has already added significantly to the range of more traditional studies of American culture. In works such as John Demos' *The Little Commonwealth* (1970), a perceptive blending of material and written sources has resulted in one of the best interdisciplinary interpretations of the early colonial period. In dealing with more contemporary themes, Tom Wolfe's *Kandy-Kolored Tangerine-Flake Streamline Baby* (1966) demonstrates how insights drawn from a study of new artifact forms are able to increase our understanding of present day American civilization. Mayer and Wade, in their *Chicago: The Growth of a Metropolis* (1969) have worked with an artifact as large and as complex as a city, while Reyner Banham has used his firsthand experience with new forms of architecture to study *Los Angeles: The Architecture of Four Ecologies* (1971). John White, in his *The American Locomotive: An Engineering History, 1830-1880* (1968) has proved that hardware history, if well done, has implications that go far beyond a particular subject, while Carl Condit's *American Building* (1968) demonstrates the success of a study combining the evidence of the physical hardware of building technology with the literature surrounding it.

The impetus to train a future generation of interdisciplinary historians sensitive to the special problems of studying material objects is gaining momentum. The pioneer "object-oriented" interinstitutional graduate programs at the University of Delaware-Winterthur Museum and the New York State Historical Association-State University College at Oneonta have led the way for other programs sponsored by The George Washington University, University of Texas, University of Connecticut, and Boston University, in conjunction with such agencies as the Smithsonian Institution, Old Sturbridge Village, and the New England Society for the Preservation of New England Antiquities.

Several theoretical models have been proposed for the study of material culture—Kubler (1961) and Garvan (1962)—but at present there is simply not enough information about any class of object to allow such theories to be either validated or disproved. Most object-oriented historians do seem to agree, however, that material culture as a discipline cannot stand apart from the written word. Both are basic sources of information, each adding to the range and depth of the other.

One of the most exciting prospects for the future is the possibility of using the interdisciplinary methods of American Studies to bring together the efforts of the university and the museum. It is ironic, that while museums have traditionally collected the objects representing only the thin upper layer of American society, it is within the reach of their critical method and point of view to discover and interpret the lives of those Americans—the craftsman, the technologist, the slave, the common man—who left no written record and whose lives will be revealed only by studying what remains of their homes, their cities, their places of work—the things they left behind. When the university is able to recognize and utilize this valuable and unique resource, truly interdisciplinary studies of American culture will be possible.

Suggested Reading

BANHAM, Reyner. *Los Angeles: The Architecture of Four Ecologies.* New York: Harper & Row, 1971.

BARLEY, M. W. *House and Home.* London: Vista Books, 1963.

BOORSTIN, Daniel J. *The Americans: The National Experience.* New York: Random House, 1965.

BUNTING, Bainbridge. *The Houses of Boston's Back Bay.* Cambridge: Harvard University Press, 1967.

CONDIT, Carl. *American Building.* Chicago: University of Chicago Press, 1968.

Contributions of the Museum of History and Technology. Washington, D. C.: The Smithsonian Institution. Random, December 1959–July 1968. Continued as *Smithsonian Studies in History and Technology.* Random, August 1969– current.

COTTER, John. *Archeological Excavations at Jamestown. . . .Virginia.* Washington, D. C.: Government Printing Office, 1959.

COTTER, John and Paul J. Hudson. *New Discoveries at Jamestown.* Washington, D. C.: Government Printing Office, 1957.

DEMOS, John. *The Little Commonwealth.* New York: Oxford University Press, 1970.

DORSON, Richard M. *American Folklore and the Historian.* Chicago: University of Chicago Press, 1971.

FLEMING, E. McClung. "Early American Decorative Arts as Social Documents," *The Mississippi Valley Historical Review* 45 (September 1958), 276-84.

FORMAN, Henry Chandlee. *The Architecture of the Old South.* Cambridge: Harvard University Press, 1948.

GARVAN, Anthony N. B. *Architecture and Town Planning in Colonial Connecticut.* New Haven: Yale University Press, 1951.

——. "Historical Depth in Comparative Culture Study," *American Quarterly* 14 (Summer 1962), 260-74.

GIEDION, Sigfried. *Mechanization Takes Command.* New York: Oxford University Press, 1948.

GLASSIE, Henry. *Pattern in the Material Folk Culture of the Eastern United States.* Philadelphia: University of Pennsylvania Press, 1968.

GOWANS, Alan. *Images of American Living: Four Centuries of Architecture and Furniture as Cultural Expression.* Philadelphia: J. P. Lippincott, 1964.

HARRINGTON, J. C. "Archaeology as an Auxilary Science to American History," *American Anthropologist* 51 (December 1955), 1121-30.

HINDLE, Brooke. *Technology in Early America: Needs and Opportunities for Study.* Chapel Hill: University of North Carolina Press, 1966.

HITCHCOCK, Henry-Russell. *Rhode Island Architecture.* Providence: Rhode Island Museum Press, 1939.

KELLY, J. Frederick. *Early Domestic Architecture of Connecticut.* New Haven: Yale University Press, 1924.

KIMBALL, Fiske. *Domestic Architecture of the American Colonies and of the Early Republic.* New York: Charles Scribner's Sons, 1922.

KOUWENHOVEN, John. *Made in America: The Arts in Modern American Civilization.* New York: Doubleday and Company, 1948.

KUBLER, George. *Shape of Time*. New Haven: Yale University Press, 1961.

MAYER, Harold M. and Richard C. Wade. Chicago: *The Growth of a Metropolis*. Chicago: University of Chicago Press, 1969.

NOÉL HUME, Ivor. *Colonial Williamsburg Archaeological Series* (Numbers 1 through 6 published). Williamsburg: Colonial Williamsburg, 1969-70.

———. *A Guide to the Artifacts of Colonial America*. New York: Alfred A. Knopf, 1970.

———. *Here Lies Virginia: An Archaeologist's View of Colonial Life and History*. New York: Alfred A. Knopf, 1963.

———. *Historical Archaeology*. New York: Alfred A. Knopf, 1969.

RAPOPORT, Amos. *House Form and Culture*. Englewood Cliffs, N.J.: Prentice Hall, 1969.

SHURTLEFF, Harold R. *The Log Cabin Myth*. Cambridge: Harvard University Press, 1939.

VOGEL, Robert M. "Industrial Archaeology—A Continuous Past," *Historic Preservation* 19 (April-June 1967), 68-75.

———. *The New England Textile Mill Survey*. Washington, D. C.: Historic American Buildings Survey, 1972.

WATERMAN, Thomas A. and John A. Burrows. *Domestic Colonial Architecture of Tidewater Virginia*. New York: Charles Scribner's Sons, 1932.

WERTENBAKER, Thomas J. *The Founding of the Middle Colonies*. New York: Charles Scribner's Sons, 1938.

WHITE, John H. *American Locomotives: An Engineering History, 1830-1880*. Baltimore: Johns Hopkins Press, 1968.

WHITEHILL, Walter M. *The Arts in Early American History: Needs and Opportunities for Study*. Chapel Hill: University of North Carolina Press, 1965.

Winterthur Portfolio. Charlottesville: University Press of Virginia. Annual, 1964-current.

WOLFE, Tom. *The Kandy-Kolored Tangerine-Flake Streamline Baby*. New York: Farrar, Straus & Giroux, 1966.

History, Anthropology, and the American Indian

by Wilcomb Washburn

Twenty years ago, at a conference on early American Indian and white relations sponsored by the Institute of Early American History and Culture at Williamsburg, William N. Fenton looked forward to the day when an Institute for American Indian History and Culture might "arise from the smoke of prairie fires" with perhaps a chair in American enthnology, a press for American Indian languages, and a lectureship in American Indian history. That era has not yet arrived but we have come a long way toward the goal. The writing of American Indian history is thriving. Organizations for those involved in the writing of Indian history have been formed. Indian studies programs have been established at a number of universities. While much of the impetus for the recent support of Indian studies comes not for historical but for racial reasons, the movement appears to be a healthy one, and one that will not die with the waning of racial animosities or concern.

Because of the wide diversity and varied histories of the numerous "tribes, bands, or other identifiable groups of American Indians" (to use the catchall phraseology of the Indian Claims Commission Act), the bulk of the ethnographic and historical literature on the American Indian is devoted to individual tribes rather than to the Indian or to Indian-white relations generally. I will cite a few examples of such works—those primarily historical in content—written by both historians and ethnologists. My main concern is, however, to suggest trends in the writing of Indian history that seem evident amidst the mountains of literature being produced, and to comment upon several problems that bedevil the enterprise.

The first and greatest problem concerns the possibility of writing a good general history of the American Indian. No historian has yet succeeded in producing an unchallengeable model. A recent attempt at a general history of the American Indian is Alvin M. Josephy, Jr.'s *The Indian Heritage of America* (New York: Alfred A. Knopf, 1968). For all its many virtues, it is perhaps too encyclopedic to create a single impression in the mind of the reader. Peter Farb's *Man's Rise to Civilization as Shown by the Indians of North America from Primeval Times to the Coming of the Industrial State* (New York: E. P. Dutton & Co., 1968) is more selective and reflects the author's imaginative concern with problems of broad popular interest (e.g., the Eskimo's adaptation to his environment, the Iroquois' primitive democracy). A weakness of Farb's book is its uncritical acceptance of the theory of cultural evolution enunciated by Elman R. Service, Leslie A. White, and others. Indeed, Service's foreword to the book makes rather extravagant claims for the extent of Farb's contribution to the theory and practice of cultural evolution. Both Josephy and Farb appeal to the general reader though their work is soundly based in the scholarly literature. Another writer whose work is based on scholarly research but who writes for the general reader is William Brandon, author of the narrative for *The American Heritage Book of Indians* (New York, 1961, and issued in paperback by Bantam Books, 1964).

D'Arcy McNickle, a Flathead Indian who is a historian teaching in an anthropology department in Canada, has written a series of slim volumes giving a general overview of the history of Indian-white relations. Beginning in 1949 with *They Came Here First: The Epic of the American Indian* (Philadelphia: Lippincott) and continuing with *Indians and Other Americans: Two Ways of Life Meet*, in conjunction with Harold E. Fey (New York: Harper & Row, 1959, rev. ed., 1970) and *The Indian Tribes of the United States: Ethnic and Cultural Survival*

Mr. Washburn is Chairman of the Department of American Studies at the Smithsonian Institution in Washington, D.C. Until 1965 he was Curator of the Division of Political History at the Smithsonian. He also is Adjunct Professor of American Studies at The American University in Washington and Consultant in Research to the American Studies graduate program at George Washington University. Mr. Washburn was educated at Dartmouth and Harvard, has taught at the College of William and Mary, and was awarded a James B. Reynolds scholarship by Dartmouth College for independent research at London and Oxford, England. He is author of numerous articles on ethnohistory, museology and colonial history, and of numerous books which include The Governor and the Rebel: A History of Bacon's Rebellion in Virginia, Red Man's Land, White Man's Law, *and most recently* The Indian in America.

Smithsonian Institution

(London: Oxford University Press, 1962, issued under the auspices of the Institute of Race Relations), McNickle has provided a valuable general—though not
detailed—guide to the entire range of Indian history. William T. Hagan's brief
survey, *American Indians*, in the Chicago History of American Civilization series
(Chicago: University of Chicago Press, 1961) is an admirable essay on the course
of Indian-white relations in the United States. Chronology is its major organizing
principle and brevity its dominating characteristic.

Despite these examples, I think it is fair to say that the tantalizing possibility
of a successful general history of the American Indian remains unfulfilled. While
historians have failed at the task of producing a synthesis, many have succeeded
admirably in dealing with specific tribes during specific eras. One can do no
more than cite a few examples from the recent past, among which are William T.
Hagan's *The Sac and Fox Indians* (Norman: University of Oklahoma Press,
1958), James C. Olson's *Red Cloud and the Sioux Problem* (Lincoln: University
of Nebraska Press, 1965), Arrell M. Gibson's *The Kickapoos: Lords of the Middle Border* (Norman: University of Oklahoma Press, 1963), and Alvin M.
Josephy, Jr.'s *The Nez Perce Indians and the Opening of the Northwest* (New
Haven and London: Yale University Press, 1965). All such studies add to our
fund of knowledge about different groups of Indians and are the building blocks
upon which a future successful general history will have to be based.

Historians with a Moral Point

Outstanding among a group of historians whose interpretation of Indian-white
relations tends to be oriented toward the government point of view is Francis
Paul Prucha. But his thorough study of *American Indian Policy in the Formative
Years: The Indian Trade and Intercourse Acts, 1790–1834* (Cambridge: Harvard
University Press, 1962) is flawed by too trusting an attitude toward the expressed verbal or written views of the federal government and by too perfunc-
tory a consideration of federal actions which failed to live up to professions of
concern for the rights and welfare of the American Indian. Prucha's ability to see
the best motives in what others regard as a bad cause was most startlingly
evident in his "Andrew Jackson's Indian Policy: A Reassessment," in the *Journal
of American History* LVI (1969), 527–539. His cool, apparently dispassionate
critique of United States Indian policy infuriates those moralists who believe
they see more clearly into the hearts of men than does Father Prucha. While
presenting a strong case against the claimed excesses of his opponents' "devil
theory" of American Indian policy, as he calls it, Prucha substitutes what his
opponents might claim to be an unrealistic "angel theory" in its stead. Prucha is
presently working on a history of United States government relations with the
Indians in the last half of the nineteenth century, and has recently prepared for
the press an impressive study of the manufacture and use of Indian peace med-
als.

Alden T. Vaughan, in his *New England Frontier: Puritans and Indians,
1620–1675* (Boston and Toronto: Little, Brown and Co., 1965), concluded,
after a thorough investigation of the sources, that "the New England Puritans
followed a remarkably humane, considerate, and just policy in their dealings
with the Indians." Vaughan's sympathetic treatment of the colonial New England authorities has aroused a reaction similar to that elicited by Father

Prucha's defense of federal Indian Policy. Not that the conflict is new. Historians from the seventeenth century to the present day have argued bitterly about the causes and effects, facts and interpretations, and rights and wrongs of the Pequot War and King Philip's War in New England. The interpretation of the events of that time is especially difficult because the bulk of the information comes from English sources alone. Those sources express not only hard facts but also vague fears, rumors, and justifications for actions taken. In his *The Northern Colonial Frontier, 1607–1763* (New York: Holt, Rinehart and Winston, 1966), Douglas Leach makes a conscious attempt to consider the importance of cultural differences. He tends to think ethnically rather than judicially in recounting the events of King Philip's War. Leach postulates a "spirit of defiance" on the part of King Philip which "tribe after tribe" soon caught and then joined "the war of extermination against the white men." No judge reviewing the evidence today would jump to so easy a conclusion.

The American Indian has attracted, in addition to historians and anthropologists, numerous intellectual and literary historians who have seen him as part of the New World context within which transplanted Europeans had to function physically, intellectually, and spiritually. Among American scholars who have recently analyzed the meaning of the American Indian in the mind of the white man, the foremost is Roy Harvey Pearce, author of *The Savages of America: A Study of the Indian and the Idea of Civilization* (Baltimore: Johns Hopkins University press, 1953, rev. ed., 1965). The Indian, in Pearce's analysis, evoked in the mind of the transplanted European both the memory of the savage heritage from which he—the white man—had emerged and the consciousness of the continuing savage obstacles which he had to overcome in order to create a civilization worthy of the name on the western shores of the Atlantic.

Henry Nash Smith, in his classic *Virgin Land: The American West as Symbol and Myth*, first printed in 1950 by Harvard University Press, and Leo Marx in his *The Machine in the Garden: Technology and the Pastoral Ideal in America* (New York: Oxford University Press, 1964) have similarly delved into the consequence of Europe's exposure to America's "savage" background. In the view of these scholars of literature, the Indian is scarcely distinguishable from the natural landscape, yet he suffuses it and it him and both the transplanted Europeans. The most recent literary examination of the impact of the Indian upon the white psyche is Leslie A. Fiedler's *The Return of the Vanishing American* (New York: Stein and Day, 1968). Fiedler's book is less about the Indian than about the European settler who confronted him, attempted to convert him, corrupted him, and eventually destroyed him. He conducts the reader on an erudite tour of the impact of the Indian on the American imagination and his discussion of the Pocahontas story is especially perceptive.

Among the younger breed of analysts of the impact of the Indian on the "mind" of America is Bernard Sheehan, whose doctoral dissertation on "Civilization and the American Indian in the Thought of the Jeffersonian Era" (University of Virginia, 1965) is currently being revised for publication. Sheehan's point of view is expressed in two *William and Mary Quarterly* articles entitled "Indian-White Relations in Early America: A Review Essay," XXVI (1969), 267–286, and "Paradise and the Noble Savage in Jeffersonian Thought," XXVI (1969),

327-359. Seeking to avoid the charge of romanticizing the Indian, he has assumed a hardnosed attitude toward any view of Indians of the past which is not consistent with his own unromantic assumptions that the historical Indian was without the special qualities—variously perceived on a value spectrum ranging from diabolical to angelic—often attributed to him. The problem of the nature of the historical Indian is much more complicated than Sheehan assumes. Writers in the literary tradition would do well to consider the anthropologist Alfred Irving Hallowell's classic essay on "The Backwash of the Frontier: The Impact of the Indian on American Culture," in Walker D. Wyman and Clifton B. Kroeber, eds., *The Frontier in Perspective* (Madison: University of Wisconsin Press, 1957).

The Anthropologist's View

The most striking feature concerning the writing of Indian history in recent times has been the emergence of the professional anthropologist as historian. Institutionally the study of the native American has become increasingly a function of the anthropology departments rather than of history departments. Because of the decline of traditional Indian cultures and the growing assimilation of the American Indian into the larger American society, any study of the Indian's distinct past must increasingly take on the character of history or sociology rather than of classical ethnography. While some young historians have been discouraged from going into the field, anthropologists are expanding their functions here as they are in archaeology, where anthropology departments are turning out more and more historical archaeologists whose dissertations are in the field of colonial history rather than on prehistoric Indian sites. The principal strength the anthropologist brings to the subject is his training in acute observation of behavior, his habit of seeing particular cultures in terms of a theoretical framework, and his ability to divest himself of his own cultural presuppositions and values in recording and analyzing the culture he is studying.

The road by which anthropologists have become historians is illustrated by the career of Wendell H. Oswalt. In *Nepaskiak: An Alaskan Eskimo Community* (Tucson: University of Arizona Press, 1963), Oswalt noted the prevalent tendency to romanticize the Eskimo by dealing with him in terms of what his life may have been. "Virtually every popular contemporary account," he wrote, "maximizes aboriginal survivals." Oswalt, in contrast, attempted to describe the 141 Eskimos he studied in "his" community along the Kuskokwim River exactly as he found them in 1956. As Oswalt continued his study of the Eskimo villagers along the Kuskokwim, he turned increasingly from the ethnographic present (of 1956) to the historical past left in the records of Russian traders and administrators, of the Greek Church, and, after Alaska was acquired by the United States, of the Moravian Church. As Oswalt noted in the introduction to his *Mission of Change in Alaska: Eskimos and Moravians on the Kuskokwim* (San Marino: Huntington Library, 1963), "I realized that no matter how many people I questioned, much of the knowledge of the aboriginal past was lost to memory. The only hope for gathering additional information seemed to lie in discovering pertinent historical records . . . . " Oswalt's technical skill in amalgamating the ethnographic and historical record of one group was applied by him to the study of ten diverse tribes (including the Kuskokwim Eskimo) in his *This Was Theirs: A Study of the North American Indian* (New York: John Wiley & Sons, 1966).

In this book he attempted to write the history of the American Indian by selecting specific tribes to represent each culture area of North America. Oswalt tells their several stories, in non-theoretical terms, both as historical summaries of their past and as descriptions of their "traditional" way of life. However, the chronologies and descriptions of several Indian tribes are juxtaposed with no attempt to generalize, except in a concluding chapter on the legal status of present-day Indians.

Harold E. Driver, author of *Indians of North America* (Chicago: University of Chicago Press, 1961, 2d ed., rev., 1969), is another of the anthropologists who have increasingly adapted historical materials to their purpose. Driver's work is organized as a comprehensive and detailed consideration of the material and social culture of the American Indian. One of its distant ancestors is Clark Wissler's *Indians of the United States*, first published in 1940, and recently reprinted in a revised edition prepared by Lucy Wales Kluckhohn (Garden City, N.Y.: Doubleday, 1966). Wissler emphasized the material culture of the American Indian above all else, though he made some generalizations about nonmaterial culture. In Wissler's book, history, when it emerges at all, tends to be anecdotal in character. Driver, on the other hand, has adopted a more comprehensive ethnological approach and, in addition, has made a more conscious effort to achieve a historical perspective. His historical chapters tend to be rather wooden recitals of basic facts which stand in uneasy contrast to the earlier chapters where he carefully analyzes housing, architecture, clothing, marriage, the family, and other topics.

Edward H. Spicer's *Cycles of Conquest: The Impact of Spain, Mexico, and the United States on the Indians of the Southwest, 1533–1960* (Tuscon: University of Arizona Press, 1962) considers one segment of the Indian population in one section of the United States. More recently, Spicer has published *A Short History of the Indians of the United States* (New York: Van Nostrand Reinhold Co., 1969), which combines documents and commentary in a compressed and readable form. In searching for an organizing principle for his history, he divides his book into chronological segments based on the legal standing of Indian societies and Indian individuals within the context of an increasingly dominant white society.

While nobody has solved the problem of producing a meaningful general history of the American Indian, perhaps the anthropologists have come closest. In addition to the books by Driver, Spicer, and Oswalt, a team of anthropologists— Robert F. Spencer, Jesse D. Jennings, *et al*—has produced a college textbook, *The Native Americans* (New York: Harper & Row, 1965) which, although written in ethnological rather than historical terms and following the culture-area approach, uses historical evidence to illustrate the ethnographic points made. The authors also make good use of archeological materials in sketching the prehistory of the American Indian. An example of the team approach to the study of American Indian history is *North American Indians in Historical Perspective*, edited by Nancy O. Lurie and Eleanor Leacock (New York: Random House, 1971), which includes chapters on areas and tribes by a number of different authors. Perhaps the team approach is the only way possible to encompass the ethnographic diversity and historical complexity of Indian history.

A number of anthropologists have focussed their talents on specific tribes for which the historical record rather than ethnographic field work provides the bulk of their data. One of the most outstanding anthropologists writing as historian is Anthony F. C. Wallace. Working within the well-documented period of Indian-white relations in Pennsylvania and New York in the eighteenth and early nineteenth centuries, Wallace has been able to bring the "culture-and-personality" approach of anthropology to the study of critical periods and key individuals in the Indian-white relationship. He described his first book, *King of the Delawares: Teedyuscung, 1700-1763* (Philadelphia: University of Pennsylvania Press, 1949, reprinted, 1970) as " . . . a biography [;] . . . it deals in discussions of emotion, motives, and states of mind—intangible matters, indeed, but the staff of which a life is made—which lie outside the province of the pure historian or ethnographer." There followed a string of brilliant technical articles in a wide variety of anthropological, scientific, and historical journals. Most recently, in *The Death and Rebirth of the Seneca: The History and Culture of the Great Iroquois Nation, their Destruction and Demoralization, and their Cultural Revival at the Hands of the Indian Visionary, Handsome Lake* (New York: Alfred A. Knopf, 1970), Wallace demonstrated how effectively the anthropological, psychological, and historical approaches can be welded together. The book's subtitle accurately reflects the amalgam of Anglo-American history, Indian tribal culture, and individual psychology, which it is Wallace's genius to be able to combine in readable form.

Two other anthropologists have distinguished themselves by the impetus they have given to ethnohistorical study. John C. Ewers has produced a staggering array of historical studies illuminated by a deep personal and professional knowledge of Plains Indians. His *The Blackfeet: Raiders on the Northwestern Plains* (Norman: University of Oklahoma Press, 1958) is one example. William N. Fenton has made fundamental contributions to our understanding of the Iroquois and of their dealings with the whites from the seventeenth century to the present. In addition to his anthropological writings, Fenton has edited Lewis Henry Morgan's *League of the Iroquois* (New York: Corinth Books, 1962) as well as Arthur C. Parker's notes on the Iroquois, *Parker on the Iroquois* (Syracuse: University of Syracuse Press, 1968), and has in preparation an English language edition of Joseph-François Lafitau's *Moeurs des sauvages amériquains* (Paris, 1724).

Among anthropologists concerned with the American Indian are several who are themselves Indians. Two of the most distinguished are Alfonso Ortiz, associate professor of anthropology at Princeton University, who has recently published *The Tewa World: Space, Time, Being and Becoming in a Pueblo Society* (Chicago: University of Chicago Press, 1969), and the late Edward P. Dozier who has written on the Pueblos, as in his *Hano: A Tewa Community in Arizona* (New York: Holt, Rinehart & Winston, 1966). Both Ortiz and Dozier are themselves Pueblo by birth and upbringing. Though writing primarily as anthropologists rather than as historians, their work—especially Dozier's—can be classified as ethnohistory because of its extensive reliance upon the record of the past—a record which reveals the remarkable continuity shown by Pueblo society in the face of successive challenges from both Indian and non-Indian forces.

Ethnohistory and Comparative Analysis

The trend to history among North American anthropologists was institutionalized early in the 1950s by the creation of the American Indian Ethnohistoric Conference (more recently called the American Society for Ethnohistory) which publishes the journal, *Ethnohistory*, and marks an increasingly close amalgamation of the historical and the ethnographic approaches to the study of the American Indian. From the historian's point of view, it is regrettable that most of the amalgamation is being performed by anthropologists and very little by historians.

Anthropological attempts at comparative analysis have been more successful than those of many historians perhaps because of the existence within the anthropological community of an agreed-upon set of categories and a distinct method for analyzing Indian cultures. An excellent example is the volume edited by Edward H. Spicer and entitled *Perspectives in American Indian Culture Change* (Chicago: University of Chicago Press, 1960), which includes studies in the acculturation of six Indian tribes by six different anthropologists. One of the contributors is Edward Dozier, who deals with Rio Grande Pueblo contact-history in five successive stages.

What is the reason for the difficulties that seem to dog the professional historian and anthropologist writing about the Indian? Robert K. Berkhofer, Jr., asserted that at the heart of the problem is the practical difficulty of reconciling a functional (synchronic) analysis of a whole culture with a historical (diachronic) analysis of the cumulative changes producing that culture. Berkhofer himself attempted to overcome the difficulty in *Protestant Missions and American Indian Response, 1787–1862* (Lexington: University of Kentucky Press, 1965). In this book he organized his data into sequences starting with the missionaries' general attitudes and assumptions, and ending with the Indians' response to the missionary. Observing the regularities in these sequences, and applying a comparative approach to the vast sum of data before him, Berkhofer attempted to avoid the "usual moral fables that masquerade as Indian history." His monograph does point to methods that should be applied by the historian in the study of Indian history, but traditional historians may assert that Berkhofer has applied a new terminology to well recognized historical, not alone sociological or anthropological, categories.

Original Documents and Oral History

The contribution of the Indian to the writing of Indian history has been minimal. Vast stores of knowledge have been lost with the death of older Indians whose recollections were never recorded on tape or on paper. Though late in the day, it is still possible to tap this source. Of primary importance is the preservation of the original document side-by-side with the ethnographic or historical commentary. Specialized studies, such as Anna Gritts Kilpatrick and Jack Frederick Kilpatrick's "Chronicles of Wolftown," Anthropological Paper No. 75, *Bureau of American Ethnology Bulletin* No. 196 (Washington, 1966), 1–111, and "Notebook of a Cherokee Shaman," *Smithsonian Contributions to Anthropology* II (1970), exemplify the respect that such documents deserve and obtain at the hands of sympathetic and scholarly observers. Stanley Vestal, in a previous generation, had felt a similar compulsion to publish many of the documents and statements of Indian and white eye-witnesses to the events he discussed in his biography of Sitting Bull. Vestal's documentary, *New Sources of Indian History, 1850-1891, The Ghost Dance, The Prairie Sioux: A Miscellany* (Norman: University of Oklahoma Press, 1934), contained these fragments which, Vestal felt, were too valuable to cast aside after he had utilized them for his biography.

A recent attempt to utilize Indian recollections to tell the history of native Americans is *Cheyenne Memories*, by John Stands in Timber and Margot Liberty, with the assistance of Robert M. Utley (New Haven and London: Yale University Press, 1967). In this book, the recollections of the Cheyennes' "historian" were taped, sorted, and annotated by sympathetic whites to form the "memories" of the published volume. The reader of these memories is, however, left without the knowledge of the original, whose preservation it is the primary responsibility of the historian to ensure. Whether this responsibility has been met by the friends of the Cheyennes' historian is open to question. It is perhaps easier to ensure the preservation of the original material in the case of graphic documents. The preservation and analysis of a fascinating graphic account of Indian life has been effected by Karen Daniels Petersen and John C. Ewers in their edition of *Howling Wolf: A Cheyenne Warrior's Graphic Interpretation of His People* (Palo Alto, California: American West Publishing Co., 1968).

The urge to discover how Indians view their history is now *de rigueur* among foundations, universities, and government officials. Yet Indian history from the Indian point of view is not an easy goal to achieve. Though oral history has gained new respectability and oral history projects dealing with the Indian have been set up in several universities in the United States, important questions remain. Can these materials be translated into formal history? Can they provide us with true and significant insights into the Indian past? Oral interviews with contemporary Indians will certainly illuminate the condition of the present-day Indian and the story of his immediate past and will record the Indian's perception of the history of his more distant past. Such interviews should be fundamental to the writing of both folk history and formal history, but their use for these purposes has not been fully demonstrated.

The voice of the Indian about his own history has recently been heard more clearly, though the use of whites as spokesmen for or collaborators with Indians has continued. Stan Steiner's *The New Indians* (New York: Harper & Row, 1968) professed to speak for the newly militant but still silent Indians. It did so, though Steiner suffered criticism from Indians who resented the fact that a white man took it upon himself, however selflessly, to speak for them. One of the first expressions of the Indian view by Indians was Vine Deloria, Jr.'s *Custer Died for Your Sins* (New York and London: Macmillan, 1969). Deloria's book marks the emergence of a group of Indian commentators on the Indian experience who self-consciously identify themselves not as anthropologists or as historians but as Indians; it is a wild swipe at the big, bad white world of anthropologists, missionaries, government functionaries, and last, but not least, Indian leaders themselves. This curious form of contemporary history, justificatory and expiatory in its intent, relies on the well-known guilt feelings of twentieth-century whites in order to be palatable to its targets. Deloria's second book, *We Talk, You Listen: New Tribes, New Turf* (New York and Toronto: Macmillan, 1970), followed on the heels of *Custer* and expresses his search for a positive philosophy—based on the potential autonomy of the tribal unit—to replace the fallen idols of his past. Noticeable again in Deloria's rhetoric is his intense preoccupation with morality as well as his zeal for practical legal solutions. He is not a historian in the traditional sense, but he gives Indians a voice and the belief that history can be written by Indians as well as by whites.

Another group of Indians have approached their history through literature rather than through history, anthropology, or opinion. Most prominent among them is N. Scott Momaday, whose novel, *House of Dawn* (New York: Harper & Row, 1968), received the Pulitzer Prize for Fiction in 1969. Momaday has looked back to, and tried to evoke the essence of his Kiowa heritage in such works as *The Journey of Tai-me* (Santa Barbara: University of California Press, 1967) and *The Way to Rainy Mountain* (Albuquerque: University of New Mexico Press, 1969). While the approach to Indian history through literature will always be insightful, the question of whether it is history still remains.

Specialized "Red Studies"?

The writing of Indian history by Indians has been provided with institutional bases by the creation of Red Studies programs in various universities, by the establishment of Indian-run colleges such as the Navajo Community College, and by the organization of the American Indian Historical Society, which publishes *The Indian Historian* as an outlet for the work of Indian historians and white supporters of the cause of Indian history. In 1970 the society published a survey of the treatment of American Indians in school textbooks titled *Textbooks and the American Indian* and *Indian Voices*, the proceedings of the first conference of Indian historians held at Princeton University in the fall of 1969. The American Indian Historical Society can justly claim to be serving history as well as the Indian people although this claim will be more fully validated as the first flush of enthusiasm for the Indian point of view is supplemented in the long run by an increasingly objective and detailed analysis of the facts of Indian history.

There are dangers in too specialized a concern with particular aspects of a larger general history, but the study of the American Indian is less subject to the dangers of overspecialization than of unconcern. The number of Indian groups is so vast, the historical record so confused, or biased, or difficult of access, the change of status and culture so rapid, the life of the Indian so inextricably mixed with the white man's presence and his goods that one needs to focus special attention upon the Indian in order to clarify his history. At the present time, that history is affected not only by ignorance of the record but by prejudices and myths inherited from earlier centuries over which new myths and prejudices have been superimposed. The sharp disagreements of historians over the meaning of the already revealed record illustrates the many problems in the field which remain to be solved. It may be that historians are constitutionally incapable of meeting the challenge posed by Indian history and that the task will be performed by anthropologists or by the Indians themselves. I am inclined to think that the job will be done by historians going over the written record with a more judicial attitude and with greater sensitivity to the implications of cultural differences than an earlier generation of historians has displayed. And prominent among those historians will be anthropologists and Indians writing not as anthropologists or as Indians but as historians dedicated to the elucidation and elaboration of the past.

Since the publication of the article here reprinted, many excellent works on the American Indian have been published. Two outstanding ones are Joseph G. Jorgensen's *The Sun Dance Religion: Power for the Powerless* (Chicago: University of Chicago Press, 1972) and Warren L. Cook's *Flood Tide of Empire: Spain and the Northwest, 1543-1819* (New Haven and London: Yale University Press, 1973). These two books strengthen the conviction expressed in the original article that the boundary between anthropology and history is an arbitrary one and that a good book dealing with the American Indian requires an author familiar with the sources and methods of both disciplines. Cook is a historian; Jorgensen an anthropologist. Each has exhaustively mined the primary sources bearing on his subject, skillfully analyzed the data, and stated new interpretations. In Cook's case, the data are primarily in written form, and Cook has dealt effectively with collections (and their custodians) all over the world. Jorgensen, on the other hand, has relied primarily on field work with living subjects—Shoshoni Indians—whose respect he earned by his concern for their dignity as well as by his respect for the truth. Cook's work is informed by a thorough understanding of anthropology and the native point of view, while Jorgensen's work carefully considers the historical evidence available. Cook's book can be classified as a history of exploration and European national rivalry, while Jorgensen's study is an anthropological treatise on the evolution of a redemptive movement—the Sun Dance—among certain reservation Indians. Yet both books illuminate the *history* of the American Indian.

Among the many solid works of traditional historical scholarship that have appeared in the last few years, often in the University of Oklahoma's Civilization of the American Indian Series, two examples may suffice: William E. Unrau's *The Kansa Indians: A History of the Wind People, 1673-1873* (Norman, 1971), and Arrell M. Gibson's *The Chickasaws* (Norman, 1971). Unrau's book was written in the face of discouraging advice that the Kansa story could probably never be told for lack of sufficient evidence. His solid research, however, uncovered the data needed to provide a coherent picture of the tragic history of that tribe.

In the literary field, perhaps the outstanding work to appear in recent years is Richard Slotkin's *Regeneration Through Violence: The Mythology of the American Frontier, 1600-1860* (Middletown, Conn.: Wesleyan University Press, 1973). Inevitably the Indian occupies a central role in the mythology of the frontier, and Slotkin comes directly to grips with the white man's perception of him. Not only in its comprehensiveness but in its sophisticated analysis Slotkin's work is a worthy companion to the books of Henry Nash Smith and Roy Harvey Pearce. Less satisfactory as intellectual history is Bernard W. Sheehan's *Seeds of Extinction: Jeffersonian Philanthropy and the American Indian* (Chapel Hill: University of North Carolina Press, 1973), which does not materially improve the dissertation version discussed in the original article.

A word about the progress of native scholarship may be in order. In the 1960s a great effort was made, by such agencies as the Office of Economic Opportunity and the Duke Oral History Project, to encourage the creation of tribal histories told from the native point of view. The results of that effort are beginning to appear. One of the first products is *The Zunis: Self-portrayals by the Zuni People*, Alvina Quam, translator (Albuquerque: University of New Mexico Press, 1972). Another, based on interviews conducted by the American Indian Research Project at the University of South Dakota, is *To Be an Indian: An Oral History*, edited by Joseph H. Cash and Herbert T. Hoover (New York: Holt, Rinehart and Winston, Inc., 1971). Although valuable contributions, these books are still not history in the technical sense, but raw material for history. One continues to await the utilization of the oral history record in true Indian history.

The Indian best known to the American public, Vine Deloria, Jr., has continued his extensive writing despite the pressure of innumerable competing demands on his time and reputation. Much of his activity, as in the compilation of the book *Of Utmost Good Faith* (San Francisco: Straight Arrow Books, 1971), has sought to make available to Indians and others the texts of treaties and agreements between the United States and the Indian tribes. At the same time he has helped to initiate legal action to secure Indian rights guaranteed under those treaties and agreements. Deloria's latest, and most powerful, statement is the book *God is Red* (New York: Grosset & Dunlap, 1973), a searching comparative study of white and red religious points of view. Deloria contrasts the white concern with time with the Indian concern with space, the white concern with dominating nature with the Indian concern with being a part of it, the white concern with history with the Indian concern with shared experience. He sees an ultimate reconciliation between the spiritual owner of the land—the Indian—and the political owner—the white man. Recent political events, such as the capture of Wounded Knee and the sacking of the BIA, are discussed in terms of the underlying moral positions of both whites and Indians. While others—both white and Indian—have hastily jumped on contemporary activist bandwagons, often at the expense of objectivity and perspective. Deloria has been able to keep himself free of too close an identification with either the establishment or the anti-establishment. Thus he has been able to maintain his integrity as a moral man and as a perceptive observer which, if one thinks about it, may serve as an appropriate definition of a historian.

Reprinted from *Pacific Historical Review,* Vol. 40, No. 3, pp. 261-281, by permission of the Branch.

Communal History in America

by Robert S. Fogarty

During the past decade there has been considerable interest in communal history as collective schemes and societies surfaced once again to suggest an alternative to our individual quests for health and happiness. Communes were founded with such exotic names as Lama, Sons of Levi, Magic Mountain, Children of Light, Atlantis I, Walden Two, and House of the Seventh Angel. Northern New Mexico was dotted with communes as formerly placid villages from Truchas to Placitas found strange and wonderful visitors descend on them in search of "community." Some of the communards had clear notions about what that meant while others believed it could be found by settling within fifty miles of the Sangre de Cristos and the Taos Pueblo.

Many of the communal ventures failed, but many were able to sustain a common life and to suggest that "community" was possible in a warring age. However, any reader of American social history knows that communes or the communitarian movement was not an invention of the Sixties, but a vibrant and enduring part of both Western and Eastern tradition. What flourished in the mountains of New Mexico and in the heart of New York and Boston had been there before—and in the same varied and colorful fashion.

Communities existed in seventeenth- and eighteenth-century America with such prosaic names as Plockhoy's Commonwealth, Society of the Women in the Wilderness of the Contented of the God-Loving Soul, and Jerusalem, while the nineteenth century saw such pedestrian efforts as Feiba-Peveli, Society of One-Mentians, Memnonia Institute, Shalam, and the Straight Edgers. And, of course, there were the Levellers of seventeenth-century England, the Adamites of twelfth-century Bohemia, the Essenes of first-century Christianity, and the Taoists of fifth-century B. C. China. So there is a substantial history of communal activity which predates the current efforts and, in fact, an enormous body of literature about that history.

A New Scholarly Interest

The present interest in new communities has had the effect of generating both scholarly and popular interest in the subject of communes (throughout this essay I'll use the terms "communes" and "communal" in place of the ponderous "communitarian"). Scholarly interest has in turn generated a growing reprint business with all the promise and problems of those ventures. There are, at present, at least three reprint projects underway and their current choices are uneven. Some valuable material has been put back into print while some discredited tales about communal life are being freely circulated without the benefit of scholarly commentary or editing. While the reprint houses were putting material back into print some university presses let valuable works on communal life go out of print.

So we are at a fortunate crossroads since there is an increasing interest in communal history and, at the same time, a growing body of both primary and secondary material—particularly on the sociology of the family, small group theory, and the possibility of a viable counter-culture. In addition, there is an emerging literature about the communes of the Sixties which lack a history as such, but have a place in a larger historical narrative.

World Perspective

Before discussing the communal tradition or the histories of individual communities in America it is essential to place such material within the larger perspective of world history. Norman Cohen's *The Pursuit of the Millennium* is a good place to begin since he outlines the development of revolutionary messianism in medieval and Reformation Europe and probes what he considers "subterranean fanaticism" as the source of modern totalitarianism. Ernest Tuveson's *Millennium and Utopia* complements Cohen's history since it carries the pursuit of the millennium into the modern progressive world of the seventeenth-century English Platonists. Notions about religious perfectibility and secular progress were often wedded in communal theory and practice and Tuveson's work is a fine guide to the source of that marriage.

German sociologist Karl Mannheim tried to understand the tension between current needs and future expectations in *Ideology and Utopia* wherein he offered a major theoretical, though occasionally misleading, historical view of communal history.

Two other works which try to comprehend the sweep of utopian thought are Joyce Oremel Hertzler's *The History of Utopian Thought* and *Utopias and Utopian Thought,* edited by Frank Manuel and originally published as a *Daedalus* volume. It contains a number of excellent essays by Lewis Mumford, Northrop Frye, Crane Brinton, and twelve other contributors. In general, the essays are scholarly, literate, and provocative pieces intended to stimulate some dialogue about the significance of ideal and real communal projects.

Another suggestive collection of essays is Sylvia Thrupp's *Millennial Dreams in Action* which probes the possibilities of using messianic and communal movements as vehicles for social analyses. Essays by Aberle, "A Note on Relative Deprivation Theory..."; Cohen, "Medieval Millenarianism"; Kaminsky, "The Free Spirit in the Hussite Revolution"; and Shepperson, "Nyasaland and the Millennium," suggest the range of the collection. A detailed study of Millenialist sects born in the wake of disasters is David Barkun's *Disaster and the Millenium*.

Frank Manuel's work is particularly valuable since his writings are suggestive for a number of fields. His *The New World of Henri Saint-Simon* and *The Prophets of Paris* are both sturdy intellectual guides to the rationalist utopian thinkers of eighteenth-century France. And the collection, *French Utopias*, edited with Fritzie Manuel, outlines French idealism from Sir John Mandeville to Pierre Teilhard de Chardin. The English tradition is the subject of W. H. G. Armytage's thorough *Heaven's Below; Utopian Experiments in England, 1560-1960*, and George Jacob Holyoake's two-volume *The History of Cooperation in England*.

General Histories and Guides

There is no single compendium of communal societies in America, but an indispensable guide to the field is the two-volume *Socialism and American Life* edited by Donald Egbert and Stow Persons in 1952 and in need of updating. Volume one contains a number of significant essays ("Terminology and Types

Antioch College

Mr. Fogarty is Associate Professor of History at Antioch College, Yellow Springs, Ohio. A specialist in the communal history of the United States, he has published articles in The Antioch Review, New England Quarterly, *and* Labor History. *In addition he has edited* American Utopianism *and* Letters From A Self-Made Merchant to His Son, *and is consulting editor for the seventeen-volume series,* The American Utopian Adventure. *He is currently working on a study of communal societies in America, 1865-1920.*

of Socialism," "Christian Communitarianism in America," "The Secular Utopian Socialists"), while the second volume has a detailed critical bibliography without equal in the field. It does not have information about every known communal venture; however, it does provide a massive array of bibliographic references about the history of socialist activity and its relationship to the arts, psychology, and social history.

Another central critical and bibliographic source is Arthur E. Bestor's *Backwoods Utopias; The Sectarian and Owenite Phases of Communitarian Socialism in America, 1663-1829.* It outlines with admirable scholarship the movement of "communitarian" thought from the early pietist settlements in the East through to the Frontier experiments led by Robert Owen at New Harmony. Bestor's books and articles have established the notion that communal societies have been "patent-office models" for social improvement, and such societies serve the cause of social reform by being test tubes for the future.

Within a larger context there is a body of literature which suggests that the whole of American life has been utopian and experimental. H. Richard Niebuhr's *The Kingdom of God in America,* Charles L. Sanford's *The Quest for Paradise,* and Ernest Tuveson's *Redeemer Nation* all examine facets of utopian thought.

Early American Communes

Although it was the early nineteenth-century Continental thinkers like Fourier and Owen who spurred the development of societies in America, there were a significant number of religiously motivated colonies who brought their pietist zeal with them either in flight from European persecution or in pursuit of the New Jerusalem. A good account of an early group, the Labadists, can be found in Bartlett James, *The Labadist Colony in Maryland,* originally published in 1899 as part of the Johns Hopkins University Studies in Historical and Political Science.

What has been called the first significant communal settlement in America—Ephrata—was founded in 1732 by the German mystic, Conrad Beissel. There is a competent biography of Beissel by W. C. Klein, *Johann Conrad Beissel, Mystic and Martinet, 1690-1768,* and an early history of Ephrata, *Chronicon Ephratense,* written by two brothers of that celibate colony, Brother Lamech and Brother Agrippa. The colony was noted for its music, and a short volume, *The Music of the Ephrata Cloister* by Julius Friedrich Sachse, reproduces some of the scores and illustrations. Sachse's two-volume *The German Sectarians of Pennsylvania, 1708-1800* and his *The German Pietists of Provincial Pennsylvania* are valuable accounts of early mystical groups whose leaders led them into solitary contemplation and communal celibacy.

The most significant Moravian settlement in America was founded at Bethlehem in 1741 and the religious roots of that collective enterprise are outlined in Joseph Mortimer Levering's *A History of Bethlehem, Pennsylvania, 1741-1892.* An intelligent and scholarly study of the Moravian settlements at Bethlehem, Pennsylvania and Herrnhut, Saxony is Gillian Lindt Gollin's prize-winning *Moravians in Two Worlds.*

Just as the German pietist groups were experiencing some difficulties the most enduring of all communal projects landed in New York. With the arrival of Ann Lee in 1775 the long history of Shakerism begins. No other set of colonies has received so much attention, so much adulation, and so much loving restoration. At the outset, however, they were vilified and treated as English spies transplanted in New York to undercut revolutionary activity.

There is nothing to match Edward Deming Andrew's scholarly efforts to catch every detail of Shaker life from the curve of their furniture to the decline of their numbers. His *The People Called Shakers* remains the standard work and there are a number of other works by Andrews which emphasize particular facets of Shaker life. For their furniture, see *Shaker Furniture,* and for music and dance, his *The Gift to be Simple.* A recently translated work by a French sociologist, at the Sorbonne, Henri Desroche, *The American Shakers* places them within a larger structure of European religious and social radicalism which Andrews ignores, but Desroche reads too much radicalism into their religious history. There is an excellent study of a single Shaker community by Thomas Clark and F. Gerald Ham, *Pleasant Hill and the Shakers.* John Patterson MacLean's *Shakers of Ohio* is another valuable local source complementing Julia Neal's study of the South Union Shakers in *By Their Fruits.*

An old but still valuable account of Shaker history written by two members of the Mount Lebanon family is Anna White and Leila S. Taylor, *Shakerism; Its Meaning and Message.* There are a number of "inside" accounts by former members and they exhibit varying degrees of hostility toward their former celibate life. Thomas Brown's *An Account of the People Called Shakers* was published in 1812 from a friendly though apostate perspective. A hostile view is presented in David Lamson's 1848 account, *Two Years Experience Among the Shakers;* however there is some interesting detail about their spiritualist phase in the Lamson book.

Their own formal history was published in 1858 by Elder Frederick Evans as *Shakers; Compendium of the Origin, History, Principles, Rules and Regulations, Government and Doctrine of the United Society of Believers in Christ's Second Appearing.* It contains simple biographies of the early leaders and a simple exposition of their faith. How one arrived at the Shaker faith can be gleaned from Evans' *Autobiography of a Shaker,* which is a fine introduction to the thought of their most learned and vigorous spokesman for the post-Civil War period.

While the Shakers were establishing their colonies on the frontier other groups were forming up. One of the most unusual was the New Jerusalem colony of Jemima Wilkinson, "The Publick Universal Friend." Her colony has been well-treated in Herbert Wisbey's *Pioneer Prophetess,* but the recently reprinted Hudson study contains too many factual errors to be of any value.

Numerous colonies were set up on the frontier and some prospered in incredible fashion. The Harmony society under the leadership of "Father" George Rapp grew from a rural settlement in Western Pennsylvania to a large and wealthy community which at one point could afford to underwrite a travelling company of the Metropolitan Opera.

Its original inspiration came from the Book of Revelation and its history has been chronicled in excellent detail by Karl J. R. Arndt. His first volume, *George Rapp's Harmony Society, 1785-1847,* records the period of Rapp's direction and their three colony locations on the Connoquenessing, Wabash, and Ohio Rivers. The second volume, *George Rapp's Successors and Material Heirs, 1847-1916,* examines its growing financial prosperity and declining spiritual fortunes through to the legal dissolution in 1916.

There are two other sources for the Harmonist history, both written by contemporaries of participants in this century-long communal enterprise. John Duss' *The Harmonists, A Personal History* and Aaron Williams' *The Harmony Society at Economy, Pennsylvania* are good accounts, with the Duss volume particularly helpful for the latter part of their history.

A Continuing History

Though some communal efforts sought separation from the world and hoped to found "little commonwealths" they were often linked to the world or each other by historical accident or common impulse. The Shakers, Harmonists, and Oneida are important not solely because they lasted, but because of their inspiration and guidance to new groups. When Robert Owen decided to found his community in America it was from the Rappites that he purchased his Indiana land. Oneida saw itself as following in the footsteps of Brook Farm and, for example, the Silkville Colony in Kansas sought advice from Oneida. The continuum between old and new communities is striking in the communal history of America.

Antebellum Charismatic Leaders

The literature about Robert Owen and his colony is extensive and two scholarly works provide the bedrock upon which a collection might be built. They are Bestor's *Blackwood Utopias,* and J. F. C. Harrison's *Quest for the New Moral World.* The former is concerned with the Owenite phase in America, while Harrison's book deals with the Owenite influence on the English reform tradition. Frank Podmore's biography, *Robert Owen* remains the standard work and Owen's autobiography, *The Life of Robert Owen* supplements the critical work.

Owen's writings were extensive and his *A New View of Society* and *The Book of the new Moral World* provide his basic views, while the appendix to his autobiography and issues of the periodical *The Millennial Gazette* provide depth to those sources. There are other biographies and accounts of life at New Harmony available, including Paul Brown's account of his time in the colony, *Twelve Months in New-Harmony,* but the cited works should provide an adequate list for a general library.

At the same time as Owen was floundering in Indiana, another English-born reformer, Frances Wright, was beginning her interracial experiment in communal living at Nashoba in Tennessee. She was the leading woman in the communal movement of her day, and William Waterman's biography, *Frances Wright,* is a sound and factual study.

After the disintegration of the New Harmony colony in 1828 there were a few scattered efforts at communities including the Mormons, but it would not be until the 1840s that the writings of the French eccentric, Charles Fourier, would take hold in America. Nicholas M. Riasanovsky's *The Teaching of Charles Fourier* presents an excellent guide to his complicated system, and Riasanovsky's book should be a standard source in any library. For those who want him untouched by rational mind, Hugh Doherty's two-volume translation of *The Passions of the Human Soul* should be sufficient. However, his collected works are available in French, *Les Oeuvres de Fourier*, in twelve volumes.

Fourier's ideas were translated for an American audience by Albert Brisbane in *The Social Destiny of Man* and in the journal, *The Phalanx*, both of which have been recently reprinted. Another reprint, Redelia Brisbane's *Albert Brisbane; A Mental Biography*, tells us less about the Fourierist movement than about the personal hegira of Fourier's chief American disciple.

For information about the varied colonies which were started under Fourierist inspiration there are some excellent collections of primary materials in John H. Noyes, *History of American Socialisms* and in my own *American Utopianism*. The most famous Fourierist colony was Brook Farm and there is a disproportionate amount of detail on that literary and educational group.

The social and intellectual ferment which led to the creation of the colony can be traced in *The Dial* and in their weekly newspaper, *The Harbinger*, while more personal statements are available in Lindsay Swift's *Brook Farm; Its Members, Scholars, and Visitors* and Marianne Orvis' *Letters from Brook Farm, 1844–1847*. Unfortunately, we still do not have an adequate history of the North American Phalanx or any other of the Fourierist efforts, though many were short-lived. Observations about certain aspects of life at the North American Phalanx can be found in the recent reprint, *Expose of the Condition and Progress of the North American*.

Although the philosophies of Owen and Fourier dominate the intellectual temper of the period there were other communities which came into existence under the leadership of charismatic figures or collective philosophy. The Methodist pietist, Dr. William Keil, led colonies in Missouri and Oregon during the Eighteen-forties and Fifties, and that history can be found in Robert Hendricks' *Bethel and Aurora*.

During the antebellum period there were varied forces at work supporting the notion of a new commonwealth and readers would do well to consult Alice Felt Tyler's *Freedom's Ferment* and Whitney Cross' *The Burned-Over District* for general background data.

Both Mormonism and Swedenborgianism were integral philosophies of the period, yet their literature more properly belongs in a discussion of religions rather than communal history. However, Marguerite Beck Block's *The New Church in the New World*, on Swedenborgianism, and Leonard Arrington's *The Great Basin Kingdom* can suggest leads on collective settlements generated by both churches.

The community way offered a solution to numerous social problems which pressed in on the reformers of the day. Some Negro leaders saw colonies as halfway stations to the white world and established settlements to aid recently freed Negroes. Jane and William Pease's *Black Utopia* looks at a number of these Canadian colonies. Wilhelm Weitling, the German Socialist, saw cooperative settlements as a solution to immigrant problems, and Carl Wittke devotes considerable space to the Communia colony in his biography, *The Utopian Communist.*

Others, like Adin Ballou, saw collective efforts bringing together the forces of reform into a unitary household. His "Practical Christianity" is outlined in his marvelous *Autobiography of Adin Ballou (1803–1890)* and the history of the successful Hopedale Community at Northampton, Massachusetts in his *History of the Hopedale Community.*

Some continued to flee European persecution and colonize in America on the older pattern and we find a Swedish colony established in Illinois at Bishop Hill by Erik Jansen in 1846. M. A. Mikkelsen's *The Bishop Hill Colony* is a thorough monograph on the group.

The most interesting of all the nineteenth-century groups was the Perfectionist commune of Oneida started by John Humphrey Noyes. There is a considerable literature about these Victorian sensualists who were viewed by the outside world as free lovers and by the modern world as the flying wedge of progressive thought. They were neither; and, while in the past they were at the mercy of newspapermen looking for juicy material, they are currently at the mercy of sociologists looking for modern morals.

Robert Allerton Parker's *A Yankee Saint* is still a good source as long as it is balanced by Maren Lockwood Carden's *Oneida: Utopian Community to Modern Corporation,* which is quite good on the community period and weak on the company history. Constance Noyes Robertson's *The Oneida Community; The Breakup, 1876–1881* uses private sources and is important for examining sexual tensions though it remains a "family" account.

There are a number of good sources about Noyes' personal development and his theology. One should begin with his partial autobiography, *The Confessions of John H. Noyes,* then proceed to George Wallingford Noyes' benevolently edited two volumes, *The Religious Experiences of John Henry Noyes* and *The Putney Experience.* Noyes' theology can be found in the community "bible," *The Berean,* and *Bible Communism,* and his sexual theory in his *Essay on Scientific Propagation.* An excellent inside view of the daily life at Oneida can be found in the *Daily Journal,* now in print.

Because of the controversial nature of Oneida there were a number of accounts published to discredit the enterprise. Some have been reprinted recently and have little historical value except to indicate that such communities have consistently raised hostility wherever they landed.

Another charismatic contemporary of Noyes was Thomas Lake Harris who combined Swedenborgianism, Christianity, Spiritualism, and Oriental mysticism into successful community structures in New York and California. There is an excellent biography of Harris and his circle by Herbert W. Schneider and George Lawton, *A Prophet and a Pilgrim.* An interesting sidelight to the Harris community is explored in *The Unknown Edwin Markham* by Louis Filler.

Whereas Harris was exotic in both his philosophy and social relations, the German colony of Amana was steady and prosaic in its success. Bertha Shambaugh's *Amana, The Community of True Inspiration* is the standard work, and a good account of Amana in 1874 can be found in Charles Nordhoff's *The Communistic Societies of the United States.* Nordhoff visited a number of colonies in his travels and viewed them with sympathy since he saw them as an alternative to the growing labor movement which he feared.

The followers of Etienne Cabet journeyed to America in 1848 in order to put into practice the cooperative socialist schemes outlined in Cabet's *Voyage en Icarie.* In Texas they found harsh weather, sickness, and bad luck and moved temporarily to Nauvoo, Illinois—in fact to the site of the recently abandoned Mormon community.

In 1857 a third community was set up at Corning, Iowa, and a splinter group established a site at Cheltenham, Missouri, at the same time. Their sturdy history is told by Albert Shaw in *Icaria, A Chapter in the History of Communism.*

The Post-Civil War Period

There is little material in print about the communities begun after the Civil War, though my own research indicates that they were as significant and as varied as those started during the height of the Fourierist and millennialist activity.

An excellent source for communities started in the industrial period is William Hinds, *American Communities and Cooperative Colonies,* the 1908 edition. The earlier 1878 and even the 1903 editions simply cannot compare with the last Hinds compilation. The 1908 edition is now back in print. Hinds was a member of the Oneida Community for all of his adult life and is particularly helpful in ferreting out information about little known groups like the Straight-Edgers and the Spirit Fruit Society.

The only other general compilation of sources for the post-Civil War period is Ernest Wooster's *Communities of the Past and Present.* His data are not always accurate, but his material suggests the range of community available to researchers.

Alexander Kent, a minister active in the reforms of the Eighteen-nineties, put together a compilation for the Department of Labor and his listing is helpful to researchers. See Alexander Kent, "Cooperative Communities in the United States," *Bulletin of the Department of Labor* 35:563–646, July, 1901. Ralph Albertson's *A Survey of Mutualistic Communistic Communities in America* could be used in conjunction with Kent's listing.

Two other works, Mark Holloway's *Heavens on Earth* and Everett Webber's *Escape to Utopia,* touch on colonies of the period, but their sources are too limited to be of significant value. For the period we must rely on individual studies of individuals and communities, and there is no better personality to begin with than Alcander Longley who was involved with at least six groups during his commune career. His *What is Communism?* is a good statement of his socialist beliefs.

Another active community organizer was the Russian emigrant William Frey, who has received a good biography at the hands of the Slavic scholar Avrahm Yarmolinsky in *A Russian's American Dream.* Warren Chase, the American anarchist, speaks of his communal experiences in *The Life-Line of the Lone One,* and James Martin's *Men Against the State* examines the earlier anarchist involvement with communities as does Madeleine Stern's biography of Stephen Pearl Andrews, *The Pantarch.*

Studies of individual communities are in short supply and histories of Shalam, Koreshan Unity, Ruskin, Rugby, and others are needed. Thomas Hughes, *Rugby, Tennessee* is a firsthand account of that heroic English colony in Tennessee while John Ballou Newbrough's *Oahspe* provided the inspiration and guidance for the New Mexican colony of Shalam. The Topolobampo colony started by the American railroad builder A. K. Owens is sketchily treated in Thomas A. Robertson's *A Southwestern Utopia,* but it is the only substantial source outside of periodical literature, though Ray Reynold's *Cat's Paw Utopia* fills in many gaps. Owens' views can be found in his *Integral Cooperation* and in Teed's *Cellular Cosmogony.*
Colonies of the Pacific Northwest have been treated in an unpublished dissertation by Charles LeWarne, and Robert Hine has surveyed the California colonies in his thorough and insightful *California's Utopian Colonies.* A study of a single California colony, the Theosophical settlement of Katherine Tingleys at Point Loma, has been written by Emmett Greenwalt in *The Point Loma Community.*

The publication of Edward Bellamy's *Looking Backward* stimulated communal thinking, and there are a number of valuable sources available about the Nationalist movement. Hine looks at the Kaweah community in his *California's Utopian Colonies,* and there are varied references to projects scattered throughout the Nationalist periodicals, *The Nationalist* and *The New Nation.* Arthur Morgan's biography, *Edward Bellamy,* remains, with Sylvia Bowman's *The Year 2000,* the standard source about Bellamy's thought. Morgan's own writings stand examination on their own utopian terms as his *Nowhere was Somewhere and The Community of the Future and the Future of Community* outline a personal perspective which has shaped the intentional community movement of this century.
And in connection with the general reform spirit of the Nineties one should look at Paul and Blanche Alyea's *Fairhope, 1894-1954,* a study of the colony devoted to Henry George's Single Tax Philosophy.
The history of the Ruskin Colony led by Julius Wayland is covered in Howard Quint's *The Forging of American Socialism;* the Christian Commonwealth in James Dombrowski, *The Early Days of Christian Socialism in America;* and the activities of the Vrooman brothers with varied communities in Ross Paulson's *Radicalism and Reform.* Elbert Hubbard and the Roycrofter group are the subjects of Freeman Champney's study, *Art and Glory.*

The Hutterite colonies deserve special notice since they have been studied so well and have been such a successful cooperative society. With the aid of the wealthy Rappite Harmony Society of Pennsylvania they established a colony in South Dakota where they grew and prospered. The standard historical account is Victor Peters, *All Things Common,* and there are a number of excellent psychological studies. Joseph W. Eaton and Robert J. Weil's *Culture and Mental Disorders; A Comparative Study of the Hutterites and Other Populations* was a

NIMH study, while Lee Emerson Deets' *The Hutterites* is a sociological account by a researcher who lived with the Hutterites.

The contrast between the secular and the religious utopians is deftly handled by Wisconsin professor Paul Conkin in his *Two Paths to Utopia*. By comparing the Hutterites with the socialist colony of Llano, Conkin brings into sharp focus the comparative values of the collectives. Llano was founded by the Socialist leader Job Harriman after his defeat in the Los Angeles mayoralty election of 1911.

There is a full account of its California and Louisiana history in Conkin, Hine, and Wooster. An off-shoot of the Llano colony was another socialist colony located in Nevada. Wilbur Shepperson's *Retreat to Nevada* is an exemplary short history of a single colony led by C. V. Eggleston.

The Twentieth Century

After 1900 we must rely almost exclusively on periodical literature and newspapers for glimpses of communities. Even the famous Helicon Hall colony of Upton Sinclair is without a history. Founded on the proceeds of the sales from *The Jungle,* the colony had a brief life, but attracted such figures as Sinclair Lewis, Allen Updegraff, Michael Williams, Edwin Bjorkman, and Frances Maule. The colony is discussed in one chapter of Sinclair's *The Autobiography of Upton Sinclair.* And the athletic House of David remains an enigma which I hope to clarify after working through their court records.

Another scattered set of colonies is briefly mentioned in an appendix to Gabriel Davidson's *Our Jewish Farmers and the Story of the Jewish Agricultural Society.*

During the Nineteen-twenties, there was a gradual growth of agrarian and decentralist notions which form much of the philosophical basis for today's communes. The work of Ralph Borsodi is slowly coming into vogue with his *This Ugly Civilization* (the primary work) and his *Flight from the City,* a personal account of his subsistence homestead in Rockland County, New York.

During the Thirties there were a number of large and small communities planned which were based on communal models and assumptions. Paul Conkin's *Tomorrow a New World* is an excellent survey of New Deal programs in new town and subsistence farming operations. As the Depression became a fact and as towns became cities, there was a slow movement toward a redefinition of community in relation to urban life. The establishment of a colony in rural Michigan is but one facet of that drive, and Joseph Cohen's *The Sunrise Community* examines the difficulties New York labor leaders had on the Michigan frontier.

An experiment on the Georgia frontier begun in 1942 still exists today after two decades of local opposition. Clarence Jordan's interracial Christian community of Koinonia at Americus, Georgia, is the subject of Dallas Lee's *The Cotton Patch Evidence.*

During the Nineteen-forties and Fifties, the commune movement was aided and sustained by the Fellowship of Intentional Communities, a loose affiliation of communal societies which met yearly to share ideas and projects. Its constitution along with other supporting statements can be found in my *American Utopianism.* Literature about the intentional community approach is available through Community Service, Inc., and a few of its publications are worth noting. Its *Handbook on Intentional Community* and *The Community Land Trust* are basic statements of principle.

Contemporary Communal Efforts

The literature about current communal groups is still too unformed to be of significant value, but there are a periodical literature, some self-conscious history, and a few good overviews. Many of the current accounts are by free-lance journalists and sociologists on the run, and we can only hope there is a Nordhoff and a Weber among them.

There is an emerging periodical literature by and about the communal lifestyle and, in fact, *Lifestyle* is devoted to looking at the general communal thrust. Recently three groups which had been publishing separate magazines (*Alternatives,* formerly *The Modern Utopian; Communitarian; Communitas*) have combined to put out *Communities* which should range widely over communal literature and philosophy.

Richard Fairfield and Consuelo Sandoval have been active in the hip communal movement and their impressions are recorded in *Communes, U.S.A.* And one community, Twin Oaks, has pieced together a history of its first four years in a *Journal of a Walden Two Commune* which hopefully other current communities will emulate. It is the first effort of the Community Publishing Cooperative and other volumes are expected to follow. A steadier view of the range of community settlements of the Sixties can be found in Ron Roberts, *The New Communes.*

There are a number of "personal trip" accounts by commune joiners and followers and Robert Houriet's *Getting Back Together* is the most readable and perceptive.

Hopefully future researchers will take Benjamin Zablocki's *The Joyful Community* as a model for their work. His study of the Bruderhoff is thorough, sympathetic, without condescension, and well written. Less satisfying is the recent effort by Rossabeth Kanter at comparative judgments in her *Commitment and Community.* Her generalizations appear—to an historian—to be based on sketchy evidence, and her generalizations about community life ought to be looked at with some caution though her theoretical framework is a striking one. And finally there is Laurence Veysey's outstanding comparative study, *The Communal Experience,* which fuses past history with current experiences by focusing on the mystical and anarchist traditions in communal societies.

There will surely be other comparative works published and there is some evidence that geographers, architects, and psychologists will bring new understanding of the plans and programs set forward by self-conscious community builders and wreckers.

Communal history abounds in excellent anecdotal material as stories about intrigue, fakery, seduction, and megalomania are mixed with tales of high purpose, social resourcefulness, and exemplary altruism. One of my favorites concerns the Llano colony which celebrated its May Day by dressing up in their best

clothes and marching through the streets of the colony bearing a red flag and
a banner with the inscription: "If you have two loaves of bread, sell one and buy
a hyacinth to feed your soul."

Works Cited

ALBERTSON, Ralph. *A Survey of Mutualistic Communistic Communities in
America.* AMS, 1973 (orig. pub. in 1936).
ALYEA, Paul and Blanche. *Fairhope, 1894-1954; The Story of a Single Tax
Colony.* Alabama, 1956.
ANDREWS, Edward D. *The Gift to be Simple; Songs, Dances and Rituals of the
American Shakers.* Dover, 1962 (orig. pub. by J. J. Augustin, 1940).
_____ . *The People Called Shakers; A Search for the Perfect Society.* Dover, 1963
(orig. pub. by Oxford, 1953).
ANDREWS, Edward D. and Faith. *Shaker Furniture, The Craftsmanship of an
American Communal Sect.* Dover, 1964 (orig. pub. by Oxford, 1937).
ARMYTAGE, W. H. G. *Heaven's Below; Utopian Experiments in England, 1560-
1960.* University of Toronto, 1961.
ARNDT, Karl J. R. *George Rapp's Harmony Society 1785-1847.* Pennsylvania,
1965.
_____ . *George Rapp's Successors and Material Heirs, 1847-1916.* Fairleigh
Dickinson, 1972.
ARRINGTON, Leonard. *The Great Basin Kingdom; An Economic History of
the Latter-Day Saints, 1830-1900.* Harvard, 1958.
BALLOU, Adin. *Autobiography of Adin Ballou, 1803-1890,* ed. by William S.
Heywood. Vox Populi Press, 1896.
_____ . *History of the Hopedale Community; From its Inception to its Virtual
Submergence in the Hopedale Parish.* Porcupine Press, 1973 (orig. pub. by
Thompson and Hill, 1897).
BARKUN, David. *Disaster and the Millenium.* Yale University Press, 1974.
BESTOR, Arthur E. *Backwoods Utopias; The Sectarian and Owenite Phases of
Communitarian Socialism in America, 1663-1829.* Pennsylvania, 1950.
BLOCK, Marguerite Beck. *The New Church in the New World; A Study of
Swedenborgianism in America.* Octagon, 1969 (orig. pub. by Holt, 1932).
BORSODI, Ralph. *Flight from the City; An Experiment in Creative Living on
the Land.* 3rd ed. Harper & Row, 1972 (orig. pub. by School of Living, 1947).
_____ . *This Ugly Civilization.* Simon and Schuster, 1929.
BOWMAN, Sylvia. *The Year 2000; A Critical Biography of Edward Bellamy.*
Bookman Associates, 1958.
BRISBANE, Albert. *The Social Destiny of Man; or, Association and Reorganiza-
tion of Industry.* B. Franklin, 1968 (orig. pub. by C. F. Stollmeyer, 1840).
BRISBANE, Redelia (Bates). *Albert Brisbane; A Mental Biography, with a
Character Study.* B. Franklin, 1969 (orig. pub. by Arena Publishing Co., 1893).
BROWN, Paul. *Twelve Months in New Harmony.* Porcupine Press, 1973 (orig.
pub. by W. H. Woodward, 1827).
BROWN, Thomas. *An Account of the People Called Shakers.* AMS, 1972 (orig.
pub. by Parker & Bliss, 1812).
CARDEN, Maren Lockwood. *Oneida; Utopian Community to Modern Corpora-
tion.* Johns Hopkins, 1969.

CHAMPNEY, Freeman. *Art and Glory; The Story of Elbert Hubbard.* Crown, 1968.

CHASE, Warren. *The Life-Line of the Lone One; or, Autobiography of the World's Child.* B. Marsh, 1857.

CLARK, Thomas and F. Gerald Ham. *Pleasant Hill and the Shakers.* Shakertown Press, 1968.

CODMAN, John Thomas. *Brook Farm; Historic and Personal Memoirs.* AMS, 1971 (orig. pub. by Arena Publishing Co., 1894).

COHEN, Joseph. *The Sunrise Community.* n.p. 1939.

COHEN, Norman. *The Pursuit of the Millennium; Revolutionary Millenarians and Mystical Anarchism of the Middle Ages.* Oxford, 1970.

COMMUNITIES. v.1–; 1971–. Communities Publications Cooperative.

COMMUNITY SERVICE, INC. *The Community Land Trust.* Community Service, Inc., 1972.

_____. *A Handbook on Intentional Communities.* Community Service, Inc., 1973.

CONKIN, Paul K. *Tomorrow a New World; The New Deal Community Program.* Cornell, 1959.

_____. *Two Paths to Utopia; The Hutterites and the Llano Colony.* Nebraska, 1964.

CROSS, Whitney. *The Burned-Over District; The Social and Intellectual History of Enthusiastic Religion in Western New York, 1800–1850.* Harper, 1965 (orig. pub. by Cornell, 1950).

DAVIDSON, Gabriel. *Our Jewish Farmers and the Story of the Jewish Agricultural Society.* L. B. Fischer, 1943.

DEETS, Lee Emerson. *The Hutterites; A Study in Social Cohesion.* (Ph.D thesis, Columbia University, 1939).

DESROCHE, Henri. *The American Shakers; From Neo-Christianity to Pre-Socialism,* tr. and ed. by John K. Savacoal. Massachusetts, 1971.

THE DIAL, v. 1-4, 1840-1846. Russell and Russell, 1961.

DOMBROWSKI, James. *The Early Days of Christian Socialism in America.* Octagon Books, 1966 (reprint of a thesis, Columbia University, 1937).

DUSS, John. *The Harmonists, A Personal History.* Porcupine Press, 1973 (orig. pub. by the Pennsylvania Book Service, 1943).

EATON, Joseph and Robert Weil. *Culture and Mental Disorders; A Comparative Study of the Hutterites and Other Populations.* Free Press, 1955.

EGBERT, Donald and Stow Persons, eds. *Socialism and American Life.* 2v. Princeton, 1952.

EVANS, Frederick W. *Shakers, Compendium of the Origin, History, Principles, Rules and Regulations, Government and Doctrine of the United Society of Believers in Christ's Second Appearing.* B. Franklin, 1972 (orig. pub. in 1859).

EVANS, George Frederick. *Autobiography of a Shaker and Revelation of the Apocalypse.* Porcupine Press, 1973 (orig. pub. in 1888).

_____. *Expose of the Condition and Progress of the North American Phalanx.* Porcupine Press, 1974.

FAIRFIELD, Richard. *Communes U.S.A.; A Personal Tour.* Penguin, 1972.

FILLER, Louis. *The Unknown Edwin Markham; His Mystery and Its Significance.* Antioch, 1966.

FOGARTY, Robert S. *American Utopianism.* F. E. Peacock, 1972.

FOURIER, Francois Marie Charles. *The Passions of the Human Soul and their Influence on Society and Civilization,* tr. by Hugh Doherty. 2v. A. M. Kelley, 1968, (orig. pub. by H. Baillière, 1851).

GOLLIN, Gillian Lindt. *Moravians in Two Worlds: A Study of Changing Communities.* Columbia University Press, 1967.

GOODMAN, Paul and Percival. *Communitas; Means of Livelihood and Ways of Life.* 2nd ed. Vintage, 1960.

GREENWALT, Emmett. *The Point Loma Community in California, 1897–1942; A Theosophical Experiment.* California, 1955.

THE HARBINGER. v. 1–8, 1845–1849. AMS, 1971.

HARRISON, John Fletcher Clews. *Quest for the New Moral World; Robert Owen and the Owenites in Britain and America.* Scribner, 1969.

HENDRICKS, Robert J. *Bethel and Aurora, An Experiment in Communism as Practical Christianity; With Some Account of Past and Present Ventures in Collective Living.* AMS, 1971 (orig. pub. by the Press of the Pioneers, 1933).

HERTZLER, Joyce Oramel. *The History of Utopian Thought.* Cooper Square, 1965, (orig. pub. by Macmillan, 1923).

HINDS, William. *American Communities and Co-operative Colonies.* Charles Kerr and Co., 1908.

HINE, Robert. *California's Utopian Colonies.* Yale, 1966 (orig. pub. by Huntington Library, 1953).

HOLLOWAY, Mark. *Heavens on Earth; Utopian Communities in America, 1680–1880.* Dover, 1966 (orig. pub. by Turnstile Press, 1951).

HOLYOAKE, George Jacob. *The History of Co-operation in England; Its Literature and Its Advocates.* 2v. AMS, 1971 (orig. pub. by Trübner, 1875–79).

HOURIET, Robert. *Getting Back Together.* Coward, McCann & Georghegan, 1971.

HUGHES, Thomas. *Rugby, Tennessee.* Macmillan, 1891.

JAMES, Bartlett B. *The Labadist Colony in Maryland.* Johns Hopkins, 1899.

KANTER, Rosabeth. *Commitment and Community; Communes and Utopias in Sociological Perspective.* Harvard, 1972.

KENT, Alexander. "Cooperative Communities in the United States". *Bulletin of the Department of Labor* 35:563–646, July, 1901.

KLEIN, Walter Conrad. *Johann Conrad Beissel, Mystic and Martinet, 1690–1768.* Pennsylvania, 1942.

LAMECH, brother and Agrippa, brother. *Chronicon Ephratense; A History of the Community of Seventh Day Baptists at Ephrata, Lancaster County, Penna.* B. Franklin, 1972 (orig. pub. by S. H. Zahm, 1889).

LAMSON, David R. *Two Years' Experience Among the Shakers.* AMS, 1971 (orig. pub. by the author, 1848).

LEE, Dallas. *The Cotton Patch Evidence.* Harper & Row, 1971.

LEVERING, Joseph Mortimer. *A History of Bethlehem, Pennsylvania, 1741–1892, with Some Account of Its Founders and their Early Activity in America.* AMS, 1971 (orig. pub. by Times Publishing Company, 1903).

LONGLEY, Alcander. *What is Communism?* 2nd ed. AMS, 1971 (orig. pub. by the Altruist Community, 1890).

LIFESTYLE. v.1–· 1971–. Madison (Ohio), *Mother Earth News.*

MACLEAN, John Patterson. *Shakers of Ohio*. Porcupine Press, 1974 (reprint of 1907 ed.).

MANNHEIM, Karl. *Ideology and Utopia; An Introduction to the Sociology of Knowledge*. Harcourt, Brace, 1936.

MANUEL, Frank. *The New World of Henri Saint-Simon*. Harvard, 1956.

_____ . *The Prophets of Paris*. Harvard, 1962.

_____ . ed. *Utopias and Utopian Thought*. Houghton, Mifflin, 1966.

MANUEL, Frank and P. Fritzie. *French Utopias: an Anthology of Ideal Societies*. Free Press, 1966.

MARTIN, James J. *Men Against the State: the Expositors of Individualist Anarchism in America, 1827-1908*. Adrain Allen Associates, 1953.

MIKKELSEN, Michael Andrew. *The Bishop Hill Colony, a Religious Communistic Settlement in Henry County, Illinois*. Porcupine Press, 1973 (orig. pub. by Johns Hopkins, 1892).

MORGAN, Arthur. *The Community of the Future and the Future of Community*. Community Service (Ohio), 1957.

_____ . *Edward Bellamy*. Columbia, 1944.

_____ . *Nowhere was Somewhere: How History Makes Utopias and How Utopias Make History*. North Carolina, 1946.

NEAL, Julia. *By Their Fruits: The Story of Shakerism in South Union, Kentucky*. Porcupine Press, 1974 (reprint of 1947 ed.).

THE NATIONALIST. v.1-3, 1889-1891. Greenwood, 1968.

THE NEW NATION. v.1-4/no. 5, 1891-1894. Greenwood, 1968.

NEWBROUGH, John Ballou. *Oahspe, the Kosmon Revelations in the Words of Jehovih and His Angel Embassadors*. Kosmon Press, 1935.

NIEBUHR, Helmut Richard. *The Kingdom of God in America*. Willett, Clark and Company, 1937.

NORDHOFF, Charles. *The Communistic Societies of the United States*. Schocken, 1965 (orig. pub. by Harper, 1875).

NOYES, George Wallingford, ed. *The Putney Experience*. Syracuse, 1973.

_____ . *The Religious Experiences of John Henry Noyes*. Syracuse, 1973 (orig. pub. in 1923).

NOYES, John H. *The Berean: a Manual for the Help of Those Who Seek the Faith of the Primitive Church*. University Microfilms, 1957 (orig. pub. by office of the Spiritual Magazine, 1847).

_____ . *Bible Communism*. Porcupine Press, 1973 (orig. pub. in 1853).

_____ . *The Confessions of John H. Noyes*. University Microfilms, 1947.

_____ . *Essay on Scientific Propagation*. University Microfilms, 1957 (orig. pub. by Oneida community, 1875?).

_____ . *History of American Socialisms*. Dover, 1966 (orig. pub. by Lippincott, 1870).

ONEIDA COMMUNITY. *Daily Journal*. 1866-1868.

ORVIS, Marianne. *Letters From Brook Farm. 1844-1847*. Porcupine Press, 1973. (orig. pub. by Vassar College, 1928).

OWEN, A.K. *Integral Cooperation: Its Practical Application*. Porcupine Press, 1974 (reprint of 1885 ed.).

OWEN, Robert. *The Life of Robert Owen*. Augustus Kelley, 1967 (orig. pub. by E. Wilson, 1857-58).

_____ . *Millennial Gazette,* Nos. 1-16, Mar. 22, 1856-Jul. 1, 1858. AMS, 1973.

_____ . *A New View of Society: or, Essays on the Principle of the Formation of the Human Character, and the Application of the Principle to Practice.* Augustus Kelley, 1972. (orig. pub. by R. Taylor & Co., 1813).

_____ . *A Supplementary Appendix to the First Volume of the Life of Robert Owen.* Augustus Kelley, 1967 (orig. pub. by E. Wilson, 1857-58).

PARKER, Robert Allerton. *A Yankee Saint: John Henry Noyes and the Oneida Community.* Porcupine Press, 1973. (orig. pub. by G. P. Putnam's sons, 1935).

PAULSON, Ross. *Radicalism & Reform: the Vrooman Family and American Social Thought, 1837-1937.* Kentucky, 1968.

PEASE, William and Jane. *Black Utopia: Negro Communal Experiments in America.* State Historical Society of Wisconsin, 1963.

PETERS, Victor. *All Things Common: the Hutterian Way of Life.* Minnesota, 1966, c1965.

THE PHALANX, Nos. 1-23, 1843-1845. AMS, 1971.

PODMORE, Frank. *Robert Owen: a Biography.* 2v. in 1. Augustus Kelley, 1968 (orig. pub. in 1906).

QUINT, Howard. *The Forging of American Socialism: Origins of the Modern Movement.* South Carolina, 1953.

REYNOLDS, Ray. *Cat's Paw Utopia.* Printed by the author, 1973.

RIASANOVSKY, Nicholas. *The Teaching of Charles Fourier.* California, 1969.

ROBERTS, Ron. *The New Communes: Coming Together in America.* Prentice-Hall, 1971.

ROBERTSON, Constance Noyes. *The Oneida Community: the Break-up, 1876-1881.* Syracuse, 1972.

ROBERTSON, Thomas A. *A Southwestern Utopia.* Ward Ritchie, 1964.

SACHSE, Julius Friedrich. *The German Pietists of Provincial Pennsylvania.* AMS, 1970 (orig. pub. by the author, 1895).

_____ . *The German Sectarians of Pennsylvania, 1708-1800: a Critical and Legendary History of the Ephrata Cloister and Dunkers.* 2v. AMS, 1971 (orig. pub. by the author, 1899-1900).

_____ . *The Music of the Ephrata Cloister.* AMS, 1971 (orig. pub. by The Society, 1903).

SANFORD, Charles. *The Quest for Paradise: Europe and the American Moral Imagination.* Illinois, 1961.

SCHNEIDER, Herbert W. and George Lawton. *A Prophet and a Pilgrim.* AMS, 1970 (orig. pub. by Columbia, 1942).

SHAMBAUGH, Bertha M. *Amana, the Community of True Inspiration.* The State Historical Society of Iowa, 1908

SHAW, Albert. *Icaria, a Chapter in the History of Communism.* Porcupine Press, 1973 (orig. pub. by G. P. Putnam's sons, 1884).

SHEPPERSON, Wilbur. *Retreat to Nevada: a Socialist Colony of World War I.* Nevada, 1966.

SINCLAIR, Upton. *The Autobiography of Upton Sinclair.* Harcourt Brace, 1962.

STERN, Madeleine. *The Pantarch: a Biography of Stephen Pearl Andrews.* Texas, 1968.

SWIFT, Lindsay. *Brook Farm, Its Members, Scholars, and Visitors.* Corinth Books, 1961.

TEED, Cyrus. *The Cellular Cosmogony; or, the Earth a Concave Sphere.* Porcupine Press, 1974 (reprint of 1905 ed.).

THRUPP, Sylvia Lettice, ed. *Millennial Dreams in Action: Studies in Revolutionary Religious Movements.* Schocken, 1970.

TUVESON, Ernest. *Millennium and Utopia: a Study in the Background of the
Idea of Progress.* California, 1949.

_____ . *Redeemer Nation: the Idea of America's Millennial Role.* Chicago, 1968.

TWIN OAKS COMMUNITY. *Journal of a Walden Two Commune: the Collected
Leaves of Twin Oaks.* Dist. by Community Pub. Cooperative, 1972.

TYLER, Alice Felt. *Freedom's Ferment: Phases of American Social History to
1860.* Minnesota, 1944.

VEYSEY, Laurence. *The Communal Experience: Anarchist and Mystical Counter-
Cultures in America.* Harper and Row, 1973.

WATERMAN, William. *Frances Wright.* AMS Press, 1972 (orig. pub. as Columbia
University Studies in history, economics and public law, CXV, 1, 1924).

WEBBER, Everett. *Escape to Utopia: the Communal Movement in America.*
Hastings House, 1959.

WHITE, Anna and Leila S. Taylor. *Shakerism: Its Meaning and Message.* AMS,
1971 (orig. pub. in 1904).

WILLIAMS, Aaron. *The Harmony Society at Economy, Pennsylvania, Founded
by George Rapp, A.D. 1805.* Augustus Kelley, 1970 (orig. pub. in 1866).

WISBEY, Herbert A., Jr. *Pioneer Prophetess: Jemima Wilkinson, the Publick
Universal Friend.* Cornell, 1964.

WITTKE, Carl. *The Utopian Communist: a Biography of Wilhelm Weitling,
Nineteenth-Century Reformer.* Louisiana, 1950.

WOOSTER, Ernest. *Communities of the Past and Present.* AMS, 1971 (orig. pub.
by Llano Colonist, c1924).

YARMOLINSKY, Avrahm. *A Russian's American Dream: a Memoir on William
Frey.* Kansas, 1965.

ZABLOCKI, Benjamin. *The Joyful Community; an Account of the Bruderhof, a
Communal Movement Now in its Third Generation.* Penguin, 1971.

© Reprinted from *Choice,* Volume 10, #4, June, 1973. *Choice* is a publication of the Association of College and Research Libraries, a division of the American Library Association.

Regional Studies in America: The Chicago Model

by Thomas J. Schlereth

Regional studies have been a useful way of comprehending American culture ever since Edward Johnson wrote his *Wonder-Working Providence of Zion's Saviour in New England* in 1654. More recent scholarship and teaching, particularly in American Studies, has continued this tradition by focusing on the culture of the South, New England, the West, and the Middle West (1). The objective in such investigations has usually been to explore the possible existence and dimensions of a regional culture as well as its relationship to the national culture.

In such a context the cultural history of Chicago from the 1870s to the 1920s provides a striking microcosm of the political, economic, literary and artistic developments in the nation at large. It offers a fertile area of study for the social scientist interested in urban history, the literary scholar working in regional literature, and the art historian intrigued by the rise of modern architecture. Ray Ginger and Hugh D. Duncan (2) have tried, with varying degrees of success, to explore the interrelations between the city's politics, economic growth, literary achievement, and architectural innovation. What I am suggesting here is a bibliographical framework that expands the Ginger-Duncan perspective by a comprehensive survey of the primary sources and secondary literature available for a systematic study of Chicago's regional culture and its relation to American history, 1871–1919.

Naturally this Chicago model is most accessible to American Studies scholars who are researching and teaching in the Middle West, but the published sources on the city are now so plentiful that one can easily do much research, or an American Studies course, on the topic in Oslo, Tokyo or Berlin. Recently British scholars developing course materials for The Open University in the United

Kingdom concurred in what social scientists have long maintained: Chicago is probably the best researched, and perhaps the best example, of a typical urban complex in the modern world. Moreover, what I also mean to suggest by this essay is the feasibility of scholars developing other interpretive frameworks using other American cities as the foci of regional inquiries: seventeenth-century Boston; eighteenth-century Baltimore or Philadelphia; early nineteenth-century Cincinnati or New Orleans; late nineteenth-century San Francisco or St. Louis; twentieth-century New York or Los Angeles.

To gain a general perspective of Chicago's development, 1871–1919, there are numerous, often highly personal, accounts of its history done by Joseph Kirkland, Lloyd Lewis and Henry Smith, Edgar Lee Masters, Wayne Andrews, Emmett Dedmon, Bessie Pierce, and more recently, Edward Wagenknecht, Finis Farr, and Stephen Longstreet (3). Pierce's three-volumes comprise the most detailed scholarly study of the period to 1893, but it has now been superseded somewhat by Harold Mayer and Richard Wade's well-written single volume, *Chicago: Growth of a Metropolis** (Chicago: University of Chicago Press: 1966) (4). Mayer, a geographer, and Wade, an historian, collaborated with Glen Holt, an historian of photography. Holt integrated their research with numerous photographs in an excellent example of how to employ visual material to document as well as illustrate an historical narrative. Holt has explained his methodology in "Chicago Through a Camera Lens: An Essay on Photography As History," published (Spring: 1971) in the Chicago Historical Society's quarterly, *Chicago History,* a publication that should be consulted for articles on music, art, economics, literature and theatre in addition to history. As should be evident from the sources I cite below, I maintain that in its general outlines, as well as in many of its specific dimensions, the Chicago story, 1871-1919, is the national story. This position is also held by such scholars as Arthur M. Schlesinger, Sr., Constance Green, Daniel Boorstin, and Howard Mumford Jones (5).

In order to review the highlights of American politics from the late nineteenth through the early twentieth century, Chicago offers excellent sources. Vernon Simpson and David Scott have collected many of them in *Chicago's Politics and Society, A Selected Bibliography** (6) which they augment with annual supplements. The rise of city bosses, ethnic politics, and the protests for social reform can be nicely studied using Chicago data. *Machine Politics, The Chicago Model** (UCP: 1947, second edition: 1968) by Harold Gosnell is the best general introduction and Joel A. Tarr, Claudius O. Johnson, Alex Gottfried and Mike Royko provide good biographical commentaries (7). A lively study of the picturesque "Lords of the Levee," principally John "The Bath" Coughlin and Hinky Dink Kenna by Lloyd Wendt and Herman Kogan (8), captures the exploits of the city's most notorious aldermen and the machinations of the infamous city council. Mayor Carter Harrison's two-volume autobiography (9) offers one personal account of the city's political life while Charles E. Merriam, University of Chicago political scientist and reform councilman, offers another in his memoirs (10).

William T. Stead's prediction *If Christ Came To Chicago* (Chicago: Laird & Lee: 1894) was but one prognosis of the need for reform in *fin de siecle* America. Chicago's Municipal Voter's League, the Civic Federation and the Union League Club (11) were various Middle Western Mugwump counterparts to the National Civil Service Reform League. Individual reformers such as Jane Addams, Francis

Willard, Clarence Darrow, Louise deKoven Bowen, Eugene Debs, Alice Hamilton and Graham Taylor (12) left descriptive reminiscences of their efforts and of the city they sought to improve. Women were particularly involved in Chicago reform and cultural uplift, and Allen Davis's new biography of Jane Addams (NY: Oxford: 1973) recreates the atmosphere in which they worked and the obstacles they had to overcome. The Arno Press has published a new edition of the 1895 *Hull House Maps and Papers* (13) which, along with data gathered in Edith Abbott's *Tenements of Chicago,* 1908–1935, (UCP: 1936) Florence Kelley's various writings and Louise deKoven Bowen's speeches (14), offers the social scientist superb primary sources for the study of urban problems. Harvey Zorbaugh, Louis Wirth, Nels Anderson and Homer Hoyt have also provided classic models (15) of such social analysis done at the University of Chicago. *Division Street, America** (NY: Pantheon: 1967) by Louis ("Studs") Terkel is a more recent and more popular example of urban sociology using Chicago as a laboratory.

As in other American cities, the boss system and its cult of ethnicity thrived, in part, because it manipulated the diverse neighborhoods of Chicago's inner city—the Irish, Germans and Scandinavians who came in the mid-nineteenth century, and the immigrants who travelled later from Italy, Russia, Austria-Hungary, the Balkans, Greece, and the Black Americans from the South. John Allswang has surveyed the immigrant history of the city in *A House For All Peoples: Ethnic Politics in Chicago, 1890-1936 (Lexington, Ky.: University of* Kentucky Press: 1971), but practically every major ethnic minority is represented in the specific monograph literature (16). To do Chicago ethnic studies, one should also visit the Polish Museum (984 Milwaukee Ave.); the Ling Long Chinese Museum (4012 S. Archer); the Maurice Spertus Museum (72 East 11th St.) and the DuSable Museum of African-American History (3806 S. Michigan).

An important chapter of the Black man's American history is likewise dramatized in Chicago, especially during and after World War I when European migration declined and Southern Blacks, encouraged by newspapers like *The Chicago Defender,* began moving up the Mississippi Valley. St. Clair Drake and Horace R. Clayton first studied this significant development (17) and more recently Harold F. Gosnell, *Negro Politicians: The Rise of Negro Politics in Chicago* (UCP: 1935, 1967) and Allan H. Spear, *Black Chicago: The Making of a Negro Ghetto, 1890–1920** (UCP: 1967) have examined its political and social consequences. William Tuttle on a scholarly level, Carl Sandburg from a

Mr. Schlereth is Assistant Professor of American Studies at the University of Notre Dame. He has taught American and European History at Grinnell College, and was a Faculty Fellow in History at the Newberry Library in Chicago in 1970–71. A member of the Organization of American Historians and the Chicago School of Architecture Foundation, Mr. Schlereth's most recent publications include Geronimo, The Last of the Apache Chiefs *(1974). He is currently engaged in research on the life of Edward Frederick Sorin.*

newsman's viewpoint, and the Chicago Race Relations Commission from a documentary perspective, have each (18) provided insight into the causes and consequences of the bloody Chicago race riot of 1919.

Chicago has always been one of the nation's more violent cities from the Fort Dearborn ambush in 1812 to the Haymarket riots of 1886 to the St. Valentine's Massacre in 1929. The Pullman strike of 1894 provides a superb case study in which are woven important strands of economic, labor, social, constitutional, business, and political history. Pullman has been examined in detail (19) from Richard T. Ely's excellent contemporary account, "Pullman, A Social Study," *Harper's New Monthly Magazine* (February: 1885) to Stanley Buder's *Pullman, An Experiment In Industrial Order and Community Planning,* 1880–1930* (NY: Oxford: 1967). For students in geographical proximity to Pullman, now a part of the city of Chicago, William Adelman of the Illinois Labor History Society has prepared an illustrated walking guide (20) to the planned company town. The Pullman Civic Organization, intent on preserving S. S. Beman's architecture, also offers guided tours of the Historic Landmark District.

Of course, Chicago's demographic, industrial, and commercial growth in the late nineteenth century is the American economic paradigm par excellence. In the hundred years from 1830 to 1930, the city grew from a settlement of fifty people to one of three and a third million. In the half century between 1840 and 1890 the rapidity of Chicago's economic development outstripped that of every other city in the world so that by 1920 only London, New York, and Berlin exceeded her in size and commercial importance. Pierce (3) has traced this expansion up to 1893, while Mayer and Wade and Dorsha Hayes's chauvinistic *Chicago, Crossroads of American Enterprise* (NY: Julian Messner: 1944) give the sweep of the city's economic history. The story is better told in assorted monographs: Harper Leech and John Carroll on Armour, Morris Werner on Rosenwald, John Tebbel on the Fields as well as the McCormicks, Medills, and the Pattersons. Forest MacDonald had done a good book on Insull (21), Sigfried Giedion's playful *Mechanization Takes Command, A Contribution To Anonymous History** (NY: Oxford: 1948, reprinted: 1969) has stimulating chapters on the Pullmans, the Armours, and the McCormicks and their role in the history of American technology.

For work in economic, political and business history, The Municipal Reference Library of the City of Chicago (Tenth Floor—City Hall), and the Chicago Historical Society (Clark at North) are excellent resources. Much documentary material on political and economic developments has been collected by Ernest W. Burgess and Charles Newcomb (census data), Homer Hoyt (land values), and Evelyn Kitagawa and Philip M. Hauser (local community sources) (22).

A number of scholars, particularly Bernard Duffey, Hugh Duncan, Dale Kramer and Henry May (23), have argued that roughly from Hamlin Garland's publication of *Crumbling Idols* in 1893 (24) to Sherwood Anderson's departure for New York in 1920, Chicago had a significant share of the nation's literary inspiration, production, and consumption. The literary awakening has also been described by the participants in a diverse crop of autobiographies: multi-volume personal accounts by Garland (25), Dreiser (26) and Anderson (27); Sandburg's nostalgic *Always the Young Strangers* (NY: Harcourt, Brace: 1953), Eunice Tietjens' *The World at My Shoulder* (NY: Macmillan: 1938), Edgar Lee Masters' *Across Spoon*

River (NY: Farrar & Rinehart: 1936); Harriet Monroe's *A Poet's Life: Seventy Years in A Changing World* (NY: Macmillan: 1938) plus Floyd Dell's amusing *Homecoming, An Autobiography* (NY: Farrar & Rinehart: 1933).

The Chicago press, equally well-remembered in the reminiscences of Ben Hecht, Melville Stone, Burton Rascoe, and Arthur Meeker (28) was perhaps the liveliest Fourth Estate in the nation between 1875 and 1925. Over a dozen dailies flourished and newspaper offices and city rooms were once a source of genuine literary talent. Eugene Field's column, "Sharps and Flats," in *The News* has been studied by Slason Thompson (29); Jean Shepherd has anthologied George Ade's "Stories of the Streets and Town" (30) and James Farrell has brought out a modern edition of *Artie And Pink Marsh, Two Novels* (Chicago: 1963) in the University of Chicago Press series on Chicago in Fiction. Of course, Finley Peter Dunn's creation of "Mr. Dooley" of Archery Road (his original was a barkeep on Dearborn Street) offers insight into the local color movement as well as American political satire. Dunne's pieces have been collected by Louis Filler and Robert Hutchinson (31). Ring Lardner (32) and his fellow raconteur Ben Hecht were also members of the Chicago press corps. Nelson Algren has written an introduction for a modern edition of Hecht's *Erik Dorn* (UCP: 1963) and *The Front Page,* a delightful play Hecht did in collaboration with Charles McArthur in 1928, has recently enjoyed a successful revival on the London and Chicago stage.

In addition to Hecht, writers like Theodore Dreiser, Carl Sandburg, Sherwood Anderson and Floyd Dell cut their literary teeth on Chicago journalism. Before this cadre of authors came into its own, an older generation had been exploring a variety of new literary topics even if they were uncertain in experimenting with new literary forms. Edmund Wilson and Guy Szuberla have sparked new interest in Henry Blake Fuller (33), whose *With the Procession**, *The Cliff-Dwellers,* and *Under the Skylights* have all been reprinted (34). Clara and Rudolf Kirk have revived Edith Wyatt while David Henry's biography of William Vaughan Moody remains the best survey of the poet-playwright's limited achievement (35).

Blake Nevius and Kenneth Jackson have worked with the numerous novels of Robert Herrick (36), who, in his *Web of Life* (NY: Macmillan: 1900) saw Chicago as a representative emblem of the American industrial age, a prototype of "all the sharp discords of the nineteenth century." In his more famous novel of 1905, *The Memoirs of an American Citizen* (Daniel Aaron has written a perceptive introduction to a Harvard University Press 1963 edition), Herrick used a fictional character, Van Harrington, not only as a typical Chicagoan but, as the book's title suggests, a representative American of the 1890s. Herrick, like Fuller, explored all the concerns that later Chicago writers would make their stock and trade: the impact of the dominant business ethos upon cultural values; the nature of urban life and its ramifications for literary art; and, the migrant experience of Americans from the country to the city.

Naturally the literature of the better known Chicago giants is the most accessible way of examining these themes as well as other representative trends in the American literature of the period (37). In paperback have been available, Dreiser's *Sister Carrie* and his triology on the city's traction-magnate Charles Yerkes (*The Titan, The Financier, The Stoic*); Upton Sinclair's *The Jungle;* Frank Norris' *The Pit;* Sherwood Anderson's *Marching Men.* Dell's *Moon Calf* (NY: A.

A. Knopf: 1920) and *Briary Bush* (NY: A. A. Knopf: 1921) are a bit harder to find but still useful for the ambience of the city's literary movement. Depending on how far one wishes to extend a study of the Chicago "school" of fiction, there is also the work of James Farrell, Richard Wright, Nelson Algren and Saul Bellow. The point, argues Bernard Duffey, the historian of *The Chicago Renaissance in American Letters* (38) is that "the group reality of twentieth-century American literature began in Chicago because in Chicago a chief strain which has favored our modern writing was first recognized."

Many of the Chicago writers were also poets and for a while the city was America's poetic center. *Poetry, A Magazine of Verse* was the movement's chief organ and remains its best primary source. The journal's success was largely the work of Harriet Monroe, a bad poet but a formidable entrepreneuse who knew how to combine philanthrophy and the arts. Her career deserves a thorough re-evaluation which could be nicely done from the Harriet Monroe Papers at the University of Chicago. (The Newberry Library in Chicago, particularly because of its extensive Middle West Authors Collection, is the best research center for manuscript study of other Chicago authors). Carl Sandburg and Vachel Lindsay were among Ms. Monroe's protégés, the best editions of their works being Sandburg's *Complete Poems* (NY: Harcourt, Brace: 1970) and Lindsay's *Collected Poems* (NY: Macmillan: 1925). The standard biographies of Sandburg and Lindsay, respectively, are by Karl Detzer and Ann Massa (39). Ms. Massa's essay is a fine example of American Studies scholarship but it does not totally supplant Edgar Lee Masters' tribute to *Vachel Lindsay, A Poet in America* (NY: Scribners: 1935) which says as much about Masters as it does about his fellow Illinoian. Masters was a man of really only one literary achievement (*The Spoon River Anthology*, NY: Macmillan: 1915) which has been recorded, as has the poetry of Lindsay and Sandburg, on the Caedamon Spoken Arts Series of Columbia Records.

In addition to *Poetry,* Francis Browne's Emersonian *Dial* (40), and Stone and Kimball's innovative *Chapbook* (41), the latter being the first of the American "little magazines," Chicago was also the birthplace of Margaret Anderson's iconoclastic *Little Review* (42). Margaret, as was her way, told her story as *My Thirty Years War* (NY: Covici-Friede: 1930) and also edited an anthology of what she considered the *Review's* best works (43).

Thus for anyone willing to look closely, Chicago's literary and poetic achievements not only paralleled currents in other parts of the country but in several instances stimulated them. For many years the East had dismissed Chicago as a muddy grain pit, a Porkopolis devoted only to "cash, cussing and cuspidors." Between 1871 and 1919, however, the city became self-conscious and self-corrective about its cultural life in various forms. Its history during these years furnishes the American Studies scholar with an abundance of cultural evidence useful for investigating important developments in late nineteenth and early twentieth century art, music and education.

Much of the city's cultural awakening revolved around preparing and executing the World's Columbian Exposition of 1893, a cultural event highly symbolic of late nineteenth-century American achievements and aspirations, yet to date only studied piecemeal (44). The fair can be used as a point of reference and a point of departure to trace trends in art, music, and popular taste. Alson J. Smith's breezy survey of *Chicago's Left Bank* (Chicago: Regnery: 1953) does this to a certain extent in his attempt to portray Chicago as a Florence to New York's Rome (45).

Smith devotes a chapter to Chicago as "The Jazz Capital" and reviews how Black talents such as Louis Armstrong, Joe "King" Oliver, "Jelly Roll" Morton and singer Bessie Smith made significant contributions to what historians (46) of music identify as the "Chicago style," a sub-species of jazz predominant in the nation, 1917–1929. The cultural and social ramifications that jazz has had on American popular music and popular taste can be examined in the Chicago context and Chadwick Hansen (47) has used the locale, in turn, to trace a reverse influence of the dominant White society upon jazz as a musical expression of the Black subculture.

From the beginning, the city's jazz was located on Chicago's South Side and not far from this musical creativity arose another, albeit quite different, cultural asset— The University of Chicago, a school founded practically overnight in 1892 with John D. Rockfeller's money, land from Marshall Field, and guided by the presidential entrepreneurship of Hebraist William Rainey Harper. Richard Storr's first volume on *Harper's University, The Beginnings* (UCP: 1966) surveys the institution's history to 1905; other monographs can be consulted to see the University as a case history of the important trends of late nineteenth-century American higher education: the rise of graduate and professional schools (48); the new emphasis of the social and behavioral sciences (49); and the increased concern to involve the university in social issues (50).

Harper recruited a faculty with such vigor and largesse that some claimed the highest degree an educator could get was a C.T.C. (Called To Chicago). Many of the giants of American intellectual history got the call, responded, and each provides an excellent biographical approach by which to study American thought at the turn of the century. Jacques Loeb has been placed in the development of American behavior psychology by Donald Flemming (51); Lloyd J. Averill (52) has argued for Shailer Mathews' place in liberal theology; R. M. Barry (53) for the role of George Herbert Mead in philosophy, and L. L. and J. Bernard (54) for Albion Small's impact in American sociology. Thorstein Veblen, of course, used his Chicago environment to write his classic *The Higher Learning in America** (Stanford, Calif.: Academic Reprints: 1954, first published 1918) as John Dewey used the University's Laboratory School (55) to gather data for his equally famous *The School And Society* (UCP: 1954, first published 1899). Joseph Dorfman relates Veblen's career to general economic theory in America and Laurence Cremin has nicely placed Dewey's work in the history of progressive education (56).

In literature, journalism and jazz, the acclaimed Chicago Renaissance was a temporary although significant phenomenon, restricted largely from the 1880s to the 1920s. In architecture the city's achievement has been constantly creative since William Jenney discovered the true skyscraper principle by using a skeleton-type construction on the ten-story Home Insurance Building in 1884–85. "The Developments in Chicago in the late 19th century," writes Hugh C. Miller, "were as consequential in world cultural history as the developments in 12th century France that produced Gothic architecture and in 15th century Italy that produced Renaissance architecture. Of these three equally significant nodal points in the history of western man, only the consequences of the Chicago School were truly global in scope" (57).

Even if this estimate approaches hyperbole, there still can be little doubt that a radical shift in urban architectural forms occurred in Chicago following the 1871 fire through a confluence of changing economic and social circumstances, technological innovations, and imaginative talent. Carl Condit has long been the dean of Chicago architectural historians surveying this amazing development. His numerous studies (58) should be supplemented by the general estimates of Sigfried Giedion, Lewis Mumford, Mark Peisch, William Jordy, and articles in the recent anthology edited by Edgar J. Kaufman (59). Naturally individual architects have been evaluated: John Wellborn Root by his sister-in-law Harriet Monroe and now by Donald Hoffman; Daniel Burnham by Charles Moore; Frederick Law Olmsted by Julius Fabos and others; and Henry Hobson Richardson by Henry Russell Hitchcock (60).

Understandably a considerable amount of scholarship has been devoted to Louis Sullivan and his brash protégé Frank Lloyd Wright. The works of Sullivan and Wright, both buildings and writings, are excellent sources for American Studies students interested in exploring the interrelations between material and verbal culture. Sullivan's extant architecture is documented in Ira Bach and Arthur Siegel's walking guides (61) and in the slide collection of the Carnegie Study of the Arts of the United States (62); his prose writings have been collected in a fine edition by Maurice English, *The Testament of Stone: Themes of Idealism and Indignation From the Writings of Louis Sullivan* (Evanston, Ill.. Northwestern University Press: 1963). Sullivan's *Kindergarten Chats** and *The Autobiography of an Idea** have also been reprinted(63). Hugh Morrison's biography(64) can be supplemented by Wright's own testimony to his hero (*Genius and the Mobocracy,** NY: Duell, Sloan, and Pearce: 1949) and especially by Sherman Paul's classic *Louis Sullivan, An Architect in American Thought** (Englewood Cliffs, N.J.: Prentice-Hall: 1962).

The literature on and by Wright forms a bibliographical essay in itself with many titles now being reprinted by the Horizon Press. Edgar Kaufman and Ben Raeburn have combined the *Writings and Buildings of Frank Lloyd Wright* (NY: Horizon: 1960) in a useful source book. Frederick Gutheim has been concerned principally with Wright's writings(65), while Martin Pawley and Yukio Futagawa and Edgar Kaufman have emphasized his buildings(66). For photographic and slide resources on Wright also see Bach, Siegel, the Carnegie Arts study, and the collections of the Frank Lloyd Wright Association in Oak Park, Illinois. Of course, Wright's influence extended far beyond Chicago and the research on his prolific work of later years is deliberately excluded in this essay. Two works that should be mentioned, however, are H. Allen Brooks, *The Prairie School: Frank Lloyd Wright and His Midwest Contemporaries* (Toronto: University of Toronto Press: 1972) and Grant C. Manson, *Frank Lloyd Wright To 1910, The First Golden Age* (NY: Reinhold Publishers: 1958). One should also note here three superb Chicago facilities for doing research in the city's architectural history: the Burnham Library in the Art Institute (Adams and Michigan); the photograph and print collection at the Chicago Historical Society (North and Clark); and the library at the Chicago Architectural Foundation, now housed in the former residence (18th and Prairie) that H. H. Richardson built for J. J. Glessner in 1886–87.

As one becomes familiar with Chicago's architectural creativity, one sees, as have Hugh Duncan and Guy Szuberla(67), certain interconnections between the literature and the architecture of the period, 1871–1919. Diverse cultural ramifications can also be explored, say, in the community planning of S. S. Beman's industrial Pullman, F. L. Olmsted's residential Riverside, or D. H. Burnham's metropolitan Plan of Chicago in 1909(68). Victoria Ranney has made *Olmsted in Chicago* (Chicago: R.R. Donnelly: 1972) her special province and provides an excellent bibliography at the conclusion of her essay. W. R. Hasbruck has written a new introduction to Burnham's grandiose Plan, recently re-issued by The Prairie School Press (Palos Park, Illinois: 1972). Carl Condit devotes a thorough chapter to the Burnham Concept in his *Chicago, 1910–1929: Building, Planning, and Urban Technology* (Chicago: UCP: 1973).

The Chicago architects determined to emphasize their innovations in their founding of the Western Association of Architects. Their publication, *The Inland Architect and Builder*—not unlike Garland's hopes for his region's contribution to literature—spoke of a West trying to assert its artistic modernity in steel and glass, those supremely modern industrial materials. The reality of that modernity is more evident in the inspiration the original "Chicago School" continues to provide for architectural practice both in Chicago and in the nation. A third generation of the city's architects represented by Ludwig Mies van der Rohe and many of his Chicago followers openly acknowledge their indebtedness to the early masters of the period, 1871–1919.

Further inquiry into Chicago's history, 1871–1919, would yield many other cultural trends with significance for the national culture. Suffice it to say that none of the national struggles, problems, and achievements during these fifty years were missing in the region that James Bryce once called "the most American part of America." Chicago was archetypal, a representative place wherein the "Age of Energy," the sobriquet Howard Mumford Jones (5) aptly uses to describe the "varieties of American experience, 1865–1915," came to something of an apex. Chicago, in this period, was not just middle America; it was America.

[Both in his essay and in the notes which follow, Mr. Schlereth has used the asterisk (*) to indicate works that are available in soft-cover editions.—Ed.]

NOTES

(1) See examples of this interest in specific American cultural areas in American Studies programs at University of Pennsylvania and Michigan State University in Robert F. Lucid, ed., "Programs in American Studies, *American Quarterly*, XXII: 2, Part 2 (Summer: 1970).

(2) *Altgeld's America, The Lincoln Ideal Versus Changing Realities** (NY: Funk Wagnalls: 1958) and *Culture and Democracy: The Struggle For Form in Society and Architecture in Chicago and the Middle West During the Life and Times of Louis H. Sullivan* (Totowa, N.J.: Bedminister Press: 1965).

(3) Respectively, *The History of Chicago*, 3 vols. (Chicago: Dibble Publishing Co.: 1892–94); *Chicago, the History of its Reputation* (NY: Harcourt, Brace: 1929); *The Tale of Chicago* (NY: G. P. Putnam's Sons: 1933); *Battle For*

Chicago (NY: Harcourt, Brace: 1946); *Fabulous Chicago* (NY: Random House: 1953); *A History of Chicago*, 3 vols. (NY: Knopf: 1937–57); *Chicago* (Norman, Oklahoma, University of Oklahoma Press: 1964); *Chicago: Personal History of America's Most American City* (New Rochelle, NY: Arlington House: 1973); *Chicago, 1860–1919* (NY: McKay: 1973).

(4) The University of Chicago Press, a cultural agency itself, has been a major publisher of data and studies about Chicago since 1894. Hereafter, in the text and in the notes, it is abbreviated UCP.

(5) *The Rise of the City, 1878–1898* (NY: Macmillan: 1933); *American Cities in the Growth of the Nation* (NY: Harper & Row: 1957) *The Americans: The National Experience* (NY: Random House: 1965); *The Age of Energy: Varieties of American Experience, 1865–1915** (NY: Viking: 1970).

(6) DeKalb, Illinois: Northern Illinois University Center for Governmental Studies: 1972.

(7) *A Study in Boss Politics: William Lorimer of Chicago* (Urbana, Ill.: University of Illinois Press: 1971); *Carter Henry Harrison I, Political Leader* (UCP: 1928); *Boss Cermak of Chicago: A Study of Political Leadership* (Seattle, Wash.: University of Washington Press: 1962); *Boss: Richard J. Daley of Chicago** (NY: Dutton: 1971).

(8) *Lords of the Levee: The Story of Bathhouse John and Hinky Dink;* (Indianapolis: Bobbs-Merrill: 1943); retitled *Bosses in Lusty Chicago** (Bloomington, Ind.: Indiana University Press: 1967).

(9) *Stormy Years: The Autobiography of Carter Henry Harrison, Five Times Mayor of Chicago* (Indianapolis: Bobbs-Merrill: 1935); *Growing Up With Chicago* (Chicago: R. F. Seymour: 1944).

(10) *Chicago: A More Intimate View of Urban Politics* (NY: Macmillan: 1929).

(11) Joan S. Miller, "The Politics of Municipal Reform in Chicago During the Progressive Era: The Municipal Voters League As a Test Case, 1896–1920" (M. A. Thesis, Roosevelt University: 1966); Bruce Grant, *Fight For A City, The Story of the Union League Club and its Time, 1880–1955* (Chicago: Rand McNally: 1955); Mark Haller, "Urban Vice and Civic Reform: Chicago in the Early Twentieth Century," in Kenneth T. Jackson and Stanley Schultz, eds., *Cities in American History* (NY: Knopf: 1972), 290–305.

(12) *Twenty Years at Hull House** (NY: Macmillan: 1910) and *Second Twenty Years at Hull House, 1909–1929* (NY: Macmillan: 1930); *Glimpses of Fifty Years: The Autobiography of an American Woman* (Chicago: H. J. Smith: 1889, re-printed by Source Book Press, New York: 1970); *The Story Of My Life* (NY: Scribners: 1932); *Growing Up With A City* (NY: Macmillan: 1926); *Walls And Bars* (Chicago: Socialist Party of America: 1927); *Exploring The Dangerous Trades* (Boston: Little, Brown: 1943); *Chicago Commons Through Forty Years* (Chicago: Chicago Commons Association: 1936).

(13) (NY: Arno Press and New York Times: 1970). Allen Davis and Mary Lynn McCree have edited a marvelous anthology, *Eighty Years at Hull House* (Chicago: Quadrangle Books: 1969) that nicely compliments the *Maps and Papers.* On Addams' male counterpart see Louise C. Wade, *Graham Taylor, Pioneer for Social Justice, 1851-1938* (UCP: 1964).

(14) *Some Ethical Gains Through Legislation* (NY: Macmillan: 1905, 1910, 1914, reprinted New York, Arno Press, 1969); *Speeches, Addresses, and Letters*

of Louise De Koven Bowen, Reflecting Social Movements in Chicago, 2 vols (Ann Arbor, Mich.: Edwards Brothers: 1937).

(15) *Gold Coast and Slum, A Sociological Study of Chicago's Near North Side* (UCP: 1929); *The Ghetto* (UCP: 1928); *The Hobo, The Sociology of the Homeless Man* (UCP: 1923); *One Hundred Years of Land Values in Chicago: The Relationship of the Growth of Chicago to the Rise in Its Land Values, 1830–1933* (UCP: 1933).

(16) See, for example, Humbert S. Nelli, *The Italians in Chicago, 1880–1930, A Study in Ethnic Mobility* (NY: Oxford: 1970); Andrew J. Townsend, *The Germans of Chicago* (UCP: 1932); Ulf Beijbom, *Swedes in Chicago, A Demographic and Social Study of the 1846–1880 Immigration* (Stockholm: Laromedelsforlaget: 1971); Philip P. Bregstone, *Chicago and its Jews, A Cultural History* (Chicago, private printing: 1933); Edward W. Levine, *The Irish and Irish Politicians: A Study of Cultural and Social Alienation* (Notre Dame, Ind.: University of Notre Dame Press: 1966).

(17) *Black Metropolis** (NY: Harcourt, Brace: 1945; Harper Torchbook Edition, 1962).

(18) *Race Riot: Chicago in the Red Summer of 1919** (NY: Atheneum: 1970); *The Chicago Race Riots, July 1919* (NY: Harcourt, Brace: 1919; reprinted 1962); *The Negro in Chicago, A Study of Race Relations and A Race Riot* (Chicago: Chicago Commission on Race Relations: 1919).

(19) On Pullman, also see Almont Lindsey, *The Pullman Strike: The Story of A Unique Experiment and of a Great Labor Upheaval* (UCP: 1942) and Colston Warne's sourcebook, *The Pullman Boycott of 1894: The Problem of Federal Intervention* (Boston: D.C. Heath: 1955).

(20) *Touring Pullman** (Chicago: Illinois Labor History Society: 1972).

(21) *Armour and His Times* (NY: Appleton-Century: 1938); *Julius Rosenwald: The Life of a Practical Humanitarian* (NY: Harper Brothers: 1939); *The Marshall Fields: A Study in Wealth* (NY: E. P. Dutton: 1947) and *An American Dynasty: The Story of the McCormicks, Medills, and Pattersons* (Garden City, N.Y.: Doubleday: 1947; reprint NY: Greenwood Press: 1958); *Insull* (UCP: 1962).

(22) *Census Data of the City of Chicago* (UCP: 1931); *One Hundred Years of Land Values in Chicago* (UCP: 1933); *Local Community Fact Book for Chicago* (UCP: 1953).

(23) *The Chicago Renaissance in American Letters* (East Lansing, Mich.: Michigan State College Press: 1954); *The Rise of Chicago As a Literary Center From 1885 to 1920, A Sociological Essay in American Culture* (Totowa, N.J.: Bedminister Press: 1964); *Chicago Renaissance, The Literary Life in the Midwest, 1900–1930* (NY: Appleton-Century: 1966); and *The End of American Innocence, A Study of the First Years of Our Time, 1912–1917** (NY: Knopf: 1959).

(24) See Robert E. Spiller's introduction and notes, *Crumbling Idols; Twelve Essays on Art Dealing Chiefly With Literature, Painting and the Drama* (Gainesville, Fla.: Scholars' Facsimiles and Reprints: 1952) or a more recent edition edited by Jane Johnson for the Belknap Press, Cambridge, Mass.: Harvard University Press: 1960).

(25) *A Daughter of the Middle Border* (NY: Macmillan: 1921); *Roadside Meetings* (NY: Macmillan: 1930); *Companions on the Trail* (NY: Macmillan: 1931).

(26) *A Book About Myself* (NY: Boni and Liveright: 1922); *Dawn: A History of Myself* (NY: H. Liveright: 1931).

(27) *A Story-Teller's Story* (N.Y.: B. W. Huebsch: 1924); *Tar: A Midwest Childhood* (NY: Boni and Liveright: 1926, reprint, Cleveland: Press of Case Western Reserve: 1969); *Sherwood Anderson's Memoirs* (NY: Harcourt Brace: 1942, reprint, Chapel Hill: University of North Carolina Press: 1969).

(28) *A Child of the Century* (NY: Simon & Schuster: 1954); *Fifty Years A Journalist* (Garden City, N.Y.: Doubleday: 1921); *Before I Forget* (Garden City, N.Y.: Doubleday: 1937); *Chicago With Love: A Polite and Personal History* (NY: A. A. Knopf: 1955).

(29) *Eugene Field: A Study in Heredity and Contradictions,* 2 volumes (NY: Scribners: 1901); *Life of Eugene Field, the Poet of Childhood* (NY: Appleton: 1927).

(30) *The America of George Ade, 1866-1944: Fables, Short Stories, Essays** (NY: Putnam: 1961); E. F. Bleiler has edited *Fables in Slang, and More Fables in Slang* (NY: Dover: 1960).

(31) *Mr. Dooley: Now and Forever* (Stanford: Academic Reprints: 1954); *Mr. Dooley on Ivrything and Iverybody** NY: Dover: 1963); On Dunne also see his autobiographical fragments and an interpretive commentary by Philip Dunne, *Mr. Dooley Remembers: The Informal Memoirs of Finley Peter Dunne* (Boston: Little, Brown: 1963).

(32) Maxwell Geismar has edited *The Ring Lardner Reader* (NY: Scribners: 1963).

(33) "Henry B. Fuller: The Art of Making It Flat," *The New Yorker* (23 May 1970); "Making The Sublime Mechanical: Henry Blake Fuller's Chicago," *American Studies, XIV:* 1 (Spring: 1973), 83–93.

(34) UCP: 1965; Ridgewood, N.J.: Gregg Press: 1968; NY: Garrett Press: 1969.

(35) "Edith Wyatt: The Jane Austen of Chicago?" *Chicago History,* I:3 (Spring: 1971), 172–78; *William Vaughan Moody, A Study* (Boston: Little, Brown: 1934).

(36) *Robert Herrick: The Development of a Novelist* (Berkeley: University of California Press: 1962); "Robert Herrick's Use of Chicago," *Midcontinent American Studies Journal, V* (1964), 24–32.

(37) Surveys that place the Chicago writers in a national context include: Larzer Ziff, *The American 1890s: The Life and Times of a Lost Generation** (NY: Viking: 1966); Jay Martin, *Harvests of Change: American Literature, 1865–1914* (Englewood Cliff, N.J.: Prentice-Hall: 1967); Warner Berthoff, *The Ferment of Realism: American Literature, 1884-1919* (NY: Free Press: 1965). Also useful is Lennox B. Grey, "Chicago and The Great American Novel; A Critical Approach to the American Epic" (Unpublished Dissertation, University of Chicago: 1935).

(38) Also see Louis Untermeyer, *The New Era in American Poetry* (NY: Holt: 1919) and Charles Blanden and Minna Mathison, *The Chicago Anthology: A Collection of Verse From the Work of the Chicago Poets* (Chicago: The Roadside Press: 1916).

(39) *Carl Sandburg: A Study in Personality and Background* (NY: Harcourt, Brace: 1941); *Vachel Lindsay, Fieldworker For the American Dream* (Bloomington, Ind.: University of Indiana Press: 1970).

(40) *The Dial* (Chicago: Jansen, McClurg: 1881–1918; New York: Dial Publishers: 1918–1929).

(41) *The Chapbook, A Miscellany and Review of Belles Lettres* (Chicago: Stone and Kimball: 1894–1896; Herbert S. Stone and Co.: 1896–1898).

(42) *The Little Review: Literature, Drama, Music, Art* (Chicago: M.C. Anderson: 1914–1929).

(43) *My Thirty Years War, An Autobiography: Beginnings and Battles to 1930* has been reprinted (NY: Horizon Press: 1969); Ms. Anderson's anthology is *The Little Review Anthology* (NY: Hermitage House: 1953).

(44) For a contemporary, illustrated portrait of the 1893 Exposition see the Bounty Books reprint of volume one of Hubert Howe Bancroft's multi-volume *The Book of the Fair, An Historical and Descriptive Presentation of the World's Science, Art and Industry, As Viewed Through the Columbian Exposition at Chicago in 1893*. There are also insights in the periodical literature: Merle Curti, "America At the World's Fairs, 1851–1893," *American Historical Review,* 55 (1950), 833–56 and Justus D. Doenecke, "Myths, Machines and Markets: The Columbian Exposition of 1893," *Journal of Popular Culture VI* (Spring: 1973), 535–549.

(45) Most studies of Chicago and the fine arts are quite uneven but ideas can be gleaned from Charles E. Russell, *The American Orchestra and Theodore Thomas* (Garden City, NY: Doubleday & Page: 1927); Lorado Taft, *The History of American Sculpture* (NY: Macmillan: 1930); Edward C. Moore, *Forty Years of Opera in Chicago* (NY: H. Liveright: 1930). Anna Morgan's *My Chicago* (Chicago: R. F. Seymour: 1918) is one place to begin for the Little Theatre movement which has also been studied by Constance D. MacKay, *The Little Theatre Movement in the United States* (NY: Holt: 1917).

(46) George D. Bushnell, Jr., "When Jazz Came to Chicago," *Chicago History, I:* 3 (Spring: 1971), 132–141.

(47) "Social Influences on Jazz Style: Chicago, 1920–1930," *American Quarterly, XII:* 4 (Winter: 1960), 493–507.

(48) Richard Storr, *The Beginnings of Graduate Education in America* (UCP: 1953).

(49) Robert Farris, *Chicago Sociology, 1920–1930* (San Francisco: Chandler Publishers: 1967); James Short, Jr., *The Social Fabric of the Metropolis: Contributions of the Chicago School of Urban Sociology* (UCP: 1971); Thomas V. Smith and Leonard White, *Chicago: An Experiment in Social Science Research* (UCP: 1929).

(50) Laurence Veysey, *The Emergence of the American University* (UCP: 1965).

(51) *The Mechanistic Conception of Life* (Cambridge: Belknap Press: 1964).

(52) *American Theology in the Liberal Tradition* (Philadelphia: Westminster Press: 1967).

(53) "A Man and A City; George Herbert Mead In Chicago," in *American Philosophy and the Future; Essays For a New Generation* ed. Michael Novak (NY: Scribners: 1968).

(54) *Origins of American Sociology: The Social Science Movement in the United States* (NY: Crowell: 1943).

(55) Ida B. DePencier, *The History of the Laboratory Schools, The University of Chicago, 1896–1965* (Chicago: Quadrangle Books: 1967).

(56) *Thorstein Veblen and His America,* rev. ed. (NY: Viking Press: 1961); *The Transformation of the School; Progressivism in American Education, 1876-1957** (NY: A. A. Knopf: 1961).

(57) *The Chicago School of Architecture** (Washington, D.C.: Department of the Interior: 1973), 1.

(58) *American Building Art: The Nineteenth Century* (NY: Oxford University Press: 1960); *American Building Art: The Twentieth Century* (NY: Oxford: 1961); *The Chicago School of Architecture, A History of Commercial and Public Building in the Chicago Area, 1875-1925** (UCP: 1964); *Chicago, 1910-1929; Building, Planning and Urban Technology* (UCP: 1973); *Chicago, 1930-1970, Building, Planning, and Urban Technology* (UCP: 1974).

(59) *Space, Time and Architecture: The Growth of a New Tradition,* 5th Ed., Revised, (Cambridge: Harvard University Press: 1967); *The Brown Decades, A Study of the Arts in America, 1865-1895* (NY: Harcourt, Brace: 1931); *The Chicago School of Architecture: Early Followers of Sullivan and Wright* (NY: Random House: 1964); *American Buildings and Their Architects: Academic and Progressive Ideals at the Turn of the Century* (Garden City, N.Y.: Doubleday: 1972), *The Rise of an American Architecture** (NY: Praeger: 1970).

(60) *John Wellborn Root* (Boston, Houghton, Mifflin: 1896, reprinted, Prairie School Press, 1966); *The Architecture of John Wellborn Root* (Baltimore: Johns Hopkins University Press: 1973); *Daniel H. Burnham, Architect, Planner of Cities* (Boston: Houghton, Mifflin: 1921); *Frederick Law Olmsted, Sr., Founder of Landscape Architecture in America* (Amherst, Mass.: University of Massachusetts: 1968); *The Architecture of H. H. Richardson and His Times,* Rev. Ed., (Hamden, Conn.: Archon Books: 1961).

(61) *Chicago On Foot, An Architectural Walking Tour** Revised, Second Edition, J. Philip O'Hara, Inc: 1973); *Chicago's Famous Buildings, A Photographic Guide**, 2nd ed. (UCP: 1969).

(62) For slides available see William H. Pierson, Jr. and Martha Davison, eds., *Arts of the United States, A Pictorial Survey* (NY: McGraw-Hill: 1960).

(63) New York: Documents of Modern Art: George Wittenborn, Inc: 1968.

(64) *Louis Sullivan, Prophet of Modern Architecture** (NY: W. W. Norton: 1935; reprinted 1962).

(65) *Frank Lloyd Wright on Architecture: Selected Writings, 1894-1940** (NY: Duell, Sloan, and Pearce: 1941). For a helpful checklist of Wright's separately published first editions see Kenneth Starosciak, *Frank Lloyd Wright, A Bibliography* (New Brighton, Minn: privately printed: 1973).

(66) *Frank Lloyd Wright: Public Buildings* (NY: Simon & Schuster: 1970); *Frank Lloyd Wright; The Early Work* (NY: Horizon Press: 1968).

(67) For Duncan's monograph see above (2); Szuberla's dissertation, "Urban Vistas and the Pastoral Garden: Studies in the Literature and Architecture of Chicago, 1893-1909" was done at University of Minnesota, 1972.

(68) On Chicago's role in urban planning see John W. Reps, *The Making of Urban America, A History of City Planning in the United States* (Princeton: Princeton University Press: 1965) and Mellier G. Scott, *American City Planning Since 1890* (Berkeley: University of California Press: 1969).

Women's Studies in the United States: Approaching Reality

by Joanna Schneider Zangrando

The focus of this essay is on the development, within the past half-dozen years, of scholarly, academically-oriented Women's Studies courses, programs, research, resources and resource repositories, publications, and communications networks.

In the mid-1960s, feminists demanded information about the social, political and economic status, roles and treatment of women in the United States, past and present. Their questions gave an urgency, unusual in academic circles, to the study of women. Their legitimate insistence on the indispensability of self-knowledge to human understanding and future behavior inspired a feminist consciousness among some scholars who began to channel their research efforts toward recovering "lost" women and celebrating outstanding heroines. Feminist needs for information, coupled with student demands for relevant education, provided both an impetus to and support for Women's Studies courses and programs throughout the United States.[1]

The pioneers in 1969-70 found few blueprints, procedural or substantive, for Women's Studies. Initially, newly-approved courses on women were offered by traditional academic departments with the expectation that a single-discipline perspective—history, sociology, or literature—was adequate. For "compensatory" purposes, to make up for previous omissions or misrepresentations, this was a necessary first step. Increasingly, however, Women's Studies advocates have indicated the long-range limitations of adding a course on "great," though long-neglected, women poets to the English curriculum, or including a special topics seminar in History on the "leaders" of the woman suffrage movement.[2] Such discrete assignments could merely replicate the traditional emphases on the contributions of famous people, those who worked within clearly-defined institutional settings or participated in military battles and political campaigns.

Increasingly, too, Women's Studies researchers, writers and teachers have moved beyond "oppression of women" as an adequate conceptual tool for understanding women's lives. The oppression model, inspired in part by articulate activists within the contemporary women's movement and in part by historical reality, has proved a useful but potentially limiting, one-dimensional conceptual framework for the study of women. The oppression model has often ignored the varied responses of women to oppression, and neglected actual changes in women's status over time. In 1946, historian Mary Beard claimed in *Woman as a Force in History* (New York: Macmillan, 1946) that the social role of women, while not in the male-defined arena, was important. To Beard, concentrating on the oppression of women prevented a full understanding of their importance as a "civilizing" force.

Those engaged in Women's Studies emphasize the need now to move beyond compensatory anthologies on women and the conceptual frameworks of "great" or "oppressed" women, as Gerda Lerner suggested in "New Approaches to the Study of Women in American History," *Journal of Social History*, 3 (Fall 1969).

Interdisciplinary Implications and Sources

The study of women in the United States cannot be restricted to one discipline. American Studies and other interdisciplinary approaches provide useful models, for Women's Studies necessarily incorporates all aspects of women's lives, and cuts across the boundaries of individual disciplines to include psychology, sociology, biology, literature, history, economics, anthropology, language, the arts, political science, and philosophy.[3]

The interdisciplinary thrust of Women's Studies was suggested as early as 1946 by Viola Klein in *The Feminine Character: History of an Ideology* (Urbana, Illinois: University of Illinois Press, 1972 edition).[4] Klein analyzed then current theories of the "feminine character" from the perspectives of biology, philosophy, psychoanalytic theory, history, anthropology, and sociology and urged an increased coordination of social science research on women's character in the future.[5] More recently, Annette K. Baxter echoed this appeal to employ an interdisciplinary approach to the study of women. In a review essay of Alice Crozier's *The Novels of Harriet Beecher Stowe* (New York: Oxford University Press, 1974) and Gail Thain Parker's *The Oven Birds: American Women on Womanhood, 1820-1920* (Garden City, New York: Anchor Books, 1972), Professor Baxter applauded the "open-ended curiosity and freedom from disciplinary bias" exercised by Crozier and Parker. Both extensive inquiry and interdisciplinary approaches contribute to the assurance "that Women's Studies can avoid the oversimplification that relegates women to a conveniently missing chapter of our history, in need only of recovery and inclusion, and can compel us to redefine that history as we redefine women."[6]

No one, acceptable way to "do" Women's Studies exists. Partly because it is a new area of study and partly because Women's Studies scholars have themselves challenged the authority of traditional sources, methods, standards of importance, and conceptualizations, it remains open to inquiry, analyses, and suggestive hypotheses. Colleges and universities provide, at least potentially, institutional settings for interdisciplinary approaches to Women's Studies.[7] But teachers, researchers and students are also dependent upon the cooperation and assistance of other institutions and professional staff. Archivists,[8] manuscript librarians, museum and historical society curators, publishers, professional journal editors all contribute to the process of gathering and sharing information crucial to an understanding of women in American culture, a topic traditionally excluded from male-dominated historical and social experiences deemed important to study.

Because women's experiences have been different from men's, many traditional sources must be carefully reexamined and used in innovative, imaginative ways. Moreover, fresh sources, often obscure, long-neglected and overlooked, must be utilized. Women's Studies scholars have developed techniques for uncovering materials, using them effectively, and sharing information about them. An impressive range and variety of sources exist, including letters, popular and professional journals, diaries, photographs, paintings, health and hospital records, travel accounts, court records, movies, newspapers, women's magazines, autobiographies, oral history interviews, family histories, household guides, economic studies, etiquette books, medical treatises, factory records, hymnals, sermons, demographic data, trade journals, women's organization records, census reports, domestic architecture, records of social habits (diet, dress) and attitudes, ephemeral women's movement literature, posters and buttons, material objects, and advertisements.

Recent family history and social mobility studies, such as John Demos' *A Little Commonwealth: Family Life in Plymouth Colony* (New York: Oxford University Press, 1970)[9] and Stephan Thernstrom's *Poverty and Progress: Social Mobility in a Nineteenth-Century City* (Cambridge, Mass.: Harvard University Press, 1964) have renewed interest in the domestic sphere to which women have, traditionally, been relegated. Women's Studies scholars have deliberately directed attention to personal, emotional relationships within the family, to the

Joanna Schneider Zangrando is Assistant Professor of American Studies at The George Washington University. A graduate of Wayne State University where she received both her B.A. and M.A. degrees, Ms. Zangrando continued her graduate work at the University of Rochester and then at The George Washington University where she received her Ph.D. in 1974. She was a Smithsonian Institution Fellow from 1968-69, and served as a museum consultant while a Fellow of the National American Studies Faculty from 1972-74. A member of the Council of the American Studies Association, Ms. Zangrando also serves as the National Coordinator of the ASA Women's Committee. She is the editor of the Newsletter *of the coordinating Committee on Women in the Historical Profession. Her scholarly publications include articles in the* American Archivist, *the* Journal of Black Studies, *and* American Quarterly *among others.*

social uses of the family, to changes in the functional and structural patterns of the family over time, and to the effects of these changes on women's roles and self-perceptions. A particularly useful study of family life, the role of women within the family, and their work outside is Virginia Yans McLaughlin's "Patterns of Work and Family Organization: Buffalo's Italians," *Journal of Interdisciplinary History* II (Autumn 1971).[10]

Women's Studies: Communications Networks, Repositories and Resource Centers

Typical of new areas of study, Women's Studies has depended upon a collective interchange of information, of a formal and informal nature. By necessity and by conscious intent, persons involved in Women's Studies have developed impressive communications networks concerned, to a large extent, with locating and relaying information about materials, repositories, and resource centers.[11]

Among the many repositories throughout the United States that house materials relevant to the study of women, the collections of several pertain directly to Women's Studies.[12] The Sophia Smith Collection was established in 1942 at Smith College, Northampton, Massachusetts. The collection consists of manuscripts, letters, diaries, journals, published and unpublished materials, essays, poems, reports, books, photographs and other primary and secondary materials, primarily in the post-1865 period. The collection reflects women's social and intellectual history: women's rights, suffrage, sex reform, birth control, education, art, literature, the professions, missionary activities, music, journalism, family life, industrial labor, peace organizations. Papers in the collection include those of: Jane Addams (1860-1935), settlement worker, reformer, organizer of the Women's International League for Peace and Freedom; Emma Goldman (1869-1940), anarchist, birth control and free speech advocate; Margaret Sanger (1882-1966), nurse, founder of the birth control movement and Planned Parenthood Federation of America; Mary Van Kleek (1883--1966), researcher and author of studies on the economic status of women, trade unions, and labor legislation. The primary and secondary materials pertain to women and their activities throughout the world.[13]

The Arthur and Elizabeth Schlesinger Library on the History of Women in America, formerly the Women's Archives, was established in 1943 at Radcliffe College, Cambridge, Massachusetts.[14] It houses perhaps the largest collection of personal, family, organization and association materials dating to the early nineteenth century.[15] A major focus of the Library has been on leaders of the women's rights movement (including oral history interviews with Jeannette Rankin and Alice Paul, two important participants in the woman suffrage campaign) and women's rights advocates (Lorine Pruette, feminist writer and teacher, and Freda Kirchwey, feminist editor and publisher of the *Nation*). The Library is the official repository of the records of the National Organization for Women (NOW), the Women's Equity Action League (WEAL), and other contemporary women's movement organizations. Microfilm publication of pre-1920 printed works on women's history, based on the Library's holdings, is now underway and micro-publication of the "Papers of the Women's Trade Union League and Its Principal Leaders" has been approved by the National Historic Publications Commission and will be funded by the National Endowment for the Humanities.[16]

The Women's History Research Center Library in Berkeley, California served, from 1968 until it was forced to close in 1974, as the only international archive of the contemporary women's movement. Two of the Library's most useful and important collections, the International Women's History Periodical Archive and the Topical Research Library contain interdisciplinary materials (newspapers, films, tapes, newsletters, course syllabi and bibliographies, periodicals) that document women's positions, past and present, in the United States and other countries.[17] The Social Welfare History Archives at the University of Minnesota Libraries (Minneapolis, Minnesota 55455) is a major repository for the historical records of national voluntary welfare organizations and the personal papers of social reform and social service leaders. The records of the American Social Health Association, the National Florence Crittenton Mission, and the Association for Voluntary Sterilization document attitudes toward sexuality, sex education, illegitimacy, prostitution, and sterilization in the twentieth century. Social service agency case records contain demographic data only recently appreciated as relevant to the study of women's lives.

Two additional repositories particularly deserve the attention of Women's Studies scholars. The Archives of Labor History and Urban Affairs at Wayne State University (Detroit, Michigan 48202) houses personal papers and other materials relating to the role of women in the labor movement. The Summer 1972 issue of the Archives *Newsletter* devoted to "Women's Collections in the Archives of Labor History and Urban Affairs" is invaluable.[18] Another major repository of materials relevant to women in the labor movement—and in almost every other activity—is the Franklin D. Roosevelt Library in Hyde Park, New York. Recently, the Library's research facilities were expanded to incorporate the papers of Eleanor Roosevelt, her correspondence, addresses, and publications which touched on almost all facets of women's lives.

Since 1970 two feminist presses—KNOW, Inc. and The Feminist Press—have published a ten-volume *Female Studies* series. These volumes constitute the most comprehensive and useful compendium of Women's Studies materials: bibliographies, syllabi, course descriptions and evaluations, essays, and information on where and by whom Women's Studies courses have been offered. *Female Studies II* (Florence Howe, ed., KNOW, Inc., 1970) contained course descriptions and bibliographies for sixty-six college courses plus five essays, primarily on literature and introductory interdisciplinary courses. The 1972 edition of *Female Studies V* (Rae Siporan, ed., KNOW, Inc.) included seventeen papers on teaching Women's Studies in several disciplines. *Female Studies VII: Going Strong—New Courses, New Programs* (Deborah Silverton Rosenfelt, ed., The Feminist Press, 1973) listed sixty courses in seventeen disciplinary areas and more than twelve in interdisciplinary areas, and included two special bibliographies: "Women, Art and Feminism" and "Anthropological Perspectives on Women." The *Female Studies* publications are themselves documents of the history of Women's Studies in the United States.[20]

Both KNOW, Inc., and The Feminist Press support education projects beyond the *Female Studies* publications, KNOW, Inc. has reprinted an impressive number of essays, articles, addresses and other literature of the contemporary women's movement. Of particular interest and usefulness are Betty Chmaj's two volumes on *American Women and American Studies*. They are "workbooks" on the status of women in American Studies, as well as handy references for Women's Studies courses, bibliographies, and essays.[21]

In addition to *Female Studies,* The Feminist Press sponsors two especially useful education projects: The Clearinghouse on Women's Studies and the quarterly *Women's Studies Newsletter.* Since 1970 the Clearinghouse has served as the major informational resource on Women's Studies. "Feminist Resources for Schools and Colleges: A Guide to Curricular Materials" (Carol Ahlum and Jacqueline M. Fralley, eds., 1973) is representative of Clearinghouse projects. First published in 1972, the *Newsletter* lists new courses and programs and publishes bibliographies and brief essays on a variety of Women's Studies topics. The press has also published books by and about women, some classics in fiction. The Feminist Press reprints include: Agnes Smedley, *Daughter of Earth*; Rebecca Harding Davis, *Life in the Iron Mills*; Mary Wilkins Freeman, *The Revolt of Mother and Other Stories*; Kate Chopin, *The Storm and Other Stories*; and Charlotte Perkins Gilman, *The Yellow Wallpaper.*[22]

Several new journals have responded to the increasing interest in Women's Studies. Among the most helpful are: *Women's Studies,* an interdisciplinary quarterly of articles and book reviews (Gordon and Breach Science Publishers, 1 Park Avenue, New York, New York 10016), and *Feminist Studies,* devoted to scholarly articles and book reviews (417 Riverside Drive, New York, New York 10025). *Women Studies Abstracts* is a quarterly annotated bibliography of recent books and articles, from over 2,000 periodicals published since July 1971 (P.O. Box 1, Rush, New York 14543). *Women's Work and Women's Studies, 1972* (KNOW, Inc., 1972) is an annotated, interdisciplinary bibliography of published and ongoing research, compiled by the Women's Center of Barnard College.[23]

Finally, the Project on the Status and Education of Women of the Association of American Colleges must be included among useful Women's Studies resource centers. Since 1971, the Project has collected and published a broad range of materials concerning women in education. In addition, the Project has periodically compiled resource guides directly useful to Women's Studies teachers and students. "Women and Film: A Resource Handbook" prepared by the Project, for example, is one of the most comprehensive collections of information on women and/in film available.[24]

Women's Studies: An Identifiable Body of Literature

Careful scrutiny of traditional myths about women and analyses of their actual status and roles over time have produced a substantial and clearly identifiable body of Women's Studies literature. Selection depends, in part, on whether one intends to "fit" women into traditional courses or categories deemed important, or whether one intends, on the basis of questioning traditional assumptions, to create new perspectives for the study of women, and men.

To separate sources of information on women's lives into discrete categories is, admittedly, arbitrary and counter-productive. To give some order to the following discussion, however, I have divided materials into several categories: documentary collections, theme-oriented histories, general histories, bibliographies and bibliographic essays, biographies and autobiographies, contemporary feminist writings, literature, behavioral and social science studies, specialized studies, government publications, anthologies, and non-print media and artifact sources.

An early and still very useful collection of documents centering on women's "proper sphere" in the United States is Aileen S. Kraditor's *Up From The Pedestal: Selected Writings in the History of American Feminism* (Chicago: Quadrangle Press, 1970). Although the documents in this publication cover the colonial through mid-twentieth century period, the strength of the collection lies in the 1830-1890s period. Kraditor's introductory essay, "Women in History and Historiography," places feminism within the conceptual framework of women's desire for autonomy and self-definition.[25] Gerda Lerner's *Black Women in White America: A Documentary History* (New York: Vintage Books, 1973) contains almost two hundred selections by black women. Underlying all of their experiences in the nineteenth and twentieth centuries is the theme of survival and strength. Informative bibliographical notes accompany the documents. Changes in work, education, reform, family life, and the roles of women from the mid-nineteenth century to the present are concisely documented by Anne Firor Scott in *The American Woman: Who Was She?* (Englewood Cliffs, New Jersey: Prentice-Hall, Inc., 1971). Scott's selections, arranged topically, emphasize the personal and social aspects of women's lives.

The most predominant theme of specific histories on women in the United States has been the organized struggle for women's rights, particularly suffrage, from the 1840s to 1920.[26] The classic, six-volume study of the women's suffrage campaign is the *History of Woman Suffrage* by Elizabeth Cady Stanton, Susan B. Anthony, Ida Husted Harper and Matilda Joslyn Gage (Rochester, New York: Fowler and Wells, 1881-1922). In *Century of Struggle: The Woman's Rights Movement in the United States* (Cambridge, Mass.: Harvard University Press, 1959) Eleanor Flexner devotes primary attention to women's organizational efforts to improve upon and expand their rights. Flexner's emphasis is on the activities of important women to whom, presumably, the Nineteenth Amendment granting woman suffrage seemed the embodiment of all of the goals of women's rights advocates.

Aileen Kraditor, in *The Ideas of the Woman Suffrage Movement, 1890-1920* (Garden City, New York: Anchor Books, 1971), traces the changes in the leadership, tactics, and goals of the suffrage movement. Suffrage advocates moved from an argument based on "justice" to the more conservative "expediency" argument. Kraditor's intellectual history places the suffrage movement within the broader reform impulse traditionally termed "progressivism." Rather than exhibiting any general consensus of opinion or recognizable ideology Kraditor contends, effectively, that the mainly native white, middle-class suffragists made serious compromises in order to obtain the vote. They used the "moral superiority of women" argument of the late nineteenth century against immigrants, black men and women, and working class Americans if it appeared expeditious to their cause.

Other writers share some of Kraditor's views on the limitations of the suffrage movement—its short-sightedness, lack of ideology, and unbounded faith in suffrage as a panacea for women's rights. They include: William O'Neill, *Everyone Was Brave: The Rise and Fall of Feminism in America* (Chicago: Quadrangle, 1969); Andrew Sinclair, *The Better Half: The Emancipation of the*

American Woman (New York: Harper & Row, 1965); and Carl N. Degler, "Revolution Without Ideology: The Changing Place of Women in America," in Robert Jay Lifton, ed., *The Woman in America* (Boston: Beacon Press, 1967 edition). While admitting the failure of a real feminist critique of society—an attack on the "conjugal family system"—Jill Conway argues, in "Women Reformers and American Culture, 1870-1930," *Journal of Social History*, Vol. 5, No. 2 (Winter 1971-1972), that American society would have been hostile to militant feminism.

Finally, two studies devote attention to pro-suffrage arguments in specific geographic regions. Political scientist Alan P. Grimes in *The Puritan Ethic and Woman Suffrage* (New York: Oxford University Press, 1967) argues that women's suffrage triumphed in the western states because it was viewed as a "civilizing force." And in the South, white women joined the suffrage movement to upgrade the status of women, and not to counter the votes of black men, according to Anne Firor Scott in *The Southern Lady: From Pedestal to Politics, 1830-1930* (Chicago: University of Chicago Press, 1970).

Women's involvement in reform movements other than women's rights is another theme prevalent in special topics studies. Although society's expectations restricted their activities primarily to the domestic sphere (so well described by Barbara Welter in "The Cult of True Womanhood: 1820-1860" and Gerda Lerner in "The Lady and the Mill Girl: Changes in the Status of Women in the Age of Jackson")[27] participation in reform movements provided opportunities for women to work together outside of the home. Angelina Grimké's *Letters to Catherine E. Beecher, in Reply to an Essay on Slavery and Abolitionism, Addressed to A.E. Grimké* (Boston: Isaac Knapp, 1938, revised by the author) documents the commitment of women to the abolition crusade. The problems encountered by women such as the Grimké sisters in that movement are described by Aileen Kraditor in *Means and Ends in American Abolitionism: Garrison and His Critics on Strategy and Tactics, 1838-1850* (New York: Vintage Books, 1969) and by Gerda Lerner in her comprehensive treatment, *The Grimke Sisters from South Carolina: Pioneers for Woman's Rights and Abolition* (New York: Schocken Books, 1971). David J. Pivar describes the participation of women in the late-nineteenth century purity reform movement in *Purity Crusade: Sexual Morality and Social Control, 1868-1900* (Westport, Conn.: Greenwood Press, 1973). Stanley Lemons portrays the important role of feminists in the social justice movement of the 1920s, a period conventionally thought devoid of active feminism, in *The Woman Citizen: Social Feminism in the 1920's* (Urbana, Illinois: University of Illinois Press, 1973). June Sochen, too, in *The New Woman: Feminism in Greenwich Village, 1910-1920* (New York: Quadrangle, 1972) discusses the "new women" activist of the early twentieth century.

Because Jane Addams was the embodiment of the turn-of-the-century social reformer, several books focus on her social settlement and peace reform efforts. Addams, herself, wrote several books, including *Twenty Years at Hull House* (New York: Signet, 1960, originally published in 1910) and *Democracy and Social Ethics* (Cambridge, Mass.: Harvard University Press, 1964). Allen Davis includes Addams in *Spearheads for Reform: The Social Settlements and the Progressive Movement, 1890-1914* (New York: Oxford University Press, 1967) and devotes *American Heroine: The Life and Legend of Jane Addams* (New York:

Oxford University Press, 1973) entirely to her. Although some of his assumptions are questionable, Christopher Lasch attempts to explain Addams' reform motivations in his critique, *The New Radicalism in America: 1889-1913, The Intellectual as a Social Type* (New York: Vintage, 1965).[28]

The subject of women and education in the United States has not been studied to any great extent. Thomas Woody's *A History of Women's Education in the United States*, published in two volumes (New York: The Science Press, 1929), is now dated. Useful information on the contemporary status of women in higher education is contained in *Academic Women on the Move* edited by Alice S. Rossi and Ann Calderwood (New York: Russell Sage Foundation, 1973).[29] The writings of individual educated women include Margaret Fuller's *Woman in the Nineteenth Century*, originally published in 1845 (Boston: Roberts Bros., 1968) and Barbara M. Cross' *The Educated Woman in America: Selected Writings of Catherine Beecher, Margaret Fuller, and M. Carey Thomas* (New York: Teachers College Press, Columbia University, 1965).

Women and the world of work is a topic of particular interest to scholars recently. William H. Chafe in *The American Woman: Her Changing Social, Economic and Political Roles, 1920-1970* (New York: Oxford University Press, 1972) attributes responsibility for their actual or potential change in status to women's economic role in the work force. Two earlier works underscore the connection between women's status and their participation in the economic world: Elizabeth A. Dexter, *Colonial Women of Affairs: Women in Business and the Professions in America before 1776* (Boston: Houghton Mifflin, 1931, 2nd ed., revised), and Julia Cherry Spruill, *Women's Life & Work in the Southern Colonies* (New York: W. W. Norton, 1972, originally published by the University of North Carolina Press in 1938).[30] Robert Smuts, *Women and Work in America* (New York: Schocken Press, 1971, 2nd ed.) and Elizabeth Faulkner Baker, *Technology and Woman's Work* (New York: Columbia University Press, 1964) are basic to an understanding of the developing relationship between work and woman's participation in the labor force.

The involvement of women in organized labor movements has been vividly described by many of the participants.[31] Among the most useful and interesting publications are: Alice Henry, *The Trade Union Woman* (New York: Appleton, 1915), Rose Schneiderman, *All For One* (New York: P. S. Ericksson, 1967), Mary Field Parton, ed., *Autobiography of Mother Jones* (Chicago: C. H. Kerr, 1925), and Rose Pesotta, *Bread Upon the Waters* (New York: Dodd-Mead, 1944). The "personal histories" of three militant, working-class, women union organizers, active in the 1930s-1940s, are in the collection of oral interviews edited by Alice and Staughton Lynd, *Rank and File: Personal Histories of Working Class Organizers* (Boston: Beacon Press, 1973).

The relationship between feminism and socialism is another theme developed in specific histories of women. Connections between the two are explicitly treated by Sheila Rowbotham in *Women, Resistance and Revolution in the Modern World* (New York: Vintage Books, 1974) and Juliet Mitchell in *Woman's Estate* (New York: Pantheon, 1971).[32]

There are several useful general histories of women in the United States suitable for introductory Women's Studies courses. Edith Hoshino Altbach's volume, *Women in America* (Lexington, Mass.: D. C. Heath and Co., 1974), focuses on unexceptional, working class women and women who remain at home. Lois Banner's *Women in Modern America: A Brief History* (New York: Harcourt Brace Jovanovich, 1974) traces the historical experiences of women from 1890 to the present. It is extremely readable, contains a brief, annotated bibliography at the end of each chapter, and effectively uses illustrated materials. *The Woman in American History* (Menlo Park, Calif.: Addison-Wesley Publishing Co., 1971) by Gerda Lerner is a basic, brief history of women from the colonial era through the twentieth century: their roles, changes in status, contributions, and society's views toward women. Mary P. Ryan's *Womanhood in America: From Colonial Times to the Present* (New York: New Viewpoints, 1975) is a thematic, interpretive treatment of sex roles, socially-prescribed images of "Womanhood," and the working toward new definitions and change in status by women over time. An extensive essay by Ann Gordon, Mari Jo Buhle and Nancy Schrom entitled "Women in American Society: An Historical Contribution," Radical America, Vol. V. No. 4 (July-August 1971) presents a variety of useful approaches to the study of women in America. A comprehensive, well-selected bibliography on women's history makes this essay especially valuable.[33]

Lucinda Cisler compiled one of the earliest, and most useful, interdisciplinary bibliographies on women. Entitled *Women: A Bibliography*, it lists historical, economic, legal and sociological studies, works of literature, biographies and autobiographies, and writings on the contemporary women's movement.[34] Another comprehensive interdisciplinary bibliography is *Women: A Selected Bibliography* (Springfield, Ohio: Wittenberg University Press, 1973), prepared by Patricia O'Connor, et al. Particularly helpful in the area of literature is Tillie Olsen's extensive and varied reading list published in the *Women's Studies Newsletter* (Winter, Spring, Summer 1973 and Winter 1974).[35] A selected bibliography on women's participation in politics from 1965 through 1974, *Women and American Politics*, is available from the Center for the American Woman and Politics, Eagleton Institute of Politics, Rutgers University (New Brunswick, New Jersey 08901). Included in *The Black Scholar*, Vol. 3, No. 4 (December 1971), is a bibliography on "The Black Women." Sheila Rowbotham's *Women's Liberation and Revolution* (Bristol, England: Falling Wall Press, 1973) is an introductory bibliography of books, articles and pamphlets on the connections between feminism and revolutionary politics throughout the world. For historians, the "Bibliography of Women's History," available from the Organization of American Historians (112 North Bryan Street, Bloomington, Indiana 47401), is a useful resource. Finally, Anne Firor Scott's essay on the status of women's history, "Women in American Life" in William H. Cartwright and Richard L. Watson, Jr., eds., *The Reinterpretation of American History and Culture* (Washington, D.C.: National Council for the Social Studies, 1973), serves as a good bibliographic resource on women and the home, at work, in education, and in reform movements.

Biographies and autobiographies constitute one of the most prevalent of published sources on women. Since the majority are about unique, outstanding individuals, often in unusual circumstances, they should be used with care. The publication of the three-volume reference work *Notable American Women: A Biographical Dictionary*, Edward T. James, editor, Janet Wilson James, associate editor, and Paul S. Boyer, assistant editor (Cambridge, Mass.: The Belknap Press of Harvard University Press) in 1971 underscores the importance that the study of women has attained. The *Dictionary* includes 1,359 biographic sketches of women—with "distinction in their own right of more than local significance" in the public arena (except for the wives of presidents)—who lived between 1607 and 1950. The bibliographic references that accompany each sketch further make the *Dictionary* an indispensable, ready reference to women of public importance.[36]

It is difficult to determine the most representative or useful biographies and autobiographies; the following selections are merely suggestive of the range and variety of these two sources. Women whose lives did not conform to prevailing social expectations include anarchist Emma Goldman, birth control crusader Margaret Sanger, socialist and communist Elizabeth Gurley Flynn, and feminist Charlotte Perkins Gilman. Emma Goldman's two-volume autobiography, *Living My Life* (New York: Dover Publications, 1970), her *Anarchism and Other Essays* (New York: Dover Publications, 1969), and Richard Drinnon's *Rebel in Paradise: A Biography of Emma Goldman* (Boston: Beacon Press, 1970, originally published by the University of Chicago Press in 1961) convey a sense of her commitment to individual freedom and of the fullness of her life.[37] Margaret Sanger related her single-minded crusade for birth control education and the legal dissemination of birth control information and devices by physicians in *My Fight for Birth Control* (New York: Farrar & Rinehart, Inc., 1931) and *An Autobiography* (New York: W. W. Norton, 1938). From a more critical perspective, David Kennedy discusses her campaign in *Birth Control in America: The Career of Margaret Sanger* (New Haven: Yale University Press, 1970). Elizabeth Gurley Flynn described her long involvement in unpopular labor and political organizations, including the I.W.W. and the socialist and communist parties, in *The Rebel Girl: An Autobiography. My First Life (1906-1926)* (rev. ed., New York: International Publishers, 1973). A turn of the century feminist and perceptive analyst of women's economic dependence within marriage, Charlotte Perkins Gilman found time to write an account of her busy, often misunderstood, life, *The Living of Charlotte Perkins Gilman: An Autobiography* (New York: Appleton Century, 1935).

The lives of individual black women are described in a number of works. Among the most informative are: Sarah Bradford, *Harriet Tubman: The Moses of Her People* (New York: Corinth Books, 1961; reprint of 1886 edition); Mary Church Terrell, *A Colored Woman in a White World* (Washington, D.C.: Ransdell Publishing Co., 1940); Alfreda Duster, ed., *Crusade for Justice: The Autobiography of Ida B. Wells* (Chicago: University of Chicago Press, 1970); Anne Moody, *Coming of Age in Mississippi* (New York: Dial Press, 1968); and Maya Angelou, *I Know Why the Caged Bird Sings* (New York: Random House, 1970).

There are a number of detailed accounts by and about women literary figures. Sylvia Plath's autobiographical novel, *The Bell Jar* (New York: Harper & Row, 1971; originally published in 1963), vividly portrays the pain she suffered, in her twentieth year, from a breakdown. Nikki Giovanni reveals other kinds of pain, and joy, in *Gemini: An Extended Autobiographical Statement on My First Twenty-Five Years of Being a Black Poet* (New York: Viking Press, 1971). Mary McCarthy's first-hand account, *Memories of a Catholic Girlhood* (New York: Harcourt, Brace, 1957), is a standard reference work for Women's Studies literature courses. For information on the life and poetry of Emily Dickinson, Richard B. Sewall's two-volume work, *The Life of Emily Dickinson* (New York: Farrar, Straus and Giroux, 1974), is very useful. In an excellent biography, Katheryn Kish Sklar analyzes Catherine Beecher's concern with the "domestic science" of homemaking and the profession of teaching for women. Sklar places Beecher and her writings within the cultural framework of the 1820s-1850s in *Catherine Beecher: A Study in Domesticity* (New Haven: Yale University Press, 1973). The life of another nineteenth-century woman, a famous actress, is described by Joseph Leach in *Bright Particular Star: The Life and Times of Charlotte Cushman* (New Haven: Yale University Press, 1970).

A pioneer in the medical and ministry professions, and a leader in the woman suffrage movement, Anna Howard Shaw related her experiences in *The Story of a Pioneer* (New York: Harper & Bros., 1915). Elizabeth Cady Stanton, one of the most publicly active suffragists, described her personal life in *Eighty Years & More: Reminiscences 1815-1897* (New York: Schocken Books, 1971). The life of another prominent suffragist is portrayed by Alma Lutz in *Susan B. Anthony: Rebel, Crusader, Humanitarian* (Boston: Beacon Press, 1959).[38] The involvement of women in other movements to improve their lives and status is discussed by Mary Anderson (first director of the Women's Bureau, Department of Labor) in *Woman at Work: The Autobiography of Mary Anderson as told to Mary Winslow* (Minneapolis: University of Minnesota Press, 1951); by Josephine Goldmark in *Impatient Crusader: Florence Kelley's Life Story* (Urbana: University of Illinois Press, 1953); by Eleanor Roosevelt in *This I Remember* (New York: Harper & Bros., 1949); and by Joseph Lash in two very detailed volumes, *Eleanor and Franklin: The Story of Their Relationship, Based on Eleanor Roosevelt's Private Papers* and *Eleanor: The Years Alone* (New York: W. W. Norton, 1971 and 1972, respectively).[39]

The oppression and secondary status of women, historically and currently, is the predominant concern of several books written from a feminist perspective. In 1948 Simone de Beauvoir described the nature of female consciousness and oppression as the "Other" in relation to make supremacy in the classic, *The Second Sex* (New York: Bantam Books, 1961; trans. and ed. by H. M. Parshley). Betty Friedan's *The Feminine Mystique* (New York: Dell, 1963) serves as the American classic of "the problem that has no name": the dichotomy between the image, or mystique, of women's lives and the reality. She discusses at length the post-World War II, media-manipulated portrayal of women as self-fulfilled wives and mothers, and criticizes the influence of Freudian psychology in fostering the "mystique."[40] Helpful to an understanding of the contemporary feminist movement and its nineteenth-century antecedents are Cellestine Ware's *Woman Power: The Movement for Women's Liberation* (New York: Tower Publications, Inc., 1970) and Roberta Salper's edited *Female Liberation: History and Current Politics* (New York: Alfred A. Knopf., 1972). Shulamith Firestone examines the factors that have given women a subservient status, from a radical feminist perspective in *The Dialectic of Sex: The Case for Feminist Revolution* (New York: Bantam Books, 1971).

In 1969 Kate Millett launched a feminist assault on the images of women created by male authors such as Henry Miller and Norman Mailer. Millett's *Sexual Politics* (Garden City, New York: Doubleday, 1969) is an indictment, incorporating sociological and psychological arguments, of male fantasy images of women. This book, too, has become a classic for feminists. For those who would attempt to counter Millett's criticisms by asking why more women literary figures have not produced more appropriate images of women, Virginia Woolf's *A Room of One's Own* (New York: Harcourt, Brace, 1929) is an excellent, forceful response. Linda Nochlin presents an equally convincing argument regarding women in art in "Why Are There No Great Women Artists?" in Vivian Gornick and Barbara Moran, eds., *Woman in Sexist Society* . . . (New York: Basic Books, 1971).

Because writing has not been viewed an appropriate full-time occupation for women until recently, much of what they have written has been discounted as unimportant. For this reason, The Feminist Press is engaged in "rediscovering" and reprinting long-forgotten literary works by women. *Life in the Iron Mills, or The Korl Woman* by Rebecca Harding Davis first appeared in the *Atlantic Monthly* in 1861. It is a relentlessly realistic portrayal of the unrelieved hardships of working class life in mid-nineteenth century America. Because Davis was not part of any supportive literary circles and because her family made demands on her time, her literary talents were never fully appreciated by her contemporaries. Her obituary described her as the mother of Richard Harding Davis![41] Much the same obscurity characterizes the lives and works of other women authors that The Feminist Press has reintroduced: Agnes Smedley, author of the autobiographical novel, *Daughter of Earth*; Mary Wilkins Freeman, author of stories about close, loyal and important relationships between women, eight of which are reprinted in *The Revolt of Mother and Other Stories*; and Charlotte Perkins Gilman, feminist critic of women's economic dependence, whose compelling short story of a woman's descent into madness, *The Yellow Wallpaper*, was first published in 1899.[42] Kate Chopin is another author whose works are being rediscovered. In her career from 1889 to 1899, Chopin devoted primary attention to short stories with a regional, Louisiana Creole focus that were generally well-received. But in 1899, public reactions of shock greeted her novel, *The Awakening*, about a woman's discovery of her sexuality and self-needs. Most contemporary reviewers felt that Chopin had exceeded the bounds of propriety accorded female writers.[43] Ann Douglas discusses those bounds, traditionally attributed to the corps of nineteenth-century women authors, in "The 'Scribbling Women' and Fanny Fern: Why Women Wrote," *American Quarterly,* Vol. XXIII, No. 1 (Spring 1971). Finally, in her thoughtful, analytical introduction to Anzia Yezierska's 1925 novel, *Bread Givers* (New York: George Braziller, 1975), Alice Kessler-Harris makes apparent the relevance of earlier works to the current thrust toward autonomy.

Recently, a number of scholars have challenged the presumption of scientific objectivity—non-manipulative and non-socially influenced—attached to sociology and psychology. Naomi Weisstein succinctly describes the bias in psychology against women in " 'Kinde, Kuche, Kirche' as Scientific Law: Psychology Constructs the Female," in Robin Morgan, ed., *Sisterhood Is Powerful* . . . (New York: Vintage Books, 1970). Phyllis Chesler develops this same theme of women as "victims" in psychiatry in *Women & Madness* (New York: Avon Books, 1972).[44] Mirra Komarovsky's *Blue Collar Marriage* (New York: Vintage Books, 1967) is an instructive sociological study about wives of blue collar workers. The views of twenty-one sociologists on manifested changes in women's behavior and status since the current feminist movement began were edited by Joan Huber in

Changing Women in a Changing Society (Chicago: University of Chicago Press, 1973; originally published in the January 1973 issue of the *American Journal of Sociology*). The roles of black women, their strengths, and the dilemmas they face are treated by sociologist Joyce A. Ladner in *Tomorrow's Tomorrow: The Black Woman* (Garden City, New York: Anchor Books, 1972). Two articles, by historians, that suggest the manipulative uses of medical science to influence women's behavior in the nineteenth century are Carroll Smith-Rosenberg's "The Hysterical Woman: Sex Roles and Role Conflicts in Nineteenth-Century America," *Social Research*, Vol. 39 (1971) and Carl N. Degler's "What Ought to Be and What Was: Women's Sexuality in the Nineteenth Century," *The American Historical Review*, Vol. 79, No. 5 (December 1974). *The Physician and Sexuality in Victorian America*, by John and Robin Haller (Urbana, Ill.: University of Illinois Press, 1974), is a more comprehensive study of the uses of science to foster social values from 1830-1900.

Charlotte Perkins Gilman's turn-of-the-century critiques of women and the economy are classic analyses of the inextricable connection between woman's status, ascribed sex roles, and economic dependence within conventional marriage. She expressed her theories for revolutionary changes in the economy and the institution of marriage—to allow women to work *and* have families—in *Women and Economics* (New York: Source Books Press, 1970 reprint) and *The Home: Its Work and Influence* (Urbana, Ill.: University of Illinois Press, 1972, reprint). More recent treatments of women's participation in the economy include Caroline Bird's *Born Female: The High Cost of Keeping Women Down* (New York: McKay, 1968); Cynthia Fuchs Epstein's *Woman's Place: Options and Limits in Professional Careers* (Berkeley: University of California Press, 1970); and Valerie Kincaid Oppenheimer's *The Female Labor Force in the United States* (Berkeley: Institute of International Studies, University of California, 1970).

A number of specialized studies that do not fit neatly into any single social or behavioral science category are included because of their usefulness to Women's Studies.[45] Leo Kanowitz has compiled an impressive amount of information on the legal rights of women in *Women and the Law: The Unfinished Revolution* (Albuquerque: University of New Mexico Press, 1969). Based on oral interviews, nineteen poor, white women from the southern Appalachian mountains and northern migrant ghettoes compellingly relate their stories of survival in Kathy Kahn's collection entitled *Hillbilly Women* (Garden City, New York: Doubleday, 1973).

Government publications are particularly helpful in determining the degree and type of women's participation in the work force and in analyzing their economic status. Since its creation in 1920, the Women's Bureau of the Department of Labor has made available studies such as Janet Hooks' *Women's Occupations Through Seven Decades* (Washington, D.C.: Government Printing Office, 1947). Occasionally, a specially-appointed President's Commission on the Status of Women publishes reports that incorporates statistics on the employment of women.[46] In addition, reports of congressional hearings on the status of women are useful.[47]

Over the last half dozen years the demand for published materials suitable for Women's Studies courses has resulted in a variety of wide-ranging and informative anthologies. Useful in the area of literature are Florence Howe and Ellen Bass, eds., *No More Masks: An Anthology of Poems by Women* (New York: Anchor Press, 1973) and John N. Miller, ed., *A World of Her Own: Writers and the Feminist Controversy* (Columbus, Ohio: Charles E. Merrill Publishing Co., 1971). Among the most comprehensive history anthologies are: Jean E. Friedman and William G. Shade, eds., *Our American Sisters: Women in American Life and Thought* (Boston: Allyn and Bacon, 1973); James L. Cooper and Sheila Mc Isaac Cooper, eds., *The Roots of American Feminist Thought* (Boston: Allyn and Bacon, 1973); and Ronald W. Hogeland, ed., *Women and Womanhood in America* (Lexington, Mass.: D. C. Heath and Co., 1973). A good anthology of writings by black women is Toni Cade's collection, *The Black Woman—An Anthology* (New York: Signet, 1970). One of the earliest, most varied, and still useful feminist perspective anthologies is Robin Morgan's *Sisterhood Is Powerful: An Anthology of Writings from the Women's Liberation Movement* (New York: Vintage Books, 1970). Also reflective of this perspective are Vivian Gornick and Barbara K. Moran, eds., *Woman in Sexist Society: Studies in Power and Powerlessness* (New York: Basic Books, 1971) and Betty and Theodore Roszak, eds., *Masculine/Feminine* (New York: Harper Colophon, 1969).[48]

Non-print media and artifact collections constitute additional Women's Studies source materials. The usefulness and creativity of film in depicting women's experiences, real and imagined, is only beginning to be appreciated.[49] "Woman and Film: A Resource Handbook" published by the Project on the Status and Education of Women of the Association of American Colleges remains the single most valuable compilation of film-related materials on women. As listings in this handbook suggest, film images of women may serve as historical documentation of women's experiences. Such images should, therefore, be analyzed as other Women's Studies materials are in terms of authenticity, biases, and social-cultural context. Mary Blewett offers some useful suggestions for classroom use of films in "Women in American History: A History Through Film Approach," *Film & History,* Vol. IV, No. 4 (December 1974).[50]

Artifact collections in museums and historical societies have been less utilized than film in recreating the experiences of women; they are, however, potentially as helpful. The briefest visit to a museum indicates that three-dimensional objects materially document the many and varied roles of women in America. Alice P. Kenney's "Women, History, and the Museum," *History Teacher,* Vol. X (August 1974) is a suggestive, but limited, discussion of the enrichment derived from studying and analyzing women's history from artifacts located in museums and historical societies. Another use of museum and historical society materials is suggested by Judy O'Sullivan's bicentennial exhibition, commissioned by SITES (Smithsonian Institution Traveling Exhibition Service), on "Workers and Allies: A Survey of Women Participating in the American Trade Union Movement, 1824-1976." The exhibit consists of fifty photographs—from newspapers, periodicals, labor publications and posters—that trace the history of women workers as individuals and as members of labor organizations.

The restored buildings of the Rappite communitarian settlement, Old Economy in Ambridge, Pennsylvania, document another dimension of women's lives. Communal living arrangements, such as the Rappites', were perceived by some nineteenth-century women as an alternative to the seemingly inevitable restriction on social relationships between the sexes to sex, motherhood, and a life of hardship thereafter.

The sources cited above indicate that Women's Studies has moved beyond un-examined, unquestioned acceptance of traditional images of women and toward a fuller understanding of the reality of women's, and men's, lives. Women's Studies is still "in process" of developing, but the integrative, interdisciplinary, information-sharing nature of the enterprise is already obvious. Recent questions, attitudes, and methods have produced interpretations of women vastly different from those that have long prevailed. There is every indication that this trend in Women's Studies will continue and will contribute, thereby, to the enrichment of all scholarly investigation, knowledge, and human development.

NOTES

1. Florence Howe discusses "the sudden and shocking apprehension—by late 1969—of the standard college curriculum as male-centered and male-biased." Tamar Berkowitz, Jean Mangi, and Jane Williamson, eds., *Who's Who and Where in Women's Studies* (Old Westbury, New York: The Feminist Press, 1974), p. vi.

2. See Elaine Hedges, "Women's Studies at a State College," *Women's Studies Newsletter*, Vol. II, No. 4 and Vol. III, No. 1 (Fall 1974-Winter 1975), for a description of the interdisciplinary, intra-university communications networks essential to establishing a Women's Studies program.

3. Interdisciplinary research, writing, and teaching about women is documented in *Female Studies* publications: volumes I-V and VIII (KNOW, Inc., Box 86031, Pittsburgh, Pennsylvania 15221; volumes VI, VIII, IX, and X (The Feminist Press, SUNY/College at Old Westbury, Box 334, Old Westbury, New York 11568).

4. In her introduction—"New Developments in Research on Women"—to the American edition of Klein's 1946 work, Janet Zollinger Giele notes new research trends in several disciplines in the 1960s.

5. The influence of the larger society's perceptions of women's proper functions on scientific and medical opinion is analyzed by Elizabeth Fee," The Sexual Politics of Victorian Social Anthropology," in Mary S. Hartman and Lois Banner, eds., *Clio's Consciousness Raised: New Perspectives on the History of Women* (New York: Harper Torchbooks, 1974). In addition, see Carroll Smith-Rosenberg and Charles Rosenberg, "The Female Animal: Medical and Biological Views of Woman and Her Roles in Nineteenth Century America," *Journal of American History,* 60 (September 1973) and Janice Law Trecker," Sex, Science and Education," *American Quarterly,* Vol. XXVI, No. 4 (October 1974).

6. Annette K. Baxter, "Women's Studies and American Studies: The Uses of the Interdisciplinary," *American Quarterly,* Vol. XXVI, No. 4 (October 1974). In 1964 David Potter noted that women have generally been ignored in interpretations of American character and culture. "American Women and the American Character," in John A. Hague, ed., *American Character and Culture* (DeLand, Florida: Everett Edwards Press, 1964). Betty Chmaj, in turn, discussed the limitations of Potter's comments in Chapter 2 of *Image, Myth and Beyond: American Women and American Studies,* Vol. Two, Betty Chmaj and Judith A. Gustafson, with Joseph W. Baunoch (Pittsburgh: KNOW, Inc., 1974).

7. Of over 2,000 institutions of higher education in the United States in 1974, 885 offered close to 5,000 Women's Studies courses. For a listing of

courses, programs, instructors and institutions see Berkowitz, Mangi and William-son, *Who's Who and Where in Women's Studies.*

8. *Ms. Archivist* is a useful newsletter for information on sources and re-positories of materials relevant to Women's Studies. For information on *Ms. Archivist,* edited by Sara Fuller, Edie Hedlin and Andy Lentz, contact: Sara Fuller, 940 Bricker Boulevard, Columbus, Ohio 43221. See also *The American Archivist* issue devoted to women in the archival professions. Vol. 36, No. 2 (April 1973).

9. In Chapter 5 entitled "Husbands and Wives," (page 82) Demos claimed that: "No aspect of the puritan household was more vital than the relationship of husband and wife."

10. See Theodore K. Rabb and Robert I. Rotberg, eds., *The Family in His-tory: Interdisciplinary Essays* (New York: Harper Torchbooks, 1971) for the McLaughlin essay plus essays by Tamara Hareven, "The History of the Family as an Interdisciplinary Field," Robert V. Wells, "Demographic Change and the Life Cycle of American Families," and Lois Banner, "On Writing Women's His-tory." Daniel J. Walkowitz explores work and family relationships in "Working-Class Women in the Gilded Age: Factory, Community and Family Life Among Cohoes, New York Cotton Workers," *Journal of Social History,* Vol. 5 (Summer 1972). Ruth Schwartz Cohen has examined another facet of working women's lives: labor-saving technological devices for the home. She suggests that techno-logically sophisticated domestic machinery was not viewed as an unmixed bless-ing by working wives, in "A Case Study of Technological and Social Change: The Washing Machine and the Working Wife," in Mary S. Hartman and Lois Banner, eds. *Clio's Consciousness Raised: New Perspectives on the History of Women* (New York: Harper Torchbooks, 1974). Another informative source on women and work is *Trade Union Women's Studies: Proceedings of the First New York Trade Union Women's Conference* (Trade Union Women's Studies, Metropoli-tan Office, New York State School of Labor and Industrial Relations, Cornell University, 7 East 43rd Street, New York, New York 10017).

11. One of the functions of the caucuses and committees organized by women in individual academic disciplines and professions has been to disseminate information about Women's Studies: new courses, research, publications. The Women's Caucus of the Modern Language Association publishes a "Research in Progress" bulletin periodically. The Sociologists for Women in Society news-letter regularly contains reviews of research and publications relevant to women in sociology. The Coordinating Committee on Women in the Historical Profes-sion publishes a newsletter that contains information on publications, as well as "New Courses" and "Research in Progress" bulletins.

12. See Elizabeth S. ten Houten, "Some Collections of Special Use for Women's History Resources in the United States," *AAUW Journal* (April 1974). Reprinted in *Ms. Archivist,* Vol. 2, No. 1 (Summer 1974). See, also, the ex-tremely useful guides compiled by Andrea Hinding, Rosemary Richardson, et al., (University of Minnesota Libraries, Minneapolis, Minnesota 55455), "Archival and Manuscript Resources for the Study of Women's History: A Beginning," and Roy Thomas (History Department, Bowie State College, Bowie, Maryland), "Guide to Manuscripts in the Library of Congress: American History, 1896-1920."

13. Two catalogs are available from the Sophia Smith Collection (Smith College, Northampton, Massachusetts 01060): iconographical resources are noted

in the "Picture Catalog of the Sophia Smith Collection" and manuscript holdings are listed in the "Catalog of the Sophia Smith Collection."

14. Two years after the woman suffrage movement went into effect,
Arthur Schlesinger, Sr., claimed that the Nineteenth Amendment signalled the
fact that women could no longer be ignored by historians. Chapter VI, "The Role
of Women in American History," in *New Viewpoints in American History* (New
York, Macmillan, 1922).

15. *Manuscript Inventories and the Catalogs of the Manuscripts, Books and
Pictures,* an index to the books, manuscripts and pictures in the Schlesinger Library collection, was published in 1973 by G. K. Hall and Co.

16. Under a 1973 Rockefeller Foundation grant, the Regional Oral History
Office, The Bancroft Library, University of California at Berkeley has under-
taken the Suffragists Oral History Project. Sets of the oral interviews with twelve
suffragists will be deposited in five libraries: Radcliffe College, Northwestern
University, the Library of Congress, New York City Public Library, the University of North Carolina (Greensboro), plus the institutional copies at the University of California, Berkeley and Los Angeles.

17. Although insufficient funding forced the Library to close, information
on microfilm projects completed and in production may be obtained from the
Women's History Research Center, Inc., 2325 Oak Street, Berkeley, California
94618. The International Women's History Periodical Archive has been trans-
ferred to the Special Collections Department of the Northwestern University
Library, Evanston, Illinois 60201, and the Topical Research Library to the Contemporary History Archive at the University of Wyoming, Laramie, Wyoming
82070.

18. *Newsletter, Archives of Labor History and Urban Affairs,* Vol. 2, No. 1
(Summer 1972).

19. In 1974 Arno Press (300 Madison Avenue, New York, New York
10017) published its third reprint series. *Women in America: From Colonial
Times to the 20th Century* consists of 59 books reprinted under the advisory
editorship of Annette K. Baxter and Leon Stein.

20. For publications information write to: KNOW, Inc., P.O. Box 86031
Pittsburgh, Pennsylvania 15221 and The Feminist Press, Box 334 Old Westbury,
New York, 11568.

21. *American Women and American Studies I* (1971) and *Image, Myth and
Beyond: American Women and American Studies II* (1974).

22. The Feminist Press plans to publish a Margaret Fuller reader and an anthology of utopian writings about women, published originally between 1880
and 1910.

23. *Women: A Journal of Liberation* (3028 Greenmount, Baltimore, Maryland 21218), within a general thematic format, reflects a commitment to the
contemporary women's movement and to revolutionary change. A new interdisciplinary quarterly, *Signs: Journal of Women in Culture and Society* (University
of Chicago Press, 11030 Langley Avenue, Chicago, Illinois 60672), has been
scheduled for initial publication in September 1975.

24. Project on the Status and Education of Women, Association of American Colleges, 1818 R Street N.W., Washington, D.C. 20009.

25. See also, Gerda Lerner, "Women's Rights and American Feminism,"
The American Scholar, Vol. 40, No. 2 (Spring 1971).

26. Two studies of non-suffrage oriented women's organizations in the early

nineteenth century are: Keith Melder, "Ladies Bountiful: Organized Women's Benevolence in Early 19th Century America," *New York History,* Vol. XLVIII (1967) and Carroll Smith-Rosenberg, "Beauty, the Beast, and the Militant Women: A Case Study in Sex Roles and Social Stress in Jacksonian America," *American Quarterly,* Vol. XXIII (October 1971).

27. *American Quarterly,* Vol. XVIII, No. 2, Pt. 1 (Summer 1966) and *Midcontinent American Studies Journal,* Vol. X, No. 1 (Spring 1969), respectively. Several articles on Victorian era societal expectations and stereotypical images of women are included in the excellent anthology edited by Mary S. Hartman and Lois Banner, *Clio's Consciousness Raised: New Perspectives on the History of Women* (New York: Harper Torchbooks, 1974). For an incisive description of the late nineteenth-century "woman of leisure" see Thorstein Veblen's "The Economic Theory of Women's Dress," *Journal of Political Economy,* Vol. XLVI (November 1894).

28. See also, Addams, *The Second Twenty Years at Hull House* (New York: Macmillan, 1930) and Mary White Ovington, a founder and active leader of the NAACP, *The Walls Came Tumbling Down* (New York: Harcourt, Brace Jovanovich, 1974).

29. See also, Jessie Bernard, *Academic Women* (University Park, Pa.: Penn State University Press, 1964).

30. Margery Davies presents an excellent analysis of women's segregation in the work force in "Woman's Place is at the Typewriter: The Feminization of the Clerical Labor Force," *Radical America,* Vol. 8, No. 4 (July-August 1974).

31. Useful information on the establishment of the Women's Trade Union League is provided by Allen Davis, "The Women's Trade Union League: Origins and Organization," *Labor History,* Vol. V, No. 1 (Winter 1964).

32. For information on the participation of women in the Socialist Party see Mari Jo Buhle's "Women and the Socialist Party, 1901-1914," *Radical America,* Vol. 4, No. 2 (February 1970).

33. *Radical America* (P.O. Box B, No. Cambridge, Massachusetts 02140) issued this essay as a separate, seventy-page pamphlet in 1972.

34. For information on this bibliography contact Lucinda Cisler: 102 West 80 Street, New York, New York 10024. For a list of American Studies articles on women, see Delores Barracano Schmidt's compilation, "Women," *American Quarterly,* Vol. XXV, No. 3 (August 1973).

35. Tillie Olsen is author of *Tell Me a Riddle* (New York: Delta Books, 1971), a collection of short stories about working class women and men.

36. June Sochen presents thirty biographical sketches of recognized feminist theoreticians in *Movers and Shakers: American Women Thinkers and Activists, 1900-1970* (New York: Quadrangle, 1973). See also, biographical excerpts from the varied lives of ten American women in Eve Merriam, ed., *Growing up Female in America* (New York: Dell, 1971).

37. Additionally useful are Alix Shulman's *Red Emma Speaks: Selected Writings and Speeches* (New York: Vintage Books, 1972) and *To the Barricades: The Anarchist Life of Emma Goldman* (New York: Crowell, 1971).

38. Alma Lutz is the author, also, of *Emma Willard, Pioneer Educator of American Women* (Boston: Beacon Press, 1964).

39. Tamara Hareven's *Eleanor Roosevelt: An American Conscience* (New York: Quadrangle, 1968) is also helpful.

40. On the basis of interviews and questionnaires, Friedan concluded that women in the 1950s had not, in fact, found self-fulfillment from their roles as wives and mothers.

41. Tillie Olsen's explanatory biographical essay, in the 1972 edition, is invaluable to an understanding of the difficulties Rebecca Harding Davis faced as an author whose primary duties and energies were not devoted to writing, but to her family.

42. *Daughter of Earth,* 1973; *The Revolt of Mother and Other Stories,* 1974; *The Yellow Wallpaper,* 1973—with afterwords by Paul Lauter, Michele Clark, and Elaine R. Hedges, respectively.

43. *The Awakening* (New York: Capricorn Books, 1964). Cynthia Griffin Wolff, "Thanatos and Eros: Kate Chopin's *The Awakening,*" *American Quarterly,* Vol. XXV, No. 4 (October 1973) and Per Seyersted, *Kate Chopin: A Critical Biography* (Baton Rouge: Louisiana State University Press, 1969) are informative on Chopin and on reactions to *The Awakening.* For a discussion of the basically conservative nature of women's literature see Gail Thain Parker's introduction to *The Oven Birds: American Women on Womanhood, 1820-1920* (Garden City, New York: Anchor Books, 1972).

44. See also, Judith Bardwick, *Psychology of Women: A Study of Bio-Cultural Conflict* (New York: Harper & Row, 1971). Sex discrimination against the participation of women in the medical profession is discussed by Barbara Ehrenreich and Deidre English in two pamphlets, *Witches, Midwives and Nurses: A History of Women Healers* and *Complaints and Disorders: The Sexual Politics of Sickness* (Old Westbury, New York: The Feminist Press, 1973).

45. The Spring 1964 issue of *Daedalus,* Vol. 93, No. 2, is devoted to "The Woman in America."

46. One example is Margaret Mead and Frances Bagley Kaplan, eds., *American Women: Report of the President's Commission on the Status of Women and Other Publications of the Commission* (New York: Scribner's 1965).

47. See, for example, United States House of Representatives, 91st Congress, 2nd Session, Hearings Before the Special Subcommittee on Education of the Committee on Education and Labor, Section 805 of H.R. 16098, "Discrimination Against Women" (Washington, D.C.: June 17, 19, 26, 29, 30, 1970).

48. Mary C. Lynn's edited collection, *Women's Liberation in the Twentieth Century* (New York: John Wiley & Sons, Inc., 1975), provides an examination of women's roles from a variety of perspectives.

49. A documentary history of the social, economic, and cultural experiences of women in the United States is incorporated in a film released in 1974, "The Emerging Woman." The film was produced by the Women's Film Project, Inc., and information on it is available from: Film Images, 17 West 60 Street, New York, New York 10023.

50. Music is another non-print media form useful in Women's Studies. Singer Helen Reddy's "I Am Woman" is an undeniably feminist statement. And oppression, aspiration, and initiative are themes apparent in the folk, soul, and rock music written and performed by Joan Baez, Janis Joplin, Roberta Flack, Joni Mitchell, among others.

Part III
General Resources
for Teaching and Research

An American Studies Bibliography: Suggested Sources for University Courses Abroad

by Donald N. Koster

[A specialist encounters numerous difficulties attempting to construct a current, judicious, and unassailable bibliography even within the confines of a narrow field. We appreciate the willingness of all of our contributors to express their convictions. We must be even more grateful to Mr. Koster, who here considers works across the entire front of American Studies. Naturally, there will be many subjective choices and no two scholars will feel the same in any field. Mr. Koster has tried to serve the foreign scholar by citing inexpensive editions where possible, and by sticking mainly to works tested by use.—Eds.]

Interdisciplinary university level courses in American Studies being offered or contemplated in various nations around the world have been traditionally hampered by difficulties in obtaining the necessary books readily and at relatively low cost. This bibliographic essay trys to suggest a nucleus of books which, wherever possible, are available in paperback editions and that, taken as a whole, range across the American experience. Notes indicate instances in which a book is out of print or, as it too often the case, not available in a paperback text edition.

Admittedly many excellent works have had to be omitted from this listing, but the need to be selective is perhaps obvious in any such attempt as this. My comments and annotations are concerned primarily with books *about* various aspects of American civilization. I begin with a group of books that are either strictly reference works or are so interdisciplinary in character as in fact to be classified under no other heading than **American Civilization.** For ready current reference *American Almanac: The U.S. Book of Facts, Statistics, and Information for 1970,* edited by B. J. Wattenburg for the Bureau of the Census, U.S. Department of Commerce, is published by Grosset and Dunlap at $2.95 [prices quoted throughout the essay are in U.S. dollars as of 1971—Ed.]. Edited by the American Council of Learned Societies and available by subscription only is the volume *Dictionary of American Biography,* published by Scribner at $290, it includes noteworthy Americans of all periods who died before 1940. Invaluable is the single-volume Library of Congress *Guide to the Study of the United States of America* (U.S. Government Printing Office, LC2.2:Un3/4, $7.00), published in 1960 and discussing in some detail representative books reflecting virtually all aspects of American life and thought. Containing extensive bibliographical notes, Max Lerner's *America As a Civilization: Life and Thought in the United States Today* (Simon and Schuster, 2 vols. at $2.45) provides a wide-ranging examination of the history, people, culture, economy, society, art, and position of the nation on the world scene. For their bibliographical importance the following journals seem to be indispensable: *America: History and Life,* published by Clio Press for the American Bibliographical Center, prints abstracts of articles, published since 1963 and concerning prehistory to present-day events in the United States and Canada, appearing in more than 500 American and Canadian and in over 1,000 foreign periodicals; *American Literature,* published by Duke University Press, includes a checklist, "Articles on American Literature Appearing in Current Periodicals," that covers about 500 foreign and domestic periodicals; and *American Quarterly,* the official journal of the American Studies Association, publishes interdisciplinary articles on all facets of American civilization as well as an "Annual Review of Books," an annotated bibliography of "Articles in American Studies," and a bibliography of writings on the theory and teaching of American Studies. Two volumes edited by Hennig Cohen, *The American Experience* and *The American Culture,* both subtitled "Approaches to the Study of the United States" (Houghton Mifflin, $4.95 each, hardcover), anthologize selected essays from the files of *American Quarterly.*

Mr. Koster is Professor of English and Director of the Program in American Civilization at Adelphi University, Garden City, Long Island, New York. For over a decade he edited American Quarterly's *annual "Articles in American Studies" and he currently edits the AQ "Annual Review of Books." He is the Bibliographer of the American Studies Association. Mr. Koster is also author of* The Theme of Divorce in American Drama, 1871–1939 *and co-author of* Modern Journalism. His Transcendentalism *in America is to appear in 1976, as will several of a series of Bibliographical Research Guides which he is editing for the Gale Research Company.*

Photo: George H. Meyer

Turning now to works on more specific aspects of American Studies, I shall mention them by categories arranged alphabetically.

For **Agriculture**, W. F. Owen's *American Agriculture: The Changing Structure* (Heath, $2.50) affords an adequate overview.

For **Art and Architecture**, Oliver W. Larkin's *Art and Life in America* (Holt Rinehart Winston, $13.95 hardcover) is a thorough, well illustrated history of American painting and sculpture from the beginnings to 1960. Also amply illustrated is E. P. Richardson's *Painting in America: From 1502 to the Present* (Crowell, $13.25 hardcover), which deals with every American painter of significance and treats all of their important works. Numerous biographical sketches and commentaries on trends, schools, and influences enrich the book. Folk art is well represented by P. C. Welsh in *American Folk Art: The Art and Spirit of a People* (Smithsonian Institution, $2.95). Architecture is ably treated in Wayne Andrews' *Architecture, Ambition, and Americans; a Social History of American Architecture*, (Free Press, $2.95), a comprehensive history from 1607 to the present. Carl W. Condit provides in *American Building* (University of Chicago Press, $10 hardcover) an excellent survey of construction methods and materials used in the United States from colonial times to the present as well as a lengthy annotated bibliography. Lewis Mumford's 1924 work *Sticks and Stones: a Study of American Architecture and Civilization*, revised in 1955 (Dover, $2.00), traces the major trends from the "medieval tradition" of seventeenth-century New England to the "machine age" to show how "architecture and civilization develop hand in hand." Emphasizing urban architecture are Vincent Scully's *American Architecture and Urbanism* (Praeger, $18.50 hardcover) with over 500 fine photographic illustrations ranging from Pueblo Indian settlements to megastructure and garden city; Christopher Tunnard and Henry H. Reed's *American Skyline: the Growth and Form of Our Cities and Towns* (New American Library, $1.25), which reviews in non-technical language seven eras of the American city pattern from the colonial to the present; and Tunnard's *Modern American City* (Van Nostrand-Reinhold, $1.75).

On **Dance**, Walter Terry's *The Dance in America* (Harper-Row, $6.95 hardcover) is, I think, still the best book on its subject because it traces its history from the beginning in every aspect of its considerable variety and is well illustrated.

Under the general heading of **Economics**, Thomas C. Cochran's *The American Business System: A Historical Perspective, 1900-1955* (Harper-Row, $1.45) reflects a synthesis of materials from economic and business history with those of other disciplines. Not only does it reveal the growth of technology and managerial enterprise but also the rise of the welfare state. Joseph Dorfman's *The Economic Mind in American Civilization* (Viking, 5 vols. at $30 the set hardcover) is a definitive study of democracy in a land founded largely on the cupidity of adventurers and developed in a mercantile and industrial mold. In a different vein in David M. Potter's *People of Plenty, Economic Abundance and the American Character* (University of Chicago Press, $1.50), a study of the effects of economic abundance on the national character. Concentrating on the functions, techniques, and responsibilities of business and industrial management is Peter F. Drucker's *The Practice of Management* (Harper-Row, $7.95 hardcover), which includes many case histories and sketches of major corporations. Based on authoritative primary and secondary sources and with an extensive critical bibliography, Foster Rhea Dulles' *Labor in America*, 3rd ed. revised (Crowell, $3.95) describes the first labor organizations, the significance of the Homestead and Pullman strikes, and the roles played in the growth of unionism by such labor leaders as Gompers, Murray, Meany, Hillman, Lewis, and Reuther. A briefer survey that may serve as a basic text useful for factual information and handy reference is Henry Pelling's *American Labor* (University of Chicago Press, $2.45). Florence Peterson's *American Labor Unions: What They Are and How They Work*, 2nd ed., revised, (Harper-Row, $6.50 hardcover) is also a comprehensive handbook, highly informative yet informal in style.

A good general history of **Education** that employs the cultural approach is *A History of Education in American Culture* (Holt Rinehart Winston, $9.95 hardcover) by R. Freeman Butts and Lawrence A. Cremin. For higher education Frederick Rudolph's *The American College and University: a History* (Random, $2.95) deals in its first part with the American college to about the Civil War; and in its second with the rise of the university. Social, political, and economic factors are ably related to higher education. Arranged chronologically from the founding of Harvard to 1948, *American Higher Education: A Documentary History* (University of Chicago Press, 2 vols., I, $2.95; II, $3.45), edited by Richard Hofstadter and Wilson Smith, is a valuable collection of representative documents while Hofstadter and Walter Metzger pioneered in their fascinating *Development of Academic Freedom in the United States* (Columbia University Press, $10 hardcover). For the general reader who wants to know how the contemporary American university operates, Jacques Barzun's *The American University; How It Runs and Where It Is Going* (Harper-Row, $2.45) provides a knowledgeable examination of our institutions of higher learning from historical and sociological points of view. John Dewey, America's most famous philosopher of education, may be represented by his best known work, *Democracy and Education* (Free Press, $2.45), and by a good collection, *Dewey on Education: Selections, with an Introduction and Notes* (Teachers College, $2.25) edited by Martin S. Dworkin.

In the field of **Folklore** Richard M. Dorson's *American Folklore* (University of Chicago Press, $2.45) covers the rise of native folk humor, regional cultures, immigrant and Negro folklore, and folk heroes. It also contains a chronological table of motifs and tale types. Alan Lomax's *The Folk Songs of North America* (Doubleday, $10 hardcover) contains all the best known folk songs of the English-speaking people of the United States. Divided into four sections—West, Southern Mountains and Backwoods, Negro South, and North—it includes music for piano and chords for guitar accompaniment. A most useful recent collection of authentic Afro-American folklore is *American Negro Folklore* (Quadrangle Books, $12.50 hardcover) compiled and edited by J. Mason Brewer. Tales, rhymes, spirituals, folk blues, and ballads are included as well as sections on superstitions, proverbs, and children's game songs.

For **Geography**, Ralph H. Brown's *Historical Geography of the United States* (Harcourt, Brace, & Jovanovich, $11.95 hardcover) places principal emphasis on past periods within time limits varying with the region considered. The eastern provinces of Canada are included in the preliminary chapters.

In the category of **Government and Politics,** *American Government and Politics* (Van Nostrand-Reinhold, $5.25 hardcover) by Harold Zink et al. is a standard college text that covers federal, state, and local government with special attention to the American style of democracy and its characteristics, flaws, and virtues. A somewhat similar text is *Government by the People: the Dynamics of American National, State, and Local Government,* 7th edition, (Prentice-Hall, $9.95 hardcover) by James M. Burns and Jack W. Peltason. Charts, tables, diagrams, and a selective bibliography assist the effort to depict American government as a lively, dynamic process.

An interesting study of the origin and development of the American tradition of political liberty is Clinton L. Rossiter's *Seedtime of the Republic* (Harcourt, Brace, & Jovanovich, 3 vols., $5.25 the set). Volume I is a background study of liberty in the colonies; Volume II deals with the "most notable thinkers" of the colonial period; and Volume III treats political theories in expression and action from 1765 to 1776. Richard Hofstadter's *The American Political Tradition and the Men Who Made It* (Random, $1.95) is a group of twelve essays that interpret our political history, ten being on individuals who were important in shaping the tradition, the two others on "The Founding Fathers" and "The Spoilsmen." Daniel J. Boorstin's *The Genius of American Politics* (University of Chicago Press, $1.50) is a revision of six public lectures analyzing the peculiar qualities of the American political system.

Government and the American Economy, 3rd edition, (Norton, $8.95 hardcover) by Merle Fainsod and Lincoln Gordon is a well integrated history of government control, regulation, and promotion that presents the economic, organizational, constitutional, and legal setting in which American enterprise has developed. Edward S. Corwin's *The President; Office and Powers, 1787-1957,* 4th edition, revised (New York University Press, $2.95), shows the development and contemporary status of the presidential power and of the office under the Constitution. The approach is partly historical, partly analytical and critical.

On diplomacy, George F. Kennan's *American Diplomacy, 1900-1950* (University of Chicago Press, $1.95; New American Library, $.75) contains essays by the former ambassador and State Department counselor on the several types of diplomacy used by the United States in the first half of the twentieth century, while *The Shaping of American Diplomacy: Readings and Documents in American Foreign Relations, 1750-1968* (Rand McNally, 2 vols., $6.35 each, hardcover), edited by William A. Williams, is an ably chosen selection of writings on each period by present-day historians, in addition to numerous contemporary documents.

Alexis de Tocqueville's famous *Democracy in America* (Random, 2 vols., $1.95 each) in the Henry Reeve texts as revised by Francis Bowen and edited by Phillips Bradley should, of course, be read. This edition contains an interesting foreword by Harold Laski, whose own *The American Democracy* (Reprint, Kelley, price not yet set) is sometimes referred to as "Tocqueville redone" from the British standpoint.

As history and literature bear the most direct testimony to the variety of men's deeds and thoughts, we may reasonably expect the largest segments of our listing to fall within those categories. For **History** I mention first four helpful reference volumes: *Concise Dictionary of American History* (Scribner, $19.50 hardcover) edited by Wayne Andrews and Thomas C. Cochran, a good one-volume abridgement of the six-volume work by James Truslow Adams; *Harvard Guide to American History* (Atheneum, $4.95), edited by Oscar Handlin et al., containing a useful index and chapters on aids to historical research, the materials of history, and historical sources; and *Encyclopedia of American History*, revised 1970 (Harper-Row, $12.50 hardcover), edited by Richard B. Morris, which provides in one handy volume the essential facts about American life and institutions, and includes biographical sketches of some 400 notable Americans.

Excellent selections of original documents include *Documents of American History*, 8th edition (Appleton, 2 vols., $4.95 each), edited by Henry Steele Commager, the first volume running from the Age of Discovery to 1898, the second volume since 1898; and *Basic Documents in American History*, revised (Van Nostrand-Reinhold, $1.95), edited by Richard B. Morris, which begins with the Mayflower Compact and extends to the present.

Recommended inclusive histories are *The Rise of American Civilization*, revised (Macmillan, 4 vols., $10.95) by Charles A. and Mary R. Beard, a historic landmark that mixes political and social facts in about equal proportion; Oscar Handlin's *The Americans: a New History of the People of the United States* (Atlantic-Little Brown, $2.45), in which the focus is on the context and on developments common to the whole population rather than on the individual. What motivated men to move, how they earned a living, their thoughts of life and death, and the ways in which they expressed themselves are the main theme. Also William Miller's *A New History of the United States*, revised (Dell, $2.45), which places emphasis on people, events, and economics. In fewer than 500 pages Miller has organized a history of considerable sweep, even if politics and war are dealt with somewhat sparsely. The bibliography is extensive and briefly annotated. Henry Bamford Parkes in *The United States of America, a history* (Knopf, $6.50 hardcover) has compressed American social and political history into a finely organized and clearly written volume in which he had made a special effort to integrate achievement in the arts with the total social structure.

For the Colonial period, William Bradford's *Of Plymouth Plantation* (Modern Library, $2.95), written between 1630 and 1650 and first published in 1856, is, of course, a classic of its kind, and this edition by Samuel Eliot Morison is a faithful transcript from the original manuscript. Morison's own *Builders of the Bay Colony*, revised (Houghton Mifflin, $2.95) provides sketches of the ten persons he believes best exemplify various aspects of life in the first fifty years of the Massachusetts Bay Colony. They are John White, Governor Winthrop, Thomas Shepard, John Hull, Henry Dunster, Nathaniel Ward, Robert Child, John Winthrop the Younger, John Eliot, and Anne Bradstreet. *The Puritan Oligarchy* (Scribner, $2.75; Grosset and Dunlap, $2.25) by T. J. Wertenbaker is of value for its clear development of Puritan influence on education, architecture, science, and town government, while Louis B. Wright's *The Cultural Life of the American Colonies, 1607-1763* (Harper-Row, $2.25) is a fine summary of colonial intellectual life in such areas as religion, literature, education, and social thought.

Although expensive, Douglas Southall Freeman's seven-volume *George Washington, A Biography* (Scribner, $15 each, hardcover) vividly reveals a figure formerly shrouded in myth and legend. Freeman begins with Washington's ancestry and continues chronologically through his presidency and brief final illness. Washington's own *Writings . . . from the Original Manuscript Sources, 1745–1799*, edited by John C. Fitzpatrick (Reprint House International, 39 vols., price not yet set, hardcover) is the most complete record available. A well written and comprehensive biography that divides its attention ably between the man and his work is Carl Van Doren's *Benjamin Franklin* (Viking, $3.95).

In *The Age of Jackson* (Little, Brown, $2.95) Arthur M. Schlesinger, Jr. presents Jacksonian democracy as the outgrowth of Jeffersonian democracy brought about by a peaceable revolution in which the non-capitalists triumphed over the entrenched capitalists, while John W. Ward in *Andrew Jackson, Symbol for An Age* (Oxford, $1.95) concentrates more on the man, who is seen as folk hero and popular symbol of an age whose principal assumptions he embodied.

For the Westward Movement Ray Allen Billington's *Westward Expansion: a History of the American Frontier*, 3rd edition, (Macmillan, $9.95 hardcover) is a revision and expansion of Turner's "Frontier Hypothesis" with an excellent seventy-five-page bibliography, while his *America's Frontier Heritage* (Holt Rinehart Winston, $2.95) reworks much of the same material. An excellent collection, with cogent introduction and full headnotes, of the most illuminating primary sources and eye-witness accounts on the great migration across the American continent is *The West: Contemporary Records of America's Expansion Across the Continent, 1607–1890* (Putnam, $2.15) edited by Bayrd Still, while a classic treatment is Walter Prescott Webb's *The Great Plains* (Grosset and Dunlap, $2.50) on which all subsequent studies have had to draw heavily.

The only book to present in brief compass the major political and military developments of the Civil War era along with border problems, non-military developments during the war, intellectual trends, anti-war efforts, religious and educational movements, propaganda methods and much else is *The Civil War and Reconstruction*, revised (Appleton, $10.95 hardcover) by James G. Randall and David Donald. Carl Sandburg's *Abraham Lincoln, the Prairie Years and the War Years*, (Dell, 3 vols., $2.95 the set) is an excellent condensation of the author's monumental six-volume work with a concentration on the man Lincoln. The standard edition of Lincoln's own *Collected Works* (Rutgers University Press, 9 vols. $115 the set, hardcover) is superbly edited by Roy P. Basler. A thorough scholarly treatment of the abolitionist movement is Louis Filler's *The Crusade Against Slavery, 1830–1860* (Harper-Row, $2.45), while John Hope Franklin's *From Slavery to Freedom: a History of Negro Americans*, 3rd edition, revised (Random, $3.45) is a comprehensive and objective work beginning a thousand years ago and tracing the record of Negroes up to their present-day life in the West Indies, Latin America, Canada, and the United States. Helpful to an understanding of present problems in the region is Wilbur J. Cash's *The Mind of the South* (Random $1.95), a cultural history based on a complex analysis of Southern psychology.

Works emphasizing immigration are Maldwyn A. Jones' *American Immigration* (University of Chicago Press, $2.45), a historical survey in which the immigrant emerges as a significant force in economic growth, social development, political alignments, the westward movement, and foreign policy. The stress of John Higham's *Strangers in the Land: Patterns of American Nativism, 1860-1925* (Atheneum, $1.95) is on the dissection of the numerous elements that formed a virulent hostility to newcomers and whose political machinations and power culminated in their great victory, the Immigration Act of 1924.

A very fine cultural history is Howard Mumford Jones' *O Strange New World, American Culture: the Formative Years* (Viking, $2.95) which, as such history must do, fuses political, religious, literary, artisitic, and sociological elements.

Intellectual history is well served by Stow Persons' *American Minds: A History of Ideas* (Holt Rinehart Winston, $8.50 hardcover) which begins with the "Colonial religious mind" of 1620-1660 and proceeds to "Liberty and Loyalty," the evolution of Civil Liberty, indicating the foremost characteristics of each successive social mind and illustrating them with a discussion of representative thinkers and movements; by Henry Steele Commager's *The American Mind: An Interpretation of American Thought and Character since the 1880s* (Yale, $3.45; Bantam, $1.65), which considers such thinkers as William James, Veblen, Turner, Beard, Parrington, Roscoe Pound, and Justice Holmes from a keenly critical viewpoint; and by Merle E. Curti's *The Growth of American Thought*, 3rd edition (Harper-Row, $12.50 hardcover), which shows the triumph of nationalism in social and political thought, and the assertion of individualism in a corporate age of applied science.

Dealing with special facets of American history are Samuel Flagg Bemis' *A Diplomatic History of the United States*, 5th edition (Holt Rinehart Winston, $14.95 hardcover), a factual narrative that runs through the cold war period and contains an extensive index; Hans Kohn's *American Nationalism: an Interpretative Essay* (Macmillan, $1.50), an analysis of the elements of such nationalism— Federal structure, the relationship between England and America, ethnic components, and finally the projection of America onto the world stage; Richard B. Lewis' *The American Adam: Innocence, Tragedy, and Tradition in the Nineteenth Century* (University of Chicago Press, $1.50), a thorough study of the American as a second Adam, particularly as this theme developed in New England and along the Atlantic seaboard, in which he is seen as innocent of the vices of older societies; Clinton L. Rossiter's *Conservatism in America*, 2nd edition, revised (Random, $1.65), the story from Cotton Mather to Robert Taft and Dwight Eisenhower, in which the author attempts a conservative theory and program for American democracy; Staughton Lynd's *Intellectual Origins of American Radicalism* (Random, $1.65), which challenges the views of Rossiter, Carl Becker, and Bernard Bailyn by showing that the dissenting tradition from the beginning raised questions that threatened private property and the authority of the state; Daniel Aaron's *Men of Good Hope: a Story of American Progressives* (Oxford, $2.50), which reflects a broad and sympathetic appreciation of social forces in American history; and W. Lloyd Warner's *American Life: Dream and Reality*, revised (University of Chicago Press, $1.95), which reveals the gap between our ideals and myths and the actuality of our history.

George R. Taylor's *The Transportation Revolution, 1815-1860* (Harper-Row, $3.75) is a very readable synthesis of materials formerly available only in specialized studies of limited scope, while Richard H. Shryock's *Medicine and Society in America: 1660-1860* (Cornell University Press, $1.75) is the best treatment of the subject for the period indicated.

Such limited but intensely current topics as violence and pacifism are admirably treated in *The History of Violence in America* (Praeger, $11.95 hardcover), edited by Hugh Davis Graham and Ted Robert Gurr, which is the unabridged Report to the National Commission on the Causes and Prevention of Violence, and Peter Brock's *Pacifism in the United States: From the Colonial Era to the First World War* (Princeton Univeristy Press, $18.50 hardcover), a monumental study that is a most valuable contribution to the literature of American reform movements.

Social history may be represented by such works as Frederick Lewis Allen's *The Big Change: America Transforms Itself, 1900-1950* (Harper-Row, $.95), a lively informal analysis of changing modes and manners with a close look at economic and political developments of the period; *The Age of Enterprise, A Social History of Industrial America* (Harper-Row, $2.45) by Thomas C. Cochran and William Miller, which traces the development of commerce, industry, labor, and agriculture from 1800 to 1930; and Foster Rhea Dulles' *A History of Recreation: America Learns to Play*, 2nd edition (Appleton, $4.50) in which organized, public recreation is used as the basis for his record of the main aspects of popular recreation. Reliable accounts of transcendentalism, Mormonism, religious and secular utopias, reform movements in education, penology and social welfare, as well as the temperance, peace, feminist, and anti-slavery crusades are to be found in Alice Felt Tyler's *Freedom's Ferment: Phases of American Social History to 1860* (Harper-Row, $2.95). The book contains a lengthy and valuable bibliography and notes.

A challenging new approach to American history is Carl N. Degler's *Out of Our Past: the Forces that Shaped Modern America*, revised (Harper-Row, $2.95), written to explain the future rather than the past. A companion volume is Degler's *Affluence and Anxiety: The United States Since 1945* (Scott Foresman, $2.75).

Finally, Michael McGiffert's capable introductions, helpful reading list, and admirably selected essays make his *The Character of Americans: A Book of Readings* revised (Dorsey, $4.50), a helpful tool in explaining the diverse nature of our people.

The American **Language** as a subject of study in itself and a means of understanding other aspects of American civilization more profoundly can well be represented by such works as George P. Krapp's *The English Language in America* (Reprinted, F. Ungar, 2 vols., $14 hardcover), a historical study reflecting the impact of the rapidly changing American society on vocabulary, names, dialects, style, spelling, and pronunciation; Albert H. Marckwardt's *American English* (Oxford, $2.25), which traces the development of the English language in America and reveals language changes as applied to the history and cultural life of the people; and Henry L. Mencken's *The American Language: an Inquiry into the*

Development of English in the United States, 4th edition and two supplements, edited by Raven I. McDavid, Jr. (Knopf, 3 vols., $38.85 the set, hardcover), a superlative achievement treating of the history and nature of the American language as distinct from the English language. Slang and dialects are studied extensively, and the lengthy indices enable the work to serve almost as a lexicon of linguistic information.

In the field of dictionaries *A Dictionary of American English on Historical Principles* (University of Chicago Press, 4 vols., $100 the set, hardcover) by W. A. Craigie and J. H. Hulbert is not only a most scholarly lexicon but also a seemingly inexhaustible anthology of American life and the American mind. An inexpensive, concise, and ably edited one-volume dictionary that avoids highly technical vocabulary is *Webster's New World Dictionary of the American Language*, 2nd edition (Popular Library, $.75). George R. Stewart's *American Place Names: A Concise and Selective Dictionary for the Continental United States of America* (Oxford, $12.50 hardcover) should also be mentioned.

A few helpful works on the **Law** may be cited, such as Edmond N. Cahn's *The Moral Decision: Right and Wrong in the Light of American Law* (Indiana University Press, $2.25), a study of the reciprocity between morals and law that specifically establishes the trend "morally but not legally liable" to "morally and therefore legally liable"; E. S. Corwin and J. W. Peltason's *Understanding the Constitution*, 5th edition (Holt Rinehart Winston, $4.25); and Robert G. McCloskey's *The American Supreme Court* (University of Chicago Press. $1.95).

Turning now to **Literature** and, first, a small group of essentially bibliographical works: Jacob Blanck's *Bibliography of American Literature* (Yale University Press, 5 vols., vols. 1–4, $20 each; vol. 5, $25 hardcover), a selective work, limited to authors who, in their own time at least, were known and read, and at present ranging alphabetically through Longfellow; Clarence Gohdes. *Bibliographical Guide to the Study of the Literature of the U.S.A.,* 3rd edition, revised (Duke University Press, $5.00 hardcover), which, while dealing primarily with American literature, also contains a list of essential tools for studying American philosophy, art, religion, history, and biography; H.M. Jones and R.M. Ludwig's *Guide to American Literature and Its Backgrounds Since 1890*, 3rd edition, revised (Harvard University Press, $2.75), which affords an excellent bibliography, reading lists of American literature since 1890, and a valuable section on backgrounds, listing general guides, reference works, histories, literary histories, works on sociology and economic history, education, science, fine and popular arts, and a critical list of magazines; W.J. Burke and Will D. Howe's *American Authors and Books, 1640 to the Present Day*, revised by Irving R. Weiss (Crown, $8.50 hardcover), an accurate reference source for biography, book digests, classified listings, awards and related information in American literature; and James D. Hart's *The Oxford Companion to American Literature*, 4th edition (Oxford, $12.50 hardcover), which treats major nonliterary aspects of the American mind and the American scene as these are reflected in and influenced by American literature. Short biographies and brief bibliographies of authors are included, with information about their style and subjects, along with summaries, definitions, and historical outlines of literary movements. A brief reference handbook for the political, social, and intellectual developments behind American literary thought is R.W. Horton and H.W. Edwards' *Backgrounds of American Literary Thought*, 2nd edition (Appleton, $3.45).

Useful inclusive histories of American literature are *Literary History of the United States*, 3rd edition (Macmillan, 2 vols., vol. I, $17.50; vol. II, Bibliography, $16.50) by Robert E. Spiller et al., unparalleled in range if uneven in merit, with an invaluable volume of bibliography; Vernon Louis Parrington's *Main Currents in American Thought* (Harcourt, Brace, & Jovanovich, 3 vols., $8.95 the set), a seminal work that investigates the social, economic, and political backgrounds of American literature with critical judgments made on the basis of social significance rather than belletristic merit; Russel B. Nye's *American Literary History from 1607* (Knopf, $3.95), a triumph of concise writing and reliable information; and Van Wyck Brooks' *Makers and Finders: A History of the Writer in America*, 1800–1915 (Dutton, 5 vols., $14 the set), which deals with an entire culture, not forgetting that a culture is a complex in which each item is significant only as it relates to the whole.

Period, thematic, or area studies helpful to the student of American literature include Daniel Aaron's *Writers on the Left; Episodes in American Literary Communism* (Discus-Avon, $1.65), a social chronicle running from 1912 to the early 1940s in which the response of a selected group of American writers to the idea of Communism is dealt with objectively; Jay B. Hubbell's *The South in American Literature, 1607–1900* (Duke University Press, $12.50 hardcover), which brings into focus many skillful writers who have been neglected and contains a wealth of biographical detail; Alfred Kazin's *On Native Grounds* (Doubleday, $1.75), an interpretation of American prose literature between 1890 and 1940 in which the author sees this body of writing as "rooted in the moral transformation of American life, thought, and manners under the impact of industrial capitalism and science"; F.O. Matthiessen's *American Renaissance: Art and Expression in the Age of Emerson and Whitman* (Oxford, $3.95), which evaluates the concepts held by Emerson, Thoreau, Hawthorne, Melville, and Whitman; William V. O'Connor's *An Age of Criticism, 1900–1950* (Regnery, $1.25), a review of the main trends in American literary criticism for the period; Henry Nash Smith's *Virgin Land; the American West as Symbol and Myth* (Random, $1.95), a study of the way in which the West of the nineteenth century influenced and molded American society, and of how the symbols and myths of the frontier were reflected in literature; Willard Thorp's *American Writing in the Twentieth Century* (Harvard University Press, $6.00 hardcover), a descriptive and historical treatment of fiction, poetry, drama, and criticism; and Robert E. Spiller's *The Cycle of American Literature* (Free Press, $1.95), which presents the theory that the cycle of life itself is the organic movement dominating American letters.

Genre studies or specialized histories are Louise Bogan's *Achievement in American Poetry, 1900–1950* (Regnery, $1.25), acute judgments of poets and their work; Edward C. Wagenknecht's *Cavalcade of the American Novel* (Holt Rinehart Winston, $9.50 hardcover), which spans the period from the beginnings to the middle of the twentieth century; Arthur Hobson Quinn's *A History of the American Drama: From the Beginning to the Civil War*, revised (Appleton, $7.50

hardcover) which, together with its companion volume, *A History of the American Drama: From the Civil War to the Present Day*, revised (Appleton, $8.00 hardcover), is the most scholarly and reliable history of its subject up to 1936, besides containing a valuable bibliography and play list; Alan S. Downer's *Fifty Years of American Drama, 1900–1950* (Regnery, $1.25), a critical overview; Gerald Weales' *American Drama Since World War II* (Harcourt, Brace, & Jovanovich, $6.50 hardcover), a critical description of plays produced since 1945, with a backward glance at playwrights of the 1920s and 1930s; Frank Luther Mott's *American Journalism: a History of Newspapers in the United States through 260 years, 1690–1950*, revised (Macmillan, $9.95 hardcover), an authoritative account arranged chronologically; and Mott's *A History of American Magazines* (Harvard University Press, 5 vols., Vols. 1–4, $12.50 each; Vol. 5, $15 hardcover), a scholarly but readable work that illustrates the main currents of American thought and feeling by analysis of magazine contents and by carefully chosen quotations from them, ranging from 1741 to 1968.

Reliable treatments of American humor are *Native American Humor* (Chandler, $4.95) edited by Walter Blair, a critical history with examples since 1809, and Constance M. Rourke's *American Humor* (Doubleday, $1.25), a psychological study of the national character as typified by the Yankee, the backwoodsman, Uncle Sam and other myths, and as revealed by American humorists from Sam Slick to Mr. Dooley and Will Rogers.

Many good anthologies of American literature exist. That which I have used with most success is *The American Tradition in Literature*, 3rd edition (Norton, 2 vols., $5.95 each), edited by E. S. Bradley et al., which spans the time from Governor Bradford to the present with nicely balanced selections from a wide range of authors. Period anthologies that are useful include *The American Puritans, their Prose and Poetry* (Doubleday, $1.75), edited by Perry Miller; *The American Transcendentalists, their Prose and Poetry* (Doubleday, $1.75), also edited by Miller, and including such figures as Theodore Parker, Margaret Fuller, George Ripley, Bronson Alcott, and Orestes Brownson; and *Modern American Poetry*, revised (Harcourt, Brace & Jovanovich, $7.95 hardcover), edited by Louis Untermeyer and providing a quite ample selection of the better modern poets beginning with Whitman. *The Oxford Book of American Verse* (Oxford, $7.50 hardcover), edited by F. O. Matthiessen, represents the work of fifty-one poets arranged chronologically over a much longer time span, with considerable space given to most of the poets.

Finally, *Landmarks of American Writing*, (Basic Books, $8.50 hardcover) edited by Hennig Cohen, is a volume of essays by thirty-three specialists that samples the American experience as reflected in literature from Irving and Cooper to Faulkner and O'Neill. Uniform in length, they were originally presented as lectures to foreign audiences of the Voice of America.

Several excellent books on American **Music** can be recommended. Gilbert Chase's *America's Music, from the Pilgrims to the Present*, revised (McGraw-Hill, $7.95 hardcover) is an inclusive history, while H. Wiley Hitchcock's *Music in the United States: A Historical Introduction* (Prentice-Hall, $2.95) covers much the same ground in less detail. Virgil Thomson's *American Music Since 1910* (Holt Rinehart Winston, $8.95 hardcover) is a new book written with critical acumen, and Joseph Machlis' *American Composers of Our Time* (Crowell, $4.95 hardcover) contains a generous amount of biographical material. Marshall Stearns' *The Story of Jazz* (Oxford, $2.95) is still the most scholarly and readable account of the genesis and history of the subject, while John Rublowsky's *Popular Music* (Basic Books, $4.95 hardcover) traces superbly the continuity of musical evolution and demonstrates the effect of technological advances on popular taste. Stanley Green's *The World of Musical Comedy*, revised (A. S. Barnes, $12 hardcover) is a reliable illustrated history of the medium as it has evolved in the United States.

The development of **Philosophy** is ably narrated in Herbert W. Schneider's *History of American Philosophy*, 2nd edition (Columbia University Press, $4.50 hardcover). Joseph L. Blau's *Men and Movements in American Philosophy* (Prentice-Hall, $8.95 hardcover) traces the course of philosophic thought through transcendentalism, idealism, pragmatism, realism, and naturalism and proves an American interest in philosophy since colonial times. Richard Hofstadter's *Social Darwinism in American Thought*, revised (Beacon, $2.95) critically appraises the impact of Darwin and Spencer on American social ideologies and philosophy, while Hans Huth's *Nature and the American: Three Centuries of Changing Attitudes* (University of California Press, $7.50 hardcover) examines ethics, philosophy, poetry, and the art of conversation from colonial days to the present. An interpretation of Americans based largely on his twenty-two years of teaching philosophy at Harvard is George Santayana's *Character and Opinion in the United States* (Norton, $1.95), and Morton G. White's *Social Thought in America* (Beacon, $2.45) deals with the intellectual pattern compounded of pragmatism, institutionalism, behaviorism, legal realism, and economic determinism that gripped America for nearly fifty years, its chief representatives being Justice Holmes, Veblen, Dewey, James Harvey Robinson, and Charles A. Beard. Two useful anthologies are *The Development of American Philosophy: A Book of Readings*, 2nd edition (Houghton Mifflin, $9.25 hardcover), edited by W. G. Muelder et al., which begins with early philosophical theology and idealism and concludes with modern philosophers such as Santayana, Edgar S. Brightman, and Sidney Hook; and *American Thought: Civil War to World War I* (Holt Rinehart Winston, $1.75), edited by Perry Miller, which presents extracts from thirteen thinkers of the period who, according to the editor's substantial introduction, expounded the crucial points of view by which Americans between 1865 and 1917 were ruled.

A comprehensive yet concise survey that traces the history of American **Religion** from colonial times to the present and includes a considerable bibliography is Clifton E. Olmstead's *Religion in America: Past and Present* (Prentice-Hall, $1.95). Henry F. May's *Protestant Churches and Industrial America* (Harper-Row, $2.25) examines the influences of American religion on the developing social thought of the industrial age (1828–1895), while Herbert W. Schneider's *Religion in Twentieth-Century America* (Atheneum, $2.95) analyzes changing trends in theological thinking as well as changes in America's religious conscience. Reflecting the shift in the United States from an inner directed life style to an outer directed one is Will Herberg's popular *Protestant, Catholic, Jew: An Essay in American Religious Sociology*, revised (Doubleday, $1.95).

A wide-ranging, informative, and generally reliable history of **Science** in America written at the layman's level is *The Story of Science in America* (Scribner, $4.95 hardcover) by L. Sprague DeCamp and Catherine C. DeCamp, while Roger Burlingame's *March of the Iron Men, A Social History of Union Through Invention* (Grosset and Dunlap, $2.65) shows the trends that shaped the United States from the invention of the printing press to 1865; the same author's *Machines That Built America* (New American Library, $.75) is also helpful. James B. Conant's *Modern Science and Modern Man* (Doubleday, $.95) is a serious discussion designed to foster understanding of the cultural significance of the new social forces at work in science.

For **Sociology**, Robin H. Williams' *American Society*, 3rd edition (Knopf, $9.95 hardcover) effectively compares American with other societies, and the present society of the United States with that of earlier periods in its history; the same author's *Strangers Next Door: Ethnic Relations in American Communities* (Prentice-Hall, $10.95 hardcover) is a well documented treatment of the subject. Two classic studies of a small, mid-Western American city are *Middletown: A Study in Contemporary American Culture* (Harcourt, Brace, & Jovanovich, $3.85) and *Middletown in Transition: A Study in Cultural Conflicts* (Harcourt, Brace, & Jovanovich, $3.95) by Robert S. and Helen M. Lynd. A well documented study reflecting the growing awareness of poverty in America from the 1840s to the present is Robert H. Bremner's *From the Depths: The Discovery of Poverty in the United States* (New York University Press, $2.95), while Michael Harrington's *The Other America: Poverty in the United States* (Penguin, $.95) is a contemporary account of the vast dimensions of want and desperation rife in this country despite its great resources; it holds that only the federal government can successfully tackle the problem. William H. Whyte's *The Organization Man* (Doubleday, $1.75) examines the rapidly growing number of men in American society who, as employees, pledge allegiance to the complex organization, be it in business, education, the church, medicine, or any other part of the modern social structure, while C. Wright Mills' *The Power Elite* (Oxford, $2.25) is a critical and provocative analysis of American society and its myths, the very rich, the warlords, and the political directorate being among the topics treated. *Class, Status, and Power*, revised (Free Press, $11.50 hardcover), edited by Reinhard Bendix and Seymour Lipset, presents a reliable group of studies in social stratification in the United States and in certain other nations.

Studies sociological, historical, or anthropological of large American racial minorities are Margaret J. Butcher's *The Negro in American Culture* (Knopf, $6.95 hardcover), a critical analysis of the contribution of Negroes to the content and characteristics of American culture, Gunnar Myrdal's *An American Dilemma* (Harper-Row, 2 vols., $3.95 each), this being a new edition of a work first published in 1944 in which the famous Swedish sociologist presents a penetrating analysis of a problem that has perplexed America for many generations; *The Negro in Twentieth-Century America* (Random, $2.95), edited by John Hope Franklin and Isidore Starr, a fine selection of essays and articles, John Collier's *The Indians of the Americas* (New American Library, $.95), the story of the Indians of the Western hemisphere from prehistoric times to the present; William T. Hagan's *American Indians* (Univerisity of Chicago Press, $1.95), which affords historical perspective on the failure of the white man-Indian relationship; and Ruth Murray Underhill's *Red Man's America: A History of Indians in the United States* (University of Chicago Press, $7.50 hardcover), an easily read account of the history and culture of the American Indian from prehistoric times to the present, grounded on recent anthropological research and having a useful bibliography.

The American Family in the Twentieth Century (Harvard University Press, $7.00 hardcover) by John Sirjamaki is a clear, concise essay that shows the American family of the present to be small, isolated from its larger kin group, and lasting only through the adult years of its spouses, if that long.

Two witty and highly readable volumes by Dixon Wecter are *The Saga of American Society: A Record of Social Aspiration, 1607-1937* (Scribner, $12.50 hardcover), a history, amply illustrated, of the leaders and activities of America's higher social circles beginning with the Virginia planters and the New England Puritans; and *The Hero in America, a Chronicle of Hero-Worship* (University of Michigan Press, $2.95) in which the aim is "to look at a few of those great personalities in public life—Washington, Franklin, Jefferson, Jackson, Lincoln, Lee, Theodore Roosevelt—from whom we have hewn out symbols of government, our ideas of what is most prizeworthy as 'American'."

Locating Major Resource Collections for Research in American Civilization

by John C. Broderick

One of the best research collections for the study of the westward movement in the United States is on the eastern seaboard, within five miles of Long Island Sound. The voluminous papers of California novelist-reformer Upton Sinclair, on the other hand, repose in the Midwest, despite Sinclair's intention to place them in Southern California. And one of the greatest collections of American literary manuscripts is in a research library noted for its medieval holdings and exquisite illuminated manuscripts.

That collection of Western Americana, of course, is at Yale University, an institution which has built impressively to the strength of its William Robertson Coe Collection. Coe's collection, in turn, derived from an interest in things Western markedly intensified by his purchase in 1910 of the Wyoming ranch of Col. William F. "Buffalo Bill" Cody. The Upton Sinclair story illustrates the effects of long political memories. About 1950, when officials of the Henry E. Huntington Library were negotiating with Sinclair for the acquisition of his library and personal papers, a prominent member of the Huntington's Board of Trustees was former President Herbert Hoover. It was Hoover's adamancy which thwarted completion of the negotiations with Sinclair and resulted in eventual location of the Sinclair archive at Indiana University's Lilly Library. The impressive American literary manuscripts at the Pierpont Morgan Library in New York City came largely through the purchase of the collection of Stephen Wakeman. And Morgan bought the collection only after long delays and considerable misgivings. According to George Hellman, who arranged the purchase, these misgivings were almost miraculously allayed when Hellman showed Morgan one of the manuscripts, Longfellow's "The Children's Hour," and remarked that the scene reminded him of Mr. Morgan and his grandchildren. Morgan read over the poem in manuscript, hit the table with his fist, and said, "I'll take the collection!"

Such vagaries as these remind us that proper things, although certainly in "proper places," to judge from the examples above, are not always in the *expected* places. American scholars gradually get used to the necessity of a careful canvass of the location and availability of research materials before committing themselves to a particular undertaking. But foreign scholars, and especially those from countries where there is centralization in a national library and state archives of most basic research materials, are frequently surprised at the extent of these materials' dispersal in the United States, a dispersal furthered by a barely concealed competitive spirit in acquisitions by university and other research libraries.

Locating for the Capstone Visit

The interest of foreign scholars in American civilization shows no signs of diminishing. For such scholars, as for Americans interested in European, Asian, or African civilization, the research visit abroad is often a capstone of one phase of study and the beginning of another, in which familiarity with the intangibles of a civilization reinforces analytical understanding. The research visit abroad therefore is always two-sided, combining unequal parts of tourism and research. While the one implies mobility and frequent changes of scene, the other requires the fixed location and the drudgery of day-by-day investigations.

In an era of limited funding, the fixed location must be properly chosen to insure the best use of available time and money. Sometimes it is specified under terms of the grant—a visiting lectureship, for example. At other times the choice

AS: AIN

Mr. Broderick is Chief of the Manuscript Division, Library of Congress, Washington, D.C. Until 1965 he was Professor of English at Wake Forest University, specializing in American cultural history; he had taught previously at the Universities of North Carolina, Texas, and Virginia. He has served as Adjunct Professor of English and bibliographic consultant at The George Washington University. Mr. Broderick is author of Whitman the Poet *and he has contributed scholarly articles to* American Literature, New England Quarterly, American Quarterly, *and* Studies in Philology. *He is a member of the Advisory Board for* Resources for American Literary Study. *For the new edition of Henry David Thoreau's writings, sponsored by the Center for Editions of American Authors, Mr. Broderick is General Editor of Thoreau's Journals. He regularly authors the lead essay on "Emerson, Thoreau, and Transcendentalism" for Duke University's annual* American Literary Scholarship.

will be made on the basis of professional considerations—to associate with leading specialists in a particular field. There will be times, however, when the scholar is free to locate himself wherever he chooses to do so. My comments are on some of the typical possibilities and the advantages a foreign scholar might find in particular locations. With a few exceptions, the emphasis will fall on historical and literary materials suitable for investigations in American Studies.

The New England States

Compact New England is inviting to the foreign student of American civilization for many reasons, not least being an informal but effective cooperative regional approach to the accumulation of source material. Thus, for example, the great John Carter Brown Library in Providence eschews the acquisition of literary and historical manuscripts in favor of books, maps, broadsides, and other such sources documenting ramifications of the macroscopic subject which its founder pursued—the European discovery, exploration, and settlement of the Western hemisphere. The library relinquishes historical manuscripts for early Rhode Island and New England history to the Rhode Island Historical Society or the Massachusetts Historical Society. Similarly, the Houghton Library at Harvard University is avowedly, though not exclusively, literary in its interests, secure in the awareness that the collections of the Massachusetts Historical Society in Boston and those of the American Antiquarian Society in Worcester, to say nothing of other special collections within the Harvard library system, amply support historical investigations.

The scholar who settles in eastern Massachusetts and its environs will find incomparable original material for "the Colonial scene" in the institutions already mentioned and in such others as the Harvard University archives or the Boston Public Library. For the Revolutionary and early National periods, the Adams family papers and the Coolidge collection of Thomas Jefferson papers at the Massachusetts Historical Society are central. The literature of nineteenth-century New England is a staple of Harvard's Houghton Library, with major collections for Emerson, Dickinson, and Longfellow, among many others. Its resources for American literary study extend far beyond New England, of course, with the James family papers and those of Thomas Wolfe, along with its voluminous theater materials, typifying resources for nineteenth- and twentieth-century investigations. For the student of more recent American political history, Houghton's Charles Sumner papers, those of Henry Cabot Lodge at the Massachusetts Historical Society, and the Supreme Court papers of Felix Frankfurter at Harvard Law School are foundation collections around which related groups cluster.

Comparisons are odious, to be sure. Nevertheless, one can hardly fail to single out the John Carter Brown Library and the American Antiquarian Society for special mention in connection with American Studies. For one thing, they are both "American" in scope, though the term means different things at the two institutions. Their comprehensiveness within chosen limits allows cultural analysis in its broadest terms of "the Early History of the Americas" (at Brown) and the civilization of the United States to the mid-nineteenth-century (at AAS). Even their apparent deficiencies—the scarcity of literary and historical manuscripts—hardly affect their standing for cultural analysis. As Robert E. Spiller pointed out at the John Carter Brown Library Conference in 1960, "Multiple playbills, newspapers, magazines, but most of all books, that share in their particular relationship to a people, a time, and a place become far more useful than the private papers of even a Shakespeare, a Locke, or a Napoleon." Concern with popular culture in its historical aspect can be implemented in an unparalleled way at the Antiquarian Society, where its collections of cookbooks, almanacs, schoolbooks, and circusiana hold a place virtually equal to that of the newspapers, fiction, and first editions.

Yale University in New Haven does not have as many supporting research centers in its vicinity, but it is within easy reach of both eastern New England and New York City. The major research strengths at Yale for American Studies are, as noted above, Western Americana—viz., the Coe and Beinecke collections, for both of which exemplary catalogs have been prepared; American literature— the special collection formed by Owen F. Aldis, supplemented by the papers of Edith Wharton, Gertrude Stein, Eugene O'Neill, Ezra Pound, and others, plus the James Weldon Johnson collection of American Negro literature; American history, both early and recent—the Benjamin Franklin, Henry L. Stimson, Edward House, Chester Bowles, and Walter Lippmann papers. As yet undeveloped, the Yale Collection of the American Musical Theater nevertheless boasts the papers and the library of Cole Porter, a promising start.

Limitations of space necessitate a more summary treatment of other localities and more frequent citation of guides and catalogs.

New York City

The voluminous resources of New York City have been summarized in two volumes: *Guide to Sources for Early American History in New York City, 1600-1800*, edited by Evarts B. Greene and Richard B. Morris (New York: Columbia University Press, 1929), and *A Guide to the Principal Sources for American Civilization, 1800-1900, in the City of New York: Manuscripts*, edited by Harry J. Carman and Arthur W. Thompson (New York: Columbia Univ. Press, 1960). Though invaluable up to a point, these volumes must be supplemented by other guides. Within the past decade reprint publishing companies have made available a number of multi-volume catalogs of special research materials, consisting of facsimile publication of catalog cards maintained by the local repository. The New York Public Library has received considerable attention in this way, with guides to the holdings of its Berg Collection (five volumes), including much American literature; its Manuscript Division (two volumes) rich in material associated with New York; and its Rare Book Division, among others. Similar catalogs exist for the American Antiquarian Society, the Boston Public Library, and the Massachusetts Historical Society, among New England repositories. The theater and dance collections of the New York Public Library and the Arthur Schomburg collection of Negro history and literature are specialized collections able to sustain numerous investigations into American civilization from different points of view. The oral history collection at Columbia University is a special resource for recent political and cultural history, and the holdings of the New York Historical Society are indispensable for the early history of New York City, with much of national history as well.

Philadelphia

There is considerable variety also in the Philadelphia area, here construed to extend to Princeton and Wilmington. The American Philosophical Society Library, one of the first in the United States to concentrate on research materials, has considerably narrowed its focus insofar as American Studies is concerned. Originally comprehensive in its acquisitions, the Society how limits its scope to the history of science, American Indian linguistics, and special areas of strength which cannot be well neglected—Benjamin Franklin, and the Society itself. Important guides have been issued to its American Indian manuscripts (Philadelphia, 1966), compiled by John F. Freeman; its archives and manuscripts (Philadelphia, 1966), edited by Whitfield J. Bell, Jr., and Murphy D. Smith; and its early pamphlets in science and medicine (Philadelphia, 1968), compiled by Simeon J. Crowther and Marion Fawcett. Photographic reprint catalogs were also issued, in 1970, of books (twenty-eight volumes) and manuscripts (ten volumes) in the Society Library. When these guides are coupled with descriptive articles in the Society's *Proceedings, Memoirs*, and other publications, the Society Library is probably the most adequately described special collection of research material in the United States. No one need arrive in Philadelphia in a state of uncertainty about resources of the American Philosophical Society Library.

Elsewhere in Philadelphia the visiting scholar will wish to acquaint himself with the resources of the Library Company of Philadelphia, the Historical Society of Pennsylvania, the Academy of Natural Sciences, and the University of Pennsylvania, which form a diversified regional resource comparable to that in Boston or New York. Collections in twentieth-century literature—F. Scott Fitzgerald, Booth Tarkington—and public affairs—John Foster Dulles, Bernard Baruch, Adlai Stevenson—may draw the foreign visitor to Princeton, whereas an interest in economic and business history, especially of the Middle Atlantic region, will draw him toward the Eleutherian Mills Historical Library in Wilmington.

The Nation's Capital

Washington, D. C., is in many respects unsurpassed and probably unsurpassable as a center for American Studies. The Library of Congress is a virtual laboratory for American Studies, its mutually supporting special and general collections the most comprehensive in the nation. "Area studies" of almost any aspect of American life can be begun and carried to virtual completion within the Library; its manuscript, music, motion picture, map, print, and other special collections are, individually, the largest in the United States. Copyright deposit requirements insure continued augmentation of its general and some special collections. For the study of popular culture its Archive of Folk Song, its graphic Americana, and its general collections are indispensable. It also has the largest collection of original material for the study of American Negro life and culture. Imaginative scholarly use of seemingly routine resources of the Library of Congress is illustrated in G. Thomas Tanselle, "Copyright Records and the Bibliographer," *Studies in Bibliography* 22 (1969), pp. 77-124. In Washington also are the vast holdings of the National Archives, official records of the Government, and the "manufacts" (as opposed to manuscripts) documenting the material culture of American life, in the custody of the Smithsonian Institution. The National

Library of Medicine and the National Agricultural Library are comprehensive specialized libraries, covering fields beyond the scope of the Library of Congress. As Dryden said of Chaucer's poetry, "Here is God's plenty." Like Dryden, this article must merely stand aside and point in wonder and admiration.

The South and Southwest

The study of the civilization of the South may best be carried on in several locations in Virginia and the Carolinas. Williamsburg, like the Winterthur Museum or the Smithsonian Institution, provides a visible model of the past to supplement more traditional research materials. For such traditional materials for early American culture the collections of Colonial Williamsburg and the College of William and Mary compete with those in Richmond—the Virginia Historical Society—and Charlottesville—especially the Tracy W. McGregor collection at the University of Virginia. The latter institution is also exceptionally strong in American literary materials through its C. Waller Barrett collection. For nineteenth-century Southern life and literature one must move further south to Durham and Chapel Hill, where the George W. Flowers Collection at Duke University and the Southern Historical Collection at the University of North Carolina, both well described, are complementary sources of regional strength. The Flowers collection is more literary, whereas the Southern Historical Collection contains much that is almost sub-literate and is uniquely valuable on that account.

Another Southern location, the University of Texas at Austin, isolated by vast Texas distances, is rapidly achieving self-sufficiency as a research center. Its American strengths are in its Latin-American holdings, documenting the Spanish, Mexican, and Texas periods of the Southwest region. Texas has also collected many American authors' papers and literary works in a burst of acquisitive activity over the past fifteen years. The recent opening of the Lyndon B. Johnson Presidential Library at Austin will make mid-twentieth-century public affairs a major new source of strength. The Johnson library is already the largest of the six existing Presidential libraries and not likely soon to be surpassed. The papers of twenty-three Presidents prior to Herbert Hoover are in the Library of Congress.

The Prairie States

In the Midwest, four research centers are outstanding for various phases of American Studies. The William L. Clements Library at Ann Arbor is, in the words of its director, a "treasure-house library" comparable to the John Carter Brown Library or the Huntington Library in California. Like others in its class, the Clements Library is comprehensive within its appointed limits, generally speaking Americana before 1860, with special strength in the period of the Revolutionary War. Its card catalog has recently been photographically reprinted in seven volumes. There are also excellent guides to some of its separate collections. In Madison, the State Historical Society of Wisconsin is an institution with a noble history, associated in large part with its founder, the legendary Lyman C. Draper, and his successor, Reuben G. Thwaites. Largely through Draper's efforts, the State Historical Society has extensive holdings on the Midwestern region, gathered in the mid-nineteenth century. For the twentieth century, the American holdings of note are in the fields of labor and social progress and in the theater and mass communications. The Society is actively collecting materials in these fields. Mass Communications includes collections on radio, television, and motion pictures, both technical and intellectual. The Newberry Library in Chicago is a general reference and research library, with some notable American strengths, chiefly Western Americana, the American Indian, and Midwestern literature. The Edward Ayer and Edward Graff collections are especially well described. Indiana University's Lilly Library is a bookman's library, with great strength in American literature and in Hispanic-American materials. Its most useful descriptive aids are a series of elaborate exhibit catalogs.

California

The foreign visitor fortunate enough to settle in California will gravitate to the San Francisco area to take advantage of the holdings of the Bancroft Library in Berkeley, the premier collection for Western history, assembled by Hubert H. Bancroft over a period of nearly forty years in the late-nineteenth century and supplemented in the twentieth. The voluminous papers of Samuel L. Clemens are also housed here. One of three projected volumes describing the Bancroft holdings appeared in the 1960s. At nearby Stanford, the Hoover Institution for War, Revolution, and Peace will occupy the student of twentieth-century international movements in the United States. In Southern California, the Henry E. Huntington Library and Art Gallery at San Marino, though better known for its holdings in English history and literature, has impressive American collections, with emphasis on California writers and California history, the Civil War, and American literary manuscripts. Much material on the American motion picture industry can be found in the Special Collections of the Library of the University of California at Los Angeles, which also holds the considerable Henry Miller papers.

Five That Are Less Conspicuous

The research centers mentioned thus far are obvious enough though the precise nature of their resources is not always well known. Five less obvious institutions actively collecting materials in American civilization are Boston University, specializing in twentiety-century Americana; Syracuse University, which is collecting widely, and particularly in archival records for economic history; Wayne State University in Detroit, which has established a labor history archives; Washington University in St. Louis, which has assembled an enviable group of American literary materials, chiefly twentieth-century; and the University of Wyoming, which has cast a wide net and caught much for the history of the West.

It is impossible in brief compass to avoid the invidious practice of naming some institutions and omitting others equally worthy of notice. Emphasis here is placed on special collections, not the multi-purpose general collections available in large university libraries. Even some special collections of note, such as Cornell's Regional History Collection, have been crowded out.

In addition to original books, manuscripts, pictorial materials, maps, and so forth, the foreign scholar should be aware of the possibilities of photoreproduction as an adjunct to research in the United States. Richard W. Hale, Jr.'s *Guide to Photocopied Historical Materials* (Ithaca, 1961) is a useful listing, though now outdated by greatly enlarged filming programs in the past decade. Early state records and early newspapers are being systematically preserved on film. Several series reproducing printed materials have been commercially issued by University Microfilms (early American books, eighteenth- and nineteenth-century American periodicals, and so forth) and the Readex Corp. (American imprints through 1880), among others. For the last-named series, a two-volume checklist prepared by Clifford K. Shipton and James E. Mooney (1970) constitutes, as its subtitle claims, "the short-title Evans."

Guides and Guidelines

Three recent or current comprehensive guides to unique material are indispensable preparations for research in American civilization. Philip M. Hamer, *Guide to Archives and Manuscripts in the United States* (New Haven, 1961), is valuable in its own right and especially valuable for its bibliographical listings. The *National Union Catalog of Manuscript Collections*, nine volumes published to date, includes reports of many collections not represented in Hamer. For literary materials, *American Literary Manuscripts*, edited by Joseph Jones (Austin, 1960), is useful and is now being revised. Guides to individual library holdings vary widely, from the bibliographically exact though incomplete *Bibliotheca Americana* describing the John Carter Brown Library collection to a pamphlet designed to accompany a microfilm edition of personal papers. The scholar might survey annual reports, guides and finding-aids issued by research libraries which he plans to visit. Unfortunately, these are likely to be fugitive items in foreign countries. A survey is best accomplished by consulting appropriate volumes of the *National Union Catalog*, where such publications will be entered under the name of the library itself. Most research libraries issue a newsletter, bulletin, or quarterly, in which descriptive articles on special collections are usually a staple. *Yale University Library Gazette, Princeton University Library Chronicle*, the *Library Chronicle* of the University of Texas are a few examples. Finally, the foreign scholar planning a visit to a research center in the United States should not hesitate to write ahead. Despite the abundance of descriptive guides, catalogs, and bibliographies, a great deal of information about special research materials exists essentially in unpublished form or quite likely in the collective memories of curators, rare book librarians, and bibliographers. The latter are, by and large, cooperative and willing to help the visiting foreign scholar to the utmost.

After all, they hope to get abroad next summer themselves.

Of the various publications issued in the past four years, the most important for locating research materials in American studies is the *Guide to the National Archives of the United States* (Washington, 1974). It supersedes the 1948 *Guide* and includes all Government records accessioned through mid-1970 (about one million cubic feet) and some gift collections, though not the material located in six Presidential libraries administered by the National Archives and Records Service. In addition to records and manuscripts, sound recordings, motion pictures, pictorial and cartographic materials form part of the holdings of the National Archives described in the 1974 *Guide.*

Additional bibliographical aid on unpublished sources can be found, especially in chapter 6, in the revised *Harvard Guide to American History,* ed. Frank Freidel (Cambridge, 1974).

There have been some significant recent additions to major resource collections, but no great change in the nature and scope of their holdings. In other words, despite occasional inflation and recession, the rich centers for research retain their centrality and continue to get richer, though at a pace sufficiently irregular to maintain a competitive market.

Surveying Journals of American Studies: A Guide for Students and Teachers

by Bernard Mergen

Scholarly journals seem to be regarded as proverbial maiden aunts. Acknowledged to be full of wisdom, they are taken for granted and generally ignored in preference to their well bound cousins in flashy jackets. The purpose of this essay is to make up for that long neglect and to list and review briefly about a hundred serial publications which I think are useful to scholars in American Studies.

Because American Studies is usually defined quite broadly, there is a real problem of selection and organization of titles. The arrangement here follows the usual distinctions between traditional disciplines. The questions I asked as I surveyed the current periodical scene were: How does this publication contribute to an understanding of American life? Do the editors and authors show an interest in the relationships among literature, the arts, and the social sciences? Does the journal attempt to provide special features such as bibliographies, illustrations, and special editions to meet the interests of a wide variety of readers?

I hope this compilation will be helpful to institutions planning new programs in American Studies and to teachers initiating their students in a variety of academic professions. For this reason, I have given the business address rather than the editorial address (when they are different) of the journals listed.

American Studies As a Discipline

One of the functions of a scholarly journal is to provide a forum for the discussion of the areas of research which its contributors claim as their own. The contributors and the editors define their interests and professional identity through the pages of the journal. *The American Quarterly* (5 issues yearly, $15.00 for membership in the American Studies Association, $10.00 for libraries, $7.50 for students, plus $2.00 for subscriptions outside the United States: Box 1, Logan Hall, University of Pennsylvania, Philadelphia, PA 19174)* has, in its own words, aided "in giving a sense of direction to studies in the culture of the United States, past and present," since 1949. Each issue has about six articles and a calendar of American Studies Association news and events in its 160 pages. Recently the editors have become much more self-conscious about theory and method in American Studies and the articles emphasize the social sciences. It remains to be seen if this attempt to define the subject of American Studies will be successful, but it is important and worthwhile. Another recent innovation is the inclusion of more photographs. There is an annual book review and bibliography issue.

American Studies (semi-annual, $2.50, student; $4.00, regular; $6.00, institutional: American Studies Department, U Kansas, Lawrence, KA 66044) first appeared in 1959 as the *Midcontinent American Studies Journal* and still serves the Midcontinent American Studies Association as a newsletter. Recently, however, it has expanded its scope and promises to be a vehicle for scholars working in areas such as urban studies and black studies. Guest editors put out the special issues. This approach helps to keep the journal responsive to changes in academic interests and opinions.

Two new periodicals with specific American Studies interests are the *Journal of American Studies* (3 yearly, $15.50 or £6.00: Cambridge University Press, 32 E. 57th Street, New York, NY 10022; or Bentley House, 2000 Euston Road, London NW1 2DB, England) and the *Canadian Review of American Studies* (2 yearly, $8.00: Canadian Association for American Studies, Strong College, Room 330, York University, Downsview, Ontario). Both carry scholarly articles and book reviews with some emphasis on Anglo-American and Canadian-American cultural relations.

Concern for the teaching of American Studies as distinct from research and for subjects neglected by traditional journals has led to the founding of three new publications. The *Red Buffalo* (quarterly; $4.00; 124 Winspear Ave., State University of New York at Buffalo, Buffalo, NY 14214) published two useful issues on the American Indian and on oral history but has now apparently ceased publication. The first issue of *Connections II* ($3.00: Lee Schiller, 406 N. State

* Prices quoted throughout are based on data available as of spring, 1974-Ed.

Mr. Mergen is Associate Professor of American Civilization at George Washington University, Washington, D.C. In 1974-75 he was a Postdoctoral Fellow at the Smithsonian Institution writing a history of shipbuilding from 1917 to 1951. He has published articles in Industrial and Labor Relations Review, South Atlantic Quarterly, *and the* Journal of Popular Culture. *Mr. Mergen previously taught at Grinnell College and was a Fulbright lecturer at the University of Göteborg in Sweden.*

Street, Ann Arbor, MI 48104) is about to appear on the subject of the "classroom." The *Connections II* group represents teachers and students who feel that traditional academic approaches to education are inadequate. *New America: A Review* (American Studies Program, University of New Mexico, Albuquerque, NM 87131) is scheduled to appear this spring. The appearance of new journals representing new regions and interest groups in American Studies can only be taken as evidence of the success of the field in the past few years.

Theory And Method In Interdisciplinary Studies

Closely related to the American Studies journals in their interest in new approaches and neglected subjects are those which focus on interdisciplinary theories and methods. *Clio: An Interdisciplinary Journal of Literature, History, and the Philosophy of History* (3 yearly; $4.50 individuals; $12.00 institutions: Greenquist Hall, University of Wisconsin-Parkside, Kenosha, WI 53140) made its appearance in 1971 to publish "critiques of literature wherein history or philosophy of history is shown operational as an ordering means, literary analysis of historical writing, and historiography that deals with the nature of historical and thus literary knowledge and narrative." Each issue has articles, reviews, and a lively editorial section. The *Journal of Interdisciplinary History* (quarterly; $12.00, individual; $16.50, institutions, plus $1.00 for foreign: The M.I.T. Press, 28 Carleton Street, Cambridge MA 02142) has, in four years, established itself as one of the foremost scholarly journals in the country. Through articles, research notes, and review articles, the editors have helped to develop several areas of research such as family history, the visual arts, and psychohistory.

History and Theory (quarterly; $8.00, individuals; $11.00, institutions: Wesleyan University, Middletown, CT 06457) contains excellent articles and review essays on the philosophy of history. *Comparative Studies in Society and History* (quarterly; $14.00 or £5.00: Cambridge University Press, 32 East 57th Street, New York, NY 10022, or Bentley House, 200 Euston Road, London NW1 2DB) is the most distinguished of the interdisciplinary journals. An international editorial board representing economic history, anthropology, sociology, history, government, and art selects articles which focus on method. There is usually one article using American data each issue. *Historical Methods Newsletter* (quarterly; $3.50, students; $5.00, individuals; $9.00, institutions: University Center for International Studies and the Department of History, University of Pittsburgh, Pittsburgh, PA 15213) has expanded rapidly in seven years and now carries several articles on quantitative methods as well as review essays, news and announcements, and descriptions of research in progress. *Computers and the Humanities* (5 issues yearly; $9.50, individuals; $20.00, institutions: Queens College Press, Flushing, NY 11367) is also concerned with quantitative methods, but in their applications to art and literature as well as history.

Literature

Among the journals focusing primarily on literature, *American Literature* (quarterly; $3.50, students; $7.00, regular; plus .40 for Canada and Pan America and .75 for other foreign: Duke University Press, P.O. Box 5597, College Station, Durham, NC 27708) is probably the most useful. Sponsored by the American

Literature Section of the Modern Language Association it contains reports of research in progress and extensive bibliographies as well as scholarly essays. Another MLA sponsored journal, *Early American Literature* (3 yearly; $5.00: Bartlett Hall, University of Massachusetts, Amherst, MA 01002) has joined the *New England Quarterly* ($8.00: Hubbard Hall, Brunswick, ME 04011) as an outlet for research on the colonial period. The latter journal, whose editorial board overlaps somewhat with both the *American Historical Review* and the *Journal of Interdisciplinary History,* is concerned with the impact of New England on the rest of the country and its articles are therefore of more than regional interest.

American Literary Realism 1870–1910 (quarterly; $3.00, U.S.; $3.50, elsewhere: Department of English, University of Texas/Arlington, Arlington, TX 76010) is one of the few journals explicitly interested in the sociology of literature. For example, Gordon Kelly's "American Children's Literature: An Historiographical Review" challenges scholars to study literature as part of the socialization process. *Genre* (quarterly; $5.00, individuals; $6.00, institutions; $7.00, foreign: Department of English, State University College, Plattsburgh, NY 12901) pursues the problem of the relation of literature to society from another direction by encouraging historical studies of particular genres and theoretical discussions of the genre concept. *Resources for American Literary Study* (2 yearly; $8.00: Department of English. University of Maryland, College Park, MD 20742) is an excellent compilation of bibliographical essays, manuscript sources, and reviews. *Eighteenth Century Studies: An Interdisciplinary Journal* (quarterly; $9.00, U.S., Canada, Pan America; $12.00 institution, plus $1.00 foreign; University of California Press, Periodicals Department, Berkeley, CA 94720) is published by the English Department of the University of California at Davis. It shows what can be done to put American Studies into a European context on a century by century basis. Finally, *Theater Survey: The American Journal of Theater History* (2 yearly; $5.00, U.S., plus .50, foreign: Department of English, Queens College, Flushing, NY 11367) usually has one article in its 120 pages on an American subject. *New Literary History* (3 yearly, $8.00, plus $.65 outside U.S.: Wilson Hall, University of Virginia, Charlottesville, VA 22903) is an interdisciplinary journal dealing with such subjects as the reasons for literary change, the definitions of periods and their uses in interpretation, and the evolution of styles, conventions, and genres.

History: Old Standards

This group of journals in history are those which have been published for more than ten years. The section following will describe some which have appeared during the past decade. *American Historical Review* (quarterly; $20.00, individual; $10.00, students; $25.00, institutions in U.S., Canada, and Mexico; $27.00, other foreign: 400 A Street, S.E., Washington, DC 20003) is, of course, the premier journal in its field. After seventy-five years in its familiar blue cocoon, it emerged in 1971 in a new format, an impressive 300 page butterfly. The transformation was due to a new press which permits the publication of illustrations. The editors have made good use of this innovation. *The Journal of American History* (quarterly; $12.00, individual; $15.00, institutional; $6.00, student: Organization of American Historians, 112 N. Bryan Street, Bloomington, IN 47401) contains exclusively American material including an excellent news and comments section which lists recent archival acquisitions.

The *William and Mary Quarterly* ($5.00, student; $8.00, regular: Institute of Early American History and Culture, Box 220, Williamsburg, VA 23185) specializes in colonial history, which is currently one of the most active fields of research in American history. Neither the *Pacific Historical Review* (quarterly; $8.00, regular; $4.00, student; $12.00, institutional, plus $1.00, foreign postage: University of California Press, Berkeley, CA 94720), nor *The South Atlantic Quarterly* ($7.00: Duke University Press, Box 6697, College Station, Durham, NC 27708) is as regional as its name suggests. Similarly, *Agricultural History* (quarterly; $5.00, student, $8.00, regular; $10.00, institutional, plus $1.00, foreign postage: University of California Press, Berkeley, CA 94720) is not as topical as its title. James Shideler's "Flappers and Philosophers and Farmers: Rural-Urban Tensions of the Twenties," for example, goes well beyond what is normally thought of as agricultural history.

The *Journal of Economic History* (quarterly; $3.00, student; $10.00, individual, U.S.; $10.50, foreign; $15.00, institutions: Graduate School of Business Administration, New York University, 100 Trinity place, New York, NY 10006) is the largest and most important publication in its field. *Business History Review* (quarterly; $8.00, teachers and students; $15.00, institutions: 214–216 Baker Library, Harvard University, Boston, MA. 02163) is less quantitative than *Explorations in Economic History* (quarterly; $10.00; address: The Kent State University Press, Kent, OH 44242) although both are interested in the social impact of business. The latter journal was formerly called *Explorations in Entrepreneurial History* and shares several members of its editorial board with *Agricultural History*. *Labor History* (quarterly; $7.00, students; $8.50, regular, plus .50 foreign postage: Bobst Library, New York University, 70 Washington Square South, New York, NY 10012) views American economic history from another perspective.

The history of science and technology is well covered by *Isis* (5 yearly; $7.50, students; $15.00, regular; $18.00, institutions, plus .50 for foreign subscriptions: Museum of History and Technology, Smithsonian Institution, Washington, DC 20560) and *Technology and Culture* (quarterly; $6.00, student; $15.00, regular, plus $1.00 foreign: University of Chicago Press, 5801 Ellis Ave., Chicago, IL 60637). The *Journal of the History of Ideas* (quarterly; $7.50, regular; $10.00, institutions, plus .50 foreign: City University of New York, Graduate Center, 33 West 42nd Street, New York, NY 10036) usually has at least one article relating to American history each issue, as does *Church History* (quarterly; $6.00, student; $10.00, regular, plus .25 foreign: American Society of Church History, 305 East Country Club Lane, Wallingford, PA 19086). *History of Education Quarterly* ($10.00, student; $12.00, individual; $15.00, institutions: School of Education, New York University, 737 East Building, Washington Square, New York, NY 10003) is a relatively new publication which has had special issues on "reform of the urban school," "the history of childhood," and "education and social change in English-speaking Canada."

Although a *Journal of Ethnic Studies* (Western Washington State College, Bellingham, WA 98225) is scheduled to appear, the three best journals on racial and ethnic minorities are: *Journal of Negro History* (quarterly; $10.00, plus .50, foreign postage: Association for the Study of Negro Life and History, 1407 Fourteenth Street, N.W., Washington, DC 20005), *The Indian Historian* (quarterly; $6.00, plus $1.00, foreign postage; The Indian Historian Press, 1451 Masonic Ave., San Francisco, CA 94117), and *Ethnohistory* (quarterly; $6.50, individual; $8.00, institutions: American Society for Ethnohistory, Arizona State Museum, The University of Arizona, Tucson, AZ 85721). *Ethnohistory* is edited by anthropologists who are interested in the problems of culture change in complex societies; one recent issue was devoted to Kentucky.

Finally, three useful journals covering special areas of history and research are: *American Archivist* (quarterly; $15.00: Society of American Archivists, Bentley Historical Library, University of Michigan, Ann Arbor, MI 48105) which contains review articles and news notes on the location of archival material; the *Quarterly Journal of the Library of Congress* ($4.50: Superintendent of Documents, U.S. Government Printing Office, Washington, DC 20402), a beautifully illustrated journal with articles on the collections of the Library and descriptions of recent acquisitions of the manuscript division; and the *Huntington Library Quarterly* ($7.50: Henry E. Huntington Library and Art Gallery, 1151 Oxford Road, San Marino, CA 91108), subtitled a "Journal for the Interpretation of English and American Civilization," which publishes research which goes well beyond its own important holdings of incunabula, American history and literature, and western history.

History: New Faces

There are almost a dozen new historical journals of note. *Perspectives in American History* (annual: $6.50: Charles Warren Center for Studies in American History, Robinson Hall, Cambridge, MA 02138) is now eight years old. It devotes each volume to one topic such as "Dislocation and Emigration." The *Journal of Social History* (quarterly; $10.00, students; $15.00, regular; $16.00 foreign: Transaction Periodicals Consortium, Rutgers University, New Brunswick, NJ 08903) is a lively journal with two or three American articles each issue. *The Family in Historical Perspective: An International Newsletter* (quarterly; $2.00: Newberry Library, Chicago, IL 60610) has published only five issues but shows promise of becoming an important publication. It contains news and research notes, course syllabi, and reviews. A much more ambitious effort, the *History of Childhood Quarterly: The Journal of Psychohistory* ($12.00, individuals; $18.00, institutions: 2315 Broadway, New York NY 10024), appeared in the summer of 1973 heralded by widespread advertising. The contributors attempt to apply psychoanalysis to both historical individuals and historical movements.

Curiously, there is still no journal of immigration history, but there is *The Immigration History Newsletter* ($3.00: Minnesota Historical Society, 690 Cedar Street, St. Paul, MN 55101) which has good reviews of meetings and recent publications. Two other specialized but valuable periodicals are: the *Journal of the History of Biology* (semiannually: $7.50, plus $1.00 outside the U.S.: Belknap Press of Harvard University, 79 Garden Street, Cambridge, MA 02138) and the *Journal of Library History, Philosophy, and Comparative Librarianship* ($12.50: School of Library Science, Florida State University, Tallahassee, FL 32306). Another regional journal which publishes articles of more than local interest is *The Western Historical Quarterly* ($7.00: Western History Association, Utah State University, Logan, UT 84322). Its bibliography of recent articles is arranged by categories such as "environment," "ethnic history," "frontier arts and crafts," and "historic preservation." The *History of Political Economy* (semiannual; $8.00: Duke University Press, 6697 College Station, Durham, NC 27708) revives an old field of interest and includes two or three articles on the United States in each issue. Finally, a new government publication, *Prologue* (quarterly; $5.00: Cashier, National Archives (GSA), Washington, DC 20408), publishes articles based on records of the Federal Government, genealogy notes, announcements of accessions, openings, and declassification of government of records.

Social Sciences

For students of American civilization, especially those interested in the total society, anthropology and sociology offer the most fruitful approaches. The *American Anthropologist* (quarterly; $16.00, students; $21.00, individuals; $30.00, institutions: 1703 New Hampshire Avenue, N.W., Washington, D.C. 20009) and *Current Anthropology* (5 yearly; $21.00, U.S.; $15.00, elsewhere: The University of Chicago Press, 5801 Ellis Avenue, Chicago, IL 60637) are essential. Anthropologists are turning increasingly to the study of complex societies and their research appears in these and journals such as *Urban Anthropology* (2 yearly; $7.50, individuals; $10.00, institutions: Institute for the Study of Man, Inc., 113 Utica Street, Brockport, NY 14420) and *Urban Life and Culture* (quarterly; $9.00, students; $10.00, individuals; $18.00, institutions: Sage Publications Inc., 275 South Beverly Drive, Beverly Hills, CA 90212, or St. George's House, 44 Hatton Garden, London EC1N8ER).

The *American Journal of Sociology* (6 yearly; $6.00, students; $10.00, individuals; $15.00, institutions, plus $1.00 for foreign subscriptions: The University of Chicago Press, 5801 Ellis Avenue, Chicago, IL 60637) and *American Sociological Review* (6 yearly; $7.00, students; $15.00, individuals; $20.00, libraries: 1722 N Street, N.W. Washington, DC 20036) are the established journals. Both include historical articles from time to time. *Youth and Society* (quarterly, $8.00, student; $10.00, individual; $15.00 institution, plus $1.50 foreign) is another of the thirty new journals founded by Sage Publications Inc. It has a distinguished editorial board which includes Kenneth Keniston, Erik Erikson, Walter Laqueur, and S.N. Eisenstadt.

Of the political science journals, *Political Science Quarterly* ($9.00, student; $12.00, regular: Academy of Political Science, 2852 Broadway, New York, NY 10025) seems closest to the interests of American studies. *Geographical Review* (quarterly; $25.00, fellows; $40.00, institutions: American Geographical Society, Broadway at 156th Street, New York, NY 10032) and *Annals of the Association of American Geographers* (quarterly; $16.00, U.S. and Canada; $17.00, elsewhere: 1710 Sixteenth Street, N.W., Washington, DC 20009) contain essays in historical and cultural geography.

Three journals which are difficult to classify because they incorporate several disciplines are: *Journal of the History of the Behavioral Sciences* (quarterly; $20.00, plus $1.00 for foreign subscriptions: Clinical Psychology Publishing Co., 4 Conant Square, Brandon, VT 05733), *Journal for the Scientific Study of Religion* (quarterly; $8.00, student; $15.00, regular: Box U68A, University of Connecticut, Storrs, CT 06268), and *Journal of Leisure Research* (quarterly; $8.00, institutions; $10.00, individuals: National Recreation and Park Association, 1601

North Kent Street, Arlington, VA. 22209). The third is the most specialized, but it contains articles and bibliographies on the concepts of time and leisure throughout history.

Society (bimonthly; $9.75, U.S.; $11.25, foreign: Box A, Rutgers—The State University, New Brunswick, NJ 08903), which was called *Trans-action* when it first appeared in 1963, and *Social Policy* (bimonthly; $6.00, students; $8.00, regular: Suite 500, 184 Fifth Avenue, New York, NY 10010) are journals of opinion and research. The former is the more attractive of the two, with more photographs and unusual topics, but the latter has the film reviews of Herbert Gans.

Art, Architecture, and Material Culture

Art Journal (quarterly; $5.00: College Art Association of America, Inc., 16 E. 52nd Street, New York, NY 10022) and *Art in America* (bimonthly; $16.50, U.S.; $19.50, foreign: 150 E. 58th St., New York, NY 10022) are attractive and interesting, with a mixture of articles and reviews on historical and contemporary subjects. *Museum News* (9 yearly; American Association of Museums, 2233 Wisconsin Avenue, N.W., Washington, DC 20007) and *Curator* (quarterly, $7.50, U.S.; foreign: The American Museum of Natural History, New York, NY 10024) are valuable for their discussions of exhibits and the use of artifacts in education.

Design and Environment (quarterly; $11.00, U.S.; $14.00, foreign: 19 West 44th Street, New York, NY 10036) is an appealing magazine with photo essays on such subjects as retirement communities in Los Angeles. It helps fill the gap caused by the demise of *Landscape* in this area of American civilization. One of the most important periodicals in the field of material culture is the *Journal of the Society of Architectural Historians* (quarterly; $12.50, student; $20.00, individuals and institutions; $22.00, foreign: Room 716, 1700 Walnut Street, Philadelphia, PA 19103). Each issue has some American material and a bimonthly *Newsletter* gives excellent coverage of meetings and research projects. *Historic Preservation* (quarterly: National Trust for Historic Preservation, 740–48 Jackson Place, N.W., Washington, DC 20006) is available by membership in the National Trust or at the price of $1.00 per copy. Like the museum journals, it illustrates the range of activities in American studies outside the classroom. A new publication devoted to architecture and material artifacts is *Pioneer America* (2 yearly; $3.00: 626 South Washington Street, Falls Church, VA 22046). It is nicely illustrated and gives attention to vernacular and folk building as well as more complex structures. *The Society for Industrial Archeology Newsletter* is sent to members of the Society ($10.00 per year: Treasurer SIA, William Penn Memorial Museum, Box 1026, Harrisburg, PA 17108) and contains information on sites and structures, museums, and recent publications.

Folklore And Popular Culture

The Journal of American Folklore (quarterly; $5.00, students; $10.00, individuals; $12.00, institutions: American Folklore Society, University of Texas Press, Austin, TX 78712) is the oldest and most generally useful publication in the field of folklore, but *Western Folklore* (quarterly: $3.00, student; $8.00, individuals; $12.00 institutions, plus $1.00 for postage outside the western hemisphere: California Folklore Society, University of California Press, Berkeley, CA 94720) and the *Journal of the Folklore Institute* (3 yearly; Dglds 27,–: Co-Libri, P.O. Box 482, The Hague 2976, The Netherlands) are both interesting. The *Journal of the Folklore Institute* is edited by Richard Dorson of the University of Indiana and has a wide variety of articles in each issue.

Ray B. Browne's *Journal of Popular Culture* (quarterly; $7.50, students; $15.00, regular: University Hall, Bowling Green University, Bowling Green, OH 43403) continues to grow in size and quality. Its special issues on folklore, circuses, carnivals, comics, and science fiction are invaluable. Among the other new journals coming out of Bowling Green University's Popular Press, The *Journal of Popular Film* (quarterly; $3.00, students; $4.00, regular: University Hall 101, Bowling Green, OH 43403) is setting higher standards in the field of film study. Two other new publications on the use of movies in historical research are *Cinema Journal* (semiannually; $4.00: Society of Cinematologists, 217 Flint Hall, University of Kansas, Lawrence, KS 66044) and *Film and History* (quarterly; $2.00, students; $5.00, individuals; $10.00, institutions: The Historians Film Committee, c/o The History Faculty, Newark College of Engineering, Newark, NJ 07102).

Potpourri

Ethnomusicology (3 yearly; $7.50, student; $12.50, individual; $15.00, institutional: 201 South Main Street, Room 513, Ann Arbor, MI 48108) contains excellent articles, bibliographies and dicographies, book and record reviews, and some ethnographic film reviews. *American Speech* (quarterly; $6.00, U.S.; $6.30, foreign: Columbia University Press, Periodicals Department, 136 South Broadway, Irvington, NY 10533) is the traditional journal of language study, while the new sociolinguistic approach is represented by *Language and Society* (Biannual; $14.50 or £4.00; Cambridge University Press, P.O. Box 92, London NW1 2DB, or 32 East 57th Street, New York, NY 10022).

Journalism Quarterly ($5.00, students; $10.00, other: School of Journalism, University of Minnesota, Minneapolis MN 55455) is an established journal "devoted to research in journalism and mass communications." *Columbia Journalism Review* (6 yearly; $9.00, plus $2.00 for foreign subscriptions: 700 Journalism Bldg., Columbia University, New York, NY 10027) has recently become one of the few journals for the serious analysis of the media.

Although it does not really fit the criteria for inclusion in this review, *The Chronicle of Higher Education* (42 issues yearly; $20.00; 1717 Massachusetts Avenue, N.W., Washington DC 20036) contains excellent coverage of news affecting the academic profession and will be valuable to anyone interested in American Studies in the context of higher education.

Feminist Studies (3 yearly, $6.00, individual; $9.00, institutional: 417 Riverside Drive, New York, NY 10025) devoted a double issue to women's history last year and has included at least one historical article in each issue.

A *Journal of Historical Geography* is scheduled to begin publication in January 1975. It will be edited by scholars at the University of Oxford and the University of Wisconsin and published by the Academic Press of London, a subsidiary of Harcourt Brace Jovanovich.

Abstracts and Reviews

The phenomenal expansion of publishing in all fields has made good reviewing and abstracting an absolute necessity. Some of the most useful abstract services are: *America: History and Life* (quarterly; $55–230, rates according to library budget: American Bibliographical Center, CLIO Press, Riviera Campus, 2040 Alameda Padre Serra, Santa Barbara, CA 93103), *Sociological Abstracts* (7 yearly; $100.00: 73 Eighth Avenue, Brooklyn, NY 11215), and *Abstracts in Anthropology* (quarterly; $35.00, plus $2.00 outside U.S. and Canada: Baywood Publishing Co., Inc., 43 Central Drive, Farmingdale, NY 11735). Of the new specialized reviews, *History: Reviews of New Books* (10 yearly; $8.00, students; $10.00, individuals; $15.00, institutions, plus $2.00 for foreign postage: Heldref Publications, 4000 Albemarle Street, N.W., Washington, DC 20016) is a 30-page journal which contains an average of 35–40 reviews of books on American history each issue. Now in its second year, *Reviews in American History* (quarterly; $14.00 individuals, plus $2.00 foreign postage: Redgrave Information Resources Corp., Dept. FO, 53 Wilton Road, Westport CT 06880) with its 160-pages of in-depth review essays (averaging 2,000 words in length) and impressive editorial board has become the premier journal of this kind.

Whatever their specialties, scholarly journals are the best sources of information on new directions in research and interpretation, and they soon become capsule histories of American intellectual life. From them, a student can quickly place himself within the boundaries of a discipline, and he can find models for his own research.

Here, then, are some periodicals which serve American Studies and which could form the nucleus of a good research library. Missing, of course, are the many excellent state and local historical journals and the growing number of journals and newsletters devoted to important individuals such as C. S. Peirce, Walt Whitman, and Ezra Pound. Despite the necessary omissions, I hope I have suggested that "last year's quarterly is more than something to wrap fish in."

Index of Titles

For the sake of simplicity and reader convenience, the following typographical practice has been adopted: roman type for book titles, roman type in quotation marks for periodical articles, and italics for periodical titles.

General Bibliography
and Author Index

The following list serves the combined purpose of an author index and a composite bibliography of all works mentioned in the foregoing essays. For each entry, imprint data is given for the most recent edition available. Where that edition is available in paperback (*), imprint data for the paperback edition is given. Books not now in print are marked (●). Page numbers follow the imprint data and are limited to the original listing of the author's name. Page references by title are in a separate title index.

---

*Aaron, Daniel. *Men of Good Hope: A Story of American Progressives.* New York: Oxford University Press, Galaxy Books, 1961. *268, 271*

*_____. *Writers on the Left: Episodes in American Literary Communism.* New York: Avon, Discus Books, 1965.

Abbott, Edith. *Tenements of Chicago, 1908-1935.* 1936. Reprint. New York: Arno Press, 1970. *226*

●Abell, Aaron I. *American Catholicism and Social Action: A Search for Social Justice, 1865-1950.* Garden City, New York: Hanover House, 1960. *19*

Abrams, Ray. *Preachers Present Arms: The Role of American Churches and Clergy in World Wars I and II, with Some Observations on the War in Vietnam.* Rev. ed. Scottsdale, Pennsylvania: Herald Press, 1969. *20*

Adams, C. C. "Introductory Notes to a Symposium on Relation of Ecology to Human Welfare."

Ecological Monographs 10 (1940): 307-10. *140*

_____. "The Relations of General Ecology to Human Ecology." *Ecology* 16 (1935):316-35.

Adams, Graham, Jr. *Age of Industrial Violence, 1900-1915: The Activities and Findings of the United States Commission on Industrial Relations.* New York: Columbia University Press, 1971. *118, 119*

*Adams, Henry. *The Education of Henry Adams.* Edited by Ernest Samuels. Boston: Houghton Mifflin, Riverside Books, 1973. *26, 27, 28, 34*

•Adams, James Truslow, ed. *Dictionary of American History.* 6 vols. 2d ed., rev. New York: Charles Scribner's Sons, 1942. *266*

Adams, John Quincy. *Memoirs of John Quincy Adams, Comprising Portions of his Diary from 1795 to 1848.* Edited by Charles Francis Adams. 12 vols. 1874-1877. Reprint. New York: Books for Libraries, 1971. *68*

•Adams, Ramon F. *The Rampaging Herd: A Bibliography of Books and Pamphlets on Men and Events in the Cattle Industry.* Norman: University of Oklahoma Press, 1959. *46*

_____. *Six Guns and Saddle Leather: A Bibliography of Books and Pamphlets on Western Outlaws and Gunmen.* Rev. ed. Norman: University of Oklahoma Press, 1969.

Adams, Sherman. *Firsthand Report: The Story of the Eisenhower Administration.* 1961. Reprint. Westport, Connecticut: Greenwood Press, 1975. *79*

*Addams, Jane. *Democracy and Social Ethics.* Edited by Anne Firor Scott. Cambridge, Massachusetts: The Belknap Press of Harvard University Press, 1964. *225, 245, 256*

•_____. *The Second Twenty Years at Hull House: September 1909 to September 1929, with a Record of a Growing World Consciousness.* New York: Macmillan, 1930.

*_____. *Twenty Years at Hull House.* 1910. Reprint. New York: New American Library, Signet Books.

Ade, George. *Artie and Pink Marsh: 1896-1897.* Edited by James Farrell. Chicago: University of Chicago Press, 1963. *228*

•Adelman, William. *Touring Pullman, A Study in Company Paternalism: A Walking Guide to the Pullman Community in Chicago, Illinois.* Chicago: Illinois Labor History Society, 1972. *227, 234*

*Ahlstrom, Sydney E. *A Religious History of the American People.* Garden City, New York: Doubleday, Image Books, 1975. *12*

*_____, ed. *Theology in America: The Major Protestant Voices from Puritanism to Neo-orthodoxy.* Indianapolis, Indiana: Bobbs-Merrill, 1967. *12*

Ahnebrink, Lars. *The Beginnings of Naturalism in American Fiction: A Study of the Works of Hamlin Garland, Stephen Crane, and Frank Norris, with Special Reference to Some European Influences, 1891-1903.* 1950. Reprint. New York: Russell and Russell, 1961. *44*

Aiken, Conrad. *Ushant: An Essay.* New York: Oxford University Press, 1971. *26, 29, 34*

*Akin, Wallace E. *The North Central United States.* Princeton, New Jersey: Van Nostrand, 1968. *53*

Albertson, Ralph. *A Survey of Mutualistic Communistic Communities in America.* 1936. Reprint. New York: AMS Press, 1973. *214, 218*

Alcock, Antony. *History of the International Labour Organisation.* New York: Octagon Books, 1971. *120*   )

Aldridge, Alfred O. *Benjamin Franklin and Nature's God.* Durham, North Carolina: Duke University Press, 1967. *15*

Alexander, Lewis. *The Northeastern United States.* 2d ed. Princeton, New Jersey: Van Nostrand, 1975. *52*

Allee, W. C., Alfred Emerson, Orlando Park, Thomas Park, and Karl P. Schmidt, eds. *Principles of Animal Ecology.* Philadelphia: Saunders, 1949. *143*

*Allen, Frederick Lewis. *The Big Change: America Transforms Itself, 1900-1950.* New York: Harper and Row, 1969. *20, 269*

*_____. *Only Yesterday: An Informal History of the Nineteen-Twenties.* New York: Harper and Row, 1957.

*_____. *Since Yesterday: The Nineteen-Thirties in America, September 3, 1929-September 3, 1939.* New York: Harper and Row, 1972. *20*

Alley, Robert S. *So Help Me God: Religion and the Presidency, Wilson to Nixon.* Richmond, Virginia: John Knox Press, 1972. *73*

Allport, Gordon W. *The Nature of Personality: Selected Papers.* 1950. Reprint. Westport, Connecticut: Greenwood Press, 1975. *30, 36*

*_____. *The Use of Personal Documents in Psychological Science.* 1942. Reprint. New York: Kraus Reprints.

Allswang, John. *A House for All Peoples: Ethnic Politics in Chicago, 1890-1936.* Lexington: University Press of Kentucky, 1971. *226*

* Altbach, Edith Hoshino. *Women in America.* Lexington, Massachusetts: D. C. Heath, 1974. *246*

* Altick, Richard. *The English Common Reader: A Social History of the Mass Reading Public, 1800-1900.* Chicago: University of Chicago Press, Phoenix Books, 1957. *177, 181*
_____. *Victorian Studies in Scarlet.* New York: W. W. Norton, 1970.

• Alyea, Paul E., and Blanche R. Alyea. *Fairhope, 1894-1954: The Story of a Single Tax Colony.* University: University of Alabama Press, 1956. *215, 218*

American Council of Learned Societies, ed. *Dictionary of American Biography.* 22 vols. and 4 suppls. with index. New York: Scribner's, 1927-1964. *262*

American Geographical Society. *Research Catalogue.* 15 vols. with map suppl. Boston: G. K. Hall, 1962. *87, 93*

American Heritage Publishing Company. *The Inaugural Story, 1789-1969.* New York, 1969. *71*

American Indian Historical Society. *Indian Voices.* Proceedings of the first conference of Indian historians, held at Princeton University, 1969. Published in 1970. *203*
_____. *Textbooks and the American Indian.* Proceedings of the first conference of Indian historians, held at Princeton University, 1969. Published in 1970. *203*

• Amis, Kingsley. *The James Bond Dossier.* New York: New American Library, 1965. *176, 181*
_____. *New Maps of Hell: A Survey of Science Fiction.* 1960. Reprint. New York: Arno Press, 1975.

• Ammon, Harry. *James Monroe: Quest for National Identity.* New York: McGraw-Hill, 1971. *74*

• Amory, Cleveland. *The Proper Bostonians.* New York: E. P. Dutton, 1947. *159, 167*

Anderson, John Q. *Louisiana Swamp Doctor: The Life and Writings of Henry Clay Lewis.* Baton Rouge: Louisiana State University Press, 1962. *42*

Anderson, Margaret C. *My Thirty Years' War: The Autobiography: Beginnings and Battles to 1930.* 1930. Reprint. New York: Horizon Press, 1969. *229*
_____, ed. *The Little Review: Literature, Drama, Music, Art.* Chicago: M. C. Anderson, 1914-1929.

*_____, ed. *The Little Review Anthology.* New York: Horizon Press, 1970.

Anderson, Mary. *Woman at Work: The Autobiography of Mary Anderson as Told to Mary N. Winslow.* 1951. Reprint. Westport, Connecticut: Greenwood Press, 1973. *249*

* Anderson, Nels. *The Hobo: The Sociology of the Homeless Man.* 1923. Reprint. Chicago: University of Chicago Press, 1975. *226*

• Anderson, Patrick. *The President's Men: White House Assistants of Franklin D. Roosevelt, Harry S. Truman, Dwight D. Eisenhower, John F. Kennedy, and Lyndon B. Johnson.* Garden City, New York: Doubleday, 1968. *71*

Anderson, Perry, and Robin Blackburn, eds. *Towards Socialism.* Ithaca, New York: Cornell University Press, 1966. *127*

• Anderson, Sherwood. *Marching Men.* New York: John Lane, 1917. *227*
_____. *Sherwood Anderson's Memoirs: A Critical Edition.* Chapel Hill: University of North Carolina Press, 1969.

*_____. *A Story-Teller's Story.* New York: Viking Press, Compass Books, 1969.

•_____. *Tar: A Midwest Childhood.* New York: Boni and LIveright, 1926.

* Andrews, Edward D. *The Gift to Be Simple; Songs, Dances and Rituals of the American Shakers.* New York: Dover, 1963. *210, 218*

*_____. *The People Called Shakers; A Search for the Perfect Society.* New enlarged edition. New York: Dover, 1963.

*_____, and Faith Andrews. *Shaker Furniture, The Craftsmanship of an American Communal Sect.* New York: Dover, 1964. *218*

* Andrews, Wayne. *Architecture, Ambition, and Americans: A Social History of American Architecture.* New York: The Free Press, 1964. *225, 263, 266*

•_____. *Battle for Chicago.* New York: Harcourt, Brace, Jovanovich, 1946.

_____, and Thomas C. Cochran, eds. *Concise Dictionary of American History.* Abridged edition. New York: Scribner's, 1962.

* Angelou, Maya. *I Know Why the Caged Bird Sings.* New York: Bantam Books, 1971. *26, 34, 248*

* Antin, Mary. *The Promised Land.* 2d ed. Boston: Houghton Mifflin, Sentry Books, 1969. *26, 34*

Apter, David, and James Joll, eds. *Anarchism Today.* London: Macmillan, 1971. *127*

* Aptheker, Herbert. *American Negro Slave Revolts.* New York: International Publishing Company, 1969. *109, 150*

*_____, ed. *A Documentary History of the Negro People in the United States.* 3 vols. New York: Citadel Press, 1951-1973.

Arky, Louis H. "The Mechanics' Union of Trade Associations and the Formation of the Philadelphia Working Men's Movement." *Pennsylvania Magazine of History and Biography* 76 (April 1952):142-76. *112*

Armytage, W. H. G. *Heaven's Below: Utopian Experiments in England, 1560-1960.* Toronto, Canada: University of Toronto Press, 1961. *208, 218*

Arndt, Karl J. R. *George Rapp's Harmony Society, 1785-1847.* Rev. ed. Rutherford, New Jersey: Fairleigh Dickinson University Press, 1972. *211, 218*

_____. *George Rapp's Successors and Material Heirs, 1847-1916.* Rutherford, New Jersey: Fairleigh Dickinson University Press, 1971.

* Arrington, Leonard J. *Great Basin Kingdom: An Economic History of the Latter-Day Saints, 1830-1900.* Lincoln: University of Nebraska Press, Bison Books, 1966. *53, 212, 218*

Ashby, Sir Eric. *Any Person, Any Study: An Essay in Higher Education in the United States.* New York: McGraw-Hill, 1971. *102*

* Auden, W. H. *The Dyer's Hand, and Other Essays.* New York: Random House, Vintage Books, 1962. *175, 181*

* Auerbach, Jerold S., ed. *American Labor: The Twentieth Century.* Indianapolis, Indiana: Bobbs-Merrill, 1969. *122, 125*

_____. *Labor and Liberty: The LaFollette Committee and the New Deal.* Indianapolis, Indiana: Bobbs-Merrill, 1966.

* Austin, Lettie J., Lewis H. Fenderson, and Sophia P. Nelson, comps. *The Black Man and the Promise of America.* Glenview, Illinois: Scott, Foresman, 1970. *148*

• Averill, Lloyd J. *American Theology in the Liberal Tradition.* Philadelphia: Westminster Press, 1967. *230*

* Bach, Ira. *Chicago on Foot: An Architectural Walking Tour.* 2d rev. ed. Chicago: J. Philip O'Hara, 1973. *231*

* Bachelard, Gaston. *The Poetics of Reverie: Childhood, Language and the Cosmos.* Boston: Beacon Press, 1971. *181*

*_____. *The Poetics of Space.* Boston: Beacon Press, 1969.

*_____. *The Psychoanalysis of Fire.* Boston: Beacon Press, 1964.

Bagrow, Leo. *Die Geschichte der Kartographie.* Berlin: Safari-Verlag, 1951. *82, 84, 91, 92*

•_____. *History of Cartography.* Rev. and enlarged by R. A. Skelton. Cambridge, Massachusetts: Harvard University Press, 1964.

_____. *Meister der Kartographie.* Berlin: Safari-Verlag, 1963.

Bailey, Thomas A. *Presidential Greatness: The Image and the Man from George Washington to the Present.* New York: Irvington Publications, 1966. *69, 78*

*_____. *Woodrow Wilson and the Great Betrayal.* New York: Quadrangle Books, 1963.

*_____. *Woodrow Wilson and the Lost Peace.* New York: Quadrangle Books, 1963.

* Bailyn, Bernard. *The Ideological Origins of the American Revolution.* Cambridge, Massachusetts: The Belknap Press of Harvard University Press, 1967. *15*

Bain, Richard E., and Judith H. Parris. *Convention Decisions and Voting Records.* 2d rev. ed. Washington, D.C.: The Brookings Institution, 1973. *70*

* Bainton, Roland H. *The Reformation of the 16th Century.* Boston: Beacon Press, 1956. *14*

Baird, Robert. *Religion in America: A Critical Abridgment.* Edited by H. W. Bowden. 1970. Reprint. Gloucester, Massachusetts: Peter Smith. *11*

Baker, Elizabeth Faulkner. *Technology and Woman's Work.* New York: Columbia University Press, 1964. *246*

Baker, Houston A., Jr. *Long Black Song: Essays in Black American Literature and Culture.* Charlottesville: University Press of Virginia, 1972. *29, 35*

Baker, Mary Roys. "Anglo-Massachusetts Trade Union Roots, 1130-1790." *Labor History* 14 (Summer 1973):352-96. *109*

Baker, Ray Stannard. *Woodrow Wilson: Life and Letters.* 8 vols. 1939. Reprint. Westport, Connecticut: Greenwood Press, 1968. *78*

* Baker, Ross, ed. *The Afro-American: Readings.* New York: Van Nostrand Reinhold, 1970. *150*

Balchin, William G. V., ed. *Geography and Man: A Practical Survey of the Life and Work of*

Man in Relation to His Natural Environment. 2d ed. 2 vols. London: New Era Publishing Company, 1955. *141*

*Baldwin, James. *The Fire Next Time.* New York: Dell, 1970. *28, 35*

*_____. *Nobody Knows My Name.* New York: Dell, 1963.

*_____. *Notes of a Native Son.* Boston: Beacon Press, 1957.

Ballou, Adin. *Autobiography of Adin Ballou, 1803-1890.* Edited by William S. Heywood. 1896. Reprint. Philadelphia: Porcupine Press, 1975. *213, 218*

_____. *History of the Hopedale Community; From Its Inception to Its Virtual Submergence in the Hopedale Parish.* 1897. Reprint. Philadelphia: Porcupine Press, 1973.

*Bancroft, George. *History of the United States from the Discovery of the Continent.* Abridged edition by Russell B. Nye. Chicago: University of Chicago Press, Phoenix Books, 1966. *11*

Bancroft, Hubert Howe. *The Book of the Fair, An Historical and Descriptive Presentation of the World's Science, Art, and Industry, As Viewed Through the Columbian Exposition at Chicago in 1893.* New York: Crown Publishers, 1972. *236*

Bancroft Library. University of California, Berkeley. *Bancroft Library Index to Printed Maps, with Supplement.* Boston: G. K. Hall, 1975. *86, 93*

*Banham, Reyner. *Los Angeles: The Architecture of Four Ecologies.* New York: Harper and Row, Harper Torchbooks, 1971. *191, 192*

*Banner, Lois. *Women in Modern America: A Brief History.* New York: Harcourt, Brace, Jovanovich, 1974. *247, 254*

*Baran, Paul A., and Paul M. Sweezy. *Monopoly Capital: An Essay on the American Economic and Social Order.* New York: Monthly Review Press, 1968. *9*

●Barbour, Hugh. *The Quakers in Puritan England.* New Haven, Connecticut: Yale University Press, 1964. *14*

*Bardwick, Judith. *Psychology of Women: A Study of Bio-Cultural Conflicts.* New York: Harper and Row, 1971. *257*

Barkun, David. *Disaster and the Millenium.* New Haven, Connecticut: Yale University Press, 1974. *208, 218*

Barley, M. W. *House and Home.* London: Vista Books, 1963. *187, 192*

Barnard, Harry. *Rutherford B. Hayes and His America.* 1954. Reprint. New York: Russell and Russell, 1967. *76*

*Barnes, Gilbert H. *The Anti-Slavery Impulse: 1830-1844.* New York: Harcourt, Brace, Jovanovich, 1964. *16*

Barnouw, Erik. *A History of Broadcasting in the United States.* 3 vols. New York: Oxford University Press, 1966-1970. *178, 181*

●_____. *Mass Communication: Television, Radio, Film, Press. The Media and Their Practice in the United States of America.* New York: Rinehart, 1956.

Barnum, Phineas T. *The Life of P. T. Barnum, Written by Himself.* Edited by Waldo R. Browne. Gloucester, Massachusetts: Peter Smith, 1962. *26, 35*

●Barry, R. M. "A Man and a City: George Herbert Mead in Chicago." In *American Philosophy and the Future: Essays for a New Generation,* edited by Michael Novak. New York: Scribner's, 1968. *230*

*Barthes, Roland. *Mythologies.* New York: Hill and Wang, 1972. *181*

_____. *Systeme de la Mode.* Paris: Editions du Seuil, 1967.

*Barzun, Jacques. *The American University: How It Runs and Where It Is Going.* New York: Harper and Row, Harper Torchbooks, 1968. *264*

_____, and Wendell H. Taylor. *A Catalog of Crime: Second Impression Corrected.* New York: Harper and Row, 1974. *176, 181*

Bassett, Margaret. *Profiles and Portraits of American Presidents and Their Wives.* Freeport, Maine: Bond Wheelwright Company, 1969. *69*

Bates, Marston. "Human Ecology." In *Anthropology Today: An Encyclopedic Inventory,* edited by A. L. Kroeber. Chicago: University of Chicago Press, 1953. *141*

_____. "The Human Ecosystem." In *Resources and Man.* Committee on Resources and Man of the Division of Earth Sciences, NAS-NRC. San Francisco: W. H. Freeman, 1969.

*_____. *Man in Nature.* 2d ed. Englewood Cliffs, New Jersey: Prentice-Hall, 1964.

Baughman, Urbanus E., and Robinson L. Baughman. *Secret Service Chief.* New York: Harper and Row, 1962. *73*

Baxter, Annette K. "Women's Studies and American Studies: The Uses of the Interdisciplinary." *American Quarterly* 26 (October 1974). *239, 253*

_____, and Leon Stein, advisory eds. *Women in America: From Colonial Times to the 20th*

Century. Reprint series of 59 books. New York: Arno Press, 1974. *255*

*Bayh, Birch. *One Heartbeat Away: Presidential Disability and Succession*. Indianapolis, Indiana: Bobbs-Merrill, 1968. *72*

*Bayliss, John F., ed. *Black Slave Narratives*. New York: Collier Books, 1970. *28, 35*

*Beard, Charles A., ed. *The Enduring Federalist*. New York: Frederick Ungar, 1959. *7, 70*

*Beauvoir, Simone de. *The Second Sex*. New York: Random House, Vintage Books, 1974. *249*

*Becker, Carl L. *The Declaration of Independence: A Study in the History of Political Ideas*. New York: Random House, Vintage Books, 1958. *15*

*Beijbom, Ulf. *Swedes in Chicago, A Demographic and Social Study of the 1846-1880 Immigration*. Chicago: Chicago Historical Society, 1971. *234*

Bell, Daniel. *The Coming of Post-Industrial Society: A Venture in Social Forecasting*. New York: Basic Books, 1973. *117, 123, 126, 127*

*_____. *The End of Ideology: On the Exhaustion of Political Ideas in the Fifties*. New York: The Free Press, 1960.

*_____. *Marxian Socialism in the United States*. Princeton, New Jersey: Princeton University Press, 1967.

•_____. *Work and Its Discontents*. Boston: Beacon Press, 1956.

•Bemis, Samuel Flagg. *A Diplomatic History of the United States*. 5th ed. New York: Holt, Rinehart, and Winston, 1965. *74, 268*

*_____. *John Quincy Adams and the Foundations of American Foreign Policy*. New York: W. W. Norton, 1973.

_____. *John Quincy Adams and the Union*. New York: Alfred A. Knopf, 1956.

Bendix, Reinhard, and Seymour Lipset, eds. *Class, Status, and Power: Social Stratification in Comparative Perspective*. 2d ed. New York: The Free Press, 1966. *274*

*Benello, C. George, and Dimitrios Roussopoulos, eds. *The Case for Participatory Democracy: Some Prospects for a Radical Society*. New York: Viking Press, Compass Books, 1971. *127*

•Bergendoff, Conrad. *The Church of the Lutheran Reformation: A Historical Survey of Lutheranism*. St. Louis, Missouri: Concordia Publishing House, 1967. *14*

Berger, Arthur A. *L'il Abner: A Study in American Satire*. New York: Twayne, 1969. *181*

*Berkhofer, Robert F. *Salvation and the Savage: An Analysis of Protestant Missions and American Indian Response, 1787-1862*. New York: Atheneum, 1972. *201*

*Berkman, Alexander. *Prison Memoirs of an Anarchist*. New York: Schocken Books, 1970. *26, 34*

Berkowitz, Tamar, Jean Mangi, and Jane Williamson, eds. *Who's Who and Where in Women's Studies*. Old Westbury, New York: The Feminist Press, 1974. *253, 254*

*Berman, Daniel M. *It Is So Ordered: The Supreme Court Rules on School Desegregation*. New York: W. W. Norton, 1966. *98*

Bernard, Jesse. *Academic Women*. University Park: Pennsylvania State University Press, 1964. *256*

•Bernard, L. L., and J. Bernard. *Origins of American Sociology: The Social Science Movement in the United States*. 1943. Reprint. New York: Russell and Russell, 1965. *230*

*Bernstein, Barton J., ed. *Towards a New Past: Dissenting Essays in American History*. New York: Random House, Vintage Books, 1969. *7*

*Bernstein, Irving. *The Lean Years: A History of the American Worker, 1920-1933*. Boston: Houghton Mifflin, Sentry Books, 1972. *120, 121*

_____. *The New Deal Collective Bargaining Policy*. 1950. Reprint. New York: Da Capo Press, 1975.

_____. *The Turbulent Years: A History of the American Worker, 1933-1941*. Boston: Houghton Mifflin, 1970.

Bernstein, Leonard. "The Working People of Philadelphia from Colonial Times to the General Strike of 1835." *Pennsylvania Magazine of History and Biography* 74 (1950):332-39. *110*

Bernstein, Samuel. *The First International in America*. New York: Augustus M. Kelley, 1962. *117*

*Berry, Brian J. L. *The Human Consequences of Urbanization: Divergent Paths in the Urban Experience of the Twentieth Century*. New York: St. Martin's Press, 1973. *164*

Bertalanffy, Ludwig von. "General System Theory: A New Approach to Unity of Science." *Human Ecology* 23 (December 1951): 302-61. *141*

Berthoff, Rowland. *British Immigrants in Industrial America, 1790-1950*. 1953. Reprint. New York: Russell and Russell, 1968. *116*

•Berthoff, Warner. *The Ferment of Realism: American Literature, 1884-1919.* New York: The Free Press, 1965. *24, 29, 33, 44, 235*

_____. "Witness and Testament: Two Contemporary Classics." In *Aspects of Narrative,* edited by J. H. Miller. New York: Columbia University Press, 1971.

*Bestor, Arthur E., Jr. *Backwoods Utopias: The Sectarian and Owenite Phases of Communitarian Socialism in America, 1663-1829.* 2d ed. Philadelphia: University of Pennsylvania Press, 1971. *111, 209, 211, 218*

Bews, J. W. *Human Ecology.* 1935. Reprint. New York: Russell and Russell, 1973. *138*

Bidwell, Percy, and John Falconer. *History of Agriculture in the Northern United States, 1620-1860.* 1925. Reprint. New York: Augustus M. Kelley, 1972. *55*

•Bier, Jesse. *The Rise and Fall of American Humor.* New York: Holt, Rinehart, and Winston, 1968. *42*

Billington, Monroe. *The South: A Central Theme?* 1969. Reprint. Gloucester, Massachusetts: Peter Smith. *16*

Billington, Ray Allen. *America's Frontier Heritage.* Albuquerque: University of New Mexico Press, 1966. *16, 19, 267*

*_____. *The Protestant Crusade, 1800-1860: A Study of the Origins of American Nativism.* New York: Quadrangle Books, 1964. *16, 19, 267*

_____. *Westward Expansion: A History of the American Frontier.* 3d ed. New York: Macmillan, 1967.

Bing, Alexander. *War-Time Strikes and Their Adjustment.* 1921. Reprint. New York: Arno Press, 1971. *119*

Binkley, Wilfred E. *American Political Parties: Their Natural History.* 4th rev. ed. New York: Alfred A. Knopf, 1963. *69, 70*

_____. *The Man in the White House: His Powers and Duties.* Baltimore: Johns Hopkins University Press, 1959.

•_____. *President and Congress.* 3d rev. ed. New York: Vintage Books, 1962.

*Bird, Caroline. *Born Female: The High Cost of Keeping Women Down.* Rev. ed. New York: David McKay Company, 1974. *251*

*Blair, Walter. *Native American Humor.* New York: Chandler Publishing Company, 1960. *42, 272*

Blake, Nelson M. *A History of American Life and Thought.* 2d ed. New York: McGraw-Hill, 1972. *174, 181*

Blanck, Jacob. *Bibliography of American Literature.* 6 vols. New Haven, Connecticut: Yale University Press, 1955-1969. *46, 270*

Blassingame, John W. "Before the Ghetto: The Making of the Black Community in Savannah, Georgia, 1865-1880." *Journal of Social History* 6 (Summer 1973):463-88. *27, 35, 166*

*_____. *The Slave Community: Plantation Life in the Antebellum South.* New York: Oxford University Press, 1973.

•Blau, Joseph L. *Men and Movements in American Philosophy.* Englewood Cliffs, New Jersey: Prentice-Hall, 1952. *13, 273*

_____, ed. *American Philosophic Addresses, 1700-1900.* New York: Columbia University Press, 1946.

*Blaustein, Albert P., and Robert Zangrando, eds. *Civil Rights and the American Negro: A Documentary History.* New York: Simon and Schuster, Touchstone-Clarion Books, 1970. *150*

•Bleiler, E. F. *Fables in Slang, and More Fables in Slang.* New York: Dover, 1960. *235*

Blewett, Mary. "Women in American History: A History Through Film Approach." *Film & History* 4 (December 1974):4. *252*

Block, Marguerite Beck. *The New Church in the New World: A Study of Swedenborgianism in America.* New York: Octagon Books, 1968. *212, 218*

•Bloom, Benjamin Samuel, et al. *Taxonomy of Educational Objectives: The Classification of Educational Goals.* New York: Longmans, Green, 1956. *100*

*Blum, John Morton. *The Republican Roosevelt.* New York: Atheneum, 1962. *13, 77*

*_____, et al. *The National Experience: A History of the United States.* 3d ed. New York: Harcourt, Brace, Jovanovich, 1973.

*Blumberg, Paul. *Industrial Democracy: The Sociology of Participation.* New York: Schocken Books, 1974. *127*

*Blumer, Herbert. *Critiques of Research in the Social Sciences: An Appraisal of Thomas and Znaniecki's "The Polish Peasant in Europe and America."* New York: Social Science Research Council, 1939. *30, 36*

Boatright, Mody C. *Folk Laughter on the American Frontier.* 1949. Reprint. Gloucester, Massachusetts, Peter Smith. *42*

*Bode, Carl. *Antebellum Culture.* (Originally *The Anatomy of American Popular Culture, 1840-1860.*) Carbondale: Southern Illinois University Press, 1970. *175, 181*

*Bogan, Louise. *Achievement in American Poetry, 1900-1950.* Chicago: H. Regnery, 1951. *271*

*Boggs, James. *The American Revolution: Pages from a Negro Worker's Notebook.* New York: Monthly Review Press, 1963. *126*

*_____. *Racism and the Class Struggle: Further Pages from a Black Worker's Notebook.* New York: Monthly Review Press, 1970.

Bogue, Donald. *The Population of the United States.* Glencoe, Illinois: The Free Press, 1959. *56*

Bok, Derek C., and John T. Dunlop. *Labor and the American Community.* New York: Simon and Schuster, 1970. *125*

*Bone, Robert. *Richard Wright.* Minneapolis: University of Minnesota Press, 1969. *29, 36*

*Bontemps, Arna, ed. *Great Slave Narratives.* Boston: Beacon Press, 1969. *28, 35*

*Boorstin, Daniel J. *The Americans: The National Experience.* New York: Random House, Vintage Books, 1967. *7, 15, 192, 225, 265*

*_____. *The Genius of American Politics.* Chicago: University of Chicago Press, Phoenix Books, 1953.

*_____. *The Lost World of Thomas Jefferson.* Boston: Beacon Press, 1960.

•Borchert, John. *Minnesota's Changing Geography.* Minneapolis: University of Minnesota Press, 1959. *53*

*Borden, Morton. *America's Ten Greatest Presidents.* 2d ed. Chicago: Rand McNally, 1961. *69*

*Borsodi, Ralph. *Flight from the City: An Experiment in Creative Living on the Land.* 3d ed. New York: Harper and Row, 1972. *216, 218*

_____. *This Ugly Civilization.* 1929. Reprint. Philadelphia: Porcupine Press, 1975.

Boulding, Kenneth E. "Economics of the Coming Spaceship Earth." In *Environmental Quality in a Growing Economy.* Baltimore: Johns Hopkins University Press, 1966. *5, 9, 141*

*_____. "Economics and Ecology." In *Future Environments of North America,* edited by F. Fraser Darling and John P. Milton. Garden City, New York: The Natural History Press, 1966.

*_____. *The Image: Knowledge in Life and Society.* Ann Arbor: University of Michigan Press, 1956.

*_____. *The Meaning of the Twentieth Century: The Great Transition.* New York: Harper and Row, 1964.

_____. *Principles of Economic Policy.* Englewood Cliffs, New Jersey: Prentice-Hall, 1958. *141*

•Bowen, Louise deKoven. *Growing Up with a City.* New York: Macmillan, 1926. *226*

•_____. *Speeches, Addresses, and Letters of Louise deKoven Bowen, Reflecting Social Movements in Chicago.* 2 vols. Ann Arbor, Michigan: Edwards Brothers, 1937.

•Bowman, Sylvia. *The Year 2000: A Critical Biography of Edward Bellamy.* New York: Bookman Associates, 1958. *215, 218*

*Bracey, John H., August Meier, and Elliott Rudwick, eds. *Black Nationalism in America.* Indianapolis, Indiana: Bobbs-Merrill, 1969. *125, 151*

*_____, eds. *Black Workers and Organized Labor.* Belmont, California: Wadsworth Publishing Company, 1971.

Braden, Charles. *Spirits in Rebellion: The Rise and Development of New Thought.* Dallas, Texas: Southern Methodist University Press, 1963. *12*

Bradford, Sarah. *Harriet Tubman: The Moses of Her People.* 1886. Reprint. Gloucester, Massachusetts: Peter Smith. *248*

Bradford, William. *Of Plymouth Plantation, 1620-1647.* Edited by Samuel Eliot Morison. New York: Alfred A. Knopf, 1952. *11, 266*

*Bradley, Edward Scully, et al., eds. *The American Tradition in Literature.* Rev. 4th ed. 2 vols. New York: W. W. Norton, 1974. *272*

*Brandon, William. *The American Heritage Book of Indians.* New York: Dell, 1961. *195*

Brant, Irving. *The Fourth President: The Life of James Madison.* Indianapolis, Indiana: Bobbs-Merrill, 1970. *74*

Brawley, Benjamin. *A Social History of the American Negro: Being a Study of the Negro Problem in the United States, Including a History and Study of the Republic of Liberia.* 1921. Reprint. New York: Johnson Reprint Corporation, 1969. *150*

*Brecher, Jeremy. *Strike!* New York: Fawcett World, Premier Books, 1974. *125*

•Bregstone, Philip P. *Chicago and Its Jews: A Cultural History.* Chicago: Private printing, 1933. *234*

Bremer, Howard F., ed. *Presidential Chronology Series.* 32 vols. Dobbs-Ferry, New York: Oceana Publications, 1967-1975. *67*

*Bremner, Robert H. *From the Depths: The Discovery of Poverty in the United States.* New York: New York University Press, 1956. *274*

*Brewer, John Mason. *American Negro Folklore.* Chicago: Quadrangle Books, 1974. *264*

Bricker, Charles. *A History of Cartography: 2500 Years of Maps and Map Makers.* London: Thames and Hudson, 1969. *83, 91*

_____. *Landmarks of Map-Making: An Illustrated Survey of Maps and Mapmakers.* London: Thames and Hudson, 1969.

*Bridenbaugh, Carl. *The Colonial Craftsman.* Chicago: University of Chicago Press, Phoenix Books, 1961. *15, 109*

*_____. *Mitre and Sceptre: Transatlantic Faiths, Ideas, Personalities, and Politics, 1689-1775.* New York: Oxford University Press, Galaxy Books, 1967.

Bridgman, Richard. *Gertrude Stein in Pieces.* New York: Oxford University Press, 1970. *29, 36*

Briggs, Asa. "History Goes to Town." *Times Literary Supplement,* December 27, 1974. *159, 167*

_____. *Victorian Cities.* New York: Harper and Row, 1963.

Brignano, Russell C. *Black Americans in Autobiography: An Annotated Bibliography of Autobiographies and Autobiographical Books Written Since the Civil War.* Durham, North Carolina: Duke University Press, 1974. *22, 32*

Brisbane, Albert. *The Social Destiny of Man; or, Association and Reorganization of Industry.* 1840. Reprint. New York: B. Franklin, 1967. *212, 218*

Brisbane, Redelia (Bates). *Albert Brisbane: A Mental Biography, with a Character Study.* 1893. Reprint. New York: B. Franklin, 1969. *212*

British Museum. Department of Manuscripts. *Catalogue of the Manuscript Maps, Charts, and Plans, and of the Topographical Drawings in the British Museum.* 3 vols. 1844-1861. Reprint. London: British Museum, 1962. *86, 93*

_____. Department of Printed Books. Map Room. *Catalogue of Printed Maps, Charts and Plans.* 15 vols. London: Trustees of the British Museum, 1967.

Brock, Peter. *Pacifism in the United States: From the Colonial Era to the First World War.* Princeton, New Jersey: Princeton University Press, 1968. *269*

Brodie, Fawn. *No Man Knows My History: The Life of Joseph Smith.* New York: Alfred A. Knopf, 1971. *12*

Brody, David. "The Emergence of Mass-Production Unionism." In *Change and Continuity in Twentieth Century America,* edited by John Braeman, Robert H. Bremner, and Everett Walters. Columbus: Ohio State University Press, 1964. *120, 121*

•_____. *Labor in Crisis: The Steel Strike of 1919.* Boston: D. C. Heath, 1963.

*Broehl, Wayne G. *The Molly Maguires.* New York: Chelsea House, 1970. 116.

Brooks, H. Allen. *The Prairie School: Frank Lloyd Wright and His Midwest Contemporaries.* Toronto, Canada: University of Toronto Press, 1972. *231*

•Brooks, Thomas R. *Picket Lines and Bargaining Tables: Organized Labor Comes of Age, 1935-1955.* New York: Grosset and Dunlap, 1968. *124*

Brooks, Van Wyck. *Makers and Finders: A History of the Writer in America, 1800-1915.* 5 vols. New York: E. P. Dutton, 1952. *271*

*Broudy, Harry S. *The Real World of the Public Schools.* New York: Harcourt, Brace, Jovanovich, 1972. *99*

*Brown, Claude. *Manchild in the Promised Land.* New York: New American Library, Signet Books, 1971. *26, 34, 148*

*Brown, J. E. *The Sacred Pipe: Black Elk's Account of the Seven Rites of the Oglala Sioux.* New York: Penguin Books, 1971. *29, 36*

Brown, Jerry Wayne. *The Rise of Biblical Criticism in America, 1800-1870: The New England Scholars.* Middletown, Connecticut: Wesleyan University Press, 1969. *18*

•Brown, Lloyd A. *Early Maps of the Ohio Valley: A Selection of Maps, Plans, and Views Made by Indians and Colonials from 1673 to 1783.* Pittsburgh, Pennsylvania: University of Pittsburgh Press, 1959. *82, 84, 91, 92*

•_____. *The Story of Maps.* Boston: Little, Brown, 1949.

Brown, Paul. *Twelve Months in New Harmony: Presenting a Faithful Acccount of the Principal Occurrences Which Have Taken Place There Within That Period.* 1827. Reprint. Philadelphia: Porcupine Press, 1973. *211, 218*

Brown, Ralph. *Historical Geography of the United States.* New York: Harcourt, Brace, Jovanovich, 1948. *51, 52, 265*

Brown, Thomas. *An Account of the People Called Shakers: Their Faith, Doctrines, and Practice.* 1812. Reprint. New York: AMS Press. *210, 218*

*Browne, Ray, and Ronald Ambrosetti, eds. *Popular Culture and Curricula.* Rev. ed. Bowling Green, Ohio: Bowling Green University Popular Press, 1972. *171, 181*

Bruce, Philip A. *Economic History of Virginia in the Seventeenth Century.* 1896. 2 vols. Reprint. Gloucester, Massachusetts: Peter Smith. *55*

*Bruce, Robert V. *1877: Year of Violence.* New York: Watts, Franklin, New Viewpoints Books, 1959. *116*

Bruner, Jerome. *The Process of Education.* Cambridge, Massachusetts: Harvard University Press, 1960. *98*

*Bryer, Jackson R., ed. *Sixteen Modern American Authors: A Survey of Research and Criticism.* Rev. ed. New York: W. W. Norton, 1973. *45*

*Buder, Stanley. *Pullman: An Experiment in Industrial Order and Community Planning, 1880-1930.* New York: Oxford University Press, 1967. *227*

Buell, Abel. *A new and correct map of the United States of North America layd down from the latest observations and best authorities, agreeable to the Peace of 1783, humbly inscribed to His Excellency the Governor of the State of Connecticut.* New Haven, Connecticut: Abel Buell, 1784. Collotype reproduction from original, in collections of New Jersey Historical Society, 1963. *91, 94*

Buhle, Mari Jo. "Women and the Socialist Party, 1901-1914." *Radical America* 4 (February 1970):2. *256*

Bunting, Bainbridge. *Houses of Boston's Back Bay: An Architectural History, 1840-1917.* Cambridge, Massachusetts: The Belknap Press of Harvard University Press, 1967. *159, 167, 187, 192*

•Bunyan, John. *Pilgrim's Progress.* Edited by James Thorpe. Boston: Houghton Mifflin, 1969. *14, 25*

Burgess, Ernest W., and Charles Newcomb. *Census Data of the City of Chicago.* Chicago: University of Chicago Press, 1933. *227*

Burke, Albert E. "Influence of Man Upon Nature—The Russian View: A Case Study." In *Man's Role in Changing the Face of the Earth,* edited by William L. Thomas et al. Chicago: University of Chicago Press, 1956. *141*

Burke, W. J., and Will D. Howe. *American Authors and Books, 1640 to the Present Day.* 3d rev. ed. New York: Crown Publishers, 1972. *270*

•Burlingame, Roger. *Machines That Built America.* New York: Harcourt, Brace, Jovanovich, 1953.

•_____. *March of the Iron Men, A Social History of Union Through Invention.* New York: Grosset and Dunlap, 1960.

Burns, James MacGregor. *John Kennedy: A Political Profile.* New York: Harcourt, Brace, Jovanovich, 1959. *78, 79*

*_____. *Roosevelt: The Lion and the Fox.* New York: Harcourt, Brace, Jovanovich, 1963.

*_____. *Roosevelt: The Soldier of Freedom.* New York: Harcourt, Brace, Jovanovich, Harvest Books, 1973.

Burns, James M., and Jack W. Peltason. *Government by the People: The Dynamics of American National, State, and Local Government.* 7th ed. Englewood Cliffs, New Jersey: Prentice-Hall, 1969. *265*

*Bushman, Richard L. *Puritan to Yankee: Character and the Social Order in Connecticut, 1690-1765.* New York: W. W. Norton, 1970. *8*

Bushnell, George D., Jr. "When Jazz Came to Chicago." *Chicago History* 1 (Spring 1971):3. *236*

*Bushnell, Horace. *Christian Nurture.* New Haven, Connecticut: Yale University Press, 1966. *18*

Butcher, Margaret J. *The Negro in American Culture, Based on Materials Left by Alain Locke.* 2d ed. New York: Alfred A. Knopf, 1972. *274*

Butt, John, ed. *Robert Owen, Prince of Cotton Spinners.* London: David and Charles, 1971. *111*

Butts, R. Freeman, and Lawrence A. Cremin. *A History of Education in American Culture.* New York: Holt, Rinehart, and Winston, 1953. *264*

*Cade, Toni, ed. *The Black Woman: An Anthology.* New York: New American Library, Mentor Books, 1974. *252*

Cady, Edwin H. *William Dean Howells: Dean of American Letters.* 2 vols. Syracuse, New York: Syracuse University Press, 1956-1958. *43*

*Cahill, Susan, and Michele F. Cooper, eds. *The Urban Reader.* Englewood Cliffs, New Jersey: Prentice-Hall, 1971. *162*

*Cahn, Edmond N. *The Moral Decision: Right and Wrong in the Light of American Law.* Bloomington: Indiana University Press, 1959. *270*

•Caldwell, Robert G. *James A. Garfield, Party Chieftain.* New York: Dodd, Mead, 1931. *76*

*Callow, Alexander B., ed. *American Urban History: An Interpretive Reader with Commentaries.* 2d ed. New York: Oxford University Press, 1973. *155, 167*

Caminos, Horacio, John F. C. Turner, and John A. Steffian. *Urban Dwelling Environments: An Elementary Survey of Settlements for the Study of Design Determinants.* Cambridge: Massachusetts Institute of Technology Press, 1969. *160, 167*

Campbell, Walter S. *The Book Lover's Southwest: A Guide to Good Reading.* Norman: University of Oklahoma Press, 1955. *46*

Cantor, Milton, ed. *Black Labor in America.* Westport, Connecticut: Negro Universities Press, 1969. *125*

*Cantor, Norman, and Michael S. Werthman, eds. *The History of Popular Culture.* 2 vols. New York: Macmillan, 1968. *172, 177, 182*

Cantwell, Robert. "The Autobiographers." *New Republic* 94 (April 27, 1938):354-56. *26, 34*

*Carden, Maren Lockwood. *Oneida: Utopian Community to Modern Corporation.* New York: Harper and Row, Harper Torchbooks, 1971. *213, 218*

Carman, Harry J., and Arthur W. Thompson, eds. *A Guide to the Principal Sources for American Civilization, 1800-1900, in the City of New York: Manuscripts and Printed Materials.*
2 vols. New York: Columbia University Press, 1960-1962. *279*

*Carmichael, Stokely, and Charles V. Hamilton. *Black Power: The Politics of Liberation in America.* New York: Random House, Vintage Books, 1967. *126*

•Carnegie, Andrew. *Autobiography of Andrew Carnegie.* Boston: Houghton Mifflin, 1920. *26, 34*

Carnegie Commission on Higher Education. *The Fourth Revolution: Instructional Technology in Higher Education.* New York: McGraw-Hill, 1972. *101, 102*

_____. *Higher Education and the Nation's Health: Policies for Medical and Dental Education.* New York: McGraw-Hill, 1970.

_____. *Less Time, More Options: Education Beyond the High School.* New York: McGraw-Hill, 1971.

_____. *The More Effective Use of Resources: An Imperative for Higher Education.* New York: McGraw-Hill, 1972.

_____. *New Students and New Places: Policies for the Future Growth and Development of American Higher Education.* New York: McGraw-Hill, 1971.

_____. *The Open-Door Colleges: Policies for Community Colleges.* New York: McGraw-Hill, 1970.

*Carpenter, Liz. *Ruffles and Flourishes: The Warm and Tender Story of a Simple Girl Who Found Adventure in the White House.* New York: Pocket Books, 1971. *71*

•Carroll, Peter N., ed. *Religion and the Coming of the American Revolution.* Waltham, Massachusetts: Ginn-Blaisdell, 1970. *15*

*Carson, Rachel. *Silent Spring.* Boston: Houghton Mifflin, Sentry Books, 1973. *139*

Carter, Everett. *Howells and the Age of Realism.* 1954. Reprint. Hamden, Connecticut: Shoe String Press, Archon Books, 1966. *44*

Carter, Paul A. *The Decline and Revival of the Social Gospel: Social and Political Liberalism in American Protestant Churches, 1920-1940.* 1956. 2d ed. Reprint. Hamden, Connecticut: Shoe String Press, Archon books, 1971. *17, 20*

_____. *The Spiritual Crisis of the Gilded Age.* DeKalb: Northern Illinois University Press, 1971.

Cartwright, Peter. *The Autobiography of Peter Cartwright.* New York: Abingdon Press, 1956. *26, 34*

*Cash, Joseph H., and Herbert T. Hoover, eds. *To Be an Indian: An Oral History.* New York: Holt, Rinehart, and Winston, 1971. *205*

*Cash, Wilbur J. *The Mind of the South.* New York: Random House, Vintage Books, 1960. *16, 267*

*Cassirer, Ernst. *The Philosophy of the Enlightenment.* Princeton, New Jersey: Princeton University Press, 1951. *15*

•Cauthen, Wilfred Kenneth. *The Impact of American Religious Liberalism.* New York. Harper and Row, 1962. *18*

*Cawelti, John G. *The Six-Gun Mystique.* Bowling Green, Ohio: Bowling Green University Popular Press, 1970. *176, 182*

*Chafe, William H. *The American Woman: Her Changing Social, Economic and Political Roles, 1920-1970.* New York: Oxford University Press, Galaxy Books, 1974. *246*

*Chambers, Whittaker. *Witness.* Chicago: H. Regnery, 1968. *26, 34*

Champagne, Robert J. "Liberty Boys and Mechanics of New York City, 1764-1774." *Labor History* 8 (Spring 1967): 115-35. *110*

•Champney, Freeman. *Art and Glory: The Story of Elbert Hubbard.* New York: Crown Publishers, 1968. *215, 219*

Chaplin, Ralph. *Wobbly: The Rough-and-Tumble Story of an American Radical.* 1948. Reprint. New York: Da Capo Press, 1972. *118*

*Chapman, Abraham, ed. *Black Voices: An Anthology of Afro-American Literature.* New York: New American Library, Mentor Books, 1968. *151*

Chase, Gilbert. *America's Music, From the Pilgrims to the Present.* Rev. ed. New York: McGraw-Hill, 1966. *272*

Chase, Warren. *The Life-Line of the Lone One; or, Autobiography of the World's Child.* 1857. Reprint. New York: AMS Press, 1972. *215, 219*

•Cherry, Conrad, ed. *God's New Israel: Religious Interpretations of American Destiny.* Englewood Cliffs, New Jersey: Prentice-Hall, 1971. *13, 15*

_____. *The Theology of Jonathan Edwards: A Reappraisal.* Gloucester, Massachusetts: Peter Smith, 1966.

•Chesler, Phyllis. *Women and Madness.* New York: Avon Books, 1973. *250*

Chessman, Caryl. *Cell 2455, Death Row.* 1954. Reprint. Westport, Connecticut: Greenwood Press, 1969. *26, 35*

*Chevalier, Michel. *Society, Manners, and Politics in the United States: Letters on North America.* Edited and with an Introduction by John William Ward. Ithaca, New York: Cornell University Press, 1970. *16*

Chicago Commission on Race Relations. *The Negro in Chicago: A Study of Race Relations and a Race Riot.* 1922. Reprint. New York: Arno Press, 1968. *227*

Chinard, Gilbert. *Honest John Adams.* 1933. Reprint. Gloucester, Massachusetts: Peter Smith. *15, 74*

*_____. *Thomas Jefferson, the Apostle of Americanism.* 2d ed., rev. Ann Arbor: University of Michigan Press, Ann Arbor Books, 1957.

Chitwood, Oliver Perry. *John Tyler, Champion of the Old South.* 1939. Reprint. New York: Russell and Russell, 1964. *75*

*Chmaj, Betty E., and Judith A. Gustafson, eds. *Image, Myth and Beyond: American Women and American Studies, 2.* Pittsburgh, Pennsylvania: KNOW, Inc., 1972. *242, 253*

*Chopin, Kate. *The Awakening.* New York: Putnam, Capricorn Books, 1964. *250*

*_____. *The Storm and Other Stories.* Edited with an Introduction by Per Seyersted. Old Westbury, New York: Feminist Press, 1974. *243*

*Chudacoff, Howard P. *The Evolution of American Urban Society.* Englewood Cliffs, New Jersey: Prentice-Hall, 1975. *160, 161, 165*

_____. *Mobile Americans: Residential and Social Mobility in Omaha, 1880-1920.* New York: Oxford University Press, 1972.

•Clark, Arthur Melville. *Autobiography, Its Genesis and Phases.* Edinburgh, 1935. Reprint. New York: Folcroft Press, 1969. *24, 33*

*Clark, Kenneth B. *Dark Ghetto: Dilemmas of Social Power.* New York: Harper and Row, Harper Torchbooks, 1965. *98, 148*

*_____. *Prejudice and Your Child.* 2d ed. Boston: Beacon Press, 1963.

•Clark, Thomas, and F. Gerald Ham. *Pleasant Hill and the Shakers.* Shakertown Press, 1968. *210, 219*

Clarke, John H., ed. *Malcolm X: The Man and His Times.* New York: Macmillan, 1969. *29, 36*

*Cleaver, Eldridge. *Soul on Ice.* New York: Dell, 1970. *29, 34, 148*

•Cleaves, Freeman. *Old Tippecanoe: William Henry Harrison and His Time.* New York: Scribner's, 1939. *75*

*Clemens, Samuel L. (Mark Twain). *The Autobiography of Mark Twain.* Edited by Charles Neider. New York: Harper and Row, 1975. *26, 34*

•_____. *Mark Twain in Eruption.* Edited by Bernard De Voto. New York: Putnam, 1968.

•_____. *Mark Twain's Autobiography.* Edited by A. B. Paine. New York: Harper and Row, 1924.

•Clocker, Theodore W. *Trade Unionism in Baltimore Before the War of 1812.* Baltimore: Johns Hopkins University Press, 1907. *110*

•Coates, Ken, and Tony Topham, eds. *Workers' Control.* London: Panther/Modern Society, 1970. *127*

•Coban, Stanley, and Lorman Ratner. *The Development of an American Culture.* Englewood Cliffs, New Jersey: Prentice-Hall, 1970. *7*

Cobb, Edith. "The Ecology of Imagination in Childhood." In *The Subversive Science: Essays Toward an Ecology of Man,* edited by Paul Shepard and Daniel McKinley. Boston: Houghton Mifflin, 1969. *31, 37, 144*

Cochran, Thomas C. *American Business in the Twentieth Century.* Cambridge, Massachusetts: Harvard University Press, 1972. *13, 263*

*_____, and William Miller. *The Age of Enterprise, A Social History of Industrial America.* Rev. ed. New York: Harper and Row, Harper Torchbooks, 1968. *269*

Codman, John Thomas. *Brook Farm: Historic and Personal Memoirs.* 1894. Reprint. New York: AMS Press, 1971. *219*

•Coffey, Joseph, and Vincent P. Rock. *The Presidential Staff.* Washington, D.C.: National Planning Association, 1961. *71*

•Cohen, Hennig, ed. *The American Culture: Approaches to the Study of the United States.* Boston: Houghton Mifflin, 1968. *42, 262, 272*

•_____. *The American Experience: Approaches to the Study of the United States.* Boston: Houghton Mifflin, 1968.

•_____. *Landmarks of American Writing.* New York: Basic Books, 1969.

*_____, and William B. Dillingham, eds. *Humor of the Old Southwest.* Athens: University of Georgia Press, 1974.

•Cohen, Joseph. *The Sunrise Community.* n.p., 1939. *216, 219*

•Cohen, Morris. *American Thought: A Critical Sketch.* New York: Macmillan, 1954. *13*

•Cohen, Norman. *The Pursuit of the Millennium: Revolutionary Millenarians and Mystical Anarchism of the Middle Ages.* New York: Oxford University Press, 1970. *207, 219*

*Cohen, Ruth Schwartz. "A Case Study of Technological and Social Change: The Washing Machine and the Working Wife." In *Clio's Consciousness Raised: New Perspectives on the History of Women,* edited by Mary S. Hartman and Lois W. Banner. New York: Harper and Row, Harper Torchbooks, 1974. *254*

Cole, Donald B. *Immigrant City: Lawrence, Massachusetts, 1845-1921.* Chapel Hill: University of North Carolina Press, 1963. *116*

Cole, Margaret. *Robert Owen of New Lanark, 1771-1858.* 1953. Reprint. New York: Augustus M. Kelley, 1975. *111*

•Cole, Marley. *Jehovah's Witnesses: The New World Society.* New York: Vantage Press, 1955. *13, 20*

Coleman, Arthur, and Garry R. Tyler. *Drama Criticism: A Checklist of Interpretation Since 1940 of English and American Plays.* Chicago: Swallow Press, 1966. *46*

*Coleman, D. C., ed. *Revisions in Mercantilism.* New York: Barnes and Noble, 1965. *110*

Coletta, Paolo E. *The Presidency of William Howard Taft.* Lawrence: The University Press of Kansas, 1973. *78*

*Collier, John. *The Indians of the Americas.* Abridged ed. New York: New American Library, Mentor Books, 1952. *274*

*Collingwood, Robin George. *The Idea of Nature.* New York: Oxford University Press, Galaxy Books, 1960. *141*

Collins, Herbert R. *Presidents on Wheels: The Complete Collection of Carriages and Automobiles Used by Our American Presidents.* Washington, D.C.: Acropolis Books, 1971. *69*

*Commager, Henry Steele. *The American Mind: An Interpretation of American Thought and Character Since the 1880's.* New Haven, Connecticut: Yale University Press, 1950. *17, 266, 268*

*_____, ed. *Documents of American History*. 2 vols. 9th ed. New York: Appleton-Century-Crofts, 1974.

Commission on Non-Traditional Study and Samuel B. Gould. *Diversity by Design*. San Francisco: Jossey-Bass, 1973. *102*

Commons, John R. "American Shoemakers, 1648-1895: A Sketch of Industrial Evolution." *Quarterly Journal of Economics* 24 (November 1909):39-84. *105, 106, 107*

_____, et al. *History of Labor in the United States*. 4 vols. 1918. Reprint. New York: Augustus M. Kelley, 1966.

_____, et al., eds. *A Documentary History of American Industrial Society*. 10 vols. 2d ed. 1910. Reprint. New York: Russell and Russell, 1958.

*Conant, James Bryant. *The American High School Today: A First Report to Interested Citizens*. New York: McGraw-Hill, 1959. *97, 274*

*_____. *The Comprehensive High School: A Second Report to Interested Citizens*. New York: McGraw-Hill, 1967.

*_____. *The Education of American Teachers*. New York: McGraw-Hill, 1963.

*_____. *Modern Science and Modern Man*. Garden City, New York: Doubleday, Anchor Books, 1959.

•_____. *Recommendations for Education in the Junior High School Years: A Memorandum to School Boards*. Princeton, New Jersey: Education Testing Service, 1960.

*_____. *Shaping Educational Policy*. New York: McGraw-Hill, 1964.

*_____. *Slums and Suburbs: A Commentary on Schools in Metropolitan Areas*. New York: McGraw-Hill, 1963.

•Condit, Carl. *American Building Art: The Nineteenth Century*. New York: Oxford University Press, 1961. *166, 191, 192, 231, 232, 263*

•_____. *American Building Art: The Twentieth Century*. New York: Oxford University Press, 1961.

*_____. *American Building: Materials and Techniques from the Beginning of the Colonial Settlements to the Present*. Chicago: University of Chicago Press, 1968.

_____. *Chicago: Building, Planning, and Urban Technology. Volume I: 1910-1929. Volume II: 1930-1970*. Chicago: University of Chicago Press, 1973 and 1974.

_____. *The Chicago School of Architecture, A History of Commercial and Public Building in the Chicago Area, 1875-1925*. Chicago: University of Chicago Press, 1964.

Condon, Thomas. *New York Beginnings: The Commercial Origins of New Netherland*. New York: New York University Press, 1968. *56*

*Cone, James H. *Black Theology and Black Power*. New York: Seabury Press, Crossroad Books, 1969. *17*

*Conkin, Paul K. *The New Deal*. 2d ed. New York: Thomas Y. Crowell, 1975. *13, 121, 216, 219*

•_____. *Puritans and Pragmatists: Eight Eminent American Thinkers*. New York: Dodd, Mead, 1968.

•_____. *Tomorrow a New World: The New Deal Community Program*. Ithaca, New York: Cornell University Press, 1959.

*_____. *Two Paths to Utopia: The Hutterites and the Llano Colony*. Lincoln: University of Nebraska Press, 1964.

Conlin, Joseph, R. *Big Bill Haywood and the Radical Union Movement*. Syracuse, New York: Syracuse University Press, 1969. *118*

_____. *Bread and Roses Too: Studies of the Wobblies*. Westport, Connecticut: Greenwood Press, 1969.

Conway, Jill. "Women Reformers and American Culture, 1860-1930." *Journal of Social History* 5 (Winter 1971-1972):2. *245*

Cook, Warren L. *Flood Tide of Empire; Spain and the Northwest, 1543-1819*. New Haven, Connecticut: Yale University Press, 1973. *204*

Cooke, Donald E. *Atlas of the Presidents*. Maplewood, New Jersey: Hammond, 1967. *68*

*Cooper, James L., and Sheila McIsaac Cooper, eds. *The Roots of American Feminist Thought*. Boston: Allyn and Bacon, 1973. *252*

Cornwell, Elmer E., Jr. *Presidential Leadership of Public Opinion*. Bloomington: Indiana University Press, 1965. *72*

Cortesão, Armando. *History of Portuguese Cartography*. Lisbon, Portugal: Junta de Investigacoes do Ultramar, 1969. Vol. 1. (Agrupamento de Estudos de Cartografia Antigua. /Publicoes/ 6). *83, 92*

Corwin, Edward S. *The President: Office and Powers, 1787-1957.* 4th ed. New York: New York University Press, 1957. *69, 265*

_____, and J. W. Peltason. *Understanding the Constitution.* 6th ed. Hinsdale, Illinois: Dryden Press, 1973. *270*

Cotter, John. *Archaeological Excavations at Jamestown. . . . Virginia.* Washington, D.C.: National Park Service, U.S. Department of the Interior, 1958. *190, 192*

_____, and Paul J. Hudson. *New Discoveries at Jamestown.* Washington, D.C.: U.S. Government Printing Office, 1957. *190, 192*

*Cowing, Cedric. *The Great Awakening and the American Revolution: Colonial Thought in the 18th Century.* Chicago: Rand McNally, 1971. *15*

Cox, James M. "Autobiography and American." In *Aspects of Narrative,* edited by J. H. Miller. New York: Columbia University Press, 1971. *25, 26, 27, 28, 33*

•Cragg, Gerald. *From Puritanism to the Age of Reason: A Study of Changes in Religious Thought Within the Church of England, 1660 to 1700.* Cambridge, Massachusetts: Cambridge University Press, 1950. *15*

Craigie, William A., and James R. Hulbert. *A Dictionary of American English on Historical Principles.* 4 vols. Chicago: University of Chicago Press, 1938-1944. Supplement, New York, 1948. *270*

Crain, Robert L. *The Politics of School Desegregation: Comparative Case Studies of Community Structure and Policy-making.* Chicago: Aldine Publishing, 1968. *98*

*Cremin, Laurence. *The Transformation of the School; Progressivism in American Education, 1876-1957.* New York: Random House, Vintage Books, 1964. *230*

Cresson, William P. *James Monroe.* 1946. Reprint. Hamden, Connecticut: Shoe String Press, Archon Books, 1971. *74*

Crèvecoeur, J. Hector de. *Letters from an American Farmer.* New York: E. P. Dutton, 1957. *16, 26, 34*

Crews, Frederick C. "Do Literary Studies Have an Ideology?" *PMLA* 85 (May 1970):423-28. *29, 36*

Crone, Gerald R. *Maps and Their Makers: An Introduction to the History of Cartography.* 4th rev. ed. London: Hutchinson, 1968. *82, 83, 91*

•Cronin, Thomas E., and Sanford D. Greenberg, eds. *The Presidential Advisory System.* New York: Harper and Row, 1969. *71*

*Cross, Barbara M., ed. *The Educated Woman in America. Selected Writings of Catherine Beecher, Margaret Fuller, and M. Carey Thomas.* New York: Teachers' College Press, Columbia University, 1965. *18, 246*

•_____. *Horace Bushnell: Minister to a Changing America.* Chicago: University of Chicago Press, 1958.

*Cross, Robert. *The Emergence of Liberal Catholicism in America.* New York: Quadrangle Books, 1968. *19*

*Cross, Whitney. *The Burned-Over District: The Social and Intellectual History of Enthusiastic Religion in Western New York, 1800-1850.* New York: Harper and Row, Harper Torchbooks, 1950. *57, 212, 219*

Crouse, Nellis M. "Causes of the Great Migration." *New England Quarterly* 5 (1937):3-36. *109*

*Crowe, Charles, ed. *The Age of Civil War and Reconstruction, 1839-1900: A Book of Interpretive Essays.* Homewood, Illinois: Dorsey Press. 1975. *17*

Crozier, Alice C. *The Novels of Harriet Beecher Stowe.* New York: Oxford University Press, 1969. *239*

*Cruse, Harold. *The Crisis of the Negro Intellectual.* New York: Morrow, 1967. *126*

Cumming, William P. *The Southeast in Early Maps, with an Annotated Check List of Printed Manuscript Regional and Local Maps of Southeastern North America During the colonial Period.* 2d ed. Chapel Hill: University of North Carolina Press, 1962. *84, 92*

_____, R. A. Skelton, and D. B. Quinn. *The Discovery of North America.* New York: McGraw-Hill, 1972. *84, 92*

•Curley, James Michael. *I'd Do It Again: A Record of All My Uproarious Years.* Englewood Cliffs, New Jersey: Prentice-Hall, 1957. *159, 167*

Curti, Merle. "America at the World's Fairs, 1851-1893." *American Historical Review* 55 (1950):833-56. *13, 236, 268*

_____. *The Growth of American Thought.* 3d ed. New York: Harper and Row, 1964.

*Curtin, Philip. *The Atlantic Slave Trade: A Census.* Madison: University of Wisconsin Press, 1969. *54*

Curtis, James C. *The Fox at Bay: Martin Van Buren and the Presidency, 1837-1841.* Lexington: University Press of Kentucky, 1970. *75*

Dakin, Edwin F. *Mrs. Eddy: The Biography of a Virginal Mind.* 1929. Reprint. Gloucester, Massachusetts: Peter Smith, 1968. *12*

*Dangerfield, George. *The Era of Good Feelings.* New York: Harcourt, Brace, Jovanovich, 1963. *74*

•Daniels, George H., ed. *Darwinism Comes to America.* Waltham, Massachusetts: Blaisdell Publishing Company, 1968. *18*

*Dansereau, Pierre. "Ecological Impact and Human Ecology." In *Future Environments of North America,* edited by F. Fraser Darling and John P. Milton. Garden City, New York: The Natural History Press, 1966. *141*

Darling, F. Fraser. "The Unity of Ecology." *The Advancement of Science* 20 (November 1963): 297-306. *141*

_____. "A Wider Environment of Ecology and Conservation." *Daedalus* 96 (Fall 1967): 1003-19.

•_____, ed. *West Highland Survey: An Essay in Human Ecology.* New York: Oxford University Press, 1955.

Darrow, Clarence. *The Story of My Life.* New York: Scribner's, 1932. *26, 34, 226*

*David, Henry. *The History of the Haymarket Affair: A Study in the American Social-Revolution and Labor Movements.* Rev. ed. New York: Macmillan, Collier Books, 1963. *116*

David, Paul T., et al. *The Politics of National Party Conventions.* Rev. ed., abridged. Edited by Kathleen Sproul. Gloucester, Massachusetts: Peter Smith, 1964. *70, 72*

_____, et al., eds. *The Presidential Election and Transition of 1960-1961.* Washington, D.C.: The Brookings Institution, 1961.

*Davidson, Basil. *The African Slave Trade: Pre-Colonial History, 1450-1850.* Boston: Little Brown, 1961. *16*

*Davidson, Edward H. *Jonathan Edwards: The Narrative of a Puritan Mind.* New York: Houghton Mifflin, 1965. *15*

•Davidson, Gabriel. *Our Jewish Farmers and the Story of the Jewish Agricultural Society.* New York: L. B. Fischer, 1943. *216, 219*

Davies, Margery. "Woman's Place Is at the Typewriter—The Feminization of the Clerical Labor Force." *Radical America* 8 (July-August 1974):4. *256*

*Davis, Allen. *American Heroine: The Life and Legend of Jane Addams.* New York: Oxford University Press, 1975. *226, 245, 256*

*_____. *Spearheads for Reform: The Social Settlements and the Progressive Movement, 1890-1914.* New York: Oxford University Press, 1967.

_____. "The Women's Trade Union League: Origins and Organization." *Labor History* 5 (Winter 1964). *256*

•_____, and Mary Lynn McCree, eds. *Eighty Years at Hull House.* Chicago: Quadrangle Books, 1969. *233*

*Davis, Charles T., and Daniel Walden, eds. *On Being Black: Writings by Afro-Americans from Frederick Douglass to the Present.* Greenwich, Connecticut: Fawcett Publications, Premier Books, 1970. *151*

*David, David B. *The Problem of Slavery in Western Culture.* Ithaca, New York: Cornell University Press, 1966. *13, 16, 109*

*_____, ed. *The Fear of Conspiracy: Images of Un-American Subversion from the Revolution to the Present.* Ithaca, New York: Cornell University Press, 1971.

*Davis, George A., and O. Fred Donaldson. *Blacks in the United States: A Geographic Perspective.* Boston: Houghton Mifflin, 1975. *167*

*Davis, Rebecca Harding. *Life in the Iron Mills; or, the Korl Woman.* Old Westbury, New York: The Feminist Press, 1973. *243, 250*

*Davis, Sammy, Jr., and Jane Boyar and Burt Boyar. *Yes I Can: The Story of Sammy Davis, Jr.* New York: Pocket Books, 1972. *23, 33*

*Davison, Kenneth E. *The Presidency of Rutherford B. Hayes.* Westport, Connecticut: Greenwood Press, 1972. *76*

Day, Mark. *Forty Acres: Cesar Chavez and the Farm Workers.* New York: Praeger, 1971. *126*

*Debs, Eugene V. *Walls and Bars.* 2d ed. Chicago: C. H. Kerr, 1973. *226*

•DeCamp, L. Sprague, and Catherine C. DeCamp. *The Story of Science in America.* New York: Scribner's, 1967. *274*

•Dedmon, Emmett. *Fabulous Chicago.* New York: Random House, 1953. *225*

•Deer, Irving, and Harriet Deer, eds. *The Popular Arts: A Critical Reader.* New York: Scribner's 1967. *174, 182*

Deets, Lee Emerson. "The Hutterites: A Study in Social Cohesion." Ph.D. dissertation, Columbia University, 1939. *216, 219*

*Degler, Carl N. *Affluence and Anxiety: America Since 1945.* 2d ed. Glenview, Illinois: Scott, Foresman, 1975. *13, 245, 251, 269*

*_____. *Out of Our Past: The Forces That Shaped Modern America.* Rev. ed. New York: Harper and Row, 1970.

_____. "Revolution Without Ideology: The Changing Place of Women in America." In *The Woman in America,* edited by Robert Jay Lifton. Boston: Beacon Press, 1967.

_____. "What Ought to Be and What Was: Women's Sexuality in the Nineteenth Century." *American Historical Review* 79 (December 1974):5.

*DeGrazia, Sebastian. *Of Time, Work, and Leisure.* Garden City, New York: Doubleday, Anchor Books, 1962. *178, 182*

•Dell, Floyd. *The Briary Bush: A Novel.* New York: Alfred A. Knopf, 1921. *228*

_____. *Homecoming: An Autobiography.* 1933. Reprint. Port Washington, New York: Kennikat Press, 1969.

•_____. *Moon Calf: A Novel.* New York: Alfred A. Knopf, 1920.

*Deloria, Vine, Jr. *Custer Died for Your Sins.* New York: Avon Books, 1970. *202, 203, 205*

*_____. *God Is Red.* New York: Dell, Delta Books, 1975.

_____. *Of Utmost Good Faith.* New York: Simon and Schuster, Straight Arrow Books, 1971.

*_____. *We Talk, You Listen: New Tribes, New Turf.* New York: Dell, Delta Books, 1972.

Demarest, D. P., Jr. "The Autobiography of Malcolm X: Beyond Didacticism." *CLA Journal* 16 (December 1972):179-87. *29, 36*

*Demos, John. *A Little Commonwealth: Family Life in Plymouth Colony.* New York: Oxford University Press, Galaxy Books, 1971. *8, 190, 191, 192, 240*

*Denney, Reuel. *The Astonished Muse.* Rev. ed. Chicago: University of Chicago Press, 1974. *173, 182*

DePencier, Ida B. *The History of the Laboratory Schools, the University of Chicago, 1896-1965.* Chicago: Quadrangle Books, 1967. *236*

Derber, Milton. *The American Idea of Industrial Democracy, 1865-1965.* Urbana: University of Illinois Press, 1970. *121, 126*

_____, and Edwin Young, eds. *Labor and the New Deal.* 1957. Reprint. New York: Da Capo Press, 1972.

Desroche, Henri. *The American Shakers: From Neo-Christianity to Pre-Socialism.* Translated and edited by John K. Savacool. Amherst: University of Massachusetts Press, 1971. *210, 219*

*Destler, Chester McArthur. *American Radicalism, 1865-1901.* New York: Quadrangle Books, 1966. *116*

•Detzer, Karl. *Carl Sandburg: A Study in Personality and Background.* New York: Harcourt, Brace, Jovanovich, 1941. *229*

•DeVoto, Bernard. *Mark Twain's America.* New York: Little, Brown, 1932. *42*

*Dewey, John. *Democracy and Education.* New York: The Free Press, 1966. *97, 230, 264*

*_____. *Dewey on Education: Selections with an Introduction and Notes.* Edited by Martin S. Dworkin. New York: Teachers' College Press, Columbia University, 1957.

*_____. *School and Society.* 2d ed. Chicago: University of Chicago Press, Phoenix Books, 1915.

Dexter, Elizabeth A. *Colonial Women of Affairs: Women in Business and the Professions in America Before 1776.* 2d rev. ed. 1931. Reprint. New York: Augustus M. Kelley, 1971. *246*

Diamond, William. "On the Dangers of an Urban Interpretation of History." In *Historiography and Urbanization,* edited by Eric F. Goldman. Baltimore: Johns Hopkins University Press, 1941. *153, 167*

Dice, Lee R. *Man's Nature and Nature's Man: The Ecology of Human Communities.* 1955. Reprint. Westport, Connecticut: Greenwood Press, 1973. *139*

Dick, William M. *Labor and Socialism in America: The Gompers Era.* Port Washington, New York: Kennikat Press, 1972. *117*

Doenecke, Justus D. "Myths, Machines and Markets: The Columbian Exposition of 1893." *Journal of Popular Culture* 6 (Spring 1973):535-49. *236*

Dombrowski, James. *The Early Days of Christian Socialism in America.* New York: Octagon Books, 1966. *215, 219*

*Donald, Aida D. *John F. Kennedy and the New Frontier.* New York: Hill and Wang, 1966. *79*

Donnan, Elizabeth, ed. *Documents Illustrative of the History of the Slave-Trade to the United States of America.* 4 vols. New York: Octagon Books, 1965. *109*

•Donovan, Robert J. *The Assassins.* New York: Popular Library, 1964. *73, 79*

•_____. *Eisenhower: The Inside Story.* New York: Harper and Row, 1956.

Dorfman, Joseph. *The Economic Mind in American Civilization, 1606-1933.* 1946-1959. Reprint. New York: Augustus M. Kelley, 1966-1969. *230, 263*

_____. *Thorstein Veblen and His America.* 1934. Reprint. New York: Augustus M. Kelley, 1964.

*Dorson, Richard M. *American Folklore.* Chicago: University of Chicago Press, 1959. *188, 192, 264*

_____. *American Folklore and the Historian.* Chicago: University of Chicago Press, 1971.

Douglas, Ann. "The 'Scribbling Women' and Fanny Fern: Why Women Wrote." *American Quarterly* 23 (Spring 1971). *250*

*Douglass, Frederick. *Narrative of the Life of Frederick Douglass, An American Slave, Written by Himself.* Edited by Benjamin Quarles. Cambridge, Massachusetts: Harvard University Press, 1960. *29, 35*

*Downer, Alan S. *Fifty Years of American Drama, 1900-1950.* Chicago: H. Regnery, 1966. *272*

Downes, Randolph C. *The Rise of Warren Gamaliel Harding, 1865-1920.* Columbus: Ohio State University Press, 1970. *78*

*Dozier, Edward P. *Hano: A Tewa Community in Arizona.* New York: Holt, Rinehart, and Winston, 1966. *200, 201*

*Drake, St. Clair, and Horace R. Cayton. *Black Metropolis: A Study of Negro Life in a Northern City.* Rev. ed. 2 vols. New York: Harcourt, Brace, Jovanovich, 1970. *166, 226*

•Draper, Theodore. *American Communism and Soviet Russia: The Formative Period.* New York: Viking Press, 1960. *120, 124*

•_____. *The Roots of American Communism.* New York: Viking Press, 1957.

•Dreseir, Theodore. *A Book About Myself.* New York: Boni and Liveright, 1922, *26, 34, 227, 228*

•_____. *Dawn: A History of Myself.* New York: H. Liveright, 1922, *26, 34, 227,*

*_____. *The Financier.* New York: New American Library, Signet Books, 1967.

•_____. *Sister Carrie.* New York: New American Library, Signet Books, 1962.

•_____. *The Stoic.* Garden City, New York: Doubleday, 1947.

*_____. *The Titan.* New York: New American Library, Signet Books.

•Drinnon, Richard. *Rebel in Paradise: A Biography of Emma Goldman.* Chicago: University of Chicago Press, 1961. *248*

*Driver, Harold E. *Indians of North America.* 2d ed., rev. Chicago: University of Chicago Press, Phoenix Books, 1969. *54, 199*

*_____, and William Massey. *Comparative Studies of North American Indians.* Philadelphia: American Philosophical Society, 1957.

Drucker, Peter F. *The Practice of Management.* New York: Harper and Row, 1954. *264*

*Duberman, Martin B., ed. *The Anti-Slavery Vanguard: New Essays on the Abolitionists.* Princeton, New Jersey: Princeton University Press, 1965. *16, 114*

*Dubofsky, Melvin. *We Shall Be All: A History of the Industrial Workers of the World.* New York: Quadrangle Books, 1974. *118*

_____. *When Workers Organize: New York City in the Progressive Era.* Amherst: University of Massachusetts Press, 1968.

*DuBois, W. E. B. *The Autobiography of W. E. B. DuBois: A Soliloquy on Viewing My Life from the Last Decade of Its First Century.* New York: International Publishers, 1969. *17, 26, 34, 166*

•_____. *Dusk of Dawn: An Essay Toward an Autobiography of a Race Concept.* New York: Schocken Books, 1968.

*_____. *The Philadelphia Negro: A Social Study.* New York: Schocken Books, 1967.

*_____. *The Souls of Black Folk: Essays and Sketches.* New York: New American Library, Signet Books, 1969.

Dubos, Rene. "Environmental Biology." *Bioscience* 14 (January 1964): 11-14. *141*

_____. "Humanistic Biology." *The American Scholar* 34 (Spring 1965): 179-98.

*_____. *Man Adapting*. New Haven, Connecticut: Yale University Press, 1965.

*_____. *So Human an Animal*. New York: Scribner's, 1968.

Duffey, Bernard. *The Chicago Renaissance in American Letters: A Critical History*. 1956. Reprint. Westport, Connecticut: Greenwood Press, 1972. *227, 229*

Dulles, Foster Rhea. *America Learns to Play*. New York: Appleton-Century-Crofts, 1940. *106, 177, 182, 264, 269*

*_____. *A History of Recreation: America Learns to Play*. 2d ed. New York: Appleton-Century-Crofts, 1965.

_____. *Labor in America: A History*. 3d ed. Northbrook, Illinois: AHM Publishing, 1966. *106*

*Dumond, Dwight L. *Antislavery: The Crusade for Freedom in America*. New York: W. W. Norton, 1966. *16*

Duncan, Hugh D. *Culture and Democracy: The Struggle for Form in Society and Architecture in Chicago and the Middle West During the Life and Times of Louis H. Sullivan*. Totowa, New Jersey: Bedminister Press, 1965. *227, 232, 237*

•_____. *The Rise of Chicago as a Literary Center from 1885 to 1920, A Sociological Essay in American Culture*. Totowa, New Jersey: Bedminister Press, 1964.

Duncan, Otis Dudley, and Leo F. Schnore. "Cultural, Behavioral, and Ecological Perspectives in the Study of Social Organization." *American Journal of Sociology* 65 (September 1959): 132-46 *142*

_____. "From Social System to Ecosystem." *Sociological Inquiry* 31 (Spring 1961):140-49. *142*

*_____. "Social Organization and the Ecosystem." In *Handbook of Modern Sociology*, edited by Robert E. L. Faris. Chicago: Rand McNally, 1964.

Dunlop, John T. "The Development of Labor Organization: A Theoretical Framework." In *Insights into Labor Issues*, edited by Richard A. Lester and Joseph Shister. New York: Macmillan, 1948. *108*

•_____. *Industrial Relations Systems*. New York: Henry Holt, 1958.

*Dunn, Delmer D. *Financing Presidential Campaigns*. Washington, D.C.: The Brookings Institution, 1972. *70*

Dunne, Finley Peter. *Mr. Dooley: Now and Forever*. Stanford, California: Academic Reprints, 1954. *228*

*_____. *Mr. Dooley on Ivrything and Iverybody*. New York: Dover, 1963.

•_____. *Mr. Dooley Remembers: The Informal Memoirs of Finley Peter Dunne*. Boston: Little, Brown, 1963.

*Dunne, John Gregory. *Delano: The Story of the California Grape Strike*. Rev. ed. New York: Farrar, Strauss and Giroux, Noonday Books, 1971. *126*

Durbin, Louise. *Inaugural Cavalcade*. New York: Dodd, Mead, 1971. *71*

•Durham, Philip. *Down These Mean Streets a Man Must Go: Raymond Chandler's Knight*. Chapel Hill: University of North Carolina Press, 1963. *182*

Duss, John. *The Harmonists: A Personal History*. 1943. Reprint. Philadelphia: Porcupine Press, 1973. *211, 219*

Duster, Alfred M., ed. *Crusade for Justice: The Autobiography of Ida B. Wells*. Chicago: University of Chicago Press, 1970. *248*

•Dwight, Sereno. *The Works of Jonathan Edwards*. 10 vols. New York: G. and C. and H. Carvill, 1830. *15*

Dyer, Brainerd. *Zachary Taylor*. New York: Barnes and Noble, 1967. *75*

Dyos, H. J. "Some Historical Reflections on the Quality of Urban Life." In *The Quality of Urban Life*, edited by Henry J. Schmandt and Warner Bloomberg, Jr. Beverly Hills, California: Sage, 1969. *157, 161, 163, 167, 168*

_____, ed. *The Study of Urban History*. New York: St. Martin's Press, 1968.

_____, and Michael Wolff, eds. *The Victorian City: Images and Realities*. 2 vols. London: Routledge and Kegan Paul, 1973. *164*

Easton, Lloyd D. *Hegel's First American Followers: The Ohio Hegelians*. Athens: Ohio University Press, 1966. *19*

•Eaton, Herbert. *Presidential Timber: A History of Nominating Conventions, 1868-1960*. New York: The Free Press of Glencoe, 1964. *70*

•Eaton, Joseph, and Robert J. Weil. *Culture and Mental Disorders: A Comparative Study of the Hutterites and Other Populations*. Glencoe, Illinois: The Free Press, 1955. *215, 219*

Eble, Kenneth E. *The Recognition and Evaluation of Teaching*. Washington, D.C.: American Association of University Professors, 1970. *103*

Edel, Leon. *Henry James*. 5 vols. Philadelphia: J. B. Lippincott, 1953-1972. *27, 35, 43*

*Edwards, Harry. *Black Students*. New York: The Free Press, 1970. *148*

*Edwards, Jonathan. "Personal Narrative." In *The American Tradition in Literature*, Vol. 1, edited by Sculley Bradley et al. 2 vols. New York: W. W. Norton, 1974. *25, 28, 33*

*Edwards, Richard, et al., eds. *The Capitalist System: A Radical Analysis of American Society*. Englewood Cliffs, New Jersey: Prentice-Hall, 1972. *126*

Egbert, Donald, and Stow Persons. *Socialism and American Life*. 2 vols. Princeton, New Jersey: Princeton University Press, 1952. *117, 208, 219*

Eggert, Gerald G. *Railroad Labor Disputes: The Beginnings of Federal Strike Policy*. Ann Arbor: University of Michigan Press, 1967. *120*

Egler, Frank E. "Pesticides in Our Ecosystem." *American Scientist* 52 (March 1964):110-36. *139, 145*

*Ehrenreich, Barbara, and Deirdre English. *Witches, Midwives, and Nurses: A History of Women Healers*. 2d ed. Old Westbury, New York: The Feminist Press, 1973. *257*

*_____. *Complaints and Disorders: The Sexual Politics of Sickness*. Old Westbury, New York: The Feminist Press, 1973.

*Eisen, Jonathan, ed. *The Age of Rock: Sounds of the American Cultural Revolution*. New York: Random House, Vintage Books, 1970. *180, 182*

Eisenhower, Dwight D. *The White House Years*. Vol. 1, *Mandate for Change, 1953-1956;* Vol. 2, *Waging Peace, 1956-1961*. Garden City, New York: Doubleday, 1963-1965. *68*

*Ekirch, Arthur. *Man and Nature in America*. Lincoln: University of Nebraska Press, Bison Books, 1973. *140*

*Eliade, Mircea. *Myth and Reality*. New York: Harper and Row, Harper Torchbooks, 1963. *181, 182*

Eliot, T. S. *Selected Essays*. New ed. New York: Harcourt, Brace, Jovanovich, 1950. *182*

*Ellis, John Tracy. *American Catholicism*. 2d ed., rev. Chicago: University of Chicago Press, 1969. *12*

•_____. *Catholics in Colonial America*. Baltimore: Helicon, 1965.

*Ellison, Ralph. *Shadow and Act*. New York: Random House, Vintage Books, 1972. *29, 36*

*Ellsworth, Lucius F. "Directory of Artifact Collections." In *Technology in Early America: Needs and Opportunities for Study*, by Brooke Hindle. Chapel Hill: University of North Carolina Press, 1966. *189*

*Elton, Charles. *Animal Ecology*. New York: Halsted Press, 1966. *137, 144*

_____. *The Ecology of Invasions by Animals and Plants*. New York: Halsted Press, 1966.

Ely, Richard T. *The Labor Movement in America*. 1890. Reprint. New York: Arno Press, 1969. *105, 227*

_____. "Pullman, A Social Study." *Harper's New Monthly Magazine* (February 1885).

English, Maurice, ed. *The Testament of Stone: Themes of Idealism and Indignation from the Writings of Louis Sullivan*. Evanston, Illinois: Northwestern University Press, 1963. *231*

*Enroth, Ronald M., et al. *The Jesus People: Old-Time Religion in the Age of Aquarius*. Grand Rapids, Michigan: William B. Eerdman's, 1972. *21*

*Epstein, Cynthia Fuchs. *Woman's Place: Options and Limits in Professional Careers*. Berkeley: University of California Press, 1970. *251*

*Equiano, Olaudah. *The Life of Olaudah Equiano, Or Gustavus Vassa, Written by Himself*. In *Great Slave Narratives*, edited by Arna Bontemps. Boston: Beacon Press, 1969. *25, 29, 34*

Erickson, Charlotte J. *American Industry and the European Immigrant, 1860-1885*. 1957. Reprint. New York: Russell and Russell, 1967. *116*

*Erikson, Erik H. *Childhood and Society*. Rev. ed. New York: W. W. Norton, 1964. *30, 31, 36, 37, 99*

*_____. "The Concept of Identity in Race Relations: Notes and Queries." In *The Negro American*, edited by T. Parsons and K. B. Clark. Boston: Houghton Mifflin, 1966.

_____. "Gandhi's *Autobiography:* The Leader as a Child." *American Scholar* 35 (Autumn 1966):362-46.

*_____. *Gandhi's Truth: On the Origins of Militant Non-Violence*. New York: W. W. Norton, 1969.

_____. "A Memorandum on Identity and Negro Youth." *Journal of Social Issues* 20 (October 1964):29-42.

_____. "Race and the Wider Identity." In *Identity: Youth and Crisis*. New York: W. W. Norton, 1968.

*Erikson, Kai T. *Wayward Puritans: A Study in the Sociology of Deviance.* New York: Wiley, 1966. *8*

*Essien-Udom, E. U. *Black Nationalism: A Search for an Identity in America.* Chicago: University of Chicago Press, Phoenix Books, 1972. *17*

*Estall, Robert. *Modern Geography of the United States.* New York: Penguin, Pelican Books, 1972. *51, 52*

Evans, Francis C. "Ecosystem as the Basic Unit in Ecology." *Science* 123 (June 22, 1956): 1127-28. *144*

Evans, Frederick W. *Shakers: Compendium of the Origin, History, Principles, Rules and Regulations, Government, and Doctrines of the United Society of Believers in Christ's Second Appearing.* 1859. Reprint. New York: B. Franklin, 1972. *210, 219*

Evans, George Frederick. *Autobiography of a Shaker and Revelation of the Apocalypse.* 1888. Reprint. Philadelphia: Porcupine Press, 1972. *219*

_____. *Expose of the Condition and Progress of the North American Phalanx.* 1853. Reprint. Philadelphia: Porcupine Press, 1974.

*Evans, Rowland, and Robert D. Novak. *Nixon in the White House: The Frustration of Power.* New York: Random House, Vintage Books, 1971. *80*

Ewers, John C. *The Blackfeet: Raiders on the Northwestern Plains.* 1958. Reprint. Norman: University of Oklahoma Press, 1967. *200*

Eyre, S. R. "Determinism and Ecological Approach to Geography." *Geography* 49 (November 1964):369-76. *142*

_____, and G. R. J. Jones, eds. *Geography as Human Ecology: Methodology by Example.* London: Edward Arnold Ltd., 1966. *144*

*Fabos, Julius Gy. *Frederick Law Olmsted, Dr., Founder of Landscape Architecture in America.* Amherst: University of Massachusetts Press, 1969. *231*

Fabre, Michel. *The Unfinished Quest of Richard Wright.* Translated by Isabel Barzun. New York: Morrow, 1973. *27, 31, 35*

Fainsod, Merle, and Lincoln Gordon. *Government and the American Economy.* 3d ed. New York: W. W. Norton, 1959. *265.*

*Fairfield, Richard. *Communes U.S.A.; A Personal Tour.* Baltimore: Penguin, 1972. *217, 219*

Falk, Robert P. *The Victorian Mode in American Fiction, 1865-1885.* East Lansing: Michigan State University Press, 1966. *44*

Falor, Paul. "Working Class Historiography." *Radical America* 3 (March-April 1969): 56-68. *106*

*Fanon, Franz. *The Wretched of the Earth.* Translated by Constance Ferrington. New York: Grove Press, 1965. *146*

•Farb, Peter, et al. *Ecology.* New York: Time-Life Books, 1970. *136, 195*

* _____. *Man's Rise to Civilization as Shown by the Indians of North America from Primeval Times to the Coming of the Industrial State.* New York: Avon, 1969. *195*

*Faris, Robert E. L. *Chicago Sociology, 1920-1932.* Chicago: University of Chicago Press, Phoenix Books, 1970. *236*

Farr, Finis. *Chicago: A Personal History of America's Most American City.* New Rochelle, New York: Arlington House, 1973. *225*

*Faulkner, Harold U. *The Quest for Social Justice: 1898-1914.* New York: Watts, Franklin, New Viewpoints Books, 1931. *174*

*Fauset, Arthur H. *Black Gods of the Metropolis: Negro Religious Cults of the Urban North.* Philadelphia: University of Pennsylvania Press, 1971. *17*

*Faust, Clarence H., and Thomas H. Johnson, eds. *Jonathan Edwards: Representative Selections.* New York: Hill and Wang, 1962. *15*

*Featherstone, Joseph. *Schools Where Children Learn.* New York: Liveright, 1971. *100*

*Fee, Elizabeth. "The Sexual Politics of Victorian Social Anthropology." In *Clio's Consciousness Raised: New Perspectives on the History of Women,* edited by Mary S. Hartman and Lois W. Banner. New York: Harper and Row, 1974. *253*

Feerick, John D. *From Failing Hands: The Story of Presidential Succession.* New York: Fordham University Press, 1965. *72*

Fenin, George, and William K. Everson. *The Western: From Silents to the Seventies.* Rev. ed. New York: Grossman, 1973. *176, 182*

•Fenno, Richard F. *The President's Cabinet: An Analysis in the Period from Wilson to Eisenhower.* Cambridge, Massachusetts: Harvard University Press, 1959. *71*

Ferm, Robert L., ed. *Issues in American Protestantism: A Documentary History from the*

Puritans to the Present. Gloucester, Massachusetts: Peter Smith, 1969. *12*

*Ferman, Louis A., Joyce L. Kornbluh, and J. A. Miller, eds. *Negroes and Jobs, A Book of Readings*. Ann Arbor: University of Michigan Press, 1968. *125*

*Feuer, Lewis F. "The Alienated Americans and Their Influence on Marx and Engels." In *Marx and the Intellectuals*, by Lewis F. Feuer. Garden City, New York: Doubleday, Anchor Books, 1969. *111*

Fiedler, Leslie A. *Love and Death in the American Novel*. Rev. ed. New York: Stein and Day, 1966. *8, 197*

*_____. *The Return of the Vanishing American*. New York: Stein and Day, 1969.

*Filler, Louis. *The Crusade Against Slavery, 1830-1860*. New York: Harper and Row, Harper Torchbooks, 1960. *16, 114, 213, 219, 267*

_____. *The Unknown Edwin Markham; His Mystery and Its Significance*. Kent, Ohio: Kent State University Press, 1966.

Fine, Sidney A. *The Automobile Under the Blue Eagle: Labor, Management, and the Automobile Manufacturing Code*. Ann Arbor: University of Michigan Press, 1963. *122*

_____. *Sitdown: The General Motors Strike of 1936-1937*. Ann Arbor: University of Michigan Press, 1969.

*Finer, Herman. *The Presidency: Crisis and Regeneration, An Essay in Possibilities*. Chicago: University of Chicago Press, 1960. *72*

*Firestone, Shulamith. *The Dialectic of Sex: The Case for Feminist Revolution*. New York: Bantam Books, 1971. *249*

*Fisch, Max H., ed. *Classic American Philosophers: Peirce, James, Royce, Santayana, Dewey, Whitehead: Selections from Their Writings*. New York: Prentice-Hall, 1966. *13*

*Fishel, Leslie H., Jr., and Benjamin Quarles. *The Black Americans: A Documentary History*. Rev. ed. Glenview, Illinois: Scott, Foresman, 1970. *150*

*Fishwick, Marshall, and Ray B. Browne, eds. *Icons of Popular Culture*. Bowling Green, Ohio: Bowling Green University Popular Press, 1970. *176, 182*

*Fite, Emerson D., and Archibald Freeman. *A Book of Old Maps, Delineating American History from the Earliest Days Down to the Close of the Revolutionary War*. New York: Dover, 1970. *85, 92*

*Fitzgerald, F. Scott. *The Crack-Up*. Edited by Edmund Wilson. New York: J. Laughlin, New Directions, 1956. *26, 35*

Fleming, E. McClung. "Early American Decorative Arts as Social Documents." *The Mississippi Valley Historical Review* 45 (September 1958):276-84. *187, 192*

*Flexner, Eleanor. *Century of Struggle: The Woman's Rights Movement in the United States*. New York: Atheneum, 1968. *244*

Flexner, James Thomas. *George Washington: Anguish and Farewell (1793-1799)*. Boston: Little, Brown, 1972. *73*

_____. *George Washington and the New Nation (1783-1793)*. Boston: LIttle, Brown, 1970.

*Flynn, Elizabeth Gurley. *The Rebel Girl: An Autobiography, My First Life, 1906-1926*. Rev. ed. New York: International Publishers, 1973. *248*

*Fogarty, Robert S., ed. *American Utopianism*. Itasca, Illinois: F. E. Peacock, 1972. *212, 217, 220*

*Fogel, Robert W., and Stanley L. Engerman. *Time on the Cross: The Economics of American Negro Slavery*. 2 vols. Boston: Little, Brown, 1974. *165*

Fogelson, Robert M. *The Fragmented Metropolis: Los Angeles, 1850-1930*. Cambridge, Massachusetts: Harvard University Press, 1967. *160, 168*

*Foner, Eric. *Free Soil, Free Labor, Free Men: The Ideology of the Republican Party Before the Civil War*. New York: Oxford University Press, Galaxy Books, 1971. *113*

*Foner, Philip S. *History of the Labor Movement in the United States*. 4 vols. 2d ed. New York: International Publishers, New World Paperbacks, 1975. *106*

*Forcey, Charles. *The Crossroads of Liberalism: Croly, Weyl, Lippmann and the Progressive Era, 1900-1925*. New York: Oxford University Press, Galaxy Books, 1967. *118*

Forman, Henry Chandlee. *The Architecture of the Old South: The Medieval Style, 1585-1850*. 1948. Reprint. New York: Russell and Russell, 1967. *187, 192*

*Forten, C. L. *Journal of Charlotte L. Forten: A Free Negro in the Slave Era*. New York: Macmillan, Collier Books, 1961. *29, 36*

Fosberg, F. R. "The Island Ecosystem." In *Man's Place in the Island Ecosystem: A Symposium*, edited by F. R. Fosberg. Bishop Museum Press, 1963. *144*

Foster, Charles I. *An Errand of Mercy: The Evangelical United Front, 1790-1837*. Chapel Hill: University of North Carolina Press, 1960. *16*

Fourier, Francois Marie Charles. *The Passions of the Human Soul and Their Influence on Society and Civilization.* Translated by Hugh Doherty. 1851. 2 vols. Reprint. New York: Augustus M. Kelley, 1968. *212, 220*

*Fox, George. *Journal.* Edited by Norman Penney. New York: E. P. Dutton, Everyman Books, 1973. *14, 25*

*Franklin, Benjamin. *The Autobiography of Benjamin Franklin.* Edited by L. W. Larrabee, et al. New Haven, Connecticut: Yale University, 1964. *23, 28, 32*

*Franklin, John Hope. *From Slavery to Freedom: A History of Negro Americans.* 4th ed. New York: Alfred A. Knopf, 1974. *109, 114, 148, 267*

*_____. *Reconstruction: After the Civil War.* Chicago: University of Chicago Press, 1961.

*_____, and Isidore Starr, eds. *The Negro in Twentieth-Century America: A Reader on the Struggle for Civil Rights.* New York: Random House, Vintage Books, 1967. *274*

Franklin, Vincent P. "Slavery, Personality, and Black Culture—Some Theoretical Issues." *Phylon* 35 (March 1974):54-63. *37*

*Frazier, E. Franklin. *The Negro Church in America.* With supplement, *The Black Church Since Frazier,* by C. Eric Lincoln. New York: Schocken Books, 1973. *12, 17*

*Fredrickson, George M. *The Inner Civil War: Northern Intellectuals and the Crisis of the Union.* New York: Harper and Row, Harper Torchbooks, 1965. *17*

•Freeman, Douglas Southall. *George Washington: A Biography.* 7 vols. New York: Scribner's, 1948-1957. *73, 267*

Freeman, Mary Wilkins. *The Revolt of Mother and Other Stories.* Old Westbury, New York: The Feminist Press, 1974. *243, 250*

•Freeman, Otis W., and Howard H. Martin, eds. *The Pacific Northwest: An Overall Appreciation.* 2d ed. New York: Wiley, 1954. *53*

Freidel, Frank B. *Franklin D. Roosevelt.* 4 vols. Boston: Little, Brown, 1952-1973. *79, 121*

_____. *The New Deal in Historical Perspective.* 2d ed. Washington, D.C.: American Historical Association, 1965.

_____, and Richard Showman, eds. *Harvard Guide to American History.* 2 vols. Rev. ed. Cambridge, Massachusetts: The Belknap Press of Harvard University Press, 1974. *284*

Freilich, Morris. "Ecology and Culture: Environmental Determinism and the Ecological Approach to Anthropology." *Anthropological Quarterly* 40 (January 1967):26-43. *142*

•Freitag, Ruth S. *Presidential Inaugurations: A Selected List of References.* 3d rev. ed. Washington, D.C.: The Library of Congress, 1969. *71*

*Friedan, Betty. The Feminine Mystique. New York: Dell, 1975. *249, 257*

Friedenberg, Edgar Z. *Coming of Age in America: Growth and Acquiescence.* New York: Random House, 1965. *99*

•Friedheim, Robert L. *The Seattle General Strike.* Seattle: University of Washington Press, 1964. *120*

*Friedman, Jean E., and William G. Shade, eds. *Our American Sisters: Women in American Life and Thought.* Boston: Allyn and Bacon, 1973. *252*

Friis, Herman. *A Series of Population Maps of the Colonies and the United States, 1625-1790.* Rev. ed. New York: American Geographic Society, 1968. *55*

*Frothingham, Octavius B. *Transcendentalism in New England: A History.* Philadelphia: University of Pennsylvania Press, 1972. *18*

*Fuchs, Estelle. *Pickets at the Gates.* New York: The Free Press, 1966. *98*

*Fuess, Claude. *Calvin Coolidge, the Man from Vermont.* Hamden, Connecticut: Archon Books, 1965. *78*

Fuller, Henry Blake. *The Cliff-Dwellers.* 1893. Reprint. Ridgewood, New York: Gregg Press, 1968.

_____. *Under the Skylights.* 1901. Reprint. New York: Mss Information Company, 1972.

*_____. *With the Procession.* Chicago: University of Chicago Press, Phoenix Books, 1965.

*Fuller, Margaret. *Woman in the Nineteenth Century.* 1855. Reprint. New York: W. W. Norton, 1971. *246*

*Fullinwider, S. P. *The Mind and the Mood of Black America: 20th Century Thought.* Homewood, Illinois: Dorsey Press, 1969. *17*

•Furman, Bess. *White House Profile, A Social History of the White House, Its Occupants and Its Festivities.* Indianapolis, Indiana: Bobbs-Merrill, 1951. *73*

Furniss, Edgar S. *The Position of the Laborer in a System of Nationalism: A Study in the Labor Theories of the Later English Mercantilists.* 1920. Reprint. New York: Augustus M. Kelley, 1965. *110*

Furniss, Norman F. *The Fundamentalist Controversy, 1918-1930.* 1954. Reprint. Hamden, Connecticut: Archon Books, 1963. *20*

Gabriel, Ralph H. *The Course of American Democratic Thought.* 2d ed. New York: Ronald Press, 1956. *13*

*Galbraith, John Kenneth. *The New Industrial State.* 2d rev. ed. Boston: Houghton Mifflin, Sentry Books, 1972. *9*

•Galenson, Walter. *The CIO Challenge to the A.F. of L.: A History of the American Labor Movement, 1935-1941.* Cambridge, Massachusetts: Harvard University Press, 1960. *121*

Ganong, William F. *Crucial Maps in the Early Cartography and Place-Nomenclature of the Atlantic Coast of Canada.* With an introduction, commentary, and map notes by Theodore E. Layng. Toronto, Canada: University of Toronto Press, 1964. *86, 93*

*Gans, Herbert J. *The Urban Villagers: Group and Class in the Life of Italian-Americans.* New York: The Free Press, 1962. *159, 168*

*Gardner, John W. *Excellence: Can We Be Equal and Excellent, Too?* New York: Harper and Row, 1971. *98, 101*

*_____. *Self-Renewal: The Individual and the Innovative Society.* New York: Harper and Row, 1964.

•Garfield, James A. *The Diary of James A. Garfield.* Edited by Harry James Brown and Frederick D. Williams. 3 vols. East Lansing: Michigan State University Press, 1967. *68*

Garland, Hamlin. *Companions on the Trail.* 1931. Reprint. New York: Somerset Publishers. *227*

•_____. *Crumbling Idols: Twelve Essays on Art Dealing Chiefly with Literature, Painting, and the Drama.* Edited by Jane Johnson. Cambridge, Massachusetts: The Belknap Press of Harvard University Press, 1960.

_____. *A Daughter of the Middle Border.* 1930. Reprint. Gloucester, Massachusetts: Peter Smith, 1960.

_____. *Roadside Meetings.* 1930. Reprint. New York: Scholarly Reprints, 1971.

•Garland, John, ed. *The North American Midwest: A Regional Geography.* New York: Wiley, 1955. *53*

•Garraty, John A. *Labor and Capital in the Gilded·Age: 1883.* Boston: Little, Brown, 1969. *116*

•Garvan, Anthony N. B. *Architecture and Town Planning in Colonial Connecticut.* New Haven, Connecticut: Yale University Press, 1951. *187, 191, 192*

_____. "Historical Depth in Comparative Culture Study." *American Quarterly* 14 (Summer 1962):260-74.

Gasper, Louis. *The Fundamentalist Movement.* The Hague: Mouton, 1963. *20*

Gatewood, Willard B., Jr. *Controversy in the Twenties: Fundamentalism, Modernism, and Evolution.* Nashville, Tennessee: Vanderbilt University Press, 1969. *20, 77*

_____. *Theodore Roosevelt and the Art of Controversy: Episodes of the White House Years.* Baton Rouge: Louisiana State University Press, 1970.

*Gaustad, Edwin S. *The Great Awakening in New England.* New York: Quadrangle Books, 1968. *12, 14, 57*

•_____. *Historical Atlas of Religion in America.* New York: Harper and Row, 1962.

*_____. *A Religious History of America.* New York: Harper and Row, 1966.

*_____. *Religious Issues in American History.* New York: Harper and Row, 1968.

*Gay, Peter. *The Enlightenment, an Interpretation: The Rise of Modern Paganism.* New York: Random House, Vintage Books, 1968. *15*

*Gayle, Addison, Jr. *Black Expression: Essays by and About Black Americans in the Creative Arts.* New York: Weybright and Talley, 1969. *151*

•Geismar, Maxwell. *The Ring Lardner Reader.* New York: Scribner's, 1963. *235*

*Genovese, Eugene D. *The Political Economy of Slavery: Studies in the Economy and Society of the Slave South.* New York: Random House, Vintage Books, 1965. *7, 8, 16, 114*

Gerlach, Arch, ed. *The National Atlas of the United States.* Washington, D.C.: U.S. Geological Survey, 1970. *51*

*Gerstenberger, Donna, and George Hendrick. *The American Novel: A Checklist of Twentieth Century Criticism.* 2 vols. Chicago: Swallow Press, 1961-1970. *46*

*_____, eds. *Third Directory of Periodicals Publishing Articles on English and American Literature and Language.* Chicago: Swallow Press, 1970. *46*

Gettys, W. E. "Human Ecology and Social Theory." *Social Forces* 18 (May 1940):469-76. *142*

Gewehr, Wesley M. *The Great Awakening in Virginia, 1740-1790.* 1930. Reprint. Gloucester, Massachusetts: Peter Smith, 1965. *14*

*Gibson, Arrell M. *The Chickasaws.* Norman: University of Oklahoma Press, 1972. *196, 204*

_____. *The Kickapoos: Lords of the Middle Border.* Norman: University of Oklahoma Press, 1963.

Gibson, William M., and George R. Petty, Jr. *Project Occult: The Ordered Computer Collation of an Unprepared Text.* New York University Press, 1970. *45*

*Giedion, Sigfried. *Mechanization Takes Command: A Contribution to Anonymous History.* New York: W. W. Norton, 1969. *185, 188, 192, 227, 231*

_____. *Space, Time and Architecture: The Growth of a New Tradition.* 5th rev. ed. Cambridge, Massachusetts: Harvard University Press, 1967.

*Gilbert, James. *Designing the Industrial State: The Intellectual Pursuit of Collectivism in America, 1880-1940.* Chicago: Quadrangle Books, 1972. *118*

Gillispie, Charles C. *Genesis and Geology: A Study in the Relations of Scientific Thought, Natural Theology, and Social Opinion in Great Britain, 1790-1850.* Santa Fe, New Mexico: William Gannon, 1970. *18*

*Gilman, Charlotte Perkins. *The Home: Its Work and Influence.* 1903. Reprint. Urbana: University of Illinois Press, 1970. *243, 248, 250, 251*

_____. *The Living of Charlotte Perkins Gilman: An Autobiography.* New York: Harper and Row, 1975.

*_____. *Women and Economics: The Economic Factor Between Men and Women as a Factor in Social Evolution.* Edited by Carl Degler. New York: Harper and Row, Harper Torchbooks, 1970.

*_____. *The Yellow Wallpaper.* Old Westbury, New York: The Feminist Press, 1973.

•Gilman, Richard. *The Confusion of Realms.* New York: Random House, 1969. *24, 29, 33*

*Ginger, Ray. *Age of Excess: American Life from the End of Reconstruction to World War I.* 2d ed. New York: Macmillan, 1975. *20, 116, 118*

*_____. *Altgeld's America: The Lincoln Ideal Versus Changing Realities.* New York: Franklin, Watts, New Viewpoints Books, 1965.

_____. *The Bending Cross: A Biography of Eugene V. Debs.* 1949. Reprint. New York: Russell and Russell, 1969.

*_____. *Six Days or Forever? Tennessee v. John Thomas Scopes.* New York: Oxford University Press, Galaxy Books, 1974.

*Ginzberg, Eli, et al. *The Middle-Class Negro in the White Man's World.* New York: Columbia University Press, 1969. *98*

*Giovanni, Nikki. *Gemini: An Extended Autobiographical Statement on My First Twenty Five Years of Being a Black Poet.* New York: Viking Press, Compass Books, 1973. *248*

Glaab, Charles N. "The Historian and the American City: A Bibliographical Survey." In *The Study of Urbanization.* New York: Wiley, 1965. *153, 158, 168*

_____. "Historical Perspective on Urban Development Schemes." In *Urban Research and Planning,* edited by Leo F. Schnore and Henry Fagin. Beverly Hills, California: Sage, 1967.

*_____, and A. Theodore Brown. *A History of Urban America.* New York: Macmillan, 1967. *161, 168*

Glacken, Clarence. *Traces on the Rhodian Shore: Nature and Culture in Western Thought from Ancient Times to the End of the Eighteenth Century.* Berkeley: University of California Press, 1973. *139*

*Glassie, Henry. *Pattern in the Material Folk Culture of the Eastern United States.* Rev. ed. Philadelphia: University of Pennsylvania Press, 1971. *56, 188, 192*

*Glazer, Nathan. *American Judaism.* Chicago: University of Chicago Press, 1972. *12*

Gleason, Philip. *The Conservative Reformers: German-American Catholics and the Social Order.* Notre Dame, Indiana: University of Notre Dame Press, 1968. *19*

Gluck, Elsie. *John Mitchell, Miner: Labor's Bargain with the Gilded Age.* 1929. Reprint. New York: AMS Press, 1971. *118*

Goen, Clarence C. *Revivalism and Separatism in New England, 1740-1800: Strict Congregationalists and Separate Baptists in the Great Awakening.* 1962. Reprint. Hamden, Connecticut: Shoe String Press, Archon Books, 1969. *14*

Gohdes, Clarence, ed. *Bibliographical Guide to the Study of the Literature of the USA.* 3d rev. ed. Durham, North Carolina: Duke University Press, 1970. *270*

•Goldberg, Arthur. *AFL-CIO: Labor United.* New York: McGraw-Hill, 1956. *125*

*Goldman, Emma. *Anarchism and Other Essays.* New York: Dover, 1970. *248*

*_____. *Living My Life: The Autobiography of Emma Goldman.* 2 vols. New York: Dover, 1970.

*Goldman, Eric. *The Tragedy of Lyndon Johnson: A Historian's Personal Interpretation.* New York: Dell, 1969. *80*

•Goldmark, Josephine. *Impatient Crusader: Florence Kelley's Life Story.* Urbana: University of Illinois Press, 1953. *249*

Gollin, Gillian Lindt. *Moravians in Two Worlds: A Study of Changing Communities.* New York: Columbia University Press, 1967. *209, 220*

*Goodman, Paul. *Growing Up Absurd: Problems of Youth in the Organized System.* New York: Random House, Vintage Books, 1960. *99*

*_____, and Percival Goodman. *Communitas: Means of Livelihood and Ways of Life.* Rev. ed. New York: Random House, Vintage Books, 1960. *220*

Gordon, Ann, Mari Jo Buhle, and Nancy Schrom. "Women in American Society: An Historical Contribution." *Radical America* 5 (July-August 1971):4. *247*

*Gornik, Vivian, and Barbara K. Moran, eds. *Woman in Sexist Society: Studies in Power and Powerlessness.* New York: New American Library, Signet Books, 1972. *252*

*Gorz, Andre. *Strategy for Labor: A Radical Proposal.* Boston: Beacon Press, 1967. *127*

*Gosnell, Harold F. *Machine Politics, The Chicago Model.* 2d ed. Chicago: University of Chicago Press, Phoenix Books, 1968. *225, 226*

*_____. *Negro Politicians: The Rise of Negro Politics in Chicago.* Chicago: University of Chicago Press, Phoenix Books, 1967.

*Gossett, Thomas F. *Race: The History of an Idea in America.* Rev. ed. New York: Schocken Books, 1965. *13*

Gottfried, Alex. *Boss Cermak of Chicago: A Study of Political Leadership.* Seattle: University of Washington Press, 1962. *225*

Gottmann, Jean. *Megalopolis: The Urbanized Northeastern Seaboard of the United States.* 1961. Reprint. New York: Kraus Reprints. *53, 56, 160, 168*

_____. *Virginia in Our Century.* Charlottesville: University Press of Virginia, 1969.

_____. "Why the Skyscraper?" *Geographical Review* (April 1966). *56*

Gould, Samuel B., and K. Patricia Cross, eds. *Explorations in Non-Traditional Study.* San Francisco:Nossey-Bass, 1972. *102*

•Gowans, Alan. *Images of American Living: Four Centuries of Architecture and Furniture as Cultural Expression.* Philadelphia: J. B. Lippincott, 1964. *188, 192*

•Graham, Aeired. *The End of Religion: Autobiographical Explorations.* New York: Harcourt, Brace, Jovanovich, 1971. *21*

•Graham, Hugh Davis, and Ted Robert Gurr, eds. *The History of Violence in America: Historical and Comparative Perspectives.* New York: Praeger, 1969. *269*

*Graham, Otis L. *The Great Campaigns: Reform and War in America, 1900-1928.* Englewood Cliffs, New Jersey: Prentice-Hall, 1971. *117*

•Grant, Bruce. *Fight for a City: The Story of the Union League Club and Its Time, 1880-1955.* Chicago: Rand McNally, 1955. *233*

Grant, Ulysses S. *Personal Memoirs of Ulysses S. Grant.* 1894. Reprint. New York: AMS Press, 1972. *26, 34*

Gray, Lewis. *History of Agriculture in the Southern United States to 1860.* 2 vols. 1933. Reprint. Gloucester, Massachusetts: Peter Smith. *55*

Grebler, Leo, et al. *The Mexican-American People: The Nation's Second Largest Minority.* New York: The Free Press, 1970. *57*

•Greeley, Andrew M. *The Catholic Experience: An Interpretation of the History of American Catholicism.* Garden City, New York: Doubleday, 1967. *12*

*Green, Constance McLaughlin. *American Cities in the Growth of the Nation.* New York: Harper and Row, 1957. *159, 168, 225*

Green, Marguerite. *The National Civic Federation and the American Labor Movement, 1900-1925.* 1956. Reprint. Westport, Connecticut: Greenwood Press, 1973. *118*

Green, Stanley. *The World of Musical Comedy: The Story of American Musical Stage as Told Through the Careers of Its Foremost Composers and Lyricists.* 2d ed. South Brunswick, New Jersey: A. S. Barnes, 1974. *273*

Greenacre, Phyllis. *Emotional Growth: Psychoanalytic Studies of the Gifted and a Great Variety of Other Individuals.* 2 vols. New York: International University Press, 1971. *31, 37*

•Greene, Evarts B., and Richard B. Morris. *Guide to Sources for Early American History in New York City, 1600-1800.* 1929. 2d ed., rev. by Richard B. Morris. New York: Columbia University Press, 1953. *279*

_____, and Virginia Harrington. *American Population Before the Federal Census of 1790.* 1932. Reprint. Gloucester, Massachusetts: Peter Smith, 1966. *55*

*Greene, John C. *Darwin and the Modern World View.* Baton Rouge: Louisiana State University Press, 1961. *18*

*_____. *The Death of Adam: Evolution and Its Impact on Western Thought*. Ames: Iowa State University Press, 1959. *18*

Greenstone, J. David. *Labor in American Politics*. New York: Alfred A. Knopf, 1969. *127*

Greenwalt, Emmett. *The Point Loma Community in California, 1897-1942: A Theosophical Experiment*. Berkeley: University of California Press, 1955. *215, 220*

Grey, Lennox B. "Chicago and the Great American Novel: A Critical Approach to the American Epic." Ph.D. dissertation, University of Chicago, 1935. *235*

*Grier, William H., and Price M. Cobbs. *Black Rage*. New York: Bantam Books, 1969. *151*

*Griffin, Clifford S. *The Ferment of Reform, 1830-1860*. New York: AHM Publishing, 1968. *16*

•_____. *Their Brothers' Keepers: Moral Stewardship in the United States, 1800-1865*. New Brunswick, New Jersey: Rutgers University Press, 1960.

•Grimes, Alan P. *The Puritan Ethic and Woman Suffrage*. New York: Oxford University Press, 1967. *245*

Grimke, Angelina. *Letters to Catherine E. Beecher, in Reply to an Essay on Slavery and Aboli-tionism, Addressed to A. E. Grimke by the Author*. 1838. Reprint. New York: Arno Press, 1969. *245*

Grimm, Harold J. *The Reformation Era, 1500-1650*. 2d rev. ed. Edited by James J. Carroll. New York: Macmillan, 1973. *14*

Grimsted, David. *Melodrama Unveiled: American Theater and Culture, 1800-1850*. Chicago: University of Chicago Press, 1968. *7, 174, 182*

_____, ed. *Notions of the Americans: 1820-1860*. New York: George Braziller, 1970.

Grob, Gerald N. "Reform Unionism: The National Labor Union." *Journal of Economic History* 14 (Spring 1954):126-42. *113, 115*

*_____. *Workers and Utopia: A Study of Ideological Conflict in the American Labor Move-ment, 1865-1900*. New York: Quadrangle Books, 1969.

Gross, Theodore L., and Stanley Wertheim. *Hawthorne, Melville, Stephen Crane: A Critical Bibliography*. New York: The Free Press, 1971. *47*

Grossman, Jonathan. *William Sylvis: Pioneer of American Labor*. New York: Octagon Books, 1972. *113*

*Grotjahn, Martin. *Beyond Laughter: A Psychoanalytical Approach to Humor*. New York: McGraw-Hill, 1957. *180, 182*

Grubbs, Frank L., Jr. *The Struggle for Labor Loyalty: Gompers, The A.F. of L. and the Pacifists, 1917-1920*. Durham, North Carolina: Duke University Press, 1968. *120*

Gruening, Ernest. "The Political Ecology of Alaska." *Scientific Monthly* 73 (December 1951): 376-86. *144*

*Grundstein, Nathan D. *Presidential Delegation of Authority in Wartime*. Pittsburgh, Pennsyl-vania: University of Pittsburgh Press, 1961. *72*

•Gunderson, Robert Gray. *The Log-Cabin Campaign*. Lexington: University of Kentucky Press, 1957. *75*

Gusdorf, Georges. "Conditions et limites de l'autobiographie." In *Formen der Selbstdarstellung*, edited by G. Reichenkron and E. Haase. Berlin: Duncker and Humblot, 1956. *24, 33*

*Gusfield, Joseph R. *Symbolic Crusade: Status Politics and the American Temperance Move-ment*. Urbana: Illinois University Press, 1966. *20*

Gustafson, James M., and Richard D. Lambert. *The Sixties: Radical Change in American Religion*. Philadelphia: American Academy of Political and Social Science, 1970. *21*

•Gutheim, Frederick, ed. *Frank Lloyd Wright on Architecture: Selected Writings, 1894-1940*. New York: Duell, Sloan and Pierce, 1941. *231*

Gutkind, Erwin A. *Community and Environment: A Discourse on Social Ecology*. New York: Haskell, 1974. *142*

Gutman, Herbert G. "Protestantism and the American Labor Movement: The Christian Spirit in the Gilded Age." *American Historical Review* 72 (October 1966):74-101. *115, 163, 165*

_____. "Work, Culture, and Society in Industrializing America, 1815-1919." *American His-torical Review* 78 (June 1973): 531-88.

*_____. "The Worker's Search for Power: Labor in the Gilded Age." In *The Gilded Age: A Reappraisal*, edited by H. Wayne Morgan. Rev. ed. Syracuse, New York: Syracuse Univer-sity Press, 1975.

_____. "The World Two Cliometricians Made: A Review-Essay." *Journal of Negro History* (January 1975). *163*

*Hagan, William T. *American Indians*. Chicago: University of Chicago Press, 1961. *196, 275*

_____. *The Sac and Fox Indians*. Norman: University of Oklahoma Press, 1958.

Hagen, Ordean A. *Who Done It? An Encyclopedic Guide to Detective, Mystery and Suspense Fiction.* New York: R. R. Bowker, 1969. *176, 182*

Hague, John A., ed. *American Character and Culture.* DeLand, Florida: Everett Edwards Press, 1964. *253*

Hale, Richard W., Jr., ed. *Guide to Photocopied Historical Materials in the United States and Canada.* Ithaca, New York: Cornell University Press, 1961. *283*

*Hall, Burton H., ed. *Autocracy and Insurgency in Organized Labor.* New York: Transaction Books, 1972. *126*

Hall, David D., ed. *Puritanism in 17th Century Massachusetts.* New York: Holt, Rinehart, and Winston, 1968. *14*

*Hall, Stuart, and Paddy Whannel. *The Popular Arts.* New York: Pantheon, 1965. *173, 182*

Haller, John S., and Robin M. Haller. *The Physician and Sexuality in Victorian America.* Urbana: University of Illinois Press, 1974. *251*

Haller, Mark. "Urban Vice and Civic Reform: Chicago in the Early Twentieth Century." In *Cities in American History,* edited by Kenneth T. Jackson and Stanley Schultz. New York: Alfred A. Knopf, 1972. *233*

*Haller, William B. *The Rise of Puritanism: or, The Way to the New Jerusalem as set forth in Pulpit and Press from Thomas Cartwright to John Lilburne and John Milton, 1570-1643.* 1938. Reprint. Philadelphia: University of Pennsylvania Press, 1972. *14*

*Hallowell, Alfred Irving. "The Backwash of the Frontier: The Impact of the Indian on American Culture." In *The Frontier in Perspective,* edited by Walker D. Wyman and Clifton B. Kroeber. Madison: University of Wisconsin Press, 1957. *54, 198*

*Hamby, Alonzo T., ed. *The New Deal: Readings in Analysis and Interpretation.* New York: Weybright, 1969. *121*

Hamer, Philip M., ed. *Guide to Archives and Manuscripts in the United States.* New Haven, Connecticut: Yale University Press, 1961. *283*

Hamilton, Holman. *White House Images and Realities.* Gainesville: University of Florida Press, 1958. *69, 75*

———. *Zachary Taylor.* 2 vols. 1951. Reprint. Hamden, Connecticut: Archon Books, 1966.

*Handlin, Oscar. *The Americans: A New History of the People of the United States.* Boston: Atlantic, Little, Brown, 1963. *7, 19, 159, 168, 266*

———. *Boston's Immigrants: A Study of Acculturation.* Rev. ed. New York: Atheneum, 1968.

———. *The Uprooted.* 2d ed. enlarged. Boston: Little, Brown, 1973.

*———, and John Burchard, eds. *The Historian and the City.* Cambridge: Massachusetts Institute of Technology Press, 1963. *156, 160, 168*

———, et al., eds. *Harvard Guide to American History.* 2 vols. Rev. ed. Cambridge, Massachusetts: The Belknap Press of Harvard University Press, 1974. *266*

Handy, Robert T. *A Christian America: Protestant Hopes and Historical Realities.* New York: Oxford University Press, 1974. *12, 16*

•———, et al., eds. *American Christianity.* New York: Scribner's, 1960. *12*

Hansen, Chadwick. "Social Influences on Jazz Style: Chicago, 1920-1930." *American Quarterly* 12 (Winter 1960):493-507. *230*

*Hansen, Marcus L. *The Atlantic Migration: 1607-1860.* New York: Harper and Row, 1951. *19*

•Hansen, Richard H. *The Year We Had No President.* Lincoln: University of Nebraska Press, 1962. *72*

*Hansen, Soren, and Jasper Jensen. *The Little Red School Book.* New York: Pocket Books, 1971. *100*

•Haraszti, Zoltan. *John Adams and the Prophets of Progress.* Cambridge, Massachusetts: Harvard University Press, 1952. *15*

*Harbaugh, William Henry. *The Life and Times of Theodore Roosevelt.* Rev. ed. New York: Oxford University Press, Galaxy Books, 1975. *77*

Hareven, Tamara. *Eleanor Roosevelt: An American Conscience.* Chicago: Quadrangle Books, 1968. *254, 256*

•Harnsberger, Caroline, ed. *Treasury of Presidential Quotations.* Chicago: Follett Publishing Company, 1964. *67*

*Haroutunian, Joseph. *Piety Versus Moralism: The Passing of New England Theology.* New York: Harper and Row, Harper Torchbooks, 1970. *18*

Harper, Ralph. *The World of the Thriller.* Cleveland, Ohio: The Press of Case-Western Reserve University, 1969. *176, 182*

Harrington, J. C. "Archaeology as an Auxiliary Science to American History." *American Anthropologist* 51 (December 1955): 1121-30. *190, 192*

*Harrington, Michael. *The Other America: Poverty in the United States.* New York: Penguin, Pelican Books, 1962. *274*

*_____. *Socialism.* New York: Bantam Books, 1973. *127*

Harris, David. *Socialist Origins in the United States, American Forerunners of Marx, 1817-1832.* Assen, the Netherlands: Van Gorcum, 1966. *112*

•Harris, Leon. *Only to God: The Extraordinary Life of Godfrey Lowell Cabot.* New York: Atheneum, 1967. *159, 168*

*Harris, Neil, ed. *The Land of Contrasts, 1880-1901.* New York: George Braziller, 1970. *7*

•Harrison, Carter H. *Growing Up with Chicago.* Chicago: R. F. Seymour, 1944. *225*

•_____. *Stormy Years: The Autobiography of Carter Henry Harrison, Five Times Mayor of Chicago.* Indianapolis, Indiana: Bobbs-Merrill, 1935.

•Harrison, John F. C. *Quest for the New Moral World: Robert Owen and the Owenites in Britain and America.* New York: Scribner's, 1969. *111, 211, 220*

Harrisse, Henry. *The Discovery of North America; A Critical Documentary, and Historic Investigation with an Essay on the Early Cartography of the New World, including Descriptions of Two Hundred and Fifty Maps or Globes Existing or Lost, Constructed before the Year 1536; to which are added a Chronology of One Hundred Voyages Westward, Projected, Attempted, or Accomplished between 1431 and 1504; Biographical Accounts of the Three Hundred Pilots who First Crossed the Atlantic; and a Copious List of the Original Names of American Regions, Caciqueships, Mountains, Islands, Capes, Gulfs, Rivers, Towns, and Harbours.* London: H. Stevens and Sons, 1892. Reprint. Amsterdam: N. Israel, 1961. *85, 92*

Hart, Francis Russell. "Notes for an Anatomy of Modern Autobiography." *New Literary History* 1 (Spring 1970):485-511. *25, 27, 33*

Hart, James D. *The Oxford Companion to American Literature.* 4th ed. New York: Oxford University Press, 1965. *174, 182, 270*

*_____. *The Popular Book: A History of America's Literary Taste.* Berkeley: University of California Press, 1950.

*Hart, John Fraser. *The Southeastern United States.* New York: Van Nostrand, Reinhold, 1967. *52, 53, 54*

*_____, ed. *Regions of the United States.* New York: Harper and Row, 1972.

*Hartman, Mary S., and Lois W. Banner. *Clio's Consciousness Raised: New Perspectives on the History of Women.* New York: Harper and Row, Harper Torchbooks, 1974. *253, 256*

*Hartz, Louis, et al. *The Founding of New Societies: Studies in the History of the United States, Latin America, South America, Canada, and Australia.* New York: Harcourt, Brace, Jovanovich, 1969. *7*

Harwell, Richard, ed. *Washington.* New York: Scribner's, 1968. *73*

•Hatch, Louis C. *A History of the Vice-Presidency of the United States.* Rev. ed. Edited by Earl L. Shoup. 1934. Reprint. Westport, Connecticut: Greenwood Press, 1970. *72*

Hauck, Richard. *A Cheerful Nihilism: Confidence and the Absurd in American Humorous Fiction.* Bloomington: Indiana University Press, 1971. *42*

Hauser, Stuart T. *Black and White Identity Formation: Studies in the Psychosocial Development of Lower Socioeconomic Class Adolescent Boys.* New York: Wiley, 1971. *30, 37*

Havlice, Patricia P. *Index to American Author Bibliographies.* Metuchen, New Jersey: Scarecrow Press, 1971. *46*

Hawley, Amos H. "Ecology and Human Ecology." *Social Forces* 22 (May 1944):398-405. *139, 142, 145*

_____. "Human Ecology." *International Encyclopedia of the Social Sciences* 4:328-337.

_____. *Human Ecology: A Theory of Community Structure.* New York: Ronald Press, 1950.

•Haycraft, Howard, ed. *The Art of the Mystery Story.* New York: Simon and Schuster, 1946. *175, 182*

•_____. *Murder for Pleasure: The Life and Times of the Detective Story.* Newly enlarged ed. New York: Biblo and Tannen, 1968.

•Hayes, Dorsha. *Chicago, Crossroads of American Enterprise.* New York: Julian Messner, 1944. *227*

Hayes, Rutherford B. *Rutherford B. Hayes: The Diary of a President, 1875-1881, Covering the Disputed Election, the End of Reconstruction, and the Beginning of Civil Service.*

Edited by T. Harry Williams. New York: David McKay Company, 1964. *68*

*Hays, Samuel P. *The Response to Industrialism, 1885-1914.* Chicago: University of Chicago Press, 1957. *114*

•Hecht, Ben. *A Child of the Century.* New York: Simon and Schuster, 1954. *228*

_____. *Erik Dorn.* Chicago: University of Chicago Press, 1963. *228*

Hedges, Elaine. "Women's Studies at a State College." *Women's Studies Newsletter* 2 and 3 (Fall 1974-Winter 1975). *253*

Heimert, Alan E. Religion and the American Mind: From the Great Awakening to the Revolution. Cambridge, Massachusetts: Harvard University Press, 1966. *15*

Helm, June. "The Ecological Approach in Anthropology." *American Journal of Sociology* 67 (May 1962):630-39. *142*

Hendrick, Burton J. *Lincoln's War Cabinet.* 1946. Reprint. Gloucester, Massachusetts: Peter Smith, 1965. *71*

Hendricks, Robert J. *Bethel and Aurora, An Experiment in Communism as Practical Christianity; With Some Account of Past and Present Ventures in Collective Living.* 1933. Reprint. New York: AMS Press, 1972. *212, 220*

Henry, Alice. *The Trade Union Woman.* 1915. Reprint. New York: B. Franklin, 1973. *246*

Henry, David. *William Vaughan Moody, A Study.* 1934. Reprint. Philadelphia: Richard West. *228*

Henry, Laurin L. *Presidential Transitions.* Washington, D.C.: The Brookings Institution, 1960. *72*

*Henson, Josiah. *Father Henson's Story of His Own Life.* New York: Corinth Books, 1962. *29, 36*

Herberg, Will. *Protestant, Catholic, Jew: An Essay in American Religious Sociology.* Rev. ed. Garden City, New York: Doubleday, Anchor Books, 1955. *19, 20, 273*

•Hermann, Augustine. *Virginia and Maryland as it is Planted and inhabited This Present Year 1670.* London, 1673. Collotype reproduction from original in John Carter Brown Library. *91, 94*

Hero, Alfred O. *The Reuther-Meany Foreign Policy Dispute.* Dobbs-Ferry, New York: Oceana Publications, 1970. *124*

•_____. *The UAW and World Affairs.* Boston: World Peace Foundation, 1965.

Herreshoff, David. *American Disciples of Marx: From the Age of Jackson to the Progressive Era.* Detroit: Wayne State University Press, 1967. *117*

*Herrick, Robert. *The Memoirs of an American Citizen.* Edited by Daniel Aaron. Cambridge, Massachusetts: Harvard University Press, 1963. *228*

_____. *The Web of Life.* 1900. Reprint. Boston: Gregg, 1970.

Hertzler, Joyce Oramel. *The History of Utopian Thought.* 1923. Reprint. New York: Cooper Square Publishers, 1965. *207, 220*

Heslop, David Alan. *The Presidency and Political Science: A Critique of the Work of Political Scientists in Three Areas of Presidential Politics.* Ann Arbor, Michigan: University Micro-films, 1969. *67*

Hesseltine, William B. *Ulysses S. Grant, Politician. 1935.* Reprint. New York: Frederick Ungar, 1957. *76*

Higgs, Robert. *The Transformation of the American Economy, 1865-1914: An Essay in Interpretation.* New York: Wiley, 1972. *116*

Higham, John. *Strangers in the Land: Patterns of American Nativism, 1860-1925.* New York: Atheneum, 1963. *19, 116, 119, 268*

*Hill, Christopher. *Society and Puritanism in Pre-Revolutionary England.* New York: Schocken Books, 1964. *110*

•Hill, Samuel S. *Southern Churches in Crisis.* Boston: Beacon Press, 1968. *16*

Hilliard, Sam B. *Hog Meat and Hoecake: Food Supply in the Old South, 1840-1860.* Carbondale: Southern Illinois University, 1972. *58*

*Hindle, Brooke. *Technology in Early America: Needs and Opportunities for Study.* Chapel Hill: University of North Carolina Press, 1968. *188, 192*

Hinds, William A. *American Communities and Cooperative Colonies.* 1908. Reprint. 3d ed. Philadelphia: Porcupine Press, 1974. *113, 214, 220*

*Hine, Robert V. *California's Utopian Colonies.* 1953. Reprint. New York: W. W. Norton, 1973. *215, 220*

Hitchcock, Henry Russell. *The Architecture of H. H. Richardson and His Times.* Cambridge: Massachusetts Institute of Technology Press, 1961. *187, 192, 231*

Hitchcock, Henry Russell. *Rhode Island Architecture.* New York: Da Capo Press, 1968.

*Hitchcock, H. Wiley. *Music in the United States: A Historical Introduction.* Englewood Cliffs, New Jersey: Prentice-Hall, 1969. *272*

•Hochfield, George, ed. *Selected Writings of the American Transcendentalists.* New York: New American Library, 1966. *18*

Hoffman, Charles. *The Depression of the Nineties: An Economic History.* Westport, Connecticut: Greenwood Press, 1970. *116*

Hoffman, Donald. *The Architecture of John Wellborn Root.* Baltimore: Johns Hopkins University Press, 1973. *231*

*Hofstadter, Richard. *The Age of Reform: From Bryan to F.D.R.* New York: Alfred A. Knopf, 1955. *7, 13, 18, 69, 116, 273*

*_____. *The American Political Tradition and the Men Who Made It.* New York: Random House, Vintage Books, 1974.

*_____. *Anti-Intellectualism in American Life.* New York: Random House, Vintage Books, 1964.

*_____. *The Progressive Historians: Turner, Beard, Parrington.* New York: Random House, Vintage Books, 1970.

*_____. *Social Darwinism in American Thought.* Boston: Beacon Press, 1955.

_____, and Walter P. Metzger. *The Development of Academic Freedom in the United States.* New York: Columbia University Press, 1955. *264*

*_____, and Wilson Smith, eds. *American Higher Education: A Documentary History.* 2 vols. Chicago: University of Chicago Press, Phoenix Books, 1968. *264*

*Hogeland, Ronald W., ed. *Woman and Womanhood in America.* Lexington, Massachusetts: D. C. Heath, 1973. *264*

*Hoggart, Richard. *The Uses of Literacy: Aspects of Working Class Life, with Special References to Publication and Entertainments.* New York: Oxford University Press, Galaxy Books, 1970. *177, 182*

Holland, Norman N. "Prose and Minds: A Psychoanalytic Approach to Non-Fiction." In *The Art of Victorian Prose,* edited by G. Lavine and W. Madden. New York: Oxford University Press, 1968. *25, 33*

*Holloway, Mark. *Heavens on Earth; Utopian Communities in America, 1680-1880.* Rev. ed. New York: Dover, 1966. *214, 220*

Holt, Glen. "Chicago Through a Camera Lens: An Essay on Photography As History." *Chicago History* (Spring 1971). *225*

Holyoake, George Jacob. *The History of Co-operation in England; Its Literature and Its Advocates.* 2 vols. 1875. Reprint. New York: AMS Press, 1972. *208, 220*

•Hooks, Janet. *Women's Occupations Through Seven Decades.* Washington, D.C.: U.S. Government Printing Office, 1947. *251*

Hoover, Dwight W. "The Diverging Paths of American Urban History." *American Quarterly* 20 (Summr 1968):296-317. *150, 153, 155, 168*

*_____. *Teacher's Guide to American Urban History.* Chicago: Quadrangle Books, 1971.

_____, ed. *Understanding Negro History.* Chicago: Quadrangle Books, 1969.

Hoover, Herbert. *Memoirs.* 3 vols. New York: Macmillan, 1951-1952. *68*

•Hopkins, Charles H. *The Rise of the Social Gospel in American Protestantism.* New Haven, Connecticut: Yale University Press, 1940. *17*

Hopkins, David M., ed. *The Bering Land Bridge.* Stanford, California: Stanford University Press, 1967. *54*

Hopkins, Richard J. "Mobility and the New Urban History." *Journal of Urban History* 1 (February 1975):217-28. *165*

*Horton, R. W., and H. W. Edwards. *Backgrounds of American Literary Thought.* 3d ed. Englewood Cliffs, New Jersey: Prentice-Hall, 1974. *271*

Houle, Cyril O. *The External Degree.* San Francisco: Jossey-Bass, 1973. *102*

*Houriet, Robert. *Getting Back Together.* New York: Avon, 1972. *217, 220*

Howe, Daniel W. *The Unitarian Conscience: Harvard Moral Philosophy, 1805-1861.* Cambridge, Massachusetts: Harvard University Press, 1970. *18*

*Howe, Florence, and Ellen Bass, eds. *No More Masks: An Anthology of Poems by Women.* New York: Doubleday, Anchor Books, 1973. *242, 251*

Howe, George Frederick. *Chester A. Arthur: A Quarter-Century of Machine Politics.* New York: Frederick Ungar, 1957. *77*

•Howe, Helen. *The Gentle Americans 1864-1960: Biography of a Breed.* New York: Harper and Row, 1965. *159, 168*

Howe, Irving, and Lewis Coser. *The American Communist Party: A Critical History.* 1962. Reprint. New York: Da Capo Press, 1974. *120*

Howe, John R., ed. *The Role of Ideology in the American Revolution.* 1970. Reprint. Glouster, Massachusetts: Peter Smith. *15*

Howells, William Dean. "Editor's Easy Chair." *Harper's Monthly* 119 (October 1909):798. *26, 32, 159, 168*

*_____. *The Rise of Silas Lapham.* New York: Macmillan, Collier Books, 1962.

Hoyt, Homer. *One Hundred Years of Land Values in Chicago: The Relationship of the Growth of Chicago to the Rise in Its Land Values, 1830-1933.* 1933. Reprint. New York: Arno Press, 1970. *226, 227*

Hubbell, Jay B. *The South in American Literature, 1607-1900.* Durham, North Carolina: Duke University Press, 1954. *271*

*Huber, Joan, ed. *Changing Women in a Changing Society.* Chicago: University of Chicago Press, Phoenix Books, 1973. *250*

Hudgins, H. C., Jr. *The Warren Court and the Public Schools: An Analysis of Landmark Supreme Court Decisions.* Danville, Illinois: Interstate Printers and Publishers, 1970. *98*

Hudson, Kenneth. *Handbook for Industrial Archaeologists: A Guide to Fieldwork and Research.* London: Baker, 1967. *190*

_____. *Industrial Archaeology: An Introduction.* Philadelphia: Dufour Editions, 1964.

*Hudson, Winthrop S. *Religion in America.* 2d ed. New York: Scribner's, 1973. *12, 13*

*_____, ed. *Nationalism and Religion in America: Concepts of American Identity and Mission.* New York: Harper and Row, 1970.

*Hughes, Emmet John. *The Living Presidency.* New York: Penguin Books, 1974. *70, 79*

•_____. *The Ordeal of Power: A Political Memoir of the Eisenhower Years.* New York: Atheneum, 1963.

*Hughes, H. S. *History as Art and as Science: Twin Vistas on the Past.* New York: Harper and Row, Harper Torchbooks, 1964. *31, 37*

Hughes, Thomas. *Rugby, Tennessee.* 1891. Reprint. Philadelphia: Porcupine Press, 1974. *215, 220*

*Hugins, Walter E. *Jacksonian Democracy and the Working Class: A Study of the New York Workingmen's Movement, 1829-1837.* Stanford, California: Stanford University Press, 1960. *12*

Hull House Residents. *Hull House Maps and Papers: A Presentation of Nationalities and Wages in a Congested District of Chicago.* New York: Arno Press, 1970. *226*

*Hunnius, Gerry. G. David Garson, and John Case, eds. *Worker's Control: A Reader on Labor and Social Change.* New York: Random House, Vintage Books, 1973. *127*

Huntington, Ellsworth. *Civilization and Climate.* 3d ed. Rev. and enlarged. Hamden, Connecticut: Archon Books, 1971. *137*

_____. *The Mainsprings of Civilization.* 1945. Reprint. New York: Arno Press, 1972.

Hurst, Michael Eliot, ed. *I Came to the City: Essays and Comments on the Urban Scene.* Boston: Houghton Mifflin, 1975. *162*

Hutchinson, John. *The Imperfect Union: A History of Corruption in American Trade Unions.* New York: E. P. Dutton, 1970. *127*

*Hutchinson, William R., ed. *American Protestant Thought: The Liberal Era.* New York: Harper and Row, Harper Torchbooks, 1968. *18*

*Huth, Hans. *Nature and the American: Three Centuries of Changing Attitudes.* Lincoln: University of Nebraska Press, 1972. *140, 273*

Huxley, Aldous O. "The Double Crisis." In *Themes and Variations.* New York: Harper and Row, 1950. *144*

_____. "The Politics of Ecology: The Question of Survival." Santa Barbara, California: Center for the Study of Democratic Institutions, 1963.

Hyman, Sidney. *The American President.* 1954. Reprint. Westport, Connecticut: Greenwood Press, 1974. *69*

*Illich, Ivan. *Deschooling Society.* New York: Harper and Row, 1972. *100*

*_____. *Tools for Conviviality.* New York: Harper and Row, 1974.

*Ingstad, Helge. *Westward to Vinland: The Discovery of Pre-Columbian Norse House Sites in North America.* New York: Harper and Row, 1972. *55*

Irving, Washington. *Knickerbocker's History of New York.* Edited by Ann C. Moore. New York: Frederick Ungar, 1959. *168*

•Isely, Bliss. *The Presidents: Men of Faith.* Rev. ed. Boston: W. A. Wilde Company, 1961. *73*

•Israel, Fred L., ed. *The State of the Union Messages of the Presidents, 1790-1966.* 3 vols. New York: Chelsea House, 1966. *68*

Jackson, Kenneth T. "Robert Herrick's Use of Chicago." *Midcontinent American Studies Journal* 5 (1964):24-32. *235*

*_____, and Stanley K. Schultz, eds. *Cities in American History.* New York: Alfred A. Knopf, 1972. *162*

*Jacobs, Harriet (Linda Brent). *Incidents in the Life of a Slave Girl.* New York: Harcourt, Brace, Jovanovich, Harvest Books, 1973. *29, 36*

*Jacobs, Norman, ed. *Culture for the Millions? Mass Media in Modern Society.* Boston: Beacon Press, 1964. *174, 182*

*Jacobson, Julius, ed. *The Negro and the American Labor Movement.* Garden City, New York: Doubleday, Anchor Books, 1968. *125*

Jaher, Frederic Cople, ed. *The Age of Industrialism in America: Essays in Social Structure and Cultural Values.* New York: The Free Press, 1968. *115*

•James, Bartlett B. *The Labadist Colony in Maryland.* 1899. Reprint. New York: Johnson Reprint Corporation, 1973. *209, 220*

*James, Edward T., et al., eds. *Notable American Women, 1607-1950: A Biographical Dictionary.* 3 vols. Cambridge, Massachusetts: The Belknap Press of Harvard University Press, 1974. *247*

*James, Henry. *The Bostonians.* Indianapolis, Indiana: Bobbs-Merrill, 1975. *26, 27, 28, 159, 168*

•_____. *Henry James: Autobiography.* Edited by F. W. Dupee. New York: Criterion Books, 1956. *34*

*James, Louis. *Fiction for the Working Man, 1830-50: A Study of the Literature Produced for the Working Classes in Early Victorian Urban England.* Baltimore: Penguin Books, 1974. *177, 182*

•James, Marquis. *The Life of Andrew Jackson.* Indianapolis, Indiana: Bobbs-Merrill, 1938. *74*

•Jeffries, Ona Griffin. *In and Out of the White House, from Washington to the Eisenhowers: An Intimate Glimpse into the Social and Domestic Aspects of the Presidential Life.* New York: W. Funk, 1960. *73*

•Jencks, Christopher, and David Riesman. *The Academic Revolution.* Garden City, New York: Doubleday, Anchor Books, 1969. *101*

*_____, et al. *Inequality: A Reassessment of the Effect of Family and Schooling in America.* New York: Harper and Row, 1973.

Jensen, Amy La Follette. *The White House and Its Thirty-Five Families.* New York: McGraw-Hill, 1970. *73*

*Jensen, Merrill, ed. *Tracts of the American Revolution, 1763-1776.* Indianapolis, Indiana: Bobbs-Merrill, 1967. *15*

•Jernegan, Marcus W. *Laboring and Dependent Classes in Colonial America, 1607-1783.* New York: Frederick Ungar, 1960. *109*

Johnpoll, Bernard K. *Pacifist's Progress: Norman Thomas and the Decline of American Socialism.* Chicago: Quadrangle Books, 1970. *120, 122*

*Johnson, Claudia ("Lady Bird"). *A White House Diary.* New York: Dell, 1971. *73*

•Johnson, Claudius O. *Carter Henry Harrison I, Political Leader.* Chicago: University of Chicago Press, 1928. *225*

Johnson, Clifton H., ed. *God Struck Me Dead: Religious Conversion Experiences and Autobiographies of Ex-Slaves.* Philadelphia: Pilgrim Press, 1969. *17*

Johnson, Hildegard. "Rational and Ecological Aspects of the Quarter Section: An Example from Minnesota." *Geographical Review* (July 1957). *57*

*Johnson, Lyndon B. *The Vantage Point: Perspectives of the Presidency: 1963-1969.* New York: Popular Library, 1972. *68*

•Joll, James. *The Anarchists.* Boston: Little, Brown, 1965. *127*

•Jones, Buford. *A Checklist of Hawthorne Criticism, 1951-1966.* Hartford, Connecticut: Transcendental Books, 1967. *47*

*Jones, Howard Mumford. *The Age of Energy: Varieties of American Experience, 1865-1915.* New York: Viking Press, Compass Books, 1971. *225, 232, 268*

*_____. *O Strange New World: American Culture: The Formative Years.* New York: Viking Press, Compass Books, 1964.

•_____, and R. M. Ludwig. *Guide to American Literature and Its Backgrounds Since 1890.* 4th rev. ed. Cambridge, Massachusetts: Harvard University Press, 1972. *270*

•Jones, Joseph, et al., eds. *American Literary Manuscripts: A Checklist of Holdings in Academic, Historical, and Public Libraries in the United States.* Austin: University of Texas Press, 1961. *283*

*Jones, Maldwyn. *American Immigration.* Chicago: University of Chicago Press, 1960. *57, 268*

•Jones, Olga. *Churches of the Presidents in Washington: Visits to Sixteen National Shrines.* 2d enlarged ed. New York: Exposition Press, 1961. *73*

•Jones, Rufus. *The Quakers in the American Colonies.* New York: W. W. Norton, 1966. *14*

•Jordan, Terry. *German Seed in Texas Soil: Immigrant Farmers in Nineteenth-Century Texas.* Austin: University of Texas Press, 1966. *53*

*Jordan, Winthrop D. *White Over Black: American Attitudes Toward the Negro, 1550-1812.* Baltimore: Penguin, Pelican Books, 1969. *8, 16, 109*

Jordy, William. *American Buildings and Their Architects: Academic and Progressive Ideals at the Turn of the Century.* Garden City, New York: Doubleday, 1972. *231*

*Jorgensen, Joseph G. *The Sun Dance Religion: Power for the Powerless.* Chicago: University of Chicago Press, Phoenix Books, 1974. *204*

*Josephy, Alvin M., Jr. *The Indian Heritage of America.* New York: Bantam Books, 1969. *195, 196*

*_____. *The Nez Perce Indians and the Opening of the Northwest.* New Haven, Connecticut: Yale University Press, 1971.

•Jouvenel, Bertrand de. "The Ecology of Social Ideas." In *The Art of Conjecture,* translated by Nikita Lary. New York: Basic Books, 1967. *141*

Kahn, Kathy. *Hillbilly Women.* Garden City, New York: Doubleday, 1973. *251*

Kallenbach, Joseph E. *The American Chief Executive: The Presidency and the Governorship.* New York: Harper and Row, 1966. *70*

Kane, Joseph Nathan. *Facts About the Presidents: A Compilation of Biographical and Historical Data.* 3d ed. New York: H. W. Wilson, 1974. *67*

*Kanowitz, Leo. *Women and the Law: The Unfinished Revolution.* Albuquerque: University of New Mexico Press, 1969. *251*

*Kanter, Rosabeth M. *Commitment and Community; Communes and Utopias in Sociological Perspective.* Cambridge, Massachusetts: Harvard University Press, 1972. *217, 220*

Kaplan, Louis. *A Bibliography of American Autobiographies.* Madison: University of Wisconsin Press, 1961. *22, 26, 32*

•Karpinski, Louis C. *Bibliography of the Printed Maps of Michigan, 1804-1880, with a Series of over One Hundred Reproductions of Maps Constituting an Historical Atlas of the Great Lakes and Michigan.* Lansing: Michigan Historical Commission, 1931. *85, 92*

•Karson, Marc. *American Labor Unions and Politics.* Carbondale: Southern Illinois University Press, 1958. *118*

Kates, Robert W., and J. F. Wohlwill, eds. "Man's Response to the Physical Environment." *The Journal of Social Issues* 22 (October 1966), Special Issue. *142*

Katz, Michael B. *Class, Schools, and Bureaucracy: The Illusion of Educational Change in America.* Rev. ed. New York: Praeger, 1975. *100*

*Kaufmann, Edgar, Jr., ed. *The Rise of an American Architecture.* New York: Praeger, 1970. *160, 168, 231*

_____, and Ben Raeburn, eds. *Frank Lloyd Wright: Writings and Buildings.* New York: Horizon Press, 1971. *231*

Kaufman, Stuart Bruce. *Samuel Gompers and the Origins of the American Federation of Labor, 1848-1896.* Westport, Connecticut: Greenwood Press, 1973. *117*

*Kazin, Alfred. *On Native Grounds: An Interpretation of Modern American Prose Literature.* Abridged, with a new postscript. New York: Harcourt, Brace, Jovanovich, 1972. *271*

Kelley, Florence. *Some Ethical Gains Through Legislation.* 1905. Reprint. New York: Arno Press, 1969. *226*

*Kelly, J. Frederick. *The Early Domestic Architecture of Connecticut.* New York: Dover, 1924. *187, 192*

*Kennan, George F. *American Diplomacy, 1900-1950.* Chicago: University of Chicago Press, Phoenix Books, 1970. *265*

*Kennedy, David. *Birth Control in America: The Career of Margaret Sanger.* New Haven, Connecticut: Yale University Press, 1970. *248*

•Kennedy, Gail, ed. *Evolution and Religion.* Boston: D. C. Heath, 1956. *20*

Kenney, Alice P. "Women, History, and the Museum." *History Teacher* 10 (August 1974). *252*

Kent, Alexander. "Cooperative Communities in the United States." *Bulletin of the Department of Labor* 35 (July 1901): 563-46. *214, 220*

Kent, George E. "Richard Wright: Blackness and the Adventure of Western Culture." *CLA Journal* 12 (1969):322-43. *29, 36*

Kerr, Clark, John T. Dunlop, Frederick Harbison, and Charles T. Myers. *Industrialism and Industrial Man.* Cambridge, Massachusetts: Harvard University Press, 1960. *108*

_____, John T. Dunlop, Frederick Harbison, and Charles T. Myers. "Postscript to *Industrialism and Industrial Men." International Labor Review* 103 (1971):519-40. *108*

Ketcham, Ralph. *James Madison: A Biography.* New York: Macmillan, 1971. *74*

Key, Valdimer Orlando. *Politics, Parties and Pressure Groups.* 5th ed. New York: Thomas Y. Crowell, 1964. *70*

Kilpatrick, Anna Gritts, and Jack Frederick Kilpatrick. "Chronicles of Wolftown." Anthropological Paper No. 75, *Bureau of American Ethnology Bulletin,* No. 196. Washington, D.C., 1966: 1-111. *201*

_____, and Jack Frederick Kilpatrick. "Notebook of a Cherokee Shaman." *Smithsonian Contributions to Anthropology* 2 (1970).

*Kimball, Sidney Fiske. *Domestic Architecture of the American Colonies and of the Early Republic.* New York: Dover, 1966. *187, 192*

•King, Martin Luther, Jr. *The Strength to Love.* New York: Pocket Books, 1963. *17*

*Kipnis, Ira. *The American Socialist Movement, 1897-1912.* New York: Monthly Review Press, 1972. *118*

Kirk, Clara, and Rudolf Kirk. "Edith Wyatt: The Jane Austen of Chicago?" *Chicago History* 1 (Spring 1971):172-78. *228*

Kirkendall, Richard S. "The Great Depression: Another Watershed in American History?" In *Change and Continuity in Twentieth Century America,* edited by John Braeman, Robert H. Bremner, and Everett Walters. Columbus: Ohio State University Press, 1964. *121*

•Kirkland, Joseph. *The Story of Chicago.* 2 vols. Chicago: Dibble Publishing Company, 1892-1894. *225*

•Kitagawa, Evelyn, and K. E. Taeuber. *Local Community Fact Book: Chicago Metropolitan Area.* Chicago: University of Chicago Press, 1960. *227*

*Kitses, Jim. *Horizons West: Anthony Mann, Budd Boetticher, Sam Peckinpah: Studies of Authorship Within the Western.* Bloomington: Indiana University Press, 1970. *176, 182*

Klapper, Joseph T. *The Effects of Mass Communication.* Glencoe, Illinois: The Free Press, 1960. *178, 182*

Klein, Philip Shriver. *President James Buchanan, A Biography.* University Park: Pennsylvania State University Press, 1962. *76*

*Klein, Viola. *The Feminine Character: History of an Ideology.* 2d ed. Urbana: University of Illinois Press, 1973. *239*

Klein, Walter Conrad. *Johann Conrad Beissel, Mystic and Martinet, 1690-1768.* Reprint. Philadelphia: Porcupine Press, 1972. *209, 220*

Kniffen, Fred B. "Folk Housing: Key to Diffusion." *Annals of the Association of American Geography* (September 1965). *53, 56*

_____. "Louisiana House Types," *Annals of the Association of American Geography* (December 1936). *56*

_____. *Louisiana: Its Land and People.* Baton Rouge: Louisiana State University Press, 1968.

*Knight, Arthur. *The Liveliest Art: A Panoramic History of the Movies.* New York: New American Library, Mentor Books, 1971. *179, 182*

*Knight, Damon. *In Search of Wonder: Essays on Modern Science Fiction.* Rev. and enlarged ed. Chicago: Publishers, 1967. *176*

*Knights, Peter R. *The Plain People of Boston, 1830-1860: A Study in City Growth.* New York: Oxford University Press, 1973. *165*

Koenig, Louis W. *The Chief Executive.* 3d ed. New York: Harcourt, Brace, Jovanovich, 1975. *70, 71*

•_____. *The Invisible Presidency.* New York: Rinehart, 1960.

*Kohl. Herbert R. *The Open Classroom: A Practical Guide to a New Way of Teaching.* New York: New York Review, 1970. *100*

Kohl, Johann Georg. *The Kohl Collection (Now in the Library of Congress) of Maps Relating to America.* Washington, D.C.: U.S. Government Printing Office, 1904. Reprint from Bibliographical Contributions to the Library of Harvard University, No. 19, 1886. *91, 94*

•Kohn, Hans. *American Nationalism: An Interpretive Essay.* New York: Macmillan, 1957. *268*

*Komarovsky, Mirra. *Blue Collar Marriage.* New York: Random House, Vintage Books, 1967. *250*

Larcom, Lucy. *A New England Girlhood.* 1890. Reprint. Gloucester, Massachusetts: Peter Smith. *26, 28, 35*

Larkin, Oliver W. *Art and Life in America.* Rev. and enlarged ed. New York: Holt, Rinehart, and Winston, 1960. *263*

•Larrabee, Eric, and Rolf Meyersohn, eds. *Mass Leisure.* Glencoe, Illinois: The Free Press, 1958. *178, 182*

*Lasch, Christopher. *The Agony of the American Left.* New York: Random House, Vintage Books, 1969. *118, 246*

*_____. *The New Radicalism in America: 1889-1913, The Intellectual as a Social Type.* New York: Random House, Vintage Books, 1965.

*Lash, Joseph. *Eleanor and Franklin: The Story of Their Relationship Based on Eleanor Roosevelt's Private Papers.* New York: New American Library, Signet Books, 1973. *79, 249*

*_____. *Eleanor: The Years Alone.* New York: New American Library, Signet Books, 1973.

Laski, Harold. *The American Democracy: A Commentary and an Interpretation.* 1948. Reprint. Chilton, New Jersey: Augustus M. Kelley, 1974. *265*

_____. *The American Presidency: An Interpretation.* 1940. Reprint. Westport, Connecticut: Greenwood Press, 1972. *70*

Laslett, John. *Labor and the Left: A Study of Socialist and Radical Influences in the American Labor Movement, 1881-1924.* New York: Basic Books, 1970. *117*

*Latham, Earl. *The Communist Controversy in Washington: From the New Deal to McCarthy.* New York: Atheneum, 1969. *124*

*Lawson, R. Alan. *The Failure of Independent Liberalism, 1930-1941.* New York: Putnam, 1972. *121*

Layng, T. E. *Sixteenth Century Maps Relating to Canada: A Checklist and Bibliography.* Ottawa: Public Archives of Canada, 1965. *86, 93*

*Leach, Douglas. *The Northern Colonial Frontier, 1607-1763.* New York: Holt, Rinehart, and Winston, 1966. *197, 249*

Leach, Joseph. *Bright Particular Star: The Life and Times of Charlotte Cushman.* New Haven, Connecticut: Yale University Press, 1970. *249*

Leary, Lewis. *Articles on American Literature Appearing in Current Periodicals.* 2 vols. *Vol. 1, 1900-1950; Vol. 2, 1950-1967.* Durham, North Carolina: Duke University Press, 1954; 1970. *45*

Leavis, F. R., and Denys Thompson. *Culture and Environment: The Training of Critical Awareness.* 1933. Reprint. New York: Barnes and Noble, 1962. *173, 183*

Leavis, Q. D. *Fiction and the Reading Public.* 1932. Reprint. Folcroft, Tennessee: Folcroft Library Editions, 1974. *173, 183*

•Lecht, Leonard A. *Manpower Needs for National Goals in the 1970's.* New York: Praeger, 1969. *125*

•Lee, Dallas. *The Cotton Patch Evidence.* New York: Harper and Row, 1971. *216, 220*

*Lee, Dorothy. *Freedom and Culture: Essays.* Englewood Cliffs. New Jersey: Prentice-Hall, 1959. *5*

Leech, Harper, and John Carroll. *Armour and His Times.* 1938. Reprint. Freeport, New York: Books for Libraries Press, 1971. *227*

•Leech, Margaret. *In the Days of McKinley.* New York: Harper and Row, 1959. *77*

Leish, Kenneth W., ed. *The American Heritage Pictorial History of the Presidents.* 2 vols. New York: American Heritage Publishing Company, 1968. *69*

Lemisch, Jesse. "Jack Tar in the Streets: Merchant Seamen in the Politics of Revolutionary America." *William and Mary Quarterly* 25 (1968):371-405. *7, 110*

_____. "Listening to the 'Inarticulate,' William Widger's Dream and the Loyalties of American Revolutionary Seamen in British Prisons." *Journal of Social History* 3 (1969):1-29.

Lemon, James T. *The Best Poor Man's Country: A Geographical Study of Early Southeastern Pennsylvania.* Baltimore: Johns Hopkins University Press, 1972. *53, 55*

Lemons, J. Stanley. *The Woman Citizen: Social Feminism in the 1920's.* Urbana: University of Illinois Press, 1973. *245*

*Lens, Sidney. *The Labor Wars: From the Molly Maguires to the Sitdowns.* Garden City, New York: Doubleday, Anchor Books, 1974. *125*

Leopold, Richard William. *Robert Dale Owen, A Biography.* 1940. Reprint. New York: Octagon Books, 1969. *112*

*Lerner, Gerda, ed. *Black Women in White America: A Documentary History.* New York: Random House, Vintage Books, 1973. *239, 244, 245, 246, 255*

*_____. *The Grimke Sisters from South Carolina: Pioneers for Women's Rights and Aboli-tion.* New York: Schocken Books, 1971.

_____. "The Lady and the Mill Girl: Changes in the Status of Women in the Age of Jackson." *Midcontinent American Studies Journal* 10, No. 1 (Spring 1969). *245*

_____. "New Approaches to the Study of Women in American History." *Journal of Social History* 3 (Fall 1969). *239*

*_____. *The Woman in American History.* Menlo Park, California: Addison-Wesley Publishing Company, 1971.

_____. "Women's Rights and American Feminism." *The American Scholar* 40, No. 2 (Spring 1971). *255*

*Lerner, Max. *America As a Civilization: LIfe and Thought in the United States Today.* 2 vols. New York: Simon and Schuster, 1967. *262*

Leuchtenburg, William E. *Franklin D. Roosevelt and the New Deal, 1932-1940.* New York: Harper and Row, 1963. *79, 121*

_____. "The New Deal and the Analogue of War." In *Change and Continuity in Twentieth Century America,* edited by John Braeman, Robert H. Bremner, and Everett Walters. Columbus: Ohio State University Press, 1964.

*Levenson, J. C. *The Mind and Art of Henry Adams.* Stanford, California: Stanford University Press, 1968. *29, 36*

Levering, Joseph Mortimer. *A History of Bethlehem, Pennsylvania, 1741-1892, with Some Account of Its Founders and Their Early Activity in America.* 1903. Reprint. New York: AMS Press, 1971. *209, 220*

Levin, David. *In Defense of Historical Literature: Essays on American History, Autobiography, Drama, and Fiction.* New York: Hill and Wang, 1967. *15, 28, 35*

*_____, ed. *Jonathan Edwards: A Profile.* New York: Hill and Wang, 1969.

Levine, Edward N. *The Irish and Irish Politicians: A Study of Cultural and Social Alienation.* Notre Dame, Indiana: Notre Dame University Press, 1966. *234*

•Levitan, Sar A., ed. *Blue Collar Workers: A Symposium on Middle America.* New York: McGraw-Hill, 1971. *125*

_____, Garth L. Mangum, and Ray Marshall. *Human Resources and Labor Markets: Labor and Manpower in the American Economy.* New York: Harper and Row, 1972.

Lewin, Kurt. "Psychological Ecology." In *Field Theory in Social Sciences,* edited by Dorwin Cartwright. 1951. Reprint. Westport, Connecticut: Greenwood Press, 1975. *142*

•Lewis, Lloyd, and Henry Smith. *Chicago, The History of Its Reputation.* New York: Harcourt, Brace, Jovanovich, 1929. *225*

*Lewis, R. W. B. *The American Adam: Innocence, Tragedy, and Tradition in the Nineteenth Century.* Chicago: University of Chicago Press, 1955. *4, 13, 268*

Lichtenstein, H. "The Dilemma of Human Identity." *Journal of the American Psychoanalytic Association* 11 (1963):173-223. *31, 37*

_____. "Identity and Sexuality: A Study of Their Relationship in Man." *Journal of the American Psychoanalytic Association* 9 (1961):179-260.

•Lillard, Richard G. *American Life in Autobiography, A Descriptive Guide.* Stanford, California: Stanford University Press, 1956. *22, 32*

Lincoln, Abraham. *Collected Works.* Edited by Roy P. Basler. 9 vols. New Brunswick, New Jersey: Rutgers University Press, 1953-1955. *267*

Lincoln, Evelyn. *My Twelve Years with John F. Kennedy.* New York: David McKay Company, 1965. *71*

*Lindbeck, Assar. *The Political Economy of the New Left: An Outsider's View.* New York: Harper and Row, 1971. *126*

Linden, George W. *Reflections on the Screen.* Belmont, California: Wadsworth Publishing Company, 1970. *179, 183*

*Lindgren, Ernest. *The Art of the Film.* New York: Macmillan, Collier Books, 1970. *179, 183*

Lindop, Edmund, and Joseph Jares. *White House Sportsmen.* Boston: Houghton Mifflin, 1964. *73*

Lindsay, Vachel. *Collected Poems.* Rev. ed. New York: Macmillan, 1925. *229*

Lindsey, Almont. *The Pullman Strike: The Story of a Unique Experiment and of a Great Labor Upheaval.* Chicago: University of Chicago Press, Phoenix Books, 1964. *116, 234*

Link, Arthur S. *Wilson.* 5 vols. Princeton, New Jersey: Princeton University Press, 1947-1965. *78*

Link, Eugene P. *Democratic-Republican Societies, 1790-1800.* New York: Octagon Books, 1965. *110*

Lister, Raymond. *How to Identify Old Maps and Globes, with a List of Cartographers, Engravers, Publishers, and Printers Concerned with Printed Maps and Globes c. 1500 to c. 1850*. Hamden, Connecticut: Archon Books; London: G. Bell, 1965. *83, 92*

*Litwack, Leon F. *North of Slavery: The Negro in the Free States, 1790-1860*. Chicago: University of Chicago Press, Phoenix Books, 1961. *114, 150*

*Lockridge, Kenneth. *A New England Town: The First Hundred Years, Dedham, Massachusetts, 1636-1736*. New York: W. W. Norton, 1970. *8*

*Lockwood, George B. *The New Harmony Movement*. 1905. Reprint. New York: Dover. *111*

Lomask, Milton. *Andrew Johnson: President on Trial*. 1960. Reprint. New York: Octagon Books, 1973. *76*

Lomax, Alan, ed. *The Folk Songs of North America*. Garden City, New York: Doubleday, 1960. *264*

*Lomax, Louis, *The Negro Revolt*. Rev. ed. New York: Harper and Row, 1971. *99*

Longley, Alcander. *What Is Communism? A Narrative of the Relief Community*. 1890. Reprint. New York: AMS Press, 1971. *214, 220*

Longstreet, Stephen. *Chicago, 1860-1919*. New York: David McKay Company, 1973. *225*

•Lorant, Stefan. *The Glorious Burden: The American Presidency*. Rev. ed. New York: Harper and Row, 1968. *69, 77*

•_____. *The Life and Times of Theodore Roosevelt*. Garden City, New York: Doubleday, 1959.   •

•_____. *The Presidency: A Pictorial History of Presidential Elections from Washington to Truman*. New York: Macmillan, 1951.

Lorwin, Lewis L. *The International Labor Movement: History, Policies, Outlook*. 1953. Reprint. Westport, Connecticut: Greenwood Press, 1973. *124*

*Lovejoy, Arthur O. *The Great Chain of Being: A Study of the History of an Idea*. Cambridge, Massachusetts: Harvard University Press, 1936. *142*

*Lovejoy, David S., ed. *Religious Enthusiasm and the Great Awakening*. Englewood Cliffs, New Jersey: Prentice-Hall, 1969. *14*

Lowenthal, David. "The American Scene." *Georgraphical Review* (January 1968). *58, 142, 143, 144*

_____. "George Perkins Marsh and the American Geographical Tradition." *Geographical Review* 43:2:207-13.

•_____. *George Perkins Marsh: Versatile Vermonter*. New York: Columbia University Press, 1958.

_____, ed. "Enviromental Perception and Behavior." University of Chicago Department of Geography Research Paper No. 109. Chicago: University of Chicago Press, 1967.

*Lowenthal, Leo. *Literature, Popular Culture, and Society*. Palo Alto, California: Pacific Books, 1968. *177, 183*

•Lowery, Woodbury. *The Lowery Collection: A Descriptive List of Maps of the Spanish Possessions Within the Present Limits of the United States, 1502-1820*. Edited with notes by Philip Lee Phillips. Washington, D.C.: U.S. Government Printing Office, 1912. *87, 95*

Lowry, Mark. "Race and Socioeconomic Well-Being: A Geographical Analysis of the Mississippi Case." *Geographical Review* (October 1970). *58*

*Lubove, Roy. *Twentieth-Century Pittsburgh: Government, Business, and Environmental Change*. New York: Wiley, 1969. *158, 169*

_____. "The Urbanization Process: An Approach to Historical Research." *Journal of the American Institute of Planners* 33 (January 1967):33-39. *169*

Lucid, Robert F., ed. "Programs in American Studies." *American Quarterly* 22 (Summer 1970). *232*

Lurie, Nancy O., and Eleanor Leacock, eds. *North American Indians in Historical Perspective*. New York: Random House, 1971. *199*

•Lutz, Alma. *Emma Willard, Pioneer Educator of American Women*. Boston: Beacon Press, 1964. *249, 256*

•_____. *Susan B. Anthony: Rebel, Crusader, Humanitarian*. Boston: Beacon Press, 1959.

Lynch, Hollis R. *The Black Urban Condition: A Documentary History, 1866-1971*. New York: Thomas Y. Crowell, 1973. *166*

*Lynch, Kevin. *The Image of the City*. Cambridge: Massachusetts Institute of Technology Press, 1960. *160, 169*

*Lynd, Robert S., and Helen M. Lynd. *Middletown: A Study in Contemporary American Culture*. New York: Harcourt, Brace, Jovanovich, 1959. *274*

*_____. *Middletown in Transition: A Study in Cultural Conflicts.* New York: Harcourt, Brace, Jovanovich, 1963.

*Lynd, Staughton. *Intellectual Origins of American Radicalism.* New York: Random House, Vintage books, 1969. *7, 110, 268*

_____. "The Mechanics in New York Politics 1774-1788." *Labor History* 5 (1964):225-46.

_____, and Alice Lynd. *Rank and File: Personal Histories of Working Class Organizers.* Boston: Beacon Press, 1973. *246*

Lynen, John F. *The Design of the Present: Essays on Time and Form in American Literature.* New Haven, Connecticut: Yale University Press, 1969. *28, 35*

•Lynes, Russell. *The Domesticated Americans.* New York: Harper and Row, 1963. *176, 183*

*_____. *The Tastemakers.* New York: Grosset and Dunlap, 1959.

Lynn, Kenneth S. *Mark Twain and Southwestern Humor.* 1960. Reprint. Westport, Connecticut: Greenwood Press, 1972. *42*

*_____, ed. *The Comic Tradition in America: An Anthology.* Garden City, New York: W. W. Norton, 1968.

Lynn, Mary C., ed. *Women's Liberation in the Twentieth Century.* New York: Wiley, 1975. *257*

•McAvoy, Thomas T. *The Great Crisis in American Catholic History, 1895-1900.* Chicago: H. Regnery, 1957. *19*

*McBrearty, James C. *American Labor History and Comparative Labor Movements, A Selected Bibliography.* Tucson: University of Arizona Press, 1973. *106*

*McCarthy, Mary. *Memories of a Catholic Girlhood.* New York: Harcourt, Brace, Jovanovich, Harvest Books, 1972. *248*

*McCloskey, Robert G. *The American Supreme Court.* Chicago: University of Chicago Press, 1960. *270*

McClure, Arthur, ed. *The Movies: An American Idiom.* Rutherford, New Jersey: Fairleigh Dickinson University Press, 1971. *179, 183*

McClure, Arthur F. *The Truman Administration and the Problems of Postwar Labor, 1945-1948.* Rutherford, New Jersey: Fairleigh Dickinson University Press, 1969. *124*

*McCord, David. *About Boston: Sight, Sound, Flavor, and Inflection.* Boston: Little, Brown, 1973. *160, 169*

McCormac, Eugene I. *James K. Polk, A Political Biography.* 1922. Reprint. New York: Russell and Russell, 1965. *75*

McCoy, Donald R. *Calvin Coolidge: The Quiet President.* New York: Macmillan, 1967. *78*

McDonald, Forrest. *Insull.* Chicago: University of Chicago Press, 1962. *227*

McFarland, Charles K. *Roosevelt, Lewis and the New Deal, 1933-1940.* Fort Worth: Texas Christian University Press, 1970. *121*

*McGiffert, Michael. *The Character of Americans: A Book of Readings.* Rev. ed. Homewood, Illinois: Dorsey Press, 1970. *269*

*MacGowan, Kenneth. *Behind the Screen: The History and Techniques of the Motion Picture.* New York: Dell, Delta Books, 1967. *179, 183*

*Machen, J. Gresham. *Christianity and Liberalism.* Grand Rapids, Michigan: William B. Eerdmans, 1923. *20*

Machlis, Joseph. *American Composers of Our Time.* New York: Thomas Y. Crowell, 1963. *273*

•MacKay, Constance D. *The Little Theatre in the United States.* New York: Holt, 1917. *236*

MacKay, Kenneth C. *The Progressive Movement of 1924.* New York: Octagon Books, 1966. *120*

•McKelvey, Blake. *American Urbanization: A Comparative History.* Glenview, Illinois: Scott, Foresman, 1973. *164*

MacKenzie, Kenneth M. *The Robe and the Sword: The Methodist Church and the Rise of American Imperialism.* Washington, D.C.: Public Affairs Press, 1961. *20*

McKenzie, Roderick D. "The Ecological Approach to the Study of the Human Community." In *The City,* edited by Robert E. Park, Ernest W. Burgess, and Roderick D. McKenzie. Chicago: University of Chicago Press, 1928. *144*

•McKissick, Floyd. *Three Fifths of a Man.* New York: Macmillan, 1969. *151*

*McKitrick, Eric L. *Andrew Johnson and Reconstruction.* Chicago: University of Chicago Press, Phoenix Books, 1960. *76*

MacLaine, Shirley. *Don't Fall Off the Mountain.* New York: W. W. Norton, 1970. *24, 33*

McLaughlin, Virginia Yans. "Patterns of Work and Family Organization: Buffalo's Italians." *Journal of Interdisciplinary History* 2 (Autumn 1971). *241*

McLean, Albert. *American Vaudeville as Ritual*. Lexington: University Press of Kentucky, 1965. *174, 183*

MacLean, John Patterson. *Shakers of Ohio: Fugitive Papers Concerning the Shakers of Ohio, with Unpublished Manuscripts*. 1907. Reprint. Philadelphia: Porcupine Press, 1965. *210, 221*

*McLoughlin, William G. *Isaac Backus and the American Pietistic Tradition*. Edited by Oscar Handlin. New York: Little, Brown, 1967. *16*

_____, ed. *The American Evangelicals, 1800-1900: An Anthology*. Gloucester, Massachusetts: Peter Smith, 1968.

McLoughlin, William G., Jr. *Modern Revivalism: Charles Grandison Finney to Billy Graham*. New York: Ronald Press, 1959. *16*

*McLuhan, H. Marshall. *The Gutenberg Galaxy: The Making of Typographic Man*. New York: New American Library, Mentor Books, 1969. *6, 8, 9, 179, 183*

*_____. *The Mechanical Bride: Folklore of Industrial Man*. Boston: Beacon Press, 1951.

*_____. *Understanding Media: The Extensions of Man*. New York: New American Library, Mentor Books, 1973.

*McManis, Douglas R. *European Impressions of the New England Coast, 1497-1620*. Chicago: University of Chicago Department of Geography, 1972. *55*

McMurry, Donald L. *Coxey's Army: A Study of the Industrial Army Movement of 1894*. 1929. Reprint. New York: AMS Press, 1970. *116*

_____. *The Great Burlington Railroad Strike of 1888: A Case History in Labor Relations*. 1956. Reprint. New York: Russell and Russell, 1973.

•McNeill, John T. *The History and Character of Calvinism*. New York: Oxford University Press, 1954. *14*

•McNickle, D'Arcy. *The Indian Tribes of the United States: Ethnic and Cultural Survival*. New York: Oxford University Press, 1962. *195*

*_____. *They Came Here First: The Epic of the American Indian*. New ed. New York: Harper and Row, 1975.

*_____, and Harold E. Fey. *Indians and Other Americans: Two Ways of Life Meet*. Rev. ed. New York: Harper and Row, 1970. *195*

McNulty, Paul James. "Labor Market Analysis and the Development of Labor Economics." *Industrial and Labor Relations Review* 19 (July 1966):538-48. *107*

_____. "Labor Problems and Labor Economics: The Roots of an Academic Discipline." *Labor History* 9 (Spring 1968): 239-61.

*McPherson, James M., et al. *Blacks in America: Bibliographical Essays*. Garden City, New York: Doubleday, Anchor Books, 1972. *166*

*McWilliams, Carey. *North from Mexico: The Spanish Speaking People of the United States*. 1949. Reprint. Westport, Connecticut: Greenwood Press, 1968. *57*

Madden, David, ed. *Tough Guy Writers of the Thirties*. Carbondale: Southern Illinois University Press, 1968. *175, 183*

*Maier, Pauline. *From Resistance to Revolution: Colonial Radicals and the Development of American Opposition to Britain, 1765-1776*. New York: Random House, Vintage Books, 1972. *110*

*Mailer, Norman. *The Armies of the Night: History as a Novel, The Novel as History*. New York: New American Library, Signet Books, 1971. *24, 26, 33*

*Malcolm X. *The Autobiography of Malcolm X*. New York: Ballantine Books, 1973. *17, 23, 24, 26, 29, 32, 148*

Malin, James. *The Grassland of North America: Prolegomena to Its History, with Addenda and Postscript*. Gloucester, Massachusetts: Peter Smith, 1967. *53, 142*

_____. "Ecology and History." *Scientific Monthly* 70 (May 1950): 295-98.

*Malone, Dumas. *Jefferson and His Time*. 5 vols. Boston: Little Brown, 1948-1974. *74*

•Manchester, William R. *Portrait of a President: John F. Kennedy in Profile*. Rev. ed. Boston: Little, Brown, 1967. *79*

Mandel, Bernard. *Samuel Gompers: A Biography*. Kent, Ohio: Kent State University Press, 1963. *116*

*Mann, Arthur M. *Yankee Reformers in the Urban Age: Social Reform in Boston, 1880-1900*. Chicago: University of Chicago Press, 1974. *159, 169*

*Mannheim, Karl. *Ideology and Utopia: An Introduction to the Sociology of Knowledge*. New York: Harcourt, Brace, Jovanovich, Harvest Books, 1955. *207, 221*

•Manning, Thomas G., ed. *The Chicago Strike of 1894: Industrial Labor in the Late Nineteenth Century.* New York: Holt, 1960. *116*

•Manross, William W. *A History of the American Episcopal Church.* 3d ed., rev. New York: Morehouse-Gorham, 1959. *12*

•Manson, Grant C. *Frank Lloyd Wright.* New York: Reinhold, 1958. *231*

*Manuel, Frank. *The New World of Henri Saint-Simon.* Notre Dame, Indiana: University of Notre Dame Press, 1963. *208, 221*

•_____. *The Prophets of Paris.* Cambridge, Massachusetts: Harvard University Press, 1962.

*_____, ed. *Utopias and Utopian Thought.* Boston: Beacon Press, 1966.

*_____, and Fritzie P. Manuel, eds. *French Utopias: An Anthology of Ideal Societies.* New York: Schocken Books, 1971. *208, 221*

*Marckwardt, Albert H. *American English.* New York: Oxford University Press, 1958. *269*

*Marcuse, Herbert. *One-Dimensional Man: Studies in the Ideology of Advanced Industrial Society.* Boston: Beacon Press, 1964.

Margalef, R. "On Certain Unifying Principles in Ecology." *The American Naturalist* 97 (November-December 1963): 357-74, *142*

•Marnell, William H. *Man-Made Morals: Four Philosophies That Shaped America.* Garden City, New York: Doubleday, 1966. *13*

*Marquand, John P. *The Late George Apley: A Novel in the Form of a Memoir.* 1937. New York: Pocket Books. *159, 169*

Marsh, George Perkins. *The Earth as Modified by Human Action: A New Edition of "Man and Nature."* New York: Charles Scribner's Sons, 1885. *132, 144*

•Marshall, F. Ray. *The Negro and Organized Labor.* New York: Wiley, 1965. *125*

•_____. *The Negro Worker.* New York: Random House, 1967.

•Marshner, F. J. *Land Use and Its Patterns in the United States.* Washington, D.C.: U.S. Government Printing Office, 1959. *57*

•Martin, Asa E. *After the White House.* State College: Pennsylvania Valley Publishers, 1951. *69*

*Martin, James J. *Men Against the State: The Expositors of Individualist Anarchism in America, 1827-1908.* Colorado Springs, Colorado: Ralph Myles, 1970. *215, 221*

•Martin, Jay. *Conrad Aiken: A Life of His Art.* Princeton, New Jersey: Princeton University Press, 1962. *29, 36, 44, 235*

*_____. *Harvest of Change: American Literature, 1865-1914.* Englewood Cliffs, New Jersey: Prentice-Hall, 1969.

•Marty, Martin E. *The New Shape of American Religion.* New York: Harper and Row, 1959. *12, 20*

*_____. *Righteous Empire: The Protestant Experience in America.* New York: Dial Press, 1970.

*_____, and Dean Peerman, eds. *New Theology No. 8.* 8 vols. New York: Macmillan, 1964-1971. *21*

*Marx, Leo. *The Machine in the Garden: Technology and the Pastoral Ideal in America.* New York: Oxford University Press, Galaxy Books, 1967. *5, 140, 197*

•Marx, Rudolph. *The Health of the Presidents.* New York: Putnam, 1961. *72*

*Masotti, Louis H., and Jeffrey K. Hadden, eds. *Suburbia in Transition.* New ed. New York: Franklin, Watts, New Viewpoints Books, 1974. *163*

Massa, Ann. *Vachel Lindsay, Fieldworker for the American Dream.* Bloomington: University of Indiana Press, 1970. *229*

*Mast, Gerald. *A Short History of the Movies.* New York: Pegasus, 1971. *179, 183*

Masters, Edgar Lee. *Across Spoon River.* 1936. Reprint. Octagon Books, 1969. *225, 227, 229*

*_____. *The Spoon River Anthology.* New ed. New York: Macmillan, 1962.

•_____. *The Tale of Chicago.* New York: Putnam, 1933.

_____. *Vachel Lindsay: A Poet in America.* 1935. Reprint. New York: Biblo and Tannen, 1969.

*Mather, Cotton. *Magnalia Christi Americana; Or, The Ecclesiastical History of New England.* Edited by Raymond J. Cunningham. New York: Frederick Ungar, 1971. *11*

•Mathews, Donald G. *Slavery and Methodism: A Chapter in American Morality, 1780-1845.* Princeton, New Jersey: Princeton University Press, 1965. *16*

•Mathison, Minna. et al., eds. *The Chicago Anthology: A Collection of Verse from the Work of the Chicago Poets.* Chicago: The Roadside Press, 1916. *235*

*Matthews, Donald R., ed. *Perspectives on Presidential Selection.* Washington, D.C.: The Brookings Institution, 1973. *70*

*Matthiessen, F. O. *American Renaissance: Art and Expression in the Age of Emerson and Whitman.* New York: Oxford University Press, Galaxy Books, 1968. *5, 41, 271, 272*
_____, ed. *The Oxford Book of American Verse.* New York: Oxford University Press, 1950.

*Matthiessen, Peter. *Sal Si Puedes: Cesar Chavez and the New American Revolution.* New York: Dell, 1973. *126*

•Maurois, Andre. *Aspects of Biography.* Translated by S. C. Roberts. New York: Frederick Ungar, 1966. *24, 27, 33*

Maxson, Charles H. *The Great Awakening in the Middle Colonies.* 1920. Reprint. Gloucester, Massachusetts: Peter Smith, 1958. *14*

•May, Ernest R., ed. *The Ultimate Decision: The President as Commander-in-Chief.* New York: George Braziller, 1960. *72*

*May, Henry F. *The End of American Innocence; A Study of the First Years of Our Time, 1912-1917.* New York: Franklin, Watts, New Viewpoints Books, 1964. *17, 227, 273*
_____. *Protestant Churches and Industrial America.* New York: Octagon Books, 1963.

•Mayer, Frederick E. *The Religious Bodies of America.* 4th ed., revised by Arthur C. Piepkorn. St. Louis, Missouri: Concordia Publishing House, 1956. *12*

*Mayer, Harold M., and Richard C. Wade. *Chicago: Growth of a Metropolis.* Chicago: University of Chicago Press, Phoenix Books, 1973. *56, 160, 165, 169, 191, 193, 225, 227*

*Mays, Benjamin E. *The Negro's God As Reflected in His Literature.* New York: Atheneum, 1968. *17*

*Mazlish, Bruce. *In Search of Nixon: A Psychohistorical Inquiry.* Baltimore: Penguin, Pelican Books, 1973. *80*

•Mazo, Earl, and Stephen Hess. *Nixon: A Political Portrait.* New York: Harper and Row, 1968. *80*

Mead, Frank S. *Handbook of Denominations in the U.S.* 6th ed. New York: Abingdon Press, 1975. *12*

•Mead, Margaret, and Frances Bagley Kaplan. *American Women: Report of the President's Commission on the Status of Women and Other Publications of the Commission.* New York: Scribner's, 1965. *257*

Mead, Sidney E. *The Lively Experiment: The Shaping of Christianity in America.* New York: Harper and Row, 1963. *12*

Mead, William, and Eric Brown. *The United States and Canada: A Regional Geography.* Atlantic Highlands, New Jersey: Humanities Press, 1962. *52*

•Meeker, Arthur. *Chicago, with Love: A Polite and Personal History.* New York: Alfred A. Knopf, 1955. *228*

Meggers, Betty. "Environmental Limitation on the Development of Culture." *American Anthropologist* 56:801-24. *138*

*Meier, August. *Negro Thought in America, 1880-1915: Racial Ideologies in the Age of Booker T. Washington.* Ann Arbor: University of Michigan Press, 1963. *17*

•_____, and Francis L. Broderick, eds. *Negro Protest Thought in the 20th Century.* Indianapolis, Indiana: Bobbs-Merrill, 1966.

•_____, et al., eds. *Black Nationalism in America.* Indianapolis, Indiana: Bobbs-Merrill, 1971.

Meine, Franklin J. *Tall Tales of the Southwest: An Anthology of Southern and Southwestern Humor, 1830-1860.* 1946. Reprint. Saint Clair Shores, Michigan: Scholarly Press, 1971. *42*

Meinig, Donald W. *The Great Columbian Plain: A Historical Geography, 1805-1910.* Seattle: University of Washington Press, 1968. *53, 57*
_____. *Imperial Texas: An Interpretive Essay in Cultural Geography.* Austin: University of Texas Press, 1969.

_____. "The Mormon Culture Region." *Annals of the Association of American Geographers* (June 1965). *53*

*_____. *Southwest: Three People in Geographical Change, 1600-1970.* New York: Oxford University Press, 1971.

Melder, Keith. "Ladies Bountiful: Organized Women's Benevolence in Early 19th-Century America." *New York History* 48 (1967). *256*

Mencken, Henry L. *The American Language: An Inquiry into the Development of English in the United States.* 4th ed. Abridged and edited by Raven I. McDavid, Jr. New York: Alfred A. Knopf, 1963. *269*

*Mendelsohn, Harold. *Mass Entertainment.* New Haven, Connecticut: College and University Press, 1966. *178, 183*

Merrens, Harry R. *Colonial North Carolina in the Eighteenth Century: A Study in Historical Geography.* Chapel Hill: University of North Carolina Press, 1964. *53, 55*

Merriam, Charles E. *Chicago: A More Intimate View of Urban Politics.* 1929. Reprint. New York: Arno Press, 1970. *225*

*Merriam, Eve, ed. *Growing Up Female in America.* New York: Dell, 1973. *256*

*Merrill, Horace Samuel. *Bourbon Leader: Grover Cleveland and the Democratic Party.* Boston: Little, Brown, 1965. *77*

*Merton, Thomas. *Mystics and Zen Masters.* New York: Dell, Delta Books, 1969. *21, 26, 34*

•_____. *The New Man.* New York: New American Library, 1971.

•_____. *The Seven Story Mountain.* New York: Doubleday, Image Books, 1970.

•Metropolitan Applied Research Center. *Racism and American Education: A Dialogue and Agenda for Action.* New York: Harper and Row, 1970. *103*

•Meyer, Donald B. *The Positive Thinkers: A Study of the American Quest for Health, Wealth and Personal Power from Mary Baker Eddy to Norman Vincent Peale.* New York: Doubleday, Anchor Books, 1965. *13, 20, 21*

_____. *The Protestant Search for Political Realism, 1919-1941.* 1960. Reprint. Westport, Connecticut: Greenwood Press, 1973.

*Meyer, Leonard B. *Music, the Arts, and Ideas: Patterns and Predictions in Twentieth Century Culture.* Chicago: University of Chicago Press, Phoenix Books, 1969. *180, 183*

*Meyers, Marvin. *The Jacksonian Persuasion: Politics and Belief.* Stanford, California: Stanford University Press, 1957. *16*

Meyersohn, Rolf. "The Sociology of Leisure in the United States: Introduction and Bibliography, 1945-1965." *Journal of Leisure Research* 1 (1969): 53-68. *183*

Meyerson, Martin, and Edward C. Banfield. *Boston: The Job Ahead.* Cambridge, Massachusetts: Harvard University Press, 1966. *160, 169*

•Middleton, Arthur P. *Tobacco Coast: A Maritime History of the Chesapeake Bay in the Colonial Era.* Newport News, Virginia: Mariners' Museum, 1953. *55*

*Mikkelsen, Michael Andrew. *The Bishop Hill Colony: A Religious, Communistic Settlement in Henry County, Illinois.* 1892. Reprint. New York: Johnson Reprint Corporation, 1973. *213, 221*

Miller, E. Joan Wilson. "The Ozark Culture Region as Revealed by Traditional Materials." *Annals of the Association of American Geographers* (March 1968). *58*

Miller, Hugh C. *The Chicago School of Architecture.* Washington, D.C.: U.S. Department of the Interior, 1973. *230*

Miller, Joan S. "The Politics of Municipal Reform in Chicago During the Progressive Era: The Municipal Voters League as a Test Case, 1896-1920." Master's thesis, Roosevelt University, 1966. *233*

*Miller, John N., ed. *A World of Her Own: Writers and the Feminist Controversy.* Columbus, Ohio: Charles E. Merrill, 1971. *252*

*Miller, Perry. *Errand into the Wilderness.* Cambridge, Massachusetts: Harvard University Press, 1975. *4, 8, 14, 17, 18, 272, 273*

*_____. *The Life of the Mind in America: From the Revolution to the Civil War.* New York: Harcourt, Brace, Jovanovich, 1970.

*_____. *Orthodoxy in Massachusetts, 1630-1650.* New York: Harper and Row, Harper Torchbooks, 1970.

*_____, ed. *The American Puritans: Their Prose and Poetry.* Garden City, New York: Doubleday, Anchor Books, 1956.

*_____, ed. *American Thought: The Civil War to World War I.* New York: Holt, Rinehart, and Winston, 1954.

*_____, ed. *The American Transcendentalists: Their Prose and Poetry.* New York: Doubleday, Anchor Books, 1957.

*_____, ed. *The Transcendentalists: An Anthology.* Cambridge, Massachusetts: Harvard University Press, 1950.

*_____, and Alan E. Heimert, eds. *The Great Awakening: Documents Illustrating the Crisis and Its Consequences.* Indianapolis, Indiana: Bobbs-Merrill, 1967. *14*

*_____, and Thomas H. Johnson, eds. *The Puritans: A Sourcebook of Their Writings.* Rev. ed. 2 vols. New York: Harper and Row, 1963.

•Miller, Robert M. *American Protestantism and Social Issues, 1919-1939.* Chapel Hill: University of North Carolina Press, 1958. *20*

*Miller, William. *A New History of the United States.* Rev. ed. New York: Dell, Delta Books, 1969. *266*

•Miller, William R. *Martin Luther King, Jr.: His Life, Martyrdom and Meaning for the World.* New York: Weybright and Talley, 1968. *17*

*Millett, Kate. *Sexual Politics.* New York: Avon, Equinox Books, 1971. *249*

Millis, Harry A., and Emily C. Brown. *From the Wagner Act to Taft-Hartley: A Study of National Labor Policy and Labor Relations.* Chicago: University of Chicago Press, 1950. *122*

*Mills, C. Wright. *The Power Elite.* New York: Oxford University Press, Galaxy Books, 1959. *274*

•Milton, John. *John Milton: A Reader's Guide to His Poetry.* Edited by Marjorie Hope Nicolson. New York: Octagon Books, 1971. *14*

•Minter, David L. *The Interpreted Design as a Structural Principle in American Prose.* New Haven, Connecticut: Yale University Press, 1969. *28, 35*

Misch, Georg. *A History of Autobiography in Antiquity.* 2 vols. 1950. Reprint. Westport, Connecticut: Greenwood Press, 1974. *24, 33*

Mitchell, David. *1919: Red Mirage, Elegy for a Lost Cause.* New York: Macmillan, 1970. *120*

*Mitchell, Juliet. *Woman's Estate.* New York: Random House, Vintage Books, 1973. *246*

Mohl, Raymond A. "Poverty, Politics and the Mechanics of New York City, 1803." *Labor History* 12 (1971):38-51. *111*

_____, and James F. Richardson. *The Urban Experience: Themes in American History.* Belmont, California: Wadsworth Publishing, 1973. *161*

Momaday, N. Scott. *House Made of Dawn.* New York: Harper and Row, 1968. *203*

•_____. *The Journey of Tai-me.* Santa Barbara: University of California Press, 1967.

*_____. *The Way to Rainy Mountain.* New York: Ballantine Books, 1972.

•Monroe, Harriet. *John Wellborn Root: A Study of His Life and Work.* 1896. Reprint. Park Forest, Illinois: Prairie School Press, 1966. *228, 229, 231*

_____. *A Poet's Life: Seventy Years in a Changing World.* Philadelphia: Richard West, 1938.

•Montgomery, David. *Beyond Equality: Labor and the Radical Republicans, 1862-1872.* New York: Alfred A. Knopf, 1967. *111, 113*

_____. "The Working Classes of the Pre-Industrial American City, 1780-1830." *Labor History* 9 (1968):3-22.

*Moody, Anne. *Coming of Age in Mississippi.* New York: Dell, 1970. *248*

*Moore, Barrington. *Social Origins of Dictatorship and Democracy: Lord and Peasant in the Making of the Modern World.* Boston: Beacon Press, 1966. *113*

Moore, Charles. *Daniel H. Burnham: Architect, Planner of Cities.* 1921. Reprint. New York: Da Capo Press, 1968. *231*

•Moore, Edward C. *Forty Years of Opera in Chicago.* New York: Horace Liveright, 1930. *236*

*Moquin, Wayne, and Charles Van Doren, eds. *A Documentary History of the Mexican Americans.* New York: Bantam Books, 1972. *126*

•Morgan, Anna. *My Chicago.* Chicago: R. F. Seymour, 1918. *236*

•Morgan, Arthur E. *The Community of the Future and the Future of the Community.* Yellow Springs, Ohio: Community Service, 1957. *215, 221*

_____. *Edward Bellamy.* 1944. Reprint. Philadelphia: Porcupine Press, 1974.

•_____. *Nowhere Was Somewhere: How History Makes Utopias and How Utopias Make History.* Chapel Hill: University of North Carolina Press, 1946.

*Morgan, Edmund S. *The Puritan Dilemma: The Story of John Winthrop.* Boston: Little, Brown, 1958. *8, 14, 15*

_____. *Roger Williams: The Church and the State.* New York: Harcourt, Brace, Jovanovich, 1967.

*_____. *Visible Saints: The History of a Puritan Idea.* Ithaca, New York: Cornell University Press, 1965.

*_____, ed. *The American Revolution: Two Centuries of Interpretation.* Englewood Cliffs, New Jersey: Prentice-Hall, 1965.

_____, ed. *The Puritan Family: Essays on Religion and Domestic Relations in Seventeenth Century New England.* Boston: The Trustees of the Public Library, 1944.

Morgan, H. Wayne. *William McKinley and His America.* Syracuse, New York: Syracuse University Press, 1963. *77*

*Morgan, Lewis Henry. *League of the Iroquois.* Secaucus, New Jersey: Citadel Press, 1972. *200*

*Morgan, Robin. *Sisterhood Is Powerful: An Anthology of Writings from the Women's Liberation Movement.* New York: Random House, Vintage Books, 1970. *250, 252*

Morgan, Ruth. *The President and Civil Rights: Policy-Making by Executive Order.* New York: St. Martin's Press, 1970. *72*

●Morin, Edgar. *The Stars.* Translated by Richard Howard. New York: Grove Press, 1960. *179, 183*

*Morison, Elting E. *Men, Machines, and Modern Times.* Cambridge: Massachusetts Institute of Technology Press, 1966. *9*

*Morison, Samuel Eliot. *Builders of the Bay Colony.* Rev. ed. Boston: Houghton Mifflin, Sentry Books, 1964. *55, 84, 92, 266*

_____. *The European Discovery of America: The Northern Voyages, A.D. 500-1600.* New York: Oxford University Press, 1971.

_____. *The European Discovery of America: The Southern Voyages, 1492-1616.* New York: Oxford University Press, 1974.

●Morland, John Kenneth. *Token Desegregation and Beyond.* Atlanta, Georgia; New York: Southern Regional Council, Anti-Defamation League of B'nai B'rith, 1963. *98*

*Morrill, Richard L., and Ernest H. Woldenberg. *The Geography of Poverty in the United States.* New York: McGraw-Hill, 1971. *58*

●Morris, George. *The CIA amd American Labor: The Subversion of the AFL-CIO's Foreign Policy.* New York: International Publishers, 1967. *124*

Morris, James O. *Conflict Within the A.F. of L.: A Study of Craft Versus Industrial Unionism, 1901-1938.* 1958. Reprint. Westport, Connecticut: Greenwood Press, 1974. *118*

Morris, Richard B. *Government and Labor in Early America.* Santa Fe, New Mexico: William Gannon, 1970. *109, 266*

*_____, ed. *Basic Documents in American History.* Rev. ed. Princeton, New Jersey: Van Nostrand, Reinhold, Anvil Books, 1965.

_____, ed. *Encyclopedia of American History.* Enlarged ed. New York: Harper and Row, 1970.

*Morrison, Hugh. *Louis Sullivan: Prophet of Modern Architecture.* 1935. Reprint. New York: W. W. Norton, 1962. *231*

●Moscowitz, Samuel. *Explorers of the Infinitive.* Cleveland, Ohio: World Publishing Company, 1963. *176, 183*

●_____. *Seekers of Tomorrow: Masters of Science Fiction.* Cleveland, Ohio: World Publishing Company, 1966.

Mott, Frank Luther. *American Journalism: A History of Newspapers in the United States Through 260 Years: 1690 to 1950.* 3d ed. New York: Macmillan, 1962. *174, 183, 272*

_____. *Golden Multitudes: The Story of Best Sellers in the United States.* New York: R. R. Bowker, 1960.

_____. *A History of American Magazines.* 5 vols. Cambridge, Massachusetts: Harvard University Press, 1930-1968.

*Mowry, George F. *The Era of Theodore Roosevelt, 1900-1912.* New York: Harper and Row, Harper Torchbooks, 1958. *77*

*Moynihan, Daniel P., and Nathan Glazer. *Beyond the Melting Pot: The Negroes, Puerto Ricans, Jews, Italians, and Irish of New York City.* 2d rev. ed. Cambridge: Massachusetts Institute of Technology Press, 1970. *19*

●Muelder, Walter G., et al., eds. *The Development of American Philosophy: A Book of Readings.* 2d ed. Boston: Houghton Mifflin, 1960. *13, 273*

Mugridge, Donald H., ed. *The Presidents of the U.S., 1789-1962: A Selected List of References.* Washington, D.C.: The Library of Congress, 1963. *67*

*Mumford, Lewis. *The Brown Decades: A Study of the Arts in America, 1865-1895.* 2d ed. New York: Dover, 1955. *7, 9, 144, 161, 231, 263*

*_____. *The City in History: Its Origins, Its Transformations, and Its Prospects.* New York: Harcourt, Brace, Jovanovich, 1968.

*_____. *The Culture of Cities.* New York: Harcourt, Brace, Jovanovich, Harvest Books, 1970.

*_____. *The Myth of the Machine.* 2 vols. New York: Harcourt, Brace, Jovanovich, 1971-1974.

*_____. *Sticks and Stones: A Study of American Architecture and Civilization.* Rev. ed. New York: Dover, 1955.

Murphy, Raymond E. *The American City: An Urban Geography.* New York: McGraw-Hill, 1974. *56*

Murray, Robert K. *The Harding Era: Warren G. Harding and His Administration.* Minneapolis: University of Minnesota Press, 1969. *78, 120*

*_____. *Red Scare: A Study in National Hysteria, 1919-1920.* New York: McGraw-Hill, 1964.

*Myrdal, Gunnar, with Richard Sterner and Arnold Rose. *An American Dilemma: The Negro Problem and Modern Democracy.* 2 vols. New York: Pantheon Books, 1975. *98, 274*

Nabokov, Vladimir. *Speak, Memory: An Autobiography Revisited.* New York: Putnam, Capricorn Books, 1970. *25, 26, 33*

•Nagel, Paul C. *One Nation Indivisible: The Union in American Thought, 1776-1861.* New York: Oxford University Press, 1964. *13*

•_____. *This Sacred Trust: American Nationality, 1798-1898.* New York: Oxford University Press, 1971.

*Nash, Roderick. *Wilderness and the American Mind.* Rev. ed. New Haven, Connecticut: Yale University Press, 1973. *7, 142*

*_____, ed. *The Call of the Wild: 1900-1916.* New York: George Braziller, 1970.

Neal, Julia. *By Their Fruits: The Story of Shakerism in South Union, Kentucky.* 1947. Reprint. Philadelphia: Porcupine Press, 1974. *210, 221*

*Needleman, Jacob. *The New Religions.* New York: Pocket Books, 1970. *21*

*Neihardt, John C. *Black Elk Speaks, Being the Life Story of a Holy Man of the Oglala Sioux.* New York: Pocket Books, 1972. *23, 24, 29, 33*

*Neill, Alexander Sutherland. *Summerhill: A Radical Approach to Child Rearing.* New York: Hart, 1960. *99*

*Nelli, Humbert S. *The Italians in Chicago, 1880-1930, A Study in Ethnic Mobility.* New York: Oxford University Press, 1973. *234*

Nelson, Hart M., et al., eds. *The Black Church in America.* New York: Basic Books, 1971. *17*

*Neufeld, Maurice F. *A Representative Bibliography of American Labor History.* Ithaca: Cornell University, New York State School of Industrial and Labor Relations, 1964. *106*

*Neusner, Jacob. *American Judaism: Adventure in Modernity.* Englewood Cliffs, New Jersey: Prentice-Hall, 1972. *21*

*Neustadt, Richard E. *Presidential Power, The Politics of Leadership.* New York: Wiley, 1960. *70*

Nevins, Allan. *Grover Cleveland, A Study in Courage.* 1932. Reprint. New York: Books for Libraries. *76, 77*

_____. *Hamilton Fish: The Inner History of the Grant Administration.* 2 vols. Rev. ed. New York: Frederick Ungar, 1957.

*Nevius, Blake. *The American Novel: Sinclair Lewis to the Present.* New York: Appleton-Century-Crofts, 1970. *46, 228*

_____. *Robert Herrick: The Development of a Novelist.* Berkeley: University of California Press, 1962.

Newbrough, John Ballou. *Oahspe, the Kosmon Revelations in the Words of Jehovih and His Angel Embassadors.* 1882. Reprint. Amherst, Wisconsin: Amherst Press. *215, 221*

•Newman, Frank. *The Report on Higher Education.* Washington, D.C.: U.S. Department of Health, Education, and Welfare, 1971. *99*

New York Public Library. *Dictionary Catalogue of the Map Division.* 10 vols. Boston: G. K. Hall, 1971. *86, 93*

•Nichol, John T. *Pentacostalism.* New York: Harper and Row, 1966. *13, 20*

*Nichols, Charles H. *Many Thousand Gone: The Ex-Slaves' Account of Their Bondage and Freedom.* Bloomington: Indiana University Press, 1969. *28, 35*

Nichols, James H. *Romanticism in American Theology: Nevin and Schaff at Mercersburg.* Chicago: University of Chicago Press, 1961. *19*

•_____, ed. *The Mercersburg Theology.* New York: Oxford University Press, 1966.

*Nichols, Roy F. *The Disruption of American Democracy.* New York: The Free Press, 1967. *75, 76*

_____. *Franklin Pierce, Young Hickory of the Granite Hills.* 2d ed. Philadelphia: University of Pennsylvania Press, 1964.

•Niebuhr, Helmut Richard. *The Kingdom of God in America.* New York: Harper and Row, Harper Torchbooks, 1959. *209, 221*

Nielson, David Gordon. "Black Ethos: The Northern Urban Negro, 1890-1930." Ph.D. dissertation, State University of New York at Binghamton, 1972. *167*

Nilon, Charles H. *Bibliography of Bibliographies in American Literature.* New York: R. R. Bowker, 1970. *46*

*Nochlin, Linda. "Why Are There No Great Women Artists?" In *Woman in Sexist Society,* edited by Vivian Gornick and Barbara Moran. New York: New American Library, 1972. *250*

Noël-Hume, Ivor. *A Guide to the Artifacts of Colonial America*. New York: Alfred A. Knopf, 1970. *190, 193*

_____. *Here Lies Virginia: An Archaelogist's View of Colonial Life and History*. New York: Alfred A. Knopf, 1963.

_____. *Historical Archaelogy*. New York: Alfred A. Knopf, 1969.

Nordenskiöld, Nils Adolf Erik, *friherre*. *Facsimile-Atlas to the Early History of Cartography with Reproductions of the Most Important Maps Printed in XV and XVI Centuries*. Translated from the Swedish by J. A. Ekelof and C. R. Markham. 1889. Reprint. New York: B. Franklin, 1967. *90, 94*

_____. *Periplus; An Essay on the Early History of Charts and Sailing Directions Translated from the Swedish Original by Francis A. Bather with Numerous Reproductions of Old Charts and Maps*. 1897. Reprint. New York: B. Franklin, 1967.

*Nordhoff, Charles. *The Communistic Societies of the United States: From Personal Visit and Observation*. Rev. ed. New York: Schocken Books, 1965. *113, 214, 221*

*Norris, Frank. *The Pit: A Story of Chicago*. New York: Grove Press, Evergreen Books, 1956. *228*

Nostrand, Richard. "The Hispanic-American Borderland: Delimitation of an American Culture Region." *Annals of the Association of American Geographers* (December 1970). *57*

Noyes, George Wallingford, ed. *John Humphrey Noyes, The Putney Community*. 1931. Reprint. Syracuse, New York: Syracuse University Press, 1973. *213, 221*

_____, ed. *The Religious Experiences of John Henry Noyes, Founder of the Oneida Community*. 1923. Reprint. Syracuse, New York: Syracuse University Press, 1973.

Noyes, John H. *The Berean: A Manual for the Help of Those Who Seek the Faith of the Primitive Church*. 1847. Reprint. New York: Arno Press, 1969. *113, 212, 213, 221*

•_____. *Bible Communism*. 1853. Reprint. Philadelphia: Porcupine Press, 1973.

•_____. *The Confessions of John H. Noyes*. Ann Arbor, Michigan: Microfilms, 1947.

•_____. *Essay on Scientific Propagation*. Ann Arbor, Michigan: University Microfilms, 1957.

•_____. *History of American Socialism*. 1870. Reprint. New York: Dover, 1966.

*Nye, Russel B. *American Literary History: 1607-1830*. Philadelphia: Philadelphia Book Company, 1970. *175, 183, 271*

*_____. *The Unembarrassed Muse: The Popular Arts in America*. New York: Dial Press, 1970.

*Nyquist, Ewald B., and Gene R. Hawes. *Open Education: A Sourcebook for Parents and Teachers*. New York: Bantam Books, 1972. *100*

O'Brien, David J. *American Catholicism and Social Reform: The New Deal Years*. New York: Oxford University Press, 1969. *19*

O'Brien, James. *A History of the New Left, 1960-1968*. Boston: New England Free Press, 1968. *126*

*O'Connor, Edwin. *All in the Family*. New York: Bantam Books, 1966. *159, 169*

*_____. *The Last Hurrah*. New York: Bantam Books, 1970.

•O'Connor, John. *The People Versus Rome: The Radical Split in the American Church*. New York: Random House, 1969. *21*

O'Connor, Patricia, Linda Headrick, and Peter Coreney. *Women: A Selected Bibliography*. Springfield, Ohio: Wittenberg University Press, 1973. *247*

*O'Connor, William V. *An Age of Criticism, 1900-1950*. Chicago: H. Regnery, 1952. *271*

O'Dea, Thomas F. *American Catholic Dilemma: An Inquiry into the Intellectual Life*. New York: Sheed and Ward, Guild Books, 1958. *12, 21*

*_____. *The Catholic Crisis*. Boston: Beacon Press, 1968.

*_____. *The Mormons*. Chicago: University of Chicago Press, Phoenix Books, 1957.

•Odegard, Peter H., ed. *Religion and Politics*. Dobbs-Ferry, New York: Oceana Publications, 1960. *73*

*Odum, Eugene P. *Ecology: The Link Between the Natural and the Social Sciences*. 2d ed. New York: Holt, Rinehart, and Winston, 1975. *136*

_____. *Fundamentals of Ecology*. 3d ed. Philadelphia: Saunders, 1971.

Office of Academic Development, State University of New York at Buffalo. *Basic Black: A Look at the Black Presence in the University Community*. Melrose, Massachusetts: Keating and Joyce, 1970. *149*

Ohmann, C. "The Autobiography of Malcolm X: A Revolutionary Use of the Franklin Tradition." *American Quarterly* 22 (Summer 1970):131-49. *23, 32*

Olmstead, Clifton E. *Religion in America, Past and Present*. Englewood Cliffs, New Jersey: Prentice-Hall, 1960. *273*

*Olmsted, Frederick Law. *The Slave States, Before the Civil War.* Edited by Harvey Wish. New York: Putnam, Capricorn Books, 1959. *16*

Olney, James. *Metaphors of Self: The Meaning of Autobiography.* Princeton, New Jersey: Princeton University Press, 1972. *24, 33*

Olsen, Tillie. "Reading List." *Women's Studies Newsletter* (Winter, Spring, Summer 1973; Winter 1974). *247, 256, 257*

*_____. *Tell Me a Riddle.* New York: Dell, Delta Books, 1971.

*Olson, James C. *Red Cloud and the Sioux Problem.* Lincoln: University of Nebraska Press, Bison Books, 1975. *196*

*O'Neill, William. *Everyone Was Brave: The Rise and Fall of Feminism in America.* Chicago: Quadrangle Books, 1969. *244*

*Oppenheimer, Valerie Kincaid. *The Female Labor Force in the United States: Demographic and Economic Factors Governing Its Growth and Changing Composition.* Berkeley: Institute of International Studies, University of California, 1970. *251*

*Ortiz, Alfonso. *The Tewa World: Space, Time, Being and Becoming in a Pueblo Society.* Chicago: University of Chicago Press, Phoenix Books, 1972. *200*

Orvis, Marianne D. *Letters from Brook Farm, 1844-1847.* Edited by Amy L. Reed. 1928. Reprint. New York: AMS Press, 1974. *212, 221*

Orwell, George. *Shooting an Elephant, and Other Essays.* New York: Harcourt, Brace, Jovanovich, 1950. *183*

*Osofsky, Gilbert. *Puttin' On Ole Massa, The Slave Narratives of Henry Bibb, William Wells Brown, and Solomon Northrup.* New York: Harper and Row, Harper Torchbooks, 1969. *28, 35*

•Oswalt, Wendell H. *Mission of Change in Alaska: Eskimos and Moravians on the Kuskokwim.* San Marino, California: Huntington Library, 1963. *198*

*_____. *Nepaskiak: An Alaskan Eskimo Community.* Tucson: University of Arizona Press, 1963.

_____. *This Was Theirs: A Study of the North American Indian.* 2d ed. New York: Wiley, 1973.

*Ovington, Mary White. *The Walls Came Tumbling Down.* 1947. Reprint. New York: Schocken Books, 1970. *256*

Owen, A. K. *Integral Cooperation: Its Practical Application.* 1885. Reprint. Philadelphia: Porcupine Press, 1974. *215, 221*

Owen, Robert. *The Life of Robert Owen.* 1857-1858. Reprint. New York: Augustus M. Kelley, 1967. *211, 221*

_____. *A New View of Society: or, Essays on the Principle of the Formation of the Human Character, and the Application of the Principle to Practice.* 1816. Reprint. New York: Augustus M. Kelley, 1972.

_____. *Robert Owen's Millennial Gazette.* 1858. Reprint. New York: AMS Press, 1973.

_____. *A Supplementary Appendix to the First Volume of the Life of Robert Owen.* 1857-1858. Reprint. New York: Augustus M. Kelley, 1967.

*Owen, Wyn F. *American Agriculture: The Changing Structure.* Lexington, Massachusetts: D. C. Heath, 1969. *263*

Ozanne, Robert. "The Labor History and Labor Theory of John R. Commons: An Evaluation in the Light of Recent Trends and Criticism." In *Labor, Management and Social Policy,* edited by Gerald G. Somers. Madison: University of Wisconsin Press, 1963. *107*

*Palmer, Robert R. *The Age of Democratic Revolution: A Political History of Europe and America, 1760-1800.* 2 vols. Princeton, New Jersey: Princeton University Press, 1969-1970. *15, 25*

•Parenti, Michael. *The Anti-Communist Impulse.* New York: Random House, 1970. *124*

Park, Robert Ezra. "Human Ecology." *American Journal of Sociology* 42 (1936). *145*

Parker, Arthur C. *Parker on the Iroquois.* Edited by William N. Fenton. Syracuse, New York: Syracuse University Press, 1968. *200*

*Parker, Gail Thain. *The Oven Birds: American Women on Womanhood, 1820-1920.* Garden City, New York: Doubleday, Anchor Books, 1972. *239, 257*

Parker, Robert Alelrton. *A Yankee Saint: John Henry Noyes and the Oneida Community.* 1935. Reprint. Philadelphia: Porcupine Press, 1972. *213, 222*

*Parkes, Henry Bamford. *The United States of America, A History.* 3d ed. New York: Alfred A. Knopf, 1968. *266*

Parkins, Almon E. *The Historical Geography of Detroit.* 1918. Reprint. Port Washington, New York: Kennikat Press, 1970. *52, 55*

_____. *The South: Its Economic-Geographic Development.* 1938. Reprint. Westport, Connecticut: Greenwood Press, 1970.

Parkman, Francis. *France and England on North America.* Introduction by Allan Nevins. 9 vols. New York: Frederick Ungar, 1965. *11*

Parmet, Herbert S. *Eisenhower and the American Crusades.* New York: Macmillan, 1972. *79*

*Parrington, Vernon L. *Main Currents in American Thought.* 3 vols. New York: Harcourt, Brace, Jovanovich, 1955. *7, 41, 271*

*Parris, Judith H. *The Convention Problem: Issues in Reform of Presidential Nominating Procedures.* Washington, D.C.: The Brookings Institution, 1972. *70*

*Parry, J. H. *The Age of Reconnaissance: Discovery, Exploration, and Settlement, 1450-1650.* New York: New American Library, Mentor Books, 1964. *55*

Parsons, James. "The Uniqueness of California." *American Quarterly* (Spring 1955). *53*

Parton, Mary Field, ed. *Autobiography of Mother Jones.* 1925. Reprint. New York: Arno Press, 1971. *246*

•Pascal, Roy. *Design and Truth in Autobiography.* Cambridge, Massachusetts: Harvard University Press, 1960. *24, 27, 33*

Pateman, Carole. *Participation and Democratic Theory.* Cambridge, England: Cambridge University Press, 1970. *127*

Paterson, John H. *North America: A Geography of Canada and the United States.* 5th ed. New York: Oxford University Press, 1975. *52*

Pattison, William. *Beginnings of the American Rectangular Land Survey System, 1784-1800.* Chicago: Chicago Geography Research Papers, 1957. *57*

•Paul, Sherman. *Louis Sullivan, An Architect in American Thought.* Englewood Cliffs, New Jersey: Prentice-Hall, 1962. *231*

Paullin, Charles O. *Atlas of the Historical Geography of the United States.* Edited by John K. Wright. 1932. Reprint. Westport, Connecticut: Greenwood Press, 1975. *51*

Paulson, Ross. *Radicalism and Reform: The Vrooman Family and American Social Thought, 1837-1937.* Lexington: University of Kentucky Press, 1968. *215, 222*

Pawley, Martin, and Christopher Woodward. *Frank Lloyd Wright: Public Buildings.* New York: Simon and Schuster, 1970. *231*

Pearce, Roy Harvey. *The Savages of America: A Study of the Indian and the Idea of Civilization.* Rev. ed. Baltimore: Johns Hopkins University Press, 1965. *197, 204*

*Peare, Catherine O. *William Penn: A Biography.* Ann Arbor: University of Michigan Press, 1966. *14*

*Pease, William, and Jane H. Pease. *Black Utopia: Negro Communal Experiments in America.* Madison: Historical Society of Wisconsin, 1972. *213, 222*

*Peckham, Morse. *Art and Pornography: An Experiment in Explanation.* New York: Harper and Row, Harper Torchbooks, 1971. *181, 183*

*Peel, Robert. *Mary Baker Eddy.* 2 vols. New York: Holt, Rinehart, and Winston, 1971-1972. *12*

*Peirce, Neal R. *The Peoples' President: The Electoral College in American History and the Direct-Vote Alternative.* New York: Simon and Schuster, Touchstone-Clarion Books, 1968. *71*

•Peisch, Mark. *The Chicago School of Architecture: Early Followers of Sullivan and Wright.* New York: Random House, 1964. *231, 237*

*Pelling, Henry. *American Labor.* Chicago: University of Chicago Press, 1960. *106, 264*

•Perlman, Mark. *Labor Union Theories in America: Background and Development.* Evanston, Illinois: Row, Peterson, 1958. *107*

Perlman, Selig. *A Theory of the Labor Movement.* 1928. Reprint. New York: Augustus M. Kelley, 1968. *107*

Perry, Ralph B. *The Thought and Character of William James.* 2 vols. 1935. Reprint. Westport, Connecticut: Greenwood Press, 1974. *18*

Persons, Stow. *American Minds: A History of Ideas.* 1958. Reprint. Huntington, New York: R. E. Krieger, 1974. *13, 268*

•Pesotta, Rose. *Bread upon the Waters.* Edited by John N. Beffel. New York: Dodd, Mead, 1944. *246*

Pessen, Edward. "The Egalitarian Myth and the American Social Reality: Wealth, Mobility and Equality in the Era of the Common Man." *American Historical Review* 76 (1971):989-1034. *112*

*_____. *Jacksonian America: Society, Personality, and Politics.* Homewood, Illinois: Dorset Press, 1969.

*_____. *Most Uncommon Jacksonians: The Radical Leaders of the Early Labor Movement.* Albany: State University of New York Press, 1967.

Peters, John L. *Christian Perfection and American Methodism.* Naperville, Illinois: Alec R. Allenson, 1956. *20*

*Peters, Victor. *All Things Common: The Hutterian Way of Life.* New York: Harper and Row, Harper Torchbooks, 1971. *215, 222*

•Petersen, Karen Daniels. *Howling Wolf: A Cheyenne Warrior's Graphic Interpretation of His People.* Palo Alto, California: American West Publishing Company, 1968. *202*

•Petersen, Svend. *A Statistical History of the American Presidential Elections.* New York: Frederick Ungar, 1968. *68*

*Peterson, Florence. *American Labor Unions: What They Are and How They Work.* 2d rev. ed. New York: Harper and Row, Harper Torchbooks, 1963. *264*

*Peterson, Merrill D. *Thomas Jefferson and the New Nation: A Biography.* New York: Oxford University Press, Galaxy Books, 1970. *74*

•Phillips, Cabell B. *The Truman Presidency: The History of a Triumphant Succession.* New York: Macmillan, 1966. *79*

•Pierce, Bessie. *A History of Chicago.* 3 vols. New York: Alfred A. Knopf, 1937-1957. *225, 227*

Pierson, William H., Jr., and Martha Davison, eds. *Arts of the United States, A Pictorial Survey.* New York: McGraw-Hill, 1960. *237*

*Pivar, David J. *Purity Crusade: Sexual Morality and Social Control, 1868-1900.* Westport, Connecticut: Greenwood Press, 1973. *245*

•Pizer, Donald. *Realism and Naturalism in Nineteenth-Century American Literature.* Carbondale: Southern Illinois University Press, 1966. *44*

•Plank, Robert. *The Emotional Significance of Imaginary Beings: A Study of the Interaction Between Psychopathology, Literature, and Reality in the Modern World.* Springfield, Illinois: Thomas, 1968. *176, 183*

*Plath, Sylvia. *The Bell Jar.* New York: Harper and Row, Bantam Books, 1975. *248*

Platt, Robert B., and George K. Reid. *Bioscience.* New York: Van Nostrand, Reinhold, 1967. *137*

•Pochmann, Henry A. *German Culture in America: Philosophical and Literary Influences, 1600-1900.* Madison: University of Wisconsin Press, 1957. *19*

Podmore, Frank. *Robert Owen: A Biography.* 2 vols. 1907. Reprint. New York: Haskell House, 1971. *211, 222*

*Poirier, Richard. *A World Elsewhere: The Place of Style in American Literature.* New York: Oxford University Press, Galaxy Books, 1966. *8*

Polk, James K. *The Diary of James K. Polk During His Presidency, 1845 to 1849.* Edited and annotated by Milo Milton Quaife. 4 vols. 1910. Reprint. New York: Kraus Reprint Company. *68*

*Pollack, Norman. *The Populist Response to Industrial America: Midwestern Populist Thought.* New York: W. W. Norton, 1966. *116*

*_____. *Teaching as a Subversive Activity.* New York: Dell, Delta Books, 1969.

Potter, David M. "American Women and the American Character." In *American Character and Culture,* edited by John A. Hague. DeLand, Florida: Everett Edwards Press, 1964. *7, 253, 263*

*_____. *People of Plenty, Economic Abundance and the American Character.* Chicago: University of Chicago Press, Phoenix Books, 1952.

Pred, Allan. "The External Relations of Cities During 'Industrial Revolution.'" University of Chicago Department of Geography Research Paper No. 76. Chicago: University of Chicago Press, 1962. *142*

*Pressly, Thomas J. *Americans Interpret Their Civil War.* New York: The Free Press, 1965. *17*

*Preston, William. *Aliens and Dissenters: Federal Suppression of Radicals, 1903-1933.* New York: Harper and Row, Harper Torchbooks, 1963. *120*

Pringle, Henry F. *The Life and Times of William Howard Taft, A Biography.* 2 vols. 1939. Reprint. Hamden, Connecticut: Archon Books, 1964. *77, 78*

*_____. *Theodore Roosevelt, A Biography.* Rev. ed. New York: Harcourt, Brace, Jovanovich, 1956.

Pritchett, V. S. "All About OUrselves." *New Statesman & Nation* 51 (May 26, 1956):601-02. *29, 36*

*Prucha, Francis Paul. *American Indian Policy in the Formative Years: The Indian Trade and*

Intercourse Acts, 1790-1834. Lincoln: University of Nebraska Press, Bison Books, 1970. *196*

_____. "Andrew Jackson's Indian Policy: A Reassessment." *Journal of American History* 56 (1969):527-39.

Ptolemaeus, Claudius. *Geographica.* Strassburg, 1513. With an Introduction by R. A. Skelton. Amsterdam: Theatrim Orbis Terrarum, 1966. *91, 94*

*Quarles, Benjamin. *The Negro in the Making of America.* Rev. ed. New York: Macmillan, Collier Books, 1969. *148*

Quinn, Arthur Hobson. *A History of the American Drama: From the Beginning to the Civil War.* 2d. ed. New York: Irvington Publishers, 1943. *271*

_____. *A History of the American Drama: From the Civil War to the Present Day.* Rev. ed. New York: Irvington Publishers, 1946.

*Quint, Howard H. *The Forging of American Socialism: Origins of the Modern Movement.* 2d ed. Indianapolis, Indiana: Bobbs-Merrill, 1964. *117, 215, 222*

*Rabb, Theodore K., and Robert I. Rotberg. *The Family in History: Interdisciplinary Essays.* New York: Harper and Row, Harper Torchbooks, 1973. *254*

Radcliffe College. The Arthur and Elizabeth Schlesinger Library on the History of Women in America. *Manuscript Inventories and the Catalogs of the Manuscripts, Books, and Pictures.* 3 vols. Boston: G. K. Hall, 1973. *255*

•Radosh, Ronald. *American Labor and United States Foreign Policy.* New York: Random House, 1969. *120, 124*

Ramsey, Gordon C. *Atatha Christie, Mistress of Mystery.* New York: Dodd, Mead, 1967. *183*

•Rand, Christopher, *Cambridge, USA: Hub of a New World.* New York: Oxford University Press, 1964. *160, 169*

Randall, James G. *Lincoln, the President,* 4 vols. New York: Dodd, Mead, 1945-1955. *17, 76*

_____, and David Donald. *The Civil War and Reconstruction.* 2d ed., rev. Boston: Little, Brown, 1973. *267*

•Ranney, Victoria. *Olmsted in Chicago.* Chicago: R. R. Donnelly, 1972. *232*

*Rapoport, Amos. *House Form and Culture.* Englewood Cliffs, New Jersey: Prentice-Hall, 1969. *190, 193*

•Rascoe, Burton. *Before I Forget.* Garden City, New York: Doubleday, 1937. *228*

•Rauschenbusch, Walter J. *Christianity and the Social Crisis.* Edited by Robert D. Cross. New York: Harper and Row, 1964. *17*

*Rayback, Joseph G. *A History of American Labor.* Rev. ed. New York: The Free Press, 1966. *106*

Rayback, Robert J. *Millard Fillmore: Biography of a President,* Buffalo, New York: H. Stewart, 1972. *75*

Red Fox, William. *The Memoirs of Chief Red Fox.* New York: McGraw-Hill, 1970. *23, 33*

Reed, John F. "Ecology in Higher Education." *Bioscience* 14 (July 1964):24. *142*

Reedy, George E. *The Presidency.* New ed. New York: Arno Press, 1975. *70*

*_____. *The Twilight of the Presidency.* New York: New American Library, Mentor Books, 1971.

*Rees, Robert A., and Earl N. Harbert, eds. *Fifteen American Authors Before 1900: Bibliographic Essays in Research and Criticism.* Madison: University of Wisconsin Press, 1971. *46*

Reeves, Thomas C. *Gentleman Boss: The Life of Chester Alan Arthur.* New York: Alfred A. Knopf, 1975. *77*

Rehmus, Charles M., and Doris B. McLaughlin, eds. *Labor and American Politics: A Book of Readings.* Ann Arbor: University of Michigan Press, 1967. *127*

*Reich, Charles. *The Greening of America: How the Youth Revolution Is Trying to Make America Liveable.* New York: Bantam Books, 1971. *21, 180*

*Reimer, Everett. *School Is Dead: Alternatives in Education.* Garden City, New York: Doubleday, Anchor Books, 1972. *100*

*Reinitz, Richard, ed. *Tensions in American Puritanism.* New York: Wiley, 1970. *14*

Renshaw, Patrick. "The Black Ghetto, 1890-1940." *Journal of American Studies* 8 (April 1974): 41-59. *167*

Reps, John W. *The Making of Urban America: A History of City Planning in the United States.* Princeton, New Jersey: Princeton University Press, 1965. *55, 56, 154, 169, 237*

_____. *Town Planning in Frontier America.* Princeton, New Jersey: Princeton University Press, 1969.

*Revel, Jean-Francois. *Without Marx or Jesus: The New American Revolution Has Begun.* New York: Dell, 1974. *21, 127*

Reynolds, Ray. *Cat's Paw Utopia.* Printed by the author, 1973. *215, 222*

Riasanovsky, Nicholas. *The Teaching of Charles Fourier.* Berkeley: University of California Press, 1969. *212, 222*

●Rich, Bennett Milton. *The Presidents and Civil Disorder.* Washington, D.C.: The Brookings Institution, 1941. *72*

*Richardson, Edgar P. *Painting in America, from 1502 to the Present.* New York: Thomas Y. Crowell, 1965. *263*

*Rickels, Milton. *George Washington Harris.* New York: Twayne Publishers, 1965. *42*

_____. *Thomas Bangs Thorpe: Humorist of the Old Southwest.* Baton Rouge: Louisiana State University Press, 1962.

*Ricoeur, Paul. *The Symbolism of Evil.* Translated by Emerson Buchanan. Boston: Beacon Press, 1969. *181, 183*

Riemar, Neal. *James Madison.* New York: Washington Square Press, 1968. *15*

●Riesman, David, and Verne A. Stadtman, eds. *Academic Transformation: Seventeen Institutions Under Pressure.* New York: McGraw-Hill, 1973. *7, 102*

Rieupeyrout, Jean-Louis. *La Grande Aventure du Western.* Paris: Editions du Cerf, 1964. *176, 183*

*Riggs, Fred W. *The Ecology of Public Administration.* New York: Asia Publishing House, 1975. *144*

Ripley, S. Dillon, and Helmut K. Buechner. "Ecosystem Science as a Point of Synthesis." *Daedalus* (Fall 1967):1192-99. *144*

Ristow, Walter W. *Guide to the History of Cartography: An Annotated List of References on the History of Maps and Map Making.* Washington, D.C.: The Library of Congress, 1973. *87, 91, 93, 94*

_____. "Recent Facsimile Maps and Atlases." *Library of Congress Quarterly Journal* 24 (July 1967):213-29.

*Roberts, Ron E. *The New Communes: Coming Together in America.* Englewood Cliffs, New Jersey: Prentice-Hall, 1971. *217, 222*

Robertson, Constance Noyes. *Oneida Community: The Break-up, 1876-1881.* Syracuse, New York: Syracuse University Press, 1972. *213, 222*

●Robertson, Thomas A. *A Southwestern Utopia.* Rev. ed. Los Angeles: Ward Ritchie Press, 1964. *215, 222*

Rodwin, Lloyd. *Housing and Economic Progress: A Study of the Housing Experiences of Boston's Middle-Income Families.* Cambridge: Massachusetts Institute of Technology Press, 1961. *160, 169*

*Rogin, Michael Paul. *The Intellectuals and McCarthy: The Radical Specter.* Cambridge: Massachusetts Institute of Technology Press, 1969. *124*

Rooney, John. "Up from the Mines and Out from the Prairies: Some Geographical Implications of Football in the United States." *Geographical Review* (January 1954). *58*

Roosevelt, Eleanor. *This I Remember.* 1949. Reprint. Westport, Connecticut: Greenwood Press, 1975. *249*

Roosevelt, Franklin D. *The Public Papers and Addresses of Franklin D. Roosevelt, 1928-1945.* 13 vols. Edited by Samuel I. Rosenman. 1938-1950. Reprint. New York: Russell and Russell, 1969. *62*

Roosevelt, Theodore. *Theodore Roosevelt: An Autobiography.* Edited by Wayne Andrews. New York: Octagon Books, 1973. *68*

●Rorty, Amelie. *Pragmatic Philosophy: An Anthology.* Garden City, New York: Doubleday, Anchor Books, 1966. *19*

*Rose, Harold M. *The Black Ghetto: A Spatial Behavioral Perspective.* New York: McGraw-Hill, 1971. *54*

_____, ed. *Geography of the Ghetto: Perceptions, Problems, and Alternatives.* De Kalb: Northern Illinois University Press, 1972.

Roseboom, Eugene H. *A History of Presidential Elections: From George Washington to Richard M. Nixon.* 3d ed. New York: Macmillan, 1970. *70*

*Rosenberg, Bernard, and David Manning White, eds. *Mass Culture: The Popular Arts in America.* Glencoe, Illinois: The Free Press, 1965. *174, 180, 183*

*Rosenfelt, Deborah Silverton, ed. *Female Studies VII: Going Strong: New Courses, New Programs.* Old Westbury, New York: The Feminist Press, 1973. *242*

*Rosengarten, Theodore. *All God's Dangers: The LIfe of Nate Shaw*. New York: Avon, 1975. *24, 33*

*Rosenthal, Raymond, ed. *McLuhan: Pro and Con*. Baltimore: Penguin, Pelican Books, 1969. *179, 183*

Rossi, Alice S., and Ann Calderwood, eds. *Academic Women on the Move*. New York: Russell Sage Foundation, 1973. *246*

*Rossiter, Clinton L. *The American Presidency*. Rev. ed. New York: Harcourt, Brace, Jovanovich, 1960. *69, 265, 268*

_____. *Conservatism in America: The Thankless Persuasion*. 2d ed. New York: Alfred A. Knopf, 1962.

_____. *Seedtime of the Republic*. 3 vols. New York: Harcourt, Brace, Jovanovich, 1953-1964.

Rosten, Leo C. *Hollywood: The Movie Colony, the Movie Makers*. 1941. Reprint. New York: Arno Press, 1974. *179, 184*

*Roszak, Betty, and Theodore Roszak, eds. *Masculine/Feminine: Readings in Sexual Mythology and the Liberation of Women*. New York: Harper and Row, 1970. *252*

*Roszak, Theodore. *The Making of a Counter Culture: Reflections on the Technocratic Society and Its Youthful Opposition*. New York: Doubleday, Anchor Books, 1969. *8, 9, 21, 101, 127, 180, 184*

* _____. *Where the Wasteland Ends: Politics and Transcendence in Post-Industrial Society*. New York: Doubleday, Anchor Books, 1973.

_____, ed. *The Dissenting Academy*. New York: Irvington, 1968.

•Roth, Robert J. *American Religious Philosophy*. New York: Harcourt, Brace, Jovanovich, 1967. *13*

Rotzel, Grace. *The School in Rose Valley: A Parent Venture in Education With Contributions from Teachers, Parents, and Children*. Baltimore: Johns Hopkins University Press, 1971. *103*

*Rourke, Constance. *American Humor: A Study of the National Character*. New York: Harcourt, Brace, Jovanovich, 1971. *7, 42, 272*

*Rowbotham, Sheila. *Women, Resistance and Revolution: A History of Women and Revolution in the Modern World*. New York: Random House, Vintage Books, 1974. *246, 247*

_____. *Women's Liberation and Revolution*. Bristol, England: Falling Wall Press, 1973.

Rowe, J. S. "The Level of Integration Concept and Ecology." *Ecology* 42 (April 1961):420-27. *144*

*Royko, Mike. *Boss: Richard J. Daley of Chicago*. New York: New American Library, Signet Books, 1971. *225*

*Rozwenc, Edwin C., ed. *The Causes of the American Civil War*. 2d ed. Boston: D. C. Heath, 1972. *16, 121*

* _____, ed. *The New Deal: Revolution or Evolution?* Rev. ed. Boston: D. C. Heath, 1959.

Rubel, Maximilien. "Notes on Marx's Conception of Democracy." *New Politics* 1 (1962):83-85. *111*

•Rubenstein, Richard L. *After Auschwitz: Radical Theology and Contemporary Judaism*. Indianapolis, Indiana: Bobbs-Merrill, 1966. *21*

* Rubin, Louis D., Jr., ed. *A Bibliographical Guide to the Study of Southern Literature*. Baton Rouge: Louisiana State University Press, 1969. *46*

Rublowsky, John. *Popular Music*. New York: Basic Books, 1967. *273*

•Rudolph, Frederick. *The American College and University: A History*. New York: Random House, Vintage Books, 1962. *264*

Rudoni, Dorothy June. *Harry S. Truman: A Study in Presidential Perspective*. Ann Arbor, Michigan: University Microfilms, 1969. *79*

*Rudwick, Elliot M. *W.E.B. DuBois: Propagandist of the Negro Protest*. New York: Atheneum, 1968. *17*

•Ruland, Richard. *The Rediscovery of American Literature: Premises of Critical Taste, 1900-1940*. Cambridge, Massachusetts: Harvard University Press, 1967. *7*

Russell, Charles E. *The American Orchestra and Theodore Thomas*. 1927. Reprint. Westport, Connecticut: Greenwood Press, 1971. *236*

Russett, Bruce M. "The Ecology of Future International Politics." *International Studies Quarterly* 11 (March 1967):12-13. *142*

'Rutman, Darrett B. *American Puritanism: Faith and Practice*. Philadelphia: J. B. Lippincott Company, 1970. *8, 14*

* _____. *The Great Awakening: Event and Exegesis*. New York: Wiley, 1970.

*_____. *Winthrop's Boston: A Portrait of a Puritan Town, 1630-1649.* 1965. Reprint. New York: W. W. Norton, 1962.

*Ruttenberg, Stanley H. *Manpower Challenge of the 1970s: Institutions and Social Change.* Edited by Jocelyn Gutchess. Baltimore: Johns Hopkins University Press, 1970. *126*

*Ryan, Mary P. *Womanhood in America: From Colonial Times to the Present.* New York: Franklin, Watts, New Viewpoints Books, 1975. *247*

Sachse, Julius Friedrich. *The German Pietists of Provincial Pennsylvania, 1694-1708.* 1895. Reprint. New York: AMS Press, 1970. *209, 222*

_____. *The German Sectarians of Pennsylvania, 1708-1800: A Critical and Legendary History of the Ephrata Cloister and the Dunkers.* 2 vols. 1899-1900. Reprint. New York: AMS Press, 1971.

_____. *The Music of the Ephrata Cloister.* 1903. Reprint. New York: AMS Press, 1971.

Salinger, Pierre, *With Kennedy.* Garden City, New York: Doubleday, 1966. *72*

*Salper, Roberta, ed. *Female Liberation: History and Current Politics.* New York: Alfred A. Knopf, 1971. *249*

Samuels, Ernest. *Henry Adams: The Major Phase.* Cambridge, Massachusetts: The Belknap Press of Harvard University Press, 1964. *27, 29, 35*

_____. *Henry Adams: The Middle Years.* Cambridge, Massachusetts: The Belknap Press of Harvard University Press, 1958.

_____. *The Young Henry Adams.* Cambridge, Massachusetts: The Belknap Press of Harvard University Press, 1948.

*Sandburg, Carl. *Abraham Lincoln: The Prairie Years and the War Years.* 3 vols. New York: Dell, 1960. *76, 226, 227, 229, 267*

_____. *Abraham Lincoln: The War Years.* 4 vols. New York: Harcourt, Brace, Jovanovich, 1939.

•_____. *The Chicago Race Riots, July 1919.* 1919. Reprint. New York: Harcourt, Brace, Jovanovich, 1969.

_____. *The Complete Poems of Carl Sandburg.* Rev. ed. New York: Harcourt, Brace, Jovanovich, 1970.

*Sandeen, Ernest R. *The Origins of Fundamentalism: Towards a Historical Interpretation.* Philadelphia: Fortress Press, 1968. *20*

_____. *Roots of Fundamentalism: British and American Millenarianism, 1800-1930.* Chicago: University of Chicago Press, 1970.

•Sanford, Charles L. *The Quest for Paradise: Europe and the American Moral Imagination.* Urbana: University of Illinois Press, 1961. *28, 35, 209, 222*

*Sanger, Margaret. *Margaret Sanger: An Autobiography.* 1938. Reprint. New York: Dover, 1971. *248*

_____. *My Fight for Birth Control.* 1931. Reprint. Elmsford, New York: Maxwell Reprint Company, 1969.

*Santayana, George. *Character and Opinion in the United States.* New York: W. W. Norton, 1967. *19, 273*

*_____. *Santayana on America.* Edited by R. C. Lyon. New York: Harcourt, Brace, Jovanovich, 1968.

•Saposs, David J. *Communism in American Unions.* New York: McGraw-Hill, 1959. *122, 124*

*Sarris, Andrew. *The American Cinema: Directors and Directions, 1929-1968.* New York: E. P. Dutton, 1969. *179, 184*

Sauer, Carl O. *The Geography of the Ozark Highland of Missouri.* 1920. Reprint. New York: AMS Press, 1971. *55*

_____. *Sixteenth-Century North America: The Land and the People as Seen by the Europeans.* Berkeley: University of California Press, 1971.

*Saxton, Alexander. *The Indispensable Enemy: Labor and the Anti-Chinese Movement in California.* Berkeley: University of California Press, 1975. *116*

•Sayre, Robert F. *The Examined Self: Benjamin Franklin, Henry Adams, Henry James.* Princeton, New Jersey: Princeton University Press, 1964. *27, 28, 29, 35, 39*

_____. "Vision and Experience in *Black Elk Speaks.*" *College English* 32 (February 1971): 509-35.

*Sayre, Wallace S., and Judith H. Parris. *Voting for President: The Electoral College and the American Political System.* Washington, D.C.: The Brookings Institution, 1970. *71*

•Scammon, Richard M., ed. *America at the Polls: A Handbook of American Presidential Elec-*

tion Statistics, 1920-1964. Pittsburgh, Pennsylvania: University of Pittsburgh Press, 1965. *68*

Schaff, Philip et al., eds. *The American Church History Series.* 13 vols. 1893-1897. Reprint. New York: B. Franklin. *11*

*_____. *The Rise of the City, 1878-1898.* New York: Franklin, Watts, New Viewpoints, 1971.

*Scheuer, Joseph F., and Edward Wakin. *The De-Romanization of the American Catholic Church.* New York: New American Library, 1966. *21*

*Schickel, Richard. *The Disney Version: The Life, Times, Art, and Commerce of Walt Disney.* New York: Avon, 1969. *179, 184*

Schlereth, Thomas J. "Regional Studies in America: The Chicago Model." *American Studies: An International Newsletter* 13 (Autumn 1974):20-34. *166*

Schlesinger, Arthur M. "The City in American History." *American Historical Review* 27 (June 1940):43-66. *14, 153, 169, 174, 175, 225, 255*

•_____. *New Viewpoints in American History.* New York: Macmillan, 1922.

*_____. *The Rise of the City, 1878-1898.* New York: Franklin, Watts, New Viewpoints, 1971.

_____, and Dixon Ryan Fox. *A History of American Life.* 13 vols. New York: Macmillan, 1927-1948. *184*

Schlesinger, Arthur M., Jr. *The Age of Jackson.* Boston: Little, Brown, 1945. *70, 74, 79, 80, 112, 267*

*_____. *The Age of Roosevelt.* 3 vols. Boston: Houghton Mifflin, Sentry Books, 1957-1960.

_____. *The Imperial Presidency.* Boston: Houghton Mifflin, 1973.

*_____. *A Thousand Days: John F. Kennedy in the White House.* New York: Fawcett, World Premier Books, 1971.

_____, and F. L. Israel, eds. *History of American Presidential Elections, 1789-1968.* 4 vols. New York: McGraw-Hill, 1971.

Schmeckebier, Laurence F., and Ray B. Eastin. *Government Publications and Their Use.* Rev. ed. Washington, D.C.: The Brookings Institution, 1969. *66*

Schmidt, Delores Barracano. "Women." *American Quarterly* 25, No. 3 (August 1973). *256*

*Schneider, Herbert W. *History of American Philosophy.* 2d ed. New York: Columbia University Press, 1963. *13, 15, 273*

*_____. *The Puritan Mind.* Ann Arbor: University of Michigan Press, 1958.

*_____. *Religion in Twentieth-Century America.* Rev. ed. New York: Atheneum, 1964.

_____, and George Lawton. *A Prophet and a Pilgrim.* 1942. Reprint. New York: AMS Press, 1972. *213, 222*

•Schneiderman, Rose. *All for One.* New York: P. S. Erickson, 1967. *246*

Schnore, Leo F. "The Myth of Human Ecology." *Sociological Inquiry* 31 (Spring 1961):128-39. *142*

_____. "Social Morphology and Human Ecology." *American Journal of Sociology* 63 (May 1958):620-34.

•Schulberg, Budd, ed. *From the Ashes: Voices of Watts.* New York: New American Library, 1967. *151*

•Schushter, Arnold. *White Power, Black Freedom: Planning the Future of Urban America.* Boston: Beacon Press, 1968. *150*

*Schweitzer, Albert. *Out of My Life and Thought: An Autobiography.* New York: Holt, Rinehart, and Winston, 1972. *143*

*Scott, Anne Firor, ed. *The American Woman: Who Was She?* Englewood Cliffs, New Jersey: Prentice-Hall, 1971. *244, 245, 247*

*_____. *The Southern Lady: From Pedestal to Politics, 1830-1930.* Chicago: University of Chicago Press, Phoenix Books, 1972.

_____. "Women in American Life." In *The Reinterpretation of American History and Culture,* edited by William H. Cartwright and Richard L. Watson. Washington, D.C.: National Council for the Social Studies, 1973.

*Scott, Mellier G. *American City Planning Since 1890.* Berkeley: University of California Press, 1969. *237*

*Scully, Vincent J. *American Architecture and Urbanism: A Historical Essay.* New York: Praeger, 1969. *263*

•Seager, Robert. *And Tyler Too: A Biography of John and Julia Gardiner Tyler.* New York: McGraw-Hill, 1963. *75*

Sears, Paul B. "Ecology: A Subversive Subject." *Bioscience* 14 (July 1964):11-13. *143*

_____. "The Ecology of Man." *Smithsonian Report for 1958-59:* 375-98. (Reprint of Condon Lecture, University of Oregon, 1957.)

_____. "Human Ecology: A Problem in Synthesis." *Science* 120 (December 1954):959-63.

•Seidman, Joel I. *American Labor from Defense to Reconversion.* Chicago: University of Chicago Press, 1953. *123*

*Seldes, Gilbert. *The Seven Lively Arts.* Cronbury, New Jersey: A. S. Barnes, 1962. *173, 184*

•Sellers, Charles Grier. *James K. Polk, Continentalist, 1843-1846.* Princeton, New Jersey: Princeton University Press, 1957-1966. *75*

_____. *James K. Polk, Jacksonian, 1795-1843.* Princeton, New Jersey: Princeton University Press, 1957-1966.

Sewell, Richard B. *The Life of Emily Dickinson.* 2 vols. New York: Farrar, Strauss and Giroux, 1974. *249*

*Sexton, Patricia Cayo, and Brendon Sexton. *Blue Collars and Hard-Hats: The Working Class and the Future of American Politics.* New York: Random House, Vintage Books, 1972. *125*

Seyersted, Per. *Kate Chopin: A Critical Biography.* Baton Rouge: Louisiana State University Press, 1969. *257*

•Shambaugh, Bertha M. H. *Amana, the Community of True Inspiration.* Iowa City: The State Historical Society of Iowa, 1908. *214, 222*

Shannon, David A. *The Decline of American Communism: A History of the Communist Party of the United States Since 1945.* 1959. Reprint. Chatham, New Jersey: Chatham Bookseller, 1971. *117, 122, 124*

*_____. *The Socialist Party of America: A History.* New York: Quadrangle Books, 1967.

*Shannon, William V. *The American Irish: A Political and Social Portrait.* Rev. ed. New York: Macmillan, Collier Books, 1974. *159, 169*

*Sharkey, Robert P. *Money, Class, and Party: An Economic Study of Civil War and Reconstruction.* Baltimore: Johns Hopkins University Press, 1959. *114*

Shaw, Albert. *Icaria: A Chapter in the History of Communism.* 1884. Reprint. Philadelphia: Porcupine Press, 1972. *214, 222*

Shaw, Anna Howard. *The Story of a Pioneer.* 1915. Reprint. Millwood, New York: Kraus Reprints. *249*

Shea, Daniel B., Jr. *Spiritual Autobiography in Early America.* Princeton, New Jersey: Princeton University Press, 1968. *25, 33*

•Sheehan, Bernard W. *Civilization and the American Indian in the Thought of the Jeffersonian Era.* Charlottesville: University Press of Virginia, 1965. *197, 204*

_____. "Indian-White Relations in Early America: Review Essay." *William and Mary Quarterly* 26 (1969):267-86.

_____. "Paradise and the Noble Savage in Jeffersonian Thought." *Willam and Mary Quarterly* 26 (1969):327-59.

*_____. *Seeds of Extinction: Jeffersonian Philanthropy and the American Indian.* New York: W. W. Norton, 1974.

Shepard, Paul. "Whatever Happened to Human Ecology?" *Bioscience* (December 1967):894. *140, 145*

Shepard, Thomas. *God's Plot: The Paradoxes of Puritan Piety; Being the Autobiography and Journal of Thomas Shepard.* Edited by Michael McGiffert and W. E. Bernhard. Amherst: University of Massachusetts Press, 1972. *25*

•Shepherd, Jean, ed. *The America of George Ade, 1866-1944: Fables, Short Stories, Essays.* New York: Putnam, 1961. *228*

*Sheppard, Harold L., and Neal Q. Herrick. *Where Have All the Robots Gone? Worker Dissatisfaction in the '70's.* New York: The Free Press, 1972. *126*

Shepperson, Wilbur S. *Retreat to Nevada: A Socialist Colony of World War I.* Reno: University of Nevada Press, 1966. *216, 222*

Shoemaker, Don, ed. *With All Deliberate Speed: Segregation-Desegregation in Southern Schools,* 1957. Reprint. Westport, Connecticut: Negro Universities Press, 1970. *98*

*Short, James F., Jr. *The Social Fabric of the Metropolis: Contributions of the Chicago School of Urban Sociology.* Chicago: University of Chicago Press, Phoenix Books, 1972. *236*

*Shrank, Jeffrey. *Teaching Human Beings: 101 Subversive Activities for the Classroom.* Boston: Beacon Press, 1972. *100*

*Shryock, Richard H. *Medicine and Society in America: 1660-1860.* Ithaca, New York: Cornell University Press, 1962. *269*

*Shulman, Alix. *Red Emma Speaks: Selected Writings and Speeches.* New York: Random House, Vintage Books, 1972. *256*
_____. *To the Barricades: The Anarchist Life of Emma Goldman.* New York: Thomas Y. Crowell, 1971.

•Shumaker, Wayne. *English Autobiography: Its Emergence, Materials, and Forms.* Berkeley: University of California Press, 1954. *24, 25, 33*

Shurtleff, Harold R. *The Log Cabin Myth: A Study of the Early Dwellings of the English Colonists in North America.* 1939. Reprint. Gloucester, Massachusetts: Peter Smith, 1967. *187, 193*

*Siegel, Arthur. *Chicago's Famous Buildings: A Photographic Guide to the City's Architectural Landmarks and Other Notable Buildings.* 2d ed. Chicago: University of Chicago Press, 1970. *231*

•Sievers, Harry J. *Benjamin Harrison.* 3 vols. Chicago: H. Regnery, 1952-1968. *77*

*Silberman, Charles E. *Crisis in Black and White.* New York: Random House, Vintage Books, 1964. *30, 36, 100, 103*
*_____. *Crisis in the Classroom: The Remaking of American Education.* New York: Random House, Vintage Books, 1970.

Silva, Ruth. *Presidential Succession.* 1951. Reprint. Westport, Connecticut: Greenwood Press, 1968. *72*

*Silver, James W. *Confederate Morale and Church Propaganda.* New York: W. W. Norton, 1967. *16*

*Simpson, Alan. *Puritanism in Old and New England.* Chicago: University of Chicago Press, Phoenix Books, 1955. *14*

•Simpson, Claude M. *The Local Colorists: American Short Stories, 1857-1900.* New York: Harper and Row, 1960. *43*

•Simpson, Vernon, and David Scott. *Chicago's Politics and Society, A Selected Bibliography.* DeKalb: Northern Illinois University Center for Governmental Studies, 1972. *225*

*Sinclair, Andrew. *The Better Half: The Emancipation of the American Woman.* New York: Harper and Row, Harper Torchbooks, 1965. *20, 244*
•_____. *Prohibition: The Era of Excess.* Boston: Little, Brown, 1962.

•Sinclair, Upton. *The Autobiography of Upton Sinclair.* New York: Harcourt, Brace, Jovanovich, 1962. *216, 222, 228*
*_____. *The Jungle.* New York: New American Library, Signet Books, 1973.

•Sinkler, George. *The Racial Attitudes of American Presidents from Abraham Lincoln to Theodore Roosevelt.* Garden City, New York: Doubleday, 1972. *72*

*Siporan, Rae L., ed. *Female Studies V.* Pittsburgh, Pennsylvania: KNOW, Inc., 1972. *242*

Sirjamaki, John. *The American Family in the Twentieth Century.* Cambridge, Massachusetts: Harvard University Press, 1953. *275*

Sizer, Theodore. *Places for Learning, Places for Joy: Speculations on American School Reform.* Cambridge, Massachusetts: Harvard University Press, 1973. *100*

*Sjoberg, Gideon. *The Preindustrial City: Past and Present.* New York: The Free Press, 1960. *164*

Skaggs, Merrill Maguire. *The Folk of Southern Fiction: A Study of Local Color Tradition.* Athens: University of Georgia Press, 1972. *43*

Skelton, Raleigh A. *Explorer's Maps: Chapters in the Cartographic Record of Geographical Discovery.* Feltham, New York: Spring Books, 1970. *82, 83, 84, 91*

*Skinner, B. F. *Beyond Freedom and Dignity.* New York: Bantam Books, 1972. *99*
*_____. *The Technology of Teaching.* Englewood Cliffs, New Jersey: Prentice-Hall, 1968.

Sklar, Katheryn Kish. *Catherine Beecher: A Study in American Domesticity.* New Haven, Connecticut: Yale University Press, 1973. *249*

*Sklar, Robert, ed. *The Plastic Age, 1917-1930.* New York: George Braziller, 1970. *7*

*Sklare, Marshell. *Conservative Judaism: An American Religious Movement.* New ed. New York: Schocken Books, 1972. *19*

Sloane, Eric. *American Barns and Covered Bridges.* New York: Funk and Wagnalls, 1954. *58*
_____. *American Yesterday.* New York: Funk and Wagnalls, 1956.
*_____. *Our Vanishing Landscape.* New York: Ballantine Books, 1975. *58*
_____. *The Seasons of America Past.* New York: Funk and Wagnalls, 1958.

Slobodkin, Lawrence B. "Aspects of the Future of Ecology." *Bioscience* 18 (January 1968): 16-23. *143*

*Slotkin, Richard S. *Regeneration Through Violence: The Mythology of the American Frontier, 1600-1860.* Middletown, Connecticut: Wesleyan University Press, 1974. *204*

*Smedley, Agnes. *Daughter of the Earth.* Old Westbury, New York: The Feminist Press, 1973. *243, 250*

*Smith, Abbott E. *Colonists in Bondage: White Servitude and Convict Labor in America, 1607-1776.* New York: W. W. Norton, 1971. *109*

•Smith, Alson J. *Chicago's Left Bank.* Chicago: H. Regnery, 1953. *230*

*Smith, David M. *The Geography of Social Well-Being in the United States: An Introduction to Territorial Social Indicators.* New York: McGraw-Hill, 1973. *58*

•Smith, Don. *Peculiarities of the Presidents: Strange and Intimate Facts Not Found in History.* Van Wert, Ohio: Wilkinson Printing Company, 1938. *67*

Smith, Elwyn A., ed. *The Religion of the Republic: Is There an American Religion?* Philadelphia: Fortress Press, 1971. *13*

*Smith, Gene. *When the Cheering Stopped: The Last Years of Woodrow Wilson.* New York: William Morrow, 1971. *78*

*Smith, Henry Nash. *Virgin Land: The American West as Symbol and Myth.* Cambridge, Massachusetts: Harvard University Press, 1970. *4, 13, 197, 204, 271*

Smith, James W., and A. Leland Jamison, eds. *Religion in American Life.* 4 vols. Princeton, New Jersey: Princeton University Press, 1961. *12*

*Smith, John E. *The Spirit of American Philosophy.* New York: Oxford University Press, Galaxy Books, 1966. *18*

Smith, Page. *John Adams.* 2 vols. 1962. Reprint. Westport, Connecticut: Greenwood Press, 1969. *74*

•Smith, Robert Collins. *They Closed Their Schools: Prince Edward County, Virginia, 1951-1964.* Chapel Hill: University of North Carolina Press, 1965. *98*

Smith, Theodore Clarke. *The Life and Letters of James Abram Garfield.* 2 vols. 1925. Reprint. Hamden, Connecticut: Shoe String Press, Archon Books, 1968. *76*

Smith, Thomas V., and Leonard D. White. *Chicago: An Experiment in Social Science Research.* 1929. Reprint. Westport, Connecticut: Greenwood Press, 1968. *236*

Smith, Timothy L. *Revivalism and Social Reform: American Protestantism on the Eve of the Civil War.* Gloucester, Massachusetts: Peter Smith, 1957. *16*

Smith-Rosenberg, Carroll. "Beauty, the Beast, and the Militant Woman: A Case Study in Sex Roles and Social Stress in Jacksonian America." *American Quarterly* 23 (October 1971). *251, 256*

_____, and Charles Rosenberg. "The Female Animal: Medical and Biological Views of Woman and Her Roles in Nineteenth Century America." *Journal of American History* 60 (September 1973). *253*

*Smuts, Robert W. *Women and Work in America.* 2d. ed. New York: Schocken Books, 1971. *246*

*Sochen, June. *Movers and Shakers: American Women Thinkers and Activists, 1900-1970.* New York: Quadrangle Books, 1974. 245, 256

*_____. *The New Woman: Feminism in Greenwich Village, 1910-1920.* New York: Quadrangle Books, 1972.

*Solomon, Barbara M. *Ancestors and Immigrants: A Changing New England Tradition.* Chicago: University of Chicago Press, Phoenix Books, 1972. *159, 169*

Sontag, Frederick, and John Roth. *American Religious Experience: The Roots, Trends, and Future of American Theology.* New York: Harper and Row, 1972. *21*

*Sontag, Susan. *Against Interpretation.* New York: Dell, Delta Books, 1967. *184*

*_____. *Styles of Radical Will.* New York: Dell, Delta Books, 1970.

Sorensen, Theodore C. *Kennedy.* New York: Harper and Row, 1965. *80*

Spate, O. H. K. "Environmentalism." In the *International Encyclopedia of the Social Sciences,* vol. 4, edited by David L. Sills. New York: Macmillan, The Free Press, 1968. *144*

*Spear, Allan H. *Black Chicago: The Making of a Negro Ghetto, 1890-1920.* Chicago: University of Chicago Press, Phoenix Books, 1969. *226*

Special Libraries Association. Geography and Map Division. Directory Revision Committee. *Map Collections in the United States and Canada, A Directory.* 2d ed. New York: Special Libraries Association, 1970. *87, 95*

Spencer, J. E., and William Thomas. *Introducing Cultural Geography.* New York: Wiley, 1973. *52*

Spencer, Robert F., et al. *The Native Americans: Prehistory and Ethnology of the North American Indians.* New York: Harper and Row, 1965. *199*

*Spencer, Samuel R., Jr. *Booker T. Washington and the Negro's Place in American Life.* Boston: Little, Brown, 1965. *17*

Spengemann, William C., and L. R. Lundquist. "Autobiography and the American Myth." *American Quarterly* 17 (Fall 1965): 92-110. *26, 27, 28, 35*

*Spicer, Edward H. *Cycles of Conquest: The Impact of Spain, Mexico, and the United States on the Indians of the Southwest, 1533-1960.* Tucson: University of Arizona Press, 1962. *199, 201*

*_____. *A Short History of the Indians of the United States.* New York: Van Nostrand, Reinhold, Anvil Books, 1969.

*_____, ed. *Perspectives in American Indian Culture Change.* Chicago: University of Chicago Press, 1975.

*Spiller, Robert E. *The Cycle of American Literature.* New York: The Free Press, 1967. *234, 271*

_____, et al. *Literary History of the United States.* 4th rev. ed. New York: Macmillan, 1974. *271*

Sprout, Harold H., and Margaret Sprout. *The Ecological Perspective on Human Affairs, with Special Reference to International Politics.* Princeton, New Jersey: Princeton University Press, 1965. *144*

•_____. *Man-Milieu Relationship Hypothesis in the Context of International Politics.* Princeton, New Jersey: Center for International Studies, Princeton University Press, 1965.

*Spruill, Julia Cherry. *Women's Life and Work in the Southern Colonies.* 1938. Reprint. New York: W. W. Norton, 1972. *246*

*Stampp, Kenneth. *And the War Came: The North and the Secession Crisis, 1860-1861.* Baton Rouge: Louisiana State University Press, 1950. *16, 17, 114, 150*

*_____. *The Era of Reconstruction, 1865-1877.* New York: Random House, Vintage Books, 1967.

*_____. *The Peculiar Institution: Slavery in the Ante-Bellum South.* New York: Random House, Vintage Books, 1964.

*Stands-in-Timber, John, and Margot Liberty. *Cheyenne Memories.* Lincoln: University of Nebraska Press, Bison Books, 1972. *202*

*Stanton, Elizabeth Cady. *Eighty Years and More: Reminiscences, 1815-1897.* New York: Schocken Books, 1971. *249*

_____, Susan B. Anthony, Ida Husted Harper, and Matilda Joslyn Gage. *History of Woman Suffrage.* 1881-1922. Reprint. New York: Arno Press, 1969. *244*

Starkey, Otis, et al. *The Anglo-American Realm.* 2d rev. ed. New York: McGraw-Hill, 1975. *52*

•Starling, Edmund W. *Starling of the White House.* New York: Simon and Schuster, 1946. *73*

*Starobin, Joseph R. *American Communism in Crisis, 1943-1957.* Berkeley: University of California Press, 1975. *124*

Starobinski, Jean. "The Style of Autobiography." In *Literary Style, A Symposium,* edited by S. B. Chatman. New York: Oxford University Press, 1971. *24, 26, 33*

Starosciak, Kenneth, and Jane Starosciak, eds. *Frank Lloyd Wright: A Bibliography Issued on the Occasion of the Destruction of the F. W. Little House.* New Brighton, Minnesota: Privately printed, 1973. *237*

Stauffer, Robert C. "Haeckel, Darwin, and Ecology." *The Quarterly Review of Biology* 32 (June 1957):138-44. *143*

Stave, Bruce M. "A Conversation with Sam Bass Warner, Jr." *Journal of Urban History* 1 (November 1974). *160, 165*

_____. "A Conversation with Stephen Thernstrom." *Journal of Urban History* 2 (February 1975):189-215.

•Stead, William T. *If Christ Came to Chicago.* Chicago: Laird and Lee, 1894. *225*

Stearn, Gerald E., ed. *Gompers.* Englewood Cliffs, New Jersey: Prentice-Hall, 1971. *117*

*Stearns, Marshall. *The Story of Jazz.* New York: Oxford University Press, Galaxy Books, 1970. *273*

*Steffens, Lincoln. *The Autobiography of Lincoln Steffens.* 2 vols. New York: Harcourt, Brace, Jovanovich, 1968. *26, 34*

*Stein, Gertrude. *The Autobiography of Alice B. Toklas.* New York: Random House, Vintage Books, 1955. *26, 27, 29, 34*

*_____. *Everybody's Autobiography.* New York: Random House, Vintage Books, 1973.

*Stein, Maurice R. *The Eclipse of Community: An Interpretation of American Studies.* Princeton, New Jersey: Princeton University Press, 1971. *6*

Stein, Meyer L. *When Presidents Meet the Press.* New York: Messner, 1969. *71*

•Steinberg, Alfred. *The Man from Missouri: The Life and Times of Harry S. Truman.* New York: Putnam, 1962. *79, 80*

•_____. *Sam Johnson's Boy: A Close-up of the President from Texas.* New York: Macmillan, 1968.

*Steiner, Stan. *La Raza: The Mexican Americans.* New York: Harper and Row, 1970. *126, 202*

*_____. *The New Indians.* New York: Harper and Row, 1975.

•Steinfield, Melvin. *Our Racist Presidents: From Washington to Nixon.* San Ramon, California: Consensus Publishers, 1972. *72*

Stephenson, William. *The Play Theory of Mass Communication.* Chicago: University of Chicago Press, 1967. *178, 184*

Stern, Madeleine. *The Pantarch: A Biography of Stephen Pearl Andrews.* Austin: University of Texas Press, 1968. *215, 222*

•Stevens, George A. *New York Typographical Union No. 6: A Study of a Modern Trade Union and Its Predecessors.* Albany: New York State Department of Labor, 1913. *110*

Stevenson, Edward L. *Terrestrial and Celestial Globes: Their History and Construction, Including a Consideration of Their Value as Aids in the Study of Geography and Astronomy.* 2 vols. 1921. Reprint. New York: Johnson Reprint Corporation, 1971. *90, 94*

*Steward, Julian H. *Theory of Culture Change: The Methodology of Multilinear Evolution.* Urbana: University of Illinois Press, 1972. *138*

Stewart, Ethelbert. "A Documentary History of the Early Organizations of Printers." *Bulletin of the Bureau of Labor, Document 61:857-1033.* Washington, D.C.: U.S. Government Printing Office, 1905. *110*

Stewart, George R. *American Place Names: A Concise and Selective Dictionary for the Continental United States of America.* New York: Oxford University Press, 1970. *58, 270*

_____. *American Ways of Life.* 1954. Reprint. New York: Russell and Russell, 1971.

_____. *U.S. 40: Cross Section of the United States of America.* 1953. Westport, Connecticut: Greenwood Press, 1973.

*Still, Bayrd. *Urban America: A History with Documents.* Boston: Little, Brown, 1974. *161, 267*

*_____, ed. *The West: Contemporary Records of America's Expansion Across the Continent, 1607-1890.* New York: Putnam, Capricorn Books, 1961.

_____, and Diana Klebanow. "The Teaching of American Urban History." *Journal of American History* 55 (March 1969): 843-47. *169*

Stoddart, D. R. "Geography and the Ecological Approach: The Ecosystem as a Geographic Principle and Method." *Geography* 50 (July 1965):242-51. *143*

Stoeffler, Ernst. *The Rise of Evangelical Pietism.* Leiden, Holland: E. J. Brill, 1965. *14*

•Stokes, Isaac. *The Iconography of Manhattan Island, 1498-1909.* 6 vols. 1915-1920. Reprint. New York: Arno Press, 1967. *92*

Stone, Albert E. "The Sea and the Self: Travel as Experience and Metaphor in Early American Autobiography." *Genre* 7 (September 1974). *27, 28, 35*

Stone, Irving. *They Also Ran: The Story of the Men Who Were Defeated for the Presidency.* New York: New American Library, 1968. *71*

Stone, Melville. *Fifty Years a Journalist.* 1921. Reprint. Westport, Connecticut: Greenwood Press, 1969. *228*

Storr, Richard. *The Beginning of Graduate Education in America.* 1953. Reprint. New York: Arno Press, 1969. *230, 236*

_____. *Harper's University: The Beginnings.* Chicago: University of Chicago Press, 1966.

*Stowe, Harriet Beecher. *Uncle Tom's Cabin.* New York: Macmillan, Collier Books, 1962. *16*

*Strout, Cushing, ed. *Intellectual History in America.* 2 vols. New York: Harper and Row, 1968. *13*

•Sturmthal, Adolf. *Worker's Councils: A Study of Workplace Organization on Both Sides of the Iron Curtain.* Cambridge, Massachusetts: Harvard University Press, 1964. *127*

*Sullivan, Louis H. *The Autobiography of an Idea.* New York: Dover, 1924. *26, 28, 34, 231*

*_____. *Kindergarten Chats.* New York: George Wittenborn, 1975.

Sullivan, William A. *The Industrial Worker in Pennsylvania, 1880-1840.* 1955. Reprint. Johnson Reprint Corporation, 1972. *112*

Sutherland, Stella H. *Population Distribution in Colonial. America.* New York: AMS Press, 1936. *55*

*Swift, Lindsay. *Brook Farm: Its Members, Scholars, and Visitors.* Secaucus, New Jersey: Citadel Press, 1973. *113, 212, 222*

*Symons, Julian. *The Detective Story in Britain.* New York: British Book Center, 1962. *175, 184*

Szuberla, Guy. "Making the Sublime Mechanical: Henry Blake Fuller's Chicago." *American Studies* 14 (Spring 1973):83-93. *228, 232, 237*

_____. "Urban Vistas and the Pastoral Garden: Studies in the Literature and Architecture of Chicago, 1893-1909." Ph.D. dissertation, University of Minnesota, 1972.

Taeuber, Conrad, and Irene B. Taeuber. *The Changing Population of the United States.* 1958. Reprint. New York: Russell and Russell, 1975. *56*

Taft, Lorado. *The History of American Sculpture.* 1924. Reprint. New York: Arno Press, 1969. *236*

Taft, Philip. *The A.F. of L. from the Death of Gompers to the Merger.* 1959. Reprint. New York: Octagon Books, 1970. *106, 116, 118, 119, 120*

_____. *The A.F. of L. in the Time of Gompers.* 1957. Reprint. New York: Octagon Books, 1970.

•_____. *Organized Labor in American History.* New York: Harper and Row, 1954.

*Tager, Jack, and Park Dixon Goist, eds. *The Urban Vision: Selected Interpretations of the Modern American City.* Homewood, Illinois: Dorsey Press, 1970. *162*

Tanis, James B. *Dutch Calvinistic Pietism in the Middle Colonies: A Study in the Life and Theology of Theodorus Jacobus Frelinghuysen.* The Hague: Martimis Nijhoff, 1967. *14*

Tannenbaum, Frank. *The Labor Movement: Its Conservative Function and Social Consequences.* 1921. Reprint. New York: Arno Press, 1969. *108*

•_____. *A Philosophy of Labor.* New York: Alfred A. Knopf, 1951.

Tanselle, G. Thomas. "Copyright Records and the Bibliographer." *Studies in Bibliography* 22 (1969):77-124. *280*

Tansley, A. G. "The Use and Abuse of Certain Vegetational Concepts and Terms." *Ecology* 16 (1935):284-307. *144*

*Taper, Bernard. *The Arts in Boston.* Cambridge, Massachusetts: Harvard University Press, 1970. *160, 169*

Tarr, Joel A. *A Study in Boss Politics: William Lorimer of Chicago.* Urbana: University of Illinois Press, 1971. *225*

*Taylor, George R. *The Transportation Revolution, 1815-1860.* Edited by H. David et al. New York: Harper and Row, Harper Torchbooks, 1968. *269*

•Taylor, Graham. *Chicago Commons Through Forty Years.* Chicago: Chicago Commons Association, 1936. *226*

*Taylor, William R. *Cavalier and Yankee: The Old South and American National Character.* New York: Harper and Row, Harper Torchbooks, 1969. *8*

Tebbel, John W. *An American Dynasty: The Story of the McCormicks, Medills, and Pattersons.* Westport, Connecticut: Greenwood Press, 1968. *227*

•_____. *The Marshall Fields: A Study in Wealth.* New York: E. P. Dutton, 1947.

Teed, Cyrus. *The Cellular Cosmogony; or, The Earth a Concave Sphere.* 1905. Reprint. Philadelphia: Porcupine Press, 1974. *215, 223*

*Teilhard de Chardin, Pierre. *The Phenomenon of Man.* Translated by Bernard Wall. New York: Harper and Row, Harper Torchbooks, 1959. *143*

ten Houten, Elizabeth S. "Some Collections of Special Use for Women's History Resources in the United States." *American Association of University Women Journal* (April 1974). *254*

*Teodori, Massimo, ed. *The New Left: A Documentary History.* Indianapolis, Indiana: Bobbs-Merrill, 1969. *126*

*Terkel, Louis. *Division Street: America.* New York: Avon, Discus Books, 1968. *226*

•Terrell, Mary Church. *A Colored Woman in a White World.* Washington, D.C.: Ransdell Publishing Company, 1940. *248*

*Terry, Walter. *The Dance in America.* Rev. ed. New York: Harper and Row, Harper Torchbooks, 1971. *263*

Thernstrom, Stephan. *The Other Bostonians: Poverty and Progress in the American Metropolis, 1880-1970.* Cambridge, Massachusetts: Harvard University Press, 1973. *5, 7, 115, 157, 163, 164, 165, 169, 240*

*_____. *Poverty and Progress: Social Mobility in a Nineteenth-Century City.* New York: Atheneum, 1969.

_____. "Up from Slavery." *Perspectives in American History* 1 (1967):434-49.

*_____. "Urbanization, Migration, and Social Mobility in Late Nineteenth-Century America. In *Towards a New Past: Dissenting Essays in American History*, edited by Barton J. Bernstein. New York: Random House, Vintage Books, 1968.

*_____, and Richard Sennett, eds. *Nineteenth-Century Cities: Essays in the New Urban History*. New Haven, Connecticut: Yale University Press, 1969. *156, 158, 159, 169*

Thomas, Benjamin P. *Abraham Lincoln, A Biography*. 1965. Reprint. New York: Modern Library, 1968. *76*

*Thomas, Hugh. *The Spanish Civil War*. New York: Harper and Row, Harper Torchbooks, 1961. *122*

Thomas, Norman C., and Hans W. Baade, eds. *The Institutionalized Presidency*. Dobbs-Ferry, New York: Oceana Publications, 1972. *71*

Thomas, Roy. "Guide to Manuscripts in the Library of Congress: American History, 1896-1920." *254*

Thomas, William I., and Florian Znaniecki. *The Polish Peasant in Europe and America*. 2 vols. New York: Octagon Books, 1974. *30, 36*

*Thomas, William L., et al., eds. *Man's Role in Changing the Face of the Earth*. Chicago: University of Chicago Press, Phoenix Books, 1971. *53, 134*

_____, ed. "Man, Time, and Space in Southern California." *Annals of the Association of American Geographers* (September 1959). *53*

Thompson, John H., ed. *Geography of New York State*. Syracuse, New York: Syracuse University Press, 1966. *53*

Thompson, Slason. *Eugene Field: A Study in Heredity and Contradictions*. 2 vols. 1901. Reprint. New York: Beekman Publishers, 1973. *228*

_____. *Life of Eugene Field, the Poet of Childhood*. New York: R. West, 1927.

Thomson, Don W. *Men and Meridians: The History of Surveying and Mapping in Canada*. 3 vols. Ottawa, Canada: R. Duhamel, Queen's Printer, 1966-1969. *85, 93*

*Thomson, Virgil. *American Music Since 1910*. New York: Holt, Rinehart, and Winston, 1971. *272*

*Thoreau, Henry David. *The Variorum Walden*. Edited by Walter Harding. New York: Washington Square Press, 1968. *26, 27, 28, 34*

Thorp, Willard. *American Writing in the Twentieth Century*. Cambridge, Massachusetts: Harvard University Press, 1960. *271*

•Thorp, William. *American Humorists*. Minneapolis: University of Minnesota Press, 1964. *42*

*Thrower, Norman J. W. *Maps and Man: An Examination of Cartography in Relation to Culture and Civilization*. Englewood Cliffs, New Jersey: Prentice-Hall, 1972. *83. 95*

•_____. *Original Survey and Land Subdivision*. Chicago: Rand McNally, 1966. *57*

•Thrupp, Sylvia Lettice, ed. *Millennial Dreams in Action: Studies in Revolutionary Religious Movements*. New York: Shocken Books, 1970. *208, 223*

•Thurston, Jarvis, et al., eds. *Short Fiction Criticism: A Checklist of Interpretation Since 1925 of Stories and Novelettes*. 1960. *46*

•Tietjens, Eunice. *The World at My Shoulder*. New York: Macmillan, 1938. *227*

*Tocqueville, Alexis de. *Democracy in America*. Edited and translated by Phillips Bradley and Henry Reeve. 2 vols. New York: Random House, Vintage Books, 1945. *16, 265*

*Toffler, Alvin. *The Culture Consumers*. New York: Random House, Vintage Books, 1973. *178, 180, 184*

*_____. *Future Shock*. New York: Bantam Books, 1971.

•Tompkins, Dorothy C. *Presidential Succession, A Bibliography*. Rev. ed. Berkeley: Institute of Government Studies, University of California Press, 1965. *72*

Tooley, Ronald V. *Maps and Map-Makers*. 5th ed. London: Batsford, 1972. *83, 91*

•Townsend, Andrew J. *The Germans of Chicago*. Chicago: University of Chicago Press, 1932. *234*

*Trachtenberg, Alan, ed. *Democratic Vistas: 1860-1880*. New York: George Braziller, 1970. 7

*_____, Peter Neill, and Peter C. Bunnell, eds. *The City: American Experience*. New York: Oxford University Press, 1971. *162*

Trecker, Janice Law. "Sex, Science, and Education." *American Quarterly* 26 (October 1974). *253*

Trent, W. P., et al. *The Cambridge History of American Literature*. 3 vols. in 1. New York: Macmillan, 1943. *45*

Trewartha, Glenn. "Types of Rural Settlement in Colonial America." *Geographical Review* (October 1946). *55*

Truman, Harry S. *Memoirs.* 2 vols. Garden City, New York: Doubleday, 1958. *68*

*Truman, Margaret. *Harry S. Truman.* New York: Pocket Books, 1974. *79*

•Tugwell, Rexford G. *The Enlargement of the Presidency.* Garden City, New York: Doubleday, 1960. *72*

•Tully, Grace F. *F.D.R., My Boss.* New York: Scribner's, 1949. *71*

*Tunnard, Christopher. *The Modern American City.* Princeton, New Jersey: Van Nostrand, Anvil Books, 1968. *263*

*_____, and Henry Hope Reed. *American Skyline: The Growth and Form of Our Cities and Towns.* New York: New American Library, Mentor Books, 1955. *154, 170, 263*

•Turner, Darwin T. *Afro-American Writers.* New York: Appleton-Century-Crofts, Goldentree Bibliography Series, 1970. *46*

*Tuttle, William M. *Race Riot: Chicago in the Red Summer of 1919.* New York: Atheneum, 1970. *226*

Tuveson, Ernest. *Millennium and Utopia: A Study in the Background of the Idea of Progress.* 1949. Reprint. Gloucester, Massachusetts: Peter Smith. *13, 207, 209, 223*

*_____. *Redeemer Nation: The Idea of America's Millennial Role.* Chicago: University of Chicago Press, Phoenix Books, 1974.

*Tyler, Alice F. *Freedom's Ferment: Phases of American Social History to 1860.* New York: Harper and Row, Harper Torchbooks, 1944. *16, 113, 212, 223, 269*

Tyler, Gus. *The Political Imperative: The Corporate Character of Unions.* Edited by Richard Eells. New York: Macmillan, 1968. *126*

Udall, Stewart L. "The Ecology of Man and the Land Ethic." *Natural History* 74 (June-July 1965):32-41. *143*

Ullman, Edward. "Amenities as a Factor in Regional Growth." *Geographical Review* (January 1954). *58*

Ulman, Lloyd. *The Rise of the National Trade Union: The Development and Significance of Its Structure, Governing Institutions, and Economic Policies.* 2d ed. Cambridge, Massachusetts. Harvard University Press, 1955. *113*

•Umans, Shelly. *The Management of Education: A Systematic Design for Educational Revolution.* Garden City, New York: Doubleday, Anchor Books, 1970. *100*

*Underhill, Ruth Murray. *Red Man's America: A History of Indians in the United States.* Rev. ed. Chicago: University of Chicago Press, Phoenix Books, 1971. *275*

Unger, Irwin. *The Greenback Era, A Social and Political History of American Finance, 1865-1879.* Princeton, New Jersey: Princeton University Press, 1964. *106, 114*

_____. "The 'New Left' and American History: Some Recent Trends in United States Historiography." *American Historical Review* 72 (July 1967):1255-57.

United States Bureau of Labor Statistics. *Problems and Policies of Dispute Settlement and Wage Stabilization During World War II.* Bulletin 1009. Washington, D.C.: U.S. Government Printing Office, 1950. *124*

_____. *Report on the Work of the National Defense Mediation Board, March 19, 1941—January 12, 1942.* Bulletin 714. Washington, D.C.: U.S. Government Printing Office, 1942.

United States Congressional Quarterly Service. *Presidential Candidates from 1788-1964, Including Third Parties, 1832-1964.* Washington, D.C.: U.S. Government Printing Office, 1964. *68*

United States Department of Agriculture. *The Look of Our Land—An Airphoto Atlas of the Rural United States.* 5 vols. Washington, D.C.: U.S. Government Printing Office, 1970-1971. *51*

United States Department of Labor. *The National Wage Stabilization Board, January 1, 1946—February 24, 1947.* Washington, D.C.: U.S. Government Printing Office, 1947. *124*

United States Library of Congress. Geography and Map Division. *The Bibliography of Cartography.* 5 vols. Boston: G. K. Hall, 1973. *89, 94*

_____. *Facsimiles of Rare Historical Maps.* 3d rev. ed. Compiled by W. W. Ristow. Washington, D.C.: U.S. Government Printing Office, 1968-1971. *91, 95*

_____. *Guide to the Study of the United States of America.* Washington, D.C.: U.S. Government Printing Office, 1960. *262*

_____. Legislative Reference Service. *Inaugural Addresses of the Presidents of the United States from George Washington, 1789, to John F. Kennedy, 1961.* Washington, D.C.: U.S. Government Printing Office, 1961. *68*

_____. Map Division. *A List of Geographical Atlases in the Library of Congress, with Bibliographic Notes.* 8 vols. Compiled by Philip Lee Phillips and Clara E. LeGear. Washington, D.C.: U.S. Government Printing Office, 1909. *86, 87, 93*

_____. *A List of Maps of America in the Library of Congress, Preceded by a List of Works Relating to Cartography*. Compiled by Philip Lee Phillips. Washington, D.C.: U.S. Government Printing Office, 1901.

_____. *United States Atlases: A List of National, State, County, City and Regional Atlases in the Library of Congress*. Compiled by Clara E. LeGear. 2 vols. Washington, D.C.: U.S. Government Printing Office, 1950-1953.

United States National Archives and Records Service. *Guide to Cartographic Records in the National Archives*. Washington, D.C.: U.S. Government Printing Office, 1971. *86, 95*

Unrau, William E. *The Kansa Indians: A History of the Wind People, 1673-1873*. Norman: University of Oklahoma Press, 1971. *204*

Untermeyer, Louis. *The New Era in American Poetry*. 1919. Reprint. New York: Scholarly Reprints, 1971. *235, 272*

_____, ed. *Modern American Poetry*. Rev. ed. New York: Harcourt, Brace, Jovanovich, 1969.

Urofsky, Melvin I. *Big Steel and the Wilson Administration: A Study in Business-Government Relations*. Columbus: Ohio State University Press, 1969. *120*

•Vale, Vivian. *Labour in American Politics*. New York: Barnes and Noble, 1971. *127*

Vance, Rupert B. *Human Geography of the South: A Study in Regional Resources and Human Adequacy*. 2d ed. 1935. Reprint. New York: Russell and Russell, 1968. *53*

•Van der Slice, Austin. *International Labor, Diplomacy and Peace, 1914-1919*. Philadelphia: University of Pennsylvania Press, 1941. *120*

*Van Deusen, Glyndon G. *The Jacksonian Era. 1828-1848*. New York: Harper and Row, Harper Torchbooks, 1959. *75*

•Van Doren, Carl. *Benjamin Franklin*. 1938. Reprint. Westport, Connecticut: Greenwood Press, 1973. *267*

Vanek, Jaroslav. *A General Theory of Labor-Managed Market Economies*. Ithaca, New York: Cornell University Press, 1970. *127*

_____. *The Participatory Economy: An Evolutionary Hypothesis and a Strategy for Development*. Ithaca, New York: Cornell University Press, 1971.

*Vaughan, Alden T. *New England Frontier: Puritans and Indians, 1620-1675*. Boston: Little, Brown, 1965. *14, 196*

_____, ed. *The Puritan Tradition in America, 1620-1730*. New York: Harper and Row, 1972.

Veblen, Thorstein. "The Economic Theory of Women's Dress." *Popular Science Monthly* 46 (November 1894). *230, 256*

*_____. *The Higher Learning in America*. New York: Hill and Wang, 1957.

Verner, Coolie. *Smith's Virginia and Its Derivatives: A Cartobibliographical Study of the Diffusion of Geographic Knowledge*. London: Map Collectors' Circle, 1968 (Map Collectors' Series #45). *85, 92*

Vestal, Stanley. *New Sources of Indian History, 1850-1891, The Ghost Dance—The Prairie Sioux: A Miscellany*. 1934. Reprint. New York: B. Franklin. *202*

*Veysey, Laurence. *The Communal Experience: Anarchist and Mystical Countercultures in America*. New York: Harper and Row, 1973. *217, 223, 236*

*_____. *The Emergence of the American University*. Chicago: University of Chicago Press, Phoenix Books, 1970.

Vogel, Robert. "Industrial Archaeology—A Continuous Past." *Historic Preservation* 19 (April-June 1967):68-75. *190, 193*

_____. *The New England Textile Mill Survey*. Washington, D.C.: Historic American Buildings Survey, 1972.

Wacker, Peter. *The Musconetcong Valley of New Jersey: A Historical Geography*. New Brunswick, New Jersey: Rutgers University Press, 1968. *56*

Wade, John Donald. *Augustus Baldwin Longstreet: A Study of the Development of Culture in the South*. Edited by M. Thomas Inge. Athens: University of Georgia Press, 1969. *42*

Wade, Louise C. *Graham Taylor, Pioneer for Social Justice, 1851-1938*. Chicago: University of Chicago Press, 1964. *233*

*Wade, Richard C. *Slavery in the Cities: The South, 1820-1960*. New York: Oxford University Press, Galaxy Books, 1967. *114*

Wagenknecht, Edward C. *Cavalcade of the American Novel, From the Birth of the Nation to the Middle of the Twentieth Century*. New York: Holt, Rinehart, and Winston, 1952. *225, 271*

_____. *Chicago*. Norman: University of Oklahoma Press, 1964.

Wagner, Henry R. *The Cartography of the Northwest Coast of America to the Year 1800*.

1937. 2 vols. in 1. Reprint. Amsterdam: N. Israel, 1968. *84, 92*

*Wakstein, Allen M., ed. *The Urbanization of America: An Historical Anthology.* Boston: Houghton Mifflin, 1970. *155, 170*

Walcutt, Charles Child. *American Literary Naturalism: A Divided Stream.* 1956. Reprint. Westport, Connecticut: Greenwood Press, 1973. *44*

*Walker, Robert H. *Everyday Life in the Age of Enterprise, 1865-1900.* New York: Putnam, Capricorn Books, 1971. *114, 184*

Walker, Williston, ed. *The Creeds and Platforms of Congregationalism.* Philadelphia: United Church Press, 1960. *14*

Walkowitz, Daniel J. "Working-Class Women in the Gilded Age: Factory, Community and Family Life Among Cohoes, New York Cotton Workers." *Journal of Social History* 5 (Summer 1972). *254*

*Wallace, Anthony F. C. *The Death and Rebirth of the Seneca: The History and Culture of the Great Iroquois Nation, Their Destruction and Demoralization, and Their Cultural Revival at the Hands of the Indian Visionary, Handsome Lake.* New York: Random House, Vintage Books, 1972. *200*

_____. *King of the Delawares: Teedyuscung, 1700-1763.* 1949. Reprint. Plainview, New York: Books for Libraries, 1973.

Walsh, Henry H. *The Christian Church in Canada.* Toronto, Canada: Ryerson Press, 1956. *13*

Walsh, Richard. "The Charleston Mechanics: A Brief Study, 1760-1776." *South Carolina Historical Magazine* 60 (1959):123-44. *110*

*Walzer, Michael. *The Revolution of the Saints; A Study of the Origins of Radical Politics.* New York: Atheneum, 1968. *110*

*Ward, Barbara. *Spaceship Earth.* New York: Columbia University Press, 1966. *143*

*Ward, David. *Cities and Immigrants: A Geography of Change in Nineteenth-Century America.* New York: Oxford University Press, 1971. *57, 159, 164, 167, 170*

_____. "A Comparative Historical Geography of Streetcar Suburbs in Boston, Massachusetts, and Leeds, England: 1850-1920." *Annals of the Association of American Geographers* 55 (Fall 1962):477-89.

*Ward, John W. *Andrew Jackson, Symbol for an Age.* New York: Oxford University Press, Galaxy Books, 1962. *16, 28, 35, 267*

_____. "Who Was Benjamin Franklin?" *American Scholar* 32 (Autumn 1963):541-53.

*Ware, Cellestine. *Woman Power: The Movement for Women's Liberation.* New York: Tower Publications, 1970. *249*

*Ware, Norman J. *The Industrial Worker, 1840-1860: The Reaction of American Industrial Society to the Advance of the Industrial Revolution.* New York: Quadrangle Books, 1964. *113, 115*

_____. *The Labor Movement in the United States, 1860-1895.* 1929. Reprint. Gloucester, Massachusetts: Peter Smith, 1959.

Warfel, Harry R., and G. Harrison Crians. *American Local-Color Stories.* 1941. Reprint. New York: Cooper Square Publishers, 1970. *43*

*Warne, Colston E., ed. *The Pullman Boycott of 1894: The Problems of Federal Intervention.* Boston: D. C. Heath, 1955. *120, 123, 234*

•_____. *Labor in Postwar America.* Brooklyn, New York: Rensen Press, 1949.

*_____. *The Steel Strike of 1919.* Boston: D. C. Heath, 1963.

_____. *War Labor Policies.* New York: Philosophical Library, 1943.

Warner, Sam Bass, Jr. "If All the World Were Philadelphia: A Scaffolding for Urban History, 1774-1930." *American Historical Review* 74 (October 1968):26-43. *5, 157, 158, 159, 161, 162, 165, 170*

*_____. *The Private City: Philadelphia in Three Periods of Its Growth.* Philadelphia: University of Pennsylvania Press, 1971.

_____. Review of S. Thernstrom and R. Sennett, eds., *Nineteenth-Century Cities. Journal of American History* 57 (December 1970):737-38.

*_____. *Streetcar Suburbs: The Process of Growth in Boston, 1870-1900.* New York: Atheneum, 1969.

*_____. *The Urban Wilderness: A History of the American City.* New York: Harper and Row, 1973.

*Warner, W. Lloyd. *American Life: Dream and Reality.* Rev. ed. Chicago: University of Chicago Press, Phoenix Books, 1962. *268*

*Warren, Harris G. *Herbert Hoover and the Great Depression.* New York: W. W. Norton, 1967. *78*

*Warshow, Robert. *The Immediate Experience: Movies, Comics, Theatre, and Other Aspects of Popular Culture.* New York: Atheneum, 1970. *173, 184*

*Washington, Booker T. *Up from Slavery: An Autobiography.* New York: Bantam Books, 1970. *17*

Washington, George. *Diaries, 1748-1799.* Edited by John C. Fitzpatrick. 4 vols. 1925. Reprint. Millwood, New York: Kraus Reprints. *68*

———. *Writings. . .from the Original Manuscript Sources, 1745-1799.* Edited by John C. Fitzpatrick. 39 vols. 1931-1944. Reprint. Westport, Connecticut: Greenwood Press, 1970. *267*

*Waterman, Thomas T., and John A. Burrows. *Domestic Colonial Architecture of Tidewater Virginia.* 1932. Reprint. New York: Dover, 1970. *187, 193*

Waterman, William. *Frances Wright.* 1924. Reprint. New York: AMS Press, 1972. *211, 223*

Watkins, Gordon S. *Labor Problems and Labor Administration in the United States During the World War.* 1920. Reprint. New York: Johnson Reprint Corporation, 1970. *120*

Watson, J. Wreford. *North America, Its Countries and Regions.* Rev. ed. New York: Praeger, 1968. *52*

Watt, Kenneth E. F., ed. *Systems Analysis in Ecology.* New York: Academic Press, 1966. *143*

*Wattenburg, B. J., ed. *American Almanac: The U.S. Book of Facts, Statistics, and Information for 1970.* New York: Grosset and Dunlap for Bureau of the Cencus, U.S. Department of Commerce, 1970. *262*

•Weales, Gerald. *American Drama Since World War II.* New York: Harcourt, Brace, and World, 1962.

Webb, R. K. *The British Working Class Reader, 1790-1848.* London: Allen and Unwin, 1955. *177, 184*

*Webb, Walter Prescott. *The Great Plains.* New York: Grosset and Dunlap, 1957. *53, 267*

•Webber, Everett. *Escape to Utopia: The Communal Movement in America.* New York: Hastings House Publishers, 1959. *214, 223*

*Weber, Brom, ed. *The Art of American Humor: An Anthology.* New York: Apollo Editions, 1970. *42*

*Weber, Max. *The Protestant Ethic and the Spirit of Capitalism.* Translated by Talcott Parsons. New York: Scribner's, 1958. *14*

*Wector, Dixon. *The Hero in America, A Chronicle of Hero-Worship.* Ann Arbor: University of Michigan Press, 1963. *275*

•———. *The Saga of American Society: A Record of Social Aspiration, 1607-1937.* 1937. Reprint. New York: Scribner's, 1970.

*Weinstein, Allen, and Frank O. Gatell, eds. *American Negro Slavery: A Modern Reader.* 2d ed. New York: Oxford University Press, 1973. *16*

*Weinstein, James. *The Corporate Idea in the Liberal State, 1900-1918.* Boston: Beacon Press, 1969. *118*

*Weisberger, Bernard. *They Gathered at the River: The Story of the Great Revivalists and Their Impact upon Religion in America.* Chicago: Quadrangle Books, 1966. *16*

*Weisstein, Naomi. "'Kinde, Kuche, Kirche' as Scientific Law: Psychology Constructs the Female." In *Sisterhood Is Powerful,* edited by Robin Morgan. New York: Vintage Books, 1970. *250*

•Welsh, P. C. *American Folk Art: The Art and Spirit of a People.* Washington, D.C.: Smithsonian Institution, 1965. *263*

Welter, Barbara. "The Cult of True Womanhood: 1820-1860." Part 1. *American Quarterly* 18 (Summer 1966). *245*

*Wendt, Lloyd, and Herman Kogan. *Bosses in Lusty Chicago: The Story of Bathhouse John and Hinky Dink.* Bloomington: Indiana University Press, 1967. *225*

•Wentz, Abdel R. *A Basic History of Lutheranism in America.* Rev. ed. Philadelphia: Fortress Press, 1964. *12*

•Werkmeister, William H. *History of Philosophical Ideas in America.* New York: Ronald Press, 1949. *13*

•Werner, Morris. *Julius Rosenwald: The Life of a Practical Humanitarian.* New York: Harper, 1939. *227*

Wertenbaker, Thomas J. *The Founding of American Civilization: The Middle Colonies.* 1938. Reprint. New York: Cooper Square Publications, 1963. *55, 193, 266*

•———. *The Puritan Oligarchy: The Founding of American Civilization.* 1947. Reprint. New York: Scribner's, 1970.

Weslager, C. A. *Dutch Explorers, Traders, and Settlers in the Delaware Valley.* Philadelphia: University of Pennsylvania Press, 1964. *56*

Wesley, William A., and Margaret W. Wesley. *The Emerging Workers: Equality and Conflict in the Mass Consumption Society.* Montreal, Canada: McGill-Queens University Press, 1971. *126*

*West, Mae. *Goodness Had Nothing to Do with It.* Rev. ed. New York: Manor Books, 1970. *26, 35*

•Whalen, Richard J. *The Founding Father: The Story of Joseph P. Kennedy.* New York: New American Library, 1964. *159, 170*

•Wheat, Carl I. *Mapping the Transmississippi West, 1540-1880.* 5 vols. San Francisco: Institute of Historical Cartography, 1957-1960. *84, 92*

•Wheat, James C., and Christian F. Brun. *Maps and Charts Published in America Before 1800, A Bibliography.* New Haven, Connecticut: Yale University Press, 1969. *84, 92*

White, Anna, and Leila S. Taylor. *Shakerism: Its Meaning and Message.* 1904. Reprint. New York: AMS Press, 1971. *210, 223*

White, Dana F. "'Back Bay Boston': A Museum Experiment with Urban History."*Museum News* 48 (March 1970):20-25. *159, 170*

White, David Manning, ed. *Pop Culture in America.* Chicago: Quadrangle Books, 1970. *174, 184*

White, John H. *American Locomotives: An Engineering History, 1830-1880.* Baltimore: Johns Hopkins University Press, 1968. *191, 193*

White, Langdon, Edwin Foscue, and Tom McKnight. *Regional Geography of Anglo-America.* 4th ed. Englewood Cliffs, New Jersey: Prentice-Hall, 1974. *52*

•White, Leonard D. *The Federalists: A Study in Administrative History.* New York: Macmillan, 1948. *70*

_____. *The Jacksonians: A Study in Administrative History, 1829-1861.* New York: Macmillan, 1954.

_____. *The Jeffersonians: A Study in Administrative History, 1801-1829.* New York: Macmillan, 1951.

*_____. *The Republican Era, 1869-1901: A Study in Administrative History.* New York: The Free Press, 1965.

White, Lynn, Jr. "The Historical Roots of Our Ecological Crisis." *Science* 155 (March 10, 1967):1203-07. *143*

*White, Morton G. *Science and Sentiment in America: Philosophical Thought from Jonathan Edwards to John Dewey.* New York: Oxford University Press, 1973. *13, 19, 273*

*_____. *Social Thought in America: The Revolt Against Formalism.* Boston: Beacon Press, 1957.

White, Ralph K. "Black Boy: A Value-Analysis." *Journal of Abnormal and Social Psychology* 42 (October 1947):440-61. *30, 36*

*White, Theodore H. *The Making of the President, 1960.* New York: New American Library, Signet Books, 1967. *80*

White, William Allen. *A Puritan in Babylon: The Story of Calvin Coolidge.* 1938. Reprint. Gloucester, Massachusetts: Peter Smith, 1973. *78*

•White, William S. *The Professional: Lyndon B. Johnson.* Cambridge, Massachusetts: Houghton Mifflin, 1964. *80*

Whitehill, Walter Muir. *The Arts in Early American History: Needs and Opportunities for Study.* Chapel Hill: University of North Carolina Press, 1965. *159, 170, 193*

_____. *Boston, A Topographical History.* 2d rev. ed. Cambridge, Massachusetts: The Belknap Press of Harvard University Press, 1968

White House Historical Association. *The Living White House.* Washington, D.C.: 1966. *26 27, 34*

_____. *The White House: An Historic Guide.* Washington, D.C.: 1969. *69*

Whitman, Walt. *Specimen Days.* Edited by A. Kazin. New York: D. R. Grodine, 1971. *34*

Whittemore, Robert C. *Makers of the American Mind.* 1964. Reprint. Plainview, New York: Books for Libraries, 1972. *13*

•Whitton, Mary O. *First First Ladies, 1789-1865, A Study of the Wives of the Early Presidents.* New York: Hastings House, 1948. *73*

*Whyte, William H. *The Organization Man.* New York: Simon and Schuster, Touchstone-Clarion Books, 1972. *274*

*Wiebe, Robert H. *Businessmen and Reform: A Study of the Progressive Movement.* New York: Quadrangle Books, 1968. *7, 17, 118*

*_____. *The Search for Order: 1877-1920*. New York: Hill and Wang, 1967.

*Wiener, Philip. *Evolution and the Founders of Pragmatism*. Philadelphia: University of Pennsylvania Press, 1972. *18*

•Willard, Frances. *Glimpses of Fifty Years: The Autobiography of an American Woman*. 1889. Reprint. New York: Source Books Press, 1970. *226*

*Willey, Basil. *The Eighteenth Century Background: Studies on the Idea of Nature in the Thought of the Period*. Boston: Beacon Press, 1961. *143*

Williams, Aaron. *The Harmony Society at Economy, Pennsylvania, Founded by George Rapp, A.D. 1805*. 1866. Reprint. New York: Augustus M. Kelley, 1971. *211, 223*

•Williams, Irving G. *The Rise of the Vice-Presidency*. Washington, D.C.: Public Affairs Press, 1956. *72*

Williams, Raymond. *The Long Revolution*. 1961. Reprint. Westport, Connecticut: Greenwood Press, 1975. *180, 184*

Williams, Robin M. *American Society: A Sociological Interpretation*. 3d rev. ed. New York: Alfred A. Knopf, 1970. *98, 274*

_____. *Strangers Next Door: Ethnic Relations in American Communities*. Englewood Cliffs, New Jersey: Prentice-Hall, 1964.

_____, and Margaret W. Ryan, eds. *Schools in Transition: Community Experiences in Desegregation*. Chapel Hill: University of North Carolina Press, 1954.

•Williams, Sylvia Berry. *Hassling*. Boston: Little, Brown, 1970. *103*

*Williams, William Appleman. *The Roots of the Modern American Empire: A Study of the Growth and Shaping of a Social Consciousness in a Marketplace Society*. New York: Random House, Vintage Books, 1970. *7, 8, 265*

*_____, ed. *The Shaping of American Diplomacy: Readings and Documents in American Foreign Relations, 1750-1968*. 2 vols. Chicago: Rand McNally, 1970.

*Wills, Garry. *Nixon Agonistes: The Crisis of the Self-Made Man*. New York: New Horizon Library, Mentor Books, 1971. *80*

Wilmerding, Lucius, Jr. *The Electoral College*. New Brunswick, New Jersey: Rutgers University Press, 1958. *70*

*Wilson, Edmund. *Classics and Commercials: A Literary Chronicle of the Forties*. New York: Farrar, Strauss and Giroux, Noonday Books, 1950. *41, 184, 228*

_____. "Henry B. Fuller: The Art of Making It Flat." *The New Yorker* (May 23, 1970).

*_____. *Patriotic Gore: Studies in the Literature of the American Civil War*. New York: Oxford University Press, Galaxy Books, 1966.

_____. *The Shores of Light: A Literary Chronicle of the Twenties and Thirties*. New York: Farrar, Strauss and Giroux, Noonday Books, 1952.

•Wilson, R. Jackson, ed. *Darwinism and the American Intellectual: A Book of Readings*. Homewood, Illinois: Dorsey Press, 1967. *18*

Winearls, Joan, and Yves Tessier, eds. *Directory of Canadian Map Collections*. Montreal: Association of Canadian Map Libraries, 1969. *87, 95*

Winch, Donald. *Economics and Policy, A Historical Survey*. London: Collins Fontana, 1972. *122*

•Windmuller, John P. *American Labor and the International Labor Movement, 1940-1953*. Ithaca, New York: The Institute of International Industrial and Labor Relations, Cornell University Press, 1954. *124*

_____. "Foreign Affairs and the AFL-CIO." *Industrial and Labor Relations Review* 9 (1956): 419-32.

_____. "The Foreign Policy Conflict in American Labor." *Political Science Quarterly* 82 (1967):205-34.

*Winslow, Ola E. *Jonathan Edwards, 1703-1758: Basic Writings*. New York: New American Library, Signet Books, 1966. *15*

_____. *Jonathan Edwards, 1703-1758: A Biography*. 1940. Reprint. New York: Octagon Books. 1973.

Winsor, Justin, ed. *Narrative and Critical History of America*. 8 vols. 1884-1889. Reprint. New York: AMS Press, 1967. *84, 92*

*Wirth, Louis. *The Ghetto*. Chicago: University of Chicago Press, Phoenix Books, 1956. *19, 226*

Wisbey, Herbert A., Jr. *Pioneer Prophetess: Jemima Wilkinson, the Publick Universal Friend*. Ithaca, New York: Cornell University Press, 1964. *210, 223*

*Wissler, Clark. *Indians of the United States*. 1940. Reprint. Rev. ed. Prepared by Lucy Wales Kluckhohn. Garden City, New York: Doubleday, 1966. *199*

Wittke, Carl. *The Utopian Communist: A Biography of Wilhelm Weitling, Nineteenth-Century Reformer.* Baton Rouge: Louisiana State University Press, 1950. *19, 213, 223*

_____. *We Who Built America: The Saga of the Immigrant.* Rev. ed. Cleveland, Ohio: Press of Western Reserve University, 1967.

*Wolf, William J. *Lincoln's Religion.* Rev. ed. Philadelphia: United Church Press, 1970. *17*

*Wolfe, Tom. *The Kandy-Kolored Tangerine-Flake Streamline Baby.* New York: Farrar, Strauss and Giroux, Noonday Books, 1965. *184, 191, 193*

*_____. *The Pump House Gang.* New York: Farrar, Strauss and Giroux, 1968.

*Wolfenstein, Martha, and Nathan Leites. *Movies: A Psychological Study.* New York: Atheneum, 1970. *179, 184*

Wolff, Cynthia Griffin. "Thanatos and Eros: Kate Chopin's *The Awakening.*" *American Quarterly* 25 (October 1973). *257*

•Wolff, Leon. *Lockout, the Story of the Homestead Strike of 1892.* New York: Harper and Row, 1965. *116*

*Wollen, Peter. *Signs and Meaning in the Cinema.* Rev. and enlarged ed. Bloomington: Indiana University Press, 1973. *179, 184*

Wolter, John A. "Geographical Libraries and Map Collections." In *Encyclopedia of Library and Information Science,* Vol. 9, 1973. *95*

Wood, Ann Douglas. "The 'Scribbling Women' and Fanny Fern: Why Women Wrote." *American Quarterly* 23 (Spring 1971). *250*

*Wood, Gordon. *The Creation of the American Republic, 1776-1787.* New York: W. W. Norton, 1972. *15*

Wood, Peter H. *Black Majority: Negroes in Colonial South Carolina from 1670 Through the Stono Rebellion.* New York: Alfred A. Knopf, 1974. *167*

•Wood, Robin. *Arthur Penn.* New York: Praeger, 1969. *184*

*_____. *Hitchcock's Films.* 2d ed. New York: Barnes and Noble, 1969.

•_____. *Howard Hawks.* Garden City, New York: Doubleday, 1968.

*Woodress, James, et al., eds. *Eight American Authors.* New York: W. W. Norton, Norton Library, 1972. *45*

•Woodson, Carter G., and Charles H. Wesley. *Negro Makers of History.* 5th rev. ed. Washington, D.C.: Associated Publishers, 1958. *148*

•_____. *The Negro in Our History.* 10th rev. ed. Washington, D.C.: Associated Publishers, 1962.

*Woodward, C. Vann. *The Burden of Southern History.* Rev. ed. Baton Rouge: Louisiana State University Press, 1968. *150, 165*

*_____. *Reunion and Reaction: The Compromise of 1877 and the End of Reconstruction.* Boston: Little, Brown, 1966.

*_____. *The Strange Career of Jim Crow.* 3d rev. ed. New York: Oxford University Press, 1974.

Woodward, David. *A Bibliography of Papers on History of Cartography in American Periodicals of Bibliographical Interest Found in the Libraries of the University of Wisconsin.* Madison: University of Wisconsin Press, Geography Department, January 1968. *88, 94*

Woody, Thomas. *A History of Women's Education in the United States.* 2 vols. 1929. Reprint. New York: Octagon Books, 1966. *246*

*Woolf, Virginia. *A Room of One's Own.* New York: Harcourt, Brace, Jovanovich, 1929. *250*

*Woolman, John. *The Journal of John Woolman.* Secaucus, New Jersey: Citadel Press, 1972. *25, 26, 33*

Wooster, Ernest. *Communities of the Past and Present.* 1924. Reprint. New York: AMS Press, 1971. *214, 223*

•Wright, Conrad. *The Beginnings of Unitarianism in America.* Boston: Beacon Press, 1955. *15*

Wright, Frank Lloyd. *The Early Works of Frank Lloyd Wright.* New York: Horizon Press, 1968. *231*

_____. *Genius and Mobocracy.* 1949. Enlarged ed. New York: Horizon Press, 1971.

Wright, H. E., and David Frey, eds. *The Quarternary of the United States.* Princeton, New Jersey: Princeton University Press, 1965. *54*

Wright, John K., and Elizabeth T. Platt. *Aids to Geographical Research: Bibliographies, Periodicals, Atlases, Gazetteers and Other Reference Books,* 2d rev. ed. 1947. Reprint. Westport, Connecticut: Greenwood Press, 1971. *81, 87, 91*

Wright, Louis B. *The Cultural Life of the American Colonies, 1607-1763.* New York: Harper, 1957. *177, 184, 266*

•_____. *Middle-Class Culture in Elizabethan England.* 1935. Reprint. Ithaca, New York: Cornell University Press, 1958.

Wright, Lyle H. *American Fiction, 1774-1850: A Contribution Toward a Bibliography.* 2d rev. ed. San Marino, California: Huntington Library, 1969. *46*

*Wright, Richard. *Black Boy, A Record of Childhood and Youth.* New York: Harper and Row, 1966. *26, 28, 29, 30, 34, 229*

*Wynes, Charles E., ed. *The Negro in the South Since 1865: Selected Essays in American Negro History.* New York: Harper and Row, Colophon Books, 1968. *151*

•Yarmolinsky, Avrahm. *A Russian's American Dream: A Memoir on William Frey.* Lawrence: University of Kansas Press, 1965. *214, 223*

*Yates, Norris W. *The American Humorist: Conscience of the Twentieth Century.* Ames: Iowa State University Press, 1964. *42*

•_____. *William T. Porter and the Spirit of the Times: A Study of the Big Bear School of Humor.* Baton Rouge: Louisiana State University Press, 1957.

Yearley, Clifton K. *Britons in American Labor: A History of the Influence of the United Kingdom Immigrants on American Labor, 1820-1914.* 1957. Reprint. Westport, Connecticut: Greenwood Press, 1974. *116*

Yeates, Maurice H., and Barry J. Garner. *The North American City.* New York: Harper and Row, 1971. *56*

•Yellowitz, Irvin. *Labor and the Progressive Movement in New York State, 1876-1916.* Ithaca, New York: Cornell University Press, 1965. *115, 118*

*_____. *The Position of the Worker in American Society, 1865-1896.* Englewood Cliffs, New Jersey: Prentice-Hall, 1969.

Yezierska, Anzia. *Bread Givers: A Struggle Between a Father of the Old World and a Daughter of the New World.* New York: George Braziller, 1975. *250*

•Yonge, Ena L. *A Catalogue of Early Globes, Made Prior to 1850 and Conserved in the United States: A Preliminary Listing.* New York: American Geographical Society, 1968. *90, 94*

Young, Alfred. "The Mechanics and the Jeffersonians, New York: 1789-1801." *Labor History* 5 (1964):247-76. *111*

*Zablocki, Benjamin. *The Joyful Community; An Account of the Bruderhof, a Communal Movement Now in Its Third Generation.* Baltimore: Penguin, Pelican Books, 1972. *217, 223*

Zahler, Helene S. *Eastern Workingmen and National Land Policy, 1829-1862.* 1941. Reprint. Westport, Connecticut: Greenwood Press, 1969. *114*

Zelinskey, Wilbur. "An Approach to the Religious Geography of the United States: Patterns of Church Membership in 1952." *Annals of the Association of American Geographers* (June 1961). *50, 54, 56, 57, 58*

_____. "Changes in the Geographic Pattern of Rural Population in the United States, 1790-1960." *Geographical Review* (October 1962). *56*

*_____. *The Cultural Geography of the United States.* Englewood Cliffs, New Jersey: Prentice-Hall, 1973.

Zieger, Robert H. *Republicans and Labor, 1919-1929.* Lexington: University of Kentucky Press, 1969. *106, 120*

_____. "Workers and Scholars: Recent Trends in American Labor Historiography." *Labor History* 13 (Spring 1971):245-66.

•Zierer, Clifford, ed. *California and the Southwest.* New York: Wiley, 1956. *53*

Ziff, Larzer. *The American 1890's: The Life and Times of a Lost Generation.* New York: Viking Press, 1966. *5, 44, 109, 116, 235*

*_____. *Puritanism in America: New Culture for a New World.* New York: Viking Press, Compass Books, 1973.

•Zink, Harold, et al. *Amrican Government and Politics; National, State, and Local.* Princeton, New Jersey: Van Nostrand, 1958. *265*

Zorbaugh, Harvey W. *Gold Coast and Slum, A Sociological Study of Chicago's Near North Side.* Chicago: University of Chicago Press, 1929. *226*

•Zube, Ervin H. *Landscapes.* Amherst: University of Massachusetts Press, 1970. *51*

Zuni People. *The Zunis: Self-Portrayals.* Translated by Alvina Quam. New York: New American Library, Mentor Books, 1974. *205*

About the Editor
Robert H. Walker is series editor of Greenwood's Contributions in American Studies. He is professor of American Civilization at George Washington University and has served as editor of the *American Quarterly* and *American Studies in the United States*. His most recent book is *American Studies Abroad,* which was published by Greenwood Press in 1975.